AUD

Auditing and Attestation

CPA Exam Review

UWorld
9111 Cypress Waters Blvd
Suite 300
Dallas, TX 75019

accounting.uworld.com/cpa-review

Permissions

The following items are utilized in this program, and are copyright property of the American Institute of Certified Public Accountants, Inc. (AICPA), all rights reserved:

- Uniform CPA Examination and Questions and Unofficial Answers, Copyright © 1991 – 2023
- Audit and Accounting Guides, Auditing Procedure Studies, Risk Alerts, Statements of Position, and Code of Professional Conduct
- Statements on Auditing Standards
- Statements on Standards for Accounting and Review Services
- Statements on Quality Control Standards
- Statements on Standards for Attestation Engagements
- Accounting Research Bulletins, APB Opinions
- Uniform CPA Examination Blueprints
- Independence Standards Board (ISB) Standards

Portions of various FASB and GASB documents, copyright property of the Financial Accounting Foundation, 401 Merritt 7, PO Box 5116, Norwalk, CT 06856-5116, are utilized with permission. Complete copies of these documents are available from the Financial Accounting Foundation. These selections include the following:

Financial Accounting Standards Board (FASB)

- The FASB Accounting Standards Codification™
- Statements of Financial Accounting Concepts
- FASB Statements, Interpretations, and Technical Bulletins

Governmental Accounting Standards Board (GASB)

- GASB Codification of Governmental Accounting and Financial Reporting Standards and GASB Statements
- GASB Concepts Statements
- GASB Interpretations and Technical Bulletins

Acknowledgements

Keeping the course materials updated and accurate would not be possible without the contribution of our team of content experts. Our team includes academics and professionals who have expertise and experience in their respective fields; several have had experience at the big 4 or have PhDs in areas related to the exam. All are passionate about helping candidates pass the exam and about UWorld's dedication to creating the highest quality materials.

For the 2024 course, the team created all new books and videos specifically designed to match the content of the 2024 AICPA Blueprints. It was a massive undertaking and could not have been possible without this team and the support of UWorld.

Auditing & Attestation

Auditing & Attestation

Introduction

Introduction

Introduction

Introduction

How to Best Use Your Course

Welcome to the UWorld CPA Review course! Our expert team is passionate about helping you succeed and have developed an award-winning program that is proven to yield results. Before you get started, please read through this guide on how to best use your course so that you can master all of the topics laid out for you in the AICPA Blueprints and ultimately pass the CPA Exam. At UWorld, our passion is to make the hard stuff easy to learn and understand.

Plan your Studies

When preparing for the CPA Exam, half the battle is setting yourself up for success with a solid plan from the get-go. This includes establishing short and long-term goals to ensure you're staying on track.

To get started, use the Study Planners in your course (located under "Study Resources"). Select a planner and customize to meet your timeframe to pass the exam. It is important to follow your planner steadily so that you can ensure you hit your goals. If you miss a day, make it up!

 Tip!

Download the app! This gives you access to everything your course offers while on-the-go.

Master the Concepts Through Active Learning

With this program, you will build your foundational knowledge and mastery of core exam topics through **active learning**. This evidence-based learning methodology centers around the principle that students retain information best when they actively participate in answering questions.

- **Begin with the Representative Task.** Read through each representative task carefully. (The Representative Tasks are from the AICPA Blueprints and are presented in our books and videos to guide you through the materials.) Pay particular attention to the words at the beginning of the task; they provide guidance on level and focus.

- **Scan the book chapter.** Do you feel confident with the material? If you do, you might want to move directly to the questions and begin to practice. If you find that you are hesitant about an area, read the book or watch the video to solidify your understanding before you practice on some questions.

- **Watch the videos.** If you prefer to absorb material on video rather than by reading the book, you will notice that the videos are deliberately set up in small segments. Our team created these segments so you can review what you need, either as part of the whole topic or for specific review of a smaller area.

- **Practice the questions.** In our question bank (our QBank) we have taken great care to provide you with very high quality questions and explanations. Each explanation not only tells you why the concept tested is important to understand, but also teaches you why the answer is correct and why the other answer choices are not correct. Images, tables, and links to definitions also help fill in gaps as you use the questions and explanations to learn by doing.

Track Your Progress and Performance

As you complete each chapter, track your progress and performance using our signature **SmartPath Predictive Technology™**. SmartPath is a data-driven platform that provides recommended targets based on previous students who have passed the CPA Exam. This is an important tool to help you study efficiently and gauge whether you are *exam-ready.* Your goal is to hit both your progress target (Questions Attempted) and performance target (Score) for each chapter. (Note that for the 2024 course, SmartPath targets are based on general performance of exam takers. We will continue to revise targets in SmartPath as we accumulate data from the 2024 exam.)

As you work through the material, don't worry about hitting your "Score" target right away and focus your efforts on hitting the "Questions Attempted" target first. This approach may feel uncomfortable, but trust that you are building your knowledge as you absorb the answer explanations.

Once you've completed all the topics in a chapter, you can go back and focus your efforts on hitting the "Score" target. If you are falling short, drill down in the Performance tab to see which topics need extra attention.

 Tip!

Don't over-study. **SmartPath™** helps determine when you can move on to the next topic.

Solidify the Concepts

Need extra help mastering the concept? Take advantage of the additional learning tools that are integrated into your course. For example, you could be working through a difficult question and find you need further explanation. No problem! There's a link to the supporting lecture right there in the question. Want to remember something for later review? Easily transfer content directly from the question to a digital flashcard. These are just a few ways we make it easy to navigate to and access the right tools you need at the right time.

These additional tools are designed to enhance your studies—**you do not necessarily need to read or watch all of this material!** Rather, use these tools as a means to improve on weak areas:

- **Video Lectures** – From the Lectures tab or directly integrated in the link at the bottom of each practice question, you have access to the profession's most motivating and effective lecturers. Lectures break down difficult topics into simplified concepts and provide helpful memory aids. These are especially recommended for visual and auditory learners.

- **Textbooks** – Digital eTextbooks are accessible side-by-side with the video lectures or in a printed format with some of our course packages. These can be used as a reference if you need further explanation of a concept. Many students also find it beneficial to follow along in the textbook while watching the lectures and either take notes directly in the physical books or by using the Notes feature and highlighting tool in the platform.

- **Digital Flashcards** – Create custom flashcards directly from your practice questions by clicking on the lightning bolt symbol. Depending on your program package, your course may also be pre-loaded with an "Expert Deck" of flashcards covering the most heavily tested topics. You can review all your cards in Study Mode or using our **Spaced-Repetition Technology.** This is an evidence-based learning method that presents cards you've marked as *difficult* more frequently, and cards you've marked as *easy* less frequently. The spacing of how and when the flashcards are introduced has been proven to increase retention and strengthen memory recall.

Get Exam-Ready

The final days leading up to the exam are a critical time in which you're going to want to review your SmartPath data and ask, "Am I *exam-ready*?" If you have hit all the targets, you are in a really good spot. However, if any areas are still marked "Needs Improvement," now is the time to focus your efforts on meeting those targets.

Finally, we recommend you **take at least one full practice exam before exam day** (click on the "Exam Sim" tab in the QBank). This allows you to hone your test-taking skills in an exam-like environment that follows the same 5-testlet, 4-hour structure as the exam.

AICPA Blueprints

The UWorld CPA Review course is based on the AICPA Blueprints, which show candidates what skills and content topics will be tested on the CPA Exam. You don't have to make tough decisions about what concepts to focus on. If you follow our methodology, you will be well on your way to passing the exam.

Let's take a look at what we mean by starting with the AICPA Blueprints. The Blueprints have four levels:

- Area
- Group
- Topic
- Representative Task

Each Representative Task also has a Skill level.

- Remembering & Understanding
- Application
- Analysis
- Evaluation (used only in AUD)

Here is a snapshot of a Blueprint with the levels and skills marked.

Area I – Business Analysis (40–50%)

Content group/topic	Remembering & Understanding	Application	Analysis	Evaluation	Representative Task
A. Current period/historical analysis, including the use of data					
1. Financial statement Analysis		✓			Determine attribute structures, format and sources of data needed to prepare financial statement analysis.
		✓			Compare current period financial statement accounts to prior periods or budget and explain variances.
		✓			Interpret financial statement fluctuations and ratios (e.g., profitability, liquidity, solvency, performance)
		✓			Use outputs (e.g., reports, visualizations)from data analytic techniques to identify patterns, trends, and correlations to explain an entity's results.
		✓			Derive the impact of transactions on the financial statements and notes to the financial statements.

BAR
Area I: Business Analysis
Group A: Current Period/Historical Analysis
Topic 1: Financial Statement Analysis

The Table of Contents of the BAR book shows how each UWorld textbook is set up to follow the order of the AICPA Blueprints, with

- Area
- Group
- Topic

In the pages of each book, we provide the Representative Tasks from the AICPA Blueprints. We did that to make a direct connection between the exam and our content. Our team deliberately focused on what the Tasks say and wrote study materials that match with the Task. There is no closer connection between what will be tested and what you are studying.

1.01 Financial Statement Analysis

Overview

A company appraises the past, present, and future execution of goals and economic fitness by performing **financial statement analysis** on its results from operations in a given period. Refer to the financial ratios used in the FAR exam for this section.

The results are viewed in relation to prior periods, budgets, and key performance indicators (ie, benchmarks). Companies **make informed decisions** using this analysis. The analysis is often presented using summaries and visualizations that present the financial data in an easy-to-understand, meaningful report.

Attribute Structures, Format, and Sources of Data

 Representative Task (Application): Determine attribute structures, format, and sources of data needed to prepare financial statement analysis.

Beyond connecting to the topics of the AICPA Blueprints, our team also differentiated the textbook content to match the skill levels of the Tasks.

- **Remembering & Understanding** tasks require you to understand the definitions and fundamentals of the topic. We have presented the information in these areas with an eye to creating clear explanations of the topics.

- **Application** tasks are more about using your knowledge in scenarios to indicate that you understand the concepts. Our authors have therefore provided examples that show you how to apply your knowledge in specific situations. Many of these examples are similar to questions that you will find on the exam.

- **Analysis** tasks require a higher level of thinking, many times leading you to choose one outcome over another or to make a decision. On the exam, these tasks will always be addressed in Task Based Simulations, or TBSs. The AICPA intentionally makes these more challenging to determine if you really know the material and can work with it as a professional. In our materials, our authors often guide you through the critical thinking required to work with TBSs.

- **Evaluation** tasks are only in the AUD section of the exam and are at the highest level of thinking. They go a step further than the Analysis level and require you to evaluate or judge different approaches or outcomes.

The CPA Exam

Within the AICPA Blueprints, there is information about how much time candidates have for each section and how many questions by question type each section contains. Question types include Multiple Choice Questions (MCQs) and Task Based Simulations (TBSs).

Section	Section Time	Multiple-Choice Questions (MCQs)	Task-Based Simulations (TBSs)
AUD – Core	4 hours	78	7
FAR – Core	4 hours	50	7
REG – Core	4 hours	72	8
BAR – Discipline	4 hours	50	7
ISC – Discipline	4 hours	82	6
TCP – Discipline	4 hours	68	7

Scoring Weight by Exam Section

The AICPA also shows candidates how the question types for each section are weighted and account for their overall score.

Section	Score Weighting	
	Multiple-Choice Questions (MCQs)	Task-Based Simulations (TBSs)
AUD – Core	50%	50%
FAR – Core	50%	50%
REG – Core	50%	50%
BAR – Discipline	50%	50%
ISC – Discipline	60%	40%
TCP – Discipline	50%	50%

Skill Allocations

As mentioned above, each Representative Task is tested at a specific Skill Level, and each part of the exam has its own weighting of the Skill Levels, as seen here.

Section	Remembering and Understanding	Application	Analysis	Evaluation
AUD – Core	30–40%	30–40%	15–25%	5–15%
FAR – Core	5–15%	45–55%	35–45%	–
REG – Core	25–35%	35–45%	25–35%	–
BAR – Discipline	10–20%	45–55%	30–40%	–
ISC – Discipline	55–65%	20–30%	10–20%	–
TCP – Discipline	5–15%	55–65%	25–35%	–

Content Allocations

The AICPA Blueprints address how coverage of the various content areas is allocated in each exam. Using the UWorld system that ties directly to the Blueprint structure, it is easy to see which topics are covered to what extent.

AUD

Content Area		Allocation
Area I	Ethics, Professional Responsibilities and General Principles	15–25%
Area II	Assessing Risk and Developing a Planned Response	25–35%
Area III	Performing Further Procedures and Obtaining Evidence	30–40%
Area IV	Forming Conclusions and Reporting	10–20%

FAR

Content Area		Allocation
Area I	Financial Reporting	30–40%
Area II	Select Balance Sheet Accounts	30–40%
Area III	Select Transactions	25–35%

REG

Content Area		Allocation
Area I	Ethics, Professional Responsibilities and Federal Tax Procedures	10–20%
Area II	Business Law	15–25%
Area III	Federal Taxation of Property Transactions	5–15%
Area IV	Federal Taxation of Individuals	22–32%
Area V	Federal Taxation of Entities (including tax preparation)	23–33%

BAR

Content Area		Allocation
Area I	Business Analysis	40–50%
Area II	Technical Accounting and Reporting	35–45%
Area III	State and Local Governments	10–20%

ISC

Content Area		Allocation
Area I	Information Systems and Data Management	35–45%
Area II	Security, Confidentiality and Privacy	35–45%
Area III	Considerations for System and Organization Controls (SOC) Engagements	15–25%

TCP

Content Area		Allocation
Area I	Tax Compliance and Planning for Individuals and Personal Financial Planning	30–40%
Area II	Entity Tax Compliance	30–40%
Area III	Entity Tax Planning	10–20%
Area IV	Property Transactions (disposition of assets)	10–20%

Exam Testlets

Each section of the 2024 exam is divided into five testlets. Two testlets cover MCQs and 3 testlets cover TBSs. Not all sections have an equal number of MCQs and TBSs, as the following chart shows.

Section	Testlet					Total	
	1	2	3	4	5		
	MCQ	MCQ	TBS	TBS	TBS	MCQ	TBS
AUD - Core	39	39	2	3	2	78	7
FAR - Core	25	25	2	3	2	50	7
REG - Core	36	36	2	3	3	72	8
BAR - Discipline	25	25	2	3	2	50	7
ISC - Discipline	41	41	1	3	2	82	6
TCP - Discipline	34	34	2	3	2	68	7

Finally, to manage your time effectively in the exam, we recommend that you:

- Use 75 seconds per multiple choice question as a benchmark.
- Allocate 15-20 minutes per task-based simulation, depending on complexity.
- Take the standard 15-minute break after the 3rd testlet; it doesn't count against your time.

To see the full AICPA Blueprints, visit
https://www.aicpa.org/becomeacpa/cpaexam/examinationcontent

We hope you found some helpful information in this introduction and that you can start the study process with confidence! As Roger always says, "You do not have to be a genius to pass the CPA Exam. If you study, you will pass!" You've got this.

AUD

Area I: Ethics, Professional Responsibilities, and General Principles

AUD 1
Ethics, Independence and Professional Responsibilities

1.01 AICPA Code of Professional Conduct

Overview

 Representative Task (Remembering & Understanding): Understand the principles, rules, and interpretations included in the AICPA Code of Professional Conduct.

 Representative Task (Application): Apply the principles, rules and interpretations included in the AICPA Code of Professional Conduct to situations.

CPAs are subject to various regulators such as the SEC or the PCAOB. Each of these agencies, organizations, regulators, and societies have rules and guidelines that affect the behavior of CPAs. One of the most comprehensive is the **AICPA Code of Professional Conduct (Code)**. Many sets of rules and codes of ethics related to accountants are largely based on the Code, which is regularly tested on the CPA exam.

The consequences of *violating the Code* will not be more severe than the **loss of the CPA's membership** in the AICPA, which is why the rules and guidelines are expressed as obligations of "members."

Note that violations of other codes of conduct (state board of accountancy) may result in a prohibition against performing certain types of services, the inability to serve certain regulated clients, or, in some cases, the suspension or loss (revocation) of the CPA certificate. This could result from the commission of a felony or the filing of a fraudulent tax return, whether for the CPA or for a client.

In addition to the Code, a CPA will consider the ethical requirements of all applicable bodies and agencies, which may include:

- State societies
- State boards of accountants and related regulatory agencies
- The SEC, PCAOB, GAO, and DOL
- Taxing authorities

The Code is organized in four parts:

- The Preface, which is applicable to all members
- Part 1, which is applicable to members in public practice
- Part 2, which applies to members in industry
- Part 3, which applies to all other members, including those retired or unemployed.

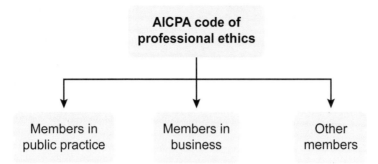

Preface

The Preface applicable to *all members* and consists of six topics:

Topic 100 – Provides:

- An overview, including an explanation of the structure of the Code
- A requirement that members adhere to the Code's rules based on an understanding of the rules and the voluntary actions of the CPA
- An indication that CPAs are expected to follow interpretations, and may be required to justify departures from them
- An indication that, when a CPA has multiple professional roles, the highest and most restrictive level of standards should be applied.

Topic 200 – Describes the structure of the **Code** and indicates its **applicability** to the services performed by a CPA. It indicates that, with few exceptions, the Code applies to **all professional services** performed by a CPA, except when rules identify services to which they do not apply.

AICPA Code of Professional Conduct

Topics and Subtopics	Applicable to Members in		
	Public Practice	Business	Other
Preface	X	X	X
Introduction	X	X	X
Integrity and Objectivity	X	X	
Independence	X		
General Standards	X	X	
Acts Discreditable	X	X	X
Fees and Other Types of Remuneration	X		
Advertising and Other Forms of Solicitation	X		
Confidential Information	X		
Form of Organization and Name	X		

Topic 300 – Describes the **principles** embedded in the Code. In the preamble, it reminds CPAs of their **responsibility of self-discipline** exceeding the simple compliance with applicable laws and regulations; responsibilities to the public, to clients, and to colleagues; and a commitment to act with honor despite the possibility of personal sacrifice that may result.

- *Responsibilities* – Requires the application of sensitive professional and moral judgment at all times and cooperation with other members of the profession to improve the art of accounting, to maintain the public's confidence in the profession, and to carry out the profession's responsibility for self-governance.

- *Public Interest* – Requires a commitment to professionalism and acting in a manner that serves the public interest and honors the trust that the public has in the accounting profession. The public interest is the collective well-being of the community of people and institutions that are served by the accounting profession, which requires the accountant to act with integrity when confronted by conflicts among various stakeholders and perform services applying integrity, objectivity, and due professional care.

- *Integrity* – Requires that the highest level of integrity be applied through the CPA's honesty and candor, within the constraints of client confidentiality, and an unwillingness to subordinate service or the public trust to personal gain or advantage.

- *Objectivity and Independence* – Requires independence, both in *fact* and in *appearance*, when performing auditing and other attestation services, for which standards require independence, and that the CPA remain free of conflicts of interest and exercise impartiality and intellectual honesty in the performance of all professional services.

- *Due Care* – Requires compliance with technical and ethical standards while continuing to endeavor to improve the CPA's competence and quality of services, which is accomplished through a commitment to learning throughout the CPA's professional life, and diligence in the provision of professional services enabling performance to the best of the CPA's ability. Due care also requires a CPA to remain competent and to understand the limitations to that competence, which may result in consultation or the referral of services, and to adequately plan and supervise all professional activities for which the CPA is responsible.

- *Scope and Nature of Services* – Requires the CPA to evaluate whether or not services can be performed in a manner consistent with the principles of the Code by practicing in a firm with appropriate quality control policies and procedures commensurate with the services being performed; making certain that services performed for an audit client do not create a conflict of interest; and that activities in which the CPA participates are appropriate for members of the CPA profession.

Topic 400 – Provides definitions of terms that are used throughout the Code.

Topic 500 – Specifies that only the Code is authoritative and that guidance provided by the staff of the Professional Ethics Division of the AICPA is nonauthoritative guidance.

Topic 600 – Indicates the status of new, revised, or pending interpretations and other guidance. It specifies that new or revised authoritative interpretations and other guidance are effective as of the last day of the month in which the pronouncement or notice is published in the Journal of Accountancy.

Part 1 – Members in Public Practice

Part 1 is applicable to members in public practice (MIPP), including government auditors. When a CPA is serving both as a MIPP and as a member in business (MIB), both Parts 1 and 2 will apply.

Part 1 presents the **conceptual framework approach** to applying the Code. It provides a member with a means of evaluating compliance with the code when confronted with a decision or other circumstance that is not directly addressed. Applying the conceptual framework approach cannot overcome a clear violation of the rules or interpretations of the Code. It can, however, assist the CPA in determining if the Code has been violated when it is not necessarily clear.

Conceptual Framework

 Representative Task (Application): Apply the Conceptual Framework for Members in Public Practice and Members in Business included in the AICPA Code of Professional Conduct to situations that could present threats to compliance with the rules included in the Code.

The conceptual framework approach involves a **3-step process.** Applying the conceptual framework approach *cannot overcome* a clear violation of the rules or interpretations of the Code. It can, however, assist the CPA in determining if the Code has been violated when it is not necessarily clear.

Threats and safeguards approach

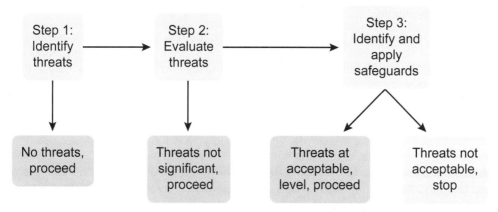

Threats

There are seven categories of threats identified in the Code. They are **not mutually exclusive** in that a single threat may fall under more than one category. Threats are evaluated both individually and in the aggregate. The threat categories are:

Self-review

The **threat of self-review** which exists when the accountant performs **some form of evaluation** of matters that were previously influenced by the accountant's judgment, such as when an accountant is performing an attest service in relation to a client's financial statements when the accountant's firm performed bookkeeping services for that client.

The self-review threat is the threat that the **accountant will assume a level of reliability** without performing an appropriate level of testing or other due diligence.

Advocacy

An advocacy threat exists when the accountant's actions effectively **promote a client's interests** or position. For example, the accountant is:

- Providing forensic accounting services to the client in a conflict with third parties.
- Providing investment advice for an officer, director, or shareholder holding 10% or more of the client's shares.
- Endorsing the products or services of a client.

Adverse Interest

The threat of an adverse interest exists when the **interests of the client are in conflict** with the interests of the accountant, which may inhibit the accountant from applying objectivity. This would be the case, for example, if the client and the accountant were involved in, or anticipating, litigation against each other.

Familiarity

The threat of familiarity results from a **close and longstanding relationship** with a client, potentially causing the accountant to become too sympathetic to the client's interests or too trusting of the client's work or products. Examples of the types of relationships that create a familiarity threat include:

- The spouse, a family member, or a close friend of an engagement team member is employed by the client.
- The member has a close and significant business relationship with an officer, director, or significant shareholder of the client.
- Senior firm personnel have a long-standing relationship with the client.

Undue Influence

The threat of undue influence results from attempts by management or others to **exercise an excessive amount of influence** over the accountant. This may involve:

- A client's threat to replace the accountant as a result of a disagreement.
- A client exerting pressure to limit an engagement to reduce fees.

Self-Interest

The threat of self-interest occurs when the accountant has the **opportunity to obtain a potential benefit** from an interest in, or another relationship with, a client. This would be the case if:

- The accountant has a financial interest in the client, the value of which may be affected by the results of the service being performed.
- The accountant enters into an arrangement that involves a contingent fee rather than one that is predetermined.
- The accountant relies excessively on the fees earned from the client.

Management Participation

The threat of **management participation** occurs when the accountant **takes on the role** of management for the client or **performs management functions** on behalf of the client.

Identification of threats to auditors' independence

Safeguards

Safeguards are **controls that eliminate or reduce threats**, ranging from prohibitions against circumstances that create threats to procedures that counteract the potential risk associated with a threat. Safeguards are considered effective if they eliminate a threat or reduce it to an acceptable level.

Three kinds of safeguards exist:

1. Safeguards created by the profession, legislation, or regulation. Examples include:
    - Ethics education, training requirements, and continuing professional education
    - Professional standards and threat of discipline
    - External reviews of a firm's quality controls
    - Legislation regulating firm's professionals
    - Licensure requirements

2. Safeguards implemented by the **client**. The client has, for example:
    - Knowledgeable and experienced managers
    - A tone at the top regarding ethical behavior and compliance
    - Effective policies and procedures for compliance and fair reporting
    - Appropriate ethics policies and procedures
    - Effective governance structure, including an active audit committee
    - Policies to prevent client from hiring a firm to provide services that would impair independence or objectivity

3. Safeguards implemented by the **firm**. Examples:
    - Strong leadership emphasizing compliance and acting in the public interest
    - Policies and procedures to implement and monitor engagement quality control
    - Designation of qualified senior manager to oversee firm's quality control system
    - Training and timely communication of firm policies and procedures
    - An effective internal disciplinary system
    - Rotation of engagement team senior personnel
    - Policies precluding partners from being compensated for selling nonattest services to attest client

In performance of any professional service, a member shall maintain **objectivity and integrity**, avoid conflicts of interest, and not knowingly misrepresent facts or subordinate their judgment to others.

Integrity and Objectivity (Topic 1.100)

In performance of any professional service, a member shall maintain **objectivity and integrity**, avoid conflicts of interest, and not knowingly misrepresent facts or subordinate their judgment to others.

Conflicts of Interest

Conflicts of interest arise when a CPA is performing professional services related to a matter for two or more clients with conflicting interests or when the interests of the CPA or the CPA's firm conflict with those of the client.

Before accepting an engagement or a relationship, the CPA should **identify a potential conflict(s)** that threaten independence and objectivity, and should continue to monitor as engagement progresses.

When an **actual conflict is identified** by any member, the Conceptual Framework should be applied and engagements should be refused or terminated if the risk of violation is unacceptably high. In evaluating possible conflicts of interest, members should ask: *Would a reasonable and informed third party conclude that a conflict exists?*

Safeguards may reduce the threat of a conflict of interest to an acceptable level. For example, maintaining separate engagement teams with clear policies and procedures for maintaining confidentiality may be an adequate safeguard to reduce the threat of a conflict of interest to a reasonable level when the conflict arises from performing services or two or more clients with conflicting interests related to the subject matter of the engagements. Additional safeguards include a regular review by a senior manager not involved in the engagement and/or consulting with third parties, such as a professional body or legal counsel.

Conflicts should be **disclosed** to clients and affected third parties, even if threats to compliance are at an acceptable level.

- General disclosure (e.g., "We audit several firms in your industry sector") may suffice.
- Specific disclosure (e.g., "We advise your closest competitor who would love to have access to your confidential information that we possess") may be needed, however.

Documenting the threat-reducing process is wise.

Members should always comply with federal (including Internal Revenue Service Circular 230), state, or local provisions that are more restrictive than the code.

Serving as a director on the board of an entity may create a conflict of interest if the entity, such as a bank, enters into or considers transactions with the CPA's clients. The member may consider limiting the relationship to a consulting arrangement, excluding transactions that may involve the CPA's clients. If, however, the CPA does serve as a director, threats and safeguards should be evaluated to make certain that threats are at an acceptable level.

Gifts and Entertainment

Offering gifts or entertainment to a client or accepting gifts or entertainment from a client may create various threats to the CPA's compliance with the Code, including threats associated with self-interest, familiarity, and undue influence.

Objectivity and integrity are threatened if the client (including its officers, directors, and 10% shareholders) give gifts or entertainment to the firm or its members (or vice versa).

A violation is presumed if:

- The member receives gifts or entertainment from a client that violate the member's or client's policies or applicable laws and regulations and
- The member knows or is reckless in not knowing of the violation.

If no rules are violated, then there is no problem if the gifts or entertainment are "reasonable in the circumstances." Factors in determining **reasonableness** include:

- The nature of the gift or entertainment
- The occasion giving rise to the gift
- The cost or value of the gift or entertainment
- The nature, frequency, and value of other gifts
- Whether the entertainment was associated with active conduct of the business

Preparing and Reporting Information

There would be a violation of the Code if a member has:

- Made, permitted, or directed another to make materially false and misleading entries in an entity's financial statements or records,

- Failed to correct misstatements when having the authority to do so,

- Signed, permitted, or directed another to sign misleading documents,

- Exercised discretion with the intent to mislead, or

- When relying on the work of others, either inside or outside the organizations, failed to ensure that the work was useful, honest, and accurate by taking into account such factors as the reputation, expertise, objectivity, and resources available to the third party.

When a member knows or has reason to know that information, he or she is associated with is misleading. The member should apply appropriate safeguards to seek to resolve the matter by getting the information correct and informing users who have already been misled by it. This process may require talking to supervisors, consulting with professional bodies, and perhaps even considering resigning. These procedures are spelled out in more detail in the next section regarding subordination of judgement.

Subordination of Judgment

Differences of opinion between a member and supervisors or other individuals within the member's organization may threaten the member's ability to comply with the integrity and objectivity rule due to the potential subordination of the member's judgment.

A supervisor, for example, may take a position that the member believes is not in compliance with standards, represents a material misstatement of facts, or violates applicable laws or regulations. In this situation, the member should:

- **Evaluate** whether the threat is at an *unacceptable level*, which occurs if the position taken would result in a material misrepresentation or legal violation. If the threat is not significant, then nothing further need be done.

- Discuss the matter with the supervisor if there is a significant threat.
  - If the discussion does not resolve the difference of opinion, the member should go over the supervisor's head.

- If, after discussion with people up the chain, the member is still worried that the right thing is not going to be done, the member should, in no particular order, invoke the following safeguards:
  - Determine whether the organization's policies and procedures have any additional requirements for reporting differences of opinion.
  - Determine whether there is a duty to report to external authorities.
  - Consult legal counsel.
  - Fully document the situation.

- If the member ultimately concludes that the threat of misrepresentation or legal violation cannot be reduced to an acceptable level, **they should consider resigning from** the firm and **taking appropriate steps** to eliminate their exposure to subordination of judgment.

- Although the code does not require the member to resign, only to *consider it*, it goes on to say that "nothing in this interpretation precludes a member from resigning from the organization at any time."

- Resigning from the firm would not necessarily discharge all obligations, such as to report to regulatory authorities or an external auditor.

Pressure to Breach the Rules

Pressure to breach the rules or ethical conflicts may arise as a result of various circumstances, but most relate to a circumstance where:

- Internal or external pressures create obstacles that interfere with following an appropriate course of action
- Conflicts arise in applying relevant professional and legal standards, such as when reporting suspected fraud may be a violation of client confidentiality rules.

Examples of pressure that could result in breach of the Integrity and Objectivity Rule include the following:

- **Conflict of interest**: Joe is a member working for ABC Sales Co. and is charged with hiring a caterer for the company's events. Joe's supervisor's uncle is a caterer and attempts to convince Joe to accept his bid over similar bids by other caterers.
- **Presentation of information**: Miko is a member working for DEF Co. and her boss strongly urges her to treat personal expenses he has incurred as business expenses so that DEF will reimburse them.
- **Due care**: Member Carlos is an auditor for the GHI accounting firm and his superiors put him in charge of the audit of JKL Corporation. They give him such a small team and such a tight deadline that it will be impossible for him to do an audit that would comply with GAAS in time. When he protests, they say: "Just shut up and get it done."
- **Financial interests**: CFO Mandy, a member of the AICPA, is preparing the annual revenue numbers for MNO Corporation. Her CEO, Tina, reminds Mandy that Tina will receive a huge bonus if revenue targets are met and that there are lots of accountants out there with the qualifications to replace Mandy.
- **Gifts or Entertainment**: Member Lia is a tax accountant for PQR Accounting. PQR hopes to be hired by Mega Corporation to prepare its tax returns. Mega's CFO, Tad, will make the hiring decision. Lia's superior, Pat, suggests strongly that Lia buy an expensive and rare vintage milk bottle that Tad collects, and to give it to him secretly.

If a member finds himself or herself under inappropriate pressure to violate the Code's rules, they may **consult with superiors or legal counsel**, escalate the matter within the organization, consider resigning, etc.

Client Advocacy

When performing certain nonattest services for a client, such as tax or consulting services, the member may be in **position to act as an advocate** for the client in supporting the client's position on accounting or financial reporting issues to other engagement team members or to standard setters or regulators. These services may **pose threats** to the member's ability to comply with the integrity and objectivity rules that should be evaluated.

Use of a Third-Party Service Provider

Use of a third-party service provider in a professional engagement may expose the third party to confidential information posing a threat to the member's ability to comply with the integrity and objectivity rules.

- Before disclosing confidential client information to a third-party service provider, the member should inform the client, preferably in writing. If the client objects, the member should either not outsource or decline the engagement.

There is no problem if the third-party service provider provides only administrative support (e.g., record storage, software application hosting, authorized e-file transmittal services).

Independence (Topic 1.200)

 Representative Task (Application): Apply the Conceptual Framework for Independence included in the AICPA Code of Professional Conduct to situations that could present threats to compliance with the rules included in the Code.

A member in public practice shall be independent in the performance of professional services when independence is required by applicable professional standards.

Independence is the ability to **act with integrity and objectivity** and applies to a *covered member and to the member's immediate family,* including the member's spouse or spousal equivalent, and all dependents, whether related or not.

Covered members include:

- Members of the attest engagement team

- Individuals in a position to influence the attest engagement

- Partners, partner equivalents, or managers providing more than 10 hours of nonattest services to the attest client with a fiscal year

- Partners or partner equivalents in the same office in which the lead engagement partner for the attest engagement practices

- The firm or the firm's employee benefit plan

- An entity controlled by any of the above or two or more of the above acting together

 For agreed-upon procedure engagements only, covered members are limited to those participating in or directly supervising the engagement and individuals consulting with the engagement team on technical or industry-related issues.

Independence in fact and in appearance is required. Independence in fact refers to independence in mind, the state of mind that enables the member to act with integrity and exercise objectivity and professional skepticism. Independence in appearance addresses the need to avoid circumstances that would make the member look like independence was lacking.

A covered member:

- Must maintain independence for attest services: examinations (including audits), reviews and agreed-upon procedure (ERA) engagements

- Does not need be independent for:
    - Compilations – Independence is expected, but not required; lack of independence must be disclosed.
    - Taxes
    - Consultations
    - F/S preparation engagements
    - Other nonattest services, such as bookkeeping or payroll

When events, circumstances, or conditions that might impair independence *are not addressed* directly in the Code, *the member is required to apply the conceptual framework approach*, applied in the same manner as the conceptual framework approach related to the Code itself.

A CPA is considering whether to accept an engagement to prepare financial statements for a new client. Which of the following statements is correct regarding the independence of the CPA?

- The CPA should be independent of the client.

- The CPA is not required to make a determination of whether the CPA is independent of the client.

- The CPA is required to disclose in the engagement report any relationships with the client's personnel.

- The CPA should obtain management's understanding regarding the benefits of an accountant being independent of a client.

Required	Not required
Attest services:	Nonattest services:
• Audits	• Financial statement preparation
• Reviews	• Tax return preparation
• Examinations	• Consulting
• Agreed-upon Procedures	• Compilations*

*Compilations do not require independence but a lack of independence must be disclosed.

Preparation engagements are *nonattest* services in which CPAs put together financial statements (F/S) and are governed by SSARS. They do not require CPAs to form an opinion or conclusion about the F/S, issue a report, or disclose relationships with client personnel. Because CPAs do not attest to the accuracy or completeness of the F/S in a preparation engagement, they **do not need to be independent.**

Accounting Firms

When a firm is part of a network of firms, all firms within that network are required to comply with the independence rules in relation to an attest client of any of the firms within that network if the use of the audit or review report for the client is not restricted. In other cases, the covered member should consider any threats to independence that the covered member knows of or has reason to believe may be created by the interests or relationships of other firms within the network.

A firm is considered to be part of a network of firms if the **firms cooperate** to enhance their ability to provide professional services through cross referrals and other means **and** has **one or more** of the following characteristics:

Characteristics of Network Firms

- A common brand name or initials that are part of the firm name
- Common control through ownership or management
- Sharing of profit and costs with the exception of certain costs such as those of operating the association and other costs that are not material to the firm
- Collaboration to create a common business strategy that member firms are held accountable for implementing
- Sharing of significant professional resources, such as systems and staff
- Uniform quality control policies monitored and enforced by the association

A member whose independence becomes impaired after the issuance of a report may reissue the report provided the member or the member's firm does not perform procedures associated with updating or dual dating the report.

An indemnification clause in an engagement letter, in which an attest client holds the member harmless from liability resulting from knowing misrepresentations by management does not impair independence. Independence would be impaired, however, if an attest firm indemnifies an attest client from liability arising directly or indirectly from the acts of the attest client. An alternative dispute resolution clause in an engagement letter would not impair independence.

Unpaid Fees

When fees for services that were performed more than one year before the date of the current-year report remain unpaid, this creates a threat to independence that cannot be reduced to an acceptable level. This is true even if the fees have not been billed to the client and if the client has signed a note for the amount owed. This does not apply, however, to unpaid fees due from a client in bankruptcy.

Financial Interests – Overview

In general, a member who possesses or has a commitment to acquire a **direct or material indirect financial interest** in an attest client creates a **self-interest threat** that cannot be reduced to an acceptable level and the member's independence would be impaired.

The same would be true if a partner or professional employee of the firm, including the partner's immediate family or any group of those individuals acting together, owned more than *5 percent* of an attest client during the period of the attest engagement.

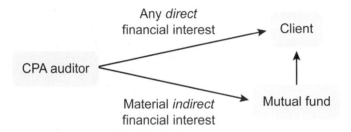

Certain other financial interests may or may not create threats to independence that cannot be reduced to acceptable level, impairing independence.

Threats to independence may be reduced to an acceptable level when a member receives an unsolicited direct or indirect financial interest in an attest client, such as through a gift that is not material to the member, if the member applies two safeguards:

- The financial interest is disposed of **within 30 days** of learning about and gaining the ability to dispose of the interest, or sooner if practicable; and

- The member does not participate on the attest engagement team during the period in which the covered member does not have the right to dispose of a material financial interest.

A CPA in charge of the external audit of a nonissuer received an unexpected inheritance that includes 100 shares of the audit client's common stock. Which of the following actions should the CPA take to avoid violating independence rules?

- Decline to accept the inheritance.
- Petition the AICPA for an independence exception from unforeseen circumstances.
- Resign from the audit firm.
- Sell or donate the stock within 30 days after receipt of ownership rights.

Is independence impaired?

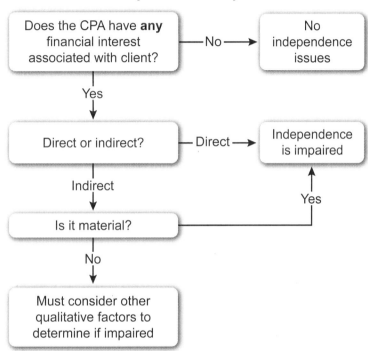

CPAs assigned to an attest engagement should not participate in the engagement if they become aware of a material (direct or indirect) unsolicited financial interest related to that client when they do not have the right to dispose of it. CPAs who become aware of—and have the rights to **dispose** of—the interest must dispose of it as soon as practical but **no later than 30 days** after receiving it.

Financial Interests – Mutual Funds

Ownership of shares of a **mutual fund** constitutes a **direct financial interest** in the mutual fund. Ownership of the underlying investments of the mutual fund are indirect. The response to these interests varies depending on the proportion of the mutual fund owned by the member and the diversity of the mutual fund's holdings.

- Ownership of 5% or less of a diversified mutual fund results in an immaterial indirect financial interest in its investments.
- Ownership of more than 5% of a diversified fund, or an ownership interest in an undiversified fund, should be evaluated to determine if the member holds a material indirect financial interest.

Financial Interests – Other

Financial interests in retirement, savings, compensation, or similar firm-sponsored plans may be direct or indirect financial interests, based on circumstances.

A partnership interest is a direct financial interest in a general or a limited partnership.

- A general partner has a direct financial interest in the partnership's financial interests.

- A limited partner has an indirect financial interest in the partnership's financial interests unless the limited partner controls the partnership, supervises or participates in the partnership's investment decisions, or has the ability to replace the general partner or participate in investment decisions, in which case the interest is direct.

An ownership interest in a limited liability company (LLC) is a direct financial interest in the LLC.

- The managing member and those with the ability to control, supervise, or participate in the LLC's investment decisions have direct financial interests in the LLC's financial interests.

- Others without the ability to control, supervise, or participate in the LLC's investment decisions have indirect financial interests.

The account owner of a Section 529 Prepaid Tuition Plan has a direct financial interest in the plan and an indirect financial interest in the underlying investments. The owner of a Section 529 Savings Plan has a direct financial interest in both the plan and its investments due to the ability to view the investment options of different plans prior to selection.

Trusts and Estates

If an estate or trust has any direct or any material indirect financial interest in an attest client, a threat to the member's independence would not be at an acceptable level if the member served as trustee of the trust, or executor or administrator of the estate, during the period of the professional engagement if any of the following also applied:

- The member had the authority to make investment decisions for the trust or estate;

- The trust or estate either owned, or was committed to acquire, an equity interest in excess of 10% of the attest client's outstanding equity securities; or

- The value of the equity interest in the attest client exceeded 10% of the total assets of the trust or estate.

When the CPA is the grantor of a trust, the trust and its investments are considered direct financial interests of the CPA, even if the trust is a blind trust, if the trust's investments ultimately revert to the CPA, or if the CPA:

- Can amend or revoke the trust;

- Has the authority to control the trust; or

- Has the ability to participate in, or supervise, the trust's investment decisions.

If none of those circumstances apply, the CPA has a direct financial interest in the trust and an indirect financial interest in the trust's underlying investments.

Participation in Employee Benefit Plans

When a CPA is a participant in an employee benefit plan that is either sponsored by an attest client or is, itself, an attest client, independence is generally impaired due to the self-interest threat. The threat would be reduced to an acceptable level, however, when the CPA is a participant in a public employee retirement plan that is sponsored by more than one governmental organization, one of which is the employer of the CPA, and the following requirements are met.:

- The CPA is required as an employee to participate in the plan, which is offered to all employees in comparable positions

- The CPA does not influence or control key aspects of the plan such as investment strategy, benefits, or other management activities

- The CPA may not serve in a role prohibited by ET 1.275, *Current Employment or Association with an Attest Client*.

When, as a result of an immediate family member's employment, that family member is a participant in a plan that is an attest client or is sponsored by an attest client, the requirements of ET 1.270, *Family Relationships with Attest Clients*, are to be complied with.

Depository, Brokerage, and Other Accounts

A firm may have funds on deposit at an attest client that is a bank or similar depository institution without impairing its independence as long as the firm concludes that the likelihood that the institution will experience financial difficulties is remote.

An individual's independence would not be impaired as long as:

- The balance on deposit is fully insured

- The aggregate of uninsured amounts is not material to the individual

- Uninsured amounts that are considered material are reduced to an amount that is not material within 30 days of when it became, or becomes, material to the individual.

When a CPA maintains **brokerage or other accounts** with an attest client that is an insurance company, investment advisor, broker-dealer, bank, or other member of the financial services industry, impairment of independence may be avoided if certain safeguards are in place:

- The attest client is providing services applying its normal terms, procedures, and requirements

- Any risk of loss, such as from the client's bankruptcy, insolvency, fraud or illegal acts, or other circumstances, is not material to the individual after considering protections from federal, state, or other insurers or from other sources.

An **insurance policy** from a stock or mutual life insurance company is not considered a financial interest unless the policy offers the policy holder an investment option. Holding such a policy would create a self-interest threat to independence only if the policy was not obtained under the issuing entity's normal terms, procedures, and requirements.

When a CPA holds an insurance policy with an investment option, independence may be impaired.

- If not obtained under the insurer's normal terms, procedures, and requirements, threats to independence would not be at an acceptable level.

- When obtained under the insurer's normal terms, procedures, and requirements, a direct financial interest would be created if the CPA participates in or oversees investment decisions and the self-interest threat would be at an unacceptable level

Loans, Leases, and Guarantees

Loans to or from an attest client, an officer or director of an attest client with decision-making ability or influence, or an individual with a beneficial ownership interest providing significant influence create a *self-interest threat* that may not be at an acceptable level. Unsecured loans that are not material to the CPA's net worth, home mortgage loans, secured loans, and student loans will not raise the threat to an unacceptable level if certain safeguards are all in place:

- The loan was obtained under the institution's normal terms, procedures, and requirements.

- The loan was obtained prior to the institution becoming an attest client; from a lender that was not an attest client but was subsequently sold to an attest client; or prior to the CPA becoming a covered member.

- The loan has been maintained as current at all times as long as the borrower has been a covered member and there have been no changes to the terms of the loan not provided for in the original agreement.

- The estimated value of collateral at least equals the outstanding balance of the home mortgage or secured loan.

Obtaining one of the following from a lending institution under its normal lending procedures, terms, and requirements would *not impair* a CPA's independence as long as the CPA is in compliance with the terms of the agreement at all times:

- Automobile loans or leases collateralized by the automobile;

- Loans fully collateralized by the cash surrender value of an insurance policy or cash deposits at the same institution; or

- Credit cards, retail installment loans, home improvement loans, and overdraft protection with an aggregate balance of no more than $10,000 after payment of the most recent monthly statement, made within the grace period.

A *lease arrangement* with an attest client would not raise threats to an unacceptable level if all the following safeguards are in place:

- The lease meets the criteria to be accounted for as an operating lease under GAAP.

- The terms and conditions are comparable to other similar leases.

- All payments are made in accordance with the lease terms.

Family Relationships with Attest Clients

Two categories of family relationships can create potential independence problems.

Family members

- Immediate family members = spouse, spousal equivalent, dependent
- Close relatives = parents, siblings, nondependent children

Immediate Family

In general, members of a CPA's immediate family, which include the CPA's spouse or spousal equivalent, and all dependents, whether related or not, are required to comply with the independence rules to avoid impairing the independence of the CPA. Any financial interests of immediate family members are attributed to the CPA, including when determining the materiality of an indirect financial interest.

Without impairing a CPA's independence, an immediate family member may:

- Be employed by an attest client provided it is not in a key position, which would create the threats of management participation, familiarity, and self-interest.

- Participate in an employee benefit plan that is an attest client or is sponsored by an attest client as long as the family member is not in a key position with the client, the plan is offered to all employees in comparable positions, the family member is not part of the plan's governance, and the family member does not participate in or oversee investment decisions.

- Participate in a retirement plan that is not an attest client or sponsored by an attest client but that holds an investment in an attest client provided:

  ○ The CPA does not participate in, and cannot influence, the attest engagement;

  ○ The family member has no other investment options available; and

  ○ If given the opportunity to invest in a nonattest client or a nonclient, the family member disposes of financial interests in the attest client as soon as is practicable, no later than 30 days after the option becomes available.

Close Relatives

Actions and circumstances related to close relatives, which are parents, siblings, and nondependent children, may also result in an impairment of a member's independence. This would be the case if a *member of the engagement team* has a close relative:

- In a key position with the attest client during the period covered by the engagement or during the period of the engagement;

- With a financial interest in the attest client that is known or believed to be material to the relative or enables the relative to exercise significant influence over the attest client.

Independence will be impaired if an *individual in a position to influence the engagement team or any partner or partner equivalent in the office of the engagement partner* has a close relative:

- In a key position with the attest client during the period covered by the engagement or during the period of the engagement

- With a financial interest in the attest client that is known or believed to be material to the relative **and** enables the relative to exercise significant influence over the attest client

Family relationships and independence

Immediate family	• Spouse or equivalent • Dependent (related or not)	Independence rules same as for CPA, except: • Employment by client OK if not in key position • Limited forms of compensation by, and investment in, client acceptable
Close relative	• Parent • Sibling • Nondependent child	Independence impaired if: • Relative in key position with client, or • Financial interest in client material to relative or gives significant influence over client

According to professional standards, which of the following circumstances will impair a CPA's independence?

- An employee at the CPA's firm who works in another state and does not work for the client that she has a material indirect financial interest in.

- The CPA has a car loan with a financial institution client.

- The CPA's dependent stepchild has a direct immaterial financial interest in the client.

- The client recently exceeded the 90-day limit for outstanding unpaid invoices due to the CPA

Independence between CPA and client can be affected by relationships between the CPA's immediate family or close relatives and the client. Close relatives include parents, siblings, and nondependent children (including stepchildren). Immediate family includes spouses and dependents (related or not). A **dependent stepchild** is therefore **immediate family**.

In determining independence, relationships between a CPA's immediate family (eg, dependents) and client are generally treated as if they existed between the CPA and client. **Direct financial interests**, even if immaterial, always **impair independence**.

Current Employment or Association with an Attest Client

When a member is employed or associated with an attest client as a director, officer, employee, promoter, underwriter, voting trustee, or trustee of a pension or profit-sharing plan during the period covered by financial statements or during the period of the professional engagement, the familiarity, management participation, advocacy, or self-review threats will be raised to an unacceptable level and independence will be impaired.

 A member may serve as an adjunct faculty member for an attest client educational institution provided the member:

- Is not in a key position with the educational institution

- Does not participate on, nor can influence, the engagement team

- Is employed by the educational institution in a nontenured or part-time position

- Is not a participant in an employee benefit plan, and

- Does not assume management responsibilities or set policy for the institution.

Threats would be at an acceptable level if a member's association with an attest client consisted of:

- Serving as an honorary director or trustee for an attest client not-for-profit organization provided the position is clearly honorary and held in name only

- Serving on the advisory board of an attest client provided the responsibilities are truly advisory in nature

- Serving as the treasurer for a mayoral campaign when the attest client is the candidate's political party or the municipality in which the candidate is running. Independence would be impaired, however, if the campaign organization itself was the attest client.

Independence will not be impaired if a CPA fails to disassociate from an attest client before becoming a covered member if certain safeguards are all met:

- The member discontinues participation in the client's employee health and welfare plans unless the client is legally required to allow the member to participate and the member pays 100% of the cost of participation on a current basis;

- The member discontinues participation in all other employee benefit plans and disposes of all vested benefits from the plan at the earliest date permitted by the plan;

- The member disposes of any direct and any material indirect financial interest in the client;

- The member collects or repays any loans to or from the client; and

- The covered member evaluates whether other relationships with the attest client create additional threats that must be addressed.

A member who leaves a CPA firm to take a key position with an attest client would potentially have created the threat of familiarity, self-interest, undue influence, or management participation. Independence will be impaired unless:

- Amounts due to the member from the firm are not material to the firm;

- The member cannot influence the firm's operations or financial position; and

- The member is not associated with the firm and does not participate, or appear to participate, in the firm's business once employed or associated with the attest client, even if compensated for doing so.

Employment with Audit Client

Prior to leaving:

- Must inform audit firm of conversations with client about possible employment
- Immediately be removed from the audit
- Once removed, the audit firm should consider whether additional work might be needed in the areas performed by the departed auditor

After employed by the audit client:

- Audit firm should consider modifying the audit plan
- Assure remaining audit team is objective
- The next annual audit should be separately reviewed by an audit firm professional uninvolved in the audit

Memberships

Although memberships do create or enhance threats associated with management participation, self-review, and self-interest, they do not necessarily impair independence.

- A pro rata share of a club's equity or debt securities held by a CPA belonging to an attest client social club would not be considered a direct financial interest if the club membership is essentially a social matter.
- Membership in an attest client trade association would not impair independence unless the CPA serves in an inappropriate position, such as a director, officer, or employee during the period covered by the financial statements subject to the attest engagement or during the period of the engagement.

Subject to those restrictions related to depository accounts and loans, membership in an attest client credit union would not impair the CPA's independence if membership was based on the CPA's qualifications or characteristics other providing professional services to the credit union.

Gifts and Entertainment

Offering a gift to, or accepting a gift from, an attest client, an individual in a key position with an attest client, or an individual with a beneficial ownership interest providing significant influence over the attest client may impair independence if the threats of undue influence or self-interest are increased to an unacceptable level.

To avoid impairing independence, the firm, a team member, or someone in a position to influence are subject to restrictions.

Gifts and entertainment—restrictions

Gifts from attest client—
only if clearly insignificant

Gifts and entertainment to attest client—
if reasonable in circumstances

Entertainment from attest client—
if reasonable in circumstances

Engagement team members and those in position to influence

In determining whether "reasonable under the circumstances," the CPA will consider factors such as the nature of the item, the occasion giving rise to it, the cost or value, similarities with other gifts or entertainment offered or accepted etc.

Actual or Threatened Litigation

Litigation, whether actual or the expressed intention to begin litigation, may create an adverse interest or a self-interest threat that could be at an unacceptable level. The materiality of such actual or threatened litigation to the CPA, the CPA's firm, and to the client should be evaluated by the CPA in making a determination. Whether or not independence is impaired will depend on the facts and circumstances surrounding each situation and will require the CPA to apply professional judgment.

Some, but not all, actual or threatened litigation between a CPA and an attest client will impair independence. Independence will not be impaired by litigation that is not related to the client's attestation engagement and is not material to either the CPA or the attest client.

Any threats to a CPA's independence due to actual or threatened litigation is eliminated when the parties reach final resolution and the matter no longer affects the relationship with the attest client. This is a matter of the CPA's professional judgment.

Performance of Nonattest Services

Many CPA firms provide a variety of nonattest services for their attest clients, the most common of which include bookkeeping; tax compliance; and nontax disbursement services; such as payroll services. The performance of nonattest services may create *self-review, management participation, or advocacy threats to independence.*

When significant threats to independence exist during either the **period** in which the professional engagement is **being performed**, or the **period covered by the financial statements** that are the subject of the attest service, they **must be reduced to an acceptable level** or independence will be impaired.

The following are examples of situations which will not prevent the CPA from performing an attest service for such a nonattest client.

- The nonattest services were performed prior to the period in which the attest services were performed
- The nonattest services relate to periods prior to the periods covered by the financial statements that are the subject of the attest services
- The financial statements for the period during which the nonattest services were performed were attested to by another CPA.

Although a CPA may not perform certain nonattest services for an attest client because they create threats to independence that cannot be reduced to an acceptable level, many nonattest services may be performed for an attest client without impairing independence. To make certain that independence is not impaired when performing nonattest services for an attest client, the CPA will address three distinct components of the Code.

The CPA will:

- Evaluate the cumulative effect of all nonattest services being performed for the client, using a conceptual framework approach, to determine if threats to independence are at an acceptable level.
- Apply the three general requirements for performing nonattest services enumerated in the Code.
- Evaluate the specific services being performed to make certain that none of them individually raise threats to independence to an unacceptable level.

Certain nonattest services, and certain conditions under which nonattest services are performed, create **threats to independence** that cannot be reduced to an acceptable level. When a CPA provides these services to a client, the management participation and self-review threats are affected.

A summary of the different types of nonattest services from the AICPA Code of Professional Conduct is provided below.

Advisory Services – The provision of advisory services to a client **does not create** unacceptable threats as long as the services are exclusively advisory in nature and the accountant does not assume any management responsibilities.

Appraisal, Valuation, and Actuarial Services – The provision of appraisal, valuation, and actuarial services **does create** unacceptable threats when a significant degree of subjectivity is involved and the amounts are material to the client's financial statements that cannot be reduced by safeguards.

Benefit Plan Administration – The assumption of management responsibilities while performing benefit plan administrative services **creates unacceptable threats** that cannot be reduced by safeguards.

Bookkeeping, Payroll, and Other Disbursements – The provision of bookkeeping, payroll and other disbursement services is **generally allowed** unless the CPA is assuming management responsibilities.

Business Risk Consulting – Business risk consulting services are **generally allowed** unless management responsibilities have been assumed. The CPA should avoid presenting business risk consideration to the board on management's behalf or making/approving any business risk decisions.

Corporate Finance Consulting – When corporate finance consulting services are provided, **advocacy threats are raised** in addition to **management participation and self-review** threats. Care must be taken to ensure that the CPA is not advocating for or acting on the client's behalf to avoid raising threats to an unacceptable level.

Executive or Employee Recruiting – Involvement in executive or employee hiring must be carefully managed to avoid problems resulting from assuming management responsibilities. The CPA should not hire or terminate client employees.

Forensic Accounting – A CPA may provide forensic accounting services, consisting of investigative services and litigation services.

Hosting – Hosting services involve services performed for an attest client to host a financial or nonfinancial information system, to provide custody or storage for the client's data or records, or to provide electronic security or backup services. The provision of hosting services **impairs independence** because the member has become a part of the client's internal control system.

Information Systems Services – A CPA performing information systems services may negatively impact independence.

Internal Audit – Internal audit services consist of assisting the client in its internal audit, or internal control activities. If the member takes responsibility for the client's internal audit activities, independence is impaired. Providing assistance to the client through the performance of other financial and operational internal audit activities does not impair independence.

Investment Advisory or Management – The provision of investment advisory or management services is allowed as long as the CPA does assume a management responsibility.

Tax Services – Tax services are generally allowed as long as the CPA does not have custody or control over client's funds and that the client employee reviews and approves tax return before filing, and, if required for filing, signs tax return. The exception is representing the client in court to resolve a tax dispute. This presents an unacceptable advocacy threat to independence.

Attestation Services and Independence

Independence requirements apply to the performance of all attest services, including services performed in accordance with attestation standards. The CPA is not required to be independent of an individual or entity engaging the CPA to perform an attestation engagement if the individual or entity is not the responsible party, the party responsible for the assertion to which the accountant is attesting.

Modifications to the independence requirements in relation to the attestation standards include:

- Restrictions on nonattest services only apply to those nonattest services performed in relation to the subject matter of the nonattest services.

- Covered members who must comply with the independence requirements in an agreed-upon procedures engagement may be limited to those participating on the engagement; those who directly supervise the engagement partner or partner equivalent; and individuals consulting with the engagement team regarding technical or industry-related issues relevant to the engagement.

For an agreed-upon procedures, the CPA performing the work, his/her direct supervisors, and any consultants who worked on the engagements may be limited to those participating on the non-attestation engagement.

General Standards (Topic 1.300)

A member should comply with the following standards for all professional engagements:

- Only accept engagements expected to be completed with **professional competency**.
- Exercise due **professional care**.
- Adequately **plan and supervise** engagements.
- Obtain **sufficient relevant data** to afford a reasonable basis for conclusions and recommendations.

A member who provides specific services, i.e., auditing, review, compilation, consulting, tax or other professional services, should comply with standards promulgated by bodies designated by Council.

Standard-setting bodies designed by council

Accounting and auditing boards	AICPA committees boards
Financial Accounting Standards Board (FASB)	Auditing Standards Board (ASB)
Public company Accounting Oversight Board (PCAOB)	Accounting and Review Services Committee (ARSC)
Governmental Accounting Standards Board (GASB)	Forensic and Valuation Services Committee
Federal Accounting Standards Advisory Board (FASAB)	Personal Financial Planning Executive Committee
International Accounting Standards Board (IASB)	Tax Executive Committee

A member may not provide positive or negative assurance that financial statements are in conformity with a financial reporting framework (GAAP, IASB, GASB, and FASAB statements) if statements contain departures from that framework having a material effect on statements taken as a whole except when unusual circumstances would make financial statements *misleading* if the requirements of the framework had been followed. Departures from GAAP are allowed under unusual circumstances, e.g., new legislation or new form of business transaction.

Acts Discreditable (Topic 1.400)

A member should NOT commit certain acts that are discreditable to the profession.

- Discrimination and harassment in employment practices
- Solicitation or disclosure of CPA Exam questions and answers
- Failure to file a tax return (including one's own personal return or his or her firm's) or failure to pay a tax liability
- Negligence in the preparation of financial statements or records
- Material departure from the audit standards of government bodies, commissions, or other regulatory agencies
- Failure to follow additional government standards over and above generally accepted auditing standards where applicable

- Improper use of indemnification and limitation of liability provisions in violation of regulatory requirements
- Confidential information obtained from employment or volunteer activities (more detail in the "Advertising and Confidentiality" lesson)
- False, misleading, or deceptive acts in promoting or marketing professional services
- Use of the CPA credential in violation of rules and regulations
- Records requests (more detail below)
- Removing client files or proprietary information from a firm after termination
- Use of confidential information obtained from a prospective client or nonclient without consent

 According to the ethical standards of the profession, which of the following actions is generally is prohibited?

- Accepting a contingent fee for representing a client in connection with obtaining a private letter ruling from the Internal Revenue Service.
- Retaining client records after the client has demanded their return.
- Revealing client tax returns to a prospective purchaser of the CPA's practice.
- Issuing a modified report explaining the CPA's failure to follow a governmental regulatory agency's standards when conducting an attest service for a client.

Record requests

	Rules	Examples
Client-provided	- *Cannot* withhold for unpaid fees, litigation, or because incomplete - Only required to provide once	- W-2s - Client's purchase invoices - Client-prepared journal/ledger
CPA-prepared	- *Can* withhold if fees due, work incomplete, or litigation - Only required to provide once	- CPA-prepared journal entries - Audit/review report - Working papers

The AICPA Code of Professional Conduct prohibits CPAs from doing anything likely to harm the reputation of the profession. **Failure to return client records** on demand is also an **act discreditable** to the profession because the records remain the property of the client even while in the CPA's possession.

Record(s) Request

There are four **types of records**:

- **Client-provided records** are records given by the client to the member.

- **Member-prepared records** are those the member was not specifically engaged to prepare and are not in the client's books and records, rendering the client's financial information incomplete. Example: adjusting, closing, combining, or consolidating journal entries and supporting schedules and documents that the member proposed or prepared as part of an engagement.

- **Member's work products** are deliverables set forth in the engagement letter, such as a tax return.

- **Working papers** are all other items prepared solely for purposes of the engagement, including items prepared by both the member (e.g., audit programs, analytical review schedules, and statistical sampling and analysis) and the client (e.g., papers prepared at the member's request and reflecting testing or other work done by the member).

The **proper treatment** of requests from clients as follows:

- Client-provided records should be delivered to the client at the client's request, even if the client has not paid its bill to the member. If records were previously made available to the client, the member may wait until payment is received to respond to a second request.

- Member-prepared records related to a completed and issued work product should be delivered to the client at the client's request, except that they may be withheld if fees are due for that specific work product.

- Work products should be delivered to the client at the client's request, except that they may be withheld under four circumstances:
  - Fees are due for the specific work product.
  - The work product is incomplete.
  - To comply with professional standards (e.g., withholding an audit report because of unresolved audit issues).
  - If threatened or outstanding litigation exists concerning the engagement or the member's work.

- Working papers are the member's property and need not be provided to the client (unless some regulation or contractual provision requires production).

Members may **charge a reasonable fee** for the time and expense incurred in copying, retrieving, and shipping records. Members should make the requested records available in any usable and accessible format. Members need not convert records that are not in electronic format to electronic format. Generally, client requests should be honored within **45 days**.

Fees and Other Types of Remuneration (Topic 1.500)

A **contingent fee** is a fee established for the performance of any service pursuant to an arrangement in which no fee will be charged unless a specified finding or result is attained, or in which the amount of the fee is otherwise dependent upon the finding or result of such service.

Members shall not receive **contingent fees for any service** performed for a client for whom he or she performs any of the following attest services:

- A financial statement audit or review,

- A financial statement compilation reasonably expected to be used by a third party that does not disclose a lack of independence, or

- An examination of prospective financial information.

Nor may a member prepare an original or amended tax return or claim for a tax refund for a contingent fee for **any client**, even nonattest clients. Examples of some **permitted contingent fees** in the tax area include:

- Representing a client before a revenue agent examining the client's income tax return
- Filing an amended federal or state income tax return claiming a refund based on a tax issue that is the subject of a test case involving a different taxpayer
- Filing an amended federal or state income tax return (or refund claim) claiming a tax refund in an amount that will be examined by a tax authority, such as the Joint Committee on Taxation
- Helping a client obtain a private letter ruling or influencing the drafting of a regulation or statute

Commissions and referral fees are prohibited for *attest* clients. For *nonattest clients*, they are permitted, but must be disclosed in writing.

Advertising and Other Forms of Solicitation (Topic 1.600)

A member may NOT engage in false, misleading, or deceptive advertising.

- Members are responsible not only for their own promotional efforts, but also for those of third parties if they are asked to perform professional services for the client or customer of a third party.

Promotional efforts are a discreditable act if they are false, misleading, or deceptive (i.e., if they contain any claim that would likely cause a reasonable person to be misled), which would be the case if they:

- Create false or unjustified expectations of favorable results
- Imply the ability to influence any court, tribunal, regulatory agency or similar body
- Contain a representation that the member will perform services for stated fees when it is likely at the time that the fees will be substantially increased

Confidential Information (Topic 1.700)

Members are not allowed to reveal confidential information without client permission. Certain exceptions exist including instances where:

- The client consents.
- Disclosure is permitted by law and authorized by the employer.
- Disclosure is required by law.

Disclosures are allowed:

- To comply with a valid and enforceable subpoena.
- In connection with a quality review under AICPA, state CPA society, or Board of Accountancy authorization.
- To initiate an ethics complaint with the AICPA, state CPA society, or state board of accountancy.
- To a member's liability insurance carrier regarding a claim.

According to the AICPA Code of Professional Conduct, which of the following statements is true with regard to confidential client information?

- Most states recognize auditor-client privilege

- An auditor may not provide confidential information to members of the auditor's firm who are not on the audit engagement team

- An auditor may allow other CPAs to see confidential information in connection with a valid program of peer review

- An auditor will generally refuse a request for confidential information made by the AICPA's professional ethics division

CPAs typically require access to highly sensitive client information. If they did not keep that information confidential, CPAs would not be entrusted with the records they need. Accordingly, the AICPA Code of Professional Conduct prohibits divulging any client information that is not available to the public, with limited exceptions.

Exceptions to rule on confidential client information

- Comply with subpoena or summons*

- Comply with quality control peer review (eg, peer review, review prior to potential sale of CPA practice)

- Comply with laws and regulations

- Initiate, pursue, or defend against actual or potential lawsuits

- Initiate or respond to complaints with AICPA ethics division or trial board

- Permit electronic preparation or submission of a client's tax return

- Secure legal advice from an attorney

*May refuse these in a state that has an accountant-client privilege statute

One exception allows that **confidential client information may be provided** for professional practice reviews (eg, **peer reviews**) authorized by the AICPA or state boards of accountancy. Without this exception, CPAs could easily avoid such reviews by citing requirements to maintain confidentiality. Everyone participating in these reviews is bound to keep the CPA's client information confidential.

Form of Organization and Firm Name (Topic 1.800)

A member may practice public accounting in any form of organization that is permitted by law or regulation with characteristics consistent with those approved in resolutions of the AICPA Council.

- Form and name should not be misleading.

- A firm cannot designate itself as "members of the AICPA" unless all of its CPA OWNERS are members of the AICPA.

- A firm name may include names of past partners.

A member may **own an interest in a separate business** that performs accounting, tax, or consulting services. If the member *controls* the separate business, then its owners and professional employees must comply with the Code where applicable (eg, commission and referral fee rules). If the member does not control the separate business, the Code will apply only to the member.

Other requirements include the following:

- Only members of a firm who are legally partners should use the designation "partner."

- If a member becomes an employee of a firm made up of one or more nonmembers, they still must comply with the code. And if the member is a partner in the firm, they are responsible for the firm's professional employees.

- Two former partners may continue to jointly perform an attest engagement, but to make it clear that a partnership no longer exists, they should present their report on plain paper (with no letterhead).

  ○ If a firm does attest work, CPAs must own a **majority** of its financial interests and must remain responsible, financially and otherwise, for a firm's attest work.

- CPAs are responsible for compliance with laws and regulations, for enrollment in an AICPA-approved practice monitoring program, for compliance with independence rules, and for compliance with all other applicable standards within their firms.

If two **firms merge**, they may use in the newly formed firm's name the name of retired or other partners in either or both of the former firms.

- A CPA member who is in partnership with non-CPAs may sign reports in the firm's name and also affix the designation "CPA" to his or her own signature if it is clear that the firm is not holding itself out as entirely comprised of CPAs.

- No misleading name that causes confusion about the legal form of the firm or its owners' identities should be used.

Part 2 – Members in Business

 Representative Task (Application): Apply the Conceptual Framework for Members in Public Practice and Members in Business included in the AICPA Code of Professional Conduct to situations that could present threats to compliance with the rules included in the Code.

Definition

Members in business (MIB) are members who are "employed or engaged on a contractual or volunteer basis in an executive, staff, governance, advisory, or administrative capacity in such areas as industry, the public sector, education, the not-for-profit sector and regulatory or professional bodies." This would include staff accountants, internal auditors, and other accountants not engaged in public practice.

MIB **do not have to worry about independence** rules. The Conceptual Framework for MIB generally tracks that of MIPP. Six of the seven threats identified for MIPP also apply to MIB: (a) adverse interest threats, (b) advocacy threats, (c) familiarity threats, (d) self-interest threats, (e) self-review threats, and (f) undue influence threats.

Topic 2.000 – Introduction

This topic indicates that this part applies to members in members in business. It also requires a conceptual framework approach to determining when threats to compliance with the Code are at an acceptable level and when they require the application of safeguards to eliminate the threat or reduce it to an acceptable level. The conceptual framework is comparable to that for members in public accounting.

Topic 2.100 – Integrity and Objectivity

As is true for members in public accounting, those in business shall maintain objectivity and integrity, avoid conflicts of interest, and not knowingly misrepresent facts or subordinate judgment in the performance of any professional service.

Topic 2.300 – General Standards

A member must comply with the following standards for all professional engagements:

- Only accept engagements expected to be completed with professional competency.
- Exercise due professional care.
- Adequately plan and supervise engagements.
- Obtain sufficient relevant data to afford a reasonable basis for conclusions and recommendations.

Topic 2.400 – Acts Discreditable

A member should NOT commit certain acts that are discreditable to the profession.

Discreditable acts may include:

- Violations of laws related to discrimination or harassment in the workplace.
- Solicitation or disclosure of CPA examination questions and answers.
- Nonpayment of a tax liability or not filing a return
- Preparing financial statements in a negligent manner
- Material departures from rules and regulations required in financial statement preparation by regulatory authorities, e.g., SEC.
- Disclosure of confidential information obtained from employment or volunteer activities.

 Susan's gift from Jessie is reasonable under the circumstances of Susan's birthday and threatens neither objectivity nor integrity. Accepting gifts or entertainment may create independence threats. If the gifts, like the coffee mug, are **reasonable** in nature, the threat may be reduced to an **acceptable** level. However, these examples of making erroneous changes, hiding financial information, and alternating documentation can threaten integrity and objectivity. Which of the following actions by a member in business would **not** threaten integrity and / or objectivity standards?

- Susan was an internal auditor for the privately-held Jonass Co. and on her birthday she accepted a gift from her company's external auditor Jessie in the form of a coffee mug emblazoned with the CPA firm's logo.
- Amber allowed her supervisor to pressure her into characterizing the tax implications of a transaction their company consummated in a manner that is completely erroneous in her view.
- Janice, who works in internal audit, hid some unflattering financial details from her employer's external auditor.
- Jen, a staff accountant at Nickleby Corporation, ordered a subordinate to back-date an IRS document.

Part 3 – Other Members

Definition

Other members are unemployed, retired, or otherwise not working in the profession, so most of the code that applies to MIPP and MIB *does not* apply to them.

Acts Discreditable

Other members are, at a minimum, not to engage in discreditable acts, including:

- Discrimination and harassment in employment practices
- Solicitation or disclosure of CPA Examination questions and answers
- Failure to file a tax return or pay a tax liability
- Improper disclosure of confidential information obtained from former employment or previous volunteer work
- False, misleading, or deceptive acts in promoting or marketing services
- Improper (misleading) use of the CPA credential

Acts Discreditable

1.02 Requirements of the SEC and PCAOB

Overview

The Securities and Exchange Commission (SEC) oversees publicly-traded (ie, issuers) companies and their auditors. The Public Company Accounting Oversight Board (PCAOB) promulgates auditing standards to be applied to the audits of public company clients. In many instances, there is alignment between the AICPA, SEC, and the PCAOB requirements.

However, in some cases, the requirements imposed on the auditors of public entities by the SEC and PCAOB are *more restrictive* than those imposed on auditors of nonpublic entities by the AICPA. For example, the auditors of public company clients are prohibited from performing almost any nonassurance services for an audit client.

 If the SEC and PCAOB issue any rules that are more restrictive than AICPA rules, they override those AICPA rules for public company audits (i.e., audits of issuers). The PCAOB developed Ethics and Independence Rules that are consistent with the legal mandates put into effect by SOX.

 Representative Task (Remembering and Understanding): Understand the ethical and independence requirements of the Securities and Exchange Commission and the Public Company Accounting Oversight Board.

 Representative Task (Application): Apply the ethical requirements and independence rules of the Securities and Exchange Commission and the Public Company Accounting Oversight Board to situations that could compromise compliance or impair independence during an audit of an issuer.

Securities and Exchange Commission (SEC) Overview

The SEC was established to protect investors, maintain markets, and facilitate the formation of companies. The **Securities Act of 1933 established initial registration requirements** for companies who wanted to sell their stock on a stock exchange.

The **Securities Exchange Act of 1934 established the SEC** and gave it the authority to require publicly held companies to issue audited financial statements, designate the acceptable basis or bases of accounting for publicly held companies, and oversee auditors of publicly held companies. The SEC has designated the PCAOB to regulate auditors of publicly held entities and to develop and maintain auditing standards applicable to their audits.

Definitions

The SEC provides key definitions of terms used in their independence rules.

Financial Reporting Oversight Role (FROR)—A role in which a person is in a position to or does exercise influence over the contents of the F/S or anyone who prepares them. Examples: director, CEO, president, CFO, COO, general counsel, CAO, controller, director of internal audit, director of financial reporting, treasurer, or any equivalent position.

Affiliate—Auditors are to be independent of the firm under audit and its affiliates. The term "affiliate" includes:

- Entities that control the entity under audit (e.g., parent corporation) or that the entity under audit controls (e.g., subsidiary corporation)
- Entities that are under common control with the entity under audit when both the entity and the entity under audit are material to the controlling entity
- An entity over which audit client audit has significant influence, unless the entity is not material to the audit client
- An entity that has significant influence over the audit client, unless the audit client is not material to the entity

Audit and Professional Engagement Period—Includes the period covered by any F/S being audited or reviewed (the "audit period") and the period of the engagement (the "professional engagement period"). The professional engagement period begins at the earlier of when the accountant signs an initial engagement letter or begins the audit and ends when the audit client or the accountant notifies the SEC that the client is no longer the accountant's audit client. The "audit and professional engagement period" doesn't include periods ended prior to the first day of the last fiscal year before the issuer first filed, or was required to file, a registration statement or report with the SEC, provided there has been full compliance with applicable independence standards in all prior periods.

Close Family Member (CFM)—A CFM is defined as a person's spouse, spousal equivalent, parent, dependent, nondependent child, and sibling.

Covered Persons—Covered persons are defined as the following partners, principals, shareholders, and employees of an accounting firm:

- Audit engagement team, which includes "all partners, principals, shareholders and professional employees participating in an audit, review, or attestation engagement of an audit client, including audit partners and all persons who consult with others on the audit engagement . . . regarding technical or industry-specific issues, transactions, or events" (comparable to AICPA "team")
- Chain of command, which includes all persons who: (a) supervise or have direct management responsibility for the audit, including at all successively senior levels through the accounting firm's chief executive; (b) evaluate the performance or recommend the compensation of the audit engagement partner; or (c) provide quality control or other oversight of the audit (PTIs)
- Any other partner, principal, shareholder, or managerial employee of the accounting firm who has provided **10 or more hours of nonaudit services (NAS)** to the audit client for the period beginning on the date such services are provided and ending on the date the accounting firm signs the report on the F/S for the fiscal year during which those services are provided, or who expects to provide 10 or more hours of NAS to the audit client on a recurring basis (10-hour persons)
- Any other partner, principal, or shareholder from an "office" of the accounting firm in which the lead audit engagement partner primarily practices in connection with the audit other partners in the office (OPIOs)

Immediate Family Member (IFM)—An IFM is a person's spouse, spousal equivalent, and dependents.

Independence Requirements

Rule 2-01 of the SEC's Regulation S-X provides specific rules regarding auditor independence in connection with public company audit clients. It also includes the SOX independence requirements. Remember that if there are any differences between the AICPA approach and the rules of the SEC or PCAOB, the latter take precedence if the audit client is a public company.

SEC independence rules are, overall, concerned with whether a relationship with or provision of a service to an audit client:

- Creates a conflict of interest for the auditor;
- Results in the accountant auditing his or her own work;
- Results in the accountant acting as an audit client's manager or employee; or
- Places the accountant in a position of being an advocate for the audit client.

To be qualified to audit a public company, a CPA must be registered and in **good standing** under the laws of his or her state and must be **independent in fact and appearance** and **capable of exercising objective and impartial judgment**.

Financial Relationships

Independence requirements limit the financial relationships between auditors and their clients. The accounting firm, any of its covered persons, or any of their immediate family members (IFMs) **may not have direct investments** in an audit client, such as owning stocks, bonds, notes, options, and so on. A "direct investment" includes one through an intermediary if:

- The firm, covered persons, or IFMs, alone or together, either supervise or participate in the intermediary's investment decisions, or
- The intermediary is a nondiversified mutual fund that has invested 20% or more its money in an audit client.

Additional financial relationships that impair independence are explained below.

Five Percent Investments—Independence is impaired if **any** partner, principal, shareholder, or professional employee of the accounting firm (and any of their IFMs or CFMs) **owns 5% or more of the client's stock**. Notice that the 5% rule applies to the individuals listed regardless of the office they work in.

Trustee of a Trust—Independence is impaired if the accounting firm or any covered persons or IFMs serve as voting trustees of a trust or executors of an estate containing an audit client's securities unless they have no authority to make investment decisions for the trust or estate.

Material Indirect Interests—As with the AICPA Code, accounting firms, covered persons, and their IFMs may not only not have direct financial interests in an audit client (whether material or immaterial), they **may not have indirect interests that are material**. It is permitted for these persons to own 5% or less of a diversified investment company, even if the company owns some shares of an audit client.

Related Entities—Independence is impaired if the firm, covered persons, or IFMs:

- Have any direct or material indirect investment in an entity that is not an audit client where:
  - An audit client has an investment in that entity that is material to the audit client and has the ability to exercise significant control over that entity, or
  - The entity has an investment in an audit client that is material to that entity and has the ability to exercise significant influence over that audit client.
- Have any material investment in an entity over which an audit client is able to exercise significant influence; or
- Have the ability to exercise significant influence over an entity that has the ability to exercise significant influence over an audit client.

Loans/Debtor Creditor Relationships—Any loan to or from an audit client, its officers or directors, or its beneficial owners (known through reasonable inquiry) of the client's equity securities where such beneficial owner has significant influence over the entity under audit, creates an independence problem.

There are **five exceptions** where loans are obtained from a financial institution under its normal lending procedures, terms, and requirements:

- Automobile loans and leases collateralized by the automobile

- Loans fully collateralized by the cash surrender value of an insurance policy

- Loans fully collateralized by cash deposits at the same financial institution

- Mortgage loans collateralized by the borrower's primary residence provided the loans were not obtained while the covered person was a covered person

- Student loans provided the loans were not obtained while the covered person in the firm was a covered person

Savings and Checking Accounts—Any savings, checking, or similar account at a bank, savings and loan, or similar institution that is an audit client creates an independence problem if the account has a balance that exceeds the amount insurable by the FDIC, except that an accounting firm may have an uninsured balance provided that the likelihood of the institution experiencing financial difficulties is remote.

Broker-Dealer Accounts—Brokerage or similar accounts maintained with a broker-dealer that is an audit client create an independence problem, if any such account includes assets other than cash or securities, or the value of assets in the accounts exceeds the amount protected by the Securities Investor Protection Corporation (SIPC), which is $500,000 for securities and $250,000 for cash.

Each of the following broker-dealer relationships impairs auditor independence with respect to a broker-dealer issuer audit client, **except**

- The auditor has a brokerage account that holds both U.S. securities and assets other than cash or securities.

- The auditor has a brokerage account that holds U.S. securities in excess of Securities Investor Protection Corporation coverage limits.

- The auditor has a brokerage account that includes assets other than cash or securities.

- The auditor has a cash balance in a brokerage account that is fully covered by the Securities Investor Protection Corporation.

CPA or CPA's firm holds brokerage account with broker-dealer issuer they are auditing

Independence is impaired if:

- Account assets include anything other than cash or securities (eg, commodities)

- Account valuations exceed amount covered by Securities Investor Protection Corporation (SIPC) or similar foreign program

A CPA's brokerage account with a broker-dealer issuer audit client **impairs independence** if the account holds anything but cash or securities or if the holdings **exceed the coverage** limits of the **Securities Investor Protection Corporation** or a similar foreign program. If the cash balance in the brokerage account is is fully covered, then there is no impairment.

Consumer Loans—Any aggregate outstanding consumer loan balance (e.g., credit card debt, retail installment loans, cell phone installment plans, and home improvement loans) greater than $10,000 owed to a lender that is an audit client creates and independence problem.

Insurance Products—Any individual policy issued by an insurer that is an audit client creates an independence problem, *unless*:

- The policy was obtained when the covered person was not a covered person in the firm; and
- The likelihood of the insurer becoming insolvent is remote.

Audit Client's Financial Relationship

If the audit client has a financial relationship with the accounting firm, then the CPAs (accounting firm) are (is) not independent in these cases:

- Investments by the Audit Client in the Accounting Firm—(a) An audit client has, or has agreed to acquire, any direct investment in the accounting firm, or (b) the audit client's officers or directors own greater than 5% of the equity securities of the accounting firm.
- Underwriting—Their firm engages an audit client to act as an underwriter, broker-dealer, market maker, promoter, or analyst for securities issued by the accounting firm.

Situations that may not impair independence

Inheritance and gifts	New audit engagement	Employee compensation and benefit plans
The individuals must dispose of the interest as soon as practicable but always less than 30 days after the person has knowledge of and the right to dispose of the interest.	A person has a financial interest that would normally impair independence but that person did not audit the client's F/S the previous year and disposes of the interest before either (a) signing an engagement letter or (b) commencing any audit procedures.	An IFM with an impermissible financial interest due to his or her employer's employee compensation or benefits program, must disposed of it as soon as practicable but always no later than 30 days after the person has the right to dispose of the financial interest.

Employment Relationships

An accountant is not independent if he or she has an employment relationship with the audit client such as those listed below.

- **Accountant's Employment at Audit Client**—A current partner, principal, shareholder, or professional employee of the accounting firm is employed by the audit client or is a member of the board of directors.
- **Certain Relatives of Accountant's Employment at Audit Client**—A CFM of a covered person is in an accounting role or FROR at an audit client.
- **Former Employee of Audit Client's Employment at Accounting Firm**—A former officer, director, or employee of an audit client becomes a partner, principal, shareholder, or professional employee of the accounting firm, unless the individual does not participate in, and is not in a position to influence, the audit of F/S covering any period he or she was employed by the audit client.
- **Former Employee of Accounting Firm's Employment at Audit Client**—The accounting firm is not independent unless the former partner, principal shareholder, or professional employee:
  - Was not a member of the audit engagement team during the one-year period preceding the date of the initiation of the audit.
  - Does not influence the accounting firm's operations or financial policies, has no capital balances in the accounting firm; and has no financial arrangement with the accounting firm other than one providing for regular payment of a fixed dollar amount (which is not dependent on the revenue, profits, or earnings of the accounting firm).

Independence requirements of Sarbanes-Oxley for audits of issuers

- Auditor must cool off for one year before taking key role with client
- Auditor cannot perform most nonaudit services for audit clients
- Auditor must report to audit committee:

  - Critical accounting policies and practices
  - Alternative accounting discussed with management
  - Material written communication between auditor and management

- Audit partner and reviewing partner must rotate off engagement every five years
- Audit committee must preapprove nonaudit services provided

Business Relationships

An accountant is not independent if at any time during the audit and professional engagement, the accounting firm or any covered person in the firm has any direct or material indirect business relationship with an audit client or with persons associated with the audit client **in a decision-making capacity**, such as an audit client's officers, directors, or beneficial owners of equity securities who have significant influence over the entity under audit.

 There is an exception to this rule. An accounting firm or covered persons can provide professional services to an audit client or buy services from a client in the **ordinary course of business** without an impermissible business relationship arising.

Prohibited Nonaudit Services

SOX provisions, as implemented by the SEC, indicate that independence is impaired if an auditor provides any of the following nine nonaudit services (NAS) to a public company audit client, unless it is reasonable to conclude that the results of these services will not be subject to audit procedures during the audit of the client's F/S:

- Bookkeeping services
- Financial information systems design and implementation
- Appraisal or valuation services
- Actuarial services
- Internal audit outsourcing services
- Management functions
- Human resources
- Broker-dealer, investment adviser, or investment banking services
- Legal services
- Expert services unrelated to the audit

Contingent Fees

An accountant is not independent if it provides any service or product to a public company audit client for a contingent fee or commission.

Audit Partner Rotation

SOX mandates that lead engagement partners and engagement quality reviewers must be rotated every five years (five on, five off). Other partners providing more than 10 hours of attest services must be rotated every seven years (seven on, two off). There are no requirements that public companies rotate audit firms. There are exemptions for firms with fewer than five public company audit clients and fewer than 10 audit partners.

Audit Committee Administration of the Audit Engagement

SOX shifts control of the audit process from the CEO and CFO to the audit committee, and an auditor is not independent unless these rules are followed. Both the **audit engagement** itself and provision of permitted **nonaudit services** (NAS) are to be **preapproved** by the **audit committee**.

Compensation

SOX provides that an accountant is not independent if any audit partner earns or receives compensation based on selling NAS to the audit client.

Quality Controls

An accounting firm's independence will not be impaired solely because a covered person is not independent, provided:

- The covered person did not know of the circumstances giving rise to the lack of independence;
- The covered person's lack of independence was corrected as promptly as possible once it became known; and
- The accounting firm has a quality control system in place that provides reasonable assurance that independence rules will be complied with.

 For firms annually auditing more than 500 companies, their quality control system provides such reasonable assurance only if it has the following features:

- Written independence policies and procedures
- An automated system tracking investments of partners and managerial employees that might impair independence
- For all professionals, a system that provides timely information about entities from which the accountant is required to maintain independence
- An annual or ongoing firm-wide training program on independence rules
- An annual internal inspection and testing program to monitor adherence to independence rules
- Notification to all firm employees of the name and title of the member of senior management responsible for compliance with independence rules
- A disciplinary mechanism to ensure compliance

Mergers and Acquisitions

Independence will not be impaired because an audit client engages in a merger or acquisition that gives rise to a relationship or service that would violate these independence rules, provided that:

- The accounting firm is in compliance with applicable independence rules throughout the period to which they apply;
- The firm has or will promptly address any conflicts that have arisen because of the merger or acquisition; and
- The firm has in place a proper quality control system.

Public Company Accounting Oversight Board (PCAOB) Overview

Congress enacted the **Sarbanes-Oxley Act (SOX)** in 2002 to **restore investor confidence** after the stock markets were alarmed by high-profile accounting scandals (eg, Enron). **SOX** created the **Public Company Accounting Oversight Board (PCAOB)** to **regulate auditors** of public companies (ie, issuers). PCAOB powers include the registration and oversight of public accounting firms that **audit issuers**.

The **five-member** board is appointed by the Securities and Exchange Commission (SEC) based on its expertise in securities laws and audit reports. Two members, and **only two members, "shall be or have been" CPAs**. Limiting the number of CPAs ensures that the board considers the needs of CPAs without favoring them over issuers, brokers, and investors.

The **PCAOB** chairperson may be one of the two CPAs if that individual has not practiced in five years prior to being appointed to the board. Board members serve a maximum of two full-time terms and may not be engaged in any other business during their terms.

Public company accounting oversight board (PCAOB) composition

Chairperson*

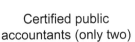

Certified public accountants (only two)

Other financial professionals

*Chairperson may be one of the two CPAs, but this individual cannot be a practicing CPA for at least five years prior to being appointed to the board.

PCAOB Responsibilities

The PCAOB has the following powers and responsibilities:

Registration of public accounting firms—U.S. and non-U.S. accounting firms that prepare audit reports of any U.S. public company (*issuer* of securities) must register with the PCAOB. (This includes non-U.S. accounting firms that play a substantial role in the preparation of such audit reports.)

Inspections of registered public accounting firms—PCAOB is directed to conduct a continuous program of inspections that assess compliance with SOA, PCAOB rules, SEC rules, and applicable professional standards. (A written report is required for each such inspection.)

- Firms that provide audit reports for more than 100 issuers—PCAOB must inspect annually.

- Firms that provide audit reports for 100 or fewer issuers—PCAOB must inspect every three years (triennially).

Standard setting—PCAOB is directed to establish auditing and related attestation, quality control, ethics and independence standards and rules to be used by registered public accounting firms in the preparation of audit reports for issuers. (The Office of the Chief Auditor and the Standing Advisory Group (SAG) assist PCAOB in establishing such auditing and professional practice standards.)

Enforcement—PCAOB has broad authority to investigate registered public accounting firms and persons associated with such firms.

- PCAOB rules require cooperation by registered public accounting firms and associated persons—must produce documents and provide testimony as directed. (PCAOB may also seek information from others, including clients of registered firms.)

- PCAOB sanctions may range from revocation of a firm's registration or barring a person from participating in audits of public companies to lesser sanctions such as monetary penalties or imposition of remedial measures, including additional training or new quality control procedures.

Funding—PCAOB's budget is funded by (1) registration and annual fees from public accounting firms and (2) an annual *accounting support fee* assessed on issuers (based on their relative monthly market capitalization).

Sarbanes-Oxley (SOX)

The Sarbanes-Oxley Act (SOX) consists of 11 key sections that impose wide-ranging and stringent requirements on issuers and their auditors. Only public, not private, companies are subject to SOX, regardless of assets or revenues. Key titles are as follows:

- **Title I (Establish the PCAOB)**—Established the PCAOB, gave standard-setting authority to the PCAOB (regarding auditing, quality control, and independence standards), and created its role in overseeing the accounting firms required to register with the PCAOB.

Powers of the PCAOB

- Registers accounting firms, allowing them to audit issuers

- Establishes audit, ethics, and quality control standards for auditors of issuers

- Investigates and disciplines violations by accounting firms

- Performs quality control inspections of registered accounting firms

- Enforces compliance with the Sarbanes-Oxley Act through administrative sanctions

- **Title II (Auditor Independence)**—Established independence requirements for external auditors, which addressed perceived conflicts of interest, including the following:

Independence requirements of Sarbanes-Oxley for audits of issuers

- Auditor must cool off for one year before taking key role with client

- Auditor cannot perform most nonaudit services for audit clients

- Auditor must report to audit committee:

  - Critical accounting policies and practices

  - Alternative accounting discussed with management

  - Material written communication between auditor and management

- Audit partner and reviewing partner must rotate off engagement every five years

- Audit committee must preapprove nonaudit services provided

- **Title III (Corporate Responsibility)**—Established requirements related to corporate responsibility to make executives take responsibility for the accuracy of financial reporting (including a requirement for certification by the entity's principal officers) and to make it illegal for management to improperly influence the conduct of an audit.

Sarbanes-Oxley (SOX) corporate responsibility requirements for issuers

- Independent audit committee hires, compensates, and communicates with auditor
- CEO and CFO certify that financial statements are fairly presented
- CEO and CFO take responsibility for internal controls and disclose deficiencies
- Officer/director prohibited from materially misleading auditor (eg, fraud)
- If earnings are restated, executive bonuses can be clawed back (ie, taken back)
- SEC may bar violators of securities laws from serving as officer/director

- **Title IV (Financial Disclosures)**—Addressed a variety of enhanced financial disclosures, the most well-known of which deals with required internal control reporting (Section 404), among other matters.

SOX: responsibilities regarding internal control of issuers

Management	<ul><li>Acknowledge responsibility for internal control</li><li>Assess effectiveness of internal control</li></ul>
Auditors	<ul><li>Understand client's control structure</li><li>Assess risk of material weakness</li><li>Evaluate and opine on design and operating effectiveness of controls</li></ul>

- **Title IX (Penalties)**—Enacted tougher fines and penalties for white-collar crime.

Criminal behaviour	Fine/Penalty
Mail and/or wire fraud	Up to 20 years imprisonment
Recklessly violates/misrepresents certification of financial reports	Up to $1 million in fines and/or up to 10 years imprisonment
Willfully violates/misrepresents certification of financial reports	Up to $5 million in fines and/or up to 20 years imprisonment
Altering, destroying, or falsifying documents in order to obstruct or influence a federal investigation	Up to $15 million in fines and/or up to 20 years imprisonment
Securities fraud	Fines and/or up to 20 years imprisonment

Independence and Ethics Rules

Independence Required

Rule 3520 provides that "a registered public accounting firm and its associated persons must be independent of the firm's audit client throughout the audit and professional engagement." No surprise there. CPAs must comply with not only PCAOB rules and SEC rules, but also "all other independence criteria applicable to the engagement."

Annual Inspections

The PCAOB registers accounting firms that audit public companies, sets standards for the audits, and inspects the registered firms. Firms performing 100 or fewer audits per year are inspected every three years. Firms performing more than 100 audits per year are inspected annually.

PCAOB inspections of firms auditing issuers

100 or fewer audits of issuers per year	More than 100 audits of issuers per year
Inspected every three years	Inspected every year

Contingency Fees and Commissions

If a firm or any affiliate provides "any service or product" to an audit client in exchange for a contingent fee or commission, independence is impaired.

 The Niblock accounting firm audited JFK, Inc., a public company. Niblock also provided tax services to JFK, receiving as its fee 20% of any tax savings JFK enjoyed because of Niblock's advice. Which of the following is true?

- Tax advice to a public company audit client is automatically forbidden and impairs independence.
- This tax advice impairs independence because of the nature of the tax advice given.
- This tax advice impairs independence because it was provided on a contingent fee basis.
- If the contingent fee had been only 10%, it would have been fine.
- Auditors of public companies **not permitted** to **provide services** to an audit client on a **contingent fee** basis. If this occurs, the auditor's **independence** would be **impaired.**

Tax Consulting

Rule 3522 puts **some limitations** on those tax services by providing that firms are not independent if during their audit engagements they provide services related to marketing, planning or opining in favor of tax transactions that are:

- **Confidential**—A "confidential transaction" is one that is offered to a taxpayer under conditions of confidentiality and for which the taxpayer has paid the advisor a fee; *or*

- **Aggressive**—An "aggressive tax position transaction" is one initially recommended by the accounting firm and a "significant purpose" of which is tax avoidance, *unless* the proposed tax treatment is at least *more likely than not* to be allowable under applicable tax laws. Examples of such impermissible aggressive transactions are ones that are the same or similar to transactions the IRS has already determined to be tax avoidance transactions. ·

Tax services prohibited for issuer audit clients

- Recommending an aggressive tax position
- Providing any tax service for person in key position with client
- Using contingent fee arrangements (even if not tax related)
- Advocating for client in a tax dispute

Tax Services for FRORs

Rule 3523 provides that public company accounting firms may also forfeit their independence by providing "any tax service" to a person in a "financial reporting oversight role" (FROR) at the audit client or to an immediate family member (IFM) (spouse, spousal equivalent, and dependents) of such a person.

- FROR is defined as a role in which a person can or does exercise influence over the contents of financial statements or anyone who prepares them. Examples of FRORs include: directors, CEOs, presidents, CFOs, COOs, general counsel, CAOs, controllers, directors of internal audit, directors of financial reporting, treasurers, or other equivalent positions.

The rule contains three exceptions. **Independence is not impaired** if the person:

- Is in an FROR only because he or she is a member of the client's board of directors.
- Is in an FROR only because of his or her relationship to an affiliate of the entity being audited where the affiliate's financial statements are not material to the consolidated financial statements of the audit client or are audited by a different audit firm.
- Was not in an FROR before a hiring, promotion or similar change in employment.

 An issuer's auditor is prohibited from providing tax services to which of the following individuals?
- The chair of the board of directors.
- The chair of the audit committee.
- The CEO.
- The CFO of an affiliate of the issuer audited by another firm.

Tax services for anyone in a key position with an issuer audit client

Prohibited, *unless* the person in the key position is:

- A director but does *not also* occupy a key *management* position
- With an affiliate whose financial statements are *immaterial* to client
- With an affiliate whose financial statements are audited by *different* firm
- Not in the position when the audit *begins*

CPAs generally cannot offer tax services to anyone in a financial reporting oversight role with an issuer audit client when the audit begins. Exceptions are allowed if the person's only role is as a director or if the **person works for either an affiliate** that is audited by another firm or for an affiliate whose financials are immaterial to the client.

Approving Permissible Tax Consulting

SOX allows certain tax consulting services to be provided to public company audit clients so long as they are pre-approved by the client's audit committee. Rule 3524 sets out the procedure for seeking such approval, requiring that the accounting firm:

- Describe in writing:
  - The scope of the service, the fee structure for the engagement, and any other related agreement between the firm and the audit client.
  - Any compensation arrangement or other agreement, such as a referral fee or fee-sharing arrangement between the firm and any person (other than the audit client) regarding the promoting, marketing, or recommending of a transaction covered by the service.
- Discuss with the audit committee the potential effects of the services on the firm's independence.
- Document the discussion.

Approving Permissible NAS

Audit firms are prohibited from providing certain non-audit services (NAS) related to internal controls over financial reporting, but allows others if pre-approved by the public company client's audit committee. The firm should:

- Describe in writing to the audit committee the scope of the service.
- Discuss and document the discussion with the audit committee the potential effects of the service on the firm's independence.

 Master Accounting Firm wishes to provide consulting services to its public company audit client, PAL Corporation. The services it wishes to provide are permitted by PCAOB rules, but Master knows that it must receive the consent of PAL's audit committee. Which of the following is not a step that Master should undertake to acquire that consent?

- Describing in writing the scope of the services to be provided
- Discuss the potential effects of provision of the services on independence
- Document the discussion with the audit committee about effects of provision of the services on independence
- Provide a list of the names of Master employees who will provide the services

The audit firm is not required to provide a list of employees who will perform the services. To provide permited NAS, the firm must describe the scope of services to the audit committee writing and discuss the impact the service could have on independence. These discussions should be documented.

Accepting New Audit Clients

Before accepting a public company as a new audit client, a registered firm must:

1. Describe in writing to the audit committee all relationships between the firm and its affiliates on the one hand and the client and its FROR employees as of the date of the communication that "may reasonably be thought to bear on independence".

2. Discuss and document with the audit committee these relationships and their potential effect on independence.

Responsibility Not to Knowingly or Recklessly Contribute to Violations

Provides that public accountants have a responsibility to not—knowingly or recklessly, by action or omission—contribute to violations of SOX, of PCAOB rules, of federal securities laws, or of professional standards.

 PCAOB rules and regulations related to engagment quality reivew procedures are covered in the Quality Control chapter.

1.03 Requirements of the GAO & DOL

Government Accountability Office (GAO) Government Auditing Standards

 Representative Task (Remembering & Understanding): Understand the ethical and independence requirements of the Government Accountability Office Government Auditing Standards.

 Representative Task (Application): Apply the ethical requirements and independence rules of the Government Accountability Office Government Auditing Standards to situations that could present threats to compliance during an audit of, or attestation engagement for, a government entity or an entity receiving federal awards.

When performing an audit of a nonfederal governmental agency or an entity receiving governmental financial assistance, the engagement is performed in accordance with **Generally Accepted Government Auditing Standards (GAGAS)** (ie, the "**Yellow Book**") and the auditor must comply with the ethical requirements of the Government Accountability Office (GAO), an agency of Congress responsible for investigating how the federal government spends taxpayer money.

With a few exceptions, the ethical principles and independence rules that apply to audits of governments and other entities that received federal financial awards are similar to GAAS. What differences do occur are due to the unique environment of governmental entities and compliance issues for federal awards. The two organizations that set rules are the GAO and the Department of Labor (DOL).

Ethical Principles

Those who audit pursuant to GAGAS are expected to audit in accordance with the following ethical and independence principles:

- **The public interest** – Integrity, objectivity, and independence are critical in performing the auditor's professional responsibilities to honor the public trust (ie, the collective well-being of the community of people and entities served.)

- **Integrity** – This includes maintaining an attitude that *is objective, fact-based, nonpartisan*, and *nonideological* regarding the audited entities and users of the audit reports.
  - Auditor integrity is important to maintaining public confidence in government.
  - Inappropriate, conflicting pressures (eg, from management or others) encountered should be resolved with decisions that are consistent with the public interest.

- **Objectivity** – This includes being independent, intellectually honest, and free of conflicts of interest as well as maintaining an attitude of impartiality.

- **Proper use of government information, resources, and positions** – Such information (which may be sensitive or classified), resources, and positions should not be used for personal gain or handled in a way that is illegal, improper, or detrimental to the interests of the audited entity or audit organization.

- **Professional behavior** – The auditor should comply with all laws, regulations, and professional obligations and avoid conduct that could bring discredit to their work.

 Applying GAGAS Ethical Requirements

Lawson CPA, LLP is performing an audit in accordance with GAGAS. In regards to ethical principles, the firm should comply with all of the following except:

- Materiality.

- Integrity.

- The public interest.

- Proper use of government information.

Generally Accepted Government Auditing Standards (GAGAS) ethical principles

- Public interest

- Integrity and objectivity

- Proper use of:

  - Government information

  - Government resources

  - Government positions

- Professional behavior

- Independence

Acting with integrity, acting with the public interest in mind, and ensuring proper use of government information are all ethical principles under Generally Accepted Government Auditing Standards. Materiality is not an ethical principle but a measure of whether a misstatement will influence users of financial information.

Independence Requirements

In all matters in a GAGAS engagement, auditors and audit organizations (AO) must be independent of the auditee. Independence comprises:

- **Independence of mind**, indicating that the auditor is free of influence that might compromise the auditor's judgment

- **Independence in appearance**, meaning no circumstances exist that would cause reasonable and informed third parties to conclude that the auditor's judgment was compromised

Independence Time Period for GAGAS Engagements

Begins at the earlier of:

- The signing of an initial engagement letter or

- Some other agreement to perform an audit

Ends at the later of:

- The formal or informal notification of the termination of the professional relationship or

- issuance of a report, whichever is later.

Internal auditors working under the direction of the audited entity's management are considered independent for purposes of reporting internally if the head of the audit organization meets **all** of the following:

- Accountable to head of the government entity or to those charged with governance;

- Reports audit results both to the head of the government entity and to those charged with governance;

- Located organizationally outside the staff or line management function of the areas being audited;

- Has access to those charged with governance; **and**

- Is sufficiently removed from political pressure to conduct audits and report findings objectively without fear of political reprisal.

If internal auditors audit external organizations, such as contractors, and no independence impairments exist, the auditor is considered an external party to the audited entities.

Independence Conceptual Framework

GAGAS incorporates an independence conceptual framework similar to the AICPA professional standards in which government auditors are expected to:

- Identify threats to independence

- Evaluate the significance of the threats, individually and collectively

- Apply safeguards to eliminate/mitigate the threats so that they are reduced to an acceptable level

Threats to Independence

There are seven categories of threats to independence in the Yellow Book. The first two here are different and the rest are very similar to the AICPA code of conduct:

- A **bias** threat occurs when the auditor is not objective with regard to the client due to political, ideological, social, or other beliefs.

- A **structural** threat occurs when the audit entity's placement within the government entity it is auditing, along with the structure of the government entity, impairs the auditor's ability to remain objective in performing the audit work and reporting the results.

- A **self-interest** threat occurs when the auditor has a financial or other interest in the entity that might affect the auditor's judgment.

- A **self-review** threat occurs when the extent of nonattest services performed by the auditor for the client raise a question as to whether the auditor will be reviewing judgments and estimates that the auditor participated in the development of.

- A **familiarity** threat occurs as a result of the duration and closeness of the relationship between the auditor and the client.

- An **undue** influence threat occurs when external sources create influence or pressure that may affect the auditor's ability to make objective judgments.

- A **management participation** threat occurs when the auditor takes on the role of management or performs management functions for the client.

Magnitude of Threats to Independence

The auditor will evaluate the magnitude (significance) of any threats, individually and in the aggregate, to determine if they are at an acceptable level. If they are not at an acceptable level (ie, threats are significant), the auditor will consider **safeguards** to mitigate or eliminate those threats.

- If safeguards are **sufficient** to reduce threats to an acceptable level, the auditor will document the analysis and may perform the audit engagement.

- If safeguards are **not sufficient**, the auditor's independence is impaired, and the auditor may not perform the engagement.

Threats to independence should be evaluated both individually and in the aggregate. Threats to independence are **not acceptable** if they either:

- Could impact the auditor's ability to perform an audit without being affected by influences that compromise professional judgment; or

- Could expose the auditor or audit organization to circumstances that would cause a reasonable and informed third party to conclude that integrity, objectivity, or professional skepticism of the audit organization, or a member of the audit team, had been compromised.

Safeguards

There are several safeguards an **auditor** can implement to eliminate the threats to independence or reduce them to an acceptable level. Examples include:

- Consulting an independent third party, such as a professional organization, a regulatory body, or another auditor

- Involving another AO to perform or re-perform part of the audit

- Having a professional staff member who was not a member of the audit team review the work performed

- Removing an individual from an audit team

In addition, the **audited entity** can also put safeguards in place, such as:

- A requirement that persons other than management ratify or approve the appointment of an AO to perform the audit (as SOX requires for public companies)

- Internal entity procedures ensuring objective choices in commissioning non audit services

- An entity governance structure that provides appropriate oversight and communications regarding the audit organization's services (comparable to the independent audit committee required by SOX for public companies)

Prohibited Nonaudit Services

If the threat to independence results from the performance of nonaudit services, the auditor will first determine if the service was prohibited. If so, independence is impaired and the auditor will not be able to perform the engagement. Prohibited nonaudit services include:

- Performing *management responsibilities,* such as strategic planning for the entity, developing entity program policies, directing employees, making decisions regarding the acquisition, use or disposition of resources, custody of assets, reporting to governance, accepting responsibility for internal controls, and voting in the management committee or board of directors

- Performing certain *accounting functions without obtaining management approval*, such as determining or changing journal entries, authorizing or approving transactions, and preparing or altering source documents*

- Providing *internal audit assistance* in the form of setting policies, strategic direction, or scope for the internal audit function, or performing internal control procedures

- Accepting *responsibility* for the design, implementation, or maintenance (DIM) of internal control, or its monitoring

- Participation in *information technology services* including the design, development, or alteration of IT systems that manage aspects of the operations that will be audited, or operating or supervising the operation of such a system

- Providing *valuation services* that materially impact information included in the financial statements

- Performing specific *additional services* related to advisory services, benefit plan administration, business risk consulting, executive or employee recruiting, and investment advisory or management

Documentation of Independence

To support the auditor's consideration of independence, documentation should include:

- Threats to independence and the safeguards applied;

- The safeguards applied if the audit organization is structurally located within a government unit and is considered independent as a result of those safeguards;

- Consideration of management's ability to oversee nonaudit services provided; and

- The understanding with the audited entity regarding the performance of nonaudit services.

- The evaluation of the significance of certain nonaudit services, including

  - Recording transactions that management has approved.

  - Preparing certain line items or sections of the financial statements based on the trial balance.

  - Posting entries that management approved.

 Applying GAGAS Independence Requirements

Forrester CPA LLP has been engaged to perform an audit in accordance with GAGAS. Management has requested the firm include the following services as part of the engagement. Which of the following services would constitute a management function under Government Auditing Standards, and result in the impairment of a CPA's independence?

- Developing entity program policies.

- Providing methodologies, such as practice guides.

- Providing accounting opinions to a legislative body.

- Recommending internal control procedures.

Management participation threats to independence:
Government Auditing Standards (GAGAS)

- Serve or recently served as a senior manager or voting board member

- Develop policy, supervise employees, authorize transactions, have custody of assets

- Recommend a candidate for a key position

- Prepare management's plan for corrective action for problems detected in audit

Under Government Auditing Standards, **participation in management decision-making** (eg, developing program policies) impairs independence. However, if an auditor merely provides *advice* to management, and if management is responsible for making final decisions, independence is not impaired.

Department of Labor (DOL) & Employee Retirement Income Security Act of 1974 (ERISA)

 Representative Task (Remembering & Understanding): Understand the independence requirements of the Department of Labor.

 Representative Task (Application): Apply the independence rules of the Department of Labor to situations when an accountant would not be considered independent during an audit of employee benefit plans.

Employee Benefit Plans (plans) are broadly regulated by the Department of Labor's (DOL's) Employee Benefits Security Administration (EBSA) pursuant to the Employee Retirement Income Security Act (ERISA) of 1974, as amended.

Statutory law provides that an accountant retained by a plan to examine plan financial information and render an opinion on the financial statements and schedules required to be contained in a plan's annual report must be "independent."

Unfortunately, despite having been strongly urged to simply adopt AICPA guidelines for independence, DOL's guidelines date to the 1970s and are **inconsistent** with some aspects of modern independence rules.

The rule specifies three types of relationships that will impair an accountant's independence. Independence is impaired by

- Commits to acquiring or has any direct **financial interest** or any material indirect financial interest in the plan during the period of the engagement, at the date of the opinion, or during the period covered by the financial statements
- Maintains **financial records** for the plan
- Has **employment ties** during the same period. This include connection as the plan sponsor, promoter, underwriter, investment advisor, voting trustee, director, officer, or employee

Independence *is not impaired* if the accountant is engaged by the plan's sponsor for a professional engagement, provided it does not involve an activity that is prohibited. In addition, independence is not impaired if the plan uses the services of an actuary that is associated with the accountant.

Applying DOL Independence Rules

In which of the following situations would an auditor who is rendering an audit opinion on the financial statements of an employee benefit plan that will be filed with the Department of Labor be considered independent?

- The auditor's spouse has obtained an immaterial direct financial interest in the employee benefit plan.

- The auditor obtained a material indirect financial interest in the employee benefit plan.

- A member of the auditor's firm was an investment advisor to the employee benefit plan during the period of professional engagement but was not providing services as of the date of the opinion.

- A member of the auditor's firm was a voting trustee of the plan in a prior year but has since disassociated from the plan and did not participate in auditing the financial statements of the plan.

Auditor independence for employee benefit plans

Independence impaired by any of the following during period of engagement or period covered by engagement:

- Direct or material indirect financial interest in the plan

- Acting as promoter, underwriter, investment advisor, voting trustee, director, officer, or employee

- Maintaining financial records for the plan

If an employee of a plan or plan sponsor left to join the accounting firm, the individual be deemed independent if the **person has completely disassociated themselves** from the plan or plan sponsor and **does not participate** in auditing financial statements of the plan covering any period of his or her employment by the plan or plan sponsor.

AUD 2
Professional Skepticism and Judgment

AUD 2: Professional Skepticism and Judgment

2.01 Professional Skepticism and Professional Judgment

Professional Skepticism and Professional Judgment

 Representative Task (Remembering & Understanding): Understand the concepts of professional skepticism and professional judgment.

Professional Skepticism

The auditor should plan and perform the audit with **professional skepticism**, which recognizes that the F/S could be materially misstated. To exercise professional skepticism, the auditor should adopt a **questioning mindset** and be on the lookout for:

- **Contradictory audit evidence** – The auditor should consider audit evidence that contradicts other audit evidence as opposed to focusing only on evidence that corroborates other audit evidence.

- **Information that indicates audit evidence may be unreliable** – Evidence that brings into question the reliability of documents (e.g., documents have been manipulated or forged) or response to inquiries (e.g., the client is lying) may require the auditor to reassess the reliability of the audit evidence.

- **Possible fraud** – The auditor should consider if conditions exist that indicate possible fraud.

- **Need for additional audit procedures** – Depending on the conditions that the auditor finds at the client, the auditor should consider if audit procedures beyond those required by GAAS should be performed.

Applying professional skepticism *reduces the risks* associated with:

- Overlooking unusual circumstances

- Drawing conclusions from audit procedures that are over-generalized

- Making decisions regarding the nature, timing, and extent of audit procedures and evaluating the results of procedures, using inappropriate assumptions

 In accordance with the structure of the AICPA Blueprints, *exercising* professional skepticism and professional judgment is also discussed in Chapter 16, *Sufficient Appropriate Evidence.*

Professional Judgment

Professional judgment reflects the auditor's application of their **training, knowledge, and experience** to make appropriate decisions about what to do given circumstances that arise during the audit. Auditors are required to exercise professional judgment in planning and performing the audit.

- Auditors develop their professional judgment through their accounting education, industry knowledge, and experience in practice.

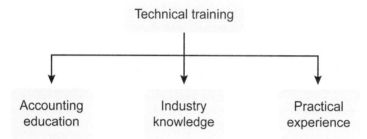

- Professional judgment is particularly necessary in making decisions related to:
  - Materiality
  - Audit risk
  - The nature, timing, and extent of audit procedures to be applied
  - Evaluations as to whether audit evidence is appropriate and sufficient
  - The evaluation of management's judgments
  - Drawing conclusions from the evidence obtained

 Professional judgment applied throughout the audit should be **adequately documented** so that an experienced auditor will understand any significant judgments made in reaching conclusions.

Which of the following ultimately determines the sufficiency and appropriateness of audit evidence to support the auditor's conclusions?

- Professional requirements.
- Professional standards.
- Professional advice.
- Professional judgment.

An application of professional judgment

Audit evidence that is... Sufficient (ie, enough) + Appropriate (ie, relevant and reliable) = Reasonable assurance

As determined by the auditor's professional judgment

It is the auditor's responsibility to determine whether the **evidence** gathered is **sufficient** and **appropriate** to support the auditor's opinion. The auditor makes this determination based on **professional judgment**. Professional judgment is the application of training, experience, and knowledge of accounting, auditing, and ethical requirements and standards to make informed decisions appropriate for the circumstances of an audit.

Auditor Biases

 Representative Task (Remembering & Understanding): Understand unconscious auditor biases and other impediments to acting with professional skepticism, including threats, incentives and judgment-making shortcuts.

Independence

In addition to being independent in appearance as is required by the independence rules covered in the AICPA's Code of Professional Conduct, auditors must also be independent in mindset.

Independence in mindset includes acting with **integrity** and **exercising objectivity** in applying professional judgment and acting with professional skepticism. Threats to professional skepticism include any relationship or circumstance that would impede the auditor's ability to exhibit an objective mindset when applying professional judgment.

 Additional coverage on threats, incentives, and judgment-making shortcuts can be found in Chapter 1.

Auditor Biases

Auditors may find it difficult to continually apply professional skepticism due to their biases, whether conscious or unconscious, and other cognitive tendencies. Cognitive biases are mental judgment-making shortcuts that may threaten the quality of the auditor's decisions. The auditor may decrease the likelihood of their decisions being influenced by a bias by actively considering their susceptibility to each of the five biases anytime they are applying their professional judgment.

Auditors are required to consider if their judgment is susceptible to any of the **five cognitive biases**.

- **Availability bias** – Auditors may place an undue amount of emphasis on events or experiences that come to mind easily (e.g., management's explanation for a fluctuation), and ignore other possibilities that are more difficult to imagine.

- **Anchoring bias** – Auditors may place an undue amount of emphasis on an early piece of information (e.g., provided by management), which causes the auditor to use that information as an anchor against which all other information is improperly evaluated. Auditors may anchor to their initial belief and be unwilling to adequately consider if subsequent information suggests a different conclusion.

- **Automation bias** – The tendency to favor output from automated systems, even when conflicting information exists about whether it is reliable or suitable for the auditor's purpose.

- **Confirmation bias** – Auditors may place an undue amount of emphasis on information that confirms their existing beliefs or expectations. For example, the auditor may expect that internal controls are operating effectively so they tend to place more weight on evidence that corroborates or confirms their belief, and they may dismiss evidence that contradicts their belief.

- **Overconfidence bias** – Auditors may overestimate their ability to make accurate risk assessments and quick judgments or decisions.

Other Impediments to Professional Skepticism

- **Human bias** (threat to objectivity) – If the auditor has a friendly relationship with client employees, the auditor may inadvertently favor the client when evaluating audit evidence. This is particularly true when there are incentives or pressure by the CPA firm to build and expand client relationships.

- **Misplaced trust in management** (threat to objectivity) – Auditors who have worked with the client in previous years may build up a trust in management that is misplaced and unwarranted. Auditors should not assume that management is honest even when their judgment is based on prior experience, nor should they assume that management is dishonest.

- **Time demands** (incentive to not take the time to apply professional judgment) – Unrealistic time budgets can result in auditors taking shortcuts in audit procedures, such as testing easily obtained evidence rather than evidence that is more difficult and time consuming to obtain and test.

An overall response to address a high assessed risk of material misstatement at the financial statement level of a nonissuer may include which of the following?

- Increasing reliance on results of internal control testing.
- Emphasizing the need for more accounting staff.
- Incorporating additional predictability into the selection of procedures.
- Providing more supervision of the audit team.

Risk of material misstatement (RMM)

If...
RMM is high

Then...
Increase professional skepticism
Increase planned audit procedures
- More thorough tests
- Rely more on year-end testing
- Assign experienced staff with specilized skills
- Close supervision required

When the RMM at the financial statement level is high, the auditor responds by decreasing detection risk (ie, the risk that a misstatement will go undetected). Detection risk can be reduced by:

- Emphasizing **professional skepticism**
- Assigning more experienced staff or specialists and **providing more supervision**
- Reducing predictability of procedures
- Changing the nature, timing, and extent of procedures (eg, more substantive procedures)

AUD 3
Audit Engagements

AUD 3: Audit Engagements

3.01 Audit Engagements

Overview of the Audit Process

There are distinct steps that occur in every audit. These steps are briefly summarized below:

Engagement Planning

- Decide whether to accept (or continue) the engagement. Recall the quality control standards regarding client acceptance/continuation issues

- Perform risk assessment procedures to address the risks of material misstatement, whether due to error or fraud

- Evaluate requirements for staffing and supervision

- Prepare the required written audit plan (sometimes called the *audit program*) that specifies the nature, timing, and extent of auditing procedures for every audit area (which is usually prepared after control risk has been assessed, so that detection risk can be appropriately set in each audit area)

Internal Control Considerations

- Obtain an understanding of internal control for planning purposes as required, emphasizing the assessment of the risk of material misstatement in individual audit areas and document the understanding of internal control

- If contemplating *reliance* on certain identified internal control strengths as a basis for reducing substantive testing, the auditor must then perform appropriate *tests of control* to determine that those specific controls are operating effectively, that is, working as intended

Substantive Audit Procedures

- Note that the word *substantive* is derived from *substantiate*, which means *to verify*. These are evidence-gathering procedures designed to verify the financial statement elements and to detect any material misstatements

- **Analytical Procedures** are evidence-gathering procedures that suggest reasonableness (or lack thereof) based on a comparison to appropriate expectations or benchmarks, such as prior year's financial statements, comparability to industry data (including ratios) or other interrelationships involving financial and/or nonfinancial data

- **Tests of Details** are those evidence-gathering procedures consisting of either of two types:

  ○ **Tests of Ending Balances** — Where the final balance is assessed by testing the composition of the year-end balance (e.g., testing a sample of individual customers' account balances that make up the general ledger accounts receivable control account balance)

  ○ **Tests of Transactions** — Where the final balance is assessed by examining those debits and credits that caused the balance to change from last year's audited balance to the current year's balance

Reporting

Conclusions are expressed in writing using standardized language to avoid miscommunication.

 Be sure to understand the components of the overall audit process. Lots of questions on the exam will evaluate the steps or documents that occur during different phases of the audit. By understanding the overall process, students are able to analyze questions to determine incorrect answers because of where they occur within the audit process.

Types of Audit Engagements

 Representative Task (Remembering & Understanding): Identify the nature, scope and objectives of the different types of audit engagements for issuers and nonissuers.

The auditor's primary role is to provide an impartial (independent) report on the reliability of management's financial statements (F/S). There are several types of audits that may be performed in relation to an entity.

Compliance Audits

Compliance audits are often performed by or for **governmental or regulatory organizations** to determine if an entity is complying with applicable laws and regulations. Entities may be chosen for audit on a random basis or may be selected due to some indication of noncompliance (eg, tax returns with unusual deductions).

Examples include:

- IRS audits
- Audits in accordance with *Generally Accepted Government Auditing Standards (GAGAS)*
- Agreed-upon procedures engagement to determine compliance with provisions of a bond or note agreement

 Compliance audits for governmental/regulatory entities and audits for compliance with laws and regulations are discussed further in other chapters.

Operational Audits

Operational (ie, performance) audits are generally performed to determine if **management's policies** are being followed appropriately, to evaluate the entity's compliance with internal controls, and to assess performance (ie, effectiveness, efficiency, and economy). Internal auditors and governmental auditors typically perform these audits, but external CPAs may also perform an operational audit as a consultant. The nature, scope, and objectives of the engagement will depend on the purpose of the audit. It can be customized as needed. Examples include:

- An internal auditor auditing a department or division of a corporation to see if it is meeting organizational goals
- A governmental auditor auditing an organization to determine the effectiveness and benefit of specific government-funded programs

Financial Audits

F/S audits are performed exclusively by CPA firms. A F/S audit is an *examination* for the purpose of giving an *objective* (ie, unbiased) *opinion* as to the *fairness of financial statement presentations* in conformity with an **applicable financial reporting framework (AFRF)**.

An AFRF is a standard or a set of criteria used to determine measurement, recognition, presentation, and disclosure of all material items appearing in the F/S. It determines the form and content of the F/S. To adhere to auditing standards, auditors must be familiar with their client's AFRF. Auditors will use the framework as a guide to help them assess if the client's F/S meet the framework's requirements.

Entity	General purpose financial reporting framework	Issued by
Public / issuer	U.S. generally accepted accounting principles (**GAAP**)	Financial Accounting Standards Board (**FASB**)
Private / nonissuer	U.S. generally accepted accounting principles (**GAAP**)	Financial Accounting Standards Board (**FASB**)
U.S. federal government	Statements of federal financial accounting standards (**SFFAS**)	Financial Accounting Standards Advisory Board (**FASAB**)
U.S. state and local government	Statements of governmental accounting standards	Governmental Accounting Standards Board (**GASB**)

There are two types of AFRFs:

- A general-purpose framework is designed to meet the common financial information objectives of a wide range of users.

- A special purpose framework (ie, other comprehensive basis of accounting—OCBOA) is a framework other than GAAP that could include the cash basis (modified cash), tax basis, regulatory agency basis, contractual basis, or an "other basis of accounting."

General purpose frameworks	Special purpose frameworks
GAAP	Income tax basis
	Cash basis
IFRS	Contractual basis
	Regulatory basis

 Auditor may have to use the International Standards on Auditing (ISA) to audit International Financial Reporting Standards (IFRS) F/S. Both ISA and IFRS are outside of the scope of the CPA exam.

Integrated Audits

Integrated audits are required for public companies to stay in compliance with the Sarbanes-Oxley Act (SOX). An integrated audit is performed exclusively by CPA firms. The typical financial audit is integrated with an audit of the internal controls over financial reporting (**ICFR**). The Public Company Accounting Oversight Board (PCAOB) auditing standards guide the integrated audit work needed by issuers.

Types of audits	Who performs?	What is evaluated?
Compliance audit	• Governmental/regulatory auditors	Compliance with laws, regulations, and contractual agreements
Operational audit	• Typically internal auditors • Governmental auditors	Compliance with internal controls and entity performance
Financial statement audit	• External auditors (only CPAs)	Compliance with an AFRF*

Applicable Financial Reporting Framework

Auditing Standards Overview

In the U.S., the primary financial reporting framework adopted for F/S presentation is **Generally Accepted Accounting Principles (GAAP)**. GAAP is a general-purpose framework that includes both **broad guidelines** and **detailed policies** and **procedures,** such as conventions and rules.

The framework defines the accounting practice at a **particular time**; it is updated regularly to stay current with changes in the business environment. The Financial Accounting Standards Board (FASB), not the AICPA, maintains GAAP in one centralized codification.

The appropriate auditing standards to be followed depend upon whether the entity is public (ie, an issuer) or private (ie, a nonissuer), as shown in the following chart:

Entity	Auditing Standard	Issued by
Private / Nonissuer	Statement on Auditing Standards (**SAS**). The current version is referred to as: • Statements on Auditing Standards: Clarification and Recodification • Clarified Auditing Standards (**AU-C**)	AICPA's Auditing Standards Board (**ASB**)
Public / Issuer	PCAOB Auditing Standards (**AS**)	Public Company Accounting Oversight Board (**PCAOB**)

Audit Standards for Nonissuers

Statements on Auditing Standards and Associated Guidance

Auditors follow generally accepted auditing standards (GAAS) when auditing private (nonissuer) entities. **GAAS** provides **broad** auditing **objectives** but does **not** include specific **procedures** that the auditor must perform. The auditor should apply **professional judgment** to determine the appropriate procedures that are necessary to achieve those objectives.

The AICPA refers to **GAAS** as authoritative professional standards in the form of **Statements on Auditing Standards**. Each statement outlines a specific topic (eg, audit documentation, planning) and is organized using *AU-C*. AU refers to "audit" and C to signify the application under the clarity standards.

SAS requires the following for auditors:

- Auditors are expected to have sufficient knowledge of the SASs to identify those applicable to the audit

- The auditor should be prepared to justify any departures from the SASs

- Materiality and audit risk also underlie the application of the SASs, particularly those related to performing the audit (evidence gathering) and reporting

Interpretive Publications consist of the appendices to the SASs, auditing interpretations of the SASs, auditing guidance included in AICPA Audit and Accounting Guides, and AICPA auditing Statements of Position.

- Interpretive publications are not considered to be auditing standards. These are issued under the authority of the ASB after all ASB members have had an opportunity to comment on the interpretive publication

- Auditors should be aware of (and consider) interpretive publications applicable to their audits. When auditors do not apply such auditing guidance, they should be prepared to explain how they complied with the SAS provisions related to such interpretive publications

Other Auditing Publications include articles in the *Journal of Accountancy* and the AICPA's *CPA Letter* (and other professional publications), continuing professional education programs, textbooks, etc.

- Other auditing publications have no authoritative status. They may be useful to the auditor in understanding and applying the SASs

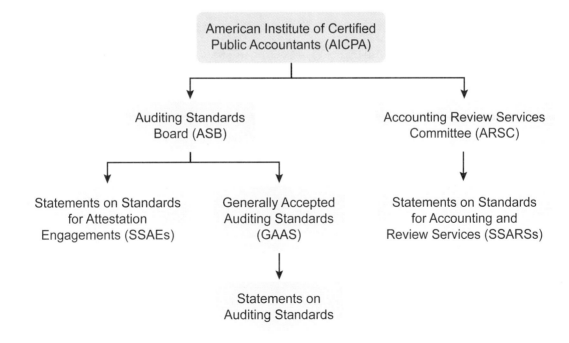

Professional Requirements

The various AICPA standards (ie, Statements on Auditing Standards, Statements on Standards for Attestation Engagements, Statements on Standards for Accounting and Review Services, and Statements on Quality Control Standards) distinguish between two types of professional requirements:

Unconditional requirements	Presumptively mandatory requirements
Must comply with the requirement without exception (indicated by "**must**" in applicable standards)	In rare circumstances, the practioner may depart from the requirement, but must document: • The justification for the departure and • How the alternate procedures performed were adequate to meet the objective of the requirement (indicated by "**should**" in applicable standards).

Purpose and Premise of an Audit

SAS are organized around four themes: (1) purpose/premise; (2) responsibilities; (3) performance; and (4) reporting (as a memory aid, remember: **PR-PR**).

The **purpose** of an audit is to provide F/S users with an opinion by the auditor on whether the F/S are **presented fairly**, in all material respects, in accordance with the applicable financial reporting framework (AFRF). An auditor's opinion enhances the degree of confidence that intended users can place in the F/S.

An audit in accordance with GAAS is conducted on the **premise** that management and, where appropriate, those charged with governance, have responsibility for:

- The preparation and fair presentation of the F/S in accordance with the AFRF, including internal controls
- Providing the auditor with all relevant information and unrestricted access to those within the entity from whom the auditor determines it necessary to obtain audit evidence

Responsibilities

Auditor responsibilities can be remembered by using the acronym **TIP**: training and professional judgment, Independence and due professional care (ethics) and finally professional skepticism.

 Additional coverage on professional skepticism, professional judgment, and auditor biases can be found in Chapter 2.01, *Professional Skepticism and Judgment.*

Training & Professional Judgment

Auditors must possess **adequate technical training**. Adequate technical training means the auditor has proper accounting education (and continuing education), industry and business knowledge, and practical experience. These skills are used to assess audit evidence and to detect irregularities in a client's response.

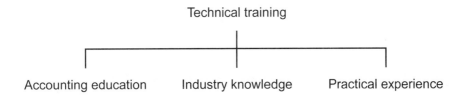

Auditor must also have the ability to exercise professional judgment in planning and performing the audit. **Professional judgment** is generally defined as the application of relevant training, knowledge, and experience to make appropriate decisions during the audit.

Independence & Other Due Care

The auditor should be **independent** in fact and appearance and comply with all other relevant requirements of the AICPA Code of Professional Conduct.

- Independence enhances the auditor's ability to act with integrity and objectivity and maintain an attitude of professional skepticism
- Independence includes the auditor, their spouse, dependent kids, or dependent relatives

There are circumstances under which an auditor will perform an audit despite a lack of independence:

- The auditor is required by law or regulation to accept the engagement
- Provides for circumstances that allow the auditor to accept the engagement

Other ethical requirements include the AICPA Code of Professional Conduct, rules of state boards of accountancy, and other relevant regulatory agencies, as well as other requirements related to F/S audits.

 Independence requirements are covered extensively under the chapter discussing the AICPA Code of Professional Conduct.

Whether they are working in public practice or in business, the AICPA Code of Professional Conduct requires CPAs to exercise due care in all their professional duties. The **due care** principle requires that CPAs **observe technical** and **ethical standards** and perform their professional responsibilities with **competence** and **diligence**.

In the case of an audit, the requirement to observe technical standards requires the auditor to follow the rules of GAAS (for a nonissuer) or the PCAOB (for an issuer). As a quality control measure, both GAAS and PCAOB standards require that **experienced auditors** (eg, managers) critically **review** the **work** and the **judgment** of **less experienced members** (ie, staff auditors) of the engagement team.

Requirements of due care

- Observe technical standards (eg, GAAP, auditing standards)
- Observe ethical standards (eg, Code of Professional Conduct)
- Strive to improve competence (eg, professional education)
- Perform duties diligently

Professional Skepticism

The auditor should plan and perform the audit with professional skepticism, which recognizes that the F/S could be materially misstated. **Professional skepticism** includes:

- Having a questioning mind

- Being alert to the possibilities of misstatement due to fraud or error

- Critically assessing audit evidence

Which of the following communications between the auditor with final responsibility for an engagement and the audit engagement team regarding the susceptibility of a client's F/S to material misstatements due to error or fraud is required by auditing standards?

- Explain all procedures to be performed to detect significant errors or fraudulent activity

- Discuss the need to maintain a questioning mind and to exercise professional skepticism throughout the audit

- Explain the firm's strategy for managing and controlling legal liability due to fraud

- Discuss the firm's policy for allocating budgeted audit hours to detect fraud

**Discussion regarding susceptibility
to material misstatements**

- External/internal fraud risk factors

- Risk of management overriding internal controls

- Circumstances indicative of earnings/financial manipulation

- Importance of professional skepticism throughout audit

- How to respond to the risk of material misstatements

The audit team should brainstorm about which areas might be more susceptible to error or fraud and how these risks may be addressed. The discussion should specifically address the importance of **maintaining professional skepticism** throughout the audit. Professional skepticism is a continuous attitude in which the auditor critically assesses audit evidence with a questioning mind. This attitude creates the viewpoint that not everything may be as it seems and is useful for detecting material misstatements due to error or fraud.

Auditors may find it difficult to continually apply professional skepticism due to their **biases**, whether conscious or unconscious, and other cognitive tendencies. Auditors must also be alert the potential effects of:

- **Misplaced Trust in Management**—Auditors who have worked with the client in previous years may build up a trust in management that is misplaced and unwarranted

- **Time Demands**—Unrealistic time budgets can result in auditors taking shortcuts in audit procedures, such as testing easily obtained evidence rather than evidence that is more difficult and time-consuming to obtain and test.

Performance

The **performance** principles are used to describe **evidence-gathering activities** (ie, fieldwork).

- To express an opinion, the auditor obtains *reasonable assurance* about whether the F/S, as a whole, are free from material misstatement, whether due to fraud or error. To obtain reasonable assurance, which is a high but not absolute level of assurance, the auditor:

  - Plans the work

  - Properly supervises any assistants

- o Determines appropriate materiality levels
- o Identifies and assesses risks of material misstatement
- o Obtains sufficient appropriate audit evidence

- The auditor is unable to obtain absolute assurance that the F/S are free from material misstatement because of **inherent limitations**, which arise from:
  - o **The Nature of Financial Reporting**—The preparation and fair presentation of F/S involves management's judgment and subjective decisions (eg, accounting estimates). Therefore, some items are subject to an inherent level of variability that cannot be eliminated with the application of audit procedures
  - o **The Nature of Audit Procedures**—There are practical and legal limitations on the auditor's ability to obtain audit evidence. For example, even though audit procedures are performed to obtain assurance that all relevant information has been obtained, the auditor still cannot be certain that management or others have provided complete information

 Which of the following statements correctly defines the term *reasonable assurance*?
- A substantial level of assurance to allow an auditor to detect a material misstatement
- A significant level of assurance to allow an auditor to detect a material misstatement
- An absolute level of assurance to allow an auditor to detect a material misstatement
- A high, but not absolute, level of assurance to allow an auditor to detect a material misstatement

Assurance hierarchy

Cost and time to achieve (vertical axis, arrow pointing up)

Absolute assurance
- Ensures 100% accuracy
- Every financial item is looked at

Reasonable assurance
- Ensures a comfortable level of accuracy
- Financial items above a threshold are tested

Limited assurance
- Ensures a low level of accuracy
- Only inquiries and analytical procedures are performed

No assurance
- Ensures no level of accuracy
- No items are tested

A **high (but not absolute) level of assurance** (reasonable assurance) gives users of financial information confidence to rely on financial reports. Financial auditors try to provide users of financial reports with a reasonable level of assurance about management's financial assertions. Assertions are management claims reported on the F/S (ie, reported revenues), like the claims of the car salesman. Investors, creditors, and other lenders are like the car buyer because they provide resources to the company based on the reported claims.

Reporting

Based on an evaluation of the audit evidence obtained, the auditor expresses, in the form of a **written report**, an opinion in accordance with the auditor's findings, or states that an opinion cannot be expressed. This **opinion** states whether the F/S are presented fairly, in all material respects, in **accordance with the AFRF.**

Audit Standards for Issuers

 Although the PCAOB issues its own auditing standards, it has significant alignment with the AICPA's guidance. The exam will often differentiate questions about the PCAOB versus AICPA standards by using the terms "issuer" and "nonissuer."

When auditing the F/S of public entities that report to the SEC and are subject to the requirements of the **PCAOB**, the auditor will have to perform an audit of internal control over financial reporting (**ICFR**) that is *Integrated* with an audit of F/S. The auditor must determine that management complied with Rules 404a & b of the Sarbanes-Oxley Act.

- Rule 404a requires the annual report to include a report on internal control (I/C) indicating *management's responsibility* for I/C and management's assessment of I/C's effectiveness

- Rule 404b requires the auditor to report on *management's assessment* of I/C (but not the efficiency or effectiveness of I/C)

PCAOB Auditing Standards

The PCAOB Auditing Standards (AS) are broken into five areas.

PCAOB auditing standards

General auditing standards	Audit procedures	Auditor reporting	Matters relating to filings under federal securities laws	Other matters associated with audits

General Auditing Standards

- General Principles and Responsibilities
  - Responsibilities and functions of the independent auditor
  - Independence
  - Training and proficiency of the independent auditor
  - Due professional care in the performance of work
- General Concepts
  - Audit risk
  - Audit evidence
  - Relationship of auditing standards to quality control standards
- General Activities
  - Supervision of the audit engagement
  - Part of the audit performed by other independent auditors
  - Dividing responsibility for the audit with another accounting firm
  - Using the work of an auditor-engaged specialist

- o Audit documentation
- o Engagement quality review

- Auditor Communications
  - o Audit committees
  - o Regarding control deficiencies in an audit of F/S

Audit Procedures

- Audit planning and risk assessment
- Auditing internal control over financial reporting
- Audit procedures
  - o In response to risks—nature, timing, and extent
  - o For specific aspects of the audit, such as fraud, illegal acts, related parties, and going concern
  - o For certain accounts or disclosures, including accounting estimates, contingent liabilities, and inventory
- Special topics, including service organization, internal audit, and predecessor auditors
- Auditor's responsibilities regarding supplemental and other information
- Concluding audit procedures including subsequent events, management representation, and evaluating the audit results
- Post-audit matters

Auditor Reporting

- Reporting on audits of F/S
- Other reporting topics, including special reports and reporting on condensed F/S

Matters Relating to Filings under Federal Securities Laws

- Responsibilities regarding filings under federal securities statutes
- Reviews of interim financial information

Other Matters Associated with Audits

- Reports on the application of accounting principles
- Compliance auditing considerations in audits of recipients of governmental financial assistance
- Reporting on whether a previously reported material weakness continues to exist

PCAOB Audit Deficiencies

An auditor's responsibilities under AS 2201 regarding the **communication** of I/C deficiencies are as follows:

- **Material weaknesses** must be communicated to management and the audit committee in writing prior to the issuance of the auditor's report on ICFR
- **Significant deficiencies** identified by the auditor must also be communicated in writing to the audit committee prior to the issuance of the auditor's report on I/C

The auditor should also communicate **control deficiencies** that are not significant deficiencies or material weaknesses to management **in writing** on a timely basis, prior to the issuance of the audit report on I/C.

3.02 Engagements Conducted under Government Accounting Office Government Auditing Standards (GAOGAS)

Overview

 Representative Task (Remembering & Understanding): Identify the nature, scope, and objectives of engagements performed in accordance with Government Accountability Office Government Auditing Standards, including single audits.

Generally Accepted Government Auditing Standards (GAGAS) (oftentimes interchangeably referred to as simply Government Auditing Standards (GAS) or the "Yellow Book") add layers of audit requirements for certain entities in addition to GAAS. That is, if GAGAS applies, so does GAAS; and if the Single Audit Act applies, then GAGAS and GAAS also apply.

The following chart breaks down these layers of audit requirements by whom they are generally applicable to, the authoritative guidance supporting them, and the organizations they're issued by.

Audit type	Applicable to	Authoritative guidance	Issued by
GAAS F/S audits	All entities requiring an F/S audit	All AU-C sections apply, except AU-C 935, *Compliance Audits,** which only apply if a government compliance audit is also required.	AICPA
GAGAS financial audits	Certain governmental entities and nongovernmental entities (eg, contractors, nonprofits) receiving / administering governmental assistance, depending on program requirements	Government Auditing Standards for financial audits	U.S. Government Accountability Office (GAO)
Single audits	Nonfederal entities (eg, cities, universities, and nonprofits) receiving major federal financial assistance (ie, ≥ $750,000 within a fiscal year)	Single Audit Act, as amended OMB Audit Requirements for Federal Awards (2 CFR 200)	Office of Management and Budget (OMB)

*PCAOB AS 6110 (and other relevant PCAOB standards) may apply instead. Also note that AU-C 935 is not applicable when an examination in accordance with attestation standards (AT-C 315) is required.

GAAS Financial Statement Audits

In an audit in accordance with GAAS ("GAAS F/S audit"), tests of compliance will be focused on **violations of laws and regulations** that have a *direct and material effect* on the amounts in the organization's F/S.

A **standard audit report** is normally issued; however, if material noncompliance is detected, it is disclosed and treated as a departure from the applicable financial reporting framework (eg, GAAP), resulting in a qualified or adverse opinion (disagreement).

GAGAS Financial Audits

All of the above GAAS requirements apply to compliance audits in accordance with GAGAS ("GAGAS financial audit"), plus more.

Required Procedures

The auditor must design the audit to provide reasonable assurance of detecting material misstatements resulting from **noncompliance with contract provisions or grant agreements** that have a *direct and material effect* on the F/S.

 Hill, CPA, is auditing the financial statements of Helping Hand, a not-for-profit organization that receives financial assistance from governmental agencies. To detect misstatements in Helping Hand's financial statements resulting from violations of laws and regulations, Hill should focus on violations that

- Could result in criminal prosecution against the organization
- Involve significant deficiencies to be communicated to the organization's trustees and the funding agencies
- Have a direct and material effect on the amounts in the organization's financial statements
- Demonstrate the existence of material weaknesses

Excerpt from GAGAS report

Compliance and Other Matters

As part of obtaining reasonable assurance about whether ABC Inc.'s financial statements are free from material misstatement, we performed tests of its compliance with certain provisions of laws, regulations, contracts, and grant agreements, **noncompliance with which could have a direct and material effect on the financial statements.** However, providing an opinion on compliance with those provisions was not an objective of our audit, and accordingly, we do not express such an opinion. The results of our tests disclosed no instances of noncompliance or other matters that are required to be reported under Government Auditing Standards.

As part of a GAAS financial statement audit, the auditor provides *reasonable assurance* that there are **no** instances of **noncompliance** with laws or regulations that have a **direct and material effect** on the financial statements. GAGAS extends this requirement to include compliance with contracts and grant agreements.

If relevant and necessary to achieve audit objectives, auditors should perform procedures to determine the following for each *finding* (ie, any matter that is required to be reported):

- **Criteria**—What are the laws, regulations, etc. that apply?

- **Condition**—What is the situation that exists?

- **Cause**—For example, is there an I/C deficiency?

- **Effect**—What are the actual or potential consequences?

Note that the consideration of I/C deficiencies may include deficiencies that result in waste or abuse.

- **Waste** is defined as "the act of using or expending resources carelessly, extravagantly, or to no purpose." It primarily relates to "mismanagement, inappropriate actions, and inadequate oversight." It can include activities that do not include abuse or a violation of law

- **Abuse** is defined as "behavior that is deficient or improper when compared with behavior that a prudent person would consider reasonable and necessary business practice given the facts and circumstances, but excludes fraud and noncompliance with provisions of laws, regulations, contracts, and grant agreements." Abuse may also include misuse of authority or position for personal financial benefit or for the benefit of a close family member or business associate

Reporting Requirements

In addition to an audit report on the F/S required by GAAS, GAGAS requires the auditor to report on:

- **Internal control**
  - Describe the **scope of the auditors' testing of I/C** over financial reporting and compliance with laws, regulations, and provisions of contracts or grant agreements
  - State whether the tests performed provided sufficient, appropriate evidence to support opinions on the effectiveness of I/C and on compliance. Note, however, that an **opinion on I/C is not required**
  - Report **significant deficiencies and material weaknesses** in I/C over financial reporting as findings

- **Compliance with laws and regulations**
  - Report identified or suspected material noncompliance or fraud

 For financial statement audits performed in accordance with generally accepted government auditing standards, auditors should report which of the following?

- All violations of private grant agreements, regardless of materiality

- Suspected illegal acts

- Significant deficiencies in internal control

- Significant changes in the entity's internal control policies

Financial audit reporting requirements

- Financial statement compliance with GAGAS

- Compliance with laws and regulations; compliance with contract provisions; instances of abuse

- Deficiencies and weaknesses in internal control

GAGAS requires an audit report on the financial statements (F/S), a written internal control report, and a report on compliance with laws and regulations. Because governments are accountable for the proper use of public resources, GAGAS imposes *supplemental reporting standards* in addition to GAAS. For example, **GAGAS** requires that **auditors report** the **scope** of their testing of **internal control** and of **noncompliance** with laws, regulations, contracts, or grants. If auditors discover **significant deficiencies** in internal control or suspect material fraud or noncompliance, they include their findings in the audit report.

The auditor should also provide written communication to the audited entity officials regarding identified or suspected noncompliance or fraud that are *less than material but warrant attention* from those charged with governance.

Material noncompliance with laws and regulations and instances of fraud should be communicated **directly to parties outside** the audited entity (eg, a federal inspector general) under two circumstances:

- If the auditee fails to communicate the issues to parties specified by law or regulation even after being notified by the auditor of the failure to do so, the auditor should notify such specified parties directly

- If the auditee fails to respond to such issues when it involves funding received directly or indirectly from a government agency, even after being notified of management's failure to respond, the auditor should report the failure directly to the funding agency

Reporting fraud or noncompliance in GAGAS audit

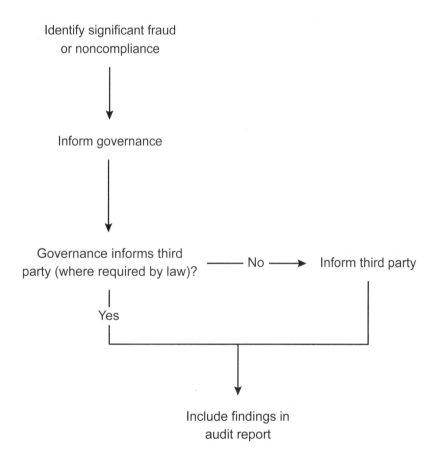

The three reports required under GAAS and GAGAS can be provided separately, or they can be combined into one or two reports (ie, one on the F/S and one combined on compliance and I/C). The following is an example from AU-C 935.

Combined Report on Compliance with Applicable Requirements & I/C Over Compliance

INDEPENDENT AUDITOR'S REPORT

[Addressee]

Report on Compliance

Opinion on [indicate the reporting level pursuant to governmental audit requirement]

We have audited Example Entity's compliance with the [identify the applicable compliance requirements or refer to the document that describes the applicable compliance requirements] applicable to Example Entity's [identify the government program(s) audited or refer to a separate schedule that identifies the program(s)] for the year ended June 30, 20X1.

We have audited Example Entity's compliance with the [identify the applicable compliance requirements or refer to the document that describes the applicable compliance requirements] applicable to Example Entity's [identify the government program(s) audited or refer to a separate schedule that identifies the program(s)] for the year ended June 30, 20X1.

In our opinion, Example Entity complied, in all material respects, with the compliance requirements referred to above that are applicable to [indicate the reporting level pursuant to governmental audit requirement] for the year ended June 30, 20X1.

Basis for Opinion

We conducted our audit of compliance in accordance with auditing standards generally accepted in the United States of America (GAAS); the standards applicable to financial audits contained in Government Auditing Standards (*Government Auditing Standards*) issued by the Comptroller General of the United States; and [*insert the name of the governmental audit requirement or program-specific audit guide*]. Our responsibilities under those standards and [insert the name of the governmental audit requirement or program-specific audit guide] are further described in the Auditor's Responsibilities for the Audit of Compliance section of our report.

We are required to be independent of Example Entity and to meet our other ethical responsibilities, in accordance with relevant ethical requirements relating to our audit. We believe the audit evidence we have obtained is sufficient and appropriate to provide a basis for our opinion. Our audit does not provide a legal determination of Example Entity's compliance with the compliance requirements referred to above.

Responsibilities of Management for Compliance

Management is responsible for compliance with the requirements referred to above and for the design, implementation, and maintenance of effective internal control over compliance with the requirements of laws, statutes, regulations, rules, and provisions of contracts or grant agreements applicable to the Example Entity's government programs.

Auditor's Responsibilities for the Audit of Compliance

Our objectives are to obtain reasonable assurance about whether material noncompliance with the compliance requirements referred to above occurred, whether due to fraud or error, and express an opinion on Example Entity's compliance based on our audit. Reasonable assurance is a high level of assurance but is not absolute assurance and therefore is not a guarantee that an audit conducted in accordance with GAAS, *Government Auditing Standards*, and [*insert the name of the governmental audit requirement or program-specific audit guide*] will always detect material noncompliance when it exists. The risk of not detecting material noncompliance resulting from fraud is higher than for that resulting from error, as fraud may involve collusion, forgery, intentional omissions, misrepresentations, or the override of internal control. Noncompliance with the compliance requirements referred to above is considered material if there is a substantial likelihood that, individually or in the aggregate, it would influence the judgment made by a reasonable user of the report on compliance about Example Entity's compliance with the requirements of the government program as a whole.

In performing an audit in accordance with GAAS, Government Auditing Standards, and [insert the name of the governmental audit requirement or program-specific audit guide], we:

Exercise professional judgment and maintain professional skepticism throughout the audit.

Identify and assess the risks of material noncompliance, whether due to fraud or error, and design and perform audit procedures responsive to those risks. Such procedures include examining, on a test basis, evidence regarding Example Entity's compliance with the compliance requirements referred to above and performing such other procedures as we considered necessary in the circumstances.

Obtain an understanding of Example Entity's internal control over compliance relevant to the audit in order to design audit procedures that are appropriate in the circumstances and to test and report on internal control over compliance in accordance with [*insert the name of the governmental audit requirement or program-specific audit guide*], but not for the purpose of expressing an opinion on the effectiveness of Example Entity's internal control over compliance. Accordingly, no such opinion is expressed.

We are required to communicate with those charged with governance regarding, among other matters, the planned scope and timing of the audit and any significant deficiencies and material weaknesses in internal control over compliance that we identified during the audit.

Report on Internal Control Over ComplianceAuditor's Responsibilities for the Audit of Com1pliance

Our objectives are to obtain reasonable assurance about whether material noncompliance with the compliance requirements referred to above occurred, whether due to fraud or error, and express an opinion on Example Entity's compliance based on our audit. Reasonable assurance is a high level of assurance but is not absolute assurance and therefore is not a guarantee that an audit conducted in accordance with GAAS, *Government Auditing Standards*, and [*insert the name of the governmental audit requirement or program-specific audit guide*] will always detect material noncompliance when it exists. The risk of not detecting material noncompliance resulting from fraud is higher than for that resulting from error, as fraud may involve collusion, forgery, intentional omissions, misrepresentations, or the override of internal control. Noncompliance with the compliance requirements referred to above is considered material if there is a substantial likelihood that, individually or in the aggregate, it would influence the judgment made by a reasonable user of the report on compliance about Example Entity's compliance with the requirements of the government program as a whole.

In performing an audit in accordance with GAAS, Government Auditing Standards, and [insert the name of the governmental audit requirement or program-specific audit guide], we:

Exercise professional judgment and maintain professional skepticism throughout the audit.

Identify and assess the risks of material noncompliance, whether due to fraud or error, and design and perform audit procedures responsive to those risks. Such procedures include examining, on a test basis, evidence regarding Example Entity's compliance with the compliance requirements referred to above and performing such other procedures as we considered necessary in the circumstances.

Obtain an understanding of Example Entity's internal control over compliance relevant to the audit in order to design audit procedures that are appropriate in the circumstances and to test and report on internal control over compliance in accordance with [*insert the name of the governmental audit requirement or program-specific audit guide*], but not for the purpose of expressing an opinion on the effectiveness of Example Entity's internal control over compliance. Accordingly, no such opinion is expressed.

We are required to communicate with those charged with governance regarding, among other matters, the planned scope and timing of the audit and any significant deficiencies and material weaknesses in internal control over compliance that we identified during the audit.

Report on Internal Control Over Compliance

A *deficiency* in internal control over compliance exists when the design or operation of a control over compliance does not allow management or employees, in the normal course of performing their assigned functions, to prevent, or detect and correct, noncompliance on a timely basis. A *material weakness* in internal control over compliance is a deficiency, or combination of deficiencies in internal control over compliance, such that there is a reasonable possibility that material noncompliance with a compliance requirement will not be prevented, or detected and corrected, on a timely basis. A *significant deficiency in internal control over compliance* is a deficiency, or a combination of deficiencies, in internal control over compliance that is less severe than a material weakness in internal control over compliance, yet important enough to merit attention by those charged with governance.

Our consideration of internal control over compliance was for the limited purpose described in the first paragraph of this section and was not designed to identify all deficiencies in internal control over compliance that might be material weaknesses or significant deficiencies in internal control over compliance. Given these limitations, during our audit we did not identify any deficiencies in internal control over compliance that we consider to be material weaknesses, as defined above. However, material weaknesses or significant deficiencies in internal control over compliance may exist that have not been identified.

Our audit was not designed for the purpose of expressing an opinion on the effectiveness of internal control over compliance. Accordingly, no such opinion is expressed.

The purpose of this report on internal control over compliance is solely to describe the scope of our testing of internal control over compliance and the results of that testing based on the [*insert the name of the governmental audit requirement or program-specific audit guide*]. Accordingly, this report is not suitable for any other purpose.

[Auditor's signature]
[Auditor's city and state]
[Date of the auditor's report]

GAGAS Performance Audits

Performance audits are primarily designed to determine the **economy, efficiency, and effectiveness** of a program in achieving its goals. Such audits also include consideration of fraud, compliance with laws and regulations, and I/C related to achieving program goals if they are significant to audit objectives. If I/C is significant to audit objectives, the auditor should:

- Obtain an understanding of I/C
- Assess I/C to the extent necessary to address audit objectives
- Evaluate I/C deficiencies and determine if such deficiencies were the cause of other audit findings (ie, any noncompliance, fraud, waste, or abuse found)

The auditor's report will include the items listed in the box below:

Included in GAGAS performance audit reports

- Objectives and scope
- Audit methodology
- Audit findings, conclusions, and recommendations
- Responsible official's views on audit findings
- Nature of confidential information omitted from the report

3.03 Other Engagements

Overview

 Representative Task (Remembering & Understanding): Identify the nature, scope and objectives of attestation engagements and accounting and review service engagements.

CPA's offer a variety of other engagements, in addition to audits, which provide the following levels of assurance:

Engagements by level of assurance

Reasonable assurance	• Audit
	• Examination
Limited assurance	• Review
	• Compilation
No assurance	• Preparation
	• Agreed-upon procedures

Statements on Standards for Attestation Engagements (SSAEs)

For an attestation engagement, the CPA leverages the Statements on Standards for Attestation Engagements (SSAEs), which is the authoritative literature issued by the AICPA's Accounting Standards Board for public companies. These are applicable when the CPA provides assurance about written representations or subject matters other than historical financial statements. CPAs must be independent to perform SSAE engagements.

To accept an attestation engagement, the CPA must possess the competency and capabilities necessary to perform the examination. This is especially important when evaluating controls at a service organization in conjunction with a SOC report because such examinations usually involve understanding IT controls and the structure of the entity's information system.

The three types of SSAE engagement can be remembered by using the word ERA: examination, review, and agreed-upon procedures.

- **Examination** - The independent CPA is engaged to provide an opinion (**positive assurance**) on the subject matter or an assertion of a responsible party that involves something **other than historical financial statements**. There are two types of examination engagements:

- ○ **Assertion-based examination** is the traditional type of examination engagement. According to AT-C section 205, the client provides a written assertion, which is the basis of the CPA's examination procedures. For example, a service organization can have a System and Organization Controls or SOC2 engagement performed over the principal service commitments and system requirements based on the Trust Service Criteria. This report can be distributed to companies who rely on the service organization.

- ○ **Direct examinations** have been in effect since 2022. The goal of this service is to allow CPA's to evaluate and report on new or emerging non-financial subject matters where there is a lot of complexity or the client lacks the expertise. The CPA can now measure or evaluate underlying subject matter (scoped area) against a criterion. AT-C section 206 does not require the responsible party (typically the client) to first measure or evaluate the underlying subject matter against the criteria or provide a written assertion. However, the responsible party must acknowledge their responsibility for the underlying subject matter.

- **Review**—The CPA is engaged to provide **limited or negative assurance** on subject matter or an assertion of a responsible party that involves something **other than historical financial statements**.

- **Agreed-Upon Procedures**—When the CPA is engaged to provide assurance in the form of "procedures and findings" on subject matter or an assertion of a responsible party that involves something other than historical financial statements. Purchasing department compliance, income tax provisioning, and due diligence procedures when buying a business are all examples of agreed-upon procedures.

Attestation engagements (ERA)		
Engagement	**Examples**	**Type of report**
Examination*	• Examining internal controls at service organization (assertion required) • Examining information *other than* historical financial statements	Opinion **(positive assurance)**
Review	• Reviewing management discussion and analysis information • Reviewing information *other than* historical financial statements	Conclusion **(negative assurance)**
Agreed-upon procedures	• Verifying cash balances in bank statements • Checking security balances	Findings **(no assurance)**

*Can be an assertion-based examination or a direct examination.

Statements on Standards for Accounting and Review Services (SSARSs)

SSARSs are applicable when the CPA is associated with the F/S of a private company, but that association is something less than a full-scope *audit engagement*.

- **Compilation**—The CPA is engaged simply to **assemble** into F/S format the financial records of a private company and issue a compilation report, without expressing any degree of assurance on the reliability of those F/S

- **Preparation Engagement**—The CPA is engaged to **prepare** the F/S of a private company without issuing any report on those F/S or expressing any form of assurance

- **Review**—The CPA is engaged to provide a **lower level of assurance** than an audit on F/S of a private company by performing limited procedures, including performing analytical procedures, and making appropriate inquiries of client personnel. The conclusion is known as "negative assurance" that the practitioner is unaware of a need for material modification

Statements on Standards for Accounting and Review Services (SSARS)

Engagement	Description	Report issues
Review	<ul><li>CPA performs inquiries and analytical procedures</li><li>*Limited assurance* provided</li><li>Independence required</li></ul>	Yes
Compilation	<ul><li>CPA assembles and reads F/S</li><li>F/S used primarily by outside parties</li><li>Independence **not** required, but must be disclosed</li></ul>	Yes
Preparation	<ul><li>CPA prepares F/S or specified F/S elements (eg, balance sheet only)</li><li>F/S used for internal purposes or by outside parties</li><li>Independence **not** required</li></ul>	No

F/S = financial statements.

Attestation engagements, as well as Accounting and Review Service engagements, are explored in detail later in the AUD text. They are introduced here so that candidates remember that the AICPA Professional Standards encompass a variety of types of standards governing different services associated with the CPA profession.

AUD 4
Terms of
Engagement

AUD 4: Terms of Engagement

4.01 Preconditions for an Engagement

Audit Firm Considerations

 Representative Task (Remembering & Understanding): Identify the preconditions needed for accepting or continuing an engagement.

Statements on Quality Control Standards

Recall the AICPA's Statements on Quality Control Standards (SQCS) that are applicable to a CPA's financial statement related services. SQCS consist of multiple elements, one of which is guidance on the acceptance of new clients or the continuation of existing ones. One of the primary purposes of SQCS is to ensure that the firm associates only with clients whose management acts with integrity (eg, provides the firm with accurate, reliable information).

Quality control for client acceptance

- Ensure association with clients whose management acts with integrity
- Provide reasonable assurance that the CPA firm:
  - Is competent to perform the engagement
  - Has needed capabilities
  - Can comply with legal and ethical requirements

Client Considerations

The auditor's objective is to accept an audit engagement involving a new or existing audit client only when the basis for the audit has been agreed upon by (1) establishing when the *preconditions for an audit* are present; and (2) confirming that a common understanding of the terms of the engagement exists between the auditor and management (and those charged with governance, as applicable).

During the acceptance process of a new client, the prospective auditor must consider a variety of factors. The auditor will want to make certain that the F/S are auditable, they can gather sufficient appropriate audit evidence and that the engagement adheres to legal and ethical standards.

Preconditions

Preconditions which must be met include the use by management of an **acceptable financial reporting framework** in the preparation of the financial statements and the agreement of management to the premise on which an audit is conducted.

Additionally, management should **acknowledge its responsibilities** for:

- The fair presentation of the financial statements

- The design and implementation of effective internal control over financial reporting

- Providing the auditor with all information relevant to the financial statements and any additional information requested by the auditor and providing access to all entity personnel relevant to the audit of the financial statements

An auditor will not wish to associate with an entity that has management who **lacks integrity**. Management has influence over every part of the day-to-day operations of the business and the financial records, and the F/S are, ultimately, the representation of management. If the auditor cannot trust the key officers of the business, all evidence related to the F/S will be subject to serious doubt.

If the preconditions are not present, the auditor should not accept the engagement; instead, the auditor should discuss the matter with management.

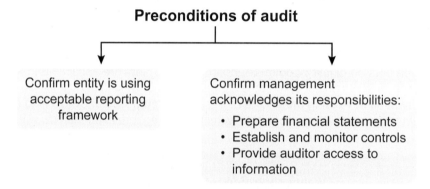

4.02 Terms of Engagement and the Engagement Letter

Initial Audits

 Representative Task (Remembering & Understanding): Identify the factors affecting the acceptance or continuance of an engagement, including communication with predecessor auditors.

AICPA Guidance

The relevant AICPA guidance is provided by AU-C 210, *Terms of Engagement*. This pronouncement addresses the auditor's responsibilities in agreeing upon the terms of the audit engagement with management (and those charged with governance, when appropriate).

Scope Limitation

A **scope limitation** imposed by the client that would require the auditor to issue a disclaimer of opinion would generally preclude the auditor from accepting the engagement. The auditor may, but is not required to, accept the engagement in such circumstances if the entity is required to have an audit by law or regulation (eg, employee benefit plans).

The auditor can accept an engagement when a scope limitation is imposed by:

- Management, but it will likely result in a qualified opinion
- Circumstances beyond management's control

Considering a scope limitation

Sufficient and appropriate audit evidence

Reasonable assurance obtained

Auditor's opinion

A scope limitation will prevent reasonable assurance and the auditor should:

- Withdraw (if possible) / not accept engagement
- Modify audit opinion (qualified or disclaimer)

Which of the following factors most likely would cause a CPA to decline to accept a new audit engagement?

- The CPA does not understand the entity's operations and industry

- Management acknowledges that the entity has had recurring operating losses

- The CPA is unable to review the predecessor auditor's working papers

- Management is unwilling to permit inquiry of its legal counsel

A **scope limitation** is a restriction that prevents an auditor from obtaining sufficient appropriate evidence to support an unmodified opinion. A client's **refusal to permit inquiry of its legal counsel** would prevent the auditor from confirming contingent legal liabilities. Because the potential effects of the management-imposed restriction are **material and pervasive**, the auditor should decline the engagement.

Timing of Engagement

Accepting an audit engagement *after the fiscal year-end* may create a **scope limitation**. The auditor should **not accept** the engagement if a scope limitation imposed by the client would **result in a disclaimer of opinion**. The auditor may accept the engagement when a scope limitation is imposed by circumstances beyond management's control.

New engagement after fiscal year close

Accept	• There are remedial procedures that can be performed for any scope limitations created by engagement timing.
Reject	• There are no remedial procedures for scope limitations caused by engagement timing. • Client has imposed scope limitations. • Audit would most likely result in a disclaimer of opinion.

Communication with Predecessor Auditor

An initial or first-year audit is when a CPA audits a company whose prior year F/S were audited by a different auditor, also known as the **predecessor auditor.** Before accepting the engagement, the auditor should request that management authorize the predecessor to respond to the auditor's inquiries.

The objective of the inquiries is to help the prospective auditor decide whether to accept the initial audit engagement. The predecessor is expected to respond fully and to indicate when the response is limited. The auditor should evaluate the predecessor's response in deciding whether to accept the engagement.

If management does not authorize the predecessor to respond or limits the predecessor's response, the auditor should consider that fact in deciding whether to accept the engagement. This could indicate issues with management's integrity.

The auditor's communication with the predecessor auditor may be written or verbal. Typical matters expected to be addressed include the following:

- Information that might bear on the integrity of management

- Any disagreements with management about accounting or auditing issues

- Communications involving those charged with governance with respect to fraud and/or **noncompliance with laws or regulations** (NOCLAR). This should also include the predecessor management's authorization to disclose suspected or identified fraud and/or NOCLAR.

- Communications involving management and those charged with governance regarding significant deficiencies in internal control
- The predecessor's understanding about: the reasons for the entity's change in auditors, the nature of the entity's related party relationships and transactions, and significant unusual transactions

Predecessor vs. successor auditor

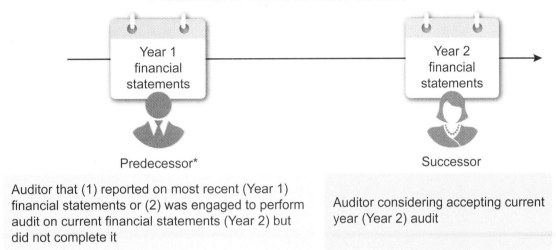

Predecessor*

Auditor that (1) reported on most recent (Year 1) financial statements or (2) was engaged to perform audit on current financial statements (Year 2) but did not complete it

Successor

Auditor considering accepting current year (Year 2) audit

*In practice, there may be two predecessor auditors if each criterion is met by a different auditing firm or CPA

It is advisable, but not required, that an auditor be allowed to review the predecessor's working papers. This process can include a review of internal controls, substantive procedures, contingencies, and subsequent events.

Recurring Audits

When a CPA firm is engaged for a recurring audit, the auditor must determine if the terms of the preceding engagement are still applicable to the current engagement. If so, the auditor should communicate the terms of engagement:

- Either in writing or orally to the management of a non-issuer. When the communication is oral, it is desirable to document the significant matters discussed (including with whom and when)
- In writing through an engagement letter to the audit committee of an issuer

It may be appropriate to revise the terms of the previous engagement. Factors that signify the terms of the preceding engagement may need to be revised include:

- Indications that management does not understand the objective and scope of the engagement
- Revised or special terms
- A significant change in the entity's size or the nature of its business
- Changes to senior management or a significant change in ownership
- Changes to legal or regulatory requirements
- A change in the AFRF or other reporting requirements

Change in the Type of Engagement

 Representative Task (Remembering & Understanding): Recall when it is acceptable to agree to management's request for a change in the type of engagement (eg, from an audit to a review).

When management requests a change in the type of engagement, the auditor must evaluate the situation to determine the most appropriate course of action. Reasonable justification would exist when there is a **change in circumstances** affecting management's requirements, or if there was a misunderstanding about the nature of the service originally requested. The resulting report should not refer to any audit procedures performed prior to changing the engagement to a review or other service.

Alternatively, the auditor may be asked to change the audit engagement to an engagement resulting in a **lower level of assurance** (prior to completing the audit engagement). The auditor should determine whether reasonable justification for doing so exists. If not, the auditor should decline the request.

If the auditor concludes **no reasonable justification** for such a change exists and management will not permit the auditor to continue the original audit engagement, the auditor should:

- Withdraw from the audit engagement, when possible
- Communicate the circumstances to those charged with governance
- Determine whether there is any legal or other obligation to report the matter to any other parties

Downgrade in engagement

Client requests change from audit to lower level of assurance engagement

↓

Does reasonable justification for change exist?

Yes →

No →

Yes:

Accountant and management should agree on and document in writing terms of the *new engagement*

↓

Accountant issues an appropriate report with *no reference to original engagement* (may include reference to procedures performed)

No:

Accountant:
- Communicates circumstances to those charged with governance
- Withdraws from engagement when possible
- Determines whether any obligation (legal or contractual) exists to report circumstances to other parties (owners)

Engagement Letter

 Representative Task (Application): Perform procedures to confirm that a common understanding of the terms of an engagement exist with management and those charged with governance.

 Representative Task (Application): Document the terms of an engagement in a written engagement letter or other suitable form of written agreement.

A common understanding of the terms of the engagement must exist between the auditor and management and those charged with governance. The auditor is required to agree upon the terms of the engagement with the client. The agreement may be with management or with those charged with governance, whichever is appropriate based on the structure of the entity.

Those charged with governance	Management
Responsible for overseeing the strategic direction of the entity and the obligations related to accountability. Examples include: • Board of directors • Audit committee • External parties, such as certain governmental agencies	Responsible for the conduct of the entity's organization. • In some cases, all of those charged with governance are also involved in managing the entity. For example, this occurs in owner-managed entities • When that is not the case, there are additional items that are communicated to those charged with governance

The auditor is required to obtain management's agreement that it understands and acknowledges its responsibilities, regardless of whether the auditor contracts with management, exclusively with those charged with governance, or exclusively with a third party.

Once the auditor has made the decision to accept the engagement, the auditor is required to send a **written engagement letter** (recommended) or a comparable written agreement to the client. In it, the auditor will confirm the scope and nature of the engagement and the responsibilities of the various parties (ie, establish an understanding with the client). The engagement letter is signed by both the client and the auditor.

The written communication includes the following sections:

- **Objective and scope** of the audit
- **Auditor Responsibilities**
  - Conducting an audit in accordance with GAAS (this doesn't guarantee that errors and fraud will be detected)
  - Informing the client of improvements in control or economy of operations that come to the auditor's attention during the engagement

- **Client (Management) Responsibilities**
  - ○ Making all records available
  - ○ Not limiting the scope of the auditor's work
  - ○ Paying the fee based on the agreed-upon method
  - ○ Preparing a fair presentation of F/S
  - ○ Designing, implementing, and maintaining (DIM) of I/C
  - ○ Providing management's representation letter

- A statement that, due to the **inherent limitations of an audit and I/C**, material misstatements may not be detected (even though the audit is properly planned and performed in accordance with GAAS)

- The identification of the Applicable Financial Reporting Framework (**AFRF**)

- Reference to the **expected form and content of the report** with an indication that the actual report may differ

- Other relevant information—**Other matters** may be referred to in the engagement letter, such as:
  - ○ Elaboration on the scope of the audit
  - ○ Matters related to the planning and performance of the audit, which can include engagement team composition and the use of internal audit or specialist
  - ○ Communication of key audit matters and the results of the engagement
  - ○ The anticipation that management will provide written representations
  - ○ The expectation that management will provide access to all information that is relevant to the preparation and fair presentation of the F/S and disclosures
  - ○ Management's agreement to inform the auditor of subsequent events and subsequently discovered facts relevant to the F/S
  - ○ Fees and billing arrangements
  - ○ A request for management's acknowledgment, evidenced by their signature on the engagement letter, of receipt of the engagement letter, and agreement to its terms
  - ○ In an initial audit, arrangements to be made with the predecessor
  - ○ Restrictions, if any, on the auditor's liability
  - ○ The auditor's obligations, if any, to provide audit documentation to other parties
  - ○ Additional services to be provided by the auditor
  - ○ Any further agreements between the auditor and the entity

Audit engagement letter

Required	• Objective and scope • Auditor and management responsibilities • Statement that some material misstatements may not be detected • Applicable financial reporting framework • Expected form and content of audit report
Included as appropriate	• Arrangements for involvement of other auditors, specialists, internal audit • Arrangement with predecessor auditor • Additional services to be performed

The auditor should not discuss in detail the audit procedures that will be performed because the procedures will vary depending on the evidence obtained during the engagement and the effectiveness of many procedures depends on the client not knowing in advance what specific evidence will be examined.

Which of the following statements would most likely appear in an auditor's engagement letter?

- Management is responsible for reporting to us any inadequate provisions for the safeguarding of assets
- We will identify internal controls relevant to specific assertions that may prevent or detect material misstatements
- Management agrees to correct all deficiencies in internal control activities identified by us
- Management is responsible for making all financial records and related information available to us.

Elements of engagement letter (FACSIMILE)

- **F**ees
- **A**uditor's responsibilities
- **C**onfirmation of engagement
- **S**cope & objective
- **I**nternal controls
- **M**anagement responsibilities
- **I**rregularities (fraud)
- **I**llegal acts
- **E**rrors

- Provide reasonable assurance
- Adhere to auditing standards
- Understand regulatory environment
- Assess internal controls

- Prepare financial statements
- Comply with laws & regulations
- Establish & monitor internal controls
- Provide auditor with relevant information

An engagement letter (EL) is used to establish an understanding between the auditor and the client about the terms of the audit. The letter includes the general responsibilities of both management and the auditor. Management responsibilities include a statement that **management will provide the auditor with all relevant information needed** (eg, all financial records) to perform the audit.

Although management is responsible for assessing an entity's internal control for the safeguard of assets and evaluate if any deficiencies exist, this is not generally *specified in* an EL. Similarly, although auditors are responsible for identifying controls specific to material assertions, the procedure is not usually specified in the EL. Management is not required to agree to correct *all* deficiencies in I/C because some of these deficiencies may not be relevant or material to financial statement accounts.

The following is an example of an engagement letter that includes those key elements that need to be communicated to ensure a common understanding between the auditor, management, and those charged with governance.

 Engagement Letter Example

Mr. John Apple, Chairman of the Audit Committee
Budget Co.
555 State Street
San Francisco, California   94133

Dear Mr. Apple,

(Objective and Scope of the Audit)

You have requested that we audit the financial statements of Budget Co., which comprise the balance sheet as of December 31, 20XX, and the related statements of income, changes in stockholders' equity, and cash flows for the year then ended, and the related notes to the financial statements. We are pleased to confirm our acceptance and our understanding of this audit engagement by means of this letter.

The objectives of our audit are to obtain reasonable assurance about whether the financial statements as a whole are free from material misstatement, whether due to fraud or error, and to issue an auditor's report that includes our opinion. Reasonable assurance is a high level of assurance but is not absolute assurance and therefore is not a guarantee that an audit conducted in accordance with auditing standards generally accepted in the United States of America (GAAS) will always detect a material misstatement when it exists. Misstatements can arise from fraud or error and are considered material if there is a substantial likelihood that, individually or in the aggregate, they would influence the judgment made by a reasonable user based on the financial statements.

(Responsibilities of the Auditor)

We will conduct our audit in accordance with GAAS. As part of an audit in accordance with GAAS, we exercise professional judgment and maintain professional skepticism throughout the audit. We also:

- Identify and assess the risks of material misstatement of the financial statements, whether due to fraud or error, design and perform audit procedures responsive to those risks, and obtain audit evidence that is sufficient and appropriate to provide a basis for our opinion. The risk of not detecting a material misstatement resulting from fraud is higher than for one resulting from error, as fraud may involve collusion, forgery, intentional omissions, misrepresentations, or the override of internal control.

- Obtain an understanding of internal control relevant to the audit in order to design audit procedures that are appropriate in the circumstances, but not for the purpose of expressing an opinion on the effectiveness of the entity's internal control. However, we will communicate to you in writing concerning any significant deficiencies or material weaknesses in internal control relevant to the audit of the financial statements that we have identified during the audit.

- Evaluate the appropriateness of accounting policies used and the reasonableness of significant accounting estimates made by management, as well as evaluate the overall presentation of the financial statements, including the disclosures, and whether the financial statements represent the underlying transactions and events in a manner that achieves fair presentation.

- Conclude, based on the audit evidence obtained, whether there are conditions or events, considered in the aggregate, that raise substantial doubt about Budget Co.'s ability to continue as a going concern for a reasonable period of time.

Because of the **inherent limitations** of an audit, together with the inherent limitations of internal control, an unavoidable risk that some material misstatements may not be detected exists, even though the audit is properly planned and performed in accordance with GAAS.

(Responsibilities of Management and Identification of the AFRF)

Our audit will be conducted on the basis that management acknowledges and understands that they have responsibility for the preparation and fair presentation of the financial statements in accordance with accounting principles generally accepted in the United States of America; for the design, implementation, and maintenance (DIM) of internal control relevant to the preparation and fair presentation of financial statements that are free from material misstatement, whether due to fraud or error; and to provide us with access to all information of which management is aware that is relevant to the preparation and fair presentation of the financial statements such as records, documentation, and other matters; additional information that we may request from management for the purpose of the audit; and unrestricted access to persons within the entity from whom we determine it necessary to obtain audit evidence.

As part of our audit process, we will request from management, written confirmation concerning representations made to us in connection with the audit.

(Other Relevant Information)

We will provide you with a **list of schedules** and information needed by our staff during the audit. It is our mutual understanding that in order to meet the audit deadlines, which we have established; your staff will provide that necessary information on a timely basis.

The **fees** for our services will be at our regular per diem rates plus out-of-pocket expenses. Invoices are payable upon presentation.

(Reporting)

We will issue a written report upon completion of our audit of Budget Co.'s financial statements. Our report will be addressed to the board of directors of Budget Co. Circumstances may arise in which our report may differ from its expected form and content based on the results of our audit. Depending on the nature of these circumstances, it may be necessary for us to modify our opinion, add an emphasis-of-matter paragraph or other-matter paragraph to our auditor's report, or if necessary, withdraw from the engagement.

Please sign and return the attached copy of this letter to indicate your acknowledgment of, and agreement with, the arrangements for our audit of the financial statements including our respective responsibilities.

Sincerely,

Roger Philip, Partner

Acknowledged and agreed on behalf of Budget Co. by

_____

(Signed) (Name and Title) (Date)

AUD 5
Requirements
for Engagement
Documentation

5.01 Requirements for Engagement Documentation

 This chapter primarily addresses audit documentation. Documentation related to other types of engagements (eg, attestation) can be found in the relevant chapters discussing those engagment types. Documentation related to specific engagement requirements (eg, internal control testing documentation) can be found in the chapter addressing that specific content.

Purposes of Audit Documentation

 Representative Task (Remembering & Understanding): Identify the elements that comprise sufficient appropriate documentation in physical or electronic form for an engagement.

Authoritative Guidance

The relevant AICPA guidance is provided by AU-C 230, *Audit Documentation*. This pronouncement states that the auditor's objective is "to prepare documentation that provides:

- A sufficient and appropriate record of the basis for the auditor's report; *and*
- Evidence that the audit was planned and performed in accordance with (GAAS) and applicable legal and regulatory requirements.

The PCAOB Auditing Standards also state that the documentation should be prepared in sufficient detail to permit an experienced auditor without prior connection to the engagement to understand the procedures performed and the conclusions reached (and to determine who performed the work and on what date).

Some PCAOB basic documentation requirements include that the audit documentation must:

- Demonstrate that the engagement complied with PCAOB standards;
- Support the basis for the auditor's conclusions regarding every relevant financial statement assertion; and
- Demonstrate that the underlying accounting records agree to or reconcile with the financial statement elements.

Definitions

Audit Documentation—the record of audit procedures performed, relevant audit evidence obtained, and conclusions reached. In practice, most CPAs refer to it as **working papers or work papers**. Audit documentation provides the **principal support** for the **auditor's opinion**.

Sufficient—refers to the **quantity** of evidence

Appropriate—refers to the **quality** of evidence in terms of its relevance and reliability

Preparing Audit Documentation

 Representative Task (Application): Prepare documentation that is sufficient to enable an experienced auditor or practitioner having no previous connection with an engagement to understand the nature, timing, extent and results of procedures performed, the significant findings and conclusions reached and the significant professional judgments made.

Working papers hold various files that detail audit procedures, evidence, and conclusions. **Working papers** might be in both paper and electronic form, with most firms using cloud-based software to retain documentation.

The auditor's workpapers are used to document that:

- The auditor complied with GAAS and any applicable legal and regulatory requirements
- The work was adequately planned and supervised
- There was an understanding of the entity and its environment, including internal control, which was obtained and evaluated as necessary to assess the risks of material misstatement and to design the audit to be responsive to those risks
- The procedures applied and the evidence obtained provide a **reasonable basis** for the **opinion** expressed

An *experienced auditor*, with no connection to the audit, should be able to review the working papers to understand the basis for the audit opinion and make sure that GAAS or other legal requirements were followed.

Proper audit documentation can

- Assist in planning and performing the engagement
- Enable engagement supervision
- Indicate who performed the work and who reviewed the work
- Support the work of the auditor
- Preserve information relevant to future engagements
- Enable internal quality reviews and external peer reviews
- Allow for review of prior period work to determine its effect on the current engagement

 For the exam, preparing documentation requires the CPA candidate to understand PCAOB and AICPA requirements listed within this chapter.

When preparing sufficient audit documentation, which of the following should the auditor include within the work papers?

- A statement indicating auditor compliance with the Code of Professional Conduct
- Copies of current licenses or certifications held by the auditor
- Definitions of tick marks (eg, symbols) used
- Evidence that the client has received copies of the working papers

---

Sufficient audit documentation should

- Indicate auditors performing the work, procedures performed, and audit timing
- Evidence that the audit met GAAS and other legal requirements
- Provide primary support for the audit report
- Summarize issues identified and professional judgments used to reach conclusions

The main purpose of audit documentation is to provide evidence supporting the audit opinion. Sufficient audit documentation exists when another experienced auditor can understand how the work performed supports the audit opinion.

Tick marks are symbols indicating the work performed to validate financial information. For example, a check mark might mean the Accounts Receivable subsidiary ledger details sum to the Accounts Receivable Balance Sheet amount. Defined tick marks allow an experienced auditor to understand the work performed.

Ownership and Confidentiality

Although audit documentation is the **auditor's property**, it is subject to the restrictions imposed by AICPA ethics rules on confidentiality. Auditors should apply appropriate controls over the audit documentation to protect the integrity of the information at all stages of the audit, to prevent unauthorized changes, and to limit access to authorized personnel. This includes establishing a formal retention policy.

Client confidentiality does not, however, prevent a CPA from providing access to other members of the auditor's firm. Other **exceptions** to confidentiality, include:

- A valid subpoena
- An IRS administrative subpoena
- A **court order**, except in those few states that have a privilege statute
- A **quality control peer review**, providing access to other accountants and the PCAOB in connection with a valid program of peer review

Working papers

- Are owned by the firm performing the audit
- Reflect compliance with GAAS
- Document work performed and conclusions reached
- Must be kept confidential
- May be shared with others only with client permission or:
    - Based on valid legal or IRS administrative subpoena
    - Under a court order
    - For audit quality peer review purposes

Common law does not recognize the concept of **privilege**, which would allow the accountant to refuse to honor a court subpoena. A small number of states have enacted privilege statutes, and the federal government now recognizes working papers developed in connection with the preparation of a tax return to be privileged in certain circumstances.

Nevertheless, privilege may not be used if the accountant has already provided some of the information requested in a subpoena. The purpose of privilege is to protect the client, not the accountant, so the accountant may not assert privilege even where privilege statutes exist if the client waives the privilege.

AICPA Audit Documentation Requirements

Audit documentation should be sufficient to permit an *experienced auditor* without prior connection to the audit to understand the following:

The nature, timing, and extent of procedures performed	The results of those procedures	The conclusions reached on significant matters	Whether the accounting records agree with the audited financial statements

At a minimum, working papers must always include:

- Reconciliation of the accounting records with the financial statements
- Audit plan detailing procedures performed during the engagement
- Documentation of the auditor's understanding of the internal control structure
- Documentation of the assessed level of control risk
- Proof of sufficient evidence to support the auditor's opinion
- Management representation letter

Other things that the audit documentation should include are:

- The **identity of the preparer** and reviewer of the audit work
- The identification of the **specific items** tested or their identifying characteristics of items in connection with the substantive procedures and any tests of control
- Abstracts or **copies of significant contracts** or agreements examined. This is necessary to understand the basis for conclusions

- **Significant audit findings or issues**. This should include actions taken to address them, the basis for conclusions reached and documented details of discussions of significant issues or findings with management including the issues discussed, and when and with whom. Examples include:

  ○ Significant matters regarding the selection, application, and consistency of accounting principles

  ○ Circumstances causing difficulty in applying necessary audit procedures

  ○ Results of audit procedures indicating a possible material misstatement

  ○ Findings that could result in modification of the audit report

- **All proposed audit adjustments** (whether or not recorded by management) that could have a material effect individually or when aggregated

- **Explanations related to information** that contradicts or was inconsistent with auditor final conclusions. This includes the rare circumstance in which the auditor departs from presumptively mandatory requirement

- The **audit report release date**

Aggregated Misstatements, Analytical Procedures, and Going-Concern Issues

Other Statements on Auditing Standards require additional specific documentation, including:

- Documentation of the nature and effect of aggregated misstatements, as well as whether the auditor's conclusion regarding materiality to the F/S (ie, are aggregated misstatements material?)

- Analytical procedures—This should include the expectation and factors (sources) considered in developing it, if not apparent. It should also include the results of the comparison of that expectation to the recorded amounts or to ratios based on recorded amounts. Any additional procedures performed (and their results) to investigate unexpected differences should also be documented

- Going-concern issues, including:

  ○ The conditions giving rise to the going concern issue

  ○ The elements of management's plan considered important to overcoming the situation

  ○ Evidence obtained to evaluate the significant elements of management's plans

  ○ The auditor's conclusion as to whether substantial doubt remains

  ○ The auditor's conclusion as to whether a "Going Concern" section should be added to the auditor's report

Quantity of Content

The quantity, type, and content of the audit documentation depends on the auditor's **professional judgment** and may include consideration of the following matters:

- The risk of material misstatement in the area involved

- The amount of judgment involved in performing the work and interpreting the results (including the nature of the audit procedures involved)

- The nature and extent of any exceptions identified

- The significance of the evidence to the assertion involved

- The need to document a conclusion not readily determinable from the documentation of the work performed

Types of Files Related to Audit Working Papers

Audit documentation can be captured in a variety of files. The **current file** contains documentation related to that year's engagement, including the audit program, reconciliations or specific analyses, and direct supporting evidence. The **permanent file** contains client documentation that has ongoing significance, applies to multiple years, and supports several audits.

Audit workpaper files	
Current file	**Permanent file**
• Audit program	• Company bylaws
• Trial balance	• Articles of incorporation
• Lead schedules	• Minutes (board, shareholder meetings)
• Auditor reconciliations	• Control flowcharts
• Auditor analysis	• Long-term debt agreements
• Responses to information requests	• Equity account analyses

When audit documentation is to be easily stored, it is added to a **bulk file**. It can include items like magnetic tables and extensive computer printouts. A **correspondence file** is used so that the audit team can conveniently review communications (letters, e-mail, etc.) related to each client organization. The **report file** contains prior years' audit reports and management letters are organized (by client) for easy review.

PCAOB Additional Documentation Requirements

For audits of *public companies* reporting to the SEC, the PCAOB has established standards for audit documentation. Although most are identical to those required by GAAS (AU-C 230), there are some additional requirements. The auditor must document:

- Audit procedures involving **inspection of documents** (including walkthroughs, tests of controls, and substantive tests of details) and identify the specific items tested (or the source and specific selection criteria); include abstracts or copies of significant contracts or agreements examined

- All **significant findings or issues** as well as any actions to address them in sufficient detail so that a reviewer can obtain a thorough understanding of the matters

- The basis for conclusions reached, including the application of accounting principles, circumstances causing modification of planned audit procedures, matters that could result in modification of the auditor's report, material misstatements, significant deficiencies or material weaknesses in internal control over financial reporting, difficulties in applying audit procedures, and disagreements among members of the engagement team about final conclusions on significant matters, among other things

Assembly and Retention of Documentation

 Representative Task (Remembering & Understanding): Identify the requirements for the assembly and retention of documentation in physical or electronic form for an engagement.

The PCAOB and AICPA have different requirements regarding the assembly and retention of documentation.

Final audit file		
Type of company	**Assembled within**	**Retained for**
Issuers (public companies)	45 days after report release date	7 years
Nonissuers (nonpublic companies)	60 days after report release date	5 years

After the documentation completion date, the auditor must not delete any audit documentation before the end of the retention period. The auditor may add to the documentation, but must document any materials added, by whom, when, reasons for the change, and the effect, if any, on the auditor's conclusions.

Simulation for Preparation of Audit Documentation

The items below represent a series of unrelated statements, questions, excerpts, and comments documented from various parts of an auditor's working paper file. For each item, select the most likely **source of the documentation** from the menu provided. Select only one source for each item. A source may be selected once, more than once, or not at all.

Menu choices for source of documentation

A   Partner's engagement review program

B   Communication with predecessor auditor

C   Auditor's engagement letter

D   Management representation letter

E   Standard financial institution confirmation request

F   Auditor's communication with the audit committee

G   Auditor's report

H   Accounts receivable confirmation

A	B
Statements	**Source**

1   Are you aware of any facts or circumstances that may indicate a lack of integrity by any member of senior management?   B

Communication with predecessor auditor

Successor auditors must communicate with the predecessor auditors before accepting an audit engagement. Inquiries with the predecessor auditor include information about the integrity of management, reasons for the change in auditor, and disagreements with management related to accounting matters. The auditor will document this communication and identify any circumstances that may indicate that members of senior management lack integrity.

2   The objective of our audit is to express an unmodified opinion on the financial statements, although it is possible that facts or circumstances encountered may preclude us from expressing an unqualified opinion.   C

Auditor's engagement letter

The auditor will prepare a written engagement letter that will include a statement as to the objective of the engagement, the expression of an opinion on the financial statements, and the fact that circumstances could preclude the expression of an opinion. The letter will confirm fees, the scope and nature of the engagement, and each party's responsibilities. It is signed by the client and the auditor and retained in the working papers.

3   Provision has been made for any material loss to be sustained in the fulfillment of, or from the inability to fulfill, any sales commitments.   D

Management representation letter

Contingencies represent gains or losses that may or may not occur in the future because of an event that has already occurred or an existing condition. Management, in its letter of representation to the auditor, will give the auditor assurance that any contingent losses (eg, losses resulting from the inability to fulfill sales commitments) have been appropriately accrued and/or disclosed. This letter is retained in the working paper file.

5   If this statement is not correct, please write promptly, using the enclosed envelope, and give details of any differences directly to our auditors.   H

Accounts receivable confirmation

An A/R confirmation is an example of audit evidence obtained directly from parties outside the entity. All types of confirmation responses are retained in the working paper file.

6   The Company has suffered recurring losses from operations and has a net capital deficiency that raises substantial doubt about its ability to continue as a going concern.   G

Auditor's report

An auditor has the responsibility to independently evaluate the going concern assumption, including evaluating management's mitigation plans and disclosure. This assessment is retained in the workpaper file as it supports the opinion that the auditors eventually selected as appropriate.

AUD 6
Communication with Management and Those Charged with Governance

6.01 Planned Scope and Timing of the Engagement

Overview

Auditor communication with those charged with governance is a requirement for GAAS and PCAOB. Remember, those charged with governance are individuals charged with the responsibility for overseeing the strategic direction of the entity and the obligations related to the accountability of the entity. This includes the board of directors and the audit committee. Management has executive responsibility for the conduct of the entity's operations.

Authoritative Guidance

The relevant AICPA guidance is provided by AU-C 260, *The Auditor's Communication with Those Charged with Governance*. This pronouncement states that the auditor's **objectives** are to:

- Communicate clearly the auditor's responsibilities related to the audit and an overview of the planned scope and timing of the audit and
- Obtain from those charged with governance information relevant to the audit

The PCAOB states **auditor objectives** regarding communication are to:

- Communicate to the audit committee the auditor's responsibilities regarding the audit and establish an understanding of the terms of the audit engagement with the audit committee
- Obtain information from the audit committee relevant to the audit
- Communicate to the audit committee information about the strategy and timing of the audit, and
- Provide the audit committee with timely and significant observations about the audit

The Communication Process

 Representative Task (Remembering & Understanding): Identify the matters related to the planned scope and timing of an engagement that should be communicated to management and those charged with governance.

 Representative Task (Application): Prepare presentation materials and supporting schedules for use in communicating the planned scope and timing of an engagement to management and those charged with governance.

During the conduct of an audit, there are several items that the auditor is required to communicate regarding the entity. In such cases, the auditor will communicate with **those charged with governance.**

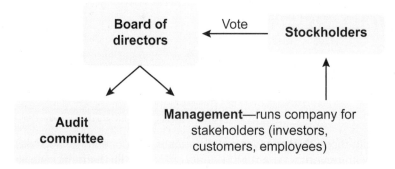

Basic Auditor Responsibility

Effective two-way communication with those charged with governance is important to having a constructive relationship, obtaining information relevant to the audit, and assisting those charged with governance in their role of overseeing financial reporting.

The auditor may choose to discuss some matters with management *before communicating* them with those charged with governance, unless that is inappropriate. For example, the auditor would not normally discuss issues involving management's competence or integrity. Likewise, the auditor may choose to discuss some matters with the internal auditor(s) before communicating the matters with those charged with governance.

Auditing standards require that auditors communicate information to those charged with governance, which may include the board of directors, the audit committee, and executive management (eg, CEO). The audit committee is an independent committee composed of board members, including at least one financial expert, and is responsible for financial reporting oversight.

Objectives of Communication

Communication with those charged with governance is intended to promote a mutual sharing of relevant information. The objectives of establishing such communication are to:

- Provide those charged with governance with information about the auditor's responsibilities regarding the audit, including an overview of the **planned scope and timing** of the engagement
- **Obtain information** (eg, regarding specific transactions or events) relevant to the audit from those charged with governance
- Provide those charged with governance with the **auditor's observations** arising from the audit that may be relevant to their role in the oversight of the financial reporting process

Matters to Be Communicated

Certain matters should be communicated to those charged with governance. While there are many matters that the auditor should communicate, the items that will be tested have been narrowed down to matters related to the following two subjects.

The planned scope and timing of the engagement – This includes communications regarding **significant risks** identified by the auditor that may require special consideration. However, the auditor should not discuss the detailed audit plan or specific audit procedures with the audit committee or management since it might reduce the effectiveness of the audit. Such communications might involve:

- **Issues of risk and materiality**
  - How will the auditor address *significant risks* of material misstatement (RMM) and areas of higher assessed RMM?
  - What factors will the auditor consider when determining *materiality*?
  - What are the entity's views of their objectives/strategies and the related *business risks* that may result in material misstatements?

- **Consequences of the auditor's work**
  - Will the auditor need to use any specialists to perform audit procedures or to evaluate results of procedures? If so, what is the nature and extent of the special skills or knowledge required?
  - Will the auditor need any assistance from the entity's internal auditors? If so, what is the nature and extent of the assistance required?
  - Is the entity aware of any matters that call for additional procedures to be performed by the auditor?

- **The entity and its environment**
  - What approach will the auditor take with respect to internal control over financial reporting (ICFR)?
  - Will the auditor be expressing an opinion on ICFR?
  - How will the auditor approach the implications for individual F/S and disclosures of significant changes in the applicable financial reporting framework (AFRF), the entity's environment, financial condition, or operations?
  - What are the attitudes, awareness, and actions of those charged with governance regarding ICFR, its effectiveness, and the detection or possibility of fraud?
  - What actions have been taken with respect to changes in law, accounting standards, corporate governance practices, etc.?
  - What actions have been taken with respect to previous communications with the auditor?

Auditor communication (GAAS)

- Communicate auditor responsibilities
- Obtain information relevant to the audit
- Provide timely communications about significant findings (eg, fraud)
- Promote useful two-way communications

Additionally, certain disagreements with management should be reported to governance, including:

Disagreements with management to be reported to governance

Matters significant to the financial statements or the audit report

- Scope of the audit
- Wording of the auditor's report
- Application of accounting principles
- Basis for management's judgments about estimates
- Disclosures to be included in the financial statements

The auditor *should not discuss* the detailed audit plan or specific audit procedures with the audit committee or management since it might reduce the effectiveness of the audit. **Deficiencies and material weaknesses in internal control (I/C)** is discussed in a later chapter.

Form, Timing & Adequacy of Communications

Those charged with governance should be informed by the auditor as to the form, timing, and expected general content of communications.

Form & Timing

Communications may be **oral** (eg, formal presentations or informal discussions) or in **writing**, and should be communicated on a timely basis. This may be during the audit or after the audit report is issued[1].

- Matters communicated orally should be documented by the auditor.
- Any written report should clearly indicate that it is intended solely for the information and use of the parties specified. That is, the report is restricted to those charged with governance, and management, if applicable.
- Written communications include the **engagement letter** (discussed in a previous chapter).
- Whether communications are oral or written may depend on various circumstances, such as:
  - Whether the matter has been resolved, was previously communicated, or is discussed in the auditor's report
  - The size, operational structure, control environment, and legal structure of the entity
  - Legal or regulatory requirements
  - The expectations of those charged with governance

Adequacy

The auditor should evaluate the adequacy of the two-way communication with those charged with governance. If communication was inadequate, the auditor should evaluate the effect on auditor's RMM assessment and the ability to obtain sufficient appropriate evidence. Adequacy may be determined based on the auditor's observations, such as:

- Were actions taken in response to the auditor's communications appropriate and timely?
- Did those charged with governance appear to be open in their communications with the auditor?
- Were they willing and capable of meeting with the auditor without management being present?
- Did those charged with governance appear to fully comprehend the matters communicated?

6.02 Internal Control Related Matters

Overview

Definitions

- **Control Deficiency**: When the design or operation of a control does not allow management or employees, in the normal course of performing their assigned functions, to prevent or detect misstatements on a timely basis

- **Deficiency in Design**: When a control necessary to meet the control objective is missing, or when the control objective is not always met, even if the control operates as designed

- **Deficiency in Operation**: When a properly designed control does not operate as designed, or when the person performing the control does not have the authority or competence to effectively perform the control

- **Significant Deficiency**: A deficiency (or combination of deficiencies) in internal control that is less severe than a material weakness, yet important enough to merit attention by those charged with governance

- **Material Weakness**: A deficiency (or combination of deficiencies) in internal control such that there is a reasonable possibility that a material misstatement of the entity's financial statements will not be prevented or detected and corrected on a timely basis

Internal control deficiency: Design or operation of a control does not prevent or detect financial misstatements	
Material weakness	• Reasonable possibility of material financial misstatement • Indicators: ○ Ineffective governance ○ Prior year financial restatements due to error or fraud ○ Material misstatements not detected by controls ○ Fraud by senior management, material or immaterial
Significant deficiency	• Less severe than material weakness • Merits attention by those charged with governance

Communicating Identified Control Deficiencies

 Representative Task (Remembering & Understanding): Identify the matters related to deficiencies and material weaknesses in internal control that should be communicated to those charged with governance and management for an engagement and the timing of such communications.

Reporting requirements for internal control matters are different for issuers versus nonissuers, as summarized in the following table:

Internal control (I/C) report	
Issuer	**Nonissuer**
<ul><li>Subject to GAAS and PCAOB</li><li>Required</li><li>I/C opinion required</li><li>All deficiencies communicated in writing</li><li>Distribution to general public</li></ul>	<ul><li>Subject to GAAS</li><li>Required</li><li>I/C opinion required—integrated audits only</li><li>Deficiencies communicated in writing<ul><li>Financial audit—material weaknesses and significant deficiencies</li><li>Integrated audit—all deficiencies</li></ul></li><li>Distribution<ul><li>Financial audit—management and those charged with governance only</li><li>Integrated audit—general public</li></ul></li></ul>

Form of Communication

Identified significant deficiencies and material weaknesses must be communicated in writing to management and those charged with governance. Certain matters may not be communicated to management when communication would be inappropriate (eg, matters that raise questions about management integrity or competence).

Lesser matters (not significant deficiencies) may be communicated to the appropriate level of operational management with the authority to take remedial action. Such lesser matters may be communicated either orally or in writing.

Timing

The required communication is best made by the "report release date" and should be made no later than **60 days following the report release date**. The "report release date" is the date that the auditor grants the entity permission to use the auditor's report in connection with the audited financial statements.

The auditor may choose to verbally communicate certain significant deficiencies and material weaknesses during the audit (eg, to permit timely correction). However, all identified significant deficiencies and material weaknesses must still be communicated in **writing no later than 60 days** following the report release date, including those matters communicated orally during the audit.

Communication on I/C for audit of nonissuer F/S
<ul><li>Provided in writing within 60 days of audit report date</li><li>Addressed to and restricted for use by client management and those charged with governance</li><li>Defines and explains identified significant deficiencies and material weaknesses</li><li>States audit was not designed to identify all significant deficiencies or material weaknesses</li><li>Specifically expresses no opinion on I/C effectiveness</li></ul>

Fraud

Fraud is an intentional use of deception that results in a **misstatement** in the financial statements. When fraud is encountered in an audit, the auditor is required to consider the potential impact on the financial statements and the audit. In addition, the auditor must report the fraud to the appropriate managerial level within the client organization.

Inconsequential **fraud** committed by a **lower-level employee** (eg, accounts payable clerk) involving immaterial **amounts** is **reported** to the appropriate level of **management** (at least one level *above* the suspected fraudster). Fraud involving *material* amounts is reported to those charged with governance (eg, audit committee).

Reporting fraud

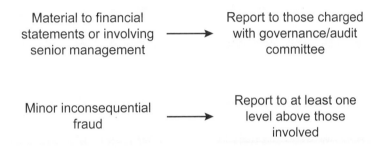

Material to financial statements or involving senior management $\longrightarrow$ Report to those charged with governance/audit committee

Minor inconsequential fraud $\longrightarrow$ Report to at least one level above those involved

Note: Fraud is not generally reported to parties outside the entity unless required by law or regulation.

Because fraud **perpetrated by** senior **management** indicates a lack of management integrity, it could lead to a modified opinion or to the auditor withdrawing from the engagement.

Other Matters

The auditor may choose to communicate other matters believed to be beneficial to the entity (including deficiencies that are not "significant deficiencies") either in writing or verbally. If communicated verbally, the auditor must document such communication.

Prepare Written Communication

 Representative Task (Application): Prepare written communication materials for use in communicating identified internal control deficiencies and material weaknesses for an engagement to those charged with governance and management.

In general, the written communication about significant deficiencies and material weaknesses should:

- State that the purpose of the audit was to express an opinion on the financial statements, not to express an opinion on the effectiveness of internal control
- State that the auditor is not expressing an opinion on the effectiveness of internal control
- State that the auditor's consideration of internal control was not designed to identify all significant deficiencies or material weaknesses
- Include the definition of the terms "material weakness" and "significant deficiency," as applicable
- Identify the matters that are considered to be material weaknesses and significant deficiencies, as applicable

The auditor may include additional statements regarding the general inherent limitations of internal control, including the possibility of management override, but such comments are not required.

- State that the communication is intended solely for the use of management, those charged with governance, and others within the organization (it should not be used by anyone other than those specified parties)—if such a communication is required to be given to a governmental authority, that specific reference may be added

 A non-issuer's previously communicated internal control deficiency has not been corrected. In which of the following situations would written communication not be required in the current year.

- Unresolved prior material weakness
- Current significant deficiency
- Unresolved prior significant deficiency
- Unresolved prior material weakness that is no longer material

Written internal control communication for nonissuers	
Include	• Unresolved prior material weaknesses or significant deficiencies • Current material weaknesses or significant deficiencies
Exclude	• Resolved prior material weaknesses or significant deficiencies • Unresolved prior issues that are no longer material weaknesses or significant deficiencies

During the engagement, the auditor must evaluate the client's resolution of any prior material weaknesses or significant deficiencies. If a prior deficiency still exists but is no longer material or significant due to changes in the client's internal control environment, it can be excluded from the current year written communications to the client.

The auditor **should not issue** a written communication stating that *no significant deficiencies* were identified. However, the auditor is permitted to add a comment that no material weaknesses were identified, perhaps as requested to submit to a governmental authority.

Management may issue a written response to the auditor's communication to indicate corrective action taken or planned or stating management's belief that the costs of correction exceed the benefits. If such a written response is included with the auditor's communication, the auditor should add a paragraph to disclaim an opinion on management's written response.

Sample Written Communication about Internal Control Deficiencies

In planning and performing our audit of the financial statements of ABC Company (the "Company") as of and for the year ended December 31, 20XX, in accordance with auditing standards generally accepted in the United States of America, we considered the Company's internal control over financial reporting (internal control) as a basis for designing our auditing procedures for the purpose of expressing our opinion on the financial statements, but not for the purpose of expressing an opinion on the effectiveness of the Company's internal control. Accordingly, we do not express an opinion on the effectiveness of the Company's internal control.

Our consideration of internal control was for the limited purpose described in the preceding paragraph and was not designed to identify all deficiencies in internal control that might be significant deficiencies or material weaknesses and therefore, there can be no assurance that all deficiencies, significant deficiencies, or material weaknesses have been identified. However, as discussed below, we identified certain deficiencies in internal control that we consider to be material weaknesses (and other deficiencies that we consider to be significant deficiencies—*add this phrase only if applicable*).

A deficiency in internal control exists when the design or operation of a control does not allow management or employees, in the normal course of performing their assigned functions, to prevent, or detect and correct misstatements on a timely basis. A material weakness is a deficiency, or a combination of deficiencies, in internal control, such that there is a reasonable possibility that a material misstatement of the entity's financial statements will not be prevented or detected and corrected on a timely basis. (We consider the following deficiencies in the Company's internal control to be material weaknesses:)

(*Describe the material weaknesses that were identified.*)

A significant deficiency is a deficiency, or a combination of deficiencies, in internal control that is less severe than a material weakness, yet important enough to merit attention by those charged with governance. (We consider the following deficiencies to be significant deficiencies in internal control:)

(*Describe the significant deficiencies that were identified.*)

This communication is intended solely for the information and use of management, (*identify the body or individuals charged with governance*), others within the organization, and (*identify any specified governmental authorities*) and is not intended to be and should not be used by anyone other than these specified parties.

AUD 7
Quality Control

AUD 7: Quality Control

7.01 Quality Control

Overview of Quality Control

Quality control criteria are in place to **ensure compliance** with professional standards, applicable regulations, and legal requirements. These controls are applied at two different levels:

- The CPA firm level
- The engagement level

These quality control standards complement those that are applied primarily at the individual level (eg, the AICPA Code of Professional Conduct).

A *system of quality control* consists of policies designed to achieve the objectives and procedures necessary to implement and monitor compliance with those quality control polices, including communication of such policies and procedures to all firm personnel.

Considerations for CPA firm quality control policies and procedures

- Firm size
- Nature of firm's practice
- Organization structure
- Costs/benefits

 Representative Task (Remembering and Understanding): Identify a CPA firm's responsibilities for its accounting and auditing practice's engagement quality.

 Representative Task (Remembering and Understanding): Explain procedures and responsibilities for managing engagement quality.

GAAS (Nonissuers) Engagement Quality Control Requirements

AICPA Guidance

An individual audit engagement is governed by GAAS, whereas a CPA firm's collective portfolio of accounting and auditing services (sometimes called the A&A practice, which involves entities' financial statements and, thereby, involves the public interest) is governed by the AICPA's Statements on Quality Control Standards (SQCS).

SQCS are issued by the AICPA's Auditing Standards Board (in particular, the section of the SQCS dealing with "A Firm's System of Quality Control" is QC10). The relevant AICPA guidance applicable to an individual audit engagement is provided by AU-C 220, *Quality Control for an Engagement Conducted in Accordance with GAAS*.

The purpose of AU-C 220 is to assist the auditor in **implementing the firm's quality control procedures** specifically at the **engagement level**. This pronouncement states that the auditor's objective is to implement quality control procedures at the engagement level that provide reasonable assurance that (a) the audit complies with professional standards and applicable legal and regulatory requirements and (b) the auditor issues an appropriate report.

Definitions

Engagement Partner—The person in the firm who is responsible for the audit engagement and its performance and for the auditor's report.

Engagement partner responsibilities

- Direction, supervision, and performance of the engagement in compliance with professional standards, applicable legal and regulatory requirements, and firm policies and procedures

- Issuance of a report that is appropriate under the circumstances

- Evaluation of the sufficiency of appropriate audit evidence to support conclusions reached and the report issued

- Consultations among engagement team members to resolve difficult or contentious matters, ensuring that:

  - An engagement quality review is performed when called for by firm policy

  - Firm policies are followed in dealing with differences of opinion among members of the engagement team

Engagement Quality Control Review—A process designed to provide an objective evaluation, before the report is released, of the significant judgments the engagement team made and the conclusions it reached in formulating the auditor's report. (The engagement quality control review process is only for those audit engagements, if any, for which the firm has determined that an engagement quality control review is required, in accordance with its policies and procedures.)

Engagement quality control review

- Objective evaluation of judgments and conclusions of the audit team

- Completed before audit report released

- Used only when dictated by firm quality control policies

- Reviewer(s) should be experienced but not on the engagement team

- Differences of opinion between engagement partner and reviewer to be settled by firm policy

Engagement Quality Control Reviewer—This is the person in the firm, a suitably qualified external person, or a team made up of such individuals, none of whom is part of the engagement team, with sufficient and appropriate experience and authority to objectively evaluate the significant judgments that the engagement team made and the conclusions it reached in formulating the auditor's report.

Engagement quality reviewer responsibilities

- Perform an objective review
- Review documentation relative to significant judgments and conclusions
- Read financial statements and audit report
- Determine if nature, timing, and extent of work is appropriate
- Determine if sufficient appropriate audit evidence supports the report

Focus of the System of Quality Control

A CPA firm is required to have a "system of quality control" for its accounting and auditing services (covering audit, attestation, compilation, and review services; note that the SQCS are not applicable to tax or consulting services) to provide reasonable assurance that engagements are performed in accordance with professional standards and applicable regulatory and legal requirements, and that the issuance of reports are appropriate in the circumstances.

- **Nature and Scope**—The policies and procedures will vary with the circumstances (eg, firm size and number of offices, complexity of services offered, and the level of experience of the professional staff)
- **Inherent Limitations**—Similar to any internal control system, a quality control system provides "reasonable" (a high, but not absolute) assurance, reflecting implicit cost-benefit trade-offs

 Which of the following actions should a CPA firm take to comply with the AICPA's quality control standards?
- Establish procedures that comply with the standards of the Sarbanes-Oxley Act
- Use attributes sampling techniques in testing internal controls
- Consider inherent risk and control risk before determining detection risk
- Establish policies to ensure that the audit work meets applicable professional standards

CPA firm's system of quality control

- Is required
- Applies to auditing and accounting engagements
- Is comprehensive
- Consists of policies and procedures
- Provides reasonable assurance that the firm
  - Complies with professional standards
  - Issues appropriate reports

SQCS outline CPA firm quality control (QC) requirements. These standards require CPA firms to establish a comprehensive QC system specific to accounting and auditing engagements, with the objective of providing *reasonable assurance* that the **firm complies with professional standards and legal and regulatory requirements** and issues appropriate reports.

Six Elements of a Quality Control System

These elements of quality control should be viewed as interrelated components:

Human Resources—Policies and procedures should address important personnel issues (including initial hiring, assignments to engagements, professional development and continuing professional education, and promotion decisions).

Ethical Requirements—Policies and procedures should address the independence of personnel as necessary (should obtain written confirmation of compliance with independence requirements from all appropriate personnel at least annually).

Acceptance and Continuance of Client Relationships and Engagements—Policies and procedures should carefully assess the risks associated with each engagement (including issues related to management integrity), and the firm should undertake only engagements that can be completed with professional competence.

Quality control for client acceptance

- Ensure association with clients whose management acts with integrity
- Provide reasonable assurance that the CPA firm
  - Is competent to perform engagement
  - Has needed capabilities
  - Can comply with legal and ethical requirements

Leadership Responsibilities for Quality—Policies and procedures should promote an internal culture that emphasizes a *commitment to quality* (sometimes called the "tone at the top"). For an individual audit engagement, the engagement partner should take responsibility for overall audit quality, although performance of certain procedures may, of course, be delegated to other members of the engagement team.

- If the engagement team identifies a **threat to independence** that safeguards may not eliminate or reduce to an acceptable level, the engagement partner is required to report the matter to the relevant person(s) in the firm to determine the appropriate action (to either eliminate the threat or withdraw from the engagement when withdrawal is allowed under applicable law or regulation)

Monitoring—Policies and procedures should provide an ongoing assessment of the adequacy of the design and the operating effectiveness of the system of quality control. Controls that are effective at one point in time may deteriorate over time owing to neglect or changed circumstances. It is important that the controls are properly monitored so that timely adjustments can be made as necessary to keep the quality control policies and procedures working effectively over time.

Engagement Performance—Policies and procedures should focus on compliance with all applicable firm and professional standards and applicable regulatory requirements and encourage personnel to consult as necessary with professional (or other) literature or other human resources within or outside of the firm for appropriate guidance.

Quality control elements for a CPA firm
(HEAL-ME)

- **H**uman resources
- **E**thical requirements
- **A**cceptance and continuance of client
- **L**eadership responsibilities for quality
- **M**onitoring
- **E**ngagement performance

Differences of Opinion

The firm should establish policies and procedures for dealing with and resolving **differences of opinion** within the engagement team, with those consulted, and between the engagement partner and the engagement quality control reviewer (including that the conclusions reached are documented and implemented and that the report is not released until the matter is resolved).

Documentation

The firm should establish policies and procedures requiring appropriate documentation of the operation of each element of the system of quality control.

GAAS engagement quality review documentation

- Reflects review date
- Provides evidence that:
    - Firm's engagement quality control procedures were performed
    - Reviewer is unaware of any unresolved or inappropriate judgments or conclusions

PCAOB on Engagement Quality Review

PCAOB Guidance

Requires an engagement quality review (and concurring approval of issuance) for engagements conducted under PCAOB standards (1) for an audit; (2) for a review of interim financial information; and (3) for an attestation engagement regarding compliance reports of brokers and dealers (or a review engagement regarding exemption reports of brokers and dealers).

Engagement Quality Reviewer

The objective of the engagement quality reviewer is to perform an **evaluation of the significant judgments** made by the engagement team and the related conclusions reached and in preparing any engagement report.

The engagement quality reviewer must be an *associated person* of a registered public accounting firm; and must have competence, independence, integrity, and objectivity:

- **Associated person of a registered public accounting firm**—Should be able to withstand any pressure from the engagement partner or others and may be someone from outside the firm; if the reviewer is from within the firm, he/she should be a partner or have an equivalent position. (There is no such requirement for a reviewer from outside the firm)
- **Competence**—Must be qualified to serve as the engagement partner on the engagement under review
- **Objectivity**—The engagement quality reviewer (and any assisting personnel) should not make engagement team decisions or assume any responsibilities of the engagement team

In addition, they must have met the **"cooling-off" restriction**.

- The person serving as engagement partner during either of the two audits preceding the audit subject to engagement quality review is not permitted to serve as engagement quality reviewer (unless the registered firm qualifies for a specific exemption to this requirement)

Engagement Quality Review Process

To evaluate the significant judgments and conclusions of the engagement team, the engagement quality reviewer should:

- Hold discussions with the engagement partner and other members of the engagement team

- Review engagement documentation

- Evaluate whether the documentation that was reviewed (1) indicates that the engagement team responded appropriately to significant risks and (2) supports the conclusions reached by the engagement team

The engagement quality reviewer **cannot express concurring approval of issuance** if there is any significant engagement deficiency where the:

- Engagement team failed to obtain sufficient appropriate evidence

- Engagement team reached an inappropriate overall conclusion

- Engagement report is not appropriate

- Firm is not independent of its client

The firm *cannot give permission to the client* to use the engagement report until the engagement quality reviewer provides concurring approval of issuance.

Documentation

Documentation should contain sufficient information to permit an experienced auditor, having no prior association with the engagement, to understand the procedures performed and conclusions reached by the engagement quality reviewer.

Documentation of an engagement quality review should be included in the engagement documentation (and be subject to other PCAOB requirements regarding retention of and changes to audit documentation).

PCAOB Standards vs. Statements on Quality Control Standards (SQCS)

Differences between the PCAOB rules and those provided by the AICPA's SQCS include the following:

- **Engagement Quality Review**—SQCS do not require an engagement quality review for any type of engagement, whereas the PCAOB establishes such a requirement

- **Cooling-off Restriction**—SQCS do not impose a "cooling-off" restriction or a requirement that the reviewer must be an associated person of a registered public accounting firm

- **Concurring Approval of Issuance**—SQCS require any engagement quality review performed be completed before the engagement report is released without requiring a concurring approval of issuance

- **Documentation Retention and Changes**—SQCS do not specifically require that engagement quality review documentation must be retained with other engagement documentation and be subject to specific policies regarding retention and changes

AUD

Area II: Assessing Risk and Developing a Planned Response

AUD 8
Planning an
Engagement

AUD 8: Planning an Engagement

8.01 Overall Engagement Strategy

 Representative Task (Remembering & Understanding): Explain the purpose and significance of the overall engagement strategy for an engagement.

Overview

According to AU-C 300, audit planning involves developing an overall audit engagement strategy for the expected conduct, timing, and scope of the audit. The overall strategy is then used to develop an audit plan that details the specific audit procedures that should be performed. The auditor's objective is to plan the audit so that it will be performed in an **effective** manner. Adequate planning helps the auditor:

- Dedicate adequate attention to critical audit items
- Solve potential problems in a timely manner
- Coordinate an efficient and effective engagement
- Select capable and competent engagement team members to address anticipated risks and allocate responsibilities to those team members
- Direct, supervise, and review team members' work

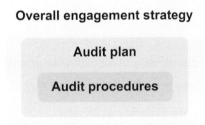

The auditor's planning-related responsibilities are virtually the same under the PCAOB standards as they are under the AICPA standards.

Overall Engagement Strategy

In establishing the overall audit strategy, the auditor should:

- Identify characteristics of the engagement that affect the scope of the audit
- Determine the reporting objectives to plan the nature and timing of communications
- Consider other factors that the auditor deems significant to the direction of the audit
- Consider the preliminary activities and relevant knowledge gained from other engagements
- Ascertain the nature, timing, and extent of resources needed to perform the engagement

Nature, Timing & Extent of Planning

Planning is an ongoing iterative process, not a one-time activity. Planning encompasses:

- Risk assessment procedures
- Understanding the applicable legal and regulatory framework
- Determination of materiality
- Involvement of specialists

The engagement partner and other key members of the engagement team should be involved in the planning of the audit. The engagement team plans the audit to be responsive to the **assessment of the risk of material misstatement (RMM)** based on the auditor's understanding of the entity and its environment, including its internal control (I/C).

The nature, extent, and timing of planning will vary with:

- The size and complexity of the entity
- The auditor's experience with the entity
- Knowledge of the entity's business and industry
- Knowledge of the entity and its environment, including I/C

Supervision & Review

The supervision and review of team members' work may depend on factors, such as:

- The size and complexity of the entity
- The area of the audit
- The assessed RMM
- The capabilities and competence of individual team members

Supervision includes:

- Tracking audit progress
- Considering the competence and capabilities of individual team members
- Addressing significant findings/issues arising during the audit and modifying the planned approach if necessary
- Identifying matters for consultation or consideration by qualified team members

Review responsibilities may be delegated to experienced team members. Such responsibilities may include considering whether:

- Work has been performed in accordance with professional standards and legal and regulatory requirements
- The nature, timing, and extent of work performed is appropriate, documented, and supports the conclusions reached
- The objectives of the procedures have been achieved, and evidence obtained is sufficient and appropriate to support the auditor's report

Specialized Skills

- The auditor should determine whether there is a need for specialized skills on the engagement

- A professional having specialized skills may be someone within or outside of the audit firm. Examples include valuation experts, appraisers, actuaries, tax specialists, IT professionals, and so on

- The auditor should be sufficiently knowledgeable about the matters involved to communicate the objectives of the work, to evaluate whether the planned procedures will meet the auditor's needs, and to evaluate the results of the procedures performed

 Prior to commencing fieldwork, an auditor usually discusses the general audit strategy with the client's management. Which of the following matters do the auditor and management agree upon at this time?

- The appropriateness of the entity's plans for dealing with adverse economic conditions

- The determination of the fraud risk factors that exist within the client's operations

- The control weaknesses to be included in the communication with the audit committee

- The coordination of the assistance of the client's personnel in data preparation

Audit process

Client acceptance/continuance

↓

Auditor communicates:
- Management responsibilities
- Auditor responsibilities
- Timing and scope of the audit
- Inquiries with management

Plan the audit
(initial strategy and plan)

↓

Obtain understanding of client, its environment & internal control

↓

Assess risk of material misstatement & design further procedures

↓

Perform tests of controls

↓

Perform substantive procedures

↓

Form an opinion

↓

Issue a report

Because audits require cooperation from management, the auditors' decisions about the nature, timing, and extent of resources to be applied will be guided in part by when records can be provided by the client. Accordingly, when setting an audit strategy, auditors will come to an agreement with management about **coordination with the client's personnel in data preparation**.

Steps in Planning the Audit

The steps in planning an audit include (**BRAINSTOPS**):

1. **Basic discussions with the client** about the nature of the engagement and the client's business and industry are performed first. In addition, the auditor meets the key employees, or new employees of a continuing client. The overall audit strategy or the timing of the audit may be discussed, but the specific audit procedures should not be.

2. **Review of audit documentation** from previous audits performed by the accounting firm (or a predecessor auditor, if available) will assist in developing an outline of the audit program.

3. **Ask about recent developments** in the company, such as mergers and new product lines, which will cause the audit to differ from earlier years.

4. **Interim F/S** are analyzed to identify accounts and transactions that differ from expectations (based on factors such as budgets or prior periods). The performance of **analytical procedures** (discussed later) is **mandatory** in the planning of an audit to identify accounts that may be misstated and that deserve special emphasis in the audit program.

5. **Nonaudit personnel** of the accounting firm who have provided services (such as tax preparation) to the client should be identified and consulted to learn more about the client.

6. **Staffing** for the audit should be determined and a meeting held to discuss the engagement.

7. **Timing** of the various audit procedures should be determined. For example, I/C testing needs to be performed early in the engagement, inventory counts need to be performed at or near the balance sheet date, and the client representation letter cannot be obtained until the end of the audit fieldwork.

8. **Outside assistance** needs should be determined, including the use of a specialist (eg, a tax practitioner, an appraiser for special valuation issues, or an IT professional) and the internal auditors of the client. We'll discuss the use of specialists and others in more detail in a later section.

9. **Pronouncements** reflecting changes in accounting principles and audit standards should be read or reviewed to assist in the development of complete audit programs fitting the unique needs of the client's business and industry.

10. **Scheduling** with the client is needed to coordinate activities. For example, client-prepared schedules need to be ready when the auditor expects to examine them, and the client needs to be informed of dates when they will be prohibited from accessing bank safe deposit boxes to ensure the integrity of counts of securities held at banks.

Planning Documentation

The auditor should address the following matters in the audit documentation: (1) the overall audit strategy; (2) the audit plan; and (3) any significant changes made to the audit strategy or the audit plan during the audit engagement, along with the reasons for any such changes.

8.02 Engagement Plan

Audit Plan/Program

 Representative Task (Application): Prepare a draft engagement plan for specific processes, accounts, or classes of transactions considering the prior period and changes in the current period.

 Representative Task (Application): Prepare supporting planning-related materials (eg, client assistance request listings, time budgets) for a detailed engagement plan starting with the prior-year engagement plan or with a template.

An audit **plan/program** (ie, a detailed audit plan) is a step-by-step **list of audit procedures**, which is **required** for every GAAS audit. It is written after sufficient planning procedures have been conducted and is designed so that:

- The planned procedures will achieve specific audit objectives, which relate to management's assertions
- It supports the auditor's conclusion

The audit plan should support the **nature, timing, and extent** of audit procedures:

- **Risk assessment procedures** are designed to provide an understanding of the entity and its environment, including I/C, in order to assess risk of material misstatement (RMM). However, on their own, they are not sufficient to support an audit opinion
- **Further audit procedures** at the relevant assertion level for each material class of transactions, account balance, and disclosure include tests of controls and substantive procedures
  - **Tests of Controls (TOC)** evaluate the operating effectiveness of I/C in preventing or detecting material misstatements. They are often used when the use of substantive procedures is not sufficient
  - **Substantive Procedures** detect material misstatements and include tests of details and substantive analytical procedures. Substantive procedures are required for all relevant assertions related to any material transaction class, account balance, and/or disclosure item

Key factors to prepare an audit program

Assess the risk of
material misstatement
(including internal controls)

Consider the client's
business environment   ⟶

Audit program:
• List of audit procedures to be performed
• Describes nature, timing, and extent of procedures
• Procedures should achieve audit objectives

Calculate materiality and
apply to audit procedures

 In addition to descriptions of the nature, timing, and extent of planned risk assessment procedures and planned further audit procedures, which of the following additional pieces of information should be documented in the engagement audit plan?

- Procedures performed to assess independence and the ability to perform the engagement

- The understanding of the terms of the engagement, including scope, fees, and resource allocation

- Other audit procedures to be performed to comply with generally accepted auditing standards

- Issues with management integrity that could affect the decision to continue the audit engagement

The audit plan provides details about how the strategy will be executed. The auditor should document the nature (eg, type of procedures), timing, and extent (ie, the area covered) of the audit procedures. Other procedures needed to comply with GAAS should also be documented. For example, if the auditor is engaged to audit an insurance company, the auditor may need an external actuary (a specialist) to help with the audit. The auditor should specify what actuarial firm will be used and the timing of their services in the audit plan.

AUD 9
Understanding an Entity and Its Environment

AUD 9: Understanding an Entity and Its Environment

9.01 External Factors

Overview

 Representative Task (Remembering & Understanding): Understand supply and demand, elasticity measures, and profit maximization (eg, marginal cost, marginal revenue).

Economics is the study of how we allocate scarce resources to satisfy unlimited wants. Microeconomics is the study of the decisions of, and interactions among, various individual economic agents (households and firms).

- Both households and firms act as buyers in the economy, providing demand for products (or goods) and services (including labor)

- Both households and firms act as sellers in the economy, providing the supply of products and services

- The interaction of demand and supply determine the price, quantity produced and consumed, and the allocation of products and services

Supply

A supply schedule for an individual producer shows the quantity of goods or services that the producer is willing to provide (supply) at alternate prices during a specified time. The graphic representation of a supply schedule presents a supply curve, which normally has a positive slope.

A supply curve shows the *direct relationship* between the price of a product or service and the quantity that a group of producers and/or sellers are willing to supply at a particular time (ie, the quantity supplied). For instance, as the price of a product increases, the quantity supplied by sellers increases.

 Economists are very specific about the usage of the terms "supply" vs. "quantity supplied." The term "supply" refers to the supply curve that can be plotted on a graph with quantity supplied on the x-axis (horizontal) and price on the y-axis (vertical). The supply curve may also be thought of as a schedule listing multiple combinations of prices and quantities supplied (eg, those for points C and D in the graph). Thus, economists would not say that higher prices increase "supply." Instead, economists would say that at higher prices, "quantity supplied" is higher. As prices increase, one moves along the supply curve to find higher quantities supplied.

The supply curve shifts if there are changes in relevant factors other than a change in price. Economists use a variety of terms to describe supply curve shifts:

- Changes in the supply curve where quantity supplied becomes larger for each and every price are described as "the supply curve shifted outward" (not upward), "the supply curve shifted to the right," or "supply increased"

- Changes in the supply curve where quantity supplied becomes smaller for each and every price are described as "the supply curve shifted inward" (not downward), "the supply curve shifted to the left," or "supply decreased"

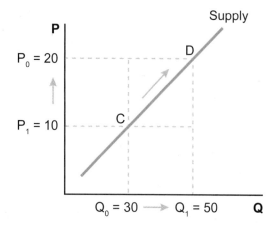

Below is a supply curve shift to the right from S_0 to S_1. Note that at a price of 20, sellers supply 70 instead of 50 units. Alternatively, for a quantity of 50, sellers charge a (lower) price of 10 instead of 20.

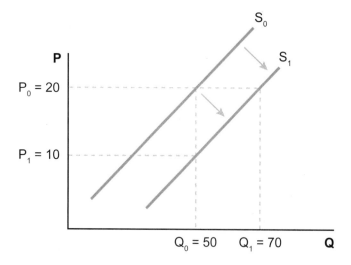

Some factors exhibit a **direct relationship** with the supply curve, meaning that increases in that factor cause the supply curve to shift outward (or supply to increase). Examples are:

- **Number of producers**—More producers normally increase the quantity supplied of a product at a given price. Entry by foreign suppliers into the U.S. auto market increases the supply of cars in the U.S.

- **Government subsidies**—Additional funding permits producers to purchase more inputs and, thus, increase quantity supplied at any given price

- **Price expectations**—If producers expect higher prices, producers will increase their quantity supplied at any given price

- **Technological advances**—Technological advances generally reduce production costs; hence, producers generally will increase their quantity supplied at any given price with an increase in technological advances

Other factors exhibit an **inverse relationship** with the supply curve, meaning that increases in that factor cause the supply curve to *shift inward* (or supply to decrease). Examples are:

- **Increases in production costs (eg, production taxes)**—If producers' costs increase, producers will decrease their quantity supplied at a given price

- **Prices of other products**—If producers may produce both product A and B, and producing A becomes more profitable, producers will decrease their quantity supplied of B at any given price

Price Elasticity of Supply

Elasticities measure the **sensitivity** of something (eg, quantity demanded) to changes in something else (eg, price). Types of elasticities include price elasticity of demand, price elasticity of supply, income elasticity of demand, and cross elasticity of demand.

The price elasticity of supply is a measure of how sensitive **quantity supplied** of a good or service is to a **change in price** or cost.

$$\text{Price elasticity of supply } (E_s) = \frac{\text{Percentage change in } \textbf{quantity supplied}}{\text{Percentage change in } \textbf{price}}$$
(elasticity of supply)

Owners of factors of production (labor, natural resources, capital, and entrepreneurship) aim to shift those factors to their most productive uses. These efforts are reflected in economic rents or surpluses, which are the excess of the payments for these factors when used most productively over their best alternative use (ie, opportunity cost).

Opportunity Cost

Opportunity cost is also known as the benefit given up from not using the resource for another purpose (the foregone benefit of a rejected alternative *not* selected).

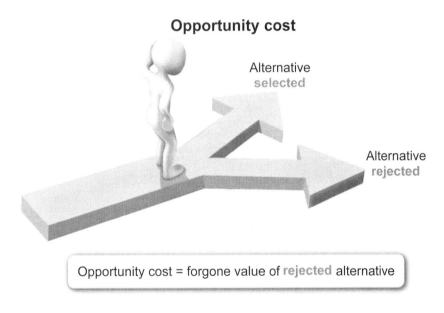

Opportunity cost

Alternative selected

Alternative rejected

Opportunity cost = forgone value of rejected alternative

For example, if a worker accepts a job paying $60,000 instead of another offering $50,000, the worker would have received an economic rent of $10,000 from accepting the higher paying job, and faced an opportunity cost of $50,000 by doing so.

For suppliers themselves, economic profit refers to the excess of the profits they are receiving over the normal profit rate in the economy. Economic profits usually result in more suppliers entering the market, and economic losses will usually result in suppliers exiting the market.

Demand

Demand is the desire, willingness, and ability to acquire a commodity. Because demand depends on having the financial ability to acquire a commodity (good or service), the quantity of a commodity for which there will be demand (quantity demanded) will be negatively associated with the price of the commodity. If other influences are held constant, the higher the price, the lower the quantity demanded, and the lower the price, the higher the quantity demanded.

A demand schedule for an **individual** shows the quantity of a commodity that will be demanded at various prices during a specified time, *ceteris paribus* (holding variables other than price constant). The graphic representation of a demand schedule presents a demand curve with a negative slope.

A market demand curve shows the *inverse relationship* between the price and the quantity of a product or service that a group of consumers are willing and able to buy at a particular time (ie, the quantity demanded). For instance, as the price of a product increases (eg, from 10 to 20), the quantity demanded by buyers decreases (eg, from 50 to 30).

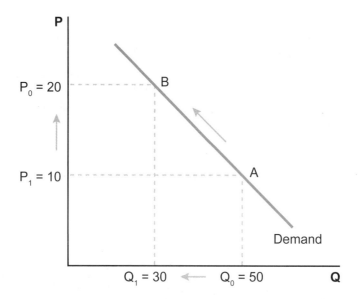

 Economists are very specific about the usage of the terms "demand" vs. "quantity demanded." The term "demand" refers to the demand curve that can be plotted on a graph with quantity demanded on the x-axis (horizontal) and price on the y-axis (vertical). The demand curve may also be thought of as a schedule listing multiple combinations of prices and quantities demanded (eg, those for points A and B in the graph). Thus, economists would not say that higher prices decrease "demand." Instead, economists would say that at higher prices, "quantity demanded" is lower. As prices increase, one moves along the demand curve to find lower quantities demanded.

Price and quantity demanded have a reliably inverse relationship; however, the precise placement of the demand curve on the graph may change regularly. These changes are known as demand curve shifts. A demand curve shifts if there are changes in relevant factors *other than a change in price*. Economists use a variety of terms to describe demand curve shifts:

- Changes in the demand curve where quantity demanded becomes larger for each and every price are described as "the demand curve shifted upward," "the demand curve shifted outward," "the demand curve shifted to the right," or "demand increased"

- Changes in the demand curve where quantity demanded becomes smaller for each and every price are described as "the demand curve shifted downward," "the demand curve shifted inward," "the demand curve shifted to the left," or "demand decreased"

Below we show an upward demand curve shift from D_0 to D_1. Note that at a price of 20, consumers are willing and able to purchase 50 instead of 30 units. Alternatively, for a quantity of 30, consumers are willing and able to pay a price of 27 instead of 20.

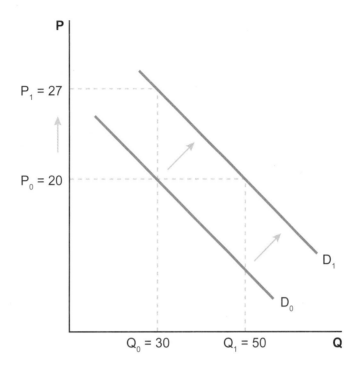

There are various reasons why demand curves may shift. Some factors exhibit a direct relationship with the demand curve, meaning that increases in that factor cause the demand curve to *shift upward* (or demand to increase). Examples are:

- **The price of a substitute good**—When product A may be an acceptable alternative to product B, an increase in the price of product A will make product B more attractive (eg, some consumers will shift from buying product A to product B). For example, an increase in the price of hamburgers will increase the demand for hot dogs

- **Expectations of price changes**—Consumers are more likely to buy now if they think prices will increase in the future. For example, if cigarette taxes are expected to double next year, some buyers will bring forward some of their purchases, increasing demand this year until the tax increase goes into effect

- **Income (for normal goods)**—For many goods (eg, cars or smartphones), when incomes increase (wealth increase), demand increases. Below we point out that not all goods are "normal goods"

- **Extent of the market**—New consumers may increase demand, therefore increasing the size of the market. For example, the removal of trade barriers by foreign governments will increase the demand for American products that can be exported. A baby boom will increase demand for baby food. A large inflow of immigrants from a country to the U.S. will increase demand for that country's ethnic food in the U.S.

Other factors exhibit an inverse relationship with the demand curve, meaning that increases in that factor cause the demand curve to *shift downward* (or demand to decrease). Examples are:

- **The price of a complement good**—When products are normally used together, an increase in the price of one of the goods decreases demand for the other. For example, an increase in the price of chips will cause a downward shift in the demand for salsa

- **Income (for inferior goods)**—For some goods (eg, used cars), when incomes increase (wealth), demand decreases as consumers shift their spending to other goods (eg, new cars)

- **Consumer boycotts**—An organized boycott will, if effective, temporarily decrease the demand for a product. For example, members of unions commonly refuse to buy from businesses that are involved in labor disputes

Changes in consumer tastes may affect demand but whether demand increases or decreases as a result depends on whether the change in tastes favors or disfavors the specific product. These are said to have an indeterminate relationship. The theory of *derived demand* predicts that demand for the resources used to produce product A is derived from the demand for product A.

Price Elasticity of Demand

Barring shifts in the demand curve, a firm expects the quantity demanded for its product to decrease as the price increases. A smaller level of sales (ie, quantity demanded) could reduce the firm's total revenue (= price × quantity). Alternatively, a higher price could increase the firm's total revenue. Whether total revenue will increase or decrease when prices change turns out to depend on the price elasticity of demand (aka elasticity of demand). This concept measures how responsive the quantity demanded (of a good or service) is to a change in price.

$$\text{Price elasticity of supply } (E_d) \text{ (elasticity of demand)} = \frac{\text{Percentage change in } \textbf{quantity demanded}}{\text{Percentage change in } \textbf{price}}$$

Elasticities are commonly computed using the "arc method" or relative to the midpoint (or average) between conditions before and after a change, instead of relative to conditions "before" the change.

$$\text{Own-price elasticity of demand} = \frac{\%\text{ change in quantity demanded of } X}{\%\text{ change in price of } X}$$

$$= \frac{\text{Change in quantity of } X}{\text{Original quantity of } X} \div \frac{\text{Change in price of } X}{\text{Original price of } X}$$

Using the formula above, price elasticities of demand technically yield negative answers (either the change in quantity demanded or the change in price will be negative while the other is positive). When interpreting price elasticities of demand, it is customary to ignore the negative sign (or to report its absolute value).

Elasticity of demand	
Elastic	• % change in quantity demanded > % change in price • Revenue declines if price increases
Unit elastic	• % change in quantity demanded = % change in price • Revenue not sensitive to price change
Inelastic	• % change in quantity demanded < % change in price • Revenue will increase if price increases

If E_d is greater than 1, demand is elastic, and total revenue will decline if the price is increased. If E_d is less than 1, demand is considered inelastic, and total revenue will increase if the price is increased. If elasticity is equal to 1, demand is said to be "unit elastic," (unitary) and total revenue is not sensitive to price changes. For example, goods that represent a larger fraction of consumers' budgets tend to be elastic (automobiles) and those that represent a smaller fraction of consumers' budgets tend to be inelastic (table salt).

Elasticities are often larger if more time elapsed while the compared changes took place. For instance, in the short run, consumers may not be able to reduce their consumption of gasoline significantly when there is an increase in gasoline prices; ie, consumers' gasoline purchases are less responsive to price changes in the short term; consumers' demand for gasoline is more inelastic over the short term.

Over longer periods, however, they can switch to more efficient cars, change their work arrangements to reduce driving needs, and reduce their consumption of gasoline. The longer they have to adjust, the more they can reduce their gasoline consumption in response to price increases (ie, consumers' gasoline purchases are more responsive to price changes in the long term; consumers' demand for gasoline is more elastic over the long term).

Income Elasticity of Demand

Income elasticity of demand measures the effect of changes in (consumer) income on changes in the quantity demanded of a product. All elasticities (not just price elasticity of demand) may be computed using the arc method.

$$\textbf{Income elasticity of demand} = \frac{\text{Percentage change in quantity demanded}}{\text{Percentage change in income}}$$

A positive income elasticity indicates a normal good, which means that as consumer income increases, the quantity demanded of the normal good also increases. A negative number indicates an inferior good, so as income increases, the quantity demanded of the inferior good will decrease. For example, if incomes increase and the quantity demanded for new cars also increases, new cars are a normal good. However, if incomes increase and the quantity demanded for used cars decreases, used cars are an inferior good.

Cross-Elasticity of Demand

Cross-elasticity of demand measures the change in the *quantity demanded of* a good to a change in the *price* of another good, and is used to determine if two different goods are substitutes (butter and margarine), which would result in a direct relationship (positive number), or complements (chips and salsa), which would result in an inverse relationship (negative number). If the coefficient is zero, the products are unrelated.

$$\textbf{Cross-elasticity of demand} = \frac{\text{Percentage change in } \textbf{quantity demanded} \text{ for product } X}{\text{Percentage change in the } \textbf{price} \text{ of product } Y}$$

For example, if the price of butter increases by 10% and the quantity demanded of margarine increases by 12%, 0.12 / 0.10 = 1.2, then their cross-elasticity of demand is positive and they are *substitutes*. However, if the price of chips increases by 10% and the quantity demanded of salsa decreases by 12%, –0.12 / 0.1 = –1.2, then their cross-elasticity of demand is negative and they are *complements*.

Marginal Cost and Marginal Revenue

Marginal Cost

Marginal cost (MC) is the dollar cost of producing **one additional unit** of physical *output*. It is computed as the difference between successive total costs or, because only variable costs change, successive total variable costs. When plotted, a marginal cost curve takes the form:

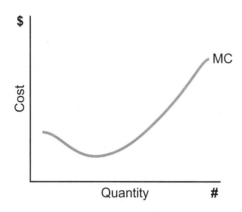

Marginal product (MP) is the change in physical output that will result from one additional unit of physical input. Notice that this measures physical output that results from physical input; it does not measure in terms of dollars. It is computed as the change in total output that results from using one additional unit of a particular factor of production (input).

Average Cost and Marginal Cost

When the marginal cost curve is combined with the average cost curves, the following results:

Average and marginal cost

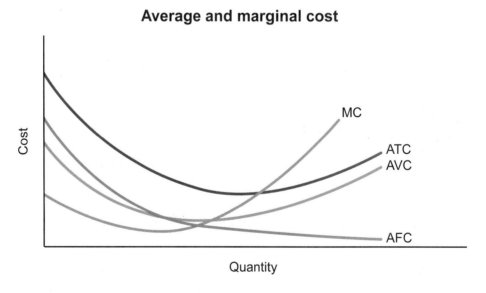

The lowest marginal cost (MC) occurs at a lower output than the lowest point on the average variable cost (AVC) or average total cost (ATC). The MC curve crosses the AVC and ATC at their respective lowest point.

Revenue and Output Concepts

Costs, as described above, are incurred in order to provide goods and services (output). The benefit derived from the sale of those goods and services (output) is commonly referred to as "revenue." Revenue concepts parallel those of cost.

Revenue—The amount earned as a result of providing goods or services.

Total Revenue (TR)—The total amount earned as a result of providing goods or services during a period. In the simplest context, it is the quantity provided (sold) multiplied by the price per unit sold.

Average Revenue (AR)—The average price (revenue) per unit for the total units sold. Average revenue is computed by dividing total revenue by the total quantity of units sold and may be expressed as AR = TR/Q.

Marginal Revenue (MR)—The dollar increase in revenue that results from the sale of one additional physical unit of output. Marginal revenue is computed as the change in total revenue as a result of selling one additional unit.

Marginal Revenue Product (MRP)—The additional dollars in revenue that will result from one additional unit of physical input. Notice that whereas this (MRP) measures revenue from input, marginal revenue (MR) measures additional revenue from output. MRP per unit of input measures the average increase in revenue attributable to each unit of input added. It is computed by dividing the marginal revenue product by the increase in the number of products (output) resulting from adding one additional unit of input.

Profit Maximization

To **maximize profits**, managers would choose levels of production (output or quantity) such that their company's **marginal revenue equals their marginal cost**. If the marginal revenue of producing one extra unit exceeds its marginal cost, it is profitable to increase production.

In the following graph, MR = MC for a quantity of 50. The total cost (TC) is $1,200 (ATC × Q = $24 × 50).

The firm would set the price at the maximum possible level given the demand curve (30), not at the marginal revenue (of about 12). Total revenue (TR) is $1,500 (P × Q = $30 × 50). Profit is $300 (TR – TC = $1,500 – $1,200).

Note that the profit maximizing quantity does not involve the minimum level of ATC (ie, where MC crosses ATC), but a slightly higher level (24).

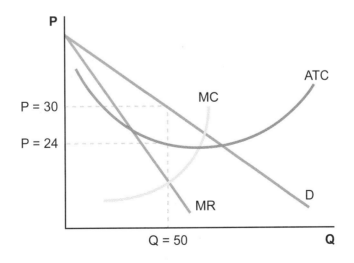

Market Equilibrium

The **equilibrium price** for a commodity is the price at which the quantity of the commodity supplied in the market is equal to the quantity of the commodity demanded in the market. Graphically, the market equilibrium price for a commodity occurs where the market demand curve and the market supply curve intersect.

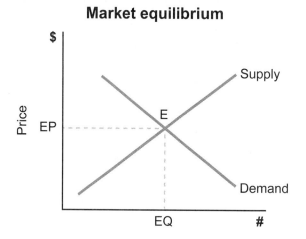

Market equilibrium

Equilibrium for the commodity occurs at the **intersection (E)** of the demand and supply curves. The equilibrium price is EP, and the equilibrium quantity is EQ. For the given supply and demand curves, at the equilibrium price (EP), the quantity of the commodity demanded (ie, that can be sold) is exactly equal to the quantity of the commodity that will be supplied at that price.

Shortages and Surpluses

Shortages and **surpluses** in quantity occur when the actual price (AP) of the commodity is less (shortage) or more (surplus) than the equilibrium price (EP).

- **Market Shortage**—The actual price is less than the equilibrium price (AP less than EP); therefore, the actual quantity supplied (QS) is less than the quantity demanded at AP (QS less than QD). A shortage equal to QD – QS exists

- **Market Surplus**—The actual price is higher than the equilibrium price (AP greater than EP); therefore, the actual quantity supplied is greater than the quantity demanded at AP (QS greater than QD). A surplus equal to QS – QD exists

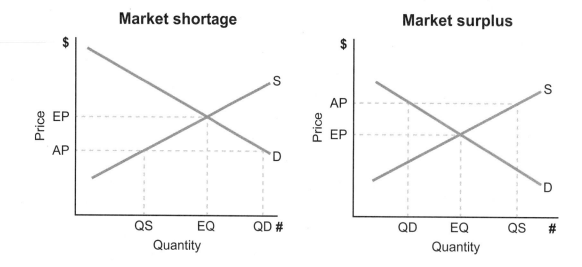

Shifts in Equilibrium

The effect of change(s) in demand and/or supply on market equilibrium depends on whether demand changes, supply changes, or both change.

- **Change in Market Demand (Only)**—An increase in market demand D1 to D2 due to an increase in the size of the market (or increased income, changes in consumer preferences, etc.) causes the demand curve to shift up and to the right. If there is no change in market supply, the results will be an increase in both the equilibrium price (EP1 to EP2) and equilibrium quantity (EQ1 to EQ2). A decrease in market demand would cause both equilibrium price and equilibrium quantity to decrease

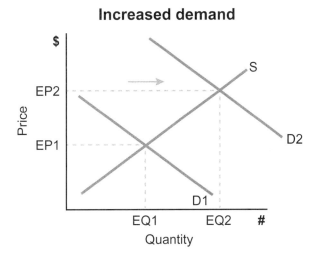

- **Change in Market Supply (Only)**—An increase in market supply (S1 to S2) due to an increase in the number of providers in the market (or lower cost of inputs, technological advances, etc.) causes the supply curve to shift down and to the right. If there is no change in market demand, the results will be a decrease in equilibrium price (EP1 to EP2) and an increase in equilibrium quantity (EQ1 to EQ2). A decrease in market supply causes a higher equilibrium price and a lower equilibrium quantity

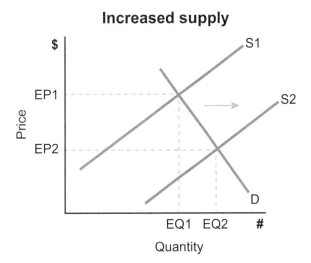

- **Changes in Both Market Demand and Market Supply**—The effect of simultaneous changes in both market demand and market supply depends on the direction of the changes (increase or decrease) and the relative magnitude of each change

  - Increases in both market demand and market supply will shift both curves to the right, resulting in a higher equilibrium quantity, but the resulting equilibrium price will depend on the magnitude of each change. The equilibrium price could remain unchanged, increase, or decrease

- Decreases in both market demand and market supply will shift both curves to the left, resulting in a lower equilibrium quantity, but the resulting equilibrium price will depend on the magnitude of each change
- The effects of a simultaneous increase in one market curve (demand or supply) and a decrease in the other market curve (supply or demand) on market price and market equilibrium can be determined only when the specific magnitude of each change is known

Governmental Influences on Equilibrium

- **Taxation and Subsidization**—As noted earlier, government taxation and subsidization have the effect of either increasing or decreasing the effective cost of production (supply). For example, a tax on a commodity at the production level increases the cost and shifts the market supply curve up and to the left. If demand remains constant, equilibrium price increases and equilibrium quantity decreases. Government subsidies have the opposite effect

- **Regulation**—Similarly, the imposition of government regulations on business tends to increase the cost of production (ie, compliance costs) and shift the market supply curve up and to the left when compared with what the market supply curve would be in the absence of regulatory costs

- **Rationing**—By imposing a rationing system, government can change market demand and thereby equilibrium in the market. Rationing would be intended to shift the demand curve down and to the left, thus lowering equilibrium price and equilibrium quantity

Price Ceilings and Floors

Government also can affect the price of a commodity through **price fiat** by establishing an (artificial) **price ceiling or price floor**. These artificial prices result in disequilibrium in the market. An imposed market ceiling (less than free-market equilibrium price) results in market supply being less than market demand at the imposed price. Market demand and market supply are not in equilibrium. An imposed market floor (greater than free-market equilibrium price) results in market supply being more than market demand at the imposed price.

For example, if government impose a **price ceiling** (eg, setting the maximum legal price at which a product or service may be sold at $7) below equilibrium (ie, $15), the quantity demanded (ie, 56) will exceed quantity supplied (ie, 24), resulting in *shortages of goods* (ie, 56 − 24 = 32 is the number of units that consumers would like to purchase at that price but are unable to; the lower line in the graph below represents the price ceiling and helps identify the various quantities).

If governments impose a **price floor** (eg, setting the minimum legal price at which a product or service may be sold at $17) above equilibrium, the quantity supplied (ie, 52) will exceed quantity demanded (ie, 28), resulting in unpurchased *surpluses of goods or services* (ie, 52 − 28 = 24 is the number of units that suppliers would like to sell at that price but are unable to; the upper line in the graph below represents the price floor and helps identify the various quantities).

Increased supply

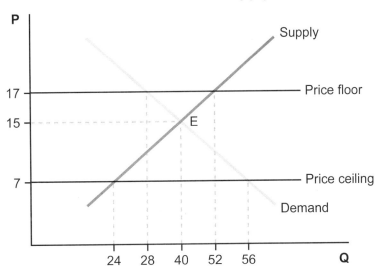

Business Cycles

 Representative Task (Remembering & Understanding): Understand the business cycles (trough, expansion, peak, recession) and leading, coincident, and lagging indicators of economic activity (eg, consumer price index, producer price index, federal funds rate, bond yields, unemployment).

Business cycles are fluctuations in economic production (output) typically lasting several years. Some business cycles have been shorter (barely a couple of years), and others longer (over a decade). Some business cycles are deep, involving large fluctuations, and others relatively shallower.

By convention, each business cycle includes one **recession** (or contraction) and one **expansion**. Each recession begins at the **peak** (or maximum level of output) from the previous expansion and ends at its trough (or minimum level of output for the recession). Each expansion begins at the **trough** of the previous recession and ends at the next peak.

The early stages of expansions are called **recoveries**. Recoveries are commonly described as having become full expansions when the previous peak is passed. Over the long term, nearly all measures of economic activity and personal well-being have grown or improved enormously in virtually every capitalist economy. However, growth has not taken place at a steady pace, but typically alternates between longer periods of strong growth and shorter periods of decline.

Business Cycle Components

Terms used in connection with the business cycle include:

- **Expansion**—Typically extended period (ie, several years) of increased economic production
  - The early stages of many expansions (ie, recoveries) during the second half of the twentieth century were marked by fast declines in unemployment rates. However, declines in unemployment have grown increasingly slower (ie, so-called **jobless recoveries**) following each of the last three recessions (ie, those of 1990–1991, 2001, and 2007–2009)

○ The final stages of many expansions during the twentieth century were marked by booming economic conditions, including GDP above potential and higher rates of inflation. Increased spending will cause a positive shift in the demand curve to the right (higher equilibrium GDP). Technological advances will also cause a positive shift in the supply curve, also resulting in a higher equilibrium GDP

- **Recession (or Contraction)**—Typically briefer periods (ie, several months or only a few years) of decreased economic production

  ○ Formally, the business cycle dating committee of the National Bureau of Economic Research (NBER, technically a non-profit) determines the beginning and end of recessions and expansions based on a variety of parameters. As a rule of thumb, economists describe recessions as periods of at least two consecutive quarters of negative growth in real GDP

  ○ During the twentieth century, many recessions followed efforts by the Federal Reserve (see section below on monetary policy) to restrain higher inflation rates through increases in interest rates

  ○ The declines in economic production during recessions are accompanied by declines in employment and increases in unemployment rates (Okun's law provides a commonly mentioned rule of thumb relating declines in GDP and increases in unemployment)

  ○ At the end of recessions, GDP is well below potential. Periods of decreased aggregate spending will shift the demand curve to the left and result in a lower equilibrium GDP. Trade wars cause a negative shift in the supply curve and also cause a decline in GDP

- **Depression**—A recession that is either particularly deep or long lasting

  ○ There is no formal agreement as to the boundary between recession and depression

  ○ For perspective, the Great Depression of 1929–1933 involved declines in real GDP of 27% and increases in unemployment rates from 3.2% to 25.2%. Since unemployment rates had declined only to 9.9% by 1941, the Great Depression is often dated as having spanned 1929–1941

  ○ In contrast, the recent Great Recession was the deepest recession since World War II and involved declines in real GDP of 4.7% and increases in unemployment rates from 4.7% to 10.1%

- **Recovery**—The early stages of an expansion, commonly thought to become a full expansion when the peak from the previous expansion is passed

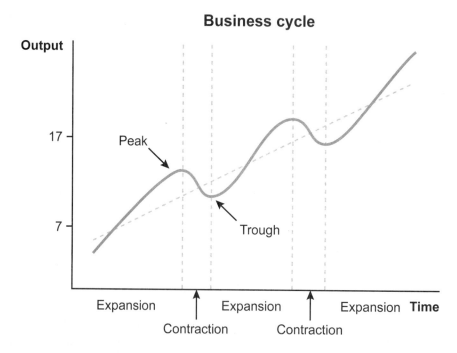

The different stages of the economy are associated with economic measures and indicators, such as GDP, unemployment, inflation, interest rates, and inventory-to-sales ratios. These relationships are outlined in the following table:

	Boom	Contraction	Recession	Expansion
GDP growth	peak	slowing	negative/low	growing
Unemployment	lowest	rising	highest	falling
Prices	rising	slowing	falling	low
Interest rates	peak	high/falling	low	low/rising
Inventory/sales	low	low/rising	high	falling

Sector Performance

Different sectors and industries in the economy perform best in different stages of the business cycle.

- **Consumer staples and utilities** are two sectors that continue to perform well in the contraction and recession phases. Examples would be food, drugs, cosmetics, tobacco, liquor, electricity, gas, and water. These goods tend to be necessities or represent a low fraction of the consumer budget. Staples and utilities have very low income elasticity; that is, there is little change in demand in relation to the change in income

- **Cyclicals and energy** do well in the early expansion stage. Examples of cyclical are savings and loans, banking, advertising, apparel, retailers, and autos. Financial firms do well because interest rates are low and rising while business and consumer borrowing grows. Other sectors do well here if they have high income elasticity; that is, the demand rises with an increase in income

- **Basic materials and technology** sectors perform well as the expansion continues. These sectors include chemicals, plastics, paper, wood, metals, semiconductors, computer hardware, and communication equipment

- In the late expansion and boom stage, the **capital goods, financial firms, and transportation sectors** do well. These sectors have high income elasticity and tend to do well when durable goods replacement increases. Examples include machinery and equipment manufacturers, airlines, trucking, railroads, and corporate or institutional banking

Which of the following statements is correct regarding an economy at the peak of the business cycle?

- The economy will be in a static equilibrium
- The economy will be at the natural rate of unemployment
- Incomes will be stable
- The rate of inflation will decrease

Stages of a business cycle	
Expansion	• Economy growing: stocks in bull market
	• Inflation nearing its target rate
	• Unemployment decreasing
Peak	• Transitionary phase: economy "overheated"
	• Excessive inflation and growth
	• Unemployment at its natural rate
Contraction	• Economy weakening: stocks in bear market
	• Unemployment increasing
	• Prices falling, deflation
Trough	• Transitionary phase: economy hits bottom
	• Low or stagnant growth
	• High unemployment

During the peak phase, the economy is becoming overheated, with both growth (ie, GDP) and inflation surpassing their "target" ranges. Businesses are no longer able to meet consumer demand, with **unemployment reaching its natural rate**. *Natural unemployment* is the rate of unemployment that will exist even when labor supply meets labor demand (ie, labor market is in equilibrium). It is the result of frictional, structural, and cyclical unemployment.

Inflation

There are three common measures of price inflation:

- The **consumer price index (CPI)** compares the price of a fixed basket of goods and services that a typical urban consumer might purchase in an earlier base period (eg, 100 in 1982–84) and the price of the same basket of goods and services at later times. The CPI is commonly used to convert "nominal" figures that are not readily comparable across years into "real" figures that use the same level of prices and are therefore more comparable

A worker earned and spent $40,000 in 2012 when the CPI was 180. The same worker earned (and spent) $50,000 in 2022 when the CPI was 230. What was the worker's real income?

Convert 2012 salary to 2022 dollars:	$40,000 × (230/180) = $51,111
Real income:	$50,000 / $51,111 = 0.978 or 97.8%

Thus, the worker's real income is 97.8% ($50,000 / $51,111) of what it used to be (ie, it fell by 2.2%)

- The **producer price index (PPI)** compares the price of a fixed basket of goods, inputs, and materials purchased by producers at the wholesale level, instead of focusing on the prices paid at the retail level by consumers

- The **GDP deflator** is the most comprehensive measure of price levels, including prices paid by all parties included in GDP instead of only consumers. The GDP deflator is the index used to convert nominal GDP into real GDP

Causes of Inflation

When aggregate spending increases, the **aggregate demand curve (AD)** moves to the **right**, causing the market equilibrium to occur at higher price levels. **Excess demand** bids up the cost of labor and other resources. Excess demand may be a result, for instance, of improved expectations by consumers or businesses, of the foreign sector, or from government fiscal and monetary policy that turned out to be too loose. According to this simplified model, the equilibrium point occurs at **higher** levels of **both prices and quantity.**

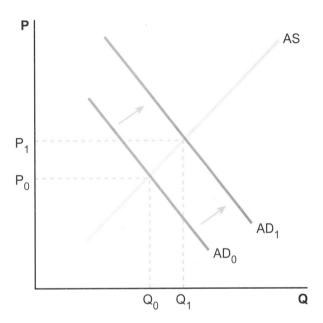

As suppliers face **increases** in input **costs** (eg, oil), the **aggregate supply curve** shifts to the **left**, causing market equilibrium to occur at a **higher price** level and **lower quantity**.

Consequences of Inflation

The occurrence of inflation, especially when unanticipated, usually has significant economic consequences. Major consequences include:

- **Lower current wealth and lower future real income**—Because of inflation, monetary items (those fixed in dollar amount) lose purchasing power. Consumers on fixed incomes, or those with incomes that do not keep pace with inflation, will reduce consumption. Similarly, creditors repaid with a fixed number of dollars will be able to purchase less. The effect of less consumption is a reduction in aggregate demand leading to lower output and higher unemployment

- **Higher interest rates**—In order to offset declines in purchasing power derived from loans, creditors increase interest rates. Higher interest rates increase the cost of borrowing, which reduces both consumer spending and business investment in capital goods. Further, lenders may tighten loan requirements, and thereby, squeeze marginal borrowers out of the market, which also would reduce spending

- **Uncertainty of economic measures**—The changing real value of the dollar makes it an uncertain measure for making economic decisions. Price increases create uncertainty about future costs, prices, profitability, and cash flows. Consequently, individuals and businesses are likely to postpone investments, which, in turn, reduces current demand and future productive capacity

Because inflation has significant adverse consequences for the economy, control of inflation is a primary economic objective of government fiscal and monetary policy.

Deflation

Deflation (or deflation rate) is the annual rate of **decrease in the price level**. Like inflation, deflation may be caused by changes in aggregate demand and/or aggregate supply.

- **Demand changes** can result in deflation when there is a significant decrease in demand (eg, as might be caused by a significant drop in consumer confidence about the economy) which results in a widespread reduction in prices by sellers in an attempt to stimulate sales

- **Supply changes** can result in deflation when there is an increase in aggregate supply (eg, as might be caused by a significant drop in cost of inputs) that significantly exceeds an increase in aggregate demand. This, too, results in sellers reducing prices in an effort to increase sales

When prices are falling, consumers have an incentive to delay purchases and businesses have an incentive to delay investments, both in anticipation of lower prices in the future. These delays create further decreases in aggregate demand, causing further reductions in prices, increased idle production capacity, increased unemployment, and reductions in wages, lending and interest rates. This cycle is called a **deflationary spiral**. If unchecked, it can have serious adverse consequences for an economy.

As with inflation, monetary and fiscal policies can be used to control deflation, primarily through spurring increased demand. Specifically, monetary policy would be implemented to increase the money supply through the Federal Reserve buying debt in the market (giving money for debt) and/or by reducing the federal funds rate to lower interest rates. Fiscal policy to control deflation would be implemented by lowering taxes and increasing government spending.

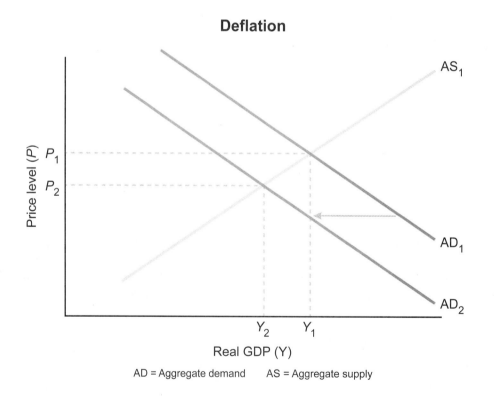

Unemployment

Economists commonly identify three or four **types of unemployment**:

- **Frictional unemployment** affects workers who are unemployed as a result of the normal turnover of workers between jobs or of new entrants into the work force. The employees can find new work relatively quickly. In a mobile society and given unavoidable "imperfections in the labor market," or "search costs" (ie, the time needed to find and compare alternative jobs and to decide that it is not worth waiting for something else better), market economies always have some of this type of unemployment, even in "full" employment

- **Structural unemployment** affects workers who lose their jobs as a result of changes in the demands for goods and services or of technological advances that reduce the need for their current skills. Addressing this type of unemployment normally requires retraining. The problem underlying this type of unemployment is not deficient aggregate demand, but the speed with which workers may be retrained to meet new demands and technologies

- **Cyclical unemployment** involves job losses resulting from the fluctuations in the business cycle. This type of unemployment is the key concern during recessions and decreases during expansions

- **Institutional unemployment.** This type of unemployment affects workers who cannot find employment as a result of government restrictions on the economy, eg, wage floors for younger workers, restrictions on the ability of small businesses to launch, etc.

Indicators of Economic Activity

Leading

In an effort to anticipate changes in the business cycle, economists and business groups have attempted to establish relationships between changes in the business cycle and other measures of economic activity that occur before a change in the business cycle. These measures of economic activity (which change before the aggregate business cycle) are called "leading indicators" and include measures of:

- Consumer expectations
- Initial claims for unemployment
- Weekly manufacturing hours
- Stock prices
- Building permits
- New orders for consumer goods
- New order for manufactured capital goods
- Real money supply
- Yield curves

Coincident Indicators

Measures of economic activity associated with changes in the business cycle that occur at approximately the same time that the economy as a whole changes are called "coincident indicators." These measures provide information about the current state of the economy and also may help identify the timing of peaks and troughs of the business cycle after they occur. Coincident indicators include measures of:

- Level of retail sales
- Current unemployment rate
- Level of industrial production
- Number of nonagricultural employees
- Personal income
- Gross domestic product (GDP)

Lagging

- Measures of economic activity associated with changes in the business cycle, but which occur after changes in the business cycle, are called lagging or trailing indicators. These lagging indicators are used to confirm elements of business cycle timing and magnitude. Lagging indicators include measures of:

- Changes in labor cost per unit of output

- Relationship between inventories and sales

- Duration of unemployment

- Commercial loans outstanding

- Relationship between consumer installment credit and personal income

- Consumer price index (CPI)

Factors Impacting Entities

 Representative Task (Application): Identify relevant factors (eg, economic, environmental, financial reporting framework, government policy, industry, regulatory, supply chain, technology) that could impact an entity, its operations, and/or the inherent risk of material misstatement.

Government Policy

While the proper role and extent of government involvement is likely to be debated indefinitely, governments are very likely to continue to regularly intervene in many aspects of the economy for the foreseeable future through **fiscal policy**, **monetary policy**, and **regulatory policy**.

Monetary Policy

Monetary policy is concerned with managing the money supply to achieve national economic objectives, including economic growth and price level stability. The Federal Reserve System can regulate the money supply (exercise monetary policy) in a number of ways:

Reserve-Requirement Changes—A bank's ability to issue check-writing deposits is limited by a reserve-requirement by the Fed on check-writing deposits. Simply put, loans made by banks are paid to borrowers by checks drawn on the lending bank. For every dollar of such checks issued as loans, the bank must have a required amount held as a reserve, either at the bank or on deposit at a Federal Reserve Bank.

- By decreasing (or increasing) the reserve requirement on check-writing deposits the Fed enables banks to increase (or requires them to decrease) the amount of loans the bank can make using check-writing deposits, and thus increase (or decrease) M1 money supply. Decreasing the requirement would affect monetary easing; increasing the requirement would affect monetary tightening

Open-Market Operations—The Fed engages in open-market operations by purchasing and selling U.S. Treasury debt obligations (eg, Treasury Bonds) from/to banks. The effect of purchasing Treasury obligations is to replace debt held by banks with additional reserves for the banks. The increase in reserves permits additional check-writing deposits (ie, lending ability) by the banks. Sale of Treasury obligations has the opposite effect. Thus, open-market purchasing implements monetary easing, while open-market sales implements monetary tightening.

Discount Rate—The rate of interest banks pay when they borrow from a Federal Reserve Bank in order to maintain reserve requirements is called the "discount rate." Borrowing from a Fed bank increases a bank's reserves with the Fed because the borrowing is credited to the bank's reserve with the Fed, not withdrawn from the Fed bank. As a result of increased reserves, banks are able to increase loans. By decreasing or increasing the discount rate, the Fed encourages or discourages borrowing from the Fed and, thereby, eases or tightens the money supply.

- The Fed's intent in making changes in the discount rate is to keep it at an appropriate "spread" below other rates available to banks. Therefore, changes in the discount rate usually follow changes in the short-term rate of interest in the broad market. Consequently, changes in the discount rate, which are widely publicized, signal Fed expectations about interest rates. For example, if the Fed increases the discount rate to maintain an appropriate spread with rising rates in the market, this tends to confirm that the Fed expects general interest rates to remain at the higher level

Monetary policy tools			
Tool	Description	Expansionary	Contractionary
Open market operations	Trade securities (usually government securities)	Buy securities	Sell securities
Discount rate	Interest rate charged to banks for short-term loans	Lower	Raise
Reserve requirements	Set percentage of bank deposits held in reserves	Decrease	Increase

Margin Requirement—The percentage of the cost of an investment in qualified (marginable) securities that an investor must pay for with his/her own funds; the percentage cost of such an investment for which the investor cannot use funds borrowed from a broker-dealer, bank, or other institution to purchase the securities.

- The margin requirement is set by the Fed, but enforced by the SEC

- Theoretically, the higher the margin requirement, the lower the investment in securities because investors must pay a larger amount of the initial cost of the securities

- Practically, however, the margin requirement currently has little effect on the level of investment because investors can borrow funds from other sources (credit cards, home equity loans, etc.) in lieu of using margin credit

Changes in the money supply, especially when accomplished through open-market operations, will affect short-term interest rates (*ceteris paribus*). For example, if other factors are held constant, an increase in the M1 money supply will lower the short-term interest rate in the market. This can be shown as follows:

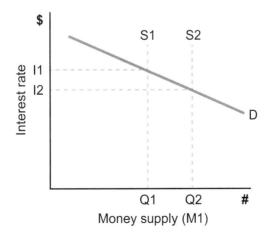

- D represents the demand for money. If the supply of money increases from Q1 to Q2, the interest rate drops from I1 to I2. At a lower interest rate, individuals and businesses are more likely to borrow to finance purchase of high cost items (eg, cars, houses, property, plant and equipment, etc.). The increase in demand (supported by more borrowing) will spur production, increase employment and raise GDP

- Similarly, if the demand for money increases, the interest rate will tend to increase. For example, large borrowings by the government will increase the demand for money and put pressure on interest rates to increase

Fiscal Policy

Fiscal policy involves governments setting, applying, and changing levels of taxes, subsidies, and government spending. The general **goal** of fiscal policy is to **maximize overall welfare**. Specific policies are often designed to aid disadvantaged population groups (eg, low-income populations) or help specific sectors (eg, strategic industries). Those goals are more easily attained when an economy is growing at its potential.

Consequently, long-term objectives of fiscal policies are designed to **stabilize output** near an economy's **sustainable GDP growth rate**. At that level of output, income growth and employment are at the highest levels that can be maintained **without creating inflationary** pressure. Growth above that level is countered with contractionary policies to stifle inflation. Growth below potential is addressed by fiscal stimulus to prevent excessive unemployment.

Objectives of fiscal policy		
	Target	**Mechanisms**
Stabilize GDP growth	Grow GDP near potential	Government spending and taxation
Better distribution of income/wealth	Support for the disadvantaged	Transfer payments and subsidies
Improve resource allocation	Direct resources to industries/ sectors	Special tax provisions or subsidies

Taken alone, an increase in government spending, a reduction in taxes, or an increase in transfer payments would be initiated to increase aggregate demand and, thus, stimulate economic activity. Conversely, taken alone, a decrease in government spending, an increase in taxes, or a reduction in transfer payments would be initiated to decrease aggregate demand and, thus, dampen economic activity.

Taken together, government fiscal policy actions are considered to be as follows:

Fiscal policy		
	Expansionary	**Contractionary**
Taxes	• *Decrease* tax rates	• *Increase* tax rates
Spending	• *Increase* transfer payments (eg, unemployment benefits)	• *Decrease* transfer payments (eg, unemployment benefits)
	• *Increase* spending on roads, bridges	• *Decrease* spending on roads, bridges

Fiscal and Monetary Policy Summary

Both fiscal and monetary policy provide means for the government to influence aggregate spending (demand). Fiscal policy is implemented through changes in government spending and/or taxes. Monetary policy is implemented primarily through control of the money supply.

- Thus, for example, governmental efforts to increase aggregate spending (and reduce unemployment, increase GDP, etc.) would include:

Action	Policy type
Increase government spending	Fiscal
Reduce taxes	Fiscal
Increase money supply	Monetary

To rein in aggregate spending the reverse types of action would be implemented. While the general effect of each type of policy action is known, the timing and net effects of the alternative forms of action are less certain.

- **Lag-time Element**—There are differences in how quickly the alternative forms of policy can be implemented and how quickly economic activity will be affected. Changes of significant magnitude in fiscal policy generally require congressional or legislative approval and may be delayed (or never approved) if there is not agreement by members of Congress or other legislators. However, once approved, changes in government spending can be implemented quickly and with an almost immediate impact on demand. Changes in tax rates, once approved, have a less immediate impact and a less certain magnitude of influence

- Generally, **changes in monetary policy** can be made **more quickly** than fiscal policy because monetary policy is changed by the Federal Reserve Board, not by legislative action. Once approved, monetary policy has an almost immediate effect on the interest rate, but the full effect on spending may not occur immediately because of the time lags inherent in ramping up (or ramping down) large-scale projects commonly sensitive to changes in the interest rate

- Of the two approaches, **monetary policy** has been the primary approach to achieving economic objectives. Changes can be approved more quickly to respond to changing economic circumstances and monetary policy changes have fewer artificial influences on the economy. Fiscal policy, on the other hand, causes a redistribution of output and income

Interest Rates

Overview

Interest is the money paid for the use of money. From the point of view of the borrower, it is the cost of borrowed funds; from the point of view of the lender, it is the revenue earned for lending money to another. It compensates the lender for deferring use of the funds and for the various risks inherent in making the loan. The greater the perceived risk in an investment or other undertaking, the greater the expected rate of return, or interest rate.

Interest is almost always expressed as an annual percentage rate, which is applied to the principal and/or other amount to determine the dollar amount of interest. Depending on the contract in a particular situation, the rate may be fixed, variable, or a combination.

- **Fixed Rate**—The percentage rate of interest does not change over the life of the loan or parts of that life. For example, in a 30-year, fixed-rate mortgage, the interest rate does not change over the 30-year life of the mortgage, regardless of the changes in rates in the market during that period

- **Variable Rate**—The percentage rate of interest can change over the life of the loan or part of that life. Generally, a change in the rate is triggered by a change in the general level of interest in the economy as measured by a macroeconomic indicator, such as the prime rate of interest. (The prime rate of interest is the rate banks charge to their most credit-worthy borrowers.) For example, in a 15-year adjustable rate mortgage, the interest rate may be related to changes in the prime rate of interest. If the prime rate goes up or down, so would the rate on the mortgage

- **Variable-to-Fixed Rate or Fixed-to-Variable Rate**—Though less common, some loans charge one kind of rate, say variable, for a portion of the life of the loan, and a different kind of rate, say fixed, for another portion of the life of the loan. For example, a 25-year mortgage may have an adjustable rate for the first 7 years, after which it carries a fixed rate

Market Interest Rate

The market rate of interest is the prevailing rate of interest paid on interest-bearing investments or charged on interest-bearing borrowings as determined by the supply and demand for funds in the market.

- The market rate of interest (ie, the prevailing rate of interest) can be different in different markets and change over time, depending on such factors as general economic conditions, expected inflation, the particular market, general type of instrument, government monetary policy, and similar macro-characteristics

- Within a given market, the rate of interest for specific instruments will depend on such factors as:
  - Credit rating of the issuer
  - Duration (length) of the instrument
  - Amount of the instrument
  - Liquidity (or marketability) of the instrument
  - Special covenants and features, if any

- Generally, the nominal (or quoted) interest rate for a security is composed of a real risk-free rate of interest, plus premiums that reflect market, entity, and instrument risks and characteristics, including inflation, risk of default, length and amount of the instrument, its marketability, and special covenants and features, if any
  - The real risk-free (inflation-free) rate of interest constitutes the interest rate that would occur if there are no risks associated with the instrument and inflation is expected to be zero
  - The inflation risk premium compensates for the adverse effects of expected inflation on the security
  - The default (or credit) risk premium compensates for the possibility that the issuer of debt will not pay interest and/or principal at the contracted time and/or in the contracted amount
  - The maturity premium compensates for the risk that longer-term fixed-rate instruments will decline in value as a result of an increase in the market rate of interest
  - The liquidity premium (also called the marketability premium) compensates for the fact that some securities cannot be converted to cash on short notice at approximate fair market value
  - Special premiums or discounts may attach to a particular instrument related to such factors as convertibility, call feature, seniority (priority claim over other securities), security provided, and other factors. The factors and the related premium/discount will depend on terms of the specific instrument

Interest Rate Concepts

While an interest rate states the cost of the use of money, not all statements of interest rate are comparable, and this is primarily due to the effects of compounding. Understanding these interest and interest rate concepts is important to both accounting and financial management.

Stated interest rate—The stated interest rate (also called the nominal or quoted interest rate) is the annual rate specified in the loan agreement or comparable contract; it does not take into account the compounding effects of frequency of payments or the effects of inflation.

Nominal interest rate, as contrasted with real interest rate, also refers to the rate of interest received before taking into account the effects of inflation.

Real interest rate, as contrasted with nominal interest rate, refers to the rate of interest after taking into account the effects of inflation on the value of funds received.

Simple interest—Simple interest is interest computed on the original principal only; there is no compounding in the interest computation. (See "Compound Interest" below.)

Compound interest—Compound interest provides that interest be paid not only on the principal, but also on any amount of accumulated unpaid interest. Compound interest pays interest on interest; simple interest does not.

Effective interest—The effective interest rate is the annual interest rate implicit in the relationship between the net proceeds from a loan and the dollar cost of the loan.

Annual percentage rate—The annual percentage rate (APR) is the annualized effective interest rate without compounding on loans that are for a fraction of a year. It is computed as the effective interest rate for the fraction of a year multiplied by the number of time fractions in a year (eg, two if semiannual, four if quarterly, and twelve if monthly).

Effective annual percentage rate—The effective annual percentage rate, also called the annual percentage yield, is the annual percentage rate with compounding.

Negative interest rate—Under a traditional (positive) interest rate agreement, a borrower (recipient) pays a lender (provider) interest for the use of funds. Under a negative interest rate agreement, the flow of benefit payment (interest) is reversed: The owner of the funds pays the recipient to hold the funds. Thus, for example, a financial institution would **charge** depositors interest to hold their money on deposit rather than **pay** them interest on those deposits as has traditionally been the case.

Term Structure of Interest Rates

The term structure of interest rates describes the relationship between long-term interest rates and short-term interest rates. The relationship is commonly plotted on a graph with the interest (yield) plotted on the vertical axis and time plotted on the horizontal axis. The resulting plot is called a "yield curve" and is used to illustrate the level of interest rates for various durations (lengths of time) as of a point in time.

Normal Yield Curve

A normal yield curve is an upward sloping curve in which short-term rates are less than intermediate-term rates, which are less than long-term rates. Historically, this curve reflects the most common relationship between short-term and long-term rates.

Long-term rates are normally higher than short-term rates because the longer period exposes securities to a greater interest rate risk; if interest rates increase, the value of outstanding fixed-rate securities will decline. Normal yield curve example:

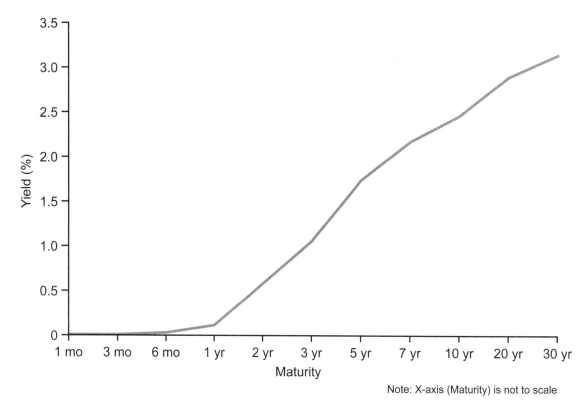

Note: X-axis (Maturity) is not to scale

Other forms of yield curves

- **Inverted (or abnormal) yield curve**—A downward-sloping curve reflecting that short- term rates are greater than intermediate-term rates, which are greater than long-term rates

- **Flat yield curve**—A horizontal curve reflecting that short-term, intermediate-term, and long-term rates are about the same

- **Humped yield curve**—A curve that increases and then decreases reflecting that intermediate-term rates are higher than both short-term and long-term rates

Bank Rate Concepts Summary

The following provides a summary of common and important bank rate concepts:

- **Federal (Fed) Funds Rate**—The interest rate at which a depository institution lends funds maintained at the Federal Reserve to another depository institution overnight without requiring collateral. The federal funds rate is generally applicable only to the most creditworthy institutions when they borrow and lend overnight funds to each other to satisfy reserve requirement shortages. When one depository institution has funds in excess of its reserve requirement needs, it may loan those funds to other institutions that have a reserve requirement shortage. The interest rate charged on those loans is the Federal Funds Rate

- **Federal (Bank) Discount Rate**—The interest rate the Federal Reserve charges on loans made by the regional Federal Reserve Banks to eligible commercial banks and other depository institutions. Banks whose reserves fall below the Fed's reserve requirement may borrow directly from the regional Federal Reserve Bank to correct their shortage. The rate charged for such borrowings is the (federal) discount rate

- **Prime (Interest) Rate**—The interest rate commercial banks charge their most creditworthy borrowers, usually large, financially sound corporations. It is one of the most widely used market lagging indicators, is a major benchmark for mortgage and credit card rates, and is often the basis for adjustable-rate loans

- **Negative Interest Rates**—A negative interest rate is one that is below zero (ie, < 0.0%). When policy or instrument terms provide for a negative interest rate, a financial institution charges depositors to hold their money on deposit rather than paying them interest on those deposits

Regulatory Policy

Governments may further influence economic activity through regulations affecting environmental issues, labor issues (eg, immigration and minimum wage laws), occupational health and safety, energy policy, health care, bank capital, lending practices, etc. On one hand, governments may choose to channel resources from disfavored sectors to favored sectors. On the other hand, governments could seek to reduce the likelihood of financial crises, for instance, by requiring banks to develop thicker capital cushions over time, or by adjusting minimum permissible mortgage down payments if other housing bubbles surfaced in the future.

Globalization

Economists use the term globalization to describe how the economies of nearly all individual countries in the world are developing increasingly deeper connections in their markets for goods, services, labor, capital, and technologies. Globalization plays a role in many deeply transformative processes that have been ongoing for several decades now. Some of the areas impacted include:

- **Increased Foreign Direct Investment (FDI)**—This occurs when companies from developed countries operate in multiple other countries, both developed and developing, operating factories, research facilities; call, service, and technical support centers; and distribution networks

- **Increased Foreign Indirect, or Portfolio, Investment**—Seeking diversification in their portfolios, international investors have been shifting growing fractions of their savings into financial (or portfolio) assets (ie, stock and bonds) denominated in the currencies of other countries

- **Falling Natural & Artificial Barriers to International Trade**—The reduction of barriers to international trade (eg, transportation, information costs, and tariffs) has resulted in many forms of greater interconnectedness across countries, including growing levels of international trade, growing levels of international business and tourism travel, and growing levels of immigrant populations worldwide, including both skilled workers and less-skilled workers

- **Increased Modernization of Developing Countries**—Companies from developed countries may once have operated in developing countries primarily to extract natural resources and to benefit from their lower labor costs. However, this is changing in some areas by increasing democratization, greater government transparency, greater openness of more business sectors to competition from the private, domestic, and foreign sectors, etc.

- **Transfer Pricing**—Transfer pricing is the cost charged by one related entity (eg, division, subsidiary) to another for the sale of goods or services. International transfer pricing can generate tax savings for the parent by assigning as much cost as possible to entities in higher-tax countries. (High cost reduces overall taxable income)

The transfer price set by a parent or subsidiary for goods or services most likely can be used by multinational companies to

- Transfer as much of the cost as allowable to the country with the lowest overall tax burden
- Transfer funds from a subsidiary located in a strong-currency country to a subsidiary located in a country with depreciating currency
- Transfer as much of the cost as allowable to the country with the highest overall tax burden
- Change the financial statements of the individual subsidiaries

International transfer pricing

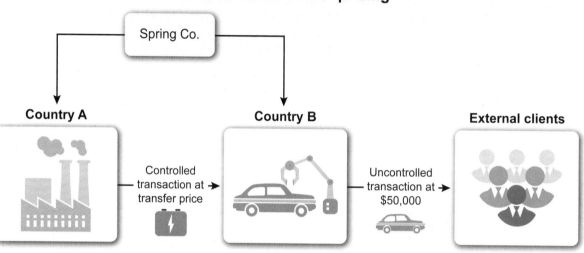

Transfer pricing is the cost charged by one **related entity** (eg, division, subsidiary) to another for the sale of goods or services. For example, the price charged by a battery division located in Country A to its final assembly division located in Country B is the transfer price.

By transferring as much of the cost as allowable to the **country with the highest overall tax burden**, any **revenue** generated in that country by the same entity (even from different activities) **is reduced**, thus reducing the overall tax burden for the entity.

Foreign Operations

Overview

There are several ways in which an entity may be involved in foreign operations. They may:

- Enter into **foreign currency transactions** with an entity in a foreign country that involves a receipt or payment in a foreign currency. The entity must determine how that transaction will be reported in U.S. dollars
- Have **financial instruments** denominated in a foreign currency (eg, a receivable or payable), meaning it will be settled by the receipt or payment of some amount of foreign currency. The amount of the receivable or payable must be converted into U.S. dollars for inclusion on the reporting entity's financial statements (F/S)

- Participate in foreign currency **exchange transactions**, such as forward exchange contracts. These transactions may be entered into for a variety of reasons but, regardless, often result in a net amount being paid or received to settle the contract, representing a liability or asset

- Have a **foreign investee** (ie, a foreign division or subsidiary) that maintains books and records in a foreign currency but will be included in the reporting entity's consolidated F/S. The F/S must be converted into U.S. dollars to include them

Exchange Rates

The exchange rates between countries' currencies are very important to any company that faces foreign competitors, regardless of whether the company is an exporter facing competitors abroad or the company faces imports from foreign competitors domestically. When a foreign country's currency weakens, products from companies from that country become cheaper for purchasers in the U.S., providing those foreign companies' products an advantage.

Fluctuations in currencies' exchange rates are ultimately based on relative changes in the supplies and demands of those currencies. Companies considering decisions regarding short-term international trade and long-term international investments face these types of (nominal and real) **exchange rate risks.**

Repatriation is the process of converting a foreign currency into your own country's currency ($US), at the current exchange rate.

Exchange rates may be expressed by dividing by either currency, for example, if €1 (ie, 1 euro) buys $1.25, the exchange rate may be expressed as €1 = $1.25, or $1 = €0.80. In a table listing multiple exchange rates for one currency, it is customary to express all exchange rates on the same basis, for example, how many units of the various foreign currencies does it take to buy $1. It is also customary to choose the "direction" of the exchange rates that ensures that most exchange rates are greater than 1 (ie, $1 = 80 yen, instead of $0.0125 = 1 yen).

Commonly cited exchange rates between currencies include:

- The **spot rate** is the exchange rate at which a financial party (a financial institution, a currency dealer, etc.) will exchange two currencies at this time (ie, "on the spot")

- The **forward rate** is the exchange rate at which a financial party will exchange two currencies at a specific future date (called the settlement date), for example, three months later

In forward markets, one currency is at a premium (discount) if its forward rate is higher (lower) than the spot rate (both rates expressed per the foreign currency), that is, if it is expected to appreciate (depreciate). For instance, according to the spot rate, 1 Kuwaiti dinar may equal $3.57, and according to the 3-month forward rate, 1 Kuwaiti dinar may equal $3.53. In this case, there is a discount since the Kuwaiti dinar will be worth less in the future (ie, it will buy fewer dollars). The size of the forward premium (or discount) is expressed in annual terms as follows:

$$\frac{\text{Forward rate} - \text{Spot rate}}{\text{Spot rate}} \times \frac{\text{Months in a year}}{\text{Months in the forward period}}$$

$$\frac{3.53 - 3.57}{3.57} \times \frac{12}{3} = -4.5\%$$

Exchange Risk

Companies with operations in more than one country bear various types of **foreign exchange (or currency) risk.**

- **Translation Risk**—A company with operations in countries with different currencies will likely have assets and liabilities in more than one currency. Translating those amounts for the F/S may result in translation (accounting) risk and are entered as gains or losses on the balance sheet as other comprehensive income (OCI)

- **Transaction Risk**—A company with operations in countries with different currencies will likely have streams of future revenues and costs in more than one currency. Thus, forecasting future earnings, expressed in the currency used where the company is headquartered, will involve one additional type of risk that is known as transaction risk

Functional Currency

When an entity enters into a transaction that will be settled through the payment or receipt of foreign currency, it is initially recognized in the **functional currency** of the entity. In general, an entity's functional currency is its **local currency**. Usually, it is also the currency in which it maintains its books and records, but that is not always the case.

Monetary assets and liabilities (eg, A/P) are remeasured using the exchange rate at the balance sheet date and settlement date to match exchange rate changes with the transactional cash flows. Foreign currency gains and losses resulting from those changes are recognized in income.

Nonmonetary assets and liabilities (eg, equipment) are remeasured at the historical exchange rate on each balance sheet date so that the carrying value does not change. This reporting reflects the asset's cost as if it had been purchased in the entity's functional currency.

- When a transaction occurs in some currency other than the functional currency, it is remeasured as if the transaction had originally occurred at the functional currency

- When the functional currency is not the same as the currency used for reporting, amounts are translated from the functional currency into the reporting currency

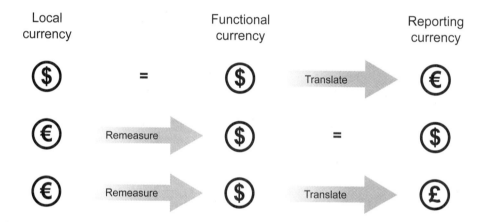

If the foreign subsidiary is *included* in the company's consolidated financial statements (F/S), it must *convert* the subsidiary's F/S from the local currency (ie, the currency in which the subsidiary's books and records are maintained) into the **parent's reporting currency**.

Translation

When the local currency is the functional currency, the parent will need to translate the F/S of the subsidiary (ie, foreign investee) into the reporting currency.

Financial statement translation process

Step 1	Translate income statement items (provides translated net income): • Revenue and expenses: weighted average rate • Gains/losses on fixed assets: rate on transaction date

Financial statement translation process

Step 2	Translate balance sheet (B/S) items: • Assets and liabilities: rate on B/S date • Contributed capital accounts and dividends: historical rates • Retained earnings (RE): rolled forward from translated net income and dividends
Step 3	Recognize translation adjustment in other comprehensive income (ie, the difference between RE calculated in Step 2 and unadjusted RE).

The normal translation process used in periods when there is not significant inflation involves applying exchange rates to F/S accounts as follows:

- Assets and liabilities are reported as of the F/S date; therefore, they are translated using the F/S date *exchange rate*
- The results of operations over a period are reported in the income statement; therefore, income statement items are translated using a *weighted average exchange rate* for that period
- Capital accounts and dividends are translated at *historical rates*
- Retained earnings are rolled forward with translated net income and dividends added to the prior ending balance

The translation adjustment is recognized in **other comprehensive income** on the parent's balance sheet. Generally, the cumulative translation adjustment remains in **accumulated other comprehensive income (AOCI)** until such time as the investment in the foreign investee is either disposed of or substantially liquidated.

Industry Analysis

Within the context of an economic system and an economic market structure, and with an understanding of the characteristics of the macro-environment in which an entity operates or may operate, an entity must assess the nature of the competition it faces (or would face) in its industry—that is, from its most direct competition. Michael Porter's five forces model provides a means of carrying out such a micro-environmental analysis.

An **industry** may be defined as the group of entities that produce goods or provide services which are close substitutes and which compete for the same customers.

Five Forces Analysis

Porter's five forces is a framework for strategic analysis that examines **an industry's competitive environment** to assess whether the conditions favor economic profits. An increase to any of the forces can potentially intensify competition within the industry and threaten economic profits.

Characteristics of Porter's five forces		
Force	**Description**	**Factors**
Threat of new entrants	Increased competition can lower profits, but barriers to entry can protect them	• Economies of scale • Brand loyalty • Switching costs • Fixed costs • Regulation
Bargaining power of supplies	Increased input costs lower profit margins	• Ease of product substitution • Concentration of suppliers • Switching costs
Bargaining power of buyers (customers)	Limited prices lower profit margins	• Customer concentration • Switching costs • Vertical integration
Threat of substitutes	Increased competition can lower sales quantities and/or prices	• Similarities in function • Utility of substitutable products
Rivalry among existing competitors	Increased competition lowers prices and profit margins	• Industry fragmentation • Degree of product differentiation • Barriers to exit

Technology

Emerging technologies can have a disruptive impact on accounting systems. Below are a few examples:

Emerging Payment Processing Systems

Historically payment services were provided by financial institutions; they were very expensive to sellers. Recent innovations in payment systems (ie, systems for processing customers' payments for goods and services) are increasingly important drivers of business success.

- Emerging payment systems are simple to use, cheaper, and seller- and user-friendly. They can reduce costs and increase online sales

- Payment system examples include Apple Pay, Samsung Pay, Walmart Pay, PayPal, Venmo, and Amazon "One-Click" payments

- Seller strategies simplify payments for customers, reduce processing fees

Internet of Things (IoT)

The Internet of things (IoT) is the widespread connection of electronic devices to the Internet. Recent news reports suggest that hackers are increasingly targeting (ie, hacking) IoT applications. The result is a real-time data stream that enables the monitoring and control of any device that is electronic. The IoT is directed at physical processes (eg, consumer applications, manufacturing, mining, energy production, and logistics and distribution).

Examples include:

- Medicine and agriculture—Real-time data feeds that monitor the status and condition of any living organism (eg, Fitbit)

- Insurance—Sensory data on road conditions, weather, traffic, driver behavior, etc.

- Banking—Monitor use and status of ATMs, physical security of offices and buildings

- Marketing—Respond in real time to customers' interests and physical proximity

Just some of the business implications include:

- Transform business processes and models

- Enables new products (eg, the Fitbit)

- New, advanced analytics—track emerging trends and interests

- New insight into production processes and customers

Accounting implications are such items as:

- Automated information collection and data streaming for audits (internal and external) and tax engagements

- Real-time managerial accounting monitoring data

- New skill sets for CPAs—Managing the IoT and the resulting "big data"

And of course there are **numerous risks** to consider:

- Privacy, intrusive devices—Previously unimagined data will become available about individuals and their behavior (eg, medical and financial data)

- Complexities of data ownership, availability, distribution, storage

- The creation and management of "big data"

Automated IT Security: Authentication

The current state of user access security (ie, authentication) is cumbersome and frustrating. Memorizing hundreds of passwords, which shouldn't be written down, to authenticate identity is increasingly obsolete in a world in which recognition technologies are accurate, cheap, and readily available.

The goal for user authentication is to have a fully integrated, multifactor security, automated system. The adoption of the IoT will lead to increasing use of automated security systems. Authentication in these systems will use multiple identifiers. Identifiers may include:

- Biometrics (eg, fingerprints, iris scans, body scans, facial recognition)

- Advanced analytics that identify system use patterns (eg, typical login times, pressure and force on keyboard and mouse)

- Objects (eg, cell phones, key cards)

- Knowledge (challenge questions)

- Contextual patterns of use that combine the above identifiers using artificial intelligence (AI)

Risks include the inevitable failures and shake-outs as vendors and users experiment with new authentication systems.

Environmental Analysis

An entity must assess the relationship between its **external environment** and its **internal characteristics**. Such an analysis is essential if an entity is to understand the possibilities, or lack thereof, of operating in the environment. Several analysis options that management can use are presented below:

SWOT Analysis

A SWOT analysis provides a framework for assessing the relationship between an entity and an operating environment by examining an entity's strengths, weaknesses, opportunities, and threats (ie, SWOT analysis) from both an internal and external perspective.

- **Strengths** include internal areas that the company excels at and with which it is able to differentiate itself from its competitors (eg, strong brand loyalty, low debt balance sheet, unique product or service)
- **Weaknesses** include internal areas requiring improvement in order to reach an entity's optimal performance level (eg, high employee turnover, high levels of debt, aging equipment)
- **Opportunities** focus on external factors that provide an advantage over competitors (eg, ability to increase market share of electric car sales due to patented cutting-edge technology)
- **Threats** also focus on external factors that represent potential harm to the entity (eg, supply chain issues in obtaining raw materials in a timely manner to meet production demands)

SWOT Matrix—The identification of strengths, weaknesses, opportunities, and threats provides the basis for constructing a matrix useful in developing an entity's strategic plans. Such a SWOT matrix takes the form:

SWOT Matrix		
	Strengths	**Weaknesses**
Opportunities	S/O Strategies	W/O Strategies
Threats	S/T Strategies	W/T Strategies

- S/O strategies utilize the entity's strengths to take advantage of opportunities in the environment
- W/O strategies pursue opportunities to overcome weaknesses
- S/T strategies utilize the entity's strengths to reduce the entity's susceptibility to external threats
- W/T strategies pursue ways to prevent the entity's weaknesses from being overcome by external threats

PEST Analysis

PEST analysis is an assessment of the **Political, Economic, Social, and Technological** elements of a macro-environment. Its purpose is to provide an understanding of those elements of an environment, typically a country or region, in which a firm operates or is considering operating.

Analysis Factors—PEST considers each of the following kinds of factors to develop a "picture" of an operating environment:

P Political	**E** Economic	**S** Social	**T** Technological
• Government policies • Tax regulations • Employment regulations • Political stability • Copyright law • Labor law • Property law • Enforcement • Social policy • Environmental policy • Trade regulations • Safety regulations	• Business cycle • Business investments • Political issues • Exchange rates • Inflation	• Productive workforce • Healthy workforce • DEI (diversity, inclusion, and equality) • Employment patterns • Job market trends • Population growth rate • Social mobility	• Automation tools • AI (artificial intelligence) • Innovation

Competitive Strategies

Cost Leadership Strategy

Under this strategy, an entity will seek to be the **low cost provider** in an industry for a given level of output. An entity will sell its product or service either at the average industry price and earn a profit higher than that of other competitors in the industry or below the average industry price so as to gain market share.

Entities acquire or maintain **cost advantages** by:

- Identifying and avoiding unnecessary costs
- Improving process efficiency
- Gaining exclusive access to lower cost inputs
- Using outsourcing in an optimal manner
- Pursuing vertical integration—moving up or down in the supply chain

Entities that successfully carry out the cost leadership strategy typically have the following kinds of strength:

- Significant capital to invest in production and logistical assets to keep cost low
- High levels of expertise in manufacturing processes
- High levels of skill in designing products for efficient manufacturing
- Efficient channels for the distribution of products

Entities that adopt the cost leadership strategy face certain risks, including:

- The possibility that other entities will be successful in adopting a cost leadership strategy and meet or beat the cost of the entity
- The possibility that technology will improve such that other firms may be able to produce at equally low cost or be able to apply new technologies to produce at an even lower cost
- The possibility that a number of firms may focus on segments of the industry and be able to separately achieve lower costs in each of those segments so that as a group they are able to control a significant portion of the industry

Differentiation Strategy

Under this strategy, an entity will seek to develop a product or service that offers unique features that are valued by customers and that those customers perceive to be better than or different from the products of competitors in the industry.

An entity expects that the value added by the quality or uniqueness of the product or service will allow the entity to charge a premium price which will more than cover the extra cost of providing the good or service. An entity may acquire or maintain differentiation by providing goods or services that are special or unique:

Product differentiation strategies

- Physical differences – individual features, quality, appearance
- Perceived differences – image, brand name, advertising
- Customer support differences – return policies, technical support

Entities that successfully carry out the **differentiation strategy** typically have the following kinds of **strengths:**

- Highly creative and skilled product/service development personnel
- Leading-edge scientific and market research capabilities
- Strong and dedicated marketing and sales personnel capable of conveying the strengths of the product or service
- A reputation for innovation, quality, and service

Firms seeking to achieve differentiation may pursue a number of **processes** to help achieve and maintain differentiation of its goods or services, including:

- Market research, so as to understand not only its customers and potential customers, but also its competitors
- New product development
- Continuous improvement of its products and processes
- Strict quality control
- Customer-oriented services (eg, delivery, financing, problem resolution, etc.)
- High level of employee training and development

Entities that adopt the differentiation strategy face certain **risks**, including:

- Changes in customer preferences or economic status
- Imitation by competitors, including the threat of "knock-offs"
- The possibility that a number of firms may focus on segments of the industry and be able to separately achieve greater differentiation in each of those segments so that as a group they are able to capture a significant portion of the industry

Focus Strategy

Under this strategy, an entity will **focus on a narrow segment** of an industry (a "niche") and within that segment seek to achieve either a cost advantage or differentiation.

- An entity seeks to identify a distinct subgroup within an industry and focus on providing goods or services that meet the distinctive needs of that subgroup

- An entity also may pursue a "quick response approach," which focuses on either being the first to bring a product to market (think "as seen on TV" products) or on providing quick delivery of the good or service to the customer. Both of these approaches are variations of focus strategy

Entities that successfully carry out the focus strategy typically have the following **strengths**:

- Outstanding market research and understanding, especially of the target subgroup

- Ability to tailor product or service development strength to the target subgroup

- High degree of customer satisfaction and loyalty

Entities that adopt the focus strategy face certain **risks**, including:

- Typically, smaller size, lower volume, and less bargaining power with suppliers

- Imitation by competitors

- Changes in targeted customers' preferences or economic status

- The possibility of an industry cost leader adapting its products or services so as to compete in the focus market

- The possibility that other entities may focus on and carve out subgroups of the targeted focus group

Supply Chain Management

A **supply chain** is the entire sequence of processes involved in the sourcing, production, and distribution of a good. Every entity that contributes in any way to the final good is part of the supply chain.

- **Supply chain management** is concerned with managing the flow of goods, services, information, and finances related to a particular product from the raw material stage through the delivery of the final output to the end user. It involves coordinating and integrating these flows both within and among entities. The primary objective of supply chain management is to meet end-user demand with the most efficient resource usage. Supply chain management often is used in the efficient management of inventory

- A key aspect of supply chain management is the **sharing of information** from final sale back through the supply chain so that all relevant parties are aware of the needs of each subsequent party in the supply chain. The intent of such sharing is to improve processes so as to reduce inventory, time, defects, and costs all along the supply chain

9.02 Internal Factors

Corporate Governance

 Representative Task (Remembering & Understanding): Understand the entity's responsibilities with respect to the corporate governance provisions of the Sarbanes-Oxley Act of 2002.

It is the role of corporate governance to make certain that the objectives of the entity are met while the legitimate needs and concerns of all stakeholders are being addressed.

- Stakeholders may include stockholders, customers, suppliers, employees, regulators, and the communities that are affected by the entity's operations or activities

- **Corporate governance** consists of the systems that are applied to control and to direct a corporation

Those responsible for governance will depend largely on the size and nature of the entity. In a small organization, governance may be the responsibility of owner-managers. In larger organizations, however, the responsibility for governance is disbursed among a variety of individuals in a somewhat more structured environment.

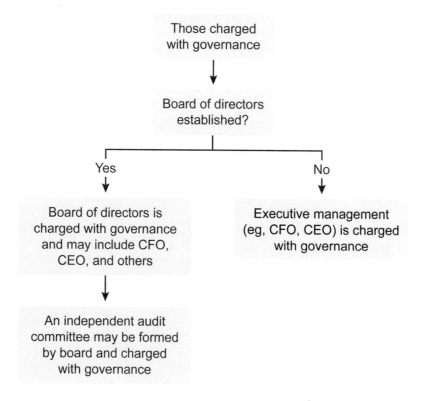

Board of Directors

In most publicly held companies, stockholders are not directly involved in its operations. They elect a **board of directors (BOD)** who in turn are responsible for **strategic planning** as well as for the selection and **oversight** of the entity's management. The board will also **monitor management** to make certain that its decisions are consistent with achieving the entity's objectives.

The **bylaws** (internal rules of the corporation) generally indicate the minimum and maximum number of directors, how they are to be selected and compensated, how often they are to meet, and the nature of their responsibilities.

The BOD fiduciary duties include:

Board of directors fiduciary duties	
Duty of loyalty	Act in entity's best interest; avoid conflict of interest
Duty of care	Act objectively; exercise independent, informed judgment; promote success
Duty of due diligence	Act with reasonable care when entering into agreements on the corporation's behalf

The typical duties of a BOD include:

- Determining or revising the entity's mission and amending its bylaws
- Strategic planning and the development of broad objectives and policies
- Selection and oversight of the chief executive
- Securing the availability of financial resources
- Budget approval, and approval of major operating and financial proposals
- Accounting to stakeholders, including making certain that reliable financial information is reported by the entity
- Providing advice to management and determining its compensation
- Establishing dividend policies

Business Judgment Rule

A director has some protection against liability when decisions do not provide the anticipated results. The business judgement rule was established as a result of case law, and it requires a director to fulfill a **fiduciary duty** to the entity by acting in good faith, being loyal, and applying due care. When they do so, the courts will not review their business decisions, regardless of the outcome. In general, directors will not be liable for their decisions unless they are guilty of fraud.

For example, if directors reasonably rely on information showing that dividends may be declared and declare such dividends when, in fact, the corporation was insolvent, the directors will not be held liable for the illegal dividends. (The shareholders will have to repay the dividends if the corporation was insolvent when the dividends were declared.)

Business judgment rule

- Applies to profit and nonprofit corporations
- Directors and officers not liable for mistakes or errors of judgment if they acted:
  - With a duty of care and loyalty
  - In good faith and on a reasonable basis

Committees of the BOD

The BOD will establish various committees to disburse the board's responsibilities.

- In some cases, committees are required to be made up of independent, or **outside directors**. These are directors who have no involvement with the entity other than in their capacity as a director
- An **inside director**, on the other hand, has some significant involvement in the entity, often as a member of management, in addition to being a director. Some entities will apply the term **executive director** exclusively to the chief executive officer (CEO), while others will apply it to any director who is also an executive, or officer, of the corporation

Audit Committee

The audit committee is required to be made up of **independent directors,** and at least one member of the audit committee is required to be a financial expert. **Responsibilities** of the audit committee include:

Audit committee responsibilities

- Oversee audit and control systems
- Monitor financial reporting process and ensure financial accuracy
- Oversee application of accounting policies
- Ensure integrity of financial statements
- Supervise internal audit function
- Recommend external auditor
- Present annual audit report to board

A **financial expert** has the attributes listed in the following box:

Audit committee financial expert attributes

- An understanding of GAAP and financial statements
- Experience preparing or auditing comparable financial statements
- Experience in accounting for estimates, accruals, and reserves
- Experience with internal accounting controls
- An understanding of audit committee duties (need not be a CPA)

Management Compensation

One of the most significant responsibilities of the BOD is the oversight of management. The board meets this responsibility through its management **compensation** policies and through **monitoring** of management.

Management compensation policies require the board to find a balance between different forms of compensation that may, on one hand, motivate management to strive to perform at the utmost level or may, on the other, cause management to find ways to maximize their own compensation at the detriment of, or at least without considering benefit to, the entity.

Monitoring Management

Internal Audit

One of the most common ways to monitor management, and often the most effective, is through internal audit. When internal auditors report directly to the audit committee of the BOD, they are more likely to be effective in helping the board monitor the performance of management, largely because the audit committee is made up exclusively of independent directors.

The Institute of Internal Auditors provides the following **definition of internal auditing**:

Internal auditing is an independent, objective assurance and consulting activity designed to add value and improve an organization's operations. It helps an organization accomplish its objectives by bringing a systematic, disciplined approach to evaluate and improve the effectiveness of risk management, control, and government processes.

External Audit

External auditors are also potentially effective in contributing to the monitoring of management. As part of their monitoring role, the independent external auditor is required **to communicate** with the **audit committee** regarding:

- Critical accounting policies and practices being used
- Alternative treatments, acceptable under GAAP, that have been discussed with management, including implications of such treatment and the public accounting firm's preference
- Any additional written communications with management, including any management letter or schedule of unadjusted differences

Sarbanes-Oxley Act of 2002 (SOX)

The Sarbanes-Oxley Act (SOX) was established by the **Public Company Accounting Oversight Board (PCAOB)** to regulate auditors of public companies, subject to SEC oversight. SOX consists of eleven key sections that impose wide-ranging and stringent requirements on issuers and their auditors.

Only public, not private, companies are subject to SOX, regardless of assets or revenues. Key titles are as follows:

- **Title I (Establish the PCAOB)**—Established the PCAOB, gave standard-setting authority to the PCAOB (regarding auditing, quality control, and independence standards), and created its role in overseeing the accounting firms required to register with the PCAOB.

Powers of the PCAOB

- Registers accounting firms, allowing them to audit issuers
- Establishes audit, ethics, and quality control standards for auditors of issuers
- Investigates and disciplines violations by accounting firms
- Performs quality control inspections of registered accounting firms
- Enforces compliance with the Sarbanes-Oxley Act through administrative sanctions

- **Title II (Auditor Independence)**—Established independence requirements for external auditors, which addressed perceived conflicts of interest, including the following:

Independence requirements of Sarbanes-Oxley for audits of issuers

- Auditor must cool off for one year before taking key role with client
- Auditor cannot perform most nonaudit services for audit clients
- Auditor must report to audit committee:
  - Critical accounting policies and practices
  - Alternative accounting discussed with management
  - Material written communication between auditor and management
- Audit partner and reviewing partner must rotate off engagement every five years
- Audit committee must preapprove nonaudit services provided

- **Title III (Corporate Responsibility)**—Established requirements related to corporate responsibility to make executives take responsibility for the accuracy of financial reporting (including a requirement for certification by the entity's principal officers) and to make it illegal for management to improperly influence the conduct of an audit.

Sarbanes-Oxley (SOX) corporate responsibility requirements for issuers

- Independent audit committee hires, compensates, and communicates with auditor
- CEO and CFO certify that financial statements are fairly presented
- CEO and CFO take responsibility for internal controls and disclose deficiencies
- Officer/director prohibited from materially misleading auditor (eg, fraud)
- If earnings are restated, executive bonuses can be clawed back (ie, taken back)
- SEC may bar violators of securities laws form serving as officer/director

- **Title IV (Financial Disclosures)**—Addressed a variety of enhanced financial disclosures, the most well known of which deals with required internal control reporting (Section 404), among other matters.

SOX: responsibilities regarding internal control of issuers	
Management	• Acknowledge responsibility for internal control • Assess effectiveness of internal control
Auditors	• Understand client's control structure • Assess risk of material weakness • Evaluate and opine on design and operating effectiveness of controls

- **Title IX (Penalties)—Enacted tougher fines and penalties for white-collar crime.**

Criminal behavior	Fine/Penalty
• Mail and/or wire fraud	• Up to 20 years imprisonment
• Recklessly violates/misrepresents certification of financial reports	• Up to $1 million in fines and/or Up to 10 years imprisonment
• Willfully violates/misrepresents certification of financial reports	• Up to $5 million in fines and/or Up to 20 years imprisonment
• Altering, destroying, or falsifying documents in order to obstruct or influence a federal investigation	• Up to $15 million in fines and/or Up to 20 years imprisonment
• Securities fraud	• Fines and/or up to 20 years imprisonment

Nature of an Entity

 Representative Task (Application): Identify the relevant factors that define the nature of an entity, including the impact on the risk of material misstatement (e.g., its operations, ownership and governance structure, investment and financing plans, selection of accounting policies and objectives and strategies).

As previously discussed, the auditor establishes an overall audit strategy dealing with the scope and timing of the audit work, conducts a preliminary risk assessment, and then develops the audit plan.

Part of that risk assessment process includes the identification of risks that will require **special audit consideration**. The auditor should consider the nature of the risks identified (e.g., whether the risk may relate to fraud, significant economic developments, the complexity of transactions, related-party transactions, subjective measurement, or nonroutine transactions that are unusual for the entity).

 Additional information related to this representative task is included in the AUD chapter entitled Assessing and Responding to Risks of Material Misstatements, Whether Due to Fraud or Error.

AUD 10
Understanding an Entity's Controls

AUD 10: Understanding an Entity's Controls

10.01 COSO Internal Control—Integrated Framework

Overview

The objective of AU-C 315 is for the auditor to identify and assess the risk of material misstatement (RMM), whether due to fraud or error, at the financial statement and relevant assertion levels. This is accomplished by understanding the entity and its environment, including internal control (I/C). This understanding will provide a basis for designing and implementing responses to the assessed risk of material misstatement (RMM).

Audit process

Client acceptance/continuance

Plan the audit
(initial strategy and plan)

Obtain understanding of client, its
environment, and internal control

For example:
- Evaluate control environment
- Identify control activities in place
- Document process followed and conclusions reached

Assess risk of material misstatement
and design further procedures

Perform tests of controls

Perform substantive procedures

Form an opinion

Issue a report

The COSO "Cube" for Internal Control

 Representative Task (Remembering & Understanding): Identify and define the components, principles, and underlying structure of the COSO internal control framework.

 Representative Task (Remembering & Understanding): Define internal control within the context of the COSO internal control framework, including the purpose, objectives, and limitations of the framework.

GAAS requires an auditor to document an understanding of an entity's internal control (I/C) design. The auditor will use this understanding to **identify control procedures** that, if implemented and operating effectively, allow for reduced substantive testing.

The auditor will first understand and evaluate the **effectiveness of management's I/C design**. If the design is effective, the auditor will determine whether the control procedures are implemented and operating effectively. The auditor will then identify situations in which **management** has **established appropriate control procedures** but **compliance** is **not enforced** (eg, invoices are not approved before payment as outlined in the control procedures). Such situations would not allow for reduced substantive testing.

Appropriate internal control procedures

- Established by management
- Designed effectively
- Implemented
- Enforced

Internal Control Framework

The most commonly used framework to benchmark internal controls in the U.S. is the Internal Control— Integrated Framework developed by the Committee of Sponsoring Organizations of the Treadway Commission (COSO). The framework helps organizations determine, evaluate, and enhance internal controls to mitigate risks and ensure that decision-making is based on reliable information.

The COSO integrated framework helps in designing, implementing, and evaluating internal control. It is often depicted as a cube to clearly see the dimensions and how everything works together.

The three dimensions capture, with respect to internal control:

- **What** is internal control (ie, its fundamental components)
- **Why** we have internal control (ie, its goals or objectives)
- **Where** we have internal control (ie, the units of analysis where we will design, implement, and test internal control)

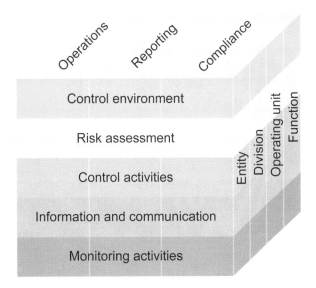

What Is Internal Control?

The first dimension of the COSO cube identifies five fundamental components of an internal control system.

- **Control Environment**—Management's philosophy toward controls, organizational structure, system of authority and responsibility, personnel practices, policies, and procedures. This component is the core or foundation of any system of internal control

- **Risk Assessment**—The process of identifying, analyzing, and managing the risks involved in achieving the organization's objectives

- **Information and Communication**—The information and communication systems that enable an organization's people to identify, process, and exchange the information needed to manage and control operations

- **Monitoring**—To ensure the ongoing reliability of information, it is necessary to monitor and test the system and its data

- **Control Activities**—The policies and procedures that ensure that actions are taken to address the risks related to the achievement of management's objectives

Components of internal controls (CRIME)	
Control activities	• Ensure achievement of objectives • Develop general controls over IT
Risk assessment	• Identify risk and consideration of fraud through clear objectives • Assess impact on internal control
Information and communication	• Generate relevant, high-quality information • Establish internal/external communication processes
Monitoring of controls	• Conduct ongoing and/or separate evaluations • Report internal control deficiencies for corrective action
Control **E**nvironment	• Establish independent governance • Commit to competence, integrity, ethics, accountability

Why Do We Have Internal Control?

The second dimension of the cube identifies the three **fundamental objectives** of a system of internal control.

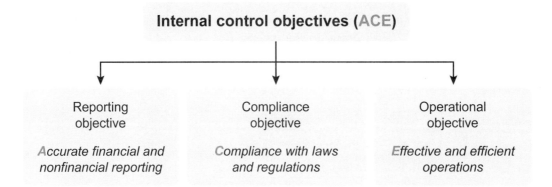

Reporting

Objectives related to the preparation of (financial or nonfinancial) reports for use by shareholders and the organization. Reporting objectives may be for internal or external objectives.

- **External financial reporting objectives** usually relate to, for example, annual financial statements, interim financial statements, or earnings releases. Characteristics of these reporting objectives include meeting shareholder requirements, being prepared in accordance with external standards such as U.S. GAAP, and/or being prepared to meet regulatory, contractual, or other agreement requirements

- **External nonfinancial reporting objectives** usually relate to internal control reports, sustainability reports, or supply change reports. Characteristics of these external nonfinancial reporting objectives are similar to the external financial reporting characteristics (see above)

- **Internal financial reporting objectives** usually relate to, for example, divisional financial reports, customer profitability analysis, and bank covenant calculations. These objectives may include staff or asset utilization, customer satisfaction measures, and/or health and safety measures. Reporting internal financial and nonfinancial information is necessary for management and the board to manage the business and support decisions regarding the business's strategic direction, operating plans, and expectations

Compliance

Compliance objectives concern complying with external laws and regulations (as opposed to the operations objectives, which include compliance with the entity's internal policies and procedures). For example, the entity must identify any laws or regulations that must be adhered to, such as human resources, taxation, and environmental compliance, or laws that apply to operations in a foreign country.

Operations

- Objectives related to the fundamental mission and vision of the entity

- Include improving financial performance, productivity, quality, environmental practices, innovation, and customer and employee satisfaction, as well as safeguarding assets (protecting and preserving assets)

Where Do We Have Internal Control?

The third dimension of the cube specifies the units and activities that must be controlled within the organization. In a business organization, accounting controls are likely to be necessary in relation to sales, production, marketing, finance, and IT. This also includes controls across different business units.

For example, The Walt Disney Company has several business segments, including media networks, parks and resorts, studio entertainment, consumer products, and interactive media. The framework ensures that adequate operations, compliance, and reporting controls are in place for the parks and resorts segments, which include sales, production, marketing, finance, etc.

COSO I/C Principles

The most recent COSO model includes 17 control principles which are organized around the five fundamental components (ie, the "what") of an internal control system.

Internal control objectives (ACE)

Control environment	Risk assessment	Control activities
1. Demonstrates commitment to integrity and ethical values	6. Specifies suitable objectives	10. Selects and develops control activities
2. Exercises oversight responsibilities	7. Identifies and analyzes risk	11. Selects and develops general controls over technology
3. Establishes structure, authority, and responsibility	8. Assesses fraud risk	12. Deploys through policies and procedures
4. Demonstrates commitment to competence	9. Identifies and analyzes significant change	
5. Enforces accountability		

Information and communication	Monitoring activities
13. Uses relevant information	16. Conducts ongoing and/or separate evaluations
14. Communicates internally	17. Evaluates and communicates deficiencies
15. Communicates externally	

Control Environment—Five Principles

The organization demonstrates a commitment to **integrity and ethical values**. Specifically, management:

- Sets and demonstrates (through actions) an ethical "tone at the top"
- Establishes and adheres to standards of conduct
- Attends to ethical failures quickly and effectively

The **board of directors** demonstrates independence of management and oversees the development and monitoring of internal control, including:

- Clear board of directors oversight and independence
- Evidence and application of relevant expertise

Management establishes, with board oversight, structures, reporting lines, and appropriate authorities and responsibilities to achieve objectives, including integrating organizational structures and services and outsourced service providers.

Competence—The organization demonstrates a commitment to attract, develop, and retain competent individuals consistent with achieving organizational objectives, including:

- Establishing policies and procedures to attract, develop, and retain competent individuals

- Assessing competencies, creating development plans to achieve needed skills and competencies, and addressing deficiencies in skills and competencies through training, hiring, or outsourcing

- Planning and preparing for turnover and succession

Accountability—The organization holds individuals accountable for their internal control responsibilities, including:

- Enforcing accountability through structures, authorities, and responsibilities

- Establishing and evaluating performance measures, incentives, rewards, and disciplinary actions for individuals

- Monitoring and considering the potential for excessive performance pressures, including unrealistic performance (eg, earnings) targets, and an excessive concern with short-term (eg, quarterly earnings) targets

 Additional content on the Control Environment can be found in the next section (10.02).

Risk Assessment—Four Principles

Objectives—The organization specifies objectives with sufficient clarity to enable the identification and assessment of risks that threaten the achievement of objectives. In so doing, the organization should consider:

- The precision of risk tolerance levels: for example, can we quantify the risk? To within what range?

- Materiality in relation to risk assessment. How big of a risk poses a threat to objectives (a loss of $10,000? $100,000? $1,000,000?)?

- Risks related to the organization's ability to comply with standards, frameworks, laws and regulations

- Risks related to operational and financial performance goals

- Risks in committing resources

Assessment—The organization identifies risks to the achievement of its objectives across the entity and analyzes risks as a basis for determining how the risk should be managed. In so doing, the organization should:

- Involve appropriate levels of management in risk assessment

- Consider and include entity, subsidiary, division, operating unit, and functional levels

- Analyze internal and external factors

- Estimate risk importance

- Develop appropriate risk responses

Risk responses

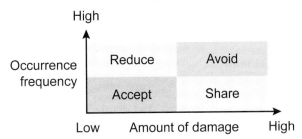

Fraud—The organization considers the potential for fraud in assessing risks to the achievement of objectives. In so doing, it:

- Considers fraud risk factors and threats
- Assesses the potential fraud influences of incentives and pressures
- Assesses opportunities that may exist in the organization for fraudsters to commit fraud
- Assesses attitudes and potential rationalizations that might be used to justify fraudulent actions

 Additional content on Fraud can be found in section 10.05.

Change Management—The organization identifies and assesses changes in the external environment (regulatory, economic, and physical environment of operation), assessing changes in the business model (new or existing business lines, rapid growth, new technologies, or acquisitions/divestitures) and changes in leadership.

Change management process

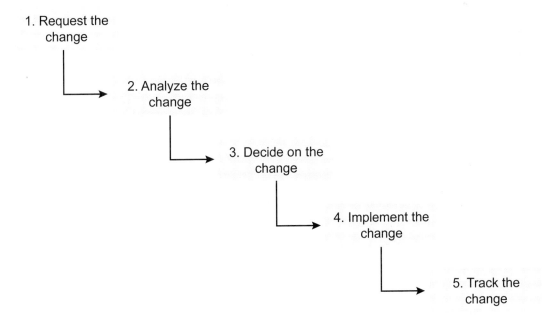

Control Activities—Three Principles

Risk Reduction—Organizational control activities mitigate (ie, reduce) the risks to the achievement of objectives to acceptable levels. The organization:

- Integrates controls with risk assessments
- Uses risk reduction analyses to determine which business processes require a control focus
- Considers how the environment, complexity, nature, and scope of operations influence risk reduction and control activities
- Evaluates a mix of potentially control activity types, including manual and automated, and preventive and detective controls
- Segregates incompatible activities and implements alternative controls where segregation is impossible

Technology Controls—The organization selects and implements general controls over technology, which support the achievement of its objectives. These activities include:

- Management understanding and determining the dependencies between business processes, automated controls, and general technology controls
- Management establishing controls to ensure the completeness, accuracy, and availability of technology and processing
- Restricting technology access rights to authorized users
- Establishing relevant security management process controls
- Establishing relevant technology acquisition, development, and maintenance process controls

Policies—The organization deploys control activities through policies and procedures that establish stakeholder expectations. Established procedures ensure the implementation of these policies. These activities include:

- Establishing policies and procedures that support the achievement of management's directives
- Establishing responsibility and accountability for executing policies and procedures
- Employing competent personnel to perform control activities in a timely manner and to take corrective action to investigate and act on control problems and issues
- Management periodically reassessing and revising policies and procedures to address changing conditions

Control activities

- Selects and develops control activities
- Selects and develops general control over technology
- Develops through policies and procedures

Information and Communication—Three Principles

Quality—Relevant, high-quality information supports the internal control processes.

These organizational processes should ensure that high-quality information supports internal control by:

- Identifying the information required to support internal control processes
- Capturing internal and external courses of data
- Transforming relevant data into information
- Producing information that is relevant, timely, current, accurate, verifiable, protected, and retained

- Considering the costs and benefits of information in relation to organizational objectives

Internal—Internal communication supports internal control processes. This includes:

- Organizational processes communicate required information to enable all personnel to understand and execute their internal control responsibilities

- Communication between management and the board of directors supports the achievement of organizational objectives

- Separate communication lines, such as an anonymous, independently monitored whistle-blower hotline, exist as a fail-safe mechanism to enable anonymous, confidential communication

- Internal communication methods are sensitive to the timing, audience, and nature of the communication

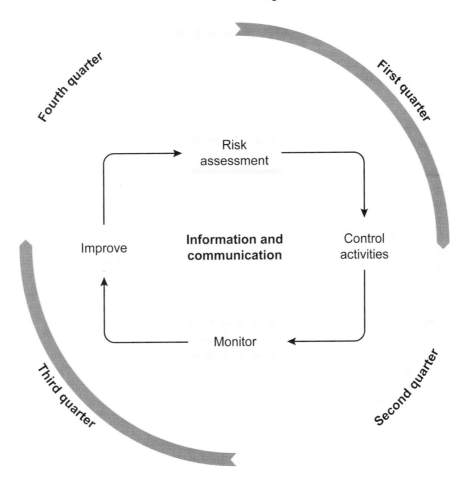

External—Communication with outsiders supports internal control processes. Organizational processes:

- Communicate relevant and timely information to external parties, including shareholders, partners, owners, regulators, customers, financial analysts, and others

- Enable inbound communications. Communication channels support the receipt of information from customers, suppliers, external auditors, regulators, financial analysts, and others

- Separate communication lines, such as a whistle-blower hotline, exist as fail-safe mechanisms to enable anonymous, confidential communication

- Communicate relevant information resulting from assessments conducted by external parties (eg, reviews of internal control) to the board of directors

- Ensure that external communication methods are sensitive to the timing, audience, and nature of the communication and to legal, regulatory, and fiduciary requirements

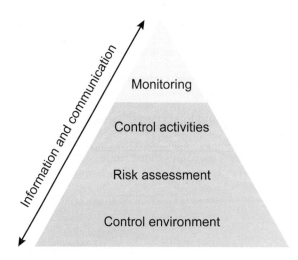

Monitoring Activities—Two Principles

Ongoing and Periodic—Ongoing and separate evaluations evaluate internal control functioning. These activities include:

- Considering the mix of ongoing and separate evaluations

- Benchmarking—considering the design and state of the existing system of internal control to establish a baseline understanding for ongoing and separate evaluations

- Developing and selecting ongoing and separate evaluations through management consideration of the rate of change of business activities and processes

- Ensuring that personnel have sufficient knowledge to conduct evaluations

- Integrating ongoing evaluations with business processes and adjusting, as needed, to changing conditions

- Providing periodic, separate evaluations for objective feedback

- Adjusting the scope and frequency of evaluations based on risk assessments

Address Deficiencies—Parties responsible for taking corrective action, including senior management and the board of directors, receive timely communication of internal control deficiencies. These activities include:

- Assessment of the results of ongoing and separate evaluations, as appropriate, by management and the board of directors

- Communication of deficiencies to those responsible for acting upon them, and to management at least one level above the identified problem

- Communication of deficiencies to senior management and the board of directors, as appropriate

- Tracking by management whether deficiencies are corrected on a timely basis

Control Categories

Controls can be understood through classification groupings. These classifications can be useful in developing and evaluating the benefits and limitations of these controls. This classification focuses on the **timing of the control relative to the potential error,** [TJ10]that is, **when** the controls are applied. A well-controlled system balances preventive and detective controls and includes corrective controls as needed.

Preventive ("before the fact") Controls

Preventive controls attempt to **stop an error or irregularity before it occurs**. They tend to be "passive" controls, that is, once established, they simply need to be activated to be effective. Examples of preventive controls include locks on buildings and doors, user names and passwords required to gain access to computer resources, and building segregation of duties into the organizational structure.

Detective ("after the fact") Controls

Detective controls attempt to **detect an error after it has occurred**. They tend to be "active" controls: that is, they must be continually performed to be effective. Examples of detective controls include data entry edits (eg, checks for missing data, values that are too large or too small), reconciliation of accounting records to physical assets (bank reconciliations, inventory counts), and tests of transactions to determine whether they comply with management's policies and procedures (audits).

- Effective detective controls, when known to the relevant constituency, often take on preventive characteristics. For example, surveillance cameras are fundamentally detective controls: They are designed to detect the commission of an unauthorized act. However, when it is known that surveillance cameras are in use, they also can serve to prevent unauthorized acts. The decrease in the number of drivers running red lights when drivers know that surveillance cameras are installed on traffic signals is an example of this phenomenon

Corrective Controls (Always Paired with Detective Controls)

These controls attempt to **reverse the effects** of the observed error or irregularity. Examples of corrective controls include maintenance of backup files, disaster recovery plans, and insurance.

Application controls	
Preventive	Designed to prevent errors and fraud from occuring
Detective	Designed to identify errors and fraud after they occur
Corrective	Designed to allow individual users to follow up on detected errors and fraud

Feedback and Feed-Forward Controls

Feedback and feed-forward controls focus on changing inputs or processes to promote desirable outcomes by comparing actual results (feedback) or projected results (feed-forward) to a predetermined standard.

- **Feedback Controls**—Evaluate the results of a process and, if the results are undesirable, adjust the process to correct the results; most detective controls are also feedback controls
- **Feed-forward Controls**—Project future results based on current and past information, and if the future results are undesirable, change the inputs to the system to prevent the outcome. Many inventory ordering systems are essentially feed-forward controls: The system projects product sales over the relevant time period, identifies the current inventory level, and orders inventory sufficient to fulfill the sales demand

General Controls and Application Controls

This classification focuses on the functional area of the control: that is, **where** the control is applied rather than **when** it is applied. The model divides information processing controls into two categories:

- **General Controls**—General controls are controls over the environment as a whole. They apply to all functions, not just specific accounting applications. General controls help ensure that data integrity is maintained
  - Examples of general controls include restricting physical access to computer resources, production and storage of backup files, and performing background checks of computer services personnel

- **Application Controls**—Application controls are controls over specific data input, data processing, and data output activities. Application controls are designed to ensure the accuracy, completeness, and validity of transaction processing. As such, they have a relatively narrow focus on those accounting applications that are involved with data entry, updates, and reporting

  ○ Examples of application controls include checks to ensure that input data is complete and properly formatted (eg, dates, dollar amounts), that account numbers are valid, and that values are reasonable (eg, that we don't sell quantities that are greater than the quantity currently in inventory)

  ○ Application controls are sometimes called "transaction controls" since they relate specifically to transaction processing

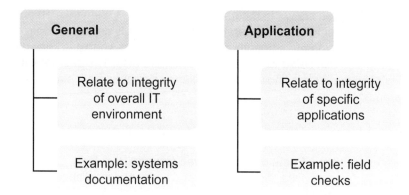

Limitations of I/C Systems

COSO identifies the following **inherent limitations** in an internal control system:

- **The suitability of objectives established as a precondition to internal control.** Internal control is the responsibility of management (not the auditors). Management may set objectives that lead to poor controls (eg, make earnings targets even if it means committing fraud)

- **Internal control depends heavily on people**. People are wonderful, fallible, imperfect creatures. Human judgment can be faulty, flawed, and biased. Breakdowns in control can occur because of human nature

- **Management may be able to, and may choose to, override internal control**. Many of the major financial reporting scandals are examples of management override, including Enron and WorldCom

- **Collusion** is an ever-present risk in internal control systems. Management, employees, and/or third parties may collude to circumvent controls. A person in the vendor maintenance group could create a fictitious vendor and collude with a person in the accounts payable group to process a fake invoice to the fictitious vendor. Both individuals would be needed to commit this type of fraud

- **External events** beyond the organization's control may lead to control failures. For example, the COVID-19 pandemic may have resulted in control issues because many companies could not maintain segregation of duties due to staffing restrictions and social distancing mandates

Deficiencies in Internal Control

An **internal control deficiency** is a shortcoming in a component or components and relevant principle(s) that reduces the likelihood of an entity achieving its objectives. Hence, a control deficiency occurs when the design or operation of a control does not allow management or employees, in the normal course of performing their assigned functions, to prevent or detect misstatements on a timely basis.

When an organization determines that an internal control deficiency exists, management must assess the severity of that deficiency (ie, classify it). Types of internal control deficiencies include the following:

- **Control Deficiency**—Defined above. The least serious of the three types of control deficiencies

- **Significant Deficiency**—A deficiency (or combination of deficiencies) in internal control that is more serious than a control deficiency but less severe than a material weakness, yet it is important enough to merit attention by those charged with governance
- **Material Weakness**—A deficiency (or combination of deficiencies) in internal control such that there is a reasonable possibility that a material misstatement of the entity's financial statements will not be prevented or detected and corrected on a timely basis

Material weakness or significant deficiency

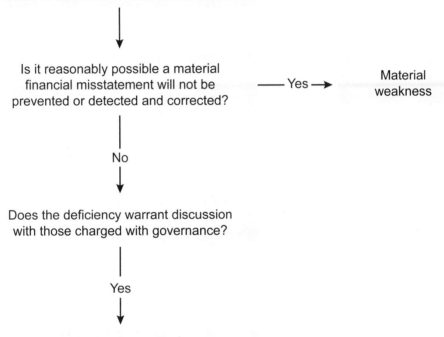

Internal controls deficiency factors

- Ineffective control oversight
- Issues noted in prior audit
- Size and complexity of entity
- Probability or size of material misstatement
- Volume of activity potentially impacted
- Nature of accounts or transactions involved

Is it reasonably possible a material financial misstatement will not be prevented or detected and corrected? —— Yes → Material weakness

No

Does the deficiency warrant discussion with those charged with governance?

Yes

Significant deficiency

 Additional coverage on internal control deficiencies can be found in Chaper 20.

Documenting I/C

Auditors are required to **document a client's I/C structure** to determine the amount of substantive testing needed. An auditor should select the documentation method that best illustrates the controls in place and helps in planning an efficient, effective audit. The **complexity and size** of the entity will most likely **influence** the form and extent of internal control **documentation**.

Factors influencing internal control documentation method

- Nature, size, and complexity of the entity
- Availability of control information from the entity
- Audit methodology and technology used

For example, the auditor can gain an understanding of the entity's control environment by documenting it with flowcharts or narratives. Questionnaires work well when the auditor has some knowledge of the controls in place and can craft appropriate questions. Decision tables/trees are appropriate for documenting the logic of a specific process.

Commonly used techniques to obtain an understanding of the I/C structure include the following (**FIND**):

Documenting internal controls (FIND)

Flowchart	<ul><li>Illustrates data flows and interactions</li><li>Segregation of duties evident</li><li>Flow between departments not evident</li></ul>
Internal control questionnaire	<ul><li>Yes/no answers only; yes = potential control</li><li>Challenging to create but easy to administer</li><li>May not identify control deficiencies</li></ul>
Narrative	<ul><li>Easy to understand</li><li>Segregation of duties may not be evident</li><li>Cumbersome</li></ul>
Decision table/tree	<ul><li>Good for decision processes</li><li>Next step depends on last answer</li><li>Not appropriate for all controls</li></ul>

Flowcharts, Diagrams & Narratives

Flowcharts and diagrams are visual depictions of the I/C structure and the client's IT system. There are several different types of flowcharts and diagrams that are commonly used to show the different aspects and levels of detail in a system, including the following:

- **Flow Charts of Business Process Cycles**—A graphical depiction of the client's accounting systems for major categories of transactions with emphasis on[SC14] the origination, processing, and distribution of important underlying accounting documents

    - *Advantages*—A fairly systematic approach that is unlikely to overlook important considerations; tailored to client-specific circumstances; fairly easy for others to review and understand; and fairly easy to update from year to year

    - *Disadvantages*—Can be rather tedious and time-consuming to prepare initially; the auditor might fail to recognize relevant internal control deficiencies by getting too absorbed in the details of documenting the client's system

- **Internal Control Questionnaires (ICQs)**—Questionnaires consisting of a listing of questions about client's control procedures and activities; a "no" answer is usually designed to indicate a control weakness

    - *Advantages*—Generic questionnaires can be prepared in advance for clients in various industry categories with every conceivable question, so that no important question related to controls is likely to be omitted; deficiencies are easily identified by a client's "no" response to any question

    - *Disadvantages*—Generic questionnaires are not tailored to client-specific circumstances and irrelevant questions are annoying to client personnel; the client personnel responding to the checklist of questions may conceal deficiencies by inaccurate answers without the auditor's knowledge

- **Narrative Write-ups**—A written memo describing the important control-related activities in the transaction cycles under consideration

    - *Advantages*—Memos can be tailored to a client's unique circumstances, can be as detailed or general as desired, and are relatively easy to prepare (and easy for reviewers to read)

    - *Disadvantages*—It is relatively easy to overlook relevant internal control issues (strengths or weaknesses) because the analysis is fairly unstructured

- **Diagrams:**
    - **Process Diagram:**
        - A business process from beginning to end
        - Which departments or groups of employees are responsible for each function
        - The interaction among departments or groups of employees
    - **Data-Flow Diagram (DFD):**
        - Depending on the level of detail, a DFD shows how data flow within a system or a specific business process
    - **Entity-Relationship (ER) Diagram:**
        - ER diagrams are typically used to describe details related to data structures, such as tables in a relational database, and how those structures relate to each other. An ER model uses three basic components to diagram data structures, as shown below
        - Entities—Any object, event, or business process that requires data storage (ie, a table)
        - Relationships—How entities are related (ie, one-to-one, one-to-many, and many-to-many)
        - Attributes—The characteristics of the entities (ie, fields in a table)

- **Decision Table/Tree** – Parts of an I/C structure may require an employee to choose from several alternative actions, depending on the conditions faced, and document such activities. This may best be accomplished by preparing a decision table that lists each possible condition and the actions that will result from each (ie, it depicts the logic of an operation or process)

Summary—Understanding the I/C Structure

An auditor performs the following procedures to obtain an understanding of an entity's internal control environment

Step 1 – Obtain an understanding of the design of all five components of the entity's I/C through the performance of risk assessment procedures

Step 2 – Document the understanding of I/C

Step 3 – Assess Risk of Material Misstatement (RMM), which consists of inherent risk (IR) and control risk (CR). RMM = IR × CR

Step 4 – Develop an audit strategy to either:

- (NOT Rely) Decide not to perform tests of controls (TofC), assessing CR at the maximum level as if the controls did not exist; or

- (RELY) Perform TofC to determine if CR is below maximum, allowing for the modification of further audit procedures (substantive tests)

Step 5 – Reassess RMM and evaluate results.

- For controls for which TofC were performed, evaluate results to reassess RMM and determine if it is appropriate to modify further audit procedures

Step 6 – Document conclusions and develop or revise audit program for further audit procedures.

 PCAOB audits are required to evaluate internal controls over financial reporting (ICFR). However, AICPA audits are only required to obtain and document an understanding of the client's I/C to assess the RMM. If the AICPA client auditor believes testing I/C will reduce substantive testing, they can choose to do so. However, in an AIPCA audit, testing of I/C is NOT required.

10.02 Control Environment, IT General Controls, and Entity-level Controls

Control Environment

 Representative Task (Remembering & Understanding): Understand the elements of an entity's control environment, including the design and implementation of IT general controls and entity-level controls.

As discussed previously, the **control environment,** which consists of **entity-level controls,** is a component of the Committee of Sponsoring Organizations (COSO) internal control (I/C) framework that sets the tone for an organization and addresses management oversight responsibilities.

Components of internal controls (CRIME)

Control activities
Risk assessment
Information and communication
Monitoring of controls
Control Environment

- Determine if internal controls are effective
- Communicate deficiencies to responsible parties

Understanding the Entity and Its Environment

The auditor's understanding of the entity and its environment consists of understanding the following:

- **Industry, regulatory, and other external factors**—There may be specific risks of material misstatement due to the nature of the business, the degree of regulation, or other economic, technical, and competitive issues

- **Nature of the entity**—This refers to the entity's operations, ownership, governance, financing, etc. (Understanding these considerations may help the auditor understand the classes of transactions, account balances, and disclosures that are relevant to the financial statements)

- **Objectives and strategies**—The auditor should obtain an understanding of the entity's objectives and strategies, including any related business risks that may cause material misstatement of the financial statements. Strategies are operational approaches by which management intends to achieve its objectives. Business risks result from circumstances that could adversely affect the entity's ability to achieve its objectives. (Note that the auditor does not have a responsibility to identify all business risks)

- **Measurement and review of the entity's financial performance**—The auditor should obtain an understanding of the entity's performance measures (and their review) and indicate aspects of the entity's performance that management considers important, which may help the auditor understand whether such pressures increase the risks of material misstatement

- **Obtain a sufficient understanding of I/C**—The auditor should perform risk assessment procedures to evaluate the design of controls relevant to the audit to identify types of potential misstatements. Note that inquiry alone is not sufficient to evaluate the design and implementation of a control. Consider factors that affect the risks of material misstatement; and design the tests of controls, if applicable, and the substantive procedures that are appropriate in the circumstances

Entity-Level Controls (ELC)

Entity-level controls deal with *company-wide issues* and set the tone of the organization, involve the assignment of authority and responsibility, and address conduct. ELCs include:

- A **mission statement** that is part of the entity's culture

- A **code of conduct** that applies to all members of the organization, including management

- **Organization charts and job descriptions** that indicate the roles and responsibilities of individuals within the organization

- The **behavior of management and executives**, which is often considered one of the more significant components

COSO control environment principles

Management and those charged with governance should:

1. Commit to integrity and ethical values
2. Exercise their oversight responsibilities
3. Establish structure, authority, and responsibility
4. Commit to competence
5. Enforce accountability

In the integrated audit of an issuer, an auditor has identified entity-level controls that are important to the conclusion as to whether the company has effective internal control over financial reporting (ICFR). Each of the following is an example of an entity-level control, **except**

- Controls over the period-end financial reporting process
- The company's risk assessment process
- Controls over the completeness of deposited cash
- Controls over management override

PCAOB auditing standards applicable to integrated audits identify several examples of entity-level controls, but those entity-level controls **do not include** the specific controls applicable to **individual elements of the financial statements** such as cash deposits.

IT Financial Reporting Systems

Organizations evaluate **information systems** based on various requirements such as the frequency of **system processing**. **Batch processing** systems **periodically** aggregate transactions and process them in a group. **Online real-time processing** systems process transactions **immediately** after they have been entered. Online real-time systems make data available more quickly than batch processing systems. The two systems differ primarily in terms of *how regularly they process transactions*; the frequency of processing is a significant differentiating requirement.

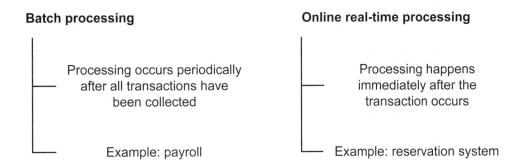

Batch processing

Processing occurs periodically after all transactions have been collected

Example: payroll

Online real-time processing

Processing happens immediately after the transaction occurs

Example: reservation system

Regardless of the type of processing system used, the auditor should obtain an understanding of how:

- The *information systems* consist of methods and records used to *record, process, summarize and report* the company's transactions to maintain accountability for the related accounts

- Individual duties and responsibilities related to I/C are established and *communicated* to involved personnel

- Transactions are initiated, authorized, and processed, including which components are performed manually and which are performed electronically

- Transactions, events, and conditions are reported

- Accountability is maintained for assets, liability, and equity, including the maintenance of records supporting information or specific items in the F/S

- The incorrect processing of transactions is identified and resolved

- Recurring and nonrecurring journal entries, unusual transactions, and other adjustments are identified and prepared

- System overrides or bypasses to controls are processed and accounted for

- Information is transferred from the processing systems to the general ledger

- Events and conditions, including depreciation and amortization of assets and collectability of receivables, are identified, and how information (ie, data) is captured

- F/S are prepared, including the development of estimates

- Information that is required to be disclosed is identified, accumulated, recorded, processed, summarized, and properly reported

IT Controls Overview

Since the auditor will usually want to rely heavily on the I/C structure of a computer-based accounting system, gaining an understanding of the I/C structure is crucial. In addition to **entity-level controls**, the operation of computer systems requires two more broad types of controls:

- **IT general controls** (ITGC)—These relate to the **overall integrity of the system**. Controls include IT governance policies, procedures, and practices (tasks and activities) established by management to provide reasonable assurance that specific objectives will be achieved

- **Application controls**—These are the policies, procedures, and activities designed to provide reasonable assurance that objectives relevant to a given **automated solution (application)** are achieved. They are designed to ensure that an individual computer application program performs properly, accepting authorized input, processing it correctly, and generating appropriate output

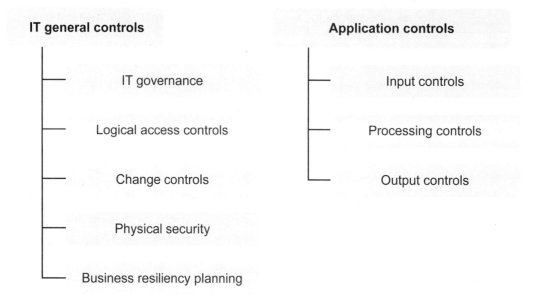

Initially, the focus of the auditor will be on understanding the general controls that relate to the overall integrity of the system. Later, the auditor may examine application controls that relate to the performance of individual computer applications.

IT Governance

IT governance is a formal structure within an entity that is overseen by the board of directors (BOD) and executive management. IT governance helps a business meet strategic goals and objectives through the management and control of IT acquisition, deployment, and use.

IT governance provides the **strategies**, **policies**, and **procedures** that are needed to meet IT objectives.

IT governance objectives	
Performance measurement	Use performance measures to asses IT projects and services
Resource management	Maintain policies and oversight to ensure cost-benefit acquisition, deployment, and use of IT resources
Risk management	Identify and minimize risk to IT assets
Strategic alignment	Align IT strategy with broader business strategies
Value delivery	Ensure IT assets and activities provide value to business and stakeholders

The board of directors and management rely on committees, especially the **IT systems steering** committee, to provide oversight, prioritize stakeholder requests, set policy, and monitor IT activities. The IT steering committee consists of management-level employees. Members' responsibilities include:

- **Prioritizing** IT projects (short- and long-range) and allocating IT resources

- **Overseeing** information systems and communicating control and risk information

- **Evaluating** IT performance

IT steering committee	
Description	A management-level committee made up of executives, key users, and advisers from various departments
Typical responsibilities	<ul><li>Prioritizes IT projects and allocates IT resources</li><li>Uses policies and standards to communicate control and risk information to the organization</li><li>Evaluates IT performance</li></ul>
Authority	Oversees day-to-day management of IT operations

IT General Controls

 Representative Task (Application): Perform procedures to obtain an understanding of how an entity has responded to risks arising from the use of IT, including identifying and testing the design and implementation of relevant IT general controls.

Logical Access Controls & Cybersecurity

Limiting access to an entity's computers and the data they hold is becoming an increasingly challenging problem. Clearly, general controls over **unauthorized access** to computers and files are of great significance in evaluating I/C in an IT environment. **Firewalls** and **user authentication** are particularly important in **networks** since the data are distributed widely; the more points of access there are, the greater the risk.

Furthermore, sensitive data should be **encrypted** to minimize the possible damage (ie, theft, alteration, or destruction of data) should the user authentication process fail. Such controls designed to protect against **cyberattacks** are referred to as **cybersecurity**.

- **Firewalls**—Another tool for establishing security is a **firewall**, which prevents unauthorized users from accessing the system and data. A firewall can be in the form of a computer program (software) or a physical device that blocks the transmission media being used (hardware)

- **User authentication**—User IDs and **passwords** are used to authenticate users (ie, they are who they say they are) and prevent others from accessing the system. Other methods of authentication might include biometrics, smartcards, security tokens, multifactor identification, and multimodal authentication. An auditor can test these procedures by entering invalid user information to see that they are rejected

  o Passwords should be changed regularly (eg, every 90 days) to make unauthorized access more difficult

  o Protocols for passwords should encourage the use of random letters, numbers, and symbols, making it more difficult for someone to guess

  o It is also considered good practice to require that individual users change assigned passwords when new accounts are created

○ Failure to remove user accounts when an employee leaves a client is a major security risk

○ A user should be locked out after a predetermined number of failed attempts to access the system (typically three attempts)

Elements of a strong password

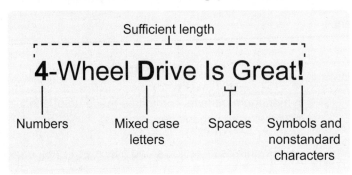

* **Encryption of data**—**Encryption** makes **data unreadable** to someone **without** knowledge of the coding method or **key**. There are two types of encryption:

  ○ **Private key encryption**—Data is encrypted and decrypted using the *same private key*.

  ○ **Public key encryption**—Data is *encrypted with a public key* and decrypted using a *private key*

* **Vulnerability testing**—Systems should be tested periodically for vulnerabilities (ie, weaknesses). This process may be manual or an automated scan

* **Penetration testing**—This involves IT personnel or an independent consultant attempting to hack the system intentionally

* **Intrusion detection**—An intrusion-detection program monitors the system to detect network break-ins

A network should also have **authorization controls**. These controls **limit** (1) **access** to certain files to authorized employees and (2) the **rights** that those individuals should have with respect to the files.

* **Role-based access controls**—This type of access control varies based on an individual's role in the organization. An auditor can test these procedures by verifying that valid roles only provide compatible access. For example, each role should be designed to prevent conflicts in **segregation of duties**. Roles should be designed to ensure the following activities are segregated

  ○ **Authorization**—The development of new programs and changes to existing programs should be performed by **systems analysts, administrators,** and **programmers**. These personnel should not be involved in the supervision of computer operations or the control and review of output. Also, since the **security administrator** controls the access to networks, programs, and data, they should not have any other responsibilities

  ○ **Recording**—**Data input clerks** and **computer operators** have the role of entering information into the computer and running the programs. These personnel should not have access to live versions of the program code that would enable them to modify programs nor should they control the output without approval

- o **Custody—Control clerks** and **librarians** review input procedures, review exception reports indicating incorrect functioning of the computer, send outputs to the proper destinations, and maintain physical storage of data. These personnel should not have the ability to create or alter programs or to operate the computers that generate the information. Also, since the **database administrator** maintains the organization's data, they should not have any programming or other operational responsibilities

- **Rule-based access controls**—This type of access control can vary based on any set rule. Rules should be set so that:
  - o Certain individuals have read-only access rights to files
  - o Authorized individuals have the rights to read, write, or edit the data in the files

- These procedures can be tested by verifying that access rules only provide compatible access

There are various types of malicious code (malware) that could infect a system. **Antivirus software** is designed to detect and potentially eliminate malicious code before damage is done and repair or quarantine files that have already been infected. It should be deployed at multiple points in an IT architecture.

Social engineering is the development of a deceptive scenario that tricks an individual into disclosing confidential information for fraudulent purposes (eg, phishing). The best defenses against social engineering are employee **training** and **security policies**.

Change Controls

Change control measures should be implemented to ensure that changes to processing programs and business processes have minimal impact.

- **Systems Development Life Cycle (SDLC)**—SDLC consists of the phases deployed in the development or acquisition of a software system. It is used to plan, design, develop, test, and implement an application system or a major modification to an application system

- **Change control** (also called change management or program changes)—After implementation, a formal change control process manages ad hoc system changes. This process requires the following steps:
  - o A **formal change request** that describes the desired change and the plans for implementation should be documented and distributed to stakeholders
  - o The formal change request will be **evaluated** to determine the impact on the project schedule and budget
  - o If the change is **authorized**, then the change is developed and **tested** to verify that the desired results have been achieved
  - o Once it has been successfully tested and approved, the change can be **implemented**

Systems documentation of new programs and alterations to existing programs ensures that IT personnel are aware of the availability and proper use of programs. Also, changes in programming personnel during projects will not interfere with the ability of other employees to understand what has been done previously. Such documentation may also assist the auditor in learning about the system.

Components of change control	
Change requests	Identify when change is needed or desired
Change analysis	Prepare cost-benefit analysis of requested change
Change decision	Based on cost-benefit analysis, management decided whether change is justified
Change implementation	Develop/implement plan for new processes/control components
Change monitoring	Monitor to ensure to change is properly executed and effective

Physical Security

Physical security consists of physical access controls and environmental controls. Physical access controls can include locks, cameras, badges, biometrics, etc. Environmental controls include temperature and humidity control, fire protection without the use of sprinklers, uninterruptable power supply, etc.

Business Continuity/Resilience Planning

The purpose of business resilience planning is to enable a business to quickly adapt and continue operations while safeguarding assets in the event of a disruption.

- **Identify the business processes of strategic importance**—These are the key processes that are responsible for both the permanent growth of the business and for the fulfillment of the business goals. Based on the key processes, the risk management process should begin with a risk assessment. The risk is directly proportional to the impact on the organization and the probability of occurrence of the perceived threat

- **Backup controls**—Copies of files and programs should be maintained to allow reconstruction of destroyed or altered files. This may include copies on the same computer, backups to removable storage media, such as disks, and off-premises backups to computers and locations outside the company. Copies may be identical, or the client may use the **grandfather-father-son** retention system. This involves the periodic saving of data versions to allow the reconstruction of records by starting with an older file and reentering lost data since that time

The three basic backup strategies, which are commonly used together, are:

- **Full**—Makes a full backup of the system's data. This complete backup takes the longest and utilizes the most backup media. Usually performed over longer time periods, such as once a week

- **Differential**—Copies only data that have changed since the last full backup. These backups are cumulative until the next full backup is complete and are typically done daily. Differential backups sacrifice completeness for speed, although as the week progresses, they, along with any required data restoration procedures, will take longer

- **Incremental**—Copies only data that have changed since the last backup of any kind, usually in increments of hours or minutes. These small increments can be restored relatively quickly but rely on the presence of a full backup. Any restoration must start with the last full backup, then load each incremental backup sequentially

Business continuity planning

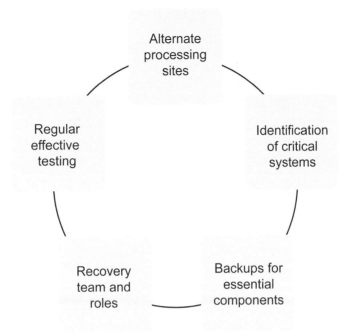

- **Planned downtime controls**—Since some downtime is inevitable, planned downtime allows maintenance so that unplanned downtime doesn't interrupt system operations

- **Checkpoints**—This is similar to grandfather-father-son, but at certain "checkpoints," the system makes a copy of the database and this "checkpoint" file is stored on a separate disk or tape. If a problem occurs, the system is restarted at the last checkpoint

- **Business continuity & disaster recovery**—The company should have plans in place that will allow operations to be restored and continued in the event of physical destruction or disabling of the site of computer operations. The configuration that represents the most complete disaster recovery plan should provide for an alternative processing site, backup and off-site storage procedures, identification of critical applications, and testing of the plan. This can be done by maintaining a(n):

  ○ **Hot site**—This is an alternate site that has computers and data ready to begin operations immediately in the event of the disaster

  ○ **Cold site**—This is an alternate site that has space available for operations but will require setup of computers and loading of data before operations can begin

  ○ **Off-site mirrored server**—This is an off-site server that is replicated from a production server in real-time, and can take over operations in a matter of seconds in the event of an outage. This is used to ensure continuous delivery of mission-critical data or services, such as those needed by government and medical applications

Disaster recovery site classifications

	❄ Cold site	🌡 Warm site	🔥 Hot site	Mirrored site
Secondary location	✓	✓	✓	✓
Equipment at location	✗	✓	✓	✓
Connectivity at location	✗	✓	✓	✓
Active before disaster	✗	✗	✓	✓
Recovery	Weeks/Months	Hours/Days	Seconds/Minutes	Seconds
Cost	$ Low	$$ Medium	$$$ High	$$$$ Very high

- **Incident response planning**—An important part of business continuity planning is the detection and response to IT security threats. An **incident response plan** is the IT-focused counterpart of the **disaster recovery plan**, which primarily addresses physical disrupters. Incident response plans address a wide variety of IT-specific threats, including service outages, data loss, and intellectual property theft. Robust incident response plans help IT staff detect technology-related threats, and offer a course of action for all significant incidents

IT Application Controls

Application controls are those applied to specific business activities within a computerized processing system to achieve financial reporting objectives. Application controls are specific to each business process cycle and refer to a client's activities. Application controls relate to data input, data processing, and data output. They are designed to prevent, detect, and correct errors in a timely manner.

They include policies and practices (eg, access controls) that provide *reasonable assurance* that specific control objectives will be achieved. Therefore, they ensure that a program performs properly, accepts only authorized input (ie, enhances security), processes it correctly, and generates appropriate output.

Because application controls are related to specific transactions, audit teams rely extensively on the effectiveness of these controls to mitigate the risk of material misstatement for account balances or classes of transactions.

Input	Processing	Output
Validity checks	Data validation	Distribution lists
Range (limit) checks	Sequence checks	Printer security
Authorization checks	Completeness checks	Storage controls
Hash amounts	Duplication checks	Confidentiality controls
Batch controls	File identification checks	Data tranmission controls

Input Controls

Input controls are designed to provide reasonable assurance that data received for processing have been **properly authorized** and **accurately entered** or converted for processing. These controls also provide the opportunity for entity personnel to correct and resubmit data initially rejected as erroneous. Errors can be avoided through:

- Observational controls

- Use of point-of-sale devices, such as scanners, to gather and record data automatically

- The use of preprinted recording forms

- Data transcription controls, such as preformatted screens, when converting data to machine-readable form

 Historically, many of the controls discussed on the exam involve verifying data that have been input to ensure the program doesn't accept inappropriate information.

As data are being entered, they should be subject to various **forms of verification** (ie, **logic tests**).

- **Field checks**—Data are validated as to the correct length and format. For example, an entry of a license plate might be verified for type (alphanumeric, so that only letters and numbers are acceptable) and length (not longer than 7)

  - **Missing data check** (Completeness check)—Data are validated to make sure that all required fields have values. For example, a timecard entry system would require that the hours worked in a day field contain a value

- **Validity checks**—Data are compared with a list of acceptable entries to be sure they match one of them. For example, a field to accept the two-letter state abbreviation will be checked against a file that lists all the acceptable choices, so that an entry of OG for the state will be rejected as invalid

- **Limit tests**—Numbers are compared to limits that have been set for acceptability. For example, the entry of a pay rate may be compared to the current minimum wage on the lower side and $50 per hour on the upper side to be sure the number entered makes sense. This is sometimes called a reasonableness test and is the closest computer equivalent to human judgment in reviewing information

- **Check digits**—Numbers with no obvious meaning, such as identification numbers, are often designed so that one of the digits is determined by a formula applied to the rest of the number. The computer applies the formula when a number is entered to determine if it is an acceptable one.

  - This control makes it difficult for someone to invent a fake number if they don't know the formula; the program will recognize a number that isn't designed so that the check digit is correct. The check digit can be either a number or letter and can be placed in any consistent position in the overall identification.

  - For example, many states have driver licenses that start with a letter which is derived from a formula applied to the numbers which follow it, and a person trying to create a fictional license will only have a 1 in 26 chance of correctly guessing the letter that should be in the first position based on the numbers.

Type of input control	Definition	Example
Field checks	Data entered is validated for proper length and format	Timecard is verified to ensure that the hours entered are numeric
Validity checks	Data entered is compared with a list of acceptable entries	State abbreviation entered is verified against list of acceptable state abbreviations
Limit tests	Data entered is compared with limits that have been set for applicability	Timecard entry is verified to make sure that hours entered do not exceed the maximum hours in day (ie, 24)
Check digits	Numbers with no obvious meaning in which one of the digits is determined by a formula applied to the rest of the number	Bank account number is verified to ensure that the number entered is a valid bank number

When using batch processing of data, manual **control totals** can be prepared and compared with computer-generated totals of entered information to ensure accuracy of inputs. These totals include:

- **Record count**—The total number of records entered into the program at that time
- **Financial total**—The total dollar amount of entries that are financial in nature
- **Hash total**—The total of values which cannot be meaningfully added together, but which serve as a way to verify the correct entry of these values
- **Other quantitative total**—The total of some column of numbers, such as check numbers or invoice numbers, that can be used to determine that all transactions have been entered as well as that a sequence has not been broken

 An entity has the following invoices in a batch:

Invoice #	Product	Quantity	Unit price
201	F10	150	$5.00
202	G15	200	$10.00
203	H20	250	$25.00
204	K35	200	$30.00

Which of the following most likely represents a hash total?

- FGHK80
- 4
- 204
- 810

A hash total is a total that has **no intrinsic meaning** but is used solely to determine that all transactions have been recorded. The total of the invoice numbers, for example, is **810**. The total does not mean anything by itself, but by computing the total of all of the invoice numbers recorded and comparing it to the total of the invoice numbers in the batch, it can be determined that all invoices have been recorded.

A program may also perform **edit checks** on batch-processed data to verify that each individual entry is appropriate; it will then generate a list of rejected transactions for review by the control clerk.

Processing Controls

Once data is input, processing controls are designed to provide reasonable assurance that data processing has been performed accurately without any omission or duplicate processing of transactions. Many processing controls are similar in nature to input controls, but they are used in the processing phases, rather than at the time input is verified.

- **Run-to-run totals** use values in the batch control record to monitor records as they move from one batch process to another batch process. They are calculated at the end of each batch process and compared to the batch control record

- **Transaction logs** track whether transactions were successfully processed or not

- **Prenumbered documents** ensure that there are no duplicate or missing records in a batch

- **Sequence checks** ensure that records in a batch are processed in correct sequential order

- A **concurrent update control** (concurrency control) helps address conflicts in a multi-user system. For example, when two people are trying to purchase tickets at the same time, it will lock one user out, so as not to oversell the tickets

- The most fundamental processing control a client can implement is **periodic system testing and evaluation** of the processing accuracy of its programs. This testing helps ensure that data are being handled or rejected appropriately, and that logical functions are correct and working

  - Computer programs can be tested using **error testing compilers** to ensure that they do not contain programming language errors

  - **Test data** exposes the program to one sample of each type of exception condition (ie, an unusual condition) likely to occur during its use

  - **Systems and software documentation** allows system analysts to verify that processing programs are complete and thorough

Output Controls

Output controls represent the final check on the results of computerized processing. Output controls are concerned with detecting errors rather than preventing errors. These controls should be designed to provide reasonable assurance that only authorized persons receive output or have access to files produced by the system.

Summary of application risks and controls

Risks/threats*—Specific programs	Application controls
Inappropriate inputs	**Input controls**
• Invalid data	• Check digit
• Poor data quality	• Validity check
• Incomplete data	• Edit test
• Inaccurate data	• Limit test
	• Financial total
	• Record counts
	• Hash total
	• Nonfinancial totals
Compromised processing integrity	**Processing controls**
• Invalid data	• Run-to-run totals
• Incomplete data	• Transaction logs
• Inaccurate data	• Prenumbered documents
• Redundant data	• Sequence checks
	• Concurrency control
	• Periodic system testing
Ineffective outputs	**Output controls**
• Inaccurate and/or incomplete data	• System testing
• Improper disposal	• Shredders
• Improper distribution of information	• Distribution lists

This is not meant to be an all-inclusive list.

Benefits of IT

The auditor should obtain audit evidence about the **accuracy and completeness** (ie, reliability) of data produced by the entity's IT system when those data are used in performing audit procedures. Thus, the primary **advantage** of IT as it relates to an audit is that a computer is not as subject to random errors as a human. That is, computers are **consistent**; they process data the same way every time.

As a result, an auditor who is able to **verify** that a computer **program** is working properly will **not** have to **test as many individual transactions** to be sure the outputs are reliable (ie, complete and accurate). An audit of a computerized system can, therefore, rely more heavily on the I/C structure and reduce the need for substantive testing, making the audit potentially more efficient. Other benefits of IT include:

- **Timeliness**—Electronic processing and updating are normally more efficient
- **Analysis**—Data can be accessed for analytical procedures more conveniently (with proper software)
- **Monitoring**—Electronic controls can be monitored by the computer system itself
- **Circumvention**—Controls are difficult to circumvent when programmed properly, and exceptions are unlikely to be permitted
- **Segregation of duties**—Security controls can prevent the performance of incompatible functions by the same individual or group through security controls in applications, databases, and operating systems

Risks of IT

There are two risks of major concern to the auditor:

- **Unauthorized access**—Disclosure, destruction, and alteration of large amounts of data are possible if unauthorized access occurs. This can cause more damage to the accounting system as a whole than in a manual system where it is difficult for one person to access, change, or destroy all the different records of the system
- **Audit trail**—The audit trail is an electronically visible trail of evidence enabling one to trace information contained in statements or reports back to the original input source. An audit trail is also important to the client for the proper functioning of the system during the year; such as monitoring activities, providing a deterrent to fraud, and answering queries by examining the source data. This would require the auditor to establish the reliability and extent of the audit trail

Other IT risks include:

- **Overreliance**—Without clear output, IT systems are often assumed to be working when they are not
- **Changes in programs**—Severe consequences without detection are possible if unauthorized program changes occur
- **Failure to change**—Programs or systems are sometimes not updated for new laws, rules, or activities
- **Manual intervention**—Knowledgeable individuals can sometimes alter files by bypassing the appropriate programs
- **Loss of data**—Catastrophic data loss is possible if appropriate controls aren't in place

The following table provides a summary of risks an entity might encounter and possible IT general controls (ITGC) the organization may implement to mitigate that risk. Table is not all-inclusive.

Risks/threats— Overall computer environment	IT general controls
Not meeting IT objectives <ul><li>Misalignment of IT strategy with business strategy</li><li>IT doesn't deliver the value it should</li></ul>	**IT governance** <ul><li>Strategic guidance</li><li>Direction (setting policies & procedures)</li><li>Monitoring</li></ul>
Unauthorized access <ul><li>Cyberattacks</li><li>Theft, alteration, or destruction of data</li><li>Malicious code</li><li>Social engineering</li><li>Misuse of data by employees</li><li>Incompatible functions (fraud/error)</li></ul>	**Access controls & cybersecurity** <ul><li>Firewalls & user authentication (lock out after 3 unsuccessful attempts)</li><li>Encryption of sensitive data</li><li>Antivirus software</li><li>Employee training</li><li>Authorization controls (limits access/rights to alter data)</li></ul>
Computer facility vulnerabilities <ul><li>Unauthorized access</li><li>Theft, physical destruction of IT assets</li><li>Environmental hazards</li><li>Fire, heat, humidity, electrical outages</li></ul>	**Physical security** <ul><li>Locks, ID badges, etc.</li><li>Cameras</li><li>Fire protection (no sprinklers)</li><li>Uninterruptable power supply (ie, battery backup) and emergency power supply (ie, generators)</li></ul>
Change risk <ul><li>Disruption of operations</li><li>Unauthorized system alterations</li><li>Uninformed IT staff</li></ul>	**Change controls** <ul><li>Systems Development Life Cycle (SDLC)</li><li>Change management</li><li>Systems documentation</li></ul>
Disruption of operations <ul><li>Accidental/intentional destruction or unauthorized alteration</li><li>Natural disasters</li></ul>	**Business resilience planning** <ul><li>Backup controls</li><li>Disaster recovery planning</li><li>Alternative processing site</li><li>Off-site storage procedures</li><li>Incident response planning</li></ul>

Which of the following sets of controls over information technology is the auditor of an issuer most likely to examine first in audit planning?

- Input controls
- Processing controls
- Output controls
- Change management controls

IT controls in the top-down approach

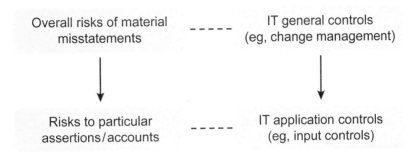

Auditors of issuers are required, and auditors of nonissuers are recommended, to use a **top-down approach to risk assessment**. When considering IT controls relating to risks of material misstatement, auditors should **first obtain an understanding of IT general controls** (eg, change management controls) and then consider application controls (ie, input, processing, and output controls).

10.03 Business Processes and the Design of Internal Controls, including the IT Environment

Business Process Cycle Overview

 Representative Task (Application): Identify and document the significant business processes and data flows that directly or indirectly impact an entity's financial statements.

 Representative Task (Application): Perform a walkthrough of a significant business process and document (eg, flowcharts, process diagrams, narratives) the flow of relevant transactions and data from initiation through financial statement reporting and disclosure.

A business process cycle is a group of essentially homogeneous transactions, that is, transactions of a particular type. Within a given cycle, control risk is essentially constant, since all transactions within that category are processed subject to the same configuration of internal control policies and procedures. A business process cycle is, therefore, the highest level of aggregation for which control risk may be viewed as a constant.

Some of the most common business processes covered on the exam include:

- Revenue/receipts
- Expenditures/disbursements
- Payroll
- Inventory, especially manufactured inventory (since purchased inventory would be similar to expenditures/ disbursements as presented here)
- Fixed assets
- Investing/financing

As part of forming an understanding of a business process, the auditor may select a few transactions to trace them through the client's accounting system (ie, a **walkthrough**). The purpose is to get some feedback as to whether the auditor has accurately understood (and documented) the way the client entity is processing transactions. The walkthrough is not considered evidence or a form of documentation and should not be confused with tests of control.

Susan is performing a walkthrough of the payroll process at Imagine Inc. Based on her procedures, she determined that the risk of material mistatement would be high because the payroll department supervisor was responsible for:

- Examining authorization forms for new employees
- Comparing payroll registers with original batch transmittal data
- Authorizing payroll rate changes for all employees
- Hiring all subordinate payroll department employees

An auditor may assess a **high level of control risk** if **segregation of duties is absent** or impaired. The functions of authorizing, recording, custody, and comparison (ARCC) should each be performed by a different person. For example, **fraud** would be a concern if the **payroll department supervisor**, who **records payroll transactions**, also **authorizes pay rate changes**. To separate these duties, human resources should authorize any pay rate changes recommended by management.

The SCARI Framework

The SCARI framework is a tool to analyze the audit considerations of internal control policies and procedures in each business process cycle. Internal controls (specifically, "control activities") should be "SCARI" to those who want to break the rules or commit fraud!

This memory aid helps students recall some basic points of emphasis that are useful to auditors in looking at the relative strength or weakness of controls in a business transaction cycle.

The SCARI Framework

S   **Segregation of Duties** – This is also referred to as separation of duties and involves separating incompatible functions to the extent possible. The same employee should not normally

1. authorize transactions (executive function),
2. have access to the related assets (custody function), and
3. perform accounting activities (record keeping function) in the ordinary course of duties

C   **Controls** (Physical Controls) – Access to assets (and to important accounting documents and computer systems) should be limited to authorized personnel. In addition, assets should be periodically counted, as appropriate, and compared to the corresponding accounting records for agreement. This is important in safeguarding assets and in establishing accountability for assets.

A   **Authorization** – Transactions should be executed in accordance with management's authorization.

R   **Reviews** (Performance Reviews) – Actual performance should be compared to appropriate budgets and forecasts. Internal data should be compared to external sources of information as appropriate. Analyses of relationships should be performed, investigated, and corrected, as needed.

I   **IT** – Information technology (IT) controls consist of two basic categories:

1. General controls, which are policies and procedures that have widespread effect on many specific applications
2. Application controls, which refer specifically to the processing of particular computer applications

Examples of Documentation

 Refer to section 10.02 for a discussion of the types of procedures that can be performed to obtain an understanding of the client's control system, including IT controls. The following section includes several images of different types of documentation. You must be able to read and understand these documents for the exam.

Flowchart Symbols

Flowcharts and business process diagrams

Symbol	Description	Symbol	Description
	Manual operation (prepare, compare, or match)		Manual input (keyboard)
	Computer operation or process (print PO)		Input or output (general ledger)
	Document (invoice, PO, error listing)		Magnetic tape (sequential access storage)
	On-page connector (to connect to another location without a connecting line)		Off-page connector (eg, from customer)
	A decision (granting credit, if/then/else)		Off-line storage (file by name, date, order number)
	Magnetic disc storage (database)		On-line storage (disc, drum)
	Start/finish		Direct access storage

Data flow diagrams

Symbol	Description	Symbol	Description
▭	Origin/destination of data	◯	Process
═══	Data storage	→	Data flow

Entity-relationship diagrams

Symbol	Description	Cardinality notation	Relationship description
▭	Entity	——	One to one
◇	Relationship	—<	One to many
◯	Attribute	>—<	Many to many

Business process flowcharts

Sales system flowchart example

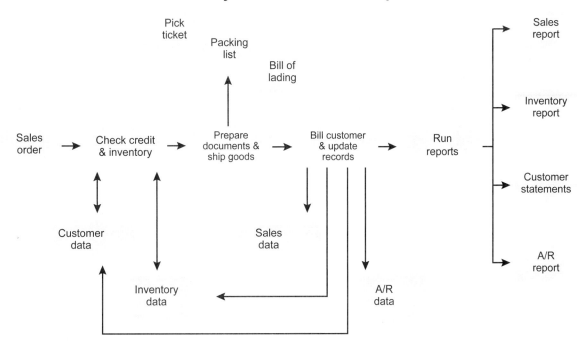

Collections process diagram example

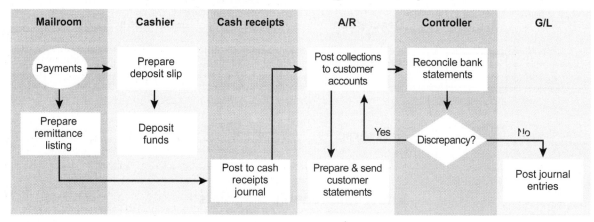

ER diagram example

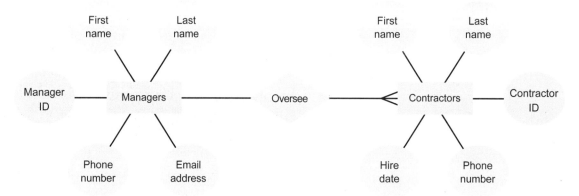

Data flow diagram example

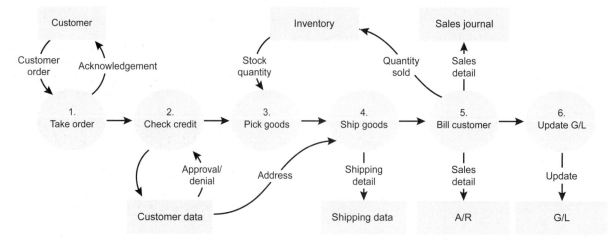

Business Process: Revenue Cycle

Overview

The revenue cycle generally consists of the following six business processes, which can be grouped into three main categories:

		Sales returns	**Collections**
Sales orders			
Credit checks	Shipping	Billing	

The following section will break out the cycle by sales and then collections.

Flow Chart of Typical Internal Controls for Sales

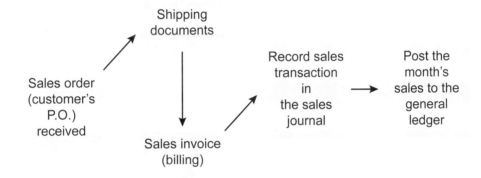

Internal Control Objectives for Sales

The objectives of internal controls in this area are to provide reasonable assurance that:

- Goods and services are provided in accordance with management's authorization (and based on approved orders)
- Terms of sale (including prices and any discounts) are in accordance with management's authorization
- Credit terms and limits are properly established (as authorized)
- Deliveries of goods and services result in accurate and timely billings
- Any sales-related discounts and adjustments (including returns) are in accordance with management's authorization

Control Considerations for Sales

The audit considerations section will be used to demonstrate how the SCARI framework is applied to different business processes.

 Although the text will include detailed examples of controls, leveraging the SCARI framework and applying it to different business processes is a better way of preparing for the exam than just memorizing the list in the book. Remember, every company is different and they could have different controls than listed.

The entity's control activities should address:

Segregation of duties (SOD)—Separate the execution (authorization), record-keeping (accounting), and custody (access) functions.

- Credit to customers should be granted by an independent department (separate from sales staff which may be paid on commission and which may have an incentive to view everyone as creditworthy)

- An independent employee should review the statements to customers

- Returns should be accounted for by an independent clerk in the shipping/receiving area

Controls (Physical Controls)

- Computer passwords should be used to limit unauthorized access to the accounting systems

- Any inventory involved should be secured with access limited to authorized personnel

Authorization—The entity's transactions should be executed as authorized by management

- Management should review the terms of sales transactions and indicate that approval on the sales invoice (billing)

- Management should usually establish general approvals of transactions within specified limits and specifically approve transactions outside of those prescribed limits

- Management should approve the entity's adjusting journal entries

Reviews (Performance Reviews)

- The entity's recorded sales should be compared to appropriate budgets and forecasts

- Related accounting documents should be compared on a timely basis—for example, sales invoices and shipping documents should be compared to verify that the sales transactions were recorded in the proper period, which is referred to as proper cutoff

IT (Information Technology)—The auditor should agree the financial statement amount(s) to the applicable general ledger account(s).

- Important accounting documents (eg, shipping documents and sales invoices) should be prenumbered and the numerical sequence should be accounted for

- An aged trial balance for accounts receivable should agree with (or be reconciled with) the general ledger control account; the aging provides important information about the quality of the receivables and the need for follow-up audit procedures

Flow chart of typical internal controls for collections

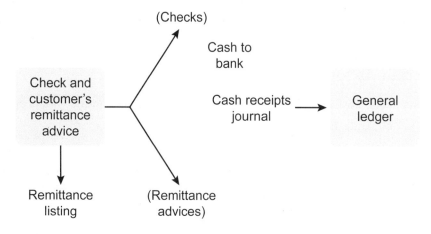

Internal Control Objectives for Collections

The objectives of internal controls in this area are to provide reasonable assurance that:

- Access to cash receipts records and accounts receivable records is limited to authorized personnel
- Detailed cash and account balance records are reconciled with control accounts and bank statements at least monthly
- All cash receipts are correctly recorded in the period received

Control Considerations for Collections

Segregation of Duties

- A listing of cash receipts (sometimes referred to as a remittance listing or log of cash receipts) is prepared upon opening the mail in the mail room; checks are restrictively endorsed immediately ("for deposit only . . . ")
- **Cash-related activities** (eg, opening the mail, making daily deposit, applying payments to customer A/R, and prepare bank reconciliation).

 Automation can also affect these processes. It can reduce expenses, increase efficiency, and decrease the incidence of errors in the process. However, it's important to consider the SOD and other control implications of using technology. Some examples include:

- **E-commerce** can potentially eliminate portions of the sales, billing, and collections processes
- A **point-of-sale (POS) system** with barcode scanners would reduce the possibility of error
- **Robotic Process Automation (RPA)** can repeat a set of tasks normally conducted by an employee using a graphical user interface (GUI). RPA could automate repetitive, rules-based tasks, such as opening an email with a sales order, extracting the data, and then entering that sales order into a computer application

Controls (Physical Controls)

- Employees with access to cash receipts should be "bonded," which is a type of insurance for which the employer pays an insurance premium and which involves background checks on the applicable employees
- Receipts should be deposited daily, not accumulated in someone's desk drawer for an occasional deposit
- Access to cash receipts (including access to documents) should be limited to those authorized
- The company might use a lockbox whereby payments from customers are directly received by the bank, thereby avoiding the company's mail room

Authorization

- Adjusting journal entries should be approved by management
- Bank reconciliations should be appropriately reviewed with the reviewer's approval indicated

Reviews (Performance Reviews)

- The initial cash receipts listing from the mail room should be compared to the total according to the cash receipts journal, and traced to that day's bank deposit to show that what was received was, in fact, deposited
- The cash accounts should be reconciled with the bank statements on a timely basis by someone not involved in handling cash receipts or updating the accounting records

IT (Information Technology)

- In general, there should be adequate documentation supporting transactions and account balances (important documents should be prenumbered and the numerical sequence properly accounted for)

- For cash transactions received on site, there should be adequate point of sale cash registers and use of prenumbered receipts

Revenue Cycle Documents & Records

Some of the documents and records (paper or electronic) that may be used to capture, distribute, and summarize information within the revenue cycle include the following:

- **Sales order**—The list of goods ordered by the customer along with the prices (from a **price list**) to be charged. Even if a customer has submitted their own purchase order, a sales order will be prepared, since these are prenumbered, making it possible to periodically verify that orders were processed

- **Pick ticket**—The list used by the warehouse clerk to gather the items ordered for shipping

- **Packing slip**—The list of all items included in a particular shipment

- **Bill of lading**—The shipping document that is signed by the courier, often a trucker, accepting goods from the shipping clerk

- **Shipping log**—List of shipments that can be used to track the status of orders

- **Sales invoice**—The bill that is prepared and sent to the customer after shipment to request payment. Before preparing a sales invoice, the billing clerk should compare the sales order and bill of lading to ensure they agree

- **Sales journal**—A special journal in which sales are posted

- **Subsidiary receivables ledger**—A ledger that lists the outstanding receivables with a separate record for each customer

- **Receiving log**—List of goods returned in the order they were returned

- **Receiving report**—Form completed by receiving personnel that indicates the quantity and condition of items returned

- **Credit memo**—Documents the return of goods and adjusts the customer's account and credit limit

- **Remittance advice (slip)**—A turnaround document included in an envelope with the check or other form of payment to indicate the purpose of the check

- **Remittance listing**—A summary of the money received that day. This may be called a prelist in some cases and is prepared by the employee first receiving the cash, which is usually the mailroom clerk

- **Cash receipts journal**—A special journal in which the remittance listings are posted

- **Deposit slip**—The document signed or stamped by the bank to acknowledge receipt of checks; it is periodically reconciled to postings into the cash receipts journal by an independent employee

- **Bank reconciliation**—Comparison of the cash balance according to the entity's records to the amount indicated by the bank that it is holding on behalf of the entity

 The use of electronic payments from customers reduces the risk associated with cash and check payment because the electronic payment goes directly to the bank and bypasses human intervention.

Business Process: Expenditures/Disbursements Cycle

The spending cycle of a business can generally be broken down into the following six business processes and grouped into three main categories:

Purchase orders			**Purchase returns**	**Cash disbursements**
Receiving	Inventory control	Accounts payable		

Internal control flowchart – purchases, accounts payable and expenditures

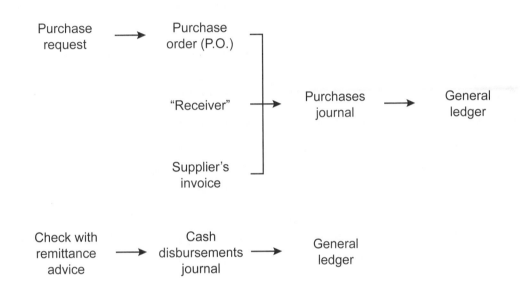

Internal Control Objectives – Purchases, Accounts Payable and Expenditures

The objectives of internal controls in this area are to provide reasonable assurance that:

- Goods and services are obtained in accordance with management's authorization and based on approved orders—considering quantity, quality, vendors, etc. This is usually handled by a separate Purchasing or Procurement department to centralize these activities

- The terms of acquisitions (including prices and quantities) are in accordance with management's authorization

- All goods and services received are accurately accounted for on a timely basis

- Adjustments to vendor accounts are made according to management's authorization

- Only authorized goods and services are accepted and paid for (and payments are timely to take advantage of any cash discounts available for prompt payment)

- Amounts payable for goods and services received are accurately recorded and properly classified

- Access to purchasing, receiving, and accounts payable records is limited to authorized personnel

- Disbursements are for authorized expenditures as approved by management

- Disbursements are recorded at the proper amounts and with the appropriate classifications

- Periodic comparisons are made between the supporting detailed accounting records (including bank reconciliations) and the general ledger control accounts

- Any adjusting journal entries for cash accounts are in accordance with management's authorization
- Access to cash and disbursement records is limited to authorized personnel

Control Considerations for Expenditures/Disbursements

Segregation of Duties

- A separate purchasing department handles the purchasing activities (after a duly approved request for goods or services has been received from the department making the request)
- The purchasing personnel (execution function) are independent of those in receiving (custody function) and in accounting (record-keeping function), including the accounts payable personnel. The accounts payable personnel should also be independent of those involved in processing the related cash disbursements
- Bank reconciliations are prepared by someone not having other involvement in handling cash receipts, cash disbursements, or record keeping

Controls (Physical Controls)

- There should be appropriate physical control over unused checks to limit access to authorized personnel
- Employees with the ability to initiate cash disbursements should be "bonded"
- Access to cash disbursements or to related documents should be limited to authorized personnel

Authorization

- All adjusting journal entries should be approved by management
- Only authorized personnel should be able to order goods and services on the company's behalf
- The department requesting the purchase of goods or services should indicate their acceptance of the goods or services received and approval, before payment is made
- Access to distribute funds, either by cash, check, or electronic should be limited to authorized personnel

Reviews (Performance Reviews)

- An appropriate employee should compare the suppliers' monthly statements with recorded payables
- An appropriate employee should compare the purchase order, "receiver," and vendor's invoice for agreement to establish that the invoice is for goods and services received and as authorized. (The invoice should be approved before payment is made and available cash discounts for prompt payment should be taken)

IT (Information Technology)

- Detailed records should be maintained to support the general ledger payable account
- Prenumbered purchase orders should be used (and the numerical sequence accounted for)
- Prenumbered checks should be used (and the numerical sequence accounted for)
- The supporting documents (including vendors' invoices) should be canceled as "paid" immediately upon payment to prevent double payments
- Two signatures should be required on checks. (Any signature plates should be kept in a secure place to prevent unauthorized use)

Expenditures/Disbursements Cycle Documents & Records

The documents and records involved in the spending cycle generally include:

- **Purchase requisition**—The internal request by the department in need for goods to be ordered by the purchasing department

- **Purchase order**—The external form mailed to the vendor to request that goods be delivered to the company. When the **purchase order** is prepared by the purchasing clerk to send to the vendor, additional copies are sent to the receiving department and the payables department
  - The receiving department copy is a **blind copy**; that is, it does not include price or quantities to ensure that the receiving department will perform an **independent count** of the goods delivered
  - The payables clerk compares the purchase order and receiving report with the vendor invoice to ensure they agree before preparing the payment voucher

- **Packing slip**—The list of all items included in a shipment

- **Bill of lading**—A shipping document that is signed by the receiving clerk, accepting goods from the courier

- **Receiving report**—The document prepared in the receiving department to note the quantity and condition of the items received. This report is signed by the courier to acknowledge the goods that have been delivered to the company

- **Receiving log**—A list of all receipts in the order they were received

- **Purchase (vendor) invoice**—The document received from the vendor indicating the goods the vendor claims to have shipped. This is the same document that is known as the sales invoice when considered from the vendor's side of the transaction

- **Invoice register**—A listing of all invoices received from vendors

- **Payment voucher**—The document prepared by the payables clerk to request that a check be issued for payment to a vendor
  - The check for payment is usually prepared by a clerk in the treasury department who doesn't have signature authority. They will provide the **unsigned check** along with the **payment voucher** and **supporting document** to the treasurer for signature. The treasurer makes sure the check **agrees** with the voucher and other documents before signing
  - Immediately after signing, the treasurer **cancels** the **supporting documents** (so that they won't accidentally be processed again), places the check in the envelope, seals it, and arranges for mailing

- **Purchase journal (or voucher register)**—A listing of all payment vouchers generated by the company

Business Process: Payroll Cycle

Overview

The personnel & payroll cycle can be broken down into three basic categories of business processes:

Hiring	**Payroll**	**Terminations**
	Time recording Cash disbursements	

These processes, however, are normally spread across four different departments to segregate the duties properly.

Department	Authorize Personnel	Recording Accounting	Custody Treasurer	Comparison Controller
Duties	Hire & fire Salary rates	Calculate pay	Signs & distributes payroll Custody of cash	Bank reconciliations

Flow chart of typical internal controls for payroll

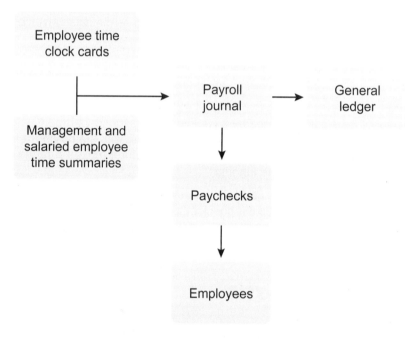

Internal Control Objectives for Payroll

The objectives of internal controls in this area are to provide reasonable assurance that:

- Payroll withholdings and deductions are based on appropriate supporting authorizations
- Compensation is made only to valid employees at authorized rates and for services actually rendered
- Gross pay, withholdings, deductions, and net pay are correctly computed
- Payroll costs and liabilities are appropriately classified and summarized in the proper periods
- Appropriate comparisons are made of personnel, payroll, and work records at reasonable intervals
- Net pay and related withholdings are remitted to the appropriate employees and agencies
- Access to sensitive personnel files and payroll records is limited to authorized personnel

Control Considerations for Payroll

Segregation of Duties

- The following activities should be performed by different personnel when circumstances permit:
  - Establishing and maintaining employee files in the personnel department
  - Timekeeping
  - Payroll preparation and updating the accounting records
  - Check distribution
  - Reconciling the payroll bank account with the general ledger account

- The treasurer should typically sign the payroll checks

- An appropriate departmental supervisor should distribute the payroll checks to employees in that department

- Unclaimed checks should be controlled. That is, they should be returned to treasury, secured, and eventually destroyed, if not claimed within an appropriate time

Controls (Physical Controls)

- Access to personnel files (containing sensitive information) should be limited to authorized personnel

- Access to payroll checks should be limited to authorized personnel

- Personnel with access to payroll checks should be bonded

Authorization

- Payroll should be authorized by a responsible official

- Payroll computations should be verified by an independent person

- Overtime payments should be approved by management

- Payroll for management should also be appropriately reviewed and approved

- Changes made to personnel information (eg, address, back account) is authorized by employee

Reviews (Performance Reviews)

- A company should maintain current and accurate payroll information (which should be periodically matched with information in the personnel files)

- The payroll checks written should be reconciled to the payroll register, serving as the supporting accounting record for each payroll period

- Other appropriate reconciliations should be made on a timely basis: for example, in a manufacturing environment, someone should reconcile the job cost time sheets to time clock cards. (For strict internal control purposes, a company should use time clocks where possible)

IT (Information Technology)

- Payroll checks should be prenumbered (and the numerical sequence accounted for)

- A company should maintain a separate checking account specifically for payroll transactions to establish more accountability and control over these important transactions

Payroll Cycle Duties, Documents & Records

- **Personnel (Human Resources)**—HR is responsible for **authorization**
  - HR is involved with personnel **records** and all **hiring forms**, including **forms** for payroll **deductions**
  - HR approves changes in **pay rates**
  - HR is also involved in the termination process. It is essential that they promptly send employee **termination notices** to the payroll department
- **Employee**—The employee prepares a **timecard** and submits it to the supervisor for authorization. The timecard is then sent to the payroll department
- **Treasurer**—The treasurer is responsible for **custody**
  - The treasurer authorizes electronic payroll distribution
  - If actual checks are used, they are submitted to the treasurer for signature and distribution to employees
  - Unclaimed checks should not be returned to the payroll department. Unclaimed paychecks should be retained until they are either distributed or voided
  - If payment of wages is in cash, employees should be required to sign a receipt for the amount received
- **Payroll accountant**—Payroll accountants are responsible for **recording**.
  - They examine and then update records based on authorization forms for hiring, firing, and pay rates received from personnel
  - They calculate payroll based on timecards and other reports approved by appropriate supervisors. They enter all timecard and wage rate information into the payroll register
  - They also prepare a payroll cost allocation based on the timecard information. The payroll cost allocation is used to distribute payroll costs over the various accounts affected
  - They prepare vouchers for payment
  - Finally, payroll is recorded in the payroll journal (or in the general ledger for smaller entities)
- **Controller**—As an overall verification of custody controls over cash, the controller should prepare monthly **bank reconciliations (comparison)** to verify that there were no errors made

Key Documents & Records

- Personnel records
- Hiritng & deduction authorization forms (W-4)
- Timecards
- Payroll register
- Paychecks
- Payroll cost allocation
- Bank reconciliations

Business Process: Production/Manufacturing Inventory Cycle

Internal Control Objectives for Production/Manufacturing Inventory

The objectives of internal controls in this area are to provide reasonable assurance that:

- The resources obtained and used in production (including raw materials, work-in-process, and finished goods) are accurately recorded on a timely basis

- Transfers of finished products to customers or others are accurately recorded

- Related expenditures are appropriately classified

- Access to all categories of inventory (and inventory-related documents) is limited to authorized personnel

- Comparisons of actual inventory on hand are made to recorded amounts at least annually

Control Considerations for Production/Manufacturing Inventory

Segregation of Duties

- To the extent possible, the company should separate the authorization of inventory- related transactions, the custody of (or access to) inventory, and the accounting recordkeeping activities

- Sales returns (inventory) should be immediately counted by the receiving clerk and a receiver (ie, a receiving document) prepared to verify the quantity and condition of the goods received

Controls (Physical Controls)

- Access to the inventory should be limited to authorized personnel (the inventory should be physically secured with access restricted to personnel having authorized keys or passcodes)

- Access to the important accounting documents, including applicable shipping documents, should be limited to authorized personnel

Authorization

- The acquisition and distribution of inventory should be consistent with management's authorization

- Management should establish general approvals of transactions within specified limits, and specifically approve transactions above those limits

- Any adjusting journal entries (including sales returns and allowances, or adjustments to inventory, such as write-downs) should be approved by management

Reviews (Performance Reviews)

- Actual inventory should be compared periodically to recorded inventory (and any unusual differences should be investigated)

- In a manufacturing context, appropriate reconciliations should be made of underlying accounting records (including applicable job order cost sheets or process cost worksheets) to the applicable inventory-related general ledger accounts

IT (Information Technology)

- The company should use prenumbered purchase orders for raw materials and components of production, along with prenumbered receivers, the receiving document. (The numerical sequence of these documents should be properly accounted for)

- The company should consider using a perpetual inventory system for items with high cost per unit

- The company should maintain adequate support for related general ledger control accounts

Production/Manufacturing Inventory Cycle Duties, Documents & Records

The results of **production planning** will determine what, how, when, and how many products will be produced in addition to the resources that will be needed to do so. This can be broken down into the following three processes:

- **Engineering**—In this process, engineers will provide the designs and specifications of products as well as the methods for producing the products. The following documents will also be prepared:

  ○ **Bill of materials**—A list of materials and parts needed for production of a product

  ○ **Operations list**—A list of the processes to perform to produce a product

- **Capital budgeting**—This process will determine the budget for resources (generally fixed assets) needed for production

- **Scheduling**—This process determines when production activities will occur while trying to meet customer demand, coordinate with the availability of materials and resources, and minimize down time. The following documents will be prepared:

  - **Production order** (or work order)—This document authorizes the production of a product, which may be initiated by a sales forecast or a sales order

  - **Production schedule**—This document specifies the timing of a production run

Business Process: Investing/Financing Cycle

Overview

The investing and financing cycle deals with transactions involving acquisition and disposal of assets other than inventory and transactions with creditors and shareholders. Since there are typically very few transactions in these areas in a typical year for a client, an auditor will often find it most efficient to ignore the I/C structure and simply test the few transactions that took place. In this case, the private company auditor may:

- Not test the controls

- Assess risk of material misstatement (RMM) at the same level as inherent risk, assuming that control risk is at the maximum level, generally resulting in a high RMM

- Reduce detection risk by performing extensive substantive tests

In those less frequent cases where a large number of transactions has occurred, the auditor may find it more efficient to rely on the I/C structure rather than test the numerous transactions that took place. In this case, the auditor will:

- Test the controls to determine their effectiveness

- Reduce RMM based on the results of the tests of controls

- Accept higher detection risk by performing only limited substantive tests

Internal Control Objectives for Investing/Financing

The objectives of internal controls in this area are to provide reasonable assurance that:

- Transactions involving investments and financing are accurately recorded and classified on a timely basis; and as authorized by management

  - **Investing**— As used here, this refers to decisions related to the composition of the company's portfolio of investment assets, both current and noncurrent

  - **Financing**—This refers to decisions related to the structure of the company's noncurrent liabilities and stockholders' equity sections of the balance sheet

- Investment assets should be reasonably secure from loss with procedures established to monitor the associated risks. Access should be limited to authorized personnel with appropriate segregation of duties

- Supporting detailed records should be maintained and compared periodically to actual investment-related assets of the company

- Any adjusting journal entries related to investment-related assets, liabilities, or stockholders' equity are approved by management

Control Considerations for Investing/Financing

Segregation of Duties

- Definitions, limits, and constraints on investment activities should be reviewed regularly by those who do not authorize transactions

- It is generally best to have an independent trustee maintain possession of securities so that they are safeguarded from all misappropriation by company employees

- Regular reconciliations to control account balances should be performed

  - The internal auditor makes a list of securities in bank safe deposit boxes and compares them with the securities listed in the records

  - The treasurer vouches the agreement of broker advices on purchases with canceled checks

  - The controller determines that debt securities are classified in the records correctly as trading securities, available-for-sale securities, or held-to-maturity securities, based on management decisions as to the intent of holding them

  - The recorded values of investments are periodically compared to current market prices

  - The investments on hand and held by custodians are periodically reconciled to their recorded amounts

Controls (Physical Controls)

- The entity maintains physical custody of investments in a secure physical location. Requiring two officers to be involved in access is common

Authorization

- Senior management should authorize investment transactions

Reviews (Performance Reviews)

- Controls should be regularly reviewed by senior management or some independent body. Senior management examines securities on hand to ensure that they are registered in the name of the company or confirms such with custodians of the investments

 With the investing/financing cycle, many of the following control activities will typically be applied by management or other employees at a very high level. This reflects the extremely large value and great danger of fraud in connection with marketable securities.

Business Process: Fixed Assets Cycle

Internal Control Objectives for Fixed Assets

The objectives of internal controls in this area are to provide reasonable assurance that:

- Transactions involving property, plant, and equipment are accurately recorded and classified; and are in accordance with management's authorization

- Estimates used in the determination of depreciation, depletion, and amortization of the assets' cost basis are reasonable and consistent over time; any changes should be properly approved

- Fixed assets are reasonably secure from loss with appropriate property insurance in force

- Supporting detailed records are maintained and periodically compared to the assets on hand

- Any adjusting journal entries related to fixed assets are approved by the management

IT System Components

 Representative Task (Application): Obtain an understanding of an entity's IT infrastructure (eg, ERP, cloud computing or hosting arrangements, custom or packaged applications) and document the procedures performed to obtain that understanding.

It is important for an auditor to understand an organization's IT structure. The identification of key IT system components stems from this process.

IT system components

Infrastructure: Physical or virtual resources that support an IT environment					
Facilities	Servers	Monitoring	Storage	Networks	Devices

Software: applications and system programs						
Operating systems	Middleware	Utilities	Databases	Web-based applications	Computer based applications	Mobile device applications

Data: Information that is generated and used by a system and software			
Files	Tables	Records	Relationships

People: Internal and external personnel involved in the management, operation, and security of an IT environment					
Board of directors	IT management	Developers	Operators	Business units	Vendors

Procedures: Processes by whicih activities are performed	
Automated	Manual

Infrastructure

Infrastructure includes the physical and virtual **hardware** that are the tangible parts of an IT system. Organizations may use infrastructure housed at their own facility (**on premises**) or at another facility connected by the Internet (**cloud**). Organizations may manage their cloud services directly or outsource them to external vendors.

Common infrastructure components include:

- **Facilities**—The physical building where IT infrastructure is found, including systems for security and environmental monitoring. Organizations may keep IT infrastructure at one or more facilities owned by them or an external vendor. Security guards and cameras monitor facilities to detect unauthorized access or disasters, such as fires

- **Server**—Servers are powerful computers that store, process, and manage data for multiple users and devices. They may be physical or virtual. Organizations may use multiple servers dedicated to performing distinct functions. For example, servers can run databases, host websites, manage email, or store files

- **Internal storage**—Hardware within a computer system that stores data inside the device for later use. Common examples of internal storage include a hard drive or video card

- **External storage devices**—Organizations may use network-attached storage devices and cloud storage for operational and backup purposes. Magnetic tape, flash drives, and external hard drives are some of the devices used for saving data outside of computers and servers

- **Networking equipment**—Networking equipment manages communications between devices, wired local area networks (LANs) or wireless local area networks (WLANs), and the Internet. Such equipment includes routers, switches, firewalls, wiring, and other security protection systems

- **End-point devices**—Hardware that allows the intended end user to interact with software and data. End-user devices include desktop computers, laptops, tablets, and even smartphones. For example, an employee can access their email through a laptop or tablet

- **Input and output devices**—These devices allow for communication between the computers and/or users. Basic input devices include a scanner, keyboard, and light pen (ie, a stylus). Certain input devices, such as barcode readers, can automate data entry and speed up business processes. Output devices include monitors, printers, and speakers

A simple, **on-premises IT infrastructure** may include the following components:

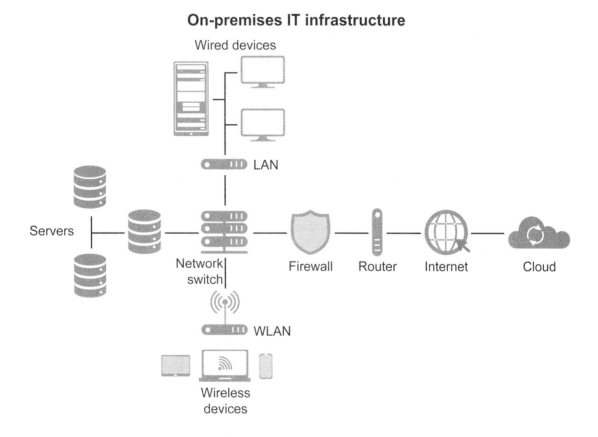

On-premises IT infrastructure

Software

Software refers to computer programs that run hardware, process data, and execute tasks. While hardware is a physical component, software includes instructions written in code. **Source code** is written in a **programming language**, which is a set of commands, instructions, and other syntax.

Software programs come in a wide range and may be categorized as:

- **Application software**—Computer programs that perform end-user functions. Applications may be web-based, computer-based, or cloud-based. Examples include operational systems, security software, enterprise resource planning (ERP) systems, accounting information systems (AIS), data analysis programs, and software to create documents or spreadsheets. Organizations may develop applications in house or purchase software made by external parties

- **System software** includes programs that run the system and direct its operations. System software, along with the supporting hardware, is used to create a **computing platform**. Despite being a vital component of the computer system, system software runs in the background and is often unnoticed by the end user. The two major categories of system software are:

  ○ **Operating system (OS)**—System software that regulates a computer's basic operations. The OS manages an application's use of computer hardware, as well as how users interact with their computers. Microsoft Windows is a well-known OS

  ○ **Utility programs** support and improve the efficiency of a computer system

System utility software

Middleware	Runtime	Database management system (DBMS)	Antivirus and antimalware
Services that help different software programs communicate with each other	Enables the execution of applications by turning programming code into machine code	Creates, reads, updates, and deletes information in a database	Protect computer systems from malicious software such as viruses, worms, and Trojans

Backup software	System monitoring and diagnostic tools	Password managers	Automation software
Creates and manages backups to prevent data loss	Monitor the performance of a computer system, including detecting and correcting problems	Securely store and manage passwords so users do not have to remember them	Automates repetitive tasks to increase productivity

Networks

A computer network is a group of connected computers, servers, network devices, or other devices that share resources. Networks can vary in size from two devices (as with home networks) to devices around the world. The **Internet** is a worldwide network that allows any computer system to link to it through an electronic gateway.

Types of networks

Local area network (LAN)	Wireless area network (WLAN)	Virtual private network (VPN)
Connects devices in a building or geographical area through hardwiring, such as Ethernet cables	Connects devices using wireless technology such as, Wi-Fi and bluetooth	Connects devices to the Internet through secure encryption

The following hardware is necessary to create and connect to a network:

- **Network switch**—Connects all the devices on an entity's computer network by moving data between the devices

- **Gateway**—A device on a network that serves as an entrance to another network. For example, to connect to the Internet, a device must first connect to a gateway computer at the Internet service provider (ISP). This computer serves as the first router, connecting to the rest of the Internet. Common gateways include:

- **Routers**—Specialized devices that receive data packets from one network and send them toward a destination network, using the best path. For example, a router may transmit data packets between a LAN or WLAN and an ISP

The Internet consists primarily of a series of routers used to transmit information between all the computers connected to the Internet. For example, when a computer in California connects to a website in Australia, there might be ten computers between them acting as intermediary routers. When parts of the Internet go down, most people never notice because the routers find another way (route) to get the information to its destination.

- **Firewall**—A computer program (software) or physical device (hardware) that prevents unauthorized users from accessing a system, thus limiting the transmission of media. The concept of a firewall is like living in a gated community: To enter, a homeowner must scan their badge to gain access to the neighborhood. In the same way, a firewall blocks unauthorized access to a company's network

Accounting Information Systems (AIS)

An information system is a formal process for gathering data, converting the data into information, and distributing that information to users. An **accounting information system (AIS)** collects, stores, and processes financial data. AIS outputs include reports that managers and other stakeholders (investors, lenders, managers, auditors, and regulators) use to make business decisions.

Accounting information systems serve three main purposes:

1. **Gather and store information** about financial activities. This includes extracting transaction data from source documents and posting entries to ledgers or journals.
2. **Supplying data to make decisions**, such as generating financial statements and managerial reports.
3. **Ensuring internal and IT application controls** are in place.

Accounting information system functions

Accounts payable	Accounts receivable	Subsidiary ledgers
General ledger	Financial statements	Taxes
Budgets	Analysis	Reconciliation

Enterprise Resource Planning (ERP)

An enterprise resource planning (ERP) system is a group of **software modules** that manage and automate business operations. ERP systems are ordinarily prebuilt (ie, packaged, off the shelf), residing **on premises** or in the **cloud**. Cloud offerings range from full web-based software-as-a service (SaaS) applications to those that only host data.

Popular ERP applications include Oracle NetSuite, Sage, Microsoft Dynamics, SAP, and Oracle JD Edwards. Each vendor offers various modules that an organization can buy and add on, based on their needs and budget.

Common ERP modules include:

Each module connects to a single **relational database,** which has a uniform data structure. A single, well-defined **data structure** provides a framework for standardization and data integrity throughout the organization. Relationships (associations) between **resources, events, and agents (REA)** create give-and-take (debit-and-credit) workflows that span ERP modules. **Unified Modeling Language (UML)** diagrams make it easier to visualize the connections between database tables; these diagrams may also be called **entity relationship diagrams (ERD)**.

Example of ERP database relationships: UML diagram

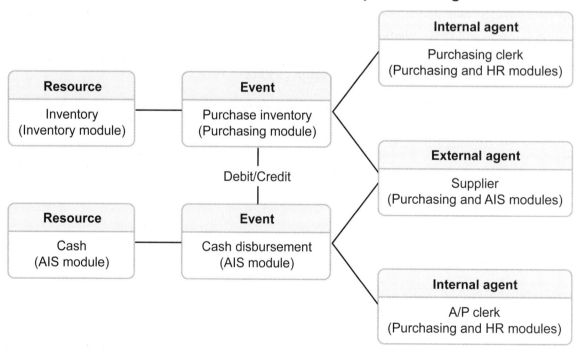

Shared data enable the exchange of information between ERP modules while preventing duplication and errors (ie, one fact, one place). Every individual within the company can access the same data from a **single source of truth**. The central collection of data for widespread use is a **fundamental ERP principle**. A single source of truth improves business insight (eg, real-time reports, dashboards), collaboration, and efficiency while lowering operational costs.

Risks of ERP systems include:

- **Implementation risks**—Implementation of a new ERP system may disrupt operations because of its pervasiveness and complexity

- **Improper segregation of duties**—A unified ERP system that joins business functions can cause an improper segregation of duties, decreasing internal controls that mitigate the risk of loss

- **Data management risks**—Complex data structures (eg, tables, relationships) used within an ERP can inhibit access to data or make changes difficult

- **Business process risks**—Use of packaged ERP software may require changes to business processes. This can increase process interdependence risk, where one business process becomes a single point of failure for the entire system

- **Financial reporting risks**—ERP systems record transactions and events that flow to financial statements. Management must ensure that the software includes internal controls to prevent, detect, and correct material misstatements

- **Security, availability, and processing integrity risks**—Unauthorized access, as well as unavailable or incorrect data, threaten the integrity of an ERP system

- **Confidentiality and privacy risks**—Disclosure of sensitive or personal information can have legal and regulatory consequences, such as lawsuits or fines

Packaged vs. Custom Software

Regardless of the system used, it will typically be categorized as packaged or custom. **Packaged applications** are purchased applications that a company can pretty much install and use. It already has the functionality the organization needs. It is often referred to as off-the-shelf software.

Custom applications are developed by, or at the behest of, an enterprise to meet specific business needs. People may refer to these systems as home-grown or developed in-house. These applications may serve similar business functions as those provided by packaged applications or fulfill a business need where no suitable packaged application is available.

Custom applications tend to be more **expensive** overall than their packaged counterparts; however, they offer more **flexibility** along with the ability to better conform with established business processes and best practices.

Custom applications can present a challenge to an auditor since they usually require the development of custom audit packages. In addition, complexities in defining the audit scope can arise when considering the custom application system and its interfaces with other applications.

	Packaged applications	Custom applications
Purpose	Mass produced for general use	Custom produced for specific use
Upfront costs	Lower	Higher
Ownership	Licensed	Wholly owned
Features	May not meet all business requirements	Should meet all business requirements
	Difficult to customize	Can alter as required
Business processes	General business processes that conform to best practices	Customized business processes
	Mature	Varies
Maturity model	Tested in a variety of settings	Tested in a development setting

Cloud Computing

Overview

Cloud computing is a method of accessing on-demand computer resources and applications over the Internet. It allows organizations to use distributed computing and storage for applications, data processing, and infrastructure services. Organizations that use cloud computing may manage the cloud service themselves, pay a third party **cloud service provider (CSP)** to supply services (infrastructure, applications, networking), or combine those two approaches.

- Traditional (on-premises) infrastructure involves using IT components within a physical **data center** or computing facility owned by the organization. This setup may be preferable when it is necessary to keep full control over infrastructure and security. Another benefit of traditional infrastructure is that the organization has access to the data in case of network issues or Internet outages. On-premises infrastructure is more expensive than the cloud as it requires organizations to maintain physical space, support staff, and technology components

- **Cloud computing IT infrastructure** has the same components as an on-premises setup; however, the organization accesses them virtually through an Internet connection. In cloud computing, hardware that would normally be physically on-site is made accessible online through a process called virtualization. **Virtualization** allows the creation of **virtual machines** that clients can access on a single physical server. For example, one physical server could host multiple virtual servers

Traditional vs. cloud computing

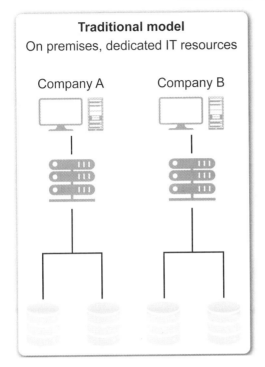

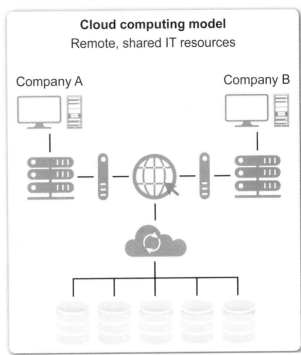

Making the decision to use a third-party service provider for cloud computing services requires weighing the advantages and disadvantages. The advantages of using a cloud service provider (CSP) include:

- **Cost savings**—Cloud computing allows the organization to save costs by not having to buy and support the same infrastructure and staff needed for an on-premises model. In addition, the organization pays only for the resources used. Cloud computing also results in tax savings because the associated costs are expensed instead of capitalized

The cost of cloud computing and applications is lower in a **multi-tenant architecture**, where a single instance of software runs on shared servers. Multi-tenancy is common with cloud-based applications sold by developers to end users. However, shared resources increase the risk of data leakage. **Single-tenant architecture**, in which a single instance of software runs on a dedicated server, is more secure but higher in cost.

Single tenant	Multi-tenant
• Hardware and software that serves one customer	• Hardware and software that serves multiple customers
• Customer can control or configure	• Customer cannot control or configure
• Stronger security	• Reduced cost
• More reliable	• Less maintenance
• Easier to back up and restore	• Efficient use of resources

- **Accessibility**—Cloud resources can be made available to a variety of end-user devices and locations, so employees no longer need to be in the office to access work resources
- **Reliability**—Because CSPs have multiple clients using their cloud services, they must keep the cloud up and running so that it is available whenever their customers need it
- **Scalability**—Cloud computing allows customers to expand or reduce their services based on changes in the business environment. It also allows for faster implementation of those services

Despite the advantages, there are potential disadvantages that need to be considered before using a CSP:

- **Downtime or outages**—When a CSP experiences downtime, outages, or technical issues, users of their cloud services might not be able to perform business processes or access company information that depends on IT resources. However, CSPs typically offer a "guaranteed uptime" with credits to compensate for lack of availability

- **Security threats**—Cloud services are high-value targets for cyberattacks such as breaches and unauthorized access by external parties. Potential users should review the contract and **service level agreement (SLA)**, along with the CSP's system and organization controls (SOC) and other compliance reports, in order to understand its system and controls

- **Limited control**—Organizations have less control over contracted cloud services than traditional IT elements that would be under their domain. An action that would take an organization a few hours to complete may take the CSP several days or weeks, depending on the issue. Even a **cloud latency**—the delay between a user organization's request and the CSP's response—can harm the organization. In addition, the setup and data migration associated with cloud computing can take extensive amounts of time and limit the company's access to its data

- **Contracts**—Cloud users must pay special attention to contracts and SLAs with cloud service providers. Data transfer costs and the use of cloud-specific technologies can lock users in with a specific cloud provider. Cloud users should carefully evaluate the agreement and develop a withdrawal plan when negotiating a contract

Cloud Computing Models

Cloud computing varies based on the type of infrastructure, software, and services the CSP offers. There are three general **delivery** models:

Cloud computing models

Infrastructure as a service (IaaS)	Platform as a service (PaaS)	Software as a service (SaaS)

- **Infrastructure as a Service (IaaS)**—For IaaS, the CSP supplies infrastructure capabilities, which include hosting the data center, servers, network devices, and storage devices. Companies using this service maintain their systems remotely through the cloud, still managing their applications and operating systems while the third party CSP provides the infrastructure. Thus, IaaS allows organizations to control their infrastructure without having to buy and support the hardware on premises. A popular IaaS provider is Amazon Web Services (AWS)

- **Platform as a Service (PaaS)**—Organizations often use PaaS cloud services to support activities related to software development, analytics, or business intelligence. Besides providing the infrastructure services of IaaS, PaaS includes operating system and data management tools hosted on the cloud

- **Software as a Service (SaaS)**—SaaS is used to supply cloud-based application access to end users. It encompasses the same services that an organization would have with a traditional on-premises solution. The CSP manages application deployment, maintenance, configuration, and the underlying IT support structures. A commonly used SaaS accounting application is NetSuite; end users access NetSuite via the Internet instead of having to download the application on a computer. **Business Process as a Service (BPaaS)**, an extension of SaaS, involves outsourcing an entire business process, such as payroll, to a third party provider offering cloud services

Differences between service models

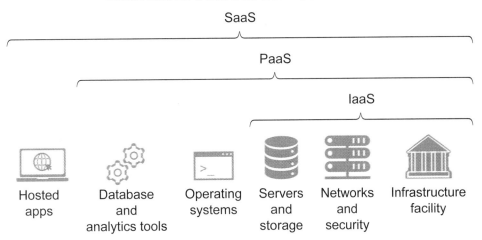

Management may not have direct access to the systems and subsystems hosted by a third party on the cloud and must rely on that CSP to keep a strong control environment. Therefore, management may require a **System and Organization Controls (SOC)** report which describes the CSP's system and controls.

Cloud Deployment Models

Cloud deployment models describe the ways cloud computing resources may be provided (ie, set up and configured). Each model offers a different level of service, cloud-hosting responsibilities, and ownership.

Cloud deployment models

Public cloud   Private cloud   Community cloud   Hybrid cloud

- **Public cloud**—In the public cloud deployment model, a third-party service provider owns and uses computing resources and allows multiple public users to share access to those resources via the Internet. Multi-tenancy associated with public cloud deployment results in cost savings, scalability, and efficiency. Popular public cloud services include Google's Cloud Platform Services, Microsoft Azure, and Amazon Web Services

- **Private cloud**—A private cloud configuration is set up for use by a single organization or single tenant. It can be managed by the organization itself or by a third-party service provider. Because only a single organization can access the resources for its internal use, private cloud deployment reduces the security risks associated with the public cloud. The private cloud owner manages the controls over data and data privacy. Costs for a private cloud are much higher than a public cloud

- **Community cloud**—A specific group of organizations with a common purpose may use a community cloud, with one of the members or a third party managing the cloud resources. For example, organizations in the health care industry might use a community cloud to share patient information; because of stringent health care legal requirements, they could configure the community cloud to ensure compliance with privacy laws specific to that business sector

- **Hybrid cloud**—Hybrid cloud deployment uses a combination of the public, private, and/or community models to fulfill specific data or processing requirements while taking advantage of the benefits of each model. For example, a company may use a public cloud service that supplies software applications while using a private cloud that hosts the data processing and storage needed for those applications

Advantages & Risks of Cloud-Based Service Arrangements

Advantages

- **Global accessibility**—Services are available to any location, including remote or home offices

- **Uniform deployment**—Users have a uniform experience and have the same version of all cloud-hosted applications

- **Centralized administration**—Administration, verification, and access can be controlled from a central location for all users and cloud-hosted applications

Risks

- **Security risks**—Cloud services are designed to be globally accessible and introduce unique identity and access management risks. Cyber threats, such as distributed denial-of-service attacks (DDoS), are also increased

- **Deployment risk**—In any cloud services arrangement, there are applications or hardware that the subscriber does not control. Updates and upgrades are controlled by the cloud services vendor

- **Service delivery risk**—Reliance on third parties for business processes introduces risks associated with the disruption of those services, which cannot be controlled by the cloud services subscriber

Financial Reporting Systems

 Representative Task (Application): Obtain an understanding of IT applications that are, directly or indirectly, the source of financial transactions or the data used to record financial transactions (eg, how the entity uses IT applications to capture, store, and process information).

The auditor is particularly concerned with information systems relevant to financial reporting. Thus, the auditor should obtain an understanding of how:

- The *information systems* consist of methods and records used to *record, process, summarize, and report* the company's transactions to maintain accountability for the related accounts

- Individual duties and responsibilities related to I/C are established and *communicated* to involved personnel

- Transactions are initiated, authorized, and processed, including which components are performed manually and which are performed electronically

- Transactions, events, and conditions are reported

- Accountability is maintained for assets, liability, and equity, including the maintenance of records supporting information or specific items in the F/S

- The incorrect processing of transactions is identified and resolved

- Recurring and nonrecurring journal entries, unusual transactions, and other adjustments are identified and prepared

- System overrides or bypasses to controls are processed and accounted for

- Information is transferred from the processing systems to the general ledger

- Events and conditions, including depreciation and amortization of assets and collectability of receivables, are identified, and how information (ie, data) is captured

- F/S are prepared, including the development of estimates

- Information that is required to be disclosed is identified, accumulated, recorded, processed, summarized, and properly reported

During a walkthrough of the revenue process, a client mentions that credit checks are initiated after the sales orders are in their ERP system. Which of the following questions would **not be helpful** in understanding the source system of financial transactions for this cycle?

- How are sales orders entered into the ERP system?

- How are sales transactions initiated?

- Do all sales orders need to go through the credit check process?

- Does a point-of-sale (POS) system interface with the ERP to provide the sales orders?

An auditor must understand the entity and its environment. This includes identifying the IT systems that support financial transactions. Whether it's through the interview, observation, or review of documentation, the auditor must determine how an entity uses **IT applications** to **capture financial information**. Although the sales orders are within the ERP system, the auditor must determine where those transactions were initiated, either within the ERP system, other systems, or on paper. Knowing if all sales go through the credit check process does not help in identifying the *source* of the transaction.

Simulation

The following section will address the remaining representative tasks using a simulation to provide an example of how the AICPA may approach a task-based simulation (TBS) within this topic.

As you review the material, make sure to consider how the exam content could be altered. For example, instead of providing a flow chart, the question could be based on a narrative or I/C questionnaire. Alternatively, the question could be focused on a different business process or IT general controls (ITGC)s.

 The AICPA uses TBS questions to evaluate higher-level thinking. As you work through these, and other simulations, make sure to use your critical thinking skills. The answers will not be as straightforward as you have seen in multiple-choice questions.

Identifying Controls

 Representative Task (Analysis): Identify and document the relevant automated and manual controls within the flow of an entity's transactions for a significant business process and consider the effect of these controls on the completeness, accuracy, and reliability of an entity's data.

You are working for Roger S.P. CPAs. The accompanying partially completed flowchart depicts part of the revenue cycle of your client, Asher, Inc. Some of the flowchart symbols are labeled to indicate controls and records.

For symbols 1 and 2, select one response from all the answer lists and determine the type of control (manual or automated) of an entity's data. Each response in the list may be selected once or not at all.

Warehouse and shipping department

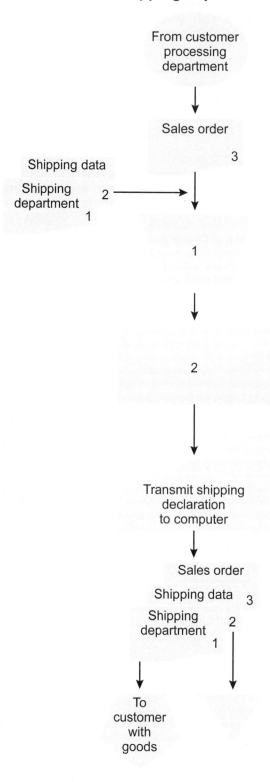

Possible Responses:

- Enter shipping data
- Verify agreement of sales order and shipping document
- Prepare aged trial balance
- To sales department
- Release goods for shipment

- Determine that customer exists
- Match customer purchase order with sales order
- Perform customer credit check
- Sales invoice
- Shipping file

Explanation:

Control	Type of control
1. Verify agreement of sales order and shipping document	Manual
2. Release goods for shipment	Automated

Testing the Design and Implementation of Controls

 Representative Task (Application): Perform tests of the design and implementation of relevant automated and manual transaction-level internal controls (eg, authorizations and approvals, reconciliations, verifications, physical or logical controls, segregation of duties).

 Representative Task (Evaluation): Conclude whether relevant automated and manual transaction-level internal controls are effectively designed and placed in operation.

Scenario

Manor Manufacturing has four manufacturing departments: extrusion, press, welding, and forging. The year under audit is Year 2. This is the second year that Manor has engaged Lotts & Files, CPAs, to perform the annual audit of its F/S.

Manor uses an in-house payroll department at its corporate headquarters to compute payroll data and authorize payments to its 517 employees. Payroll for salaried, commissioned, and hourly employees is processed biweekly. Rates and working conditions for hourly manufacturing employees are negotiated during the union contract negotiations, typically on an annual basis. In general, rate changes for other employees occur 90 days after their hire date and then once annually on June 30.

The controller indicates that nothing has changed in payroll processing since the previous year's audit. Based on documentation from this prior audit, a questionnaire will be developed to obtain an understanding of Manor's I/C and assess the risk of material misstatement.

Using the information provided, amend the underlined sentence in the questionnaire to help test the design and implementation of the control.

Draft Questionnaire

Manor Manufacturing
Internal Control Questionnaire—Payroll Segment
May 5, Year 2

Question	Yes	No
Are the employees who perform each of the following payroll functions independent of the other listed functions?		
• Calculating hours worked	○	○
• Preparing payroll data	○	○
• Approving final payroll amounts	○	○
• Reconciling payroll account	○	○

Excerpt from Prior Year Work Paper

Manor Manufacturing
Payroll Overview

Prepared by: Rick Lotts
Date: May 2, Year 1
Assisted by: Jan Aman
Date: April 27, Year 1
Reviewed by: BC
Date: January 2, Year 2

Each Manor employee is paid biweekly at latest by the Friday following the end of the pay period under one of three models: hourly, salary, and salary with a commission element. When year-end changes, vacation or sickness among personnel involved in completion of the payroll, or holidays do not interfere, payroll usually is processed before this deadline.

Hourly employees are paid based on their hourly rates with a premium for the second shift. They receive time and half for more than 40 hours up to 48 hours and double time for more than 48 hours in a work-week. The work week begins with the start of shift change (3:00) on Sunday for second shift and the end of shift change (3:30) on Sunday for the first shift.

Salaried staff aside from sales staff are paid a base salary based on attendance.

Sales staff are paid a base salary. They also get a commission ultimately based on collected sales revenues over an annual minimum. Rather than wait until the annual minimum is reached, a conservatively annualized projection of sales to date is made each month and compared to the annual minimum. If the projection is over the annual minimum, payments for that month are made in the first pay period of the next month. Sales staff receive a commission calculation statement each month.

When the sales staff separate from the company, the advance is not paid, but commissions accrue on previously made sales. These commissions are paid once payment is received from the related customers. If the sales staff separate from the company, with a net negative balance due to unpaid invoices, whether the advance is excused is decided on a case by case basis.

Options for Updating Questionnaire

a. Communicating new hire and separation information

b. Communicating separation information and approving salary, commission rates, and wage rates

c. Communicating new hire information and approving salary, commission rates, and wage rates

d. Communicating new hire and separation information and approving salary, commission rates, and wage rates

e. No Update - Keep "calculating hours worked"

Explanation

Duties are properly segregated when different people perform authorization, recording, or reconciling activities or have custody of assets. This section of the I/C questionnaire should be designed to ask if these functions are properly segregated. **"Communicating new hire and separation information and approving salary, commission rates, and wage rates"** would be the best question to assess the design on the control.

Function	Associated payroll activities
Authorize	Authorize salaries, commission rates, wage rates, the addition of newly hired employees to payroll, and the removal of those who have separated from the company
Record	Process payroll data (including information regarding hours worked and paid time off)
Have custody (ie, cash)	Approve distribution of cash from payroll account
Reconcile	Reconcile payroll account

The auditor would want to know that the **authorization** function is **performed by** someone who **does not record, reconcile, or have custody of asset**s and that the function's activities **include the addition and removal of employees** from payroll, as well as the **approval of salary** amounts, **commission rates, and hourly wage rates**. This segregation of duties helps ensure that valid employees are paid the approved amounts.

Documenting Conclusions

Based on the procedures performed and the evidence gathered, the auditor must conclude whether relevant automated and manual transaction-level internal controls are effectively designed and placed in operation.

Remember that this focus on procedures during this phase of the audit is to determine if the controls were **designed effectively and implemented.** Testing internal controls for operating effectiveness will occur later on in the process.

Payroll process

Control	Procedures performed & results	Conclusion
Processing new hire and separation information and approving salary, commission rates, and wage rates are segregated.	**When:** December 13, 2023 **Client Name:** June Cleaver, Human Resources **Procedures Performed:** Ava Costales, Senior Auditor, met with J. Cleaver to go over how employees are added and removed. During this process, she explained that the company limits her access to only adding users to the system and entering an individual's termination date. She stated that she did not have access to approve salaries, commissions rates, or wages, as this approval comes from the business. During the meeting, she logged into the PAS system and added a new employee, Dan Stone, who starts next week. J. Cleaver noted that once the employee is created, the salary and rate information must be entered by the individual's manager. She also went to the "Enter Salary & Wages" area in the system. Although she could see data, she did not have access to enter any salary or pay rate information.	Control was design effectively and was implemented.

10.04 Implications of Using a Service Organization

Overview

AICPA Guidance

The relevant AICPA guidance is provided by AU-C 402, *Audit Considerations Relating to an Entity Using a Service Organization*. The standard states that the user auditor's objectives, when the user entity uses the services of a service organization, are to:

- Obtain an understanding of the nature and significance of the services provided and their effect on the user entity's internal control relevant to the audit sufficient to assess the risks of material misstatement

- Design and perform audit procedures that are responsive to those risks

Definitions

Complementary User Entity Controls—Controls that management of the service organization assumes, in the design of its service, will be implemented by user entities, and which, if necessary to achieve the control objectives stated in management's description of the service organization's system, are identified as such in that description.

Service Auditor—A practitioner who reports on controls at a service organization.

Service Organization—An organization or segment of an organization that provides services to user entities that are relevant to those user entities' internal control over financial reporting.

Subservice Organization—A service organization used by another service organization to perform some of the services provided to user entities that are relevant to those user entities' internal control over financial reporting. (This SAS also applies to subservice organizations.)

Type 1 Report—Report on management's description of a service organization's system and the suitability of the design of controls.

Type 2 Report—Report on management's description of a service organization's system and the suitability of the design and operating effectiveness of controls.

User Auditor—An auditor who audits and reports on the financial statements of a user entity.

User Entity—An entity that uses a service organization and whose financial statements are being audited.

System and Organization Controls (SOC) Engagements

 Representative Task (Remembering & Understanding): Understand the differences between SOC 1® and SOC 2® engagements.

 Representative Task (Application): Identify and document the purpose and significance of an entity's use of a service organization, including the impact of using a SOC 1® Type 2 report in an audit of an entity's financial statements.

Service organizations (SO) are entities that provide services (eg, payroll, webhosting) to other entities. User entities will often use SO because they provide benefits such as cost savings and expertise. This outsourcing arrangement is significant because the user entity no longer has control over the activities performed by the SO.

For the purposes of the AUD exam, the services of a SO are relevant to the audit of a user entity when those services (and the controls over those services) affect the user entity's internal control over financial reporting.

 Let's say an audit client uses an SO to process payroll. That means that internal controls related to the payroll process will be performed by the SO, not the audit client. The client and the auditor need to understand the design of internal controls at the SO.

System and Organization Controls (SOC) reports provide assurance about a service organization's I/C relevant to the user entity. The user auditor can obtain a SOC report from the SO or the subservice organization.

 Which of the following standards applies to obtaining an understanding of the nature and materiality of transactions processed by a service organization for a nonissuer user entity's financial reporting processes?

- Statements on Auditing Standards
- Statements on Standards for Accounting and Review Services
- Statements on Standards for Consulting Services
- Statements on Standards for Attestation Engagements

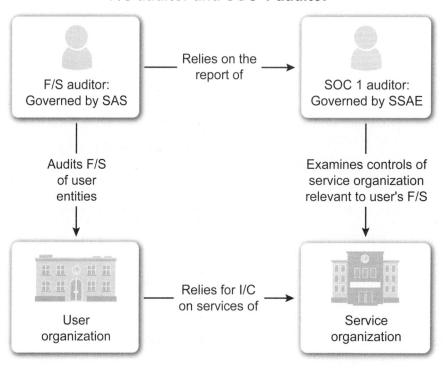

F/S auditor and SOC 1 auditor

The CPA **performing** a SOC 1 engagement (ie, works for the Service Organization) is governed by SSAE. However, the auditor **using** that SOC 1 report in a F/S audit is **governed by SAS**.

SSARS cover certain review engagements, preparations, and compilations, not audits or examinations of service organization controls. *Statements on Standards for Consulting Services* cover consulting engagements, not audits or examinations of service organization controls.

There are two primary categories of SOC examinations that are addressed in this chapter.

SOC 1®

SOC 1® reports—These reports address I/C relevant to the **user entity's financial reporting**. The reports help auditors of user entities understand or evaluate the SO's I/C over financial reporting. For example, controls reviewed might be ones that ensure a hospital's customers are properly billed.

SOC 1® is a **restricted report**. Intended users include the service organization, user entities, and user entity auditors.

Examples of service organizations who may need a SOC1® report

Transaction, payment, and payroll processors	Investment custodian or trust service providers	Retirement and employee benefit plan processors
Health insurance claim processors	Loan or mortgage servicers	SaaS, PaaS, and IaaS cloud service providers

SOC 2®

SOC 2® reports—These reports provide assurance on the service organization's controls over **trust services criteria (TSC)** (ie, security, availability, processing integrity, confidentiality, and privacy of the user entity's data). The SO can customize the SOC 2 engagement to include security and whichever additional TSC their user entities might want.

 For example, an SO providing cloud computing infrastructure services would likely have a SOC 2® report to provide assurance to its customers that their infrastructure is secure and available.

SOC 2® is also a **restricted report**. Intended users must have a direct relationship with the service organization and sufficient knowledge to understand the report. Direct relationships include user entities and user auditors, business partners and their auditors, prospective user entities and business partners, as well as regulators.

SOC 2® reports help user entities understand a service organization's system and controls. The use of SO may expose user entities to regulatory, operational, or financial risks. A SOC 2® report helps the user entity fulfill its oversight responsibilities. Prospective user entities may request a SOC 2® report prior to signing an agreement with a service organization.

Examples of service organizations who may need a SOC2® report

Customer support	Data centers	IT management and support services
Health insurance claim processors	Financial technology services (FinTech)	SaaS, PaaS, and IaaS cloud service providers

Service organization's controls are designed, implemented, and operated to provide reasonable assurance of achieving . . .

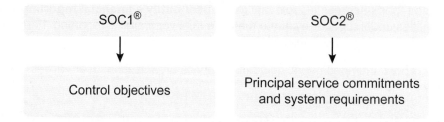

This difference in terminology is key in determining what is needed. From an external audit perspective, the SOC 1 control objectives are key.

Types of Reports

The service organization auditor can issue one of two types of reports:

	Type 1	Type 2
Examination scope →	As of a specified date	Throughout a period
Service organization management describes the system and asserts. . . →	Controls were suitably designed	Controls were suitably designed and operated effectively
Service auditor evaluates. . . →	Description of system and suitability of design of controls	Description of system, suitability of design of controls, and operating effectiveness of controls

A SOC 1® engagement is what user auditor cares most about. If the user organization is an **issuer or a nonissuer relying on controls**, the **SOC 1, the Type 2 report** would be the **most relevant**.

Service auditors report on the service organization's controls using a System and Organization Controls (SOC) report. All of the following information is contained in both Type 1 and Type 2 SOC reports except

- Information about tests performed
- Nature and scope of the audit work performed
- Management's acknowledgment of responsibility for internal controls
- Supporting services provided by another service company

Subject matter of System and Organization Controls (SOC) reports		
	SOC 1	**SOC 2**
Type 1	Design of controls relevant to user's **financial reporting**	Design of controls relevant to user's **operations**
Type 2	Design *and operating effectiveness* of controls relevant to user's **financial reporting**	Design *and operating effectiveness* of controls relevant to user's **operations**

Both SOC 1 and SOC 2 reports include the client's *management acknowledgment of responsibility* for the SO's I/C. Both types of reports also include information about the *nature and scope of the work* performed. Both types of SOC reports have a Type 1 and Type 2 report. Only a Type 2 report contains information about **tests performed** because only Type 2 reports include the **service auditor's opinion** on the controls' operating effectiveness.

Summary of SOC 1 and SOC 2

Examination	Reports on internal controls over:	Type	Control coverage	Users
SOC 1	Financial reporting	1	Design	• User entities
		2	Design and operating effectiveness	• User auditors
SOC 2	• Security • Availability • Processing integrity • Confidentiality • Privacy	1	Design	
		2	Design and operating effectiveness	• Management • Regulators

User Auditor Responsibilities

 Representative Task (Application): Use a SOC 1® Type 2 report to determine the nature and extent of testing procedures to be performed in an audit of an entity's financial statements.

A **SOC 1®** report provides assurance about the **service organization's controls** relevant to the **user entity's financial reporting**. If a CPA auditing the F/S of an entity that uses the services of the service organization for I/C intends to **rely on those controls**, the auditor will likely ask to see a SOC 1, **Type 2** report. This will allow the auditor to determine whether the service organization's controls that relate to the user entity's financial reporting operate effectively.

If the auditor determines it is *not possible* to provide reasonable assurance regarding a particular assertion using substantive testing alone, the auditor should determine if related internal controls are reliable. If the assertion relates to a process (eg, payroll) provided by a service organization that has not provided a SOC 1 report, the auditor will determine whether the entity under audit has established its own controls over the services of the service organization.

 For example, an entity using a payroll processing firm may establish controls (eg, reconciliation, recalculation) over the data transmitted to and from the service organization that would prevent material misstatements.

- If the auditor determines that those controls are operating effectively, the auditor may be able to obtain reasonable assurance and issue an unmodified opinion
- If the auditor is unable to obtain reasonable assurance on assertions relating to the client's payroll processing, the auditor must issue a disclaimer of opinion

Obtain an Understanding of the Services Provided by a Service Organization

When the user auditor intends to rely on the controls at the SO, those controls must be subjected to **tests of controls**, which may be accomplished by one or more of the following:

The user auditor should:

- Evaluate the design and implementation of relevant controls at the user entity related to the service organization's services
- Determine whether a sufficient understanding of the nature and significance of the service organization's services and their effect on the user entity's internal control relevant to the audit have been obtained to assess the risks of material misstatement

If the user auditor is **unable to obtain a sufficient understanding** from the user entity, the user auditor should obtain that understanding by:

- Obtaining and reading the service auditor's Type 1 or Type 2 report
- Contacting the service organization (through the user entity) to obtain specific information, or visiting the service organization and performing necessary procedures about relevant controls
- Using another auditor to perform procedures to provide the necessary information about controls at the service organization

Using a Type 1 or Type 2 report to support the user auditor's understanding

- The user auditor should be satisfied about (1) the service auditor's professional competence and independence and (2) the standards that the service auditor followed in issuing the report

- The user auditor should (1) evaluate whether the report provides sufficient appropriate evidence for understanding the user entity's relevant internal controls and (2) determine whether any complementary user entity controls identified by the service organization are relevant in assessing the risks of material misstatement

 A client uses a service organization to process its payroll. Which of the following statements is correct regarding the user auditor's use of the service auditor's report on internal controls placed in operation?

- The user auditor can use the service auditor's report to jointly determine the materiality level
- The user auditor can use the service auditor's report without inquiring about the service auditor's reputation
- The service auditor's report should be referred to in the report of the user auditor
- The user auditor can use the service auditor's report as audit evidence for the client's internal controls

Considerations when using a service auditor's SOC report

- Competency and independence of service auditor
- Adequacy of standards under which the report was issued
- Alignment of SOC report period with audit period
- Relevancy of report information to client's internal controls
- Materiality of client financial information managed by service organization

When an audit client uses an SO to process financial transactions (eg, payroll), the **user's auditor may use a SOC 1 report** to assess the client's ICFR. Any SOC 1 report will include the SO management's description of ICFR and the SO auditor's opinion on the ICFR design's suitability to meet control objectives. *Before using* the SOC 1 report as audit evidence, the user auditor should inquire about the SO auditor's reputation and professional competency. The user auditor should use the SOC 1 report *only* if the SO auditor is reputable.

The *user auditor* is solely responsible for the audit opinion regarding the client's financial statements. Therefore, the user auditor must determine materiality based on the client's ICFR and possibly information from the SOC 1 report. The user auditor's report should *not* reference the SO auditor's SOC report. This action could be interpreted as indicating a shared responsibility for the client auditor's procedures and resulting opinion.

Responding to the Assessed Risks of Material Misstatement

The user auditor should determine whether sufficient appropriate audit evidence is available at the user entity; and, if not, perform further audit procedures at the service organization.

- When the user auditor's risk assessment includes an expectation that controls at the SO are operating effectively, the user auditor should obtain evidence about such operating effectiveness by either obtaining a Type 2 report or performing appropriate tests of controls at the service organization (or using another auditor to perform those tests of controls)

- A user entity may outsource some or all of its finance function to a service organization. In that case, a significant portion of the audit evidence resides at the service organization. Necessary substantive procedures may be performed at the service organization by the user auditor or by the service auditor on the user auditor's behalf. The user auditor is still responsible for obtaining sufficient appropriate audit evidence

The user auditor should inquire of the user entity's management as to whether they are aware of any **fraud**, noncompliance with laws and regulations, or **uncorrected misstatements** at the SO affecting the financial statements of the user entity.

Reporting Issues to the User Auditor

Modified Opinion

If the user auditor is **unable to obtain sufficient appropriate audit evidence** about the services provided by the service organization relevant to the user entity's financial statements, the user auditor should **modify the opinion for a scope limitation**.

The user auditor may refer to the service auditor in the user auditor's report containing a modified opinion if that reference would be relevant to understanding the user auditor's modification. The user auditor should indicate that such reference does not change the user auditor's responsibility for that opinion.

Unmodified Opinion

The user auditor should not refer to the service auditor in the user auditor's report containing an unmodified opinion. The user auditor is responsible for the opinion expressed, and *no division of responsibility* is permitted.

10.05 Limitations of Controls and Risk of Management Override

Overview

 Representative Task (Remembering & Understanding): Understand the limitations of internal controls and the potential impact on the risk of material misstatement of an entity's financial statements.

 Representative Task (Application): Identify and document the risks associated with management override of internal controls and the potential impact on the risk of material misstatement of an entity's financial statements

Inherent Limitations of Internal Controls

Internal controls can provide only *reasonable assurance* of achieving an entity's objectives. That is, even with an effective system of I/C, the following **inherent limitations (COP)** may result in failures (ie, fraud and error):

- *Collusion*—Control activities that depend on segregation of duties will not be effective if those engaged in the segregated functions conspire with one another
- *Override by management*—Since management designs and implements the system of I/C, they are able to override it
- *Poor human judgment and errors*—If control procedures are erroneously applied, they will not be effective. I/C cannot be expected to prevent mistakes in human judgment

 Additional information on the limitations of a system of internal control can be found under section 10.01.

Segregation of Duty (SOD)

SODs are intended to **reduce the opportunity for errors or fraud**. Remember that greater **management oversight** is necessary when an organization's small size prevents segregation of incompatible duties (eg, same person collects and deposits cash and reconciles bank and cash balances).

Ideally, the following categories of functions should be performed by different individuals:

Segregation of duties: ARCC

Each performed by
a different person
{
Authorization
Recordkeeping
Custody
Comparison/reconciliation

For smaller entities that may have difficulty assigning these functions to multiple personnel, compensating controls include:

Compensating controls for conflicts of interest in small entities*

- Strong tone at the top (ie, corporate culture)

- Independent management review/monitor internal control system

- Random selection of transactions/reconciliations for comparison to supporting documents (or strong internal audit function)

- Effective and anonymous whistleblower program

*Source: COSO's Internal control over Financial Reporting—Guidance for Smaller Public companies, Executive Summary

Fraud Risk Factors (Fraud Triangle)

Due to the nature of fraud, the risk of not detecting it is higher than the risk of not detecting errors. Furthermore, the risk of not detecting *management fraud* is higher than the risk of not detecting employee fraud, since management is generally in a better position to **override controls and conceal it.**

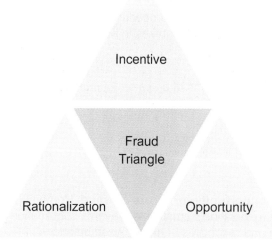

There are three conditions (ie, the *fraud triangle*) that are generally assumed to be present whenever fraud occurs. These risk factors should be considered by the auditor when assessing fraud risk.

- **Motivation**—Individuals generally have a reason or motivation to commit fraud, such as an **incentive** of personal gain or **pressure** to meet certain objectives to prevent getting fired

- **Opportunity**—A lack of effective internal controls allows for the opportunity to commit fraud. Individuals (particularly management) may have the authority to override controls or the ability to circumvent controls (eg, through collusion). If the employee at the cash register is alone and knows the cameras don't work, he would have the opportunity to commit fraud

- **Rationalization**—Individuals who commit fraud usually rationalize their behavior as justified. Some rationalizations (attitudes) include:
  - This isn't really wrong—It's a small amount and no one would even notice
  - Revenge—They are justified in "getting even" with the company
  - They have no choice since the repercussions of not perpetrating the fraud would be too severe (eg, the stock price will not meet an earnings expectation) and they will lose their job

Defining and Categorizing Fraud

COSO defines fraud as "any intentional act or omission designed to deceive others, resulting in the victim suffering a loss and/or the perpetrator achieving a gain" (COSO Executive Summary).

COSO Fraud Categories and Risks

COSO defines four categories of fraud, as follows:

Category	Definition	Examples
Financial reporting fraud	An intentional misstatement of accounting information. Often includes a goal of improving financial results by overstating income or assets, understating losses or expenses, or misleading disclosures.	Improper revenue recognition through backdating agreements (recognizing unshipped goods as sales) or channel stuffing (shipping more products to retailers than they request or can sell)
Nonfinancial reporting fraud	Manipulating nonfinancial reports, including environmental, health, safety, production, quality, or customer reports. Falsifications or nonfinancial reports often result from management setting unrealistic performance targets.	Volkswagen installed software that effectively falsified the information about pollution emissions from its U.S. cars.
Misappropriation of assets	Theft or misuses of tangible or intangible assets by employees, customers, vendors, hackers, or criminal organizations	Vendors submitting inflated or fictitious invoices or employees stealing tangible or intangible assets
Other illegal acts and corruption	Violations of laws or regulations that may have a material impact on the financial statements	Bribes, kickbacks, "gratuities" (ie, gifts to purchasing agents)

Inherent Limitations of an Audit Procedures

Due to inherent limitations in the audit process itself, most audit evidence is **persuasive** rather than conclusive. Inherent limitations of the audit process include the following items.

Nature of Financial Reporting. The preparation and fair presentation of F/S involves management's judgment and subjective decisions (eg, accounting estimates). Therefore, some items are subject to an inherent level of variability that cannot be eliminated with the application of audit procedures.

Nature of Audit Procedures. There are practical and legal limitations on the auditor's ability to obtain audit evidence. For example:

- Even though audit procedures are performed to obtain assurance that all relevant information has been obtained, the auditor still cannot be certain that management or others have provided complete information

- Audit procedures may be ineffective at detecting intentional misstatements that may be concealed (ie, fraud)

- The auditor is not given specific legal powers (eg, the power of search) that would be required in an official investigation into wrongdoing

Timeliness of Financial Reporting and the Balance between Benefit and Cost. The relevance and value of information tends to diminish over time. It is also impracticable to address all information. Therefore, it is expected that the auditor will form an opinion on the F/S within a reasonable period of time to balance the benefits of the audit with its cost. This makes it necessary for the auditor to:

- Plan the audit so that it will be performed in an effective manner

- Direct a larger proportion of audit effort to areas expected to contain risks of material misstatement

- Use testing and other means of examining populations for misstatements

AUD 11
Materiality

AUD 11: Materiality

11.01 Materiality for the Financial Statements as a Whole

Overview

 Representative Task (Remembering & Understanding): Understand materiality, including qualitative considerations, as it relates to the financial statements and related disclosures as a whole.

When the auditor expresses an opinion regarding the fair presentation of the financial statements (F/S) in accordance with the applicable financial reporting framework (AFRF), it is based on whether the F/S:

- Contain a material misstatement that will influence users, or
- Are materially misstated as a whole.

To express such an opinion, the auditor is required to understand what is, or is not, **material** and to establish **quantitative measures** of what would be considered material in various circumstances.

Authoritative Guidance

AU-C 320, *Materiality in Planning and Performing an Audit*, provides that the concept of **materiality** is often incorporated in the principles underlying an FRF in the context of the preparation and fair presentation of the F/S.

The relevant PCAOB guidance is provided by *Consideration of Materiality in Planning and Performing an Audit*. The auditor's responsibilities regarding materiality under the PCAOB standards are very similar to those under AICPA standards, although the PCAOB standard does not use the term "performance materiality."

Such frameworks may discuss materiality differently, but they generally indicate that:

- Misstatements and omissions are considered **material** if there is a substantial likelihood that, individually or in the aggregate, they would influence the judgment of a reasonable user based on the F/S
- **Judgments** about materiality consider:
  - Both **quantitative and qualitative** information
  - Surrounding circumstances, including the size and nature of misstatements
  - The needs of F/S users as a group, rather than the effects of misstatements on individual users

Materiality

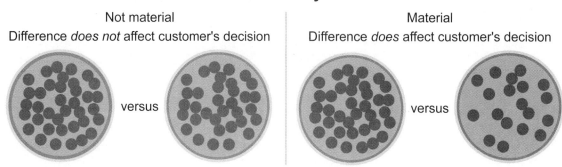

Not material
Difference *does not* affect customer's decision

versus

Material
Difference *does* affect customer's decision

versus

Materiality Levels

The auditor's measurement of materiality is a matter of **professional judgment**, considering the anticipated needs of F/S users. It is applied in planning the engagement as well as in its performance.

When **planning** an audit, an auditor determines the nature, timing, and extent of testing based on an assessment of the risk of material misstatement (RMM). To assess RMM, the auditor must first make a preliminary judgment about what sort of misstatement is material.

Materiality in preliminary audit planning

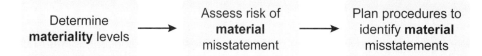

Determine **materiality** levels ⟶ Assess risk of **material** misstatement ⟶ Plan procedures to identify **material** misstatements

Materiality is **quantitatively measured** by applying a percentage to some benchmark. **Common benchmarks** include categories of income, such as profit before tax, total revenue, gross profit, total equity, or total assets. The percentage to be applied to the benchmark is a matter of **professional judgment** and considers the nature of the benchmark

The selection of an appropriate benchmark will be influenced by a variety of factors, such as:

- The elements of the F/S (eg, assets, liabilities, etc.)
- Items on the F/S that are expected to be of particular interest to the users
- The nature of the entity, including its level of maturity, its industry, and the economic environment in which it operates
- The entity's ownership structure and how it is financed (eg, solely by debt or equity)
- The volatility of the benchmark

A few examples of frequently used general guidelines follow (these are not specifically identified in the AICPA auditing standards, however):

- 5% to 10% of net income or earnings before taxes
- 0.50% to 2% of the larger of net sales or total assets
- 5% of owners' equity for private companies

The auditor should consider that **qualitative matters**, such as the surrounding circumstances and perceived risks, might affect the auditor's judgment of what is material to the users. There are too many factors to list here, but two examples include:

- A lower materiality threshold may apply to public companies owing to *more exposure to litigation* and because the owners of private companies may be closer to the day-to-day operations and, therefore, have different information needs

- A lower materiality threshold may apply to a company in an *unstable industry*, which is by nature more susceptible to business failure

When the materiality level is different based on the benchmarks from the various F/S, the **smallest aggregate dollar amount** is generally selected.

- For example, if the materiality level is identified as $10 million on the balance sheet and $3 million on the income statement, the auditor will consider items in the audit to be material if they individually or collectively could result in a misstatement of $3 million or more.

There is an **inverse relationship** between *audit risk* and the *materiality* consideration.

- Assessment of risk as low indicates that an item is less likely to influence users of the F/S; thus, a larger misstatement to such an item will have less effect than a smaller misstatement on a more sensitive item. Therefore, when risk is low, materiality can be set at a higher level

- Assessment of risk as high indicates that an item is more likely to influence users of the F/S; thus, a small misstatement to such an item will have a greater impact on users than a larger misstatement on a less sensitive item. Therefore, when risk is high, materiality would be set at a low level, such that a small misstatement would potentially be considered material

An auditor of a nonissuer is most likely to conclude that a misstatement identified during an audit that is below the quantitative materiality limit is qualitatively material if it

- Changes the company's operating results from a net loss to a net income
- Arises from a transaction cycle with controls that were determined to be operating effectively
- Is the first time a misstatement has arisen from the relevant transaction cycle
- Decreases management's incentive compensation for the period

Evaluating materiality of a misstatement

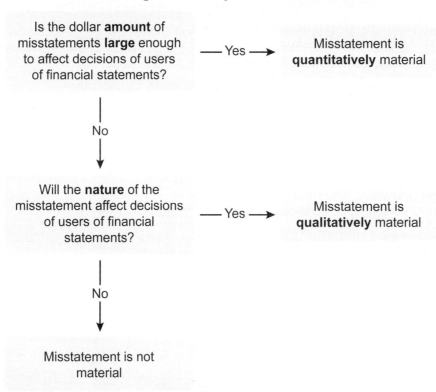

A misstatement may be material because it involves a large dollar **amount** (ie, **quantitative materiality**). However, the **nature** of a misstatement may also make it **qualitatively** material even when the dollar amount involved is below quantitative materiality. For example, an investor's judgments about a company are likely to be affected by whether that company is profitable, even if the profit is small.

Materiality Revisions

During the engagement, the auditor may become aware of issues that will **change the measurement of materiality**. If, for example, materiality was measured as a percentage of sales and, as a result of audit procedures applied, the auditor determines that sales were overstated, the auditor will propose an adjustment to materiality accordingly.

- The decrease in the benchmark will result in a decrease in the measurement of what is material
- This may also result in a decrease to the materiality level assigned to one or more specific classes of transactions, account balances, or disclosures
- Previously identified misstatements that were considered immaterial may have to be reevaluated in relation to the reduced measurement

If materiality was to be measured at 5% of sales and the client's trial balance indicated sales of $5,000,000, a misstatement under $250,000 would not be considered material. A proposed adjustment reducing sales to $4,500,000 due to an overstatement found would reduce the measurement of materiality to $225,000. Thus, a misstatement between $225,000 and $250,000 would now be considered material.

Materiality Documentation Requirements

The auditor is required to document:

- Materiality for the F/S taken as a whole
- Materiality for specific classes of transactions, account balances, or disclosures, if appropriate
- Performance materiality
- Revisions to any of the materiality measurements occurring during the engagement

Calculate Materiality for the F/S as a Whole

Representative Task (Application): Calculate materiality for an entity's financial statements as a whole.

The AICPA and PCAOB auditing standards do not provide specific criteria to calculate materiality. However, there are commonly used benchmarks that the auditor can leverage. When selecting a benchmark and the associated percentage, the auditor should take into consideration **qualitative factors**. For example, if a client has high fraud risk or a history of material misstatement, an auditor might select a percentage which results in a lower level of materiality.

Calculating Materiality for F/S as a Whole

Reuse Clothing Inc., a for-profit company, is a recurring audit client for AuditsRus, LLP. The auditors have determined that 3-5% of net income before taxes would be an appropriate benchmark for materiality. During the prior year audit, a material mistatement was discovered related to fraud.

Using the information below, calculate the most appropriate materialilty level for the F/S as a whole.

Key financial information

- Net income before taxes: $4,500,000
- Net income: $3,510,000

Materiality calculations based on NIBT

$4,500,000*.03 = $135,000
$4,500,000*.04 = $180,000
$4,500,000*.05 = $225,000

Based on the history of fraud and material mistatement, the auditor should select **the more conservative benchmark percentage** after considering qualitative factors. The auditor should set **$135,000** (3% of net income before taxes) as the overall materiality level.

Materiality for Classes of Transactions, Account Balances, and Disclosures

 Representative Task (Application): Calculate the materiality level (or levels) to be applied to classes of transactions, account balances and disclosures in an audit of an issuer or nonissuer.

In certain situations, an auditor may determine that misstatements of an amount lower than overall materiality would influence the judgment of a reasonable financial statement user. In those situations, the auditor can apply **performance materiality** to assess the risk of material misstatement and determine the nature, timing, extent of further audit procedures for specific classes of transactions, account balances, or disclosures.

Performance materiality considers that a misstatement that is immaterial, in relation to the F/S as a whole, may reach materiality when combined with other identified misstatements. Performance materiality is **lower** than materiality at the F/S level. It is estimated at an amount such that it is probable that the aggregate of uncorrected and undetected misstatements will not reach the level of F/S materiality.

Determining performance materiality is not just a mathematical calculation but involves the extensive use of **professional judgment**. Guidance for calculating performance materiality can be found in the next section.

 An auditor has set the materiality level for the financial statements as a whole at $125,000. Which of the following misstatements would the auditor most likely consider material?

- The client did not record $47,000 in trade accounts payable at year end
- The client did not disclose $45,000 of related party transactions in the footnotes
- The client misclassified $42,000 of supplies expense as miscellaneous expense
- The client's estimate of the allowance for doubtful accounts is $40,000 more than the auditor's estimate

Risks in related party transactions

- May not be arm's-length transactions
- Increased risk of fraud
- Not disclosed in financial statements

Related party transactions pose a heightened risk of fraud because the parties' relationship provides greater opportunity for collusion and manipulation of transactions (eg, selling a building to the entity above market value).

Companies are required to disclose related party transactions **regardless of materiality** because financial statement users need to understand the nature of related party transactions and their effects on financial statements. Auditors are responsible for performing procedures that identify related parties and related transactions and for evaluating whether these transactions have been properly accounted for and disclosed.

A misstatement is considered material if it meets either a quantitative threshold (eg, materiality of $125,000) or is qualitatively material (eg, related parties, fraud). Because none of these individual misstatements ($47,000, $42,000, and $40,000) meet either criteria (ie, below the threshold, not qualitatively material), none of them are considered material.

11.02 Tolerable Misstatement & Performance Materiality

Understand Tolerable Misstatement & Performance Materiality

 Representative Task (Remembering & Understanding): Understand the use of tolerable misstatement or performance materiality in an audit.

The auditor determines **performance materiality** during planning. This considers that a misstatement that is immaterial in relation to the F/S as a whole may be material when combined with other identified misstatements.

Thus, **performance materiality is lower than materiality** at the F/S level. It is estimated at an amount such that it is probable that the aggregate of uncorrected and undetected misstatements will not reach the level of F/S materiality. Applying the concept of performance materiality to a particular sample is called **tolerable misstatement.** It is the maximum error in the population that the auditor is willing to accept.

- In practice, performance materiality (tolerable misstatement) typically falls between **50** and **75%** of the overall materiality. The auditor may opt for a lower performance materiality for high-risk areas

Tolerable misstatement is the amount that an incorrect F/S item can differ from the correct amount without having an effect of the fair presentation of the F/S taken as a whole. Tolerable misstatement is usually set for a particular audit procedure at less than F/S materiality so that when the results of all audit procedures are aggregated, the required overall assurance will be attained.

- Performance materiality and tolerable misstatement are sometimes used interchangeably. Both terms relate to the **maximum amount** of an error or misstatement that an auditor is willing to accept for a specific class of transactions, account balances, and/or disclosures before deciding that the F/S are materially misstated

Unlike materiality over the entire F/S as a whole, performance materiality and tolerable misstatement can vary based on the area (ie, Accounts receivable versus Long-term Debt) from which the sample is selected.

 Holding other planning considerations equal, a decrease in the amount of misstatement in a class of transactions that an auditor could tolerate most likely would cause the auditor to

- Apply the planned substantive tests prior to the balance sheet date
- Perform the planned auditing procedures closer to the balance sheet date
- Increase the assessed level of control risk for relevant financial statement assertions
- Decrease the extent of auditing procedures to be applied to the class of transactions

Auditing standards state that **decreasing the tolerable amount of misstatement** will require the auditor to do one or more of the following: (1) perform auditing procedures **closer to the balance sheet date**; (2) select a more effective auditing procedure; or (3) increase the extent of a particular auditing procedure.

Calculate Tolerable Misstatement & Performance Materiality

 Representative Task (Application): Determine tolerable misstatement or performance materiality for the purposes of assessing the risk of material misstatement and determining the nature, timing, and extent of further audit procedures in an audit of an issuer or nonissuer.

 Dewey Inc. is a reoccurring public audit client for AuditsRUs, LLP. The auditors have determined overall materiality at the F/S level is $30,000. The audit firm typically sets tolerable misstatement at 50–75% of overall materiality. The prior year's cash balance was $250,000. Due to the nature of the industry, the cash account is highly susceptible to fraud and error. That indicates there is a high risk for uncorrected and undetected issues. Determine the most appropriate tolerable misstatement for the cash account.

Materiality Calculation

Cash and Cash Equivalents	$30,000*.50 = $15,000

To determine tolerable misstatement:

- Identify overall materiality. The amount of $30,000 was given

- Determine the applicable percentage. Based on professional judgment, the auditor would select the lower percentage of 50% because of the higher risk associated with the cash account. This will result in a smaller tolerable misstatement

- Calculate the tolerable misstatement for the cash account. This is $15,000.

AUD 12
Assessing and Responding to Risks of Material Misstatements, Whether Due to Fraud or Error

12.01 Assessing and Responding to Risks of Material Misstatements, Whether Due to Fraud or Error

Overview of Audit Process

The audit process begins with client acceptance. Audit planning is performed after the client acceptance phase is completed and is used to develop an **audit strategy** for **risk assessment procedures**, tests of controls, and substantive procedures. The auditor should consider information obtained during the initial phases of the audit to develop a strategy that is appropriate to the client. This chapter begins at the **assessing and responding to RMM** phase of the audit process.

Audit process

Client acceptance/continuance

Plan the audit
(initial strategy and plan)

Obtain understanding of client, its
environment and internal control

Assess risk of material misstatement
and design further procedures

Perform tests of controls

Perform substantive procedures

Form an opinion

Issue a report

Develop a Detailed Audit Plan/Program

The auditor should prepare a written audit plan/program that specifies the nature, timing, and extent of further audit procedures to be performed, and the auditor should document the conclusions about control risk in planning the audit:

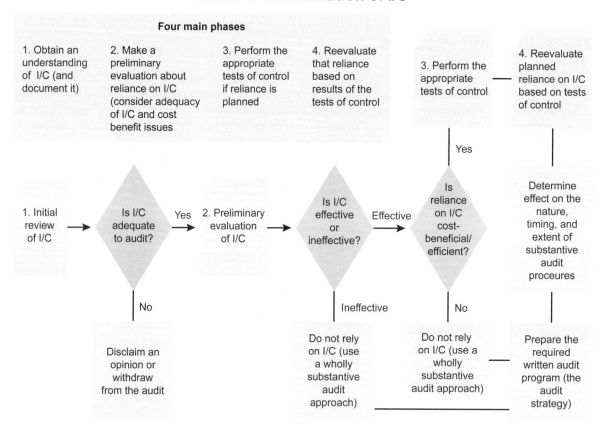

Auditor's consideration of I/C

Four main phases

1. Obtain an understanding of I/C (and document it)
2. Make a preliminary evaluation about reliance on I/C (consider adequacy of I/C and cost benefit issues
3. Perform the appropriate tests of control if reliance is planned
4. Reevaluate that reliance based on results of the tests of control
3. Perform the appropriate tests of control
4. Reevaluate planned reliance on I/C based on tests of control

Audit Risk

Representative Task (Application): Determine risk of material misstatement, whether due to fraud or error, at the financial statement level and relevant assertion level for each significant class of transactions, significant account, and disclosure.

Audit risk is the risk that the auditor expresses an **inappropriate audit opinion** when the financial statements are materially misstated. Audit risk is a function of the risks of material misstatement and detection risk.

The presence of audit risk is indicated in the auditor's report by reference to *reasonable assurance,* meaning that **audit risk cannot be reduced to a zero probability** (which would imply "absolute assurance") owing to the inherent limitations of an audit. *Reasonable assurance* is a high, but not absolute, level of assurance.

Risk of Material Misstatement (RMM) Defined

A **material misstatement** exists when incorrect financial statement information can negatively impact users' financial decisions. The **risk of material misstatement (RMM)** exists when the client's control risk is high (eg, internal control [I/C] procedures are missing or ineffective). RMM exists at two levels:

- **RMM at the Overall Financial Statement Level**—This refers to risks that are "pervasive" in the financial statements and that potentially affect many assertions

- **RMM at the Assertion Level**—The auditor assesses RMM at the assertion level for the purpose of determining the nature, timing, and extent of further audit procedures to obtain sufficient appropriate audit evidence. RMM at the assertion level consists of two components: (1) inherent risk; and (2) control risk

Audit Risk Model

- At the assertion level, **audit risk** consists of three component risks: (1) inherent risk (IR), (2) control risk (CR), and detection risk (DR).

- **Inherent Risk (IR)**—The probability that a material misstatement would occur in the particular audit area in the absence of any internal control policies and procedures

- **Control Risk (CR)**—The probability that a material misstatement that occurred in the first place would not be detected and corrected by internal controls that are applicable

- **Detection Risk (DR)**—The probability that a material misstatement that was not prevented or detected and corrected by internal control was not detected by the auditor's substantive audit procedures (ie, an undetected material misstatement exists in a relevant assertion)

Auditors use the **audit risk model** to plan and execute audit testing. The model can be broken into three steps:

1. **Audit Risk**—First, auditors determine how much risk they are willing to accept that the opinion they issue on the F/S will be more favorable than is appropriate

Audit risk model

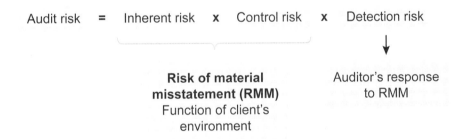

1. **Risk of Material Misstatement (RMM)**—Auditors then determine the risk that the F/S are materially misstated. RMM is a function of inherent risk and control risk

Impact of risk on audit testing

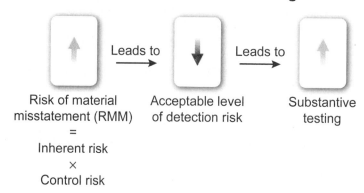

Risk of material misstatement (RMM)
=
Inherent risk
×
Control risk

Note: If the RMM decreases, the acceptable level of detection risk increases and substantive testing decreases.

3. **Detection Risk**—Finally, in response to the assessed RMM, auditors adjust the risk (ie, detection risk) that they will not identify a material misstatement; they do this by changing the nature, timing, and extent of audit testing (ie, substantive procedures). The higher the RMM, the less detection risk auditors will be able to tolerate while holding audit risk. As the acceptable level of detection risk decreases, the extent of substantive testing should increase

Audit Risk Components

The component risks do not necessarily have to be quantified; for example, they could be assessed qualitatively as high, medium, or low. Each component is considered from left to right in order: audit risk is set, then inherent risk is assessed, then control risk is assessed, and finally the implications for the appropriate level of detection risk are considered.

Detection risk is the only component risk that is specifically the auditor's responsibility. Inherent risk arises because of the particular audit area under investigation, and control risk reflects management's responsibility to design and implement internal controls.

- If IR and CR are seen by the auditor as too high, the auditor must compensate by decreasing DR

- If IR and CR are perceived as low, the auditor may consider accepting a higher DR

 The auditor must "assess" inherent risk and control risk, but the auditor actually makes the decisions that, in effect, result in some level of detection risk. This should be taken into consideration in the auditor's assessment of the risk of material misstatement.

As discussed, increasing or decreasing DR is accomplished by adjusting the **nature, timing, and/or exten**t of the auditor's substantive audit procedures. These might be viewed as the auditor's three strategic variables that, in effect, "set" DR based on the auditor's professional judgment about the following:

- **Nature**—What specific audit procedures to perform (perhaps shifting the relative emphasis placed on the "soft evidence" analytical procedures versus the "hard evidence" tests of details)?

- **Timing**—When will the procedures be performed? At an "interim" date (prior to year end) or at the "final" date (after year end when the books have been closed) and the auditor is actually auditing the numbers that the entity intends to report in its financial statements?

- **Extent**—Are large samples required for the auditor's test work or can somewhat smaller sample sizes be justified? How extensively should substantive procedures be performed?

An auditor concludes that there is a heightened risk of a material misstatement. Which of the following is an appropriate action that an auditor can take?

- Decrease materiality and increase acceptable detection risk level

- Only decrease materiality

- Only increase acceptable detection risk level

- Do not change materiality or the acceptable detection risk level

Audit risk = risk of material misstatement (RMM) × detection risk

If...
RMM is high

Then...
Planned audit procedures increased:
- More thorough tests
- Rely more on year end testing
- Assign experienced staff with specilized skills
- Close supervision required

In order to...
Decrease detection risk

When the risk of material misstatement (RMM) is high, the auditor has a **lower acceptable detection risk level.** Setting the acceptable detection risk at a low level means performing more audit procedures than would be performed when setting acceptable detection risk level high.

Materiality is a threshold used by auditors to determine which items need to be investigated further (ie, items at or above the threshold are investigated). In addition to performing more audit procedures, an auditor can **decrease the materiality threshold** in response to a heightened RMM. Decreasing the threshold means that more items are evaluated by auditors than when the threshold is higher.

Obtain Understanding of Entity's Internal Controls

Representative Task (Application): Determine appropriate procedures to assess the operating effectiveness of relevant controls.

Obtaining an understanding of internal control in general (including IT controls) can be found in Chapter 10 along with the associated AICPA Blueprint Representative Tasks. This section focuses on determining whether operating effectiveness of a specific entity's controls can be relied upon.

AICPA Guidance

The primary relevant AICPA guidance is provided by AU-C 315, *Understanding the Entity and Its Environment and Assessing the Risks of Material Misstatement*. This pronouncement states that the auditor's objective is to "identify and assess the risks of material misstatement, whether due to fraud or error, at the financial statement and relevant assertion levels through understanding the entity and its environment, including its internal control, thereby providing a basis for designing and implementing responses to the assessed risks of material misstatement."

Additional relevant guidance is provided by AU-C 330, *Performing Audit Procedures in Response to Assessed Risks and Evaluating the Audit Evidence Obtained*. The auditor's objective is "to obtain sufficient appropriate audit evidence regarding the assessed risks of material misstatement through designing and implementing appropriate responses to those risks."

Understand Entity's I/C and RMM

Unlike issuer audits, nonissuer F/S audits do *not* require an opinion on the entity's internal control (I/C) over financial reporting (ICFR). However, an auditor **must** gain and document an **understanding** of the entity's **I/C** to assess the risk of material misstatement (RMM).

GAAS requires the auditor to test only those controls to be relied on to reduce the RMM. When ICFR *cannot* be relied upon to reduce the RMM, extensive substantive procedures (not tests of controls) will be performed to determine if the entity's accounting system effectively generates materially correct financial information.

Audit process

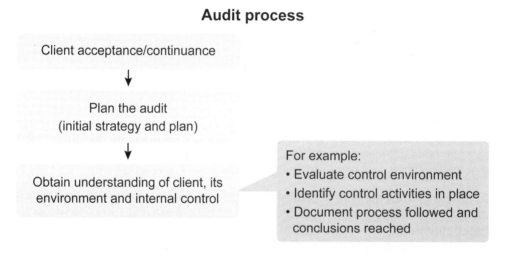

The auditor's internal control analysis tends to focus on the entity's major **transaction cycles** (ie, business processes). A transaction cycle is a **group of homogeneous transactions**; that is, transactions of the same type. A specific transaction cycle is the **highest level of aggregation** about which meaningful generalizations of control risk can be made, since control risk is constant within that transaction cycle.

Each transaction within a specific transaction cycle is captured, processed, and recorded subject to the same set of internal control policies and procedures. Typical business processes include the following:

- Revenue/receipts
- Expenditures/disbursements
- Payroll
- Financing/investing activities
- Inventory, especially if inventory is manufactured, rather than purchased

The auditor may initially consider whether reliance on specific internal control strengths within transaction cycles is appropriate. In doing so, they should consider the **adequacy of controls** (regarding design effectiveness). The following list represents some additional auditor considerations:

- ○ Consider the possible types of errors or problems that could occur
- ○ Consider the kinds of procedures that would prevent and/or detect such errors or problems
- ○ Determine whether such controls are in place
- ○ Evaluate the implications of any identified weaknesses

Specific procedures designed to obtain an understanding include:

- **Inquiries of Management and Others**—The auditor should obtain information from inquiries made of management and others, including internal auditors, production and marketing personnel, those charged with governance, and outsiders (such as external legal counsel or valuation experts used by the entity)
- **Observation and Inspection**—The auditor's risk assessment procedures should include observation of entity operations, inspection of documents (eg, internal control manuals), reading reports prepared by management and those charged with governance (eg, minutes of meetings), and visits to the entity's facilities

Analytical procedures may also be performed in planning to assist the auditor in understanding the entity and its environment and identify specific risks relevant to the audit.

As part of this process, the auditor should review information about the entity and its environment obtained in **prior periods**. The auditor should consider whether changes may have affected the relevance of that information (perhaps by making inquiries or performing a walkthrough of transactions through the entity's systems).

Finally, the **audit team** should discuss the susceptibility of the entity's F/S to material misstatements.

- **Key Members Should Be Involved in the Discussion**—But professional judgment is required to determine who should be included in that discussion. (For a multilocation audit, there may be multiple discussions for key members at each major location)
  - ○ **Objective of This Discussion**—The purpose of the discussion is for members of the audit team to understand the potential for material misstatements of the financial statements (due to error or fraud) in specific areas assigned to them and how their work may affect other parts of the audit
  - ○ **The Discussion Should Include Critical Issues**—Such matters include the areas of significant audit risk, the potential for management override of controls; important controls; materiality at the financial statement level and the relevant assertion level; etc.

If I/C is perceived to be **ineffective**, the auditor would assess control risk at the maximum level. The auditor should document the basis for conclusions about internal control either way, whether internal control is perceived to be effective or ineffective.

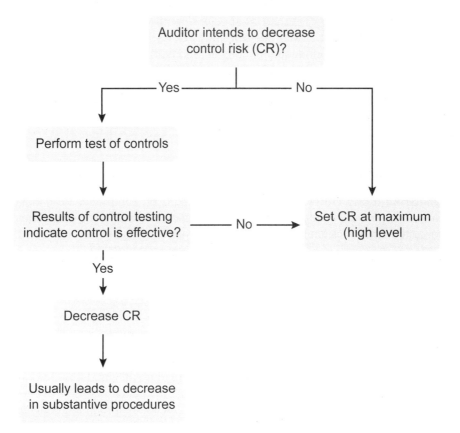

Assess and Respond to Risk of Material Misstatement (RMM)

 Representative Task (Analysis): Assess risks of material misstatement, whether due to fraud or error, at the financial statement level and develop a response by leveraging the combined knowledge and understanding of the engagement team.

 Representative Task (Analysis): Assess the potential impact of identified risks of material misstatement at the relevant assertion level for each significant class of transactions, significant account, and disclosure, considering the controls the auditor intends to test.

 Representative Task (Analysis): Analyze the risk of material misstatement, including the potential impact of individual and cumulative misstatements, to provide a **basis for developing** planned audit procedures.

 Risk assessment procedures include determining the risk of material misstatement **due to fraud**. Coverage of fraud and illegal acts can be found at the end of this section.

The auditor should identify and assess the risks of material misstatement (RMM) at the F/S level and at the relevant assertion level related to classes of transactions, account balances, and disclosures.

Audit process

Client acceptance/continuance

Plan the audit
(initial strategy and plan)

Obtain understanding of client, its
environment and internal control

↓

Analytical procedures
performed to identify:
• Inconsistencies
• Abnormal fluctuations

Assess risk of material misstatement
and design further procedures

Assessing RMM

As part of identifying and assessing the RMM, the auditor should consider the following items:

- **Internal Control Considerations**—A weak control environment (such as management's lack of competence) may have pervasive financial statement effects and require an overall response by the auditor. The auditor's understanding of internal control may also raise questions about the auditability of the entity's financial statements (eg, sufficient appropriate evidence may not be available)

- **Significant Risks**—These are risks that the auditor believes require special audit consideration. The auditor should consider the nature of the risks identified (eg, whether the risk may relate to fraud, significant economic developments, the complexity of transactions, related-party transactions, subjective measurement, or nonroutine transactions that are unusual for the entity)

- **Risks for Which Substantive Procedures Alone Do Not Provide Sufficient Appropriate Audit Evidence**—The auditor should evaluate the design and implementation of controls over such risks, since it is not possible to reduce detection risk to an acceptably low level with substantive procedures by themselves: for example, when IT is a significant part of the entity's information system and transactions are initiated, authorized, recorded, processed, and reported electronically without an audit trail

- **Revision of Risk Assessment**—Risk assessment is an iterative process and the assessment of risks may change as additional evidence is obtained. (For example, when performing tests of controls, evidence may be obtained that controls are ineffective, or when performing substantive procedures, misstatements may be detected that suggest that controls are ineffective)

Simulation (Analysis-level task)

You have been assigned to the audit of the Year 2 financial statements of Sangeeta, Inc., a nonissuer. The audit is now in the planning stage. Which of the following is the factor *most likely* to increase the risk of material misstatement? Enter "Yes" for only one factor and enter "No" for the remaining three factors.

	Potential risk factor	Yes/No
1	The company has begun to focus on a strategic advertising plan so that it may expand its domestic market into other states.	
2	During Year 2, management issued additional long-term debt with complex financial covenants.	
3	Sangeeta is organized in two divisions, which serve the major markets of the company's products.	
4	The new CFO was an audit manager for the predecessor audit firm.	

Answer and explanation

	Potential Risk Factor	Yes/No
1	The company has begun to focus on a strategic advertising plan so that it may expand its domestic market into other states.	No

Expanding operations into new markets may increase RMM if it increases the size and complexity of the company's operations. However, the creation of a strategic advertising plan with the intent of expanding into a new market does not in itself present additional risks.

2	During Year 2, management issued additional long-term debt with complex financial covenants.	Yes

An **increase in debt**, particularly with complex financial covenants, **would most likely increase RMM**. When debt carries financial covenants (eg, current ratio must be above a certain level), management may be motivated to misstate financial results to ensure the entity is not in violation of the covenants. This motivation increases the risk of fraud. In addition, one or more covenants may simply be overlooked, thus creating a misstatement if the company turns out to be in violation.

3	Sangeeta is organized in two divisions, which serve the major markets of the company's products.	No

If the company was previously undivided, a separation into two divisions, like any major change, could result in errors (accounting and otherwise) and therefore additional RMM as the organization adjusts. However, there is no indication that the division is a recent change for Sangeeta. Entities with two divisions do not inherently have greater RMM than those with a single division.

4	The new CFO was an audit manager for the predecessor audit firm.	No

The new CFO's background as an audit manager for the predecessor audit firm does not increase, and may actually decrease, RMM. Having previously audited the entity, the CFO would be knowledgeable about accounting policies and practices relevant to the entity and the industry, thus decreasing the likelihood of misstatement due to error. In addition, coming from the predecessor audit firm does not affect the CFO's risk of being incentivized to misstate results.

Responding to RMM

 Representative Task (Application): Determine a response to risks of material misstatement at the financial statement level (eg, maintaining professional skepticism, engagement team supervision, incorporating elements of unpredictability), considering the auditor's understanding of the control environment.

After identifying the RMM, the auditor plans audit procedures to respond to those risks. Those procedures can be categorized as follows:

Categories of audit tests used to address risk of material misstatement		
Types	**Purpose**	**Example**
Control tests	Determine the operating effectiveness of I/C	Testing a sample of invoices to determine whether they were properly approved
Substantive testing: Analytical procedures	Identify unexpected relationships between recorded amounts and other data	Comparing dollar amounts of sales invoices in current year with previous year's invoices
Substantive testing: Tests of details	Determine conclusively if a material misstatement has occurred and by how much	Inspecting a sample of invoices to determine whether they were properly recorded

Procedures that function as more than one type of test are known as **dual-purpose tests**. For example, an auditor could draw a sample of invoices and, while reviewing them, ascertain whether they were properly authorized (a test of controls) and whether they were correctly recorded in accordance with the dates, terms, and amounts on the invoices (a test of details). Dual-purpose tests provide an efficient means of obtaining additional evidence.

As the RMM increases:

- The auditor may assign more **experienced staff** to the engagement; provide closer supervision; use specialists; use more unpredictable audit procedures; and/or make appropriate changes in the nature, timing, or extent of further audit procedures

- The auditor's strategy in using a *substantive approach* or a *combined approach* may be influenced to use both tests of controls (regarding the operating effectiveness of controls) and substantive procedures

Substantive procedures must be performed to some degree for all relevant assertions related to each material class of transactions, account balance, or disclosure (ie, the auditor cannot rely totally on the effectiveness of the entity's internal controls).

When substantive procedures alone do not provide sufficient appropriate evidence at the relevant assertion level, the audit should perform **tests of controls (TOC)**. For example, when the entity uses IT extensively and no audit trail exists.

Documentation

Risk assessment documentation requirements include the following:

Risk assessment documentation
• An understanding of key aspects of the entity, its environment, and its internal control components
• The assessed level of the risk of material financial misstatement
• The basis for the assessment
• Who participated in the assessment
• When and how the assessment was conducted
• Risks identified that require tests of controls

Other Engagements

 Representative Task (Application): Determine procedures to satisfy the requirements and objectives of an attestation engagement.

 Representative Task (Application): Determine procedures to satisfy the requirements and objectives of an accounting and review services engagement.

 Representative tasks related to determining procedures to satisfy the requirements and objectives of attestation engagements and accounting and review service engagements can be found in Chapters 24 and 25, respectively.

Audit Data Analytic Procedures

 Representative Task (Analysis): Use outputs from audit data analytic procedures (eg, reports and visualizations) to identify transactions that may have a higher risk of material misstatement and interpret the results to develop planned audit procedures.

An auditor is auditing the Year 4 financial statements of a laptop manufacturer to assess sales (revenue) for **unexpected variations**. The goal is to determine the nature, timing, and extent of audit procedures related to sales and to determine if valuation issues exist in the printer inventory. The company began operations in Year 1, Quarter 2.

The auditor has the following **expectations** for Year 4:

- Poor sales in Quarter 1 due to a labor strike at the manufacturing plant
- Improved sales paralleling prior year patterns starting in Quarter 2 as the strike was settled at the end of Quarter 1
- Strong Quarter 4 sales due to holiday gift-giving

The auditor plots the quarterly sales for the past four years. This analysis indicated:

- A decline in sales in early Year 4, as expected
- A slower than expected return to normal volume for Quarters 2 and 3
- Very strong sales in Quarter 4 (more than expected)

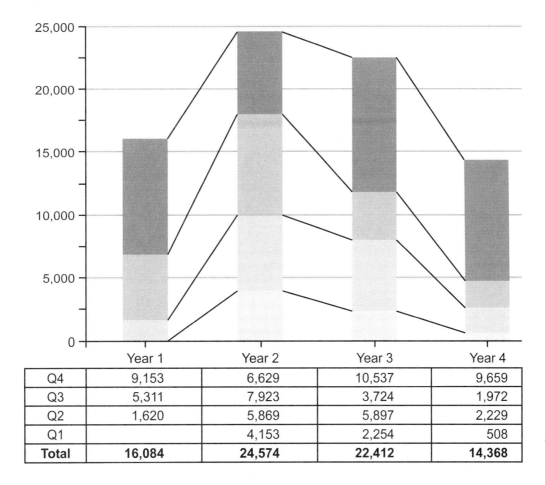

	Year 1	Year 2	Year 3	Year 4
Q4	9,153	6,629	10,537	9,659
Q3	5,311	7,923	3,724	1,972
Q2	1,620	5,869	5,897	2,229
Q1		4,153	2,254	508
Total	**16,084**	**24,574**	**22,412**	**14,368**

Impact of Year 4 Audit Planning—Given that Quarter 4 sales increased significantly, more than expected, the auditor prepared a comparison between Quarter 3 and Quarter 4 for the four years, as follows:

	Year 1	Year 2	Year 3	Year 4
Q3 to Q4 Change	72%	(16%)	109%	390%

Although there is clearly variation in the change in sales between Quarter 3 sales and Quarter 4 sales for each of the four years, the increase in Year 4 is significant enough to warrant increased concern over a material misstatement or fraud. The auditor should **increase substantive testing** in the revenue cycle.

Perform Tests of Controls (TOC)

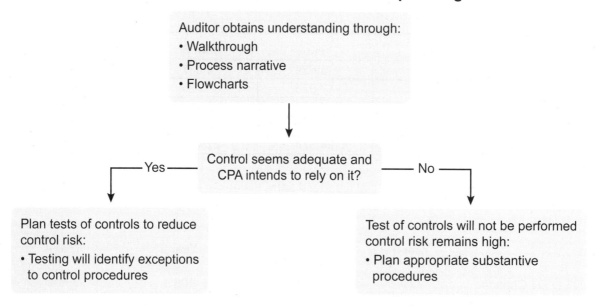

Reliance on I/C means the same thing as assessing **control risk** at *less than the maximum level* for purposes of accepting a somewhat *higher level of detection risk*. If reliance is planned, the auditor should **perform tests of controls (TOC)**, but only for those specific control policies and procedures (strengths that justify accepting a somewhat higher level of detection risk) on which reliance is planned.

Circumstances that warrant performing tests of control (associated with a reliance strategy) include any time that the:

- Auditor's risk assessment **includes an expectation** regarding the operating effectiveness of controls
- Performance of substantive procedures alone does not limit audit risk to an acceptably low level

- Verify that the controls that *looked good on paper* (design effectiveness) were actually working as intended throughout the period (operating effectiveness)

Reasons to test controls

- To lower the assessed risk of material misstatement
- More efficient than substantive testing
- To reduce the amount of substantive testing
- Substantive tests cannot provide audit evidence
- Controls appear to be reliable
- Controls are well designed
- Relevant to management assertions
- Required for all issuer and nonissuer integrated audits

Examples of TOC include:

- **Inspection of Records/Documents**—Examining records or documents, whether internal or external, whether paper or electronic, or other media
- **Inspection of Tangible Assets**—Physical examination of the assets either by being physically present or by using remote observation tools
- **Observation**—Looking at a process or procedure being performed by others. Note that observation provides the auditor with direct knowledge, but it is limited to a point in time (ie, the point in time the auditor is viewing the process)
- **Inquiry**—Seeking information of knowledgeable persons inside or outside the entity and evaluating their responses. Note that inquiry alone does not provide sufficient appropriate audit evidence either for substantive purposes or for tests of controls
- **Confirmation**—Obtaining a representation directly from a knowledgeable third party
- **Recalculation**—Checking the mathematical accuracy of documents
- **Reperformance**—The auditor's execution of procedures or controls originally performed as part of the entity's internal controls

When a control is applied on a transaction basis (eg, matching approved purchase orders to suppliers' invoices) and if the control operates frequently, the auditor can use **audit sampling techniques** to test operating effectiveness; when a control is applied on a periodic basis (eg, monthly reconciliation of the accounts receivable subsidiary ledger to the general ledger), the auditor should perform procedures appropriate for testing smaller populations.

When an auditor increases the assessed level of control risk because certain control activities were determined to be ineffective, the auditor most likely would increase the:

- Level of detection risk

- Extent of tests of details

- Level of inherent risk

- Extent of tests of controls

Process for understanding internal control (I/C) and assessing control risk (CR)

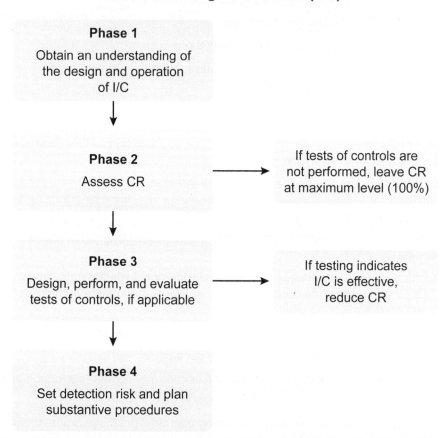

To make an initial assessment of CR, the auditor must understand internal control and evaluate its *design*. If CR is initially assessed as low, the auditor will test controls to determine whether they are, in fact, *effective in operation*. If those tests show that the **controls** are **not effective**, the auditor will then reassess CR as high, opt **not** to **rely on controls**, and likely increase substantive procedures, especially **tests of details**.

Perform Substantive Procedures

 Representative Task (Application): Determine appropriate substantive procedures to test relevant assertions for each significant class of transactions, significant account and disclosure

 Additional coverage on analytical procedures and tests of details can be found in Chapter 18.

Substantive procedures are audit procedures that are directly related to the F/S elements and disclosures. Recall that the word *substantive* is derived from *substantiate*, which means *to verify*. The auditor should **design the substantive procedures** to be responsive to the **assessed risks of material misstatements**.

Audit process

Client acceptance/continuance

Plan the audit
(initial strategy and plan)

Obtain understanding of client, its
environment and internal control

Assess risk of material misstatement
and design further procedures

Perform tests of controls

Perform substantive procedures   Test account balances, send lawyer legal letter, send confirmations, perform cutoff procedures, scan client journals, etc.

The auditor's substantive procedures should include the following related to the **financial reporting** process:

- Agree the financial statement information to the underlying accounting records
- Examine material journal entries and other adjustments made during the preparation of the financial statements
- Additional procedures responsive to the planned level of detection risk include using substantive analytical procedures

There are two primary types of substantive procedures:

- **Analytical Procedures**—Those evidence-gathering procedures that suggest *reasonableness* (or *unreasonableness*) based upon a **comparison to appropriate expectations** or benchmarks, such as the prior year's financial statements, comparability to industry data (including ratios) or other interrelationships involving financial and/or nonfinancial data

Substantive tests using analytical procedures

- Optional
- Begin with expectations developed using relevant, reliable data
- Used to verify reasonableness of accounts/assertions
- Can have results that vary significantly from expectations, causing:
  - Increase in assessed risk of material misstatement
  - Likely decrease in acceptable level of detection risk
  - Likely increase in amount of substantive tests of details

- **Tests of Details**—Those evidence-gathering procedures consisting of either of two types:
  - **Tests of Ending Balances**—Where the final balance is assessed by testing the composition of the year end balance (eg, testing a sample of individual customers' account balances that make up the general ledger accounts receivable control account balance)
  - **Tests of Transactions**—Where the final balance is assessed by examining those debits and credits that caused the balance to change from last year's audited balance to the current year's balance

Planning and Performing Substantive Procedures

Substantive procedures are designed to be responsive to the assessed RMM. The auditor should **perform substantive procedures** for all **relevant assertions** related to each material class of transactions, account balance, and disclosure (regardless of the assessed risk of material misstatement), since there are inherent limitations to internal controls, and the assessment of risk is judgmental.

Substantive testing decreases detection risk

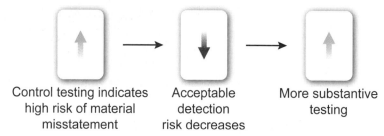

Control testing indicates high risk of material misstatement → Acceptable detection risk decreases → More substantive testing

In stating that the financial statements are consistent with GAAP, management makes several **assertions** (which are implicit or explicit statements of fact). For each management assertion related to each account, auditors have one or more audit objectives. For each of these objectives, an auditor will plan one or more procedures (eg, tracing, observation) to test the assertion.

Historically, the auditing standards discussed five traditional financial statement assertions (and the PCAOB standards still focus on these five assertions):

- Existence/occurrence;
- Completeness;
- Rights and obligations;

- Valuation and allocation; and
- Presentation and disclosure.

AICPA Professional Standards classify assertions in two separate categories for the auditor's consideration, related to:

- Account balances (and related disclosures) at period end;
- Classes of transactions and events (and related disclosures) for the period under audit.

Account Balance Assertions

There are six assertions specific to **account balances** (and related disclosures) at period-end:

- **Existence**—That the assets, liabilities, and equity interests exist
- **Completeness**—That all assets, liabilities, and equity interests that should have been recorded have been recorded. There are no omissions, and all appropriate disclosures have been included
- **Rights and Obligations**—That the entity holds or controls the rights to its assets, and the liabilities are the obligations of the entity. Any restrictions on the rights to the assets or obligations for the liabilities must be disclosed
- **Accuracy, Valuation, and Allocation**—That assets, liabilities, and equity interests are included in the financial statements at appropriate amounts (relative to the requirements of GAAP) and any resulting valuation or allocation adjustments are appropriately recorded. Related disclosures have been appropriately measured and described
- **Classification**—Assets, liabilities, and equity interests have been recorded in the proper accounts
- **Presentation**—Assets, liabilities, and equity interests are appropriately aggregated or disaggregated and clearly described. Related disclosures are relevant and understandable

Classes of Transactions and Events

There are six assertions about classes of transactions and events during the period (and related disclosures).

- **Occurrence**—That transactions and events that have been recorded have occurred. In other words, they are properly recorded and valid
- **Completeness**—That all transactions and events that should have been recorded have been recorded. There are no omissions
- **Cutoff**—That transactions and events have been recorded in the correct accounting period. Note that there are only two ways to record a transaction in the wrong period. One is by recording a transaction prematurely, which violates the "occurrence" assertion; and the other is to record a transaction belatedly, which violates the "completeness" assertion
- **Accuracy**—That amounts and other data have been recorded appropriately, and that all related disclosures have been appropriately measured and described
- **Classification**—That transactions and events have been recorded in the proper accounts
- **Presentation**—Transactions and events are appropriately aggregated or disaggregated and clearly described. Related disclosures are relevant and understandable

Which of the following management assertions is an auditor most likely testing if the audit objective states that all inventory on hand is reflected in the ending inventory balance?

- The entity has rights to the inventory
- Inventory is properly valued
- Inventory is properly presented in the financial statements
- Inventory is complete

Testing management assertions

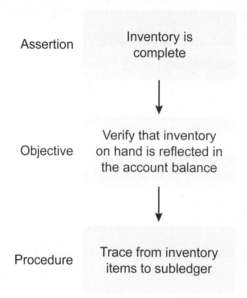

For the assertion that **inventory is complete**, one audit objective will be to verify that all inventory on hand is reflected in the ending inventory balance (ie, no inventory items were left out of the count).

To test the completeness of inventory, the auditor will trace from physical inventory items to the inventory subledger. In practice, this is usually accomplished by tracing tags on individual inventory items to the year end inventory count sheets and tying the amounts in the count sheets to the inventory subledger.

Timing of Substantive Procedures

Substantive tests may be performed at an interim date (before year end) or at final (at or after year end). Remember, performing substantive procedures at an interim date increases detection risk. The auditor should perform additional substantive procedures (or substantive procedures combined with tests of control) to mitigate the increased risk and provide a reasonable basis for extending the audit conclusions from the interim date to year end.

It is not necessary to rely on internal controls (ie, test the operating effectiveness of controls) to extend the audit conclusions from the interim date to year end. However, the auditor should consider whether only performing additional substantive procedures is sufficient.

In which of the following circumstances is substantive testing of accounts receivable before the balance sheet date most appropriate?

- The client has a new sales incentive program in place
- Internal controls during the remaining period are effective
- There is a high turnover of senior management
- It is a first engagement of a new client

Factors influencing interim substantive testing

- Effectiveness of internal controls
- Availability of needed information at year end
- Purpose of the test
- Assessed risk of material misstatement
- Type of account or transactions
- Cost and ability to control audit risk between interim and year end
- Predictability of year end balances after interim testing

When it is possible to perform substantive testing prior to the balance sheet date while still gathering sufficient appropriate evidence to provide reasonable assurance, an auditor may do so. If tests indicate that **internal controls in the remaining period are effective**, the auditor will have greater confidence in the final balance. However, even if internal controls are effective, the auditor will still need to perform some substantive testing covering the remaining period for all material balances. That testing may be relatively limited.

Extent of Substantive Procedures

Determine the implications to sample sizes (considering the planned level of detection risk, materiality, tolerable misstatement, expected misstatement, and the nature of the population).

Additional coverage on sampling can be found in Chapter 17.

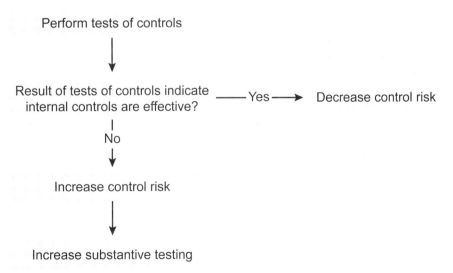

Effect of increasing control risk

Perform tests of controls

↓

Result of tests of controls indicate internal controls are effective? —— Yes ⟶ Decrease control risk

| No

↓

Increase control risk

↓

Increase substantive testing

Simulation—Assessing RMM (Analysis-level Task)

An auditor should design and perform substantive procedures for the relevant management assertions associated with Accounts Receivable (A/R). The goal of these procedures is to provide sufficient appropriate audit evidence that A/R are reported according to the appropriate financial reporting framework (eg, GAAP).

Below is a list of some audit procedures related to the client's accounts receivable assertions. For each assertion, select the audit procedure from the menu that would provide the most appropriate audit evidence.

1	Audit assertions	Audit procedure
2	Accounts receivable represent all amounts owed to the entity at the balance sheet date.	
3	The entity has legal right to all accounts receivable at the balance sheet date.	
4	Accounts receivable are stated at net realizable value.	

Menu Choices

Select an option below

Analyze the relationship of accounts receivable and sales and compare it with relationships for preceding periods.

Perform sales cutoff tests to obtain assurance that sales transactions and corresponding entries for inventories and cost of goods sold are recorded in the same and proper period.

Review the accounts receivable aging report to see the time between the balance sheet date and when the associated sales occurred.

Obtain an understanding of the business purpose of transactions that resulted in accounts receivable balances.

Review loan agreements for indications of whether accounts receivable have been factored or pledged.

Analyze unusual relationships between monthly accounts rec eivable balances and monthly accounts payable balances.

Confirm accounts receivable balances at year end with customers.

Verify any accounts receivable amounts associated with loans to officers or employees.

Solution

1	Audit assertions	Audit procedure
2	Accounts receivable represent all amounts owed to the entity at the balance sheet date.	**Perform sales cutoff tests**

Management asserts that all amounts owed are reflected in the A/R account balance (ie, the completeness assertion). The auditor should verify sales transactions, along with related inventory and COGS transactions, before and after both the beginning and the end of the audit year. This test provides evidence that sales are recorded in the proper period and are accompanied by entries to either cash or A/R. Validating sales resulting in A/R allows the auditor to determine which of those receivables are still outstanding, providing evidence that the A/R balance is complete.

| 3 | The entity has legal right to all accounts receivable at the balance sheet date. | **Review loan agreements** |

Some entities sell (ie, factor) or pledge their A/R in order to obtain immediate cash rather than waiting to receive customer payments. Such agreements indicate situations where the entity has given up the right to receive A/R payments. To obtain audit evidence that the entity has legal right to all A/R at the balance sheet date (ie, the rights and obligations assertion), the auditor should review loan agreements for indications of factoring or pledging A/R.

| 4 | Accounts receivable are stated at net realizable value. | **Review A/R aging report** |

Some sales on credit (ie, A/R) will not result in customer payments. Therefore, entities will estimate nonpayment situations based on historical, industry, or economic information. The amount of A/R estimated to be uncollectible is recorded in the allowance for credit losses contra account and a credit loss expense is recorded, matching the expense of extending credit with the associated sales revenue. This contra account netted with the A/R balance provides the net realizable value for A/R. To obtain evidence that A/R are stated at net realizable value (ie, valuation and allocation assertion), the auditor should evaluate the information supporting the allowance for credit losses account balance. One way to accomplish this is to review the A/R aging report, looking for significantly past-due accounts. This will provide the auditor with information to determine if the estimated allowance for credit losses balance reasonably represents uncollectible accounts.

Differences between AICPA and PCAOB Risk Assessment Standards

A summary of fundamental differences between the PCAOB risk assessment standards and the AICPA Auditing Standards Board risk assessment standards includes the following:

- The PCAOB risk assessment standards apply to **integrated audits of issuers** (encompassing both the company's financial statements and internal control over financial reporting), whereas the AICPA risk assessment standards apply solely to audits of nonissuers' financial statements

- The PCAOB standards tended to provide more **specific guidance** in certain areas (such as the engagement partner's responsibilities) that were originally addressed in somewhat more general terms in the AICPA standards; however, the AICPA's clarified auditing standards are now very similar to PCAOB auditing standards in these areas

- A more significant difference involves the treatment of "assertions" in their respective standards dealing with the topic of audit evidence. The PCAOB focuses on the five traditional financial statement assertions while the current AICPA standard classifies twelve assertions into two broad categories: (1) account balances (and related disclosures) at the period end (for which there are six assertions) and (2) transactions and events (and related disclosures) for the period (for which there are six assertions)

Detecting Fraud

 Representative Task (Application): Determine the pressures, incentives, and opportunities for fraud (eg, fraudulent financial reporting, misappropriation of assets) that could lead to the risk of material misstatement.

AICPA Guidance

The relevant AICPA guidance is provided by AU-C 240, *Consideration of Fraud in a Financial Statement Audit*. This pronouncement states that the auditor's objectives are to: (1) identify and assess the risks of material misstatement due to fraud; (2) obtain sufficient appropriate audit evidence regarding the assessed risks of material misstatement due to fraud, through designing and implementing appropriate responses; and (3) respond appropriately to fraud or suspected fraud identified during the audit.

Definitions

Fraud—An intentional act by one or more individuals among management, those charged with governance, employees, or third parties, involving the use of deception that results in a misstatement in the financial statements.

Fraud Risk Factors—Events or conditions that (a) indicate an incentive or pressure to perpetrate fraud; (b) provide an opportunity to commit fraud; or (c) indicate attitudes or rationalizations to justify a fraudulent action.

Significant Unusual Transactions—Significant transactions that are outside the normal course of business for the entity or that otherwise appear to be unusual due to their timing, size, or nature.

Auditor's Responsibility

In general, the auditor is required to design (plan) the audit to provide "reasonable assurance" of detecting misstatements that are material to the financial statements. In particular, the auditor should specifically assess the **risk of material misstatement due to fraud** (in addition to error) and design the audit procedures to be responsive to that risk assessment. That risk assessment should be performed at both the financial statement level and the assertion level.

Fraud detection audit steps

Gain an understanding of fraud

↓

Hold engagement team
brainstorming session

↓

Identify risks of material misstatement
(RMM) due to fraud

↓

Determine nature and timing
of tests to detect fraud

↓

Evaluate results of tests

↓

Document

↓

Report

Gain an Understanding of Fraud

Brainstorming

Key audit team members must have a **brainstorming** discussion to consider how and where the financial statements might be susceptible to material misstatement owing to fraud and to emphasize the importance of maintaining professional skepticism. That discussion should consider such matters as the following:

- Known internal and external fraud risk factors relevant to the entity
- The risk of management override of controls
- Indications of "earnings management"
- The importance of maintaining professional skepticism throughout the engagement
- How the auditor might respond to the risk of material fraud

Misstatements

There are two types of misstatements relevant to the auditor's consideration of fraud:

1. **Fraudulent Financial Reporting**—This Involves **misstatements** that are **intended to deceive** F/S users, such as management override of controls, recording fictitious journal entries, concealing facts, and altering underlying records to achieve the deception. There is often collusion here as well.

2. **Misappropriation of Assets**—This Involves **theft of assets** causing the F/S to be misstated (often due to false entries intended to conceal the theft). Misappropriation of assets often involves embezzlement of receipts, stealing physical assets or intellectual property, and diverting the entity's assets for personal use.

Fraud Risk Factors

Examples of risk factors related to **financial reporting** that the auditor should consider include:

- **Incentive/Pressure**—Reasons that management might be motivated to commit fraudulent financial reporting

  - **Financial Stability/Profitability**—When the entity is threatened by deteriorating economic conditions (for example: operating losses threaten bankruptcy; recurring negative cash flows from operations; vulnerability to rapid changes due to technology or other factors; increasing business failures in the industry; or the entity reports unusual profitability relative to others in the industry)

  - **Excessive Pressure to Meet the Expectations of Outsiders**—Senior management may face significant pressure to meet external expectations (for example: there are overly optimistic press releases; the entity is only barely able to meet the stock exchange's listing requirements; the entity is having difficulty meeting debt covenants; or the entity must obtain additional outside financing to retool production to be competitive)

- **Opportunities**—Circumstances that might give management a way to commit fraudulent financial reporting.

  - **Nature of the Industry or the Entity's Operations**—For example: significant unusual transactions with related parties; ability to dominate suppliers or customers in a certain industry sector; unnecessarily complex transactions close to year end raise "substance over form" issues; significant bank accounts or business operations in "tax-haven" jurisdictions with no clear business justification; major financial statement elements that involve significant estimates by management that are difficult to corroborate

  - **Ineffective Monitoring of Management**—For example, domination of management by a single person or small group without compensating controls, or ineffective oversight by those charged with governance

  - **Complex or Unstable Organizational Structure**—For example, organization consists of unusual legal entities; high turnover of senior management, counsel, or board members

  - **Internal Controls Are Deficient**—For example, inadequate monitoring of controls; high turnover rates in accounting, internal auditing, and information technology staff; ineffective accounting and information systems. (There are significant deficiencies that rise to the level of material weaknesses)

- **Attitudes/Rationalizations**—Attitudes, behaviors, or justifications of management that might be associated with fraudulent financial reporting:

  - Lack of commitment to establishing and enforcing ethical standards

  - Previous violations of securities laws (or other regulations)

  - Excessive focus by management on the entity's stock price

  - Management's failure to correct reportable conditions

  - Pattern of justifying inappropriate accounting as immaterial

  - Management has a strained relationship with the predecessor or current auditor

Risk factors of fraudulent financial reporting	
Motivation (incentive/pressure)	• Threats to entity's financial stability • Entity's performance linked to executive compensation • Pressure to meet financial benchmarks
Opportunity	• Weak internal controls • Ineffective oversight by governance • Ineffective staff, or high turnover
Attitude/ rationalization	• Ethical standards not communicated or enforced • Aggressive or unrealistic forecasts/expectations • History of violating SEC rules

Examples of risk factors related to **misappropriation of assets** that the auditor should consider include:

- **Incentive/Pressure**—An employee or member of management might be motivated to commit the misappropriation for a variety of reasons, such as the following: employees who have access to cash (or other assets susceptible to theft) may have personal financial problems, or they may have adverse relationships with the entity under audit (perhaps in response to anticipated future layoffs or recent decreases to their benefits or compensation levels)

- **Opportunities**—Circumstances that might give someone a way to commit the misappropriation include the following:
  - When assets are inherently vulnerable to theft—For example, there are large amounts of liquid assets on hand, or inventory items are small, but valuable
  - Inadequate internal control over assets—For example, there is inadequate segregation of duties, inadequate documentation or reconciliation for assets, or inadequate management understanding related to information technology

- **Attitudes/Rationalizations**—The individual perpetrating the misappropriation might possess attitudes or justifications they might use to rationalize improper behaviors and avoid any feelings of remorse for this misconduct. Generally, the auditor cannot normally observe these attitudes, but should consider the implications of such matters when they are discovered. The following might be of interest to the auditor:
  - The employee's behavior indicates dissatisfaction with the entity under audit
  - There are changes in the employee's behavior or lifestyle that are suspicious
  - The employee exhibits a disregard for internal control related to assets by overriding existing controls or failing to correct known deficiencies

Identify RMM Due to Fraud

The auditor should use **professional judgment** in considering the individual or collective effects of the risk factors and recognize that the effects of these risk factors vary widely. Specific controls may *mitigate* the associated risks, and specific control deficiencies may add to the risks.

To obtain information needed to identify the risks of material fraud the auditor emphasizes **inquiry** and **analytical procedures**.

- **Inquiry**—The auditor should question management personnel about their knowledge of fraud, suspected fraud, allegations of fraud, and any significant unusual transactions (including related-party involvement); inquire about specific controls that management has implemented to mitigate fraud risks; and inquire about management's communications with those charged with governance about fraud-related issues. The auditor may also choose to question others (eg, audit committee, internal auditors, operating personnel, in-house legal counsel) about fraud-related issues

- **Analytical Procedures**—The auditor should perform analytical procedures involving revenue accounts, in particular. In general, the auditor should consider whether any unexpected results associated with analytical procedures might have been intentional

Determine Nature, Timing, and Extent of Procedures

Auditors should plan procedures specifically to address **management override of internal control**. Management override means that upper management may not be affected by controls that are imposed on subordinates throughout the organization. (Therefore, management may be able to sidestep those controls without leaving an audit trail for discovery.)

- **Examine Adjusting Journal Entries**—The auditor should be especially attentive to nonstandard journal entries (involving unusual accounts or amounts and those involving complex issues or significant uncertainty). Likewise, the auditor should also be especially attentive to journal entries near the end of the reporting period (both for the fiscal year and any applicable interim reporting periods, such as quarterly reports)

- **Evaluate Accounting Estimates for Bias**—The auditor should consider performing a "retrospective review," which means evaluating prior years' estimates for reasonableness in light of facts occurring after those estimates were made. In other words, did later events support or refute the appropriateness of management's estimates in prior periods? That may affect the auditor's perception of the reliability of management's estimates in the current period

- **Evaluate the Business Rationale for Any Unusual Transactions**—The auditor should look for appropriate authorization of any unusual transactions by those charged with governance

Conditions may be discovered during fieldwork that cause the assessment of these risks in the planning stage to be modified. Factors that might cause the auditor's concerns to increase include the following examples:

- There are discrepancies in the accounting records, including inaccuracies or unsupported balances

- There is conflicting or missing evidence including missing documents or the absence of original documents that should be available (perhaps only photocopies are available)

- There is a problematic relationship between the auditor and the entity, including restricted access of the auditor to records or personnel and undue time pressures imposed by management

Evaluating Misstatements for Fraud

As part of evaluating identified misstatements in the F/S, the auditor should consider whether such misstatements might be **indicative of fraud**. For example, the auditor might consider the organizational level involved. If a misstatement may be the result of fraud involving management, the auditor should reevaluate the assessment of material fraud risk and the auditor's response to the assessed risks.

Substantive testing: possible fraud

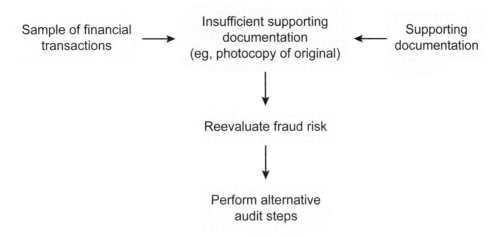

Adjust Nature, Timing, and Extent of Procedures

In response to the **fraud risk assessment**, the auditor may conclude that the planned procedures should be modified or that control risk should be reconsidered. The auditor might make some **overall responses** (at the financial statement level, such as assigning more experienced staff to the engagement) and make other responses at the assertion level (by designing audit procedures for which the nature, timing, and extent of those procedures are responsive to the assessed risks of fraud).

- **Overall Responses**—The auditor may decide to assign more experienced personnel or information technology specialists to the engagement. The auditor should incorporate a degree of "unpredictability" in audit testing, whether at the financial statement level or the assertion level (eg, unannounced visits to some locations for inventory counts) or selecting some items for testing that are below materiality levels

- **Responses at the Assertion Level**—The auditor may decide to increase the emphasis on audit procedures that provide a stronger basis for conclusions or to confirm the terms of sales transactions, in addition to receivable balances; the auditor may move important audit testing to year end, instead of performing those tests at an interim date; and/or the auditor may increase sample sizes for audit testing

If the misstatement is (or may be) the result of fraud and the effect could be material to the financial statements (or if the auditor has been unable to evaluate the materiality involved):

- **Attempt to obtain additional evidence** to determine the facts as to the cause and whether the financial statements are misstated. Discuss the issues and any further investigation required with an appropriate level of management (at least one level above those believed to be involved) and with those charged with governance (especially if senior management appears to be involved)

- If the auditor encounters circumstances related to fraud that call into question whether it is appropriate to continue the audit, the auditor should determine the **applicable professional and legal responsibilities** and consider whether it is appropriate to withdraw from the engagement

  ○ If the auditor withdraws, then the matter should be discussed with management and those charged with governance

  ○ Circumstances that may call into question the auditor's ability to continue the audit include the following: (a) the entity does not take appropriate action regarding fraud; (b) audit evidence suggests that there is a significant risk of pervasive fraud; and (c) the auditor has significant concerns about the competence or integrity of management or those charged with governance

Required Documentation

The auditor should document the following matters related to the consideration of fraud in the financial statement audit:

- The discussion among engagement personnel about fraud in planning the audit, including how and when the discussion occurred, the team members who participated, and the subject matter discussed;

- The procedures performed to obtain information necessary to assess the risks of material fraud;

- Specific risks of material fraud that were identified at the financial statement level and at the assertion level, including a description of how the auditor responded to those identified risks (including the linkage of audit procedures to the risk assessment);

- Reasons supporting the auditor's conclusion if revenue recognition was not identified as a fraud risk contrary to the presumption that revenue recognition is a fraud risk;

- The results of procedures performed to further address the risk of management override of controls;

- Other conditions and analytical relationships that caused the auditor to perform additional auditing procedures; and

- The nature of any communication about fraud made to management, those charged with governance, regulators, and others.

Required Communications

The auditor's communication of fraud issues with management (or those charged with governance) may be written or oral but should be timely. As indicated above, such communication should be documented in the audit documentation.

- If the fraud is **not material** to the financial statements and **senior management is not involved** in the fraud, the appropriate level of management (which is usually considered to be at least one level above where the fraud is believed to have occurred) should be notified. Determining the appropriate level of management for such communication is a matter of judgment, and includes consideration of the likelihood of collusion within management

- If the **fraud is material** to the financial statements or if **senior management is involved** in the fraud, those charged with governance should be notified

- The auditor should consider whether any identified fraud risk factors may constitute a "significant deficiency" (or material weakness) regarding internal control that should be reported to senior management and those charged with governance

- **Other Matters Related to Fraud**—The auditor may choose to discuss a variety of other matters with those charged with governance, including the following:

  - Concerns about the adequacy of management's assessment of the entity's controls to prevent and detect fraud

  - Failure by management to respond appropriately to identified fraud or to address identified significant deficiencies in internal control

  - Concerns about the entity's control environment, including the competence or integrity of management

  - Concerns about management's efforts to "manage earnings"

  - Concerns about the authorization of transactions that do not appear to be within the normal course of the entity's business

Which of the following statements is correct concerning an auditor's responsibility to report fraud?

- The auditor is required to communicate to the client's audit committee all minor fraudulent acts perpetrated by low-level employees, even if the amounts involved are inconsequential

- The disclosure of material management fraud to principal stockholders is required when both senior management and the board of directors fail to acknowledge the fraudulent activities

- Fraudulent activities involving senior management of which the auditor becomes aware should be reported directly to the SEC

- The disclosure of fraudulent activities to parties other than the client's senior management and its audit committee is not ordinarily part of the auditor's responsibility

Reporting fraud

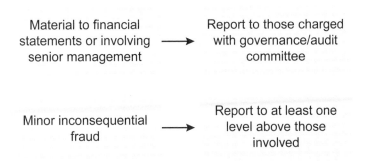

Note: Fraud is not generally reported to parties outside the entity unless required by law or regulation.

Auditors are required to investigate all instances of fraud and communicate knowledge or suspicion of fraud to the appropriate level of management or governance on a timely basis. Unless required by law, regulation, or appropriate public authorities, **auditors do not ordinarily disclose fraudulent activities** to parties other than management and the audit committee.

Fraud involving senior management should always be **communicated to those charged with governance**, including the audit committee but not the SEC. Minor instances of fraud that are clearly inconsequential should be communicated to at least one level above those involved but not to the audit committee. If senior management and the board of directors refuse to acknowledge fraud that is material to the financial statements, the best course of action is to withdraw from the engagement, not to disclose it to principal shareholders. Disclosing that information violates the CPA's responsibility of client confidentiality.

Whistleblowing

Informing others (outside) the entity such as regulatory and enforcement authorities, is ordinarily prohibited by the auditor's confidentiality requirements, although the duty of confidentiality may be overridden by law or regulation (or the requirements of audits for governmental entities). Accordingly, it would be appropriate for the auditor to seek legal guidance when facing such circumstances. The auditing (and ethical) standards historically have identified four basic exceptions to the auditor's confidentiality requirements:

- The auditor must respond truthfully to a valid legal subpoena

- The auditor must comply with applicable legal and regulatory requirements (including complying with the SEC's 8-K requirements about important matters, such as the entity's decision to change auditors)

- A predecessor auditor must respond appropriately to the successor auditor's inquiries when the former client has given permission for the predecessor auditor to respond to the auditor's questions

- The auditor must report fraud to the applicable funding agency under the requirements of government auditing standards

Illegal Acts

AICPA Guidance

The relevant AICPA guidance is provided by AU-C 250, *Consideration of Laws and Regulations in an Audit of Financial Statements*. This pronouncement states that the auditor's objectives are to:

1. obtain sufficient appropriate audit evidence regarding material amounts and disclosures about laws and regulations generally recognized to have a direct effect on the financial statements;

2. perform specified audit procedures that may identify instances of noncompliance with other laws and regulations that may have a material effect on the financial statements; and

3. respond appropriately to noncompliance (or suspected noncompliance) with laws and regulations identified during the audit.

Definition

Legal and Regulatory Framework: Those laws and regulations to which an entity is subject; noncompliance may result in fines, litigation, or other consequences that may have a material effect on the financial statements.

Auditor Responsibility

The essence of the auditor's responsibility is to obtain reasonable assurance that the financial statements are free from material misstatement, whether caused by fraud or error, considering the applicable legal and regulatory framework.

- **Inherent Limitations**—The auditor cannot be expected to detect all noncompliance with all laws and regulations, since that is a legal determination and because many laws focus on an entity's operations instead of on the financial statementsThe SAS distinguishes between two categories of considerations:

- Laws and regulations having a direct effect on the amounts and/or disclosures in the financial statements—The auditor should obtain sufficient appropriate audit evidence regarding material amounts and disclosures

- Other laws and regulations not having a direct effect on the financial statements—The auditor should perform specified audit procedures that may identify noncompliance that may have a material effect on the financial statements

Audit procedures to identify illegal acts

- Read the minutes
- Inquire of management, in-house counsel, and external legal counsel concerning litigations, claims, and assessments
- Perform substantive tests of details of classes of transactions, account balances, or disclosures
- Examine large or unusual transactions

Auditor's Consideration of Compliance with Laws and Regulations

In obtaining an understanding of the entity and its environment, the auditor should obtain an understanding of the entity's applicable legal and regulatory framework and how the entity is complying with that framework.

- If information suggests **possible noncompliance**, the auditor should obtain an understanding of the circumstances of the act involved and gather further information to evaluate the financial statement effect. The auditor should also evaluate the implications of noncompliance to other aspects of the audit engagement, including risk assessment and the reliability of written representations

- If the auditor **suspects noncompliance**, the auditor should discuss the matter with management (at least one level above those suspected to be involved) and with those charged with governance, as appropriate

- If **unable to obtain sufficient information** as to compliance, the auditor should evaluate the effect of the lack of sufficient appropriate audit evidence on the auditor's report (and consider the need for obtaining legal advice)

Reporting of Identified or Suspected Noncompliance

Reporting Noncompliance to Those Charged with Governance—The auditor should communicate with those charged with governance any noncompliance with laws and regulations (unless it is clearly inconsequential). When management or those charged with governance is involved, the auditor should communicate to the next higher level of authority. If no higher level of authority within the entity exists, the auditor should consider obtaining legal advice.

Reporting Noncompliance in the Auditor's Report—If a material effect on the financial statements has not been appropriately reported, the auditor should modify the opinion (expressing either a qualified or adverse opinion). If the auditor has been prevented from obtaining sufficient appropriate audit evidence to evaluate the financial statement impact of the matter, the auditor should modify the opinion (expressing either a qualified opinion or disclaimer of opinion) for a scope limitation.

Reporting Noncompliance to Regulatory/Enforcement Authorities—The auditor should determine whether there is a responsibility to report the matter to parties outside the entity, which may take priority over confidentiality responsibilities. The auditor should consider obtaining legal advice about this issue.

If the entity refuses to accept a modified opinion and if withdrawal is possible under applicable law or regulation, the auditor may **withdraw from the engagement** and inform those charged with governance of the reasons in writing. Likewise, if the entity does not take the appropriate corrective action regarding noncompliance issues, the auditor may withdraw if such action is permitted by applicable law or regulation.

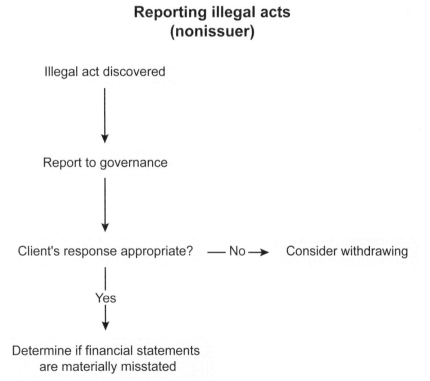

**Reporting illegal acts
(nonissuer)**

Illegal act discovered

Report to governance

Client's response appropriate? —— No ➔ Consider withdrawing

Yes

Determine if financial statements
are materially misstated

AUD 13
Planning For and Using the Work of Others

AUD 13: Planning For and Using the Work of Others

13.01 Planning For and Using the Work of Others

Overview

 Representative Task (Remembering & Understanding): Identify the factors to consider in determining the extent to which an engagement team can use the work of the internal audit function, IT auditor, auditor's specialist, management's specialist, or a component auditor.

 Representative Task (Application): Determine the nature and scope of the work of the internal audit function, IT auditor, auditor's specialist, management's specialist, or component auditor.

 Representative Task (Application): Perform and document procedures to determine the extent to which an engagement team can use the work of the internal audit function, IT auditor, auditor's specialist, management's specialist, or a component auditor.

An auditor may use the work of others in an audit to help perform audit procedures and gather evidence. An auditor may use the work of others to aid in:

- Valuation of complex financial instruments
- Actuarial calculations of liabilities for employee benefits
- Valuation of environmental liabilities and cleanup costs
- Estimation of oil and other mineral reserves
- Interpretation of contracts, laws, and regulations; and so forth

Parties that assist auditors in performing audit procedures and gathering evidence include:

- **Internal auditors.** They can provide audit evidence or direct assistance
- **IT auditors**. They can evaluate the client's IT system
- **Auditor's Specialists.** They can provide expertise that the auditor does not possess and are hired by the auditor (or work for the auditor firm)
- **Management's Specialists.** They also can provide expertise that the auditor does not possess but are hired (or work for) the client
- **Component auditors.** They can assist with a group financial audit
- Using the work of others comes with certain responsibilities for the **direction** and **supervision** of such individuals. There are also factors for the auditor to consider, such as their competence, objectivity, the nature and scope of their work, documentation, and reporting requirements.

Internal Auditors

AICPA Guidance

The relevant AICPA guidance is provided by AU-C 610, *Using the Work of Internal Audit*. This pronouncement requires the auditor to obtain an understanding of the role of the internal audit function while obtaining an understanding of the entity and its environment (ie, during the planning stage), including its internal controls. Based on that understanding, the auditor may conclude that the work of the internal audit function may provide audit evidence.

The internal auditor can assist the external auditor in a variety of areas, which include:

- **Gaining an understanding of the internal control structure**. The internal auditor will be a useful source of information about the structure

- **Testing controls**. The internal auditor can obtain evidence for review by the external auditor

- **Substantive testing**. The internal auditor can pull appropriate documents and assist the external auditor in locating assets to prove their existence

To use the work of internal auditors, the auditor will need to evaluate:

- The **objectivity and competence** of internal auditors and the internal audit function

- Whether the internal audit function applies a **systematic and disciplined approach** that includes quality control in the performance of its responsibilities

Competence

The external auditor will evaluate the **knowledge** and **skills** of the internal audit function and individual internal auditors to determine if their skills are sufficient to enable them to perform with the appropriate level of quality. There are several **factors** that enhance such competency.

- Resources (eg, money, staff, etc.) available to the internal audit function, relative to the size of the entity and the nature of its operations

- Policies related to the hiring, training, and matching of internal auditors with engagements

- Availability of technical training and experience

- Achievement of professional designations (eg, Certified Internal Auditor) based on established professional standards

- Demonstrated knowledge of the entity's AFRF and knowledge specific to the industry and the entity's financial reporting

- Membership in professional associations establishing relevant professional standards and requirements for the continuing education of its members

A *deficiency in objectivity* cannot be compensated for by *strength in competency*, nor vice versa. To judge both **competence and objectivity**, the external auditor may also consider:

- Entity policies and procedures, along with the status of internal audit within the organization

- Discussions with management

- The external auditor's previous dealings with the internal auditor

- The internal auditor's compliance with professional internal auditing standards

Objectivity

The external auditor will also need to determine whether internal auditors are objective:

- Free of bias or conflicts of interests

- Subject to the undue influence of others such that the professional judgment of internal auditors may be overridden or otherwise affected

When performing an **evaluation of the objectivity** of the internal audit function and of individual internal auditors, the external auditor should keep in mind **that neither can be independent** in relation to the entity.

The **level of authority** to which internal auditors report will significantly affect objectivity, as follows:

- Objectivity is *enhanced* when internal auditors report to those charged with governance or an officer with appropriate authority

- Objectivity is *impaired* when internal auditors report to management, although this can be mitigated if the internal auditors have access to those charged with governance

- Constraints or restrictions on internal auditors, such as restrictions on communications with the external auditors, *impair* objectivity

- The level at which employment and remuneration decisions related to internal auditors are made also affects objectivity

- Objectivity is *enhanced* when internal auditors participate in professional associations that impose professional standards related to objectivity on their members or when the entity's internal policies are designed to achieve comparable objectives

Internal auditor's objectivity

Promotes objectivity

Board of directors

Senior management (eg, CEO) — Audit committee

Lower-level managers — Internal audit function

Impairs objectivity

Board of directors

Senior management (eg, CEO)

Management — Internal audit function

Systematic & Disciplined Approach

When considering using the work of the internal audit function in obtaining audit evidence, it is essential that the work is performed applying a **systematic and disciplined approach** that includes an element of **quality control**. When such an approach is not applied, neither a high level of competence nor the strong support of the internal audit function's objectivity can compensate.

Internal Auditor Judgment

Regardless of the level of objectivity, competence, or the application of a systematic and disciplined approach, the external auditor will not rely on the internal audit function or internal auditors in relation to any matters that require the application of the **auditor's judgment**.

This includes significant judgments, such as:

- Assessing the RMM
- Evaluating the sufficiency of tests performed
- Evaluating management's assumptions as to substantial doubt as to whether the entity is a going concern
- Evaluating significant estimates
- Evaluating the adequacy of disclosures or any other issues that may affect the external auditor's report on the F/S

The work of the internal audit function may:

- Include **tests of controls and/or substantive tests**. The external auditor may be able to use the results of such tests to modify the nature or timing, or to reduce the extent, of the respective tests that the auditor had planned to perform
- Be **applied to a component of a group** for which the external auditor is the group auditor. The external auditor may be able to use the results of those procedures, for example, to reduce the number of components to which audit procedures are applied
- Be used to **obtain evidence** regarding the tracing of transactions through the accounting information system to determine if information is being properly and accurately captured and summarized for reporting purposes and regarding compliance with regulatory requirements

Assessing internal audit	
Competence	• Internal auditor education, certification, experience • Departmental policies & practices • Supervision • Documentation & report quality
Objectivity	• Organization status/reporting level • Policies maintaining organizational objectivity
Competence and objectivity	• Institute of Internal Auditors (IIA) guidelines

Direct Assistance in Performing Audit Procedures

Prior to using internal auditors to provide *direct assistance* in the performance of audit procedures, the external auditor will obtain **written representation** from management or those charged with governance *indicating* that:

- The internal auditors will be allowed to follow the instructions of the external auditor; and
- The entity will not intervene in the work performed for the external auditor by the internal auditors.

The amount of direction, supervision, and review will be based on the external auditor's evaluation of the objectivity and competence of the internal auditors.

- Review procedures will include testing some of the work performed by the internal auditor
- The external auditor will instruct internal auditors to bring identified accounting and auditing issues to their attention
- The auditor should remain alert to any indications that prior evaluations of the internal auditor's objectivity or competence are no longer appropriate

An entity has an internal audit staff that the external auditor assessed to be both competent and objective. Which of the following statements is correct about the **external auditor's** use of the internal auditors to provide direct assistance in performing tests of controls?

- The auditor cannot rely on any of the work of the internal auditors

- The internal auditors should not be performing any audit procedures that the auditor is able to perform

- The auditor can use internal auditors to assess control risk, but cannot rely on their tests of controls

- The auditor should direct, supervise, and review the work performed by the internal auditors

Internal audit assistance	
Allowed if internal audit is deemed competent and objective	• To reduce the amount of external auditor's testing • To test controls • To map flow of data • Under the external auditor's supervision
Not allowed	• For matters requiring external auditor judgement • To test areas with high risk of material misstatement • To reduce external auditor responsibility • If there is a threat to internal audit objectivity

An external F/S auditor may rely on internal auditors to perform audit work in certain areas after determining that the internal auditors are competent and objective. For example, auditors often rely on internal auditors to help gain an understanding of and/or test I/C. However, the external auditor still has *sole responsibility* for the audit report, and must **direct, supervise, review, and evaluate *all* audit work**. The external auditor should also re-perform some of the internal audit work to validate the results.

Documentation

The external auditor will document the results of the evaluation of:

- The objectivity of the internal audit function and the internal auditors, including the status of each within the organization and entity policies and procedures that support objectivity

- The competence of the internal audit function and the internal auditors

- The application of a systematic and disciplined approach by the internal audit function, including quality control, but only if using the work of the internal audit function to obtain audit evidence

When using the work of the internal audit function to **obtain audit evidence**, the external auditor will document the:

- Nature and extent of the work used and the basis for the decision to use it

- Period covered by the work performed by the internal audit function and the results of the work

- Procedures performed to evaluate the adequacy of the work of the internal audit function, including procedures applied in re-performing some of the work

- Basis for concluding that the external auditor was adequately involved in the engagement

When using internal auditors to **provide direct assistance** to the external auditor in performing audit procedures, documentation will include:

- Threats to the objectivity of the internal auditors and safeguards that eliminated the threats or reduced them to an acceptable level
- The level of competence of the internal auditors providing direct assistance
- The basis for deciding on the nature and extent of work to be performed by internal auditors
- The nature and extent of the review performed by the external auditor in relation to work performed by internal auditors
- Working papers prepared by internal auditors providing direct assistance to the external audit in the performance of audit procedures
- The basis for concluding that the external auditor was adequately involved in the engagement

IT Auditors

Many organizations rely on complex IT systems throughout the financial reporting process. Because *financial auditors* may have a limited understanding of IT systems, they commonly rely on **assistance** from **IT auditors** in both **planning** and **performing procedures**. This is particularly appropriate when the IT system is especially complex, newly implemented, or custom designed for the client.

IT auditors may be employed by the audit firm or the client as part of the internal audit function, or they may be external specialists that are called upon to assist in select audit situations.

- If they are part of the **audit firm**, they would be viewed as part of the audit staff performing an engagement
- If the IT auditor is **employed by the client**, any resulting work they perform would be subject to the same evaluation as that of an internal auditor
- If the IT auditor is an **external specialist**, any resulting work they perform would be subject to the same evaluation as that of a specialist

An IT auditor can assist the auditor with:

- Obtaining an understanding of the IT system, including its general and application controls, and the effect on the audit
- Identifying and assessing IT risks as well as control deficiencies
- Designing and performing tests of IT controls and substantive tests through the computer using computer-assisted auditing techniques (CAATs)
- Determining the effect of outsourced IT activities and evaluating controls that mitigate any associated risks
- Preparing system audit documentation (eg, system flowcharts, data flow diagrams, process diagrams, etc.)

IT auditor may assist financial auditor in:

- Obtaining understanding of the IT system, including controls
- Assessing risk of material misstatement related to IT
- Designing and performing tests of controls
- Designing and performing substantive tests
- Preparing audit documentation (eg, data flow diagrams)

Specialists

AICPA Guidance

The relevant AICPA guidance is provided by AU-C 620, *Using the Work of an Auditor's Specialist*. This pronouncement states that the **auditor's objectives** are to determine: (1) whether to use the work of an auditor's specialist; and (2) whether the work of the auditor's specialist is adequate for the auditor's purposes.

Definitions

Auditor's Specialist: An individual or organization possessing expertise in a field other than accounting or auditing, whose work in that field is used by the auditor to assist the auditor in obtaining sufficient appropriate audit evidence.

Management's Specialist: An individual or organization possessing expertise in a field other than accounting or auditing, whose work in that field is used by the entity to assist the entity in preparing the financial statements (F/S).

Circumstances

Circumstances sometimes arise in an audit when the work of a **specialist** is needed (remember, internal audit is *not considered* to be a specialist). For example:

- A gemologist may be required for an audit of a jewelry store to verify the **valuation** of inventory
- A land surveyor might be needed to help gauge the **quantity** of property owned by the client

Requirements

Although the specialist will often be performing tasks that the auditor is not personally capable of performing, the **auditor must understand** the **methods** and **assumptions** underlying the specialist's work, and must be able to **evaluate** the **results** of that work. The specialist, in turn, must understand the way the auditor will be utilizing the specialist's work to provide **corroborative evidence** to support the auditor's opinion. These understandings should be documented.

Audit requirements when using a specialist:

- Evaluate the specialist's competence and objectivity
- Create a written agreement for nature, scope, and objective of work
- Evaluate the work of the specialist
- Verify any relationships with the client are appropriate
- Assess the risk of material misstatement with the subject matter

The auditor should carefully consider the specialist's **competence and objectivity**.

- **Competence** may be demonstrated by licenses, reputation, and the quality of written reports
- **Objectivity** depends on the specialist not having any relationship with the client that would impair the specialist's independence
  - An auditor may still utilize the work of a specialist who lacks objectivity but must consider the situation in gauging the level of persuasiveness of the evidence received from the specialist

The auditor will **evaluate the adequacy** of the work of the specialist, including:

- The *relevance and reasonableness* of the specialist's findings and conclusions and their consistency with the audit evidence

- The specialist's use of *significant assumptions and methods*, which the auditor should understand and evaluate

- The specialist's use of *source data*, in which case the auditor will evaluate its relevance, accuracy, and completeness

If the **work is not adequate**, the auditor and the auditor's specialist should agree on any further work to be performed, or the auditor should perform additional audit procedures that are appropriate to the circumstances (which could include engaging another auditor's specialist). If the auditor is unable to resolve the matter, it could constitute a **scope limitation** that would result in a **modified opinion**.

The auditor must be cautious about references to the work of the specialist in the audit report. Since it is not appropriate to divide responsibility for the opinion with someone who is not also an auditor, the auditor must **not refer** to the specialist in the audit report if it contains an **unmodified/unqualified** opinion.

- The auditor may refer to the work of a specialist if it is relevant to the understanding of a modification to the auditor's opinion

- When referring to the work of a specialist, the auditor should indicate in the report that the reference does not reduce the auditor's responsibility for the opinion

In using the work of a specialist, an auditor may refer to the specialist in the auditor's report if, as a result of the specialist's findings, the auditor

- Desires to disclose the specialist's findings, which imply that a more thorough audit was performed

- Makes suggestions to management that are likely to improve the entity's internal control

- Corroborates another specialist's findings that were consistent with management's assertions

- Adds an explanatory paragraph to the auditor's report to emphasize an unusually important subsequent event

Disclosing the work of a specialist	
Unmodified opinion	No reference is made to the specialist
Modified opinion	<ul><li>Add explanatory language indicating that the use of a specialist:</li><li>Does not reduce the auditor's responsibility for the audit opinion and</li><li>Helps users understand critical matters in the financial statements</li></ul>

Circumstances may arise in an audit that require the work of a **specialist**. The auditor **may not refer** to the specialist in the audit report if the report contains an *unmodified (ie, unqualified)* opinion. This may imply that the auditor is attempting to share responsibility for the opinion or that a more thorough audit was performed.

The auditor can refer to the specialist (in an **explanatory paragraph**) *only* when the audit report is **modified** and *only* if the disclosure is **relevant to the reader's understanding** of the specialist's findings.

For example, a real estate developer might purchase property *after the report date* but before the release date (ie, a subsequent event) and discover ground contamination that requires the use of a specialist to quantify the potential legal issues. If the opinion refers to the specialist, the auditor should indicate that the reference **does not reduce** the auditor's responsibility for the opinion.

Component Auditors & Group Financial Audits

A component auditor is an auditor involved in part of a **group audit engagement**. For example, a company may have subsidiaries (ie, components) whose F/S are audited by other firms (ie, component auditors).

The component auditors provide opinions on each component separately and the group auditor provides an opinion on the group (eg, parent company) F/S. In that case, the group auditor must decide whether to **assume responsibility** for the component auditor's work. The group engagement auditor must **evaluate component auditors**, taking into consideration the items in the box below:

The group engagement auditor should **obtain sufficient appropriate audit evidence** regarding the component *without* using any of the work of the component auditor when:

- The component auditor does not meet independence requirements, or
- The group engagement auditor has reservations about other matters.

Reporting Requirements

If the group auditor decides to **assume responsibility** for the work of a component auditor, they **should not** make any **reference** to the component auditor. If, however, the group auditor determines that it will **refer** to the component auditor as a means of indicating a **division of responsibility**:

- The component auditor must have complied with GAAS
- The component auditor's report cannot be restricted

The group auditor should:

- Clearly indicate in the report that the component was not audited by the group auditor but the component auditor. Such indication should include the magnitude of the portion of the F/S audited by the component auditor
- Present the component auditor's report together with the report on the group F/S
- Consider whether modifications to the component auditor's report may necessitate modifications to the group auditor's report

Using the work of a component auditor

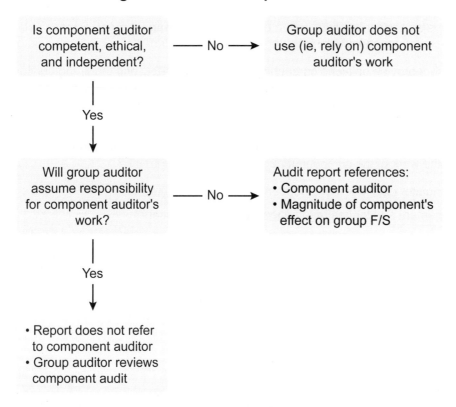

If the F/S of a component were prepared in accordance with a financial reporting framework (FRF) that is different from the FRF applicable to the group F/S, no reference should be made unless:

- The measurement, recognition, presentation, and disclosure criteria incorporated into the FRF used for the component are similar to those applicable to the FRF applied to the group F/S; and

- The group auditor has obtained evidence indicating that adjustments made to convert the component's F/S to the FRF used in the group F/S are appropriate.

AUD 14
Specific Areas of
Engagement Risk

AUD 14: Specific Areas of Engagement Risk

14.01 An Entity's Compliance with Laws and Regulations

Overview

 Representative Task (Remembering & Understanding): Understand the accountant's responsibilities with respect to laws and regulations that have a direct effect on the determination of material amounts or disclosures in an entity's financial statements for an engagement.

 Representative Task (Remembering & Understanding): Understand the accountant's responsibilities with respect to laws and regulations that are fundamental to an entity's business but do not have a direct effect on the entity's financial statements in an engagement.

AICPA Guidance

Noncompliance with applicable laws and regulations (ie, illegal acts) is defined as acts of omission or commission by the entity, either intentional or unintentional, which are contrary to the prevailing laws or regulations. Such noncompliance may result in fines, litigation, or other consequences that may have a material effect on the F/S.

The relevant AICPA guidance is provided by AU-C 250, *Consideration of Laws and Regulations in an* Audit of Financial Statements. This pronouncement states that the auditor's objectives are to:

- Obtain sufficient appropriate audit evidence regarding material amounts and disclosures about laws and regulations generally recognized to have a direct effect on the F/S

- Perform specified audit procedures that may identify instances of noncompliance with other laws and regulations that may have a material effect on the F/S

- Respond appropriately to noncompliance (or suspected noncompliance) with laws and regulations identified during the audit

Management's Responsibility

It is **management's responsibility** to ensure that an entity's operations are conducted in accordance with the provisions of laws and regulations. An **auditor's primary concern** of noncompliance (ie, illegal acts) is whether it results in a material misstatement. AU-C 240 states that a material misstatement may occur due to errors, fraud, and illegal acts with a direct effect on financial statement amounts.

Inherent limitations: The auditor cannot be expected to detect all noncompliance with all laws and regulations, since that is a legal determination and because many laws focus on an entity's operations instead of on the F/S. (Note that the personal misconduct of management, those charged with governance, or others is outside the meaning of the term *noncompliance*.)

Audit Procedures

 Representative Task (Application): Perform tests of compliance with laws and regulations that have a direct effect on material amounts or disclosures in an entity's financial statements in an engagement.

 Representative Task (Application): Perform tests of compliance with laws and regulations that are fundamental to an entity's business, but do not have a direct effect on the entity's financial statements for an engagement.

In obtaining an understanding of the entity and its environment, the auditor should obtain an understanding of

- The entity's applicable legal and regulatory framework; *and*
- How the entity is complying with that framework.

The SAS distinguishes between two categories of considerations:

- **Laws and regulations having a direct effect on the amounts and/or disclosures in the financial statements.** Here, the auditor should obtain sufficient appropriate audit evidence regarding material amounts and disclosures

- **Other laws and regulations *not having* a direct effect on the financial statements.** Here, the auditor should perform specified audit procedures that may identify noncompliance that may have a material effect on the financial statements. The specified audit procedures include inquiry of management and those charged with governance about compliance issues, inspection of any correspondence with regulatory authorities, reading minutes, and so forth

 If specific information comes to an auditor's attention that implies noncompliance with laws that could result in a material, but indirect effect on the financial statements, the auditor should:

- Seek the advice of an informed expert as to possible contingent liabilities
- Apply audit procedures directed to ascertaining whether compliance has occurred
- Report the matter to an appropriate level of management at least one level above those involved
- Discuss the evidence with the client's audit committee

AU-C 250 requires the auditor to **apply audit procedures** specifically designed to determine whether an illegal act has occurred when such information comes to his/her attention. The remaining answer choices would all occur *after initial procedures* had confirmed the existence of the illegal act(s).

If information suggests **possible noncompliance,** the auditor should obtain an understanding of the circumstances of the act involved and gather further information to evaluate the financial statement effect. The auditor should also evaluate the implications of noncompliance to other aspects of the audit engagement, including risk assessment and the reliability of written representations.

If the auditor **suspects noncompliance**, the auditor should discuss the matter with management (at least one level above those suspected to be involved) and with those charged with governance, as appropriate.

If **unable to obtain sufficient information** as to compliance, the auditor should evaluate the effect of the lack of sufficient appropriate audit evidence on the auditor's report (and consider the need for obtaining legal advice).

Audit procedures to identify illegal acts

- Read the minutes

- Inquire of management, in-house counsel, and external legal counsel concerning litigations, claims, and assessments

- Perform substantive tests of details of classes of transactions, account balances, or disclosures

- Examine large or unusual transactions

Reporting of Identified or Suspected Noncompliance

The auditor should communicate with **those charged with governance** any noncompliance with laws and regulations (unless it is clearly inconsequential). When management or those charged with governance is involved, the auditor should communicate to the **next higher level of authority**. If no higher level of authority within the entity exists, the auditor should consider obtaining legal advice.

If a **material effect** on the F/S has not been appropriately reported, the auditor should **modify the opinion** (expressing either a qualified or adverse opinion). If the auditor has been prevented from obtaining sufficient appropriate audit evidence to evaluate the F/S impact of the matter, the auditor should modify the opinion (expressing either a qualified opinion or disclaimer of opinion) for a scope limitation.

The auditor should determine whether there is a responsibility to **report the matter to parties outside** the entity, which may take priority over confidentiality responsibilities. The auditor should consider obtaining legal advice about this issue.

If the entity refuses to accept a modified opinion and if withdrawal is possible under applicable law or regulation, the auditor may withdraw from the engagement and inform those charged with governance of the reasons in writing. Likewise, if the entity does not take the appropriate corrective action regarding noncompliance issues, the auditor may withdraw if such action is permitted by applicable law or regulation.

 During the audit of a nonissuer client, the auditor determined that management had given illegal bribes to municipal officials during the year under audit and for several prior years. The auditor notified the client's board of directors, but the board decided to take no action because the amounts involved were immaterial to the financial statements. Under these circumstances, the auditor should

- Add an explanatory paragraph emphasizing that certain matters, while not affecting the unmodified opinion, require disclosure

- Report the illegal bribes to the municipal official at least one level above those persons who received the bribes

- Consider withdrawing from the audit engagement and disassociating from future relationships with the client

- Issue a qualified opinion or an adverse opinion with a separate paragraph that explains the circumstances

Reporting illegal acts
(nonissuer)

```
            ┌─────────────────────────┐
            │  Illegal act discovered │
            └─────────────────────────┘
                        │
                        ▼
            ┌─────────────────────────┐
            │   Report to governance  │
            └─────────────────────────┘
                        │
                        ▼
    ┌──────────────────────────────┐         ┌─────────────────────┐
    │ Client's response appropriate?│── No ──▶│ Consider withdrawing│
    └──────────────────────────────┘         └─────────────────────┘
                        │
                       Yes
                        │
                        ▼
            ┌─────────────────────────────┐
            │ Determine if financial      │
            │ statements are materially   │
            │ misstated                   │
            └─────────────────────────────┘
```

Auditors of nonissuers are required to **report illegal acts** to those charged with **governance** unless the acts are clearly inconsequential. If those charged with governance do not take appropriate action, the auditor should **consider withdrawing** from the engagement. Even if an illegal act has no material effect on the financial statements, the entity's inaction may call into question the **integrity of management** or those charged with governance.

If the auditor is satisfied as to management's integrity and decides not to withdraw, there is no need to reference the illegal acts in the audit report because they are immaterial. Because the illegal acts do not have a material effect on the financial statements, a qualified or adverse opinion would be inappropriate. Note that the auditor *may* need to report the illegal acts to the appropriate agency if the client receives federal financial assistance, but no such assistance is indicated in this case.

*Note: If the **client were an issuer**, the board of directors would have to be notified within one business day of the auditor's discovery. If the board failed to notify the SEC by the next business day, the auditor would need to withdraw or notify the SEC.*

Documentation

The auditor should document the identified or suspected noncompliance and the results of the discussion with management, those charged with governance, and others, as applicable. Such documentation might include:

- Copies of records or documents
- Minutes of the discussion with management, those charged with governance, and others

14.02 Accounting Estimates

Overview

 Representative Task (Remembering & Understanding): Recognize the potential impact of lower complexity and higher complexity significant accounting estimates on the risk of material misstatement, including the indicators of management bias.

AICPA Guidance

Many items that are required to be reported or disclosed in the F/S may not be subject to precise measurement as of the F/S date. As a result, these items require the use of an accounting estimate. An **accounting estimate** is an approximation of a F/S element, item, or account.

AU-C 540 *Auditing Accounting Estimates, Including Fair Value Accounting Estimates and Related Disclosures* provides guidance and requirements relative to the auditor's responsibility for such accounting estimates, including fair value measurements.

Auditing Approaches

When auditing accounting estimates, a combination of approaches may be used, including:

- Reviewing and testing management's process, including the method of measurement, assumptions made, and the data used
- Developing an estimate Independently
- Reviewing subsequent events up to the date of the auditor's report
- Testing the effectiveness of internal controls related to accounting estimates

The auditor's main concern is to **determine** the **reasonableness** of the **estimates** and the related **disclosures** made by management. In evaluating the reasonableness of estimates, auditors normally concentrate on assumptions that are subjective (ie, higher risk) and more susceptible to bias (and fraud).

In evaluating an entity's accounting estimates, one of the auditor's objectives is to determine whether the estimates are

- Prepared in a satisfactory control environment
- Consistent with industry guidelines
- Based on verifiable objective assumptions
- Reasonable in the circumstances

An auditor is responsible for **evaluating the reasonableness** of accounting estimates made by management in the context of the financial statements taken as a whole. While it is advantageous to have accounting estimates prepared in a satisfactory control environment, this is *not required*. There are few industry guidelines with respect to accounting estimates. In many circumstances the assumptions may be quite subjective (ie, may not be objective).

Understanding Management's Process

The auditor's initial step is to understand the **process used by management** to prepare significant estimates. The auditor will consider estimates when performing risk assessment procedures to understand the entity and its environment.

In doing so, the auditor will obtain an understanding of:

- The requirements of the applicable financial reporting framework (AFRF)
- How management determines when estimates are necessary
- How management develops accounting estimates and the data on which they are based

Management Bias

The auditor must:

- Determine whether the accounting estimates are reasonable in relation to the AFRF or are misstated
- Determine if disclosures are in compliance with the AFRF
- Evaluate management's decisions and judgments for potential management bias

Management bias is inherent in subjective decisions and may be intentional or unintentional. Professional skepticism will be very important in evaluating any of the following indicators of possible management bias:

Testing for management bias
• Review any arbitrary or subjective changes in estimates or methods
• Examine events that may indicate an estimate is misstated
• Assess management's estimation efforts addressing uncertainty
• Review fair value estimates inconsistent with observable market assumptions
• Test significant assumptions that favor management objectives or indicate a pattern of optimism or pessimism

Assessing the Risks of Material Misstatement

Based on this understanding, the auditor will evaluate the risk of material misstatement (RMM) of estimates. All accounting estimates are subject to a degree of estimation uncertainty, which results in RMM. The degree of that estimation uncertainty depends on:

- The nature of the estimate

- The subjectivity of assumptions used

- The availability of a generally accepted method or model to arrive at the estimate

In evaluating the reasonableness of an entity's accounting estimates, an auditor most likely concentrates on key factors and assumptions that are

- Stable and not sensitive to variation

- Objective and not susceptible to bias

- Deviations from historical patterns

- Similar to industry guidelines

Lower-risk estimates	Higher-risk estimates
• Estimates related to transactions and activities that are not complex	• Estimates involving the outcome of litigation Estimates of fair value for securities that are not publicly traded
• Estimates related to routine transactions	• Fair value estimates formulated:
• Estimates based on readily available, reliable data (eg, published market values)	○ Using a complex or sophisticated model
• Fair value estimates measured:	○ Involving assumptions or inputs that are not observable
○ Using simple and easily applied approaches	
○ Under generally accepted models that use observable inputs/assumptions	

There are a number of techniques the auditor can use to evaluate reasonableness. In general, the auditor should concentrate on estimates that represent the **highest risk of misstatement**. Such estimates have underlying assumptions that are subjective and therefore more susceptible to management bias. Higher-risk estimates include those that:

- Differ from expectations (ie, deviate from historical patterns)

- Lack stability or objectivity (ie, are subject to management bias)

- Contradict industry guidelines and averages

Additional topics related to Accounting Estimates are covered in Chapter 19, including: Procedures to Respond to RMM and Evaluation of Evidence, Disclosures, and Management Bias

PCAOB Requirements

PCAOB Guidance and Overview

PCAOB Auditing Standard No. 43 addresses accounting estimates, including fair value measurements. This standard:

- Requires auditors to give greater attention to **potential management bias** involving accounting estimates as follows:
  - Requires a discussion among audit team members (ie, **brain-storming**) about the potential for management bias
  - Emphasizes the importance of exercising **professional skepticism**
  - Requires auditors to consider contradictory evidence as well as corroborating evidence regarding assertions related to such estimates
  - Requires auditors to identify significant assumptions (and evaluate their reasonableness) related to estimates, including those that are susceptible to bias
  - Requires auditors to obtain an understanding of management's analysis of "critical accounting estimates"
  - Requires auditors to evaluate whether data was appropriately used and whether any change in the source of data is appropriate
- Extends key requirements in the fair value standard to other significant accounting estimates to achieve a more uniform approach to substantive testing
  - Describes the auditor's responsibilities for testing the methods, data, and significant assumptions used by the company in developing the estimate
  - Describes the auditor's responsibilities for evaluating the company's methods for developing the estimate, including whether the methods conform with the requirements of the applicable financial reporting framework and are appropriate in the circumstances
- Integrates requirements with the PCAOB's risk assessment standards to emphasize estimates having greater RMM
  - Addresses risk factors to identify significant accounts and disclosures associated with accounting estimates
  - Acknowledges that it might be impossible to design effective substantive procedures alone that would provide sufficient appropriate audit evidence when dealing with accounting estimates that involve complex models or processes
- Provides more specific requirements when auditing the fair value of financial instruments
  - Requires a determination of whether pricing information obtained from third parties (eg, pricing services and brokers or dealers) provides sufficient appropriate audit evidence
  - Requires the auditor to obtain an understanding of how any unobservable inputs were determined and to evaluate their reasonableness

Additional Specific Considerations

To test accounting estimates, the auditor should perform one or more of the following:

- Test the company's process for developing the accounting estimate
- Develop an independent expectation for comparison
- Evaluate evidence from events occurring after the measurement date

When the company **changed the method** used to determine the accounting estimate, the auditor should evaluate the appropriateness of the change.

When evaluating the reasonableness of **significant assumptions**, the auditor should determine whether the company has a *reasonable basis* for significant assumptions used.

- Significant assumptions are those that are important to the recognition for measurement of an accounting estimate (eg, assumptions that are sensitive to variation, susceptible to manipulation or bias, involve unobservable data, or depend on the company's intent and ability to carry out specific actions)

The auditor should also determine whether the significant assumptions are **consistent** with the following, when applicable:

- Relevant industry and other external factors, including economic factors

- The company's objectives, strategies, and business risks

- External market information

- Relevant historical or recent experience

- Other significant assumptions used by the company in other estimates tested by the auditor

Critical accounting estimates are accounting estimates where the:

- Nature of the estimate is material due to the levels of subjectivity and judgment necessary to account for **highly uncertain matters** or the susceptibility of such matters to change

- Impact of the estimate on financial condition or operating performance is material

- The auditor should obtain an understanding of management's analysis of the sensitivity of its significant assumptions to change when evaluating the reasonableness of the significant assumptions and potential for bias

14.03 Related Parties and Related Party Transactions

Overview

 Representative Task (Application): Perform procedures to identify related party relationships and transactions, including consideration of significant unusual transactions and transactions with executive officers.

AICPA Guidance

The relevant AICPA guidance is provided by the clarified SAS, AU-C 550, *Related Parties*. This pronouncement states that the auditor's objectives are to obtain:

- An understanding of related-party relationships and transactions to address fraud risk factors and evaluate whether the F/S achieve fair presentation
- Sufficient appropriate audit evidence about whether related-party relationships and transactions are properly identified, accounted for and adequately disclosed in the F/S

Definitions

Financial Accounting Standards Board (FASB) definition of **related party**:

"Affiliates of the enterprise; entities for which investments are accounted for by the equity method by the enterprise; trusts for the benefit of employees, such as pension and profit-sharing trusts that are managed by or under the trusteeship of management; principal owners of the enterprise; its management; members of the immediate families of principal owners of the enterprise and its management; and other parties with which the enterprise may deal if one party controls or can significantly influence the management or operating policies of the other to an extent that one of the transacting parties might be prevented from fully pursuing its own separate interests."

AICPA definition of **arm's-length transaction**:

"A transaction conducted on such terms and conditions between a willing buyer and a willing seller who are unrelated and are acting independently of each other and pursuing their own best interests."

Historical Cost Principle

The historical cost principle in accounting is based on the notion of an **exchange price** negotiated in an **arms-length transaction**, which results in an accurate measure of the value exchanged. However, related parties could potentially set the transaction price at whatever value they wish, without regard to the "real" economic value or even engage in fraudulent transactions.

As a result, auditors have **multiple responsibilities for related party transactions** and the RMM arising from such transactions. They must ensure that related parties are fully identified and that related party transactions served a business purpose and are adequately accounted for and disclosed.

Risk Assessment

The auditor should assess the **risk of material misstatement (RMM)** that could result from the entity's related-party relationships and transactions. The auditor should view any significant related-party transactions outside the entity's normal course of business as **significant risks**.

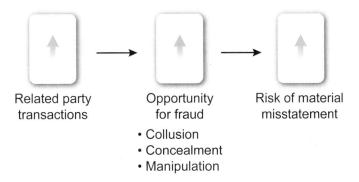

Related party
transactions

Opportunity
for fraud

- Collusion
- Concealment
- Manipulation

Risk of material
misstatement

As part of the risk assessment procedures, the auditor should:

- **Inquire of management** and others within the entity about:
  - The identity of the entity's related parties
  - The nature of the relationships involved
  - The business purpose of entering into a transaction with a related party (instead of an unrelated party)
  - Whether the entity entered into, modified, or terminated any transactions with related parties; if so, the type and business purpose of the transactions

- Inquire about (and perform other risk assessment procedures) to **obtain an understanding** of the applicable controls established to:
  - Identify and account for such related-party relationships and transactions
  - Authorize and approve significant transactions with related parties, as well as those that may be significant unusual transactions. (The risk of management override of controls is higher when management has significant influence with parties with whom the entity does business.)

- Inquire about any related-party transactions that were **not subject to established controls** for authorization and approval; inquire about the reasons for any such exceptions
  - Examples of arrangements that may indicate **undisclosed** related-party relationships
    - Participation in partnerships with other parties
    - Agreements with other parties having conditions outside the normal course of business
    - Guarantees involving other parties
  - Examples of transactions that may be significant unusual transactions (ie, **outside the normal course of business**)
    - Complex equity transactions (restructurings or acquisitions)
    - Transactions with offshore entities
    - Sales transactions with unusually large discounts
    - Transactions with circular arrangements (such as repurchase agreements)

- Examine documents for **unusual or large transactions** (such as investment transactions) and transactions that have terms or conditions that are inconsistent with prevailing market conditions (such as loans with abnormal interest rates or without stated maturity dates):

  ○ Guarantees of loans (either payable or receivable) might be identified on confirmations of such loans

  ○ Transactions with major customers, suppliers, borrowers, or lenders might indicate undisclosed relationships

  ○ Invoices from law firms might indicate work performed for related parties or related-party transactions

- **Remain alert** for any indications of related-party relationships or transactions that management has failed to disclose to the auditor. The auditor should be attentive to such matters when

  ○ Reviewing bank confirmations and other records or documents

  ○ Reading the minutes of meetings of those charged with governance

  ○ Significant unusual transactions are identified

- **Share relevant information** about related parties with the members of the engagement team

 Which of the following procedures most likely could assist an auditor in identifying related party transactions?

- Performing tests of controls concerning the segregation of duties
- Evaluating the reasonableness of management's accounting estimates
- Reviewing confirmations of compensating balance arrangements
- Scanning the accounting records for recurring transactions

Transactions that suggest related-party involvement

- Loans at zero or unusually low interest rates
- Sales at prices far above or below fair market or appraised value
- Large, nonrecurring transactions occurring very close to the balance sheet date
- Loan guarantees

Routine testing such as evaluating segregation of duties or testing management's estimates is not likely to identify related-party transactions, so additional audit work is required to specifically search for related-party activity.

For example, if a compensating balance on a loan is maintained for the benefit of a principal stockholder, it could be an indication that the entity may be indebted to that stockholder. Reviewing terms of the loan included on a confirmation may provide evidence of such an arrangement.

Response to Risk Assessment

When there is a **significant risk** about related-party transactions or they are required to be disclosed, the auditor should :

- Read the contracts or agreements
- Determine that the transaction terms are consistent with management's explanations
- Verify that the transactions have been appropriately accounted for and disclosed
- Verify appropriate authorization and approval for the transactions

Additional substantive procedures that may be performed when a significant risk of improper accounting or inadequate disclosure exists include:

- Confirm business purpose, terms, or amounts with related parties

- Inspect evidence in the possession of the related party or other parties

- Confirm (or discuss) information with intermediaries, such as banks or others

- Review the F/S to evaluate **financial capability** of related-party for material receivables, guarantees, and other obligations

The auditor should evaluate whether the identified related-party relationships and transactions have been **appropriately accounted for** and **properly disclosed** and whether the F/S achieve *fair presentation* regarding those related-party relationships and transactions. The **substance** of the transactions is normally *more important* than their legal form.

If the auditor identifies related-party transactions **not previously disclosed** by management, the auditor should:

- Communicate relevant information to members of the engagement team

- Ask management to identify all transactions with the newly identified related party

- Inquire about why the entity's controls did not identify the related-party relationship

- Perform appropriate substantive audit procedures

- Reconsider the risk that there may be other undisclosed related-party relationships

- Evaluate whether management's failure to disclose the matter might have been intentional

If the auditor identifies related-party transactions that are **required to be disclosed** or are considered to be a **significant risk**, the auditor should determine whether those transactions have been appropriately authorized. The auditor should also inspect any underlying agreements to evaluate the business purpose and whether the terms are consistent with management's explanations or whether the business rationale might suggest fraud

In auditing related party transactions, an auditor ordinarily places primary emphasis on

- The probability that related-party transactions will recur

- Confirming the existence of the related parties

- Verifying the valuation of the related-party transactions

- The adequacy of the disclosure of the related-party transactions

Auditors are responsible for identifying related-party transactions and obtaining evidence to determine whether management has properly **identified, disclosed, and presented** the transactions in the financial statements. Confirming *known* related parties would not help in identifying *unknown* related parties, which is the underlying audit risk.

Communication

The auditor should communicate with those **charged with governance** any significant matters involving the entity's related parties and inquire about any concerns those charged with governance may have about relationships or related-party transactions.

Documentation

The auditor should include in the audit documentation the names of the identified related parties and the nature.

14.04 Uniform Guidance for Single Audits

Government Auditing Standards

 Representative Task (Remembering & Understanding): Understand when an entity is required to have a single audit in accordance with the audit requirements of the Uniform Guidance, including the identification of federal awards and major programs.

 Additional topics related to Uniform Guidance for Single Audits are covered under Chapter 19.06. That coverage is related to testing transactions for federal awards.

Government Auditing Standards (also known as Generally Accepted Government Auditing Standards or GAGAS) are issued by the U.S. Government Accountability Office (in GAO's Yellow Book) under the authority of the Comptroller General of the United States.

GAGAS must be followed when required by applicable law, regulation, or agreement. These standards may apply to a variety of different governmental engagements, including financial audits, performance audits, and attestation engagements.

Primary Reporting Differences between GAGAS and GAAS

Government Auditing Standards require a written report on:

Reports on GAGAS financial statement audits: requirements in addition to GAAS	
Internal control	• Scope of testing • Material weaknesses and significant deficiencies identified
Compliance with laws, regulations, contracts	• Scope of testing • Significant noncompliance or fraud identified *or* suspected

An independent auditor is issuing an audit report for a governmental entity and plans to issue separate reports on internal control over financial reporting and compliance with laws and regulations. The auditor should do which of the following?

- Report to the governing authority that separate reports will be issued

- Issue the same opinion in each report

- Obtain permission from the audit committee to issue separate reports

- State in the audit report that separate reports will be issued

The auditor may issue a **combined report or separate reports** but **should disclose** in the audit report what the auditor is doing. Unless the contract with the client specifies a single report, the auditor generally does not need to get permission from the audit committee to issue separate reports. Note that the same opinion might not be appropriate for each report.

Single Audit Act

The **Single Audit Act** is applicable to state and local governmental entities that have expenditures of federal assistance (grants) aggregating at least **$750,000** in a given year. It imposes certain requirements on such entities and their auditors that go beyond GAAS and even GAGAS.

Government standards require specific consideration of the **internal control structure** established to ensure compliance with the laws and regulations applicable to the financial assistance and issuance of a separate report on internal control.

Report requirements for compliance audits performed in conjunction with a finacial statement audit

GAAS F/S audit

1. Financial statements

2. Internal control
3. Compliance with laws and refulations

GAGAS financial audit

4. Schedule of federal award expenditures
5. Schedule of findings and questioned costs
6. Summary of audit results for F/S, I/C, and compliance

Single audit

Benefits of a Single Audit

Efficiency—A single coordinated audit of the aggregate federal financial assistance provided to a state or local governmental entity (with emphasis on the entity's major programs) is intended to result in greater efficiency compared to the alternative, which would be having multiple audits of the entity conducted on a grant-by-grant basis.

Added Requirements—A single coordinated audit of the aggregate federal financial assistance involves more than just a financial statement audit. Specific consideration of internal control over compliance is required for major programs, and additional testing is also required for major programs regarding the entity's compliance with applicable laws, regulations, or other requirements applicable to major programs.

Multiple Reports—The auditor should issue reports on (a) the fairness of the entity's financial statements (and schedule of expenditures of federal awards - SEFA); (b) internal control over financial reporting; (c) internal control over compliance; and (d) compliance with applicable laws, regulations, and other requirements. If audit findings were identified, the auditor should also prepare a Schedule of Findings and Questioned Costs.

Management Requirements

- Prepare the F/S along with a schedule of expenditures of federal awards

- Prepare a *corrective action plan* to respond to any current-year audit findings and any prior-year audit findings that remain unresolved

- Submit certain necessary forms, including the audit report to the designated Federal Audit Clearinghouse on a timely basis

Auditor Requirements

- Identify each *major program* to be audited based on appropriate **risk assessment considerations** (and materiality should be determined separately for each major program)

- Evaluate whether the F/S and schedule of expenditures of federal awards (SEFA) are fairly presented using appropriate criteria

- Obtain an appropriate **understanding of internal control** over the federal assistance programs and assess internal control over designated major programs

- Evaluate the entity's **compliance** with applicable laws, regulations, or other requirements having a direct and material effect on designated major programs

- Report any identified audit findings, including material instances of noncompliance with applicable laws, regulations, or other requirements involving designated major programs; identified instances of fraud; and significant deficiencies in internal controls over designated major programs

 After performing a compliance audit of an entity that received federal funds, what conclusion would the auditor draw if the entity does not have adequate documentation to support $5 million in operating expenses paid from federal program funds?

- The entity spent $5 million in operating expenses that were not approved
- The entity spent $5 million of government funds for services that were not required
- Questioned costs of $5 million for operating expenses have been identified
- The entity submitted unauthorized invoices for expenses

The auditor must also provide opinions on whether the schedule of expenditures of federal awards is fairly stated and on the entity's compliance with laws, regulations, or grants that may affect the major programs identified. In addition, the audit **report** will include a schedule (ie, list) of findings and **questioned costs** related to federal awards. **Questioned costs** are those costs singled out as **problematic** by the auditor.

Single Audit Act Opinions

As mentioned above, when reporting on compliance in an audit under the Single Audit Act, the auditor provides **reasonable assurance** that the entity complied with all laws, regulations, grants, and contracts. If there is **noncompliance** that has a **direct** and **material effect** on the assistance program, the auditor will issue either a **qualified** or **adverse** opinion on compliance, **depending** on the **pervasiveness** of its effects.

Opinions on compliance under Single Audit Act

Unmodified   No material noncompliance

Qualified   Noncompliance has material, but *not* pervasive, effect on financial assistance program

Adverse   Noncompliance has a material *and* pervasive effect on financial assistance program

Disclaimer   Auditor unable to obtain sufficient and appropriate evidence to support an opinion

Note that a **disclaimer of opinion** should be issued only when an auditor was unable to form an opinion in accordance with the relevant standards (eg, scope limitation). It is not an appropriate response to discovered instances of material noncompliance.

AUD

Area III: Performing Further Procedures and Obtaining Evidence

AUD 15
Use of Data and Information

AUD 15: Use of Data and Information

15.01 Requesting, Preparing, and Transforming Data

Extract, Transform, Load Process (ETL)

 Representative Task (Remembering & Understanding): Determine attribute structures, format, and sources of data needed when making a data extraction request to complete planned procedures.

To analyze data effectively and efficiently, auditors often need to **extract, transform, and load (ETL)** data from a client's accounting system. Extracted data that is not usable for analysis due to errors and formatting issues must be transformed. After extraction, an auditor must prepare the data for audit data analytics (ADAs).

For example, assume a retailer wants to analyze sales trends across its entire business. The sales data for its online and brick-and-mortar storefronts are stored in separate systems and in different fields and formats. The retailer also wants to incorporate data from social media and online weather sources to determine if these data affect sales trends. Accomplishing this task, requires ETL.

1. **Extract**—This involves **gathering data** from various sources. These data could reside in internal or external systems that are developed and supported by different vendors, hosted on different computer hardware, and managed by different employees. In our example, we begin by collecting sales data from the different internal systems, as well as social media and weather data from online sources.

2. **Transform**—This involves **converting the raw data** gathered from the extract phase into a consistent, useful format for loading the data into the target database. (See additional discussion on this step later in the chapter.)

3. **Load**—This involves **inserting** the transformed data into the **target database** for analysis. The target database could be a data mart, data warehouse, data lake, or other form of data repository. The data is now ready to be analyzed.

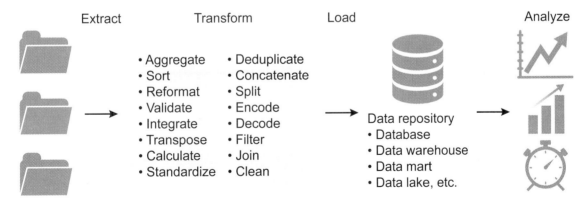

An accountant is analyzing a company's supply chain issue. Which of the following actions would the accountant most likely take when extracting raw data from different internal and external sources into a usable database?

- Identify unusual shipping and receiving delays

- Assess relevance of a government supply chain database

- Sort delivery data to identify the number of on-time deliveries

- Reformat vendor supply chain data to be consistent

Objectives for extract, transform, and load phases

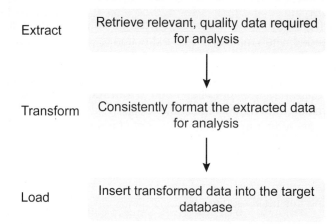

Assessing the *relevance* of a data source (such as a government supply chain database) is part of the **extraction phase**. Data must pertain to the purpose of the data extraction request in order to provide useful information to the user. The accountant should also consider **data quality**. Quality data are reasonably accurate, complete, valid, timely, and consistently measured and formatted.

Data Extraction Requests

Sometimes end users cannot extract the data they need themselves. In this case, they must **request the data** from the IT department. Requesting the data may be an interactive process, wherein the end user requests the data and then refines the request over several attempts.

When requesting data, the following should be considered:

- What data are needed (eg, tables, fields, records), and why are they needed?

- What is the business purpose of the data request?

- How often are the data needed (quarterly, monthly, yearly)?

- What is the desired format of the data (eg, spreadsheet, text file, document)?

- Who is the intended audience for the data?

- Which tool will be used to analyze and process the data?

- What are the risks to data integrity? For example, if the data are incomplete, consider mitigation strategies, such as supplementing your request with additional data

Descriptions of Data

A **data description** is metadata that defines the data within a dataset or data repository. This description allows users to **understand** the **nature** of the data, the **purpose** of the data, what determines **membership** (ie, whether a data point is included or excluded), and the **limitations** of the data. To be sure that a description is useful and accurate, it should meet certain criteria[1]:

- The **purpose** of the data—This helps users understand whether the data are **relevant** to their intended use. The dataset is complete and accurate, and includes:
  - The **population** of events or instances—Users of the data need to understand the factors that determined the inclusion or exclusion of certain data points (ie, members or records of data)
  - The **nature** of elements—Each data element (ie, attribute or field) is a characteristic of an event or instance that should be carefully defined to avoid misunderstanding. For example, data on "course attendance" might include a count of students physically present, but they might also include students who are virtually present. Hence, the data would differ depending on how course attendance is defined and measured
  - The **sources** of the data—Understanding the source of data helps users evaluate the credibility of the source. For instance, data from free online sources may be more biased than data obtained from commercial data providers
  - The accuracy, correctness, or **precision of measurement**—To properly use the data, the user needs to understand the precision of measurement of the data. For example, monetary units expressed in millions may lack the precision needed to accurately forecast inventory purchases
  - The **uncertainty** inherent in the data—Some data may be based on estimates or other uncertainty (eg, a weather forecast states there is a 75% chance of rain). In such cases, information regarding the measure of uncertainty, such as the credibility of those who calculated estimates, should be provided. Other indicators may include standard deviation, historical variations, margin of error, and range of possible values
  - **Date or period of occurrence**—Addressing the time or period of data collection helps users understand whether the data are relevant and current

- Other factors or characteristics—Any other factors that help a user understand the data should be identified. Examples include data classification (ie, sensitive, confidential, internal, or public), who can access the data, who owns the data, and retention requirements
  - **It identifies or refers to other information that has not been included but is necessary to understand the data. For example, GAAP rules would not be included in a description, but a reference should be made to GAAP for financial data based on such rules**

Data Structures

Data may be structured, semistructured, or unstructured:

- **Structured**—Data that has a specific format or schema, such as tables with fields and records. Structured data are stored in relational databases or spreadsheets that may have input masks to ensure the data are formatted correctly. An input mask is a string expression created by the developer which defines the type of input allowed for a given field (ie, to help ensure valid input). Since structured data are predefined, they can be searched, sorted, and analyzed easily using SQL, Python, or other languages or tools. Examples include data found in enterprise resource planning (ERP) systems, accounting information systems (AIS), and customer relationship management (CRM) systems
- **Semistructured**—Data that have a partial structure but are not as defined as structured data. Semistructured data may contain metadata, or tags, which make it easier to organize than unstructured data. Examples include email, comma-separated values (CSV) files, Internet of Things (IoT) sensor data, web server logs, and HTML-, XML-, and XBRL-tagged text

---

[1] *As defined by the Assurance Services Executive Committee of the AICPA in Criteria for Describing a Set of Data and Evaluating Its Integrity, 2020.*

- **Unstructured**—Raw data that do not have an obvious, predefined format. They are seemingly without form and therefore difficult to search. Examples include text, PDFs, video, audio, and photos. Extracting the implicit structure of unstructured data is an important application of data mining

The following terms are important in understanding the **basics of data structure**:

- **Bit**—A single switch in a computer that is either on (1) or off (0)
- **Byte**—A group of 8 bits representing a character
- **Character**—A letter, number, punctuation mark, or special character
- **Alphanumeric**—A character that is either a letter or number
- **Field**—Represents an **attribute** (**characteristic**) of an entity, person, event, etc., such as a name or phone number (ie, a group of related characters representing a unit of data). A field may also be referred to as an **element** of data or a **column** in a table
- **Record**—A collection (**row**) of attributes (fields) related to an entity, person, event, etc., in a file/table/ dataset. A record is sometimes referred to as a *tuple* in a database. It can also be referred to as a **member** of a dataset
- **File**—A group of logically related records (eg, contact info for all employees)
    - ○ **Master File**—A permanent source that is used as an ongoing reference and that is periodically updated
    - ○ **Detail File**—A file listing a group of transactions which may be used to update a master file. This is also frequently called a transaction file
- **Dataset**—A collection of data (eg, a file or a table in a file) that shares common characteristics or relationships
- **Database**—A stored collection of related files
- **Data Repository**—A broad term that may refer to a **population** of data, as well as the supporting infrastructure that stores the data, makes the data available for use, and organizes the data. Data held within a data repository can be used for further analysis and reporting. Specific types of data repositories include **data warehouses**, **data lakes**, and **data marts**. We'll take a closer look at the different types of data repositories in the next section
- **Data Dictionary**—Sometimes hidden data that describe the logical structure of a database, including information such as titles, descriptions, and format of fields (ie, data types) as well as the relationships that exist between the data. It will also tell you who has the permissions needed to access specific data. This type of data is called **metadata** (ie, "data about data")

Data Formats (Types of Data)

Data type refers to the specific *format* and *size* of data that can be stored in a field. It also limits the kind of data that can be stored (eg, numbers, text, dates, images). Identifying the data type for each field is important when designing a database. It helps users search and sort records, perform calculations, and compare the value of fields. Every database has its own specific data types. Here are some of the most common:

Data types	
Integer	Whole numbers with positive, negative, or zero values (ie, no decimals)
Decimal	Numbers with decimals (eg, currency)
String (or text)	Alphanumeric characters, spaces, or special characters (eg, /, &)
Boolean	Binary values that represent true/false data
Date/time	Dates and times
BLOB	Binary large objects (eg, videos, audio files, images)

Data Sources

Data sources can be internal and/or external. Internally sourced data are referred to as primary data whereas externally sourced data are called secondary data.

Internal/Primary Data	External/Secondary Data
Data collected by the organization itself	**Data collected by others for various purposes**
• Accounting data	• Industry data
• Customer data	• Government data
• Employee data	• Census data
• Marketing data	• Social media
• Supplier data	
• Shipping data	

Organizations capture data from the above sources through a wide variety of manual, electronic, and automated equipment and/or processes. These include:

- **Application Programming Interfaces (APIs)**—APIs are software interfaces that allow two or more computer systems or software applications to communicate and share data. An API is an automated set of rules in computer code; fields from one system's database are either copied or extracted and are then imported into another system using the API

- **Artificial Intelligence (AI)**—Computer systems that can simulate human intelligence by making connections between data points, then using those connections to perform tasks such as visual perception, speech and facial recognition, and translation

- **Character Recognition**—Optical character recognition (OCR), optical mark reading (OMR), and intelligent character recognition (ICR) automatically capture and extract data from documents such as receipts, checks, forms, IDs, and contracts. This reduces the need for manual data entry

- **Digital Signatures**—Digital signatures allow users to sign documents or approve workflows over the Internet via an application or email. A digital signature is encrypted, geolocated, and time-stamped to authenticate the signer's identity. Sensitive applications may require a digital certificate issued by a third party, such as a bank or government entity, to supply proof of identity

- **Electronic Data Interchange (EDI)**—EDI is the computer-to-computer exchange of documents in a standard electronic format between business partners

- **File Import**—Data stored in different databases or applications can be shared between them by extracting (ie, exporting) the data from one location, then importing (ie, loading) them into another

- **Image and Video Capture**—Image captures can be photos taken by a camera, waves displayed on a monitor, or videotape recordings

- **Keying and Forms**—Data can be manually keyed directly into a database or input using electronic forms. Such forms may be on paper or a part of computer, web, and mobile applications. It is generally best to avoid human-entered data since automating this process improves data accuracy, system efficiency, and human happiness

- **Machine Learning**—A type of artificial intelligence in which computer systems learn and adapt without receiving explicit instructions, but instead by using algorithms and statistical models to analyze and draw inferences from patterns in data

- **QR and Barcodes**—QR and barcodes include metadata that is recognized by a device. For example, when a QR code is read by a camera on a mobile device, it takes users to a link on a webpage and stores data about the number of times the code was used. Barcodes can be applied to almost any object (eg, documents, equipment, inventory) and linked to software for tracking; for example, the codes may be read by a laser reader or decoded using a mobile device application

- **Robotic Process Automation (RPA)**—Software technology may also be used to build, deploy, and manage software robots that automate manual tasks

- **Sensors**—Sensors can track data points that relate to weather or environmental conditions. For example, sensor or IoT devices may capture temperature, humidity, pressure, weight, water, gas, or chemical levels

- **Swipe/Chip/NFC Cards**—Swipe cards may be credit cards or cards that allow users to enter restricted areas. Credit, debit, and prepaid cards may also use a chip for contact transactions or wireless near-field communication (NFC) technology for contactless payments

- **Voice Capture**—Conversations or voice messages can be captured using cloud-based technology or on-site call-recording devices

- **Web and Screen Scrapers**—Web scraping means using a tool to extract content and data from a website. Screen scraping refers to harvesting information shown on a digital display for reuse

 Representative Task (Application): Determine methods to transform (eg, preparing, cleaning, scrubbing) data to complete planned procedures.

Transforming Data

Data extracted from different sources are often not usable for analysis due to errors, **inconsistencies, or formatting** issues. Thus, a series of transformations prepare the data for loading into the target database.

At a high-level, the objectives of the transformation phase are to:

- Remove errors and inconsistencies in the extracted data

- Correct mismatches and ensure that columns are in the same order

- Ensure that the data are in the same format

- Enrich datasets by including additional information

Data Cleaning and Standardization

Data cleaning is a step in the transformation process and involves **deleting** or **correcting** extracted data that are incomplete, inaccurate, irrelevant, incorrectly **formatted**, or duplicated. For example, if dates are sometimes in the MMDDYYYY format and sometimes in the DDMMYYYY format, it may cause the auditor's analytic tools (eg, generalized audit software, spreadsheet application) to misinterpret (or be unable to analyze) the data.

Cleaning client data for audit data analytics

Invoice #	Date	Amount
254987	12/15/Year 1	$2,154.33
254988	12/15/Year 1	8,215.11
#MNGJU	1/1/1900	#VALUE!
254990	16/12/Year 1	4198.78
254991	12/16/Year	1943.12
254992	12/17/Year 1	11038.29

Reformat date

Consider deleting

Data standardization involves merging the formats of data from different systems into one. Examples of these data transformations include the following:

- **Aggregating**—Involves summarizing or grouping data (eg, summarizing total sales by store or region)

- **Calculating and Deriving**—Involves calculating new values from existing data. For example, creating new, from existing, variables to calculate total cost, profit margin, or total sales

- **Cleaning**—Leading and trailing zeroes and nonprintable characters should be removed where appropriate because they can cause problems with data analysis. Nonprintable characters include white spaces, page breaks, line breaks, and tabs. This will happen especially when numbers or dates were stored as text in the source files, eg, in CSV files, but need to be analyzed as numeric values

- **Decoding and Recoding**—Involves standardizing codes for data. One source system may represent customer status as "AC" for active, or "IN" for inactive, whereas another system may represent the same customer status as "1" (active) or "0" (inactive). In the transformation phase, the data would be **decoded** and then **recoded** for a consistent format

- **Deduplicating or "Deduping"**—Involves identifying and removing duplicate records or columns

- **Encoding**—Involves assigning free form values to the data to make them compatible with the target database. Examples include changing NULL values to 0 or changing "M" to "male" and "F" to "female"

- **Filtering**—Involves removing extraneous fields and records. For example, if the source data have three columns (eg, job code, age, salary), then the selection, ie, the filter, may extract only two fields (eg, job code and salary) or the selection could omit records where salary is missing (ie, null)

- **Joining**—Involves connecting multiple data points using a primary key. For example, combining weather data from online sources with internal sales data to forecast sales

- **Removing Headings or Subtotals**—Involves removing unnecessary headers or subtotals. Useful in creating structured data tables for relational databases

- **Sorting Data**—Involves rearranging the data into a useful order (eg, ascending, descending, or custom)

- **Splitting**—Involves dividing data into separate fields or columns. For example, a column with employees' full names can be split into two columns to separate the first and last names

- **Standardizing**—Involves formatting the data into tables to match the format of the target database. For example, a field in one source system may be numeric and the same column in the target system may be text. Furthermore, the extracted source data could be in different formats for each data type; hence, all the extracted data should be converted into a standardized format. Specific formatting issues include:

  ○ **Date/Time Conversion**—There are many issues surrounding dates because the Gregorian date system is problematic, and there are many different date and time formats. For example, one source may store dates as Month DD, YYYY while another system uses MM/DD/YYYY

  ○ **Numbers**—Numbers can be misinterpreted, particularly if manually entered (eg, "7" versus "seven"). In addition, negative numbers may require reformatting (eg, negative signs vs. parentheses). Also, any data with accounting characters may require reformatting to raw form (eg, "123.45", not "$123.45")

  ○ **International Characters and Encoding**—When working with data across countries, it is likely that you will encounter accent marks or special characters or invisible computer characters (eg, line breaks, tabs, returns). These special characters may need to be removed before analysis

  ○ **Languages and Measures**—Like international characters, data may contain different words or measures that have the same meaning. For example, cheese or fromage. To analyze the data, you will need to convert these different words for consistency

- **Transposing**—Involves inverting rows and columns. For example, columns and rows can be switched, ie, rows become columns or vice versa, or the data can be pivoted by turning multiple columns into multiple rows or vice versa

Measurement Scales

 Representative Task (Remembering & Understanding): Explain the characteristics and uses of different measurement scales (eg, nominal, ordinal, interval, ratio, continuous, discrete).

Overview

Multiple measurement scales can be used for data. A measurement scale quantifies or "qualifies" data variables. Ideally, the measurement scale used is matched to the type of data collected.

There are four types of measurement scales: nominal, ordinal, interval, and ratio. Nominal and ordinal scales are typically used to measure **qualitative** data in **discrete increments,** whereas interval and ratio scales are used to measure **quantitative** data in **continuous** increments. Discrete increments could be **"brown" or "white,"** or, "0", "1", or "2". Continuous increments could be between, for example, "0.00" and "1000.00".

Characteristics of a Measurement Scale

A measurement scale can be described using four characteristics: identity, magnitude, intervals, and absolute zero.

- **Absolute Zero**—Only ratio scales have this attribute. Ratio scales include a zero value which represents the absence of the measured variable (eg, no size, no color, etc.).

- **Equal Intervals**—This refers to a scale which reflects a consistent order; specifically, the difference between each level on the scale is the same (eg, each level increases by 1 increment). Interval scales have this property; they have identity, magnitude, and equal intervals.

- **Identity**—This assigns a number to each variable value in the dataset. For example, assume a questionnaire asks for the person's eye color with the options being brown, green, hazel, or blue. We could assign the values of 1, 2, 3, and 4 for each color, respectively. This scale is used to identify the discrete levels of a variable and is a characteristic of a "nominal" scale (see description below).

- **Magnitude**—This refers to the direction of the measurement scale. For example, an ordinal scale shows size in either an ascending (least to most) or descending (greatest to smallest) order. Ordinal scales have both identity and magnitude characteristics.

Levels of Data Measurement

- **Nominal**—Nominal scales **categorize data** into mutually exclusive groups using non-numeric (ie, quantitative, not qualitative) variables. For example, "What color are your eyes?"

- **Ordinal**—Ordinal scales rank items based on the degree of occurrence of variable values, in either ascending or descending order, often using terms such as *very likely, highly likely, less likely*, etc. Often, such scales are used in marketing research, advertising, and customer satisfaction surveys. For example, "How likely are you to return to our restaurant?" Ordinal scales permit statistical analysis such as modes and medians.

- **Interval**—Interval scales identify which attribute is greater or smaller, and also the distance (or extent) of differences in values. For example, a numeric grading scale, which is also converted to a letter grade, reflects the cutoff for each letter grade and shows the distance between each cutoff point. Such scales permit the calculations of means, medians, modes, ranges, and measures of variability, including standard deviations.

- **Ratio**—The ratio scale extends the interval scale and has all four characteristics of a measurement scale: identity, magnitude, equal interval, and the absolute value property. Examples include length, weight, and time scales. For example, marketing researchers could use a ratio scale to show price information or the number of customers. For example, such a scale could represent, "How much money do you spend weekly on groceries?"

Characteristics of measurement scales

	Named	Ordered	Put into equal intervals, added, and subtracted	True zero point as origin
Nominal	✓			
Ordinal	✓	✓		
Interval	✓	✓	✓	
Ratio	✓	✓	✓	✓

Relational Database Components

 Representative Task (Remembering & Understanding): Explain the components of a relational database (eg, tables, records, fields/ attributes, primary and foreign keys, normalization).

A **relational database** is a **collection of structured** in which certain data points are associated with (ie, related to) one another. The basic elements of a relational database are as follows:

- **Table**—A table in a relational database with rows and columns. Each row is an **individual record** while each column describes a **field or attribute**

  ○ Tables hold information about a specific entity or an **association** between entities. An entity is a group of objects with similar characteristics; an association is a related link between two tables

- **Record**—A record is a single entry or instance in a table

- **Fields/Attributes**—Attributes are the *column fields* in a relational database table; they hold detailed information the organization wants to keep about an entity or association. The attributes function like column headers in a spreadsheet. For example, in a sales table, attributes may include the sales ID#, date of the sale, and dollar amount of the sale

- **Primary Key**—Each table must have at least one attribute that uniquely identifies an individual record. The primary key should be data about a record that cannot be duplicated and will not change (eg, social security number, EIN). If there are no naturally occurring unique data, the primary key may be system generated (eg, customer ID, employee ID). Every record must have a primary key so that it can be linked to other tables

- **Foreign Key**—A foreign key is a table's primary key, which is added to another table, creating an association. For example, consider a sales table with a primary key of Sale# and a customer table with a primary key of Customer#. The sales table would include the foreign key field Customer# to associate the sale with a specific customer

- **Association**—Tables in a database may be related by different associations. Three of the fundamental relationships, or associations, between data tables are:

Relationship	Example
One to one (1:1)	For every department, there is only one manager.
One to many (1:M)	For every manager, there are many employees.
Many to many (M:M)	Employees may provide services to many clients, and clients may receive services from many employees.

Database normalization involves creating tables for storing data in a **relational database**. It splits one table with multiple fields (ie, denormalized) into multiple related tables with fewer fields. Storing data this way **reduces data duplication** and **improves data consistency** because updates to data need to be made in only one table. Tables in relational databases are connected by the **primary key** in one table to a **foreign key** in another table.

Denormalized table

Cust. ID	Name	Address	City	State	Zip	Inv no.	Inv date	Ship date	Inv amt	Item no.	Qty	Price	Ext. price
4526	Bob Lee	14 Main St.	Eek	AK	99578	558496	2/1/XX	2/5/XX	145	125A	5	20	100
4526	Bob Lee	14 Main St.	Eek	AK	99578	558496	2/1/XX	2/5/XX	145	254B	3	15	45

Normalized table

Customers

	Customer ID	Name	Address	City	State	Zip
Primary key →	4526	Bob Lee	14 Main St.	Eek	AK	99578

Invoices

Invoice number	Invoice date	Ship date	Invoice amount	Customer ID	
558496	2/1/XX	2/5/XX	145	4526	← Foreign key

Note: Tables are joined primary key to foreign key.

15.02 Reliability of Data and Information

Data Reliability

 Representative Task (Application): Perform procedures (eg, agreeing information to original sources such as general ledger, subledger, or external information sources, validating search or query criteria used to obtain data) to validate the reliability (completeness, accuracy, authenticity, and susceptibility to management bias) of data and information obtained.

Data Validation for Integrity

After each ETL phase, a series of **data validations** should be performed to ensure that the data have integrity. **Data integrity** refers to ensuring that the data accurately reflect, ie, represent, the business events underlying them and that any anomalies are rectified.

- Note that **data quality** is a **subset** of data integrity. Quality data are accurate, complete, consistent, valid, and timely. Data integrity includes those characteristics in addition to relevance. That is, data that have integrity are relevant and useful in addition to being complete, accurate, consistent, valid, and timely

Users need to ensure that data contain all records needed from the source (ie, **completeness**), that the transformed data are **consistent** with the source data, and that the data **loaded** into the target source properly. Incorrect or invalid data can skew analysis and lead to inaccurate conclusions.

Input Controls

The objective of input controls is that the input of data is accurate and as authorized. Data validation controls are a subset of input controls and focus particularly on establishing the validity of data prior to (or at the time of) data input.

Common controls used for **data validation purposes** that involve computer edit routines to identify errors in data include the following:

Input controls: logic tests		
Type of input control	**Definition**	**Example**
Field checks	Data entered is validated for proper length and format	Timecard entry is verified to ensure that the hours entered are numeric
Validity checks	Data entered is compared with a list of acceptable entries	State abbreviation entered is verified against list of acceptable state abbreviations
Limit tests	Data entered is compared with limits that have been set for applicability	Timecard entry is verified to make sure that hours entered do not exceed the maximum hours in day (ie, 24)
Check digits	Numbers with no obvious meaning in which one of the digits is determined by a formula applied to the rest of the number	Bank account number is verified to ensure that the number entered is a valid bank number

Examples of overall input controls include:

- **Comparisons** are made to verify that all the appropriate data were input
- **Record Count**—Comparing the number of records that were actually input to the number of records that were supposed to be input
- **Batch Totals**—Totals that are subject to meaningful interpretation (eg, the day's cash withdrawals at a specific ATM location)
- **Hash Totals**—Totals that have no meaningful interpretation as such, even though a total can be arithmetically determined (eg, adding up employees' social security numbers to verify that no employees were omitted from a payroll application)

Whenever the control procedures flag a data-input error, there should be specific procedures to fix the error and resubmit the data for input.

Processing Controls

The objective is that the processing of data is accurate and as authorized. Specific controls include:

- **Logic Checks**—The various logic checks identified above as input controls may also be used as processing controls (eg, limit tests, etc.)
- **Control totals**, especially batch totals and hash totals, may also be used as processing controls, as described above with respect to input control
- **Limit on Processing Time**—A predetermined limit for computer processing time can be specified; if that limit is exceeded, the program will terminate
- **Checkpoint/Restart**—For particularly long processing runs, there can be built-in checkpoint/restart locations; if the program crashes, it can be resumed without having to go back to the beginning
- **Error Resolution Procedures**—Whenever the control procedures flag a data processing error, there should be specific procedures to fix the problem and resume processing

Audit Data Standards (ADS)

To make the ETL process easier, the AICPA has developed voluntary Audit Data Standards (ADS). The ADS provide:

- **A Uniform Data Model**—If implemented by an entity, the ADS help standardize the formatting of essential audit data in files and fields to avoid the time-consuming processes mentioned above. Even if the entity has not implemented the ADS, the auditor can map the entity's data to the ADS and automate the standardization of subsequent data extractions

- **Standards for Data Requests**—The ADS provide questionnaires for the entity to answer each time data are provided. The answers to the questions will help the auditor understand the data and any exceptions to the ADS that may exist

- **Automated Data Validation Procedures**—Such procedures help the auditor evaluate the completeness and integrity of data extracted and received. These tests include, for example:
  - Checking that all **files** and data **fields** requested have been received
  - Checking the range of **dates** on the data to be sure the data are for the dates requested
  - Checking **control totals** (eg, record counts, financial totals, hash totals) to determine whether all data requested have been received
  - Counting the number of **blank values** by field
  - Counting the records that contain fields with **incorrect formatting**

 An auditor has received a file containing sales data extracted from a continuing client's electronic sales journal. Which of the following procedures would be most effective in verifying that all the data were extracted?

- Trace physical sales invoices to the extracted file
- Compare the extracted sales data with sales data from the prior year
- Ask the client to explain the steps taken in the extraction process
- Calculate a financial total in the extracted data and compare it to the source data

Control totals

	Check number	Payee	Amount	Account code
	1001	Philipp Corporation	$ 500	307
Record	1002	Rog Enterprises	3,000	602
count = 3	1003	Ruiz Company	600	302
	3006		$4,100	1211
	Hash total		Financial total	Hash total

To verify that the source data were properly and completely extracted, an auditor can **calculate and compare control totals** (eg, hash total, financial total) for the source and extracted files. For example, if the total dollar amount of sales (a financial total) in an extracted file matches the amount in the sales journal, it is likely that all transactions were successfully extracted.

Tracing invoices to the extracted file would not verify that the extracted data matches the source data. Because prior-year sales are only a rough indicator of what can be expected in the current year, comparing sales in the extracted file to the prior year would not provide evidence that the extracted file is complete. Asking the client to explain the data extraction process might help explain discrepancies identified using control totals but would not provide sufficient evidence of the completeness.

15.03 Data Analytics

Audit Data Analytics (ADAs) Overview

 Representative Task (Application): Describe how to apply automated tools and techniques to process, organize, structure, or present data in a given context to generate useful information that can be used as evidence.

AICPA Guidance

The AICPA's *Guide to Audit Data Analytics* (Guide) defines ADAs as follows: "The science and art of discovering and analyzing patterns, identifying anomalies, and extracting other useful information in data underlying or related to the subject matter of an audit through analysis, modeling, and visualization for the purpose of planning or performing the audit."

Note: The AICPA's Guide does not address using ADAs as tests of control. The Guide does not establish any auditor requirements beyond those associated with the AICPA's Statements on Auditing Standards.

Purpose of Data Analytics

Data analytics can be used to **create valuable insight**, foster innovation, and make better decisions. It all starts with asking the right questions. The purpose of data analytics is to:

- Solve a problem
- Manage risk
- Increase market share
- Increase internal audit efficiency or effectiveness
- Increase other operational efficiencies/effectiveness
- Analyze changing trends and consumer behavior

Data can be extracted, both *internally and externally*, for every facet of operations to gain insights that are then used to strategize and drive an organization's decisions to meet its goals and solve its problems.

Much of the same data and many of the same tools used to drive client decisions are valuable resources to the auditor as well. The auditor can mine an entity's data (as well as external data) to **discover relevant patterns** and **anomalies** and **analyze** such information **through modeling** and **visualization** to gain a deeper understanding of the business and its environment, assess the risks, and plan the audit accordingly.

Uses of audit data analytics	
Risk assessment	• Analytical procedures • Tests of controls
Substantive procedures	• Analytical procedures • Tests of details

 Audit data analytics would be **least** useful in

- Planning the audit for a new client

- Performing substantive procedures when the reliability of internal data is questionable

- Performing risk assessment procedures when inherent risks are high

- Forming a conclusion on the audit of a client that operates in a volatile industry

An audit data analytic (ADA) is a procedure used to help the auditor **discover patterns and identify anomalies** that may require further investigation. It can be used in all phases of an audit, including risk assessment procedures, tests of controls, substantive analytical procedures, tests of details, and formation of an audit opinion.

Auditors should consider the **relevance and reliability** of the data being used. This includes examining the nature and source of the data, the processes used to produce the data, and whether additional audit procedures are needed to verify the reliability of the data. If the data are unreliable, the conclusions produced by the ADA may mislead the auditor; therefore, the auditor would use alternative procedures.

Types of Data Analytics

There are four main types of data analytics. An auditor, however, would generally be focused on the first three here:

- **Descriptive Analytics** focuses on *what has happened*

- **Diagnostic Analytics** aims to tell you *why something happened*

- **Predictive Analytics** tell you *what should happen* based on past patterns and trends

- **Prescriptive Analytics** use the other three types of analytics to tell you *what to do* to get to the results desired

Which of the following types of audit techniques would be most useful for assessing the probability of an audit client's ability to continue as a going concern?

- Descriptive analytics
- Diagnostic analytics
- Predictive analytics
- Prescriptive analytics

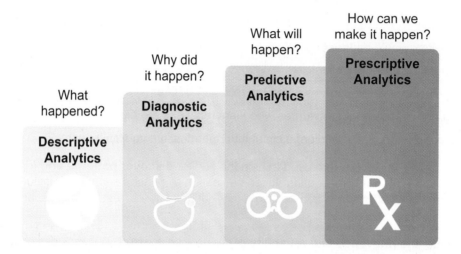

A tremendous amount of data underlies large organizations' financial reporting. Efficient auditing of that data often requires using data analytics to perform procedures on whole populations (eg, recorded sales), including descriptive, diagnostic, and predictive analytics.

Because testing the going-concern assumption involves estimating the probability of a *future* event, **predictive analytics** would be the most useful. Prescriptive analytics are used to determine how to achieve an organization's goals; they are commonly used by management, not financial statement auditors.

Data Analytic Techniques and Visualizations

Representative Task (Analysis): Perform procedures using outputs (eg, reports, visualizations) from audit data analytic techniques to determine relationships, trends, or notable items in the data and identify the appropriate audit response.

Data analytics is the process of examining, cleaning, organizing, and modeling data with the goal of drawing conclusions/insights to support strategic planning and decision-making. **Data visualization** is the graphic representation and communication of those insights, making it easier for management to detect patterns, trends, and outliers in big data.

Techniques

- **Affinity Grouping Analysis**—Identifying the nature and frequency of relationships (associations) between variables
- **Cluster Analysis** (aka segmentation analysis)—Grouping data by similarities (ie, attributes) in a way that shows the structure/relationships/differences between the data (eg, customers can be segmented by location, demographics, or common interests to facilitate target marketing)

- **Comparative Analysis**—Comparing the relationships between variables over two or more periods

- **Cross-sectional Regression Analysis**—A regression analysis that uses data from one period of time or a point in time to make predictions

- **Decision Tree** (aka classification analysis)—Dividing up a dataset in a way that shows the sequential/hierarchical relationship between events, decisions, or objects

- **Estimation Analysis**—Making predictions (ie, estimations) based on historical data

- **Market Basket Analysis**—Analyzing sales combinations to identify past customer behaviors to predict future customer behavior

- **Ratio Analysis**—Calculating ratios to discover relationships among financial and nonfinancial data

- **Regression Analysis**—Using statistical analysis to examine the relationship between one or more independent variables (ie, predictors) and a dependent variable

- **Sentiment Analysis**—Using natural language processing (NLP) and text analysis to identify and categorize opinions and emotions in text (eg, social media), determining whether the writer's attitude is positive, negative, or neutral

- **Time-series Regression Analysis**—A regression analysis that uses data from multiple past periods to predict trends

- **Trend Analysis**—Analyzing changes in data over time to look for trends (a type of comparative analysis)

Company X's data analytics department uses many types of data visualization to present data analytics to management. Which type of data analytics technique is illustrated in the image below?

- Cluster analysis

- Trend analysis

- Sentiment analysis

- Regression analysis

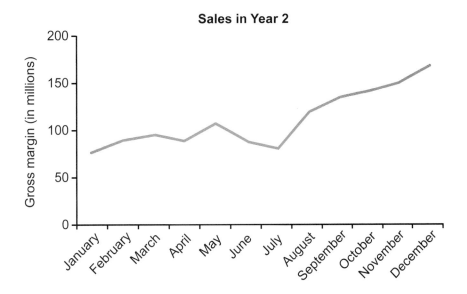

The **image** above is an example of trend analysis, which analyzes changes in data **over time** to identify patterns (a type of comparative analysis).

Visualizations

Visualization is the use of various types of **graphics** (for example, charts, scatter diagrams, trend lines), tables, or combinations thereof in formats such as dashboards.

- The **purpose** of such visualization techniques is to **make relationships** of interest in very large datasets more easily identifiable

- The **form and content** of such graphics and/or tables when performing ADAs require the auditor's professional judgment

Data visualization boils down to four basic **presentation types**: comparison, composition, distribution, and relationship. Some techniques, such as regression analysis, are generally associated with certain visualizations, like a scatterplot, which shows both distribution and relationship.

Most visualizations, however, are a matter of judgment as to which options to combine to best communicate the results of a data analytic. The user should not need to read too much to understand the visualization.

The following are some examples of the use of visualizations from the AICPA's ADA Guide.

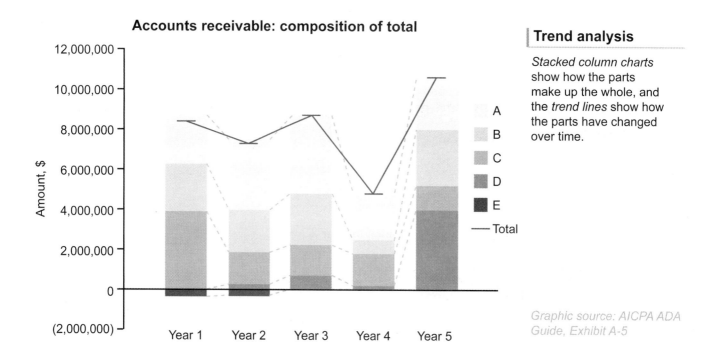

Trend analysis

Stacked column charts show how the parts make up the whole, and the *trend lines* show how the parts have changed over time.

Graphic source: AICPA ADA Guide, Exhibit A-5

Liquidity ratios

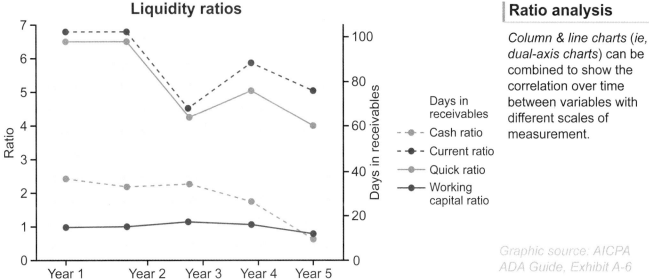

Ratio analysis

Column & line charts (ie, dual-axis charts) can be combined to show the correlation over time between variables with different scales of measurement.

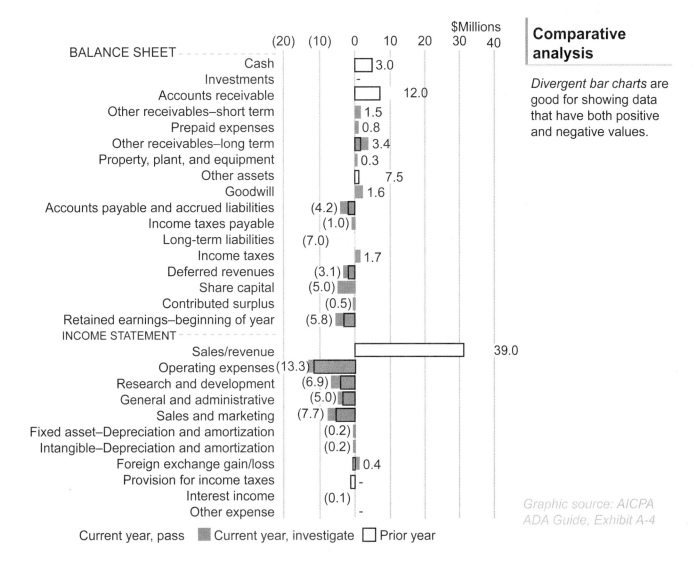

Comparative analysis

Divergent bar charts are good for showing data that have both positive and negative values.

AICPA Five-Step Approach to Using ADAs

The Guide identifies a five-step approach applicable to using ADAs, as follows:

Step #1—Plan the ADA

Procedures should include:

- **Describing the objective** of an ADA. Recall that ADAs may be used for risk assessment or substantive purposes

  - **Risk assessment procedures** involve obtaining an understanding of the entity and its environment, including the entity's internal control, to identify and assess risks of material misstatement

  - **Substantive procedures** are designed to detect material misstatements at the relevant assertion level. These can be classified as either tests of details or substantive analytical procedures

- **Brainstorming potential ADAs**, which involves the audit team's discussion of where the potential ADAs and related objectives can be applied

- **Developing an understand**ing of the relationship between specific audit assertions and ADAs

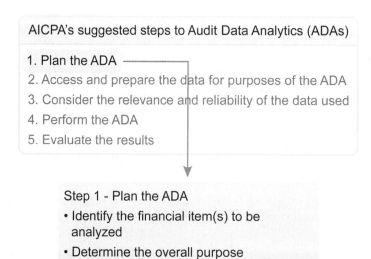

AICPA's suggested steps to Audit Data Analytics (ADAs)

1. Plan the ADA
2. Access and prepare the data for purposes of the ADA
3. Consider the relevance and reliability of the data used
4. Perform the ADA
5. Evaluate the results

Step 1 - Plan the ADA
- Identify the financial item(s) to be analyzed
- Determine the overall purpose
- Specify objective(s)
- Determine the data population to be used
- Identify the ADA techniques (eg, tools, visuals)

Step #2—Access and Prepare the Data for Use in an ADA

Request and access the data from a client or third party in relation to the objectives of the ADA. Determine the relevant characteristics of the data and the related technology. The auditor should consider the following factors related to the requested data:

- **Data Storage**—Auditors should understand and document where the data are stored prior to extraction

- **Extraction Methodologies**—Auditors should understand and document how the data were extracted and by whom

- **File Types**—Auditors should understand and document the types of files they are requesting and using.

- **Metadata**—Characteristics that provide context and additional information about the data (such as file name, file type, file size, creation date/time, last modification date/time, and identification of who can access and/or update the data)

Auditors need to understand and document:

- The accounting system(s) and the flow of transactions with an emphasis on the entity's business processes
- How the IT general controls and application controls affect the integrity of the data

The data are then prepared for use in the ADA (ie, ETL). Note that errors in the data may indicate that controls over the data are not operating effectively.

- **Blank Fields**—Should verify that blank fields are appropriate and not a result of missing data
- **Field Format Inconsistency**—Should identify and correct inconsistencies in data fields (for example, some data may be presented as month-day-year, whereas other data in the same field could be presented as day-month-year)
- **Field-type Mistakes**—Should identify and correct instances where fields contain the wrong type of data; for example, an intended numerical field might consist of letters (text) instead of numbers

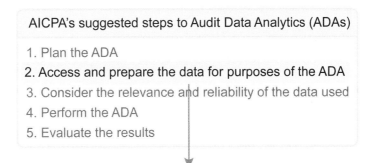

Step #3—Consider the Relevance and Reliability of the Data

Data should have the following attributes:

- **Accuracy**—Data are free from significant errors
- **Completeness**—Data contain all the requisite data (that is, there are no omissions of data that should be present)
- **Consistency**—Data fields are well defined and managed
- **Freshness**—Data contain the most up-to-date changes/additions
- **Timeliness**—Data are available when needed
- **Clarity and Relatedness**—Data fields are clearly defined and related to the objective(s) being tested

Consider the **integrity of the data** (with emphasis on accuracy and completeness over the data's life cycle). Determine whether data have been protected whenever acquired and/or delivered.

- Determine whether files are encrypted to protect access to data
- Critically examine a dataset and the procedures used to obtain the data to understand where it originated (regarding freshness, timeliness, and clarity and relatedness)

Identify procedures directed at ensuring the accuracy and completeness of the dataset, such as:

- **Reconciliations**—Prepare or review reconciliations of underlying data
- **Sequence Checks**—Verify the appropriateness of the sequence; gaps may indicate possible omissions
- **Record Counts**—Verify that the appropriate number of records are accounted for

Consider the impact of changes to the environment that may increase the risks of errors in the data—for example, changes in management or changes in the accounting system (such as an ERP system).

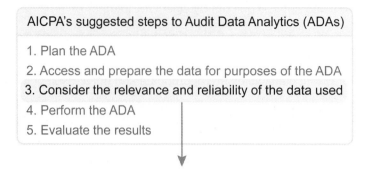

AICPA's suggested steps to Audit Data Analytics (ADAs)

1. Plan the ADA
2. Access and prepare the data for purposes of the ADA
3. Consider the relevance and reliability of the data used
4. Perform the ADA
5. Evaluate the results

Step 3 - The auditor will consider:
• Nature of data
• Source of data
• Process to produce data
• Procedures needed to verify data

Step #4—Perform the ADA

Simple ADAs might be used to test journal entry posting, cash accounts, accounts receivable, accounts payable, and inventory. The auditor should identify and address any "notable items."

The Guide defines a notable item as follows:

"An item identified from the population being analyzed that has one or more characteristics that, for the relevant assertions, may do the following: (a) Be indicative of a risk of material misstatement that (i) was not previously identified (a new risk) or (ii) is higher than originally assessed by the auditor; (b) provide information that is useful in designing or tailoring procedures to address risks of material misstatement."

- When a large number of notable items is identified, the auditor may use a grouping and filtering process to identify characteristics of interest common to the groups; the auditor should perform appropriate procedures to address the risks of each group

- When a small number of notable items is identified, the auditor may perform manual risk assessment procedures; further audit procedures should be responsive to the assessed risks of material misstatement

When using ADAs in forming an overall conclusion, the auditor may decide it appropriate to revise previous risk assessments and perform further audit procedures in response.

Step #5—Evaluate the Results

The auditor should develop preliminary conclusions or recommendations for an ADA. The auditor should then evaluate whether the ADA has been appropriately planned and performed. If not, the auditor should refine and re-perform the ADA.

The auditor should document the performance and results of the ADAs; any screenshots of graphics necessary to support the auditor's work should also be retained.

Performing the ADA and evaluating the results

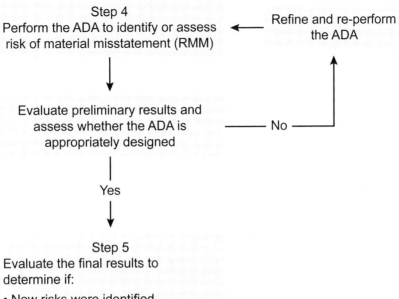

Step 4
Perform the ADA to identify or assess risk of material misstatement (RMM)

Refine and re-perform the ADA

Evaluate preliminary results and assess whether the ADA is appropriately designed

No

Yes

Step 5
Evaluate the final results to determine if:

• New risks were identified

• Modifications to the assessed RMM are needed

• Modifications to audit procedures are needed to address the RMM

AUD 16
Sufficient Appropriate Evidence

AUD 16: Sufficient Appropriate Evidence

16.01 Sufficient Appropriate Evidence

Overview

AICPA Guidance

AU-C 330, *Performing Audit Procedures in Response to Assessed Risks and Evaluating the Audit Evidence Obtained*, requires the auditor to obtain **sufficient appropriate audit evidence** by designing and performing audit procedures to address the assessed risks of material misstatement (RMM). This should be done in a manner that is not biased toward evidence that is corroborative over evidence that is contradictory.

AU-C 500, *Audit Evidence*, helps the auditor determine whether the audit evidence obtained is, in their professional judgment, sufficient and appropriate. As a basis for this conclusion, the auditor will consider the results of the audit procedures performed. The nature, extent, and timing (NET) of such procedures will affect the **persuasiveness** of the audit evidence.

Definitions

Audit Evidence—Information used by the auditor in arriving at the conclusion on which the auditor's opinion is based. Audit evidence is information to which audit procedures have been applied and consists of information that corroborates or contradicts assertions in the financial statements.

Accounting Records—The records of initial accounting entries and supporting records (eg, checks, invoices, contracts, the general and subsidiary ledgers, etc.).

Other Information—Information obtained from *external information sources.* For example, minutes of board of directors' meetings; confirmations; information in developing an understanding of the entity and its environment (eg, comparable data about competitors to use for benchmarking purposes); and information prepared by *management's specialist.*

Audit Evidence

 Representative Task (Application): Determine the sources of sufficient appropriate evidence (eg, obtained from management specialists, obtained from external sources, developed by the audit team from internal or external sources).

Sources of Information

 On the exam, you may be asked to evaluate which information provides the *most reliable* audit evidence. You should consider the source (external sources are less likely to be biased than internal sources), the form (hardcopy or electronic document is more reliable than inquiry evidence), and how the evidence was obtained (auditor's direct knowledge as opposed to evidence obtained indirectly or by inference).

Information to be used as audit evidence may come in different forms: oral (inquiries), visual (observation), paper documents, and electronic documents or data. The form of the information will determine the procedures necessary to evaluate the information. In addition to the client's accounting records, additional sources of information include:

- **External Information Source**—An external party that provides information that is either used by the entity in preparing the F/S or the auditor as audit evidence, when such information is suitable for use by a broad range of users (eg, A/R confirmation). It does not include a party acting as a specialist or service organization with respect to that information

- **Management's Specialist**—An external party with expertise in a field other than accounting or auditing (eg, engineering or actuarial services) that is used by the entity to assist in preparing the F/S

- **Auditor's Specialist**—An internal/external party that may develop information to be used as audit evidence such as developing an independent expectation of warranty expense

Audit evidence

- Supports the audit opinion
- Includes:
    - Accounting records that support the financial information
    - Other information that either confirms or contradicts management assertions
- Sufficient
- Considers cost-benefit relationship in obtaining evidence
- Persuasive rather than conclusive
- Relevant
- Reliable
- Based on professional judgment

Evaluating Audit Evidence

 Representative Task (Analysis): Exercise professional skepticism and professional judgment while analyzing information to be used as audit evidence, taking into account its relevance and reliability, authenticity and whether such information corroborates or contradicts the assertions in the financial statements.

 Representative Task (Evaluation): Conclude whether sufficient appropriate evidence has been obtained to achieve the objectives of the planned procedures.

The auditor should **evaluate information** to be used as audit evidence by considering:

- The relevance and reliability of the information, including the source from which it was obtained
- Whether the information corroborates or contradicts F/S assertions

Such evaluation should include:

- Determining whether the information is sufficiently precise and detailed for the auditor's purposes

- Obtaining evidence regarding the accuracy and completeness of the information, if necessary

 In accordance with the structure of the AICPA Blueprints, *understanding* professional skepticism and professional judgment are discussed in Chapter 2, *Professional Skepticism and Judgment*, as well as in this chapter.

As discussed in a previous chapter, the auditor should apply professional skepticism and professional judgment to evaluate both the **sufficiency and appropriateness** of audit evidence.

One of the most significant judgments made during an audit is considering when the auditor has gathered sufficient, appropriate evidence on which to base their opinion.

Sufficient and Appropriate

"Sufficient" refers to the **quantity** of evidence, whereas "appropriate" refers to the **quality** of evidence in terms of its relevance and reliability. The quantity of evidence required (ie, sufficiency) is directly related to the risk of misstatement (the greater the risk, the more evidence is needed) and inversely related to the quality of evidence (the higher the quality, the less evidence is needed).

The auditor may appropriately consider the **cost of information** relative to its usefulness, although cost alone is not a valid basis for omitting an audit procedure.

In evaluating **sufficiency and appropriateness**, the auditor should consider:

- Previous audit experience

- The auditor's understanding of the entity and its environment

- The significance and likelihood of potential misstatements

- The effectiveness of management's responses and controls

- Whether any instances of fraud or error were identified

Professional judgment is also used to evaluate the **persuasiveness** of contradictory and corroborative information. The relevance of contradictory information should be considered even when it comes from a source that is less reliable than the source of corroborative information.

Persuasiveness of audit evidence			
	Measure of:	**Affected by:**	**Relationship to testing:**
Sufficiency	*Quantity* of evidence	Risks of material misstatement (RMM) Quality of audit evidence obtained	Extent
Appropriateness	*Quality* of evidence	*Relevance* and *reliability* of audit evidence	Nature Timing

In response to an increased level of assessed **risk of material misstatement**, an auditor of a nonissuer would generally

- Not make changes to the nature, timing, or extent of further audit procedures

- Increase the emphasis on professional skepticism when gathering and evaluating audit evidence with the audit team

- Perform more substantive audit procedures at an interim date instead of at period end

- Perform additional tests of controls at an interim date to eliminate the need for substantive tests at period end

Audit risk = risk of material misstatement (RMM) × detection risk

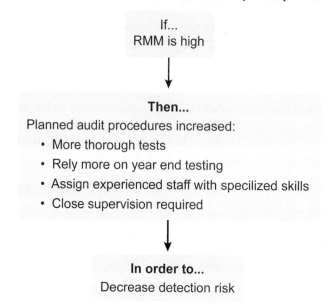

When planning and executing an audit, auditor identifies and assesses the risk of material misstatement (RMM) at the financial statement level and at the level of individual management assertions. RMM is the risk that the financial statements contain one or more *material misstatements*. When RMM is high, the auditor responds by **decreasing detection risk** (ie, risk that a misstatement will go undetected). This is done by:

- **Emphasizing professional skepticism when gathering evidence**

- Assigning more experienced staff or specialists

- Providing more supervision

- Reducing predictability of procedures

- Changing the nature, timing, and extent of procedures (eg, more substantive procedures)

Relevance and Reliability

Relevance—Information to be used as audit evidence is relevant if it is **timely** and **supports** or **contradicts** a relevant management assertion. For example, an audit data analytic (ADA) can use commodity pricing data to assess recorded revenue, but the time periods for the data and the revenue must be aligned.

Reliability—The reliability of audit evidence is directly related to the **nature** of the audit evidence, the **source** from which it is obtained, the **conditions** under which it is developed and acquired, and its **form**. The reliability of information is affected by its accuracy, completeness, authenticity, and susceptibility to management bias.

The following Statements on Auditing Standards (SAS) guidelines offer further clarification of reliable evidence:

- Evidence obtained directly by the auditor is more reliable than evidence obtained indirectly or by inference (eg, observation of the application of a control is more reliable than inquiry of entity personnel about the application of a control)

- Evidence is more reliable when obtained from external parties because it is less susceptible to management bias than evidence from internal sources

- Evidence generated internally is more reliable when the related controls are effective

- Evidence is more reliable when it exists in documentary form (whether paper or electronic)

- Evidence provided by original documents is more reliable than evidence based on photocopies/facsimiles (faxes) or scanned documents

Ranking Reliability

Audit evidence, ranking from the most reliable to the least, may come from the following sources:

- **Auditor Developed**—Audit evidence obtained directly by the auditor (eg, observing a control being applied) is more reliable than evidence obtained indirectly or by inference (eg, inquiring about the application of a control). For example, the auditor may:
  - Develop information to be used as audit evidence (eg, the auditor may have accumulated data on industry trends)
  - Use a specialist to assist in developing audit evidence
  - Produce audit evidence using automated tools and techniques to analyze information provided by management or external parties

- **External Information Sources (Outside)**—Information obtained directly from independent sources outside the entity (eg, data, confirmations received from banks) is less susceptible to management bias and is, therefore, generally more reliable than evidence received from inside the entity. Keep in mind that such evidence received from outsiders can be compromised due to collusion

- **Management**—Management may provide information obtained from the financial reporting process as well as information obtained from outside of the accounting records (eg, risk management system). Management may also have a specialist provide information that will be used as audit evidence
  - **Outside/Inside**—Evidence that originated outside the entity but provided from inside the entity (eg, a bank statement provided by the client) is more reliable than information that is both received from the entity and prepared by the entity. This evidence is less reliable than evidence received directly from outsiders since management or other employees may have the ability to alter external documents within the client's control
  - **Inside**—Internally generated audit evidence is less reliable than evidence obtained directly by the auditor or received from outsiders, since such documents are the most susceptible to alteration by the client
    - **Original documents** are **more reliable** than audit evidence transformed into electronic form (eg, photocopies, facsimiles, etc.). Further audit procedures may be necessary to determine the reliability of such information. This may include verifying the authenticity of the documents or testing the controls over the document's transformation and maintenance
    - **Documents**, whether paper or electronic, are **more reliable than oral** evidence
    - The **reliability** of internally generated documents **depends** on the operating effectiveness of the **controls** over their preparation and maintenance

Reliability of audit evidence

Category	Source	Example
1. Auditor developed	Directly obtained by auditor	Inventory observation
2. Outside	Obtained directly from outsider	Bank confirmations
3. Outside/Inside	Prepared by outsider but obtained from client	Bank statements
4. Inside	Prepared by client	Client sales invoices

Persuasiveness (arrow pointing up)

Audit evidence is usually "persuasive" (or suggestive) and is rarely "conclusive" (or compelling). The auditor should not be satisfied with evidence that is less than persuasive. Generally, though, the lower the acceptable level of detection risk (DR), the the higher the level of persuasiveness needed to reduce the chances of a material misstatement going undetected.

Which of the following procedures would yield the most competent evidence?

- A scanning of trial balances
- An inquiry of client personnel
- A comparison of beginning and ending retained earnings
- A recalculation of credit loss expense

The hierarchy* of audit evidence

Less reliable and less persuasive (arrow pointing down)

- Generated/obtained directly by auditor (eg, observation)
- Received directly from parties outside the entity under audit (eg, A/R confirmations)
- Generated externally but received from entity under audit (eg, bank statement)
- Generated internally by entity under audit (eg, client-generated invoices)

*There are exceptions to the ranking.

The most **competent**, reliable audit evidence is obtained directly by the auditor. For example, competent **audit evidence** supporting credit loss **expense** exists when the **auditor's recalculation** results in the **same F/S expense amount**. Scanning trial balances does *not* provide any audit evidence. Inquiry of client personnel is one of the *least competent* forms of audit evidence. The client may not be able to answer the audit question or may answer deceitfully. A comparison of beginning and ending retained earnings (R/E) balances does not provide any audit evidence about the accuracy of the R/E amount on the F/S.

AUD 17
Sampling Techniques

AUD 17: Sampling Techniques

17.01 Sampling Techniques

Overview

AICPA Guidance

The relevant AICPA guidance is provided by AU-C 530, *Audit Sampling*. This pronouncement states that the auditor's objective is to provide a reasonable basis for the auditor to draw conclusions about the population from which the sample is selected.

Definitions

Sampling—The selection and evaluation of **less than 100% of the population** of audit relevance such that the auditor expects the items selected to be representative of the population.

Attribute Sampling—Sampling for purposes of deciding whether internal controls are working as designed (tests of controls).

Variables Sampling—Sampling for purposes of deciding whether account balances (such as inventory or receivables) are fairly stated (substantive tests of details).

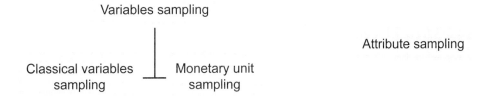

Variables sampling

Classical variables sampling | Monetary unit sampling

Attribute sampling

Primarily used in:
- Tests of details
- Reaching conclusions in terms of **dollar amounts** (quantitative)

Primarily used in:
- Tests of controls
- Reaching conclusions in terms of **rate of occurrence** (qualitative)

Note: Monetary unit sampling uses the probability proportional to size (PPS) selection method.

Sampling Approaches

Representative Task (Remembering & Understanding): Understand the purpose and application of sampling techniques, including the use of automated tools and audit data analytic techniques to identify significant events or transactions that may impact the financial statements.

Auditors select items from a population using either **statistical or nonstatistical sampling**.

- **Statistical sampling** uses the law of probability when selecting a sample size and allows auditors to quantitatively evaluate sample results and measure sampling risk. Because statistical sampling allows auditors to quantify sampling risk, it is preferable over nonstatistical sampling for an audit-level engagement

- An example of a statistical sampling method is classical variables sampling (CVS). In CVS, each item (eg, transaction) has an equal chance of being selected, regardless of dollar amount

- **Nonstatistical sampling** is any sampling method that does not allow the auditor to make a statistical evaluation of the sampling results (eg, haphazard or judgmental sampling). The sampling risk is unmeasurable because the results of the sample cannot be quantitatively evaluated. An example of nonstatistical sampling is using auditor judgment to select items when testing the year-end physical inventory

Statistical	Nonstatistical
• Uses the law of probability	• Does *not* use law of probability
• Probability of selection is known	• Judgement may be used to select items
• Quantifies sampling risk	• Does *not* quantify sampling risk
• Generally used when population is large	• Generally used when population is small

Use of Sampling

Sampling is used both in the **tests of controls** and in **substantive testing.**

- During the **internal control phase** of the audit, the auditor will perform **tests of controls** on a sample basis to determine the operating effectiveness of controls they plan to rely on

- During the **substantive testing phase** of the audit, the auditor will perform **tests of details** of transactions, accounts, and disclosures on a sample basis to obtain sufficient appropriate audit evidence to support management assertions

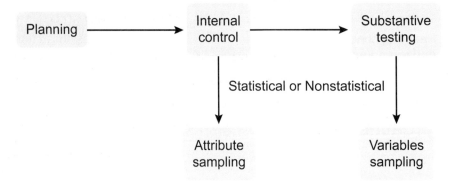

Sampling is not practical for all parts of the audit. In gaining an understanding of the internal control structure and documenting the understanding, the auditor cannot simply look at a part of the structure and use that as a basis for claiming understanding of the entirety. During substantive testing, the application of analytical procedures to some accounts cannot be considered evidence applicable to all the accounts.

Sampling Risk

 Representative Task (Application): Use sampling techniques to extrapolate the characteristics of a population from a sample of items.

Sampling risk is the risk that the sample may not be truly representative of the population. In other words, it is the chance of an erroneous conclusion that the auditor takes by examining a subset of the population, rather than the entire population. There are two types of errors:

- **Type I Errors (False Rejection)**
  - Type I errors relate to **efficiency**. The auditor will probably achieve the appropriate conclusions, although not in the most efficient manner (perhaps taking more than one sample, maybe at the urging of the client who has faith in the effectiveness of the internal control or the fairness of the financial statement element)

- **Type II Errors (False Acceptance)**
  - Type II errors relate to **effectiveness**. The auditor may have failed to meet the overall objective, which is to limit audit risk to an acceptably low level. (The client will have no incentive to argue about this conclusion, so the auditors will not have any reason to take a second look)

 Which of the following would be a consideration in planning an auditor's sample for a test of controls?
- Preliminary judgments about materiality levels
- The auditor's allowable risk of assessing control risk too high
- The level of detection risk for the account
- The auditor's allowable risk of assessing control risk too low

Risk type	Internal control testing	Substantive testing
Type I	Assessing RMM too high	Incorrect rejection
Type II	Assessing RMM too low	Incorrect acceptance

When planning samples, auditors consider sampling risk—forming an incorrect conclusion because procedures were performed on less than 100% of a population. The allowable risk of assessing control risk too low is the **greatest concern with sampling** tests of controls. In Type 2 risk, the sample results lead an auditor to conclude that internal controls operate effectively when they don't. The consequence is overreliance on the client's internal controls and reduced audit procedures, resulting in undetected misstatements and an ineffective audit.

Nonsampling Risk

Nonsampling risk refers to reaching **wrong conclusions** because of reasons **other than sampling**. It reflects **human errors** made by the auditors themselves and is managed through firm quality control measures, such as staff education and supervision.

Selecting **inappropriate audit procedures** is a nonsampling risk. For example, auditors cannot reveal *unrecorded* receivables by confirming only *recorded* receivables. Auditors must use professional judgment to create an adequate audit plan. Applying the most pertinent audit procedures is important to detecting misstatements.

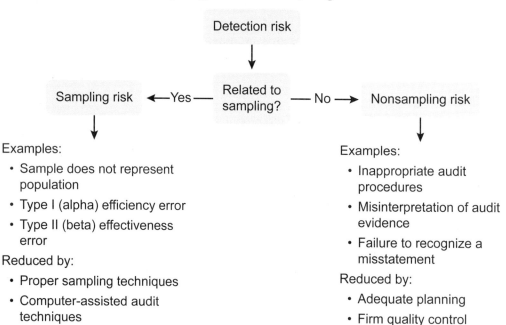

Sampling vs. nonsampling risk

Naturally, an auditor is more concerned about an audit being **ineffective** than inefficient. In particular, when the cost of additional testing is low, the auditor will often allow higher risks of assessing control risk too high and incorrect rejection.

 The diagram below depicts the auditor's estimated deviation rate compared with the tolerable rate, and also depicts the true population deviation rate compared with the tolerable rate.

		True state of population	
		Deviation rate exceeds tolerable rate	**Deviation rate is less than tolerable rate**
Auditor's estimate based on sample results	**Deviation rate exceeds tolerable rate**	I.	II.
	Deviation rate is less than tolerable rate	III.	IV.

As a result of tests of controls, the auditor assesses risk of material misstatement too high and thereby increases substantive testing. This is illustrated by quadrant:

- I
- II
- III
- IV

Sampling risks in tests of controls

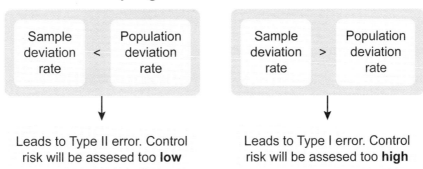

| Sample deviation rate | < | Population deviation rate | | Sample deviation rate | > | Population deviation rate |

Leads to Type II error. Control risk will be assesed too **low**

Leads to Type I error. Control risk will be assesed too **high**

Note: Errors occurred because sample did not represent the population.

Sampling risk is the possibility an auditor will draw a conclusion from a **sample** that **differs** from the true **population**. Auditors sample tests of controls to evaluate if the client deviates from prescribed controls more than is tolerable.

Situation II would cause the auditor to assess the risk of misstatement too high. In the sample, the auditors found the **deviation rate** was *higher* than **tolerable**. However, in the true population, the deviation rate is *less* than tolerable. Assessing the **risk of misstatement** too high leads to a Type I error, audit inefficiency (ie, more substantive testing than necessary).

In situations I and IV, the results in the sample and the true state of the population are the same. Therefore, sampling led the auditor to the correct conclusion. Situation III would draw the auditor to an incorrect conclusion. If the deviation rate in the sample was less than tolerable but the opposite occurs in the true population, the risk of misstatement would be assessed too low. This leads to Type II error affecting the effectiveness of the audit (ie, not enough substantive testing).

Attribute Sampling

 Representative Task (Remembering & Understanding): Identify the appropriate population of items to sample to meet the objectives of the planned procedures.

 Representative Task (Application): Determine the appropriate sampling method to be used in order to accomplish the objective (control, attribute, test of detail) of the planned procedures.

In general, attribute sampling is used to **test internal controls**. The auditor examines control activities to ensure that the client does not deviate from the control more often than the auditor considers tolerable.

There are various types of attribute sampling. These include:

- **Attribute sampling**, or fixed sample-size attribute sampling, used to estimate the rate of deviations in the population

- **Stop-or-go sampling** (sequential sampling) is a special type of attribute sampling which allows the auditor to stop when sufficient data is gathered. It is appropriate when the expected deviation rate is low and may provide the auditor with the most efficient sample size in an attribute sampling plan. The sample is selected in several steps and each step relies on the results of the previous step. By electing sequential samples, the auditor may stop sampling if no deviations are found

- **Discovery sampling** is also a special type of attribute sampling and is used when the expected deviation rate is very low, near zero. The sample size in this method is usually large enough to find at least one deviation if it exists. Discovery sample sizes and discovery sampling tables are designed to measure the probability of at least one error occurring in a sample if the error rate in the population exceeds the tolerable rate

To determine the **appropriate attribute sample size**, the auditor considers three key factors (ie, TEA):

1. **Tolerable deviation rate:** percentage of time for which a control can be violated and still lead the auditor to believe it is operating effectively

2. **Expected population deviation rate:** percentage of time for which the auditor expects the control was violated

3. **Acceptable level of risk of overreliance:** risk that the sample will cause the auditor to incorrectly rely on the control

Note: For the auditor to rely on a control, the sample deviation rate must be lower than the tolerable deviation rate.

In assessing the tolerable rate of deviations of a test of controls that was performed using statistical sampling, an auditor should consider that

- Deviations from pertinent controls do not affect the risk of material misstatement in the accounting records

- Deviations from pertinent controls at a given rate ordinarily result in misstatements at a lower rate

- When the degree of assurance desired in a sample is high, the auditor should allow for a high level of sampling risk

- Increasing the number of items selected for the test of controls usually increases the tolerable rate of deviations

| Control not followed 20% of time | ≠ | Account balance misstated* by 20% |

*Misstatement rate is usually lower than control deviation rate

Tests of controls are used to test the **rate of deviation** from a prescribed control. The **tolerable rate** (TR) is the **maximum deviation** rate an auditor is willing to accept before concluding the control is ineffective. If auditors decide the TR for a cash control tested is 10%, it means that in any given sample, the control is considered ineffective if the deviation is above 10%. However, even when the deviation rate for the control is above the TR, it does not mean the account balance is more than 10% misstated. When considering the TR (ie, maximum rate) of deviation, auditors should consider that although a *control deviation* may be high, it **does not necessarily imply that the rate of misstatement is high.**

Risks

The risks associated with attribute sampling are the **risk of assessing RMM too high**, which will result in an *inefficient* engagement, and the **risk of assessing RMM too low**, which will result in an *ineffective* engagement.

The risk of an ineffective engagement is greater since that means that users will rely on financial statements (F/S) that should not be relied on. As a result, the auditor will seek to reduce the risk of assessing RMM too low by making certain that the sample size is appropriate.

Attribute Sampling for Tests of Controls

When performing tests of controls, the form of sampling that is typically used is **attribute sampling.** Remember, attribute sampling cannot be used to verify a quantity or dollar amount, since it only provides information on the **presence or absence of something**, not its size.

Sampling applies to tests of controls when the auditor needs to decide **whether a rate of deviation is equal to or less than a tolerable rate**. However, sampling does not apply to risk assessment procedures performed to obtain an understanding of internal control.

Furthermore, sampling concepts may not apply to some tests of controls, such as the following: (1) tests of automated application; (2) analyses of controls for determining appropriate segregation of duties or other analyses that do not examine documentary evidence of performance; (3) tests of certain documented controls or analyses of the effectiveness of security and access controls; or (4) tests directed toward obtaining audit evidence about the operation of the control environment or accounting system.

The "**attribute**" or **characteristic** that the auditor is looking to find is a deviation from the proper application of the internal control activity being tested. For example, the auditor, while gaining an understanding of the internal control structure, might have identified a control activity requiring the authorization by an officer of all purchase requisitions.

If the auditor considers this a potential strength and wants to rely on the control, it must be tested to determine its operating effectiveness. The auditor will pull a sample from the population of purchase requisitions and determine how many items in the sample did not include proper authorization. Failure to authorize is the attribute, or **deviation**, being sought.

It is considered a **deviation** when the client cannot provide the document the auditor wishes to examine, as well as when the document fails to demonstrate the application of the control being tested.

- For each deviation that is identified, the auditor should consider the **qualitative** issues as well as the quantitative. If a deviation gives evidence of **fraud** committed by an employee, the auditor must consider the **broader implications** of that employee's impact on company operations and financial information as a whole, not limited to the specific control being tested

- When a deviation from control is identified, this doesn't mean there is a misstatement in the F/S as a result. For example, the failure of a purchase to be properly authorized does not mean it wasn't correctly processed and accounted for in the financial records. **Deviation** at a particular **rate** will usually result in actual **misstatements** at a much **lower rate**

Attribute sampling is appropriate for tests involving **re-performance** or **inspection**, where there is an identifiable population of documents or records from which the auditor can select a sample, but it is **not** normally appropriate for tests involving **inquiry** or **observation,** since each inquiry usually is made only once, and sample observations can rarely be performed randomly through the year so as to be representative of the entire year.

As a result of control testing, a CPA has decided to reduce control risk. What is the impact on substantive testing sample size if all other factors remain constant?

- The sample size would be irrelevant

- The sample size would be higher

- The sample size would be lower

- The sample size would be unaffected

Effect of control risk on substantive testing sample size

Tests of controls findings	Control risk	Substantive testing sample size
Internal controls are not effective	Increased	Higher
Internal controls are effective	Reduced	Lower

Control risk, a part of risk of material misstatement (RMM), is the probability that a client's internal controls do not prevent, detect, or correct misstatements. Auditors perform tests of controls to assess control risk, then decide how much substantive testing is necessary. There is a **direct relationship between control risk and the sample size** used in substantive testing.

The more confident an auditor is that internal controls prevent, detect, and correct misstatements, **the smaller the substantive testing sample size** needed to obtain sufficient audit evidence.

Steps for Attribute Sampling

There are eight steps involved in attribute sampling, as follows:

1. **Identify the Sampling Objective**—That is, the purpose of the test.

2. **Define What Constitutes an Occurrence**—Sometimes called a deviation or error when a control procedure of interest was not properly performed.

3. **Identify the Relevant Population**

   - Specify the relevant time period

   - Specify the sampling unit—what it is that the auditor is selecting (eg, sales transactions)

4. **Determine the Sampling Method**—How the specific items (or transactions) are to be selected for the sample.

   - **Statistical sampling approaches**

     ○ Random number—Each transaction has the same probability of being selected (the best approach)

     ○ Systematic—For example, selecting every 100th item

   - **Judgmental sampling approaches** (not appropriate for attribute sampling)

     ○ Block—A group of contiguous items (eg, the sales transactions for the entire month of June)

     ○ Haphazard—Arbitrary selection, with no conscious biases. Subconscious biases may exist without the auditor's awareness, however

5. **Determine the Sample Size**—Factors affecting sample size in an attribute sample include:

   - The **tolerable rate of error** has an inverse relationship to sample size. When a control is not significant, and, as a result, the auditor is not as concerned about whether or not it is being followed properly, the auditor will use a smaller sample size, which is less likely to be representative of the population

   - The **expected rate of error** has a direct relationship to sample size. When the auditor expects that a control is not operating as intended, the auditor will seek a sample size that is adequately large to make certain that there are likely to be a representative number of exceptions in the sample to reflect the error rate in the population

- The **acceptable risk** of assessing RMM too low has an inverse relationship to sample size. When a high assessment of RMM is acceptable, the auditor is not concerned about errors that will result from the control not being applied properly and is less likely to be concerned about an accurate measure of the degree to which it is not being complied with

Effect on sample size

Tolerable rate ↓	Sample size ↑
Confidence level (reliability) ↑	Sample size ↑
Deviation rate ↑	Sample size ↑
Population size ↑	Sample size ↑
Allowance (precision) (more accurate) ↓	Sample size ↑

6. **Select the Sample**—Identify the occurrences associated with all the items in the sample.

7. **Evaluate the Sample Results**—This means make a decision as to whether the auditor can rely on the effectiveness of the internal control procedure under consideration.

   - Calculate the observed deviation rate = (# errors)/n

   - Determine the point estimate, the best single indicator of the percentage of times that the control procedure was performed as designed in the population (ignoring, for the moment, the uncertainty surrounding whether the sample is truly representative of the population)

   - Calculate a confidence interval for the achieved upper precision limit (in view of the actual errors observed). There are AICPA tables to determine the achieved upper precision limit

   - Compare the achieved upper precision limit to the stated tolerable rate; the auditor can only rely on the internal control procedure if the error rate, based on the upper bound of the confidence interval (the achieved upper precision limit from the tables), is less than or equal to the stated tolerable rate

   - Consider the qualitative characteristics of the internal control deviations for any implication for the rest of the audit

   - Make the appropriate decision—Should the auditor rely on the specific control procedure (ie, assess control risk at less than the maximum) or not?

8. **Document the Auditor's Sampling Procedures**

Attribute Sampling Example

Suppose that an auditor specified the following parameters for a statistical sampling application related to internal controls in the revenue/receipts transaction cycle:

Acceptable risk of overreliance on internal control (a Type 2 error):	5%*
Estimated population deviation rate	1%
Tolerable deviation rate	5%

The auditor is willing to rely on the control procedure if the statistical test indicates that the control is working as prescribed at least 95% of the time.

Identify the required sample size using the following AICPA table for attribute sampling.

Statistical sample sizes for tests of controls						
5% risk of overreliance						
Expected population	**Tolerable rate**					
Deviation rate	**2%**	**3%**	**4%**	**5%**	**6%**	**7%**
0.25	236	157	117	93	78	66
0.50	*	157	117	93	78	66
0.75	*	208	117	93	78	66
1.00	*	*	156	93	78	66
1.25	*	*	156	124	78	66

*Sample size is too large to be cost-effective for most audit applications.

*__Note__: This table has been adapted from material copyrighted by the American Institute of Certified Public Accountants, Inc.

Solution—The 5% **risk of overreliance** determines the applicable page of the AICPA tables. The 5% **tolerable rate** determines the applicable column of the AICPA table. The 1% **estimated population deviation rate** determines the applicable row of the AICPA table. The resulting sample size is **93**.

 An auditor is performing attribute testing on a sample of fifty documents that results in three deviations. If the tolerable rate is 7%, the expected population deviation rate is 5%, and the allowance for sampling risk is 1%, the auditor will most likely

- Increase the level of control risk because the tolerable rate plus the allowance for sampling risk exceeds the expected population deviation rate

- Accept the sample results and reduce control risk because the sample deviation rate plus the allowance for sampling risk exceeds the tolerable rate

- Accept the sample results and reduce control risk because the sample deviation plus the allowance for sampling risk is less than or equal to the tolerable rate

- Increase the level of control risk because the sample deviation rate plus the allowance for sampling risk exceeds the tolerable rate

Evaluating results of control testing

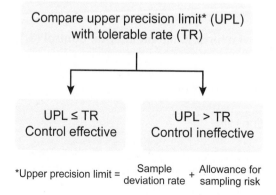

Compare upper precision limit* (UPL) with tolerable rate (TR)

UPL ≤ TR
Control effective

UPL > TR
Control ineffective

*Upper precision limit = Sample deviation rate + Allowance for sampling risk

Auditors test controls primarily by using attribute sampling to identify deviations from control procedures. Before testing a control, the auditor develops a tolerable deviation rate (ie, the percentage of time a control can be violated and still be considered effective).

After the sample is tested, the sample deviation rate is added to the allowance for sampling risk to calculate the upper precision limit (UPL), an estimate of the maximum deviation rate that likely exists within an entire population. If the UPL is less than or equal to the tolerable rate, the control is considered effective. In this scenario, calculations are as follows:

Calculate sample deviation rate $\qquad \dfrac{3 \text{ Number of deviations}}{50 \text{ Sample size}}$ = .06 or 6%

Calculate upper precision limit $\qquad$ 6% + 1% Allowance for sampling risk (given) = 7%

Compare to tolerable rate $\qquad$ Tolerable rate (given) 7% = 7%

Because the UPL equals the tolerable rate, the control is considered effective and the level of control risk can be reduced. Note: The expected population deviation rate (5%) is used to calculate sample size, not evaluate results.

Variables Sampling

During the substantive testing phase, the auditor will be testing the details of transactions and accounts in order to determine if the individual account balances are materially correct. To do so, they must use sampling to estimate the numerical value of the account balance, and this is known as **variables estimation sampling** or **sampling for variables**.

Of course, the estimate resulting from sampling for variables is not going to exactly equal the account balance, so the estimate will be expressed with an amount to be added and subtracted to determine the range of amounts within which the value of the population is likely to fall. This is known as the **precision** of the results or the precision range. As long as the account balance is within the acceptable precision range, the auditor will consider the sample to support the account balance.

The normal sampling unit for a population of documents is each individual document. When the dollar values on the various documents are widely different from each other, the auditor may **stratify** the sample by dividing the documents into different groups based on approximate values, using larger sample sizes for the more important large documents and smaller sample sizes for the documents with smaller dollar amounts, since they are less significant in determining whether the account being audited is materially correct.

Types of Variables Sampling

There are a variety of variables sampling methods, including:

Mean-per-Unit Estimation—The auditor determines the average value of the items in the sample and then multiplies this average by the number of items in the population to estimate the total numerical value of the population.

Projected misstatement: mean-per-unit estimation

Population per books:
1 million items totaling $90 million

Sample: 50 items
Total actual value: $5,000

→

Project average
per item:
$100 ($5,000/50)

Projected population:
$100 million (1 million × $100)

Projected misstatement:
$10 million
($100 million − $90 million)

- **Difference Estimation**—The auditor determines the average dollar amount by which the audited amounts exceed the book amounts in the sample (or vice versa), and assumes that this average difference applies to the entire population, so that the difference per item is multiplied by the number of items in the population, and the result is added to (or subtracted from) the total book amount.

- **Ratio Estimation**—This approach involves identifying the ratio of the audit values and book values for the sampled items. It is useful when the dollar amount of the differences between the audit and the book values is expected to be proportional to the book values.

 The auditor determines the ratio of the audited amounts to the book amounts in the sample (audited amount divided by book amount), and then multiplies the total book amount by this ratio. Assume that 3 invoices are pulled from a population of 100 invoices (with a total account balance of $3,000 on the books). The 3 invoices have recorded amounts of $40, $20, and $27, respectively, but when the auditor examines the support, they find the correct values are $42, $24, and $27, respectively. The evaluation under the 3 methods would be as follows:

Mean-per-Unit Estimation: $42 + $24 + $27 = $93 / 3 = $31. With a mean-per-unit of $31, the population of 100 invoices is estimated at $31 × 100 = $3,100.

Difference Estimation: $2 + $4 + $0 = $6 / 3 = $2. With an average excess of audited amount over book amount of $2, the population of 100 invoices should be increased by $2 × 100 = $200, estimating the population at $3,000 + $200 = $3,200.

Ratio Estimation: 1.05 + 1.20 + 1.00 = 3.25 / 3 = 1.08 (rounded). With an average ratio of audited amount to book amount of 1.08, the population is estimated to have a value of $3,000 × 1.08 = $3,240

Risks

The risks associated with variables sampling are concluding that:

- An item contains a misstatement when it does not (the risk of incorrect rejection), which will result in an inefficient engagement, and

- An item does not contain a misstatement despite the fact that it does (the risk of incorrect acceptance) which will result in an ineffective engagement.

The risk of an ineffective engagement is greater since that means that users will rely on F/S that should not be relied on. As a result, the auditor will seek to reduce the risk of incorrect acceptance by making certain that the sample size is appropriate.

Steps of Variables Sampling

The eight basic steps in a variables sampling plan are practically the same as in attribute sampling:

1. **Identify the Sampling Objective**—The purpose of "variables sampling" is to determine the inferred audit value of a population of interest (eg, for accounts receivable or inventory).

2. **Identify the Relevant Population:**

    -   Specify what constitutes the sampling unit

    -   Be careful to assure that conclusions are properly extended to the appropriate population (ie, completeness of the population)

3. **Select the Specific Sampling Technique**—The choices are difference estimation, ratio estimation, mean-per-unit estimation, or probability-proportionate-to-size sampling.

4. **Calculate the Sample Size**—Four factors enter into the determination of **sample size**: three of them parallel factors used in attribute sampling, and the fourth is specific to sampling for variables. The factors are:

    -   **Tolerable Misstatement**—This refers to the amount by which an account can differ from the recorded value without being considered materially misstated. It is based on the auditor's determination of the materiality level. The larger the tolerable misstatement, the smaller the sample size. Tolerable misstatement combined for all audit tests should not exceed financial statement materiality. Tolerable misstatement for any specific audit procedure will generally be less than financial statement materiality

    -   **Expected Misstatement**—This is the amount by which the auditor expects the account to be misstated. It is based on previous audits as well as information gathered while obtaining an understanding of internal control structure. The larger the expected misstatement, the larger the sample size

    -   **Allowable Risk of Incorrect Acceptance**—This refers to the risk the auditor is willing to take of accepting the account value as materially correct and have it be materially misstated. It is based on the auditor's overall willingness to accept audit risk as well as the assessed level of risk of material misstatement, since the auditor may be willing to accept greater detection risk when RMM is low. The larger the allowable risk of incorrect acceptance, the smaller the sample size

    -   **Standard Deviation**—This is the variability of the dollar values of the individual items in the population. It is usually based on previous audits or a tiny sample of the items in the current population. The larger the standard deviation, the larger the sample size (as discussed earlier, when standard deviation is extremely high, it may be appropriate to stratify the sample or use PPS (probability proportional to size) sampling instead)

    -   The basic formula, based on classical statistics:

$$n = (S * Z\text{-coefficient} * N/A)^2$$

    -   where:

        o   n represents the sample size to be determined

        o   S represents the estimated population standard deviation (related to the variability of the population)

        o   Z-coefficient represents a measure of reliability for some level of specified "confidence" (typically about 2)

        o   N represents the size of the population (number of accounts or items of inventory, etc.)

        o   A represents the specified allowance for sampling risk, related to the statistical concept of "precision"

Note: It is very unlikely that the AICPA will require calculations of sample size. However, they frequently test these concepts. In particular, they might ask questions related to the factors that influence the sample size and whether that influence is directly or inversely related. The formula identified above is a useful way to keep these relationships straight.

5. **Determine the Method of Selection**—Random (the preferred approach) or systematic.

6. **Conduct the Sample**

7. **Evaluate the Sample** and project to population:

- Calculate a point estimate (the implied audit value) for the population based on the sample's audited values

- Construct a confidence interval to determine whether to accept or reject the client's recorded balance as consistent with the audit evidence

8. **Document the Auditor's Sampling Procedures and Judgments.**

An auditor established a $60.000 tolerable misstatement for an asset with an account balance of $1,000,000. The auditor selected a sample of every twentieth item from the population that represented the asset account balance and discovered overstatements of $3,700 and understatements of $200. Under these circumstances, the auditor most likely would conclude that

- There is an unacceptable high risk that the tolerable misstatement exceeds the sum of actual overstatements and understatements.

- There is an unacceptably high risk that the actual misstatements in the population exceed the tolerable misstatements because the total projected misstatement is more than the tolerable misstatement.

- The asset account is fairly stated because the total projected misstatement is less than the tolerable misstatement.

- The asset account is fairly stated because the tolerable misstatement exceeds the net of projected actual overstatements and understatements.

Difference estimation in variables sampling

Total projected misstatement = (Sample audited amount – Sample book amount) × Population

Projected misstatement > Tolerable misstatement	High risk
Projected misstatement < Tolerable misstatement	Low risk

Variables sampling techniques are appropriate when an auditor is estimating a numerical amount. In **difference** estimation, auditors **calculate** the amount by which the **sample value** differs from **book value** and assume that the error rate is consistent throughout the entire population. The **total projected misstatement** is the *gross* audited sample difference applied to 100% of the population.

In this scenario, there is an **unacceptably high risk of misstatement** because the total projection is higher than is tolerable. The over- and understatements are **not netted** because the goal is to determine how far the sample numbers deviate from actual, no matter whether positive or negative.

Overstatements	$ 3,700
Understatements	200
Gross sample to book difference	$ 3,900
Sample size	Every twentieth
Sample size as a % of population (ie, 1 / 20)	5%
Multiplier to project sample to population	20
Total projected misstatement ($3,900 × 20)	$78,000
Tolerable misstatement	$60,000

Probability Proportional to Size Sampling (PPS)

Sampling Unit

PPS sampling defines the sampling unit to be an **individual dollar** associated with the F/S element involved. (Variations of this approach are referred to as dollar-unit sampling or monetary-unit sampling.) For example, suppose accounts receivable consists of 7,500 customer accounts having a total balance of $3,000,000. The population is viewed as consisting of 3,000,000 individual items (dollars) rather than 7,500 accounts.

However, when an individual dollar is selected as part of the sample, it attaches to the related account or logical record, which is then examined in its entirety. Accordingly, the probability that an individual account will be selected is "proportional" to that individual account's balance relative to the total for all accounts.

PPS sampling is **more conservative** than variables sampling and is more likely to reject an account balance. This is particularly the case for a population that contains several misstatements. As a result, this method is best for populations that are *not believed* to contain a large number of misstatements.

This type of sampling is particularly useful for:

- Confirming accounts receivable or loans receivable

- Tests of pricing of investments securities or inventory

- Tests of fixed-asset additions where existence is the primary risk

This type of sampling is generally NOT appropriate for:

- Confirming accounts receivable when there are a large number of unapplied credits

- Inventory test counts and price tests when the auditor anticipates a significant number of misstatements that could be overstatements or understatements

- Converting inventory from FIFO to LIFO

- Populations without individual recorded amounts

- Any application in which the primary objective is to estimate an amount

Advantages of PPS Sampling over Variables Estimation

- Larger accounts automatically have a greater chance of being selected, and individual accounts exceeding the sampling interval are always selected, so the method automatically stratifies the population

- The method accommodates populations with items that vary widely in value without any need to compute standard deviation

- A sample can be designed more easily and sample selection can begin before the final and full population is available

Disadvantages of PPS Sampling over Variables Estimation

- The method is not useful in detecting understated accounts, since smaller accounts have a proportionately smaller chance of being selected

- Special methods must be used in order to deal with zero or negative accounts, since they will ordinarily never be selected under this approach

- Identified understatements require special consideration, and large understatements may lead to invalid projections or conclusions

- Larger anticipated misstatements require larger sample sizes, often making classical variables sampling more efficient

Classical variables sampling   vs.   Probability proportional to size

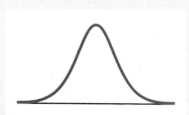

- Items treated as sample unit regardless of dollar value
- Standard deviation for population needed
- All items have equal chance of selection
- Especially useful to detect understatements

- Treats each dollar value as sampling unit
- Standard deviation for population *not* needed
- Larger items have a higher chance of selection
- Especially useful to detect overstatements

Projecting Misstatement Example

In a probability-proportional-to-size sample with a sampling interval of $10,000, an auditor discovered that a selected account receivable with a recorded amount of $5,000 had an audited amount of $4,000. If this were the only misstatement discovered by the auditor, the projected misstatement of this sample would be

- $1,000
- $2,000
- $5,000
- $10,000

Projecting misstatement to interval using PPS* sampling

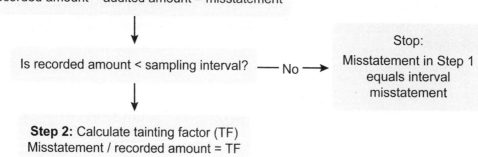

Step 1: Calculate item misstatement amount
Recorded amount − audited amount = misstatement

Is recorded amount < sampling interval? —— No ——▸ Stop: Misstatement in Step 1 equals interval misstatement

Step 2: Calculate tainting factor (TF)
Misstatement / recorded amount = TF

Step 3: Project misstatement to interval using TF
TF × sampling interval = projection

*Probability-proportional-to-size

Probability-proportional-to-size (PPS) sampling is used to:

- **select items** from the population
- **estimate errors** (ie, misstatements) in the population

To select items, the population is first organized. An item (eg, invoice) will be selected each time the interval amount is reached (eg, one item picked for every $10,000 in the population). Once all the selections have been made, auditors will evaluate them. If no errors are noted, auditors can conclude that the population is fairly stated.

To estimate any errors in the population, auditors first project the error to each interval. Errors need to be projected (ie, extrapolated) only when the recorded amount is less than the interval. If the recorded amount is greater than the interval, no projection is needed for that sample because the error already represents the actual misstatement (ie, already extrapolated). Next, auditors add the errors in each interval; the sum is the estimated population error.

The steps are as follows:

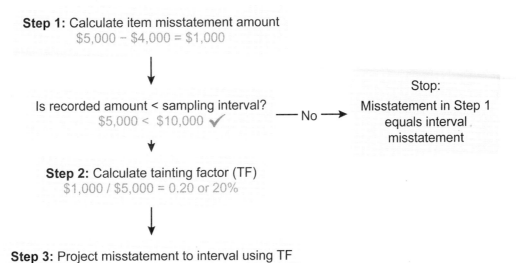

Step 1: Calculate item misstatement amount
$5,000 − $4,000 = $1,000

Is recorded amount < sampling interval?
$5,000 < $10,000 ✓ — No → Stop: Misstatement in Step 1 equals interval misstatement

Step 2: Calculate tainting factor (TF)
$1,000 / $5,000 = 0.20 or 20%

Step 3: Project misstatement to interval using TF
20% × $10,000 = $2,000

In this scenario, this was the only error discovered. Therefore, there are no other intervals to add, and the total error is $2,000.

AUD 18
Procedures to Obtain Sufficient Appropriate Evidence

18.01 Test of Controls and Test of Details

Overview of Testing to Address Risk of Material Misstatement

After identifying the risks of material misstatement, an auditor plans audit procedures to respond to those risks. These procedures can be categorized as follows:

- **Tests of Controls**—Test the operating effectiveness of I/C for preventing or detecting material misstatements
- **Substantive Analytical Procedures**—Examine the relationship between recorded amounts (eg, annual sales) and other information (eg, COGS [cost of goods sold]) to identify unusual relationships, which may indicate misstated amounts
- **Tests of Details**—Directly identify misstatements (eg, identify unrecorded expenses by tracing a sample of receiving reports)

Procedures that function as more than one type of test are known as **dual-purpose tests**. For example, an auditor could draw a sample of invoices and, while reviewing them, ascertain whether they were properly authorized (a test of controls) and whether they were correctly recorded in accordance with the dates, terms, and amounts on the invoices (a test of details). Dual-purpose tests provide an efficient means of obtaining additional evidence.

Categories of audit tests used to address risk of material misstatement

Types	Purpose	Example
Control tests	Determine the operating effectiveness of I/C	Testing a sample of invoices to determine whether they were properly approved
Substantive testing: Analytical procedures	Identify unexpected relationships between recorded amounts and other data	Comparing the dollar amounts of sales invoices in current year with previous year's invoices
Substantive testing: Tests of details	Determine conclusively if a material misstatement has occurred and by how much	Inspecting a sample of invoices to determine whether they were properly recorded

Tests of Controls (TOC)

 Representative Task (Application): Use observation and inspection to obtain evidence.

 Representative Task (Application): Use recalculation (manually or using automated tools and techniques) to test the mathematical accuracy of information to obtain evidence.

Representative Task (Application): Use re-performance to independently execute procedures or controls to obtain evidence.

 Representative Task (Application): Inquire of management and others to gather evidence and document the results.

 Representative Task (Analysis): Analyze responses obtained during structured interviews or informal conversations with management and others, including those in non-financial roles, and ask relevant and effective follow-up questions to understand their perspectives and motivations.

Tests of controls (TOC) are audit procedures designed to **evaluate the operating effectiveness of controls** in preventing or detecting and correcting material misstatements at the *assertion level*.

When an auditor believes that the nature, timing, or extent of substantive testing can be limited due to effective I/C, the auditor must perform tests of controls to verify that they are operating effectively as designed and intended. Based on those tests, the auditor draws a conclusion as to whether the controls can be relied on for the entire period for which controls were tested.

Reasons to test controls

- To lower the assessed risk of material misstatement
- More efficient than substantive testing
- To reduce the amount of substantive testing
- Substantive tests cannot provide audit evidence
- Controls appear to be reliable
- Controls are well designed
- Relevant to management assertions
- Required for all issuer and nonissuer integrated audits

The auditor may choose **not to test** relevant controls when the assessed RMM or the substantive testing sample sizes remain unchanged regardless of test results. In such a situation, control testing would be an inefficient use of audit resources.

Examples of TOC

- **Observation** (eg, observation of inventory count, observation of control activities)—The auditor can observe activities physically or remotely with the use of technology (eg, a drone). Note that observation provides the auditor with direct knowledge, but it is limited to a *point in time* (ie, the point in time the auditor is viewing the process)

- **Inspection of tangible assets** (eg, inventory items)—The auditor can inspect assets (physically or remotely) to verify that they are in appropriate condition and that they are the same as described by the entity

- **Inspection (examination) of records or documents** (eg, invoice for an equipment purchase transaction)—The auditor can inspect electronic and paper documents (manually or with automated techniques) to determine if they have been interpreted and recorded properly

- **Recalculation** (eg, checking the mathematical accuracy of documents or records)—The auditor may recalculate information included in the F/S, manually or using generalized audit software (more on this later). An example would be recalculating depreciation expense and accumulated depreciation to compare it to the client's amounts

- **Re-performance** (eg, re-performing the aging of accounts receivable)—The auditor can re-perform processes to determine the outcome and compare that outcome to information provided by the client. For example, the auditor can re-perform an internal control procedure to determine if the procedure would be effective in preventing a material misstatement from occurring or detecting it so that it can be corrected on a timely basis

- Inquiry (eg, written inquiries and oral inquiries)—The auditor can make inquiries of management and others, including those external to the entity (note that this does not constitute a confirmation). Inquiries may be written or oral and may be used to learn about:

  ○ The entity and its environment, including its internal control

  ○ Accounting policies and procedures, such as capitalization policies and how estimates are developed

  ○ How balances were derived, including the sources used for developing measurements or the methodology for determining balances

  ○ Any other matters that the auditor believes a response to which will provide audit evidence

Timing of TOC

When the auditor identifies a significant risk of material misstatement (RMM) but plans to rely on the effectiveness of controls that mitigate that risk, the auditor should test those controls in the **current period**.

When obtaining evidence about the effectiveness of controls for an **interim period**, the auditor should determine what evidence is required for the remaining period. If planning to rely on controls that have changed since last tested, the auditor should test those controls currently.

If planning to rely on controls that have not changed since last tested, the auditor should test the operating effectiveness of those controls at least every third year (ie, no more than two years should pass before retesting such controls).

Extent of TOC

When a control is applied on a **transaction basis** (eg, matching approved purchase orders to suppliers' invoices) and if the control operates frequently, the auditor should use **audit sampling techniques** to test operating effectiveness.

When a control is applied on a **periodic basis** (eg, monthly reconciliation of the accounts receivable subsidiary ledger to the general ledger), the auditor should **perform procedures** appropriate for testing smaller populations.

Tests of Operating Effectiveness of Internal Controls

 Representative Task (Analysis): Perform tests of operating effectiveness of internal controls, including the analysis of exceptions to identify deficiencies in an audit of financial statements or an audit of internal control.

If the risk assessment is based on an expectation that controls are operating effectively, the auditor should test the **operating effectiveness of controls** that have been determined to be suitably designed to prevent or detect material misstatements.

Tests of these controls alone are not normally sufficient to base an audit opinion on; therefore, **further audit procedures**, including **substantive tests**, will be required. Thus, tests of controls will be performed when a combination of tests of controls and a decreased scope of substantive tests is **more cost effective** than performing more extensive substantive tests.

The overall approach here, as it relates to controls is to:

- Identify controls that are relevant to specific assertions that are likely to prevent or detect material misstatements, and

- Perform tests of controls to evaluate the effectiveness of those controls

To test the effectiveness of the design and operation of a control, the auditor must consider:

- *How* the control was applied

- The *consistency* with which it was applied

- *By whom* it was applied

 Which of the following actions should the auditor take in response to discovering a deviation from the prescribed internal control procedure?

- Make inquiries to understand the potential consequence of the deviation

- Assume that the deviation is an isolated occurrence without audit significance

- Report the matter to the next higher level of authority within the entity

- Increase sample size of tests of controls

Internal control testing

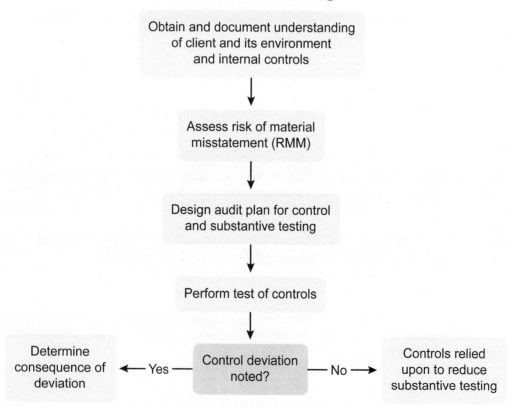

To determine a client's risk of material misstatement (RMM), an auditor must obtain and document an understanding of that client's internal control design. To determine substantive testing needed, the auditor must test the controls that are likely to reduce RMM.

The tests of controls may reveal deviations from prescribed procedures (eg, expense approval procedure not followed). When a **deviation** is **discovered**, the auditor should **make inquiries** to **determine** the **consequences** of the deviation. The auditor may decide that the consequences are insignificant if other procedures provide compensating controls.

Tests of Details

 Representative Task (Analysis): Perform tests of details, including the analysis of exceptions, to identify potential misstatements in an audit of financial statements.

Substantive audit procedures are used to **detect material misstatements** for all relevant assertions related to each material class of transactions, account balances, and disclosures. Substantive procedures are required for each material transaction class, account balance, and disclosure item. There are two categories of substantive tests:

- **Tests of Details**—These are the relatively precise (but usually rather expensive, labor-intensive) procedures (that suggest whether the client's recorded amounts are right or not)
- **Analytical Procedures**—Evaluations of financial information through analysis of plausible relationships among both financial and nonfinancial data

Selection of Procedures

The decision by the auditor as to what tests of details to apply will depend on the **level of detection risk** that is acceptable and the availability of appropriate evidence. For example, observation may not be possible for an intangible asset (eg, goodwill). Observation may also not be necessary when the RMM is low and the auditor is willing to accept evidence obtained from other sources.

In selecting appropriate audit procedures, the auditor may consider the relationship between **cost and usefulness**. However, in situations where there is no appropriate alternative procedure, difficulty or expense are not valid reasons for choosing to omit necessary audit procedures.

Timing of Procedures

Since the balances at the F/S date often depend heavily on transactions occurring near the end of the year, the auditor must be careful about the decision to perform substantive tests at interim dates. This can increase incremental audit risk and should be avoided unless the acceptable level of detection risk is relatively high or the accounts are such that year end balances are reasonably predictable.

Interim Testing

Factors influencing **interim substantive testing** include:

- Effectiveness of internal controls
- Availability of needed information at year end
- Purpose of the test
- Assessed risk of material misstatement

- Type of account or transactions

- Cost and ability to control audit risk between interim and year end

- Predictability of year end balances after interim testing

In some cases, tests of details cannot be performed until after the close of the fiscal year under audit. Examples include the search for unrecorded liabilities (since the auditor must know what was recorded to perform the search) and obtaining a management representation letter (since it must be dated as of the audit completion date). Other tests must be performed as close to the balance sheet date as possible (eg, counts of inventory and marketable securities on hand).

18.02 Analytical Procedures

Analytical Procedures—Overview

Analytical procedures are audit procedures that involve the auditor **developing an expectation** based on knowledge that may have been obtained from a variety of sources.

- This expectation is then compared to client representations. The degree to which they match will provide the auditor with evidence as to the reliability of management's representation
- The reliability of the expectation is generally a function of the source of information used by the auditor to develop it

AICPA Guidance

The relevant AICPA guidance is provided by AU-C 520, *Analytical Procedures*. This pronouncement states that the auditor's objectives are to:

- Obtain relevant and reliable audit evidence when using substantive analytical procedures
- Design and perform analytical procedures near the end of the audit that assist the auditor when forming an overall conclusion about whether the F/S are consistent with the auditor's understanding of the entity

Purpose and Timing

Analytical procedures serve three distinct purposes:

- They are useful as a risk assessment procedure for **planning purposes** (required)
  - These tests of reasonableness involve analyzing trends and interrelationships. The key is developing a *meaningful expectation* by which to judge the reasonableness of the client's recorded amount
- They are useful (but not required) as a form of substantive evidence (and, in this context, are referred to as "substantive analytical procedures")
- They are required to be performed near the end of the audit to assist the auditor when forming an overall conclusion about the financial statements

Using analytical procedures		
Planning (risk assessment)	Required	• To enhance understanding of the entity • To identify high risk accounts/assertions
Substantive testing	Optional	• Verify reasonableness of accounts/assertions
Overall review	Required	• Confirm that F/S are consistent with overall understanding of entity • Ensure all unexpected amounts/relationships have been explained

An auditor's decision whether to apply analytical procedures as substantive tests usually is determined by the

- Availability of documentary evidence that should be verified
- Extent of accounting estimates used in preparing the financial statements
- Precision and reliability of the data used to develop expectations
- Number of transactions recorded just before and just after the year end

Factors affecting reliability of data used to develop expectations for analytical procedures

- Source (eg, inside or outside the entity)
- Comparability (eg, broad industry data vs. niche within an industry)
- Nature/relevance (eg, budgets include expectations vs. goals)
- Internal controls (eg, over the preparation of budgets)

When analytical procedures are used to test individual account balances (ie, substantive procedures), it is essential that the **data** from which expectations are developed are **reliable** and sufficiently **precise**. For example, suppose an auditor wants to use substantive analytical procedures to test payroll expense by comparing it with an average for similar companies in the industry. If the figure used for the average is derived from a twenty-year-old dataset, the analytical procedure may not be useful because the data are likely outdated and therefore unreliable.

Analytical Procedures

 Representative Task (Analysis): Perform substantive analytical procedures, including developing an expectation, on an account balance to provide evidence to support an identified assertion.

 Representative Task (Analysis): Perform analytical procedures near the end of an audit engagement that assist the auditor when forming an overall conclusion about whether the financial statements are consistent with the auditor's understanding of the entity.

 Representative Task (Application): Determine the suitability of substantive analytical procedures to provide evidence to support an identified assertion.

Analytical procedures include manual or automated "scanning" to **review accounting data** to identify **unusual items** to be tested further. Automated tools and techniques, including audit data analytics, may be especially useful in identifying significant or unusual items.

There are five basic **types of comparisons** that may be performed as analytical procedures:

- **Client vs. Industry**—A client's financial data can be expected to have some plausible relationship to industry averages. A client's sales, for example, may tend to rise and fall at the same time the revenues of competitors in the industry change

- **Related Accounts**—Certain accounts are closely associated with each other and have a range of expected relationships. Interest expense, for example, should approximate the weighted average of liabilities for the period to the weighted average effective interest rate paid by the entity

- **Actual vs. Budget**—Results during the year should have a plausible relationship to budgets, allowing for the inevitable variances. Actual payroll expenses, for example, should be reasonably close to budgets for payroll, given the control management has over the level of hiring

- **Financial vs. Nonfinancial**—Certain nonfinancial measures are clearly associated with dollars of revenues or costs. Number of passenger miles flown during the year, for example, should have a predictable relationship to airline revenues

- **Current Year vs. Prior Year**—In the absence of extreme changes in the company and with appropriate adjustments for normal growth and changes to the entity's environment, income statement amounts for the current period should be closely associated with those from previous years of the company. Rent expense, for example, will be similar to the previous year in the absence of major changes in company size or alteration of the ratio of purchased to leased assets

 Which of the following actions is an analytical procedure that an auditor most likely would use while auditing a company's notes payable?

- Performing calculations to determine if the company is in compliance with debt covenants

- Multiplying the average outstanding loan balance by the interest rate and comparing the result to interest expense actually recorded

- Sending a confirmation to the lender requesting verification of the loan's outstanding balance

- Reviewing the details of the company's loan and interest expense accounts to determine that all payments were properly recorded

Analytical procedure for interest expense: using an expectation based on debt balances

Analysis of year 1 debt		Income statement for year ended 12/31/year 1	
Average total long-term debt	$10,000,000	Sales	$12,000,000
		COGS	9,000,000
Average interest rate	7%	**Gross profit**	$ 3,000,000
		SG&A expenses	600,000
Expected interest expense	$ 700,000 ?	Depreciation expense	100,000
		Operating income	$ 2,300,000
		Interest expense	300,000
		Gain on sale of equipment	50,000
		Income before tax	$ 2,050,000
		Provision for income tax	800,000
		Net income	$ 1,250,000

Analytical procedures involve **developing an expectation** about what financial amounts should be and comparing that expectation with actual recorded amounts. Because there is a predictable **relationship** between the balance of **debt** (eg, notes payable) and the **interest** incurred on that debt, an auditor will likely employ substantive **analytical procedures** to test this relationship. For example, the auditor may **multiply** the average outstanding **loan balance** by the **interest rate** and compare the result with **recorded interest expense**. If the relationship is not in the expected range, the auditor will increase tests of details.

Further Considerations

The AICPA states that the effectiveness and efficiency of substantive analytical procedures depends on the following four factors or considerations:

- **Nature of the assertion:** Analytical procedures may be particularly effective (compared to tests of details) in detecting omissions of transactions (regarding the "completeness" assertion). Tests of details may not be effective in detecting omissions when there are no underlying source documents associated with unrecorded transactions

- **Plausibility and predictability of the relationship:** The auditor's expectation improves with the increased predictability of an account balance or ratio. Predictability is affected by several considerations:

  - Relationships in a stable environment are usually more predictable than those in a dynamic environment

  - Relationships involving income statement accounts tend to be more predictable than those involving balance sheet accounts (since the income statement deals with a period of time rather than a single moment in time)

  - As management discretion increases, the predictability of an account balance or ratio tends to decrease

Relationships used in analytical procedures must be predictable

Less predictable	More predictable
←	→
• Unstable environment	• Stable environment
• More management discretion	• Less management discretion
• Represent point in time (balance sheet)	• Represent whole period (income statement)

- **Availability and reliability of data:** Analytical procedures are improved as the reliability of the data used increases. The following considerations tend to enhance the reliability of the data used:

  - When data have been subject to audit testing (either currently or in the past), the reliability of the data is enhanced

  - When data have been obtained from independent external sources (rather than from the client entity), the reliability of the data is enhanced

  - When data obtained from the client entity are developed under conditions of effective internal control (rather than ineffective internal control), the reliability of the data is enhanced

- **Precision of the expectation:** The likelihood of detecting a misstatement increases as the level of aggregation of the data decreases

  - Relationships of interest to the auditor may be obscured by the noise in the data at high levels of aggregation of the data

  - For example, simply comparing the current year's sales in total to the prior year's total sales is a high level of aggregation; a more precise analysis (at a lower level of aggregation) would be analyzing the sales by month broken down by product line

Performing Analytical Procedures

Steps constituting the auditor's performance of substantive analytical procedures include:

- Determine the suitability of the analytical procedures for the identified assertions involved

- Evaluate the reliability of the data used to develop the auditor's expectation

- Develop the auditor's expectation of the recorded amounts (or ratios) and evaluate whether the expectation is sufficiently precise

- Compare the recorded amounts (or ratios) to the auditor's expectation
- Determine whether any difference relative to the auditor's expectation requires further investigation (such as inquiry of management or other actions)

Selected Ratios

Common ratios used for analytical procedures include:

Relationships used in analytical procedures

Profitability	Asset utilization	Liquidity
• Gross margin ratio • Return on assets	• Inventory turnover • Receivable turnover	• Current ratio • Quick ratio (acid test)

Debt utilization	Market
• Debt-to-total assets ratio • Debt-to-equity ratio	• Price-to-earnings ratio • Sales-to-cash flow ratio

Documentation Requirements

The following items should be included in the audit documentation:

- The overall responses to address the assessed risk of misstatement at the F/S level
- The nature, timing, and extent of the further audit procedures
- The linkage of those procedures with the assessed risks at the relevant assertion level
- The results of the audit procedures
- The conclusions reached in the current audit about the operating effectiveness of controls tested in a prior audit

Task-Based Simulation

 Representative Task (Evaluation): Evaluate and investigate differences resulting from analytical procedures (eg, fluctuations or relationships that are inconsistent with other information or expected values).

Holiday Manufacturing Co. prepared financial statements for the year ended December 31, Year 5, along with various ratios calculated using the financial statements for Years 3, 4, and 5. Sales are all on account and are stated net of returns and discounts. The total assets and the balances for receivables and inventory at December 31, Year 5, were materially the same as the balances at December 31 in Years 3 and 4.

Rows 2 through 5 represent an auditor's observed changes in certain financial statement ratios or amounts from the prior year's ratios or amounts. For each row, select the most likely explanation for the observed change from the list provided, considering the impact of explanations for the observed change(s) in the previous row(s).

1	Observed change	Most likely explanation
2	Accounts receivable turnover decreased substantially from the prior year.	List 1
3	Inventory turnover increased substantially from the prior year.	List 2
4	Allowance for credit losses as a percentage of accounts receivable decreased from the prior year.	List 3
5	Long-term debt increased from the prior year, but interest expense increased a larger-than-proportionate amount than long-term debt.	List 4

LIST 1

Year 5 beginning accounts receivable balance was much smaller than the ending balance.

Sales increased in Year 5.

Year 5 beginning accounts receivable balance was much larger than the ending balance.

Sales decreased in Year 5.

LIST 2

Inventory items purchased and sold at the end of Year 5 were recorded in Year 6.

Inventory purchases early in Year 6 were incorrectly recorded as received in Year 5.

Inventory items were purchased and recorded as expense in Year 5 before being sold.

Sales caused the cost of goods sold to increase.

LIST 3

Sales increased in Year 5.

Year 5 beginning accounts receivable balance was much smaller than the ending balance.

Credit policies were relaxed in Year 5.

Management changed estimation procedures to increase net income.

LIST 4

All short-term debt was converted to long-term debt.

Existing long-term debt was replaced with long-term debt at a higher interest rate.

Long-term debt was refinanced because interest rates changed.

New long-term debt in Year 5 carried a lower interest rate.

1	Observed change

2 **Answer: Sales decreased in Year 5.**

A/R turnover = Sales / Average A/R

The introductory information states that A/R balances remained materially the same in Years 3, 4, and 5. Therefore, the auditor might have expected A/R turnover to remain consistent as well. However, A/R turnover decreased substantially in Year 5. A/R turnover will decrease if there is a decrease in sales or an increase in average A/R. In this case, because the A/R balance was consistent, average A/R did not change. Instead, sales must have decreased in Year 5.

3 **Answer: Inventory items were purchased and recorded as expense in Year 5 before being sold.**

Inventory turnover = Cost of goods sold / Average inventory

The introductory information states that inventory balances remained materially the same, so the auditor might expect the Year 5 inventory turnover ratio to also remain consistent. However, this ratio increased substantially between Years 4 and 5. Because the inventory balance was consistent, the average inventory portion of this ratio did not change. Therefore, COGS must have increased.

The auditor must consider whether the increase in COGS could be due to an increase in sales. Although the change in sales was not given, the decrease in the A/R turnover ratio (Row 2) was due to a decrease (not an increase) in sales; this indicates that the increase in COGS is not due to a sales increase. However, COGS would be overstated (ie, increased) if inventory purchases were incorrectly recorded as expense (ie, debit A/P and credit COGS).

In response to this analytical procedure, the auditor might plan for increased substantive testing associated with COGS.

4   **Answer: Management changed estimation procedures to increase net income.**

Percentage of allowance-to-A/R ratio = (Allowance for credit losses / A/R) × 100

The allowance for credit losses account is a contra account associated with A/R. Given a materially consistent A/R balance for three years, the auditor would likely expect a consistent percentage for the allowance-to-A/R ratio. In this scenario, the percentage decreased in Year 5, meaning the allowance for credit losses account must have decreased.

A Year 5 decrease in allowance for credit losses may be due to a reduction in Year 5 credit loss expense (ie, debit credit loss expense and credit allowance for credit losses). Because the allowance account is an indicator of the A/R balance not expected to be paid, a decrease in the allowance account might be due to *improved* (not relaxed) credit policies or collection efforts. However, the allowance is based on an estimate, which management might change to decrease credit loss expense and increase net income.

While the auditor may consider control tests to determine changes in credit policies or collection efforts, the audit program will likely include increased substantive testing of management's credit loss expense calculation because the calculation is based on an estimate.

5   **Answer: Existing long-term debt was replaced with long-term debt at a higher interest rate.**

Ratio of interest expense to long-term debt = Interest expense / Long-term debt

Long-term debt increased in Year 5, but the ratio of debt interest expense to debt increased by a greater percentage. In other words, if long-term debt increased by 15%, the increase in long-term debt interest expense may have been 17%.

An interest expense increase proportionately higher than the increase in long-term debt may indicate that old long-term debt has been paid and new long-term debt with a higher interest rate has been negotiated. This is the most likely explanation from the options presented, but the auditor would also need to determine if the unexpected interest expense increase might have been created by variable rate debt instruments.

18.03 External Confirmations

AICPA Guidance

The relevant AICPA guidance is provided by AU-C 505, *External Confirmations*. This pronouncement states that the auditor's objective is "to design and perform external confirmations to obtain relevant and reliable audit evidence."

Confirmations as Audit Evidence

 Representative Task (Application): Confirm significant account balances and transactions using appropriate tools and techniques (eg, confirmation services, electronic confirmations, manual confirmations) to obtain relevant and reliable evidence.

 Representative Task (Analysis): Analyze external confirmation responses to determine the need for follow-up or further investigation.

External confirmations are audit evidence obtained as a direct written response to the auditor from a third party ("the confirming party"), either in paper form or by electronic or other medium (eg, through the auditor's direct access to information held by a third party).

External confirmations are considered **more reliable sources of audit evidence** because they are obtained directly from parties outside the entity and are in documentary form.

The hierarchy* of audit evidence

Less reliable and less persuasive

- Generated/obtained directly by auditor (eg, observation)
- Received directly from parties outside the entity under audit (eg, A/R confirmations)
- Generated externally but received from entity under audit (eg, bank statement)
- Generated internally by entity under audit (eg, client-generated invoices)

*There are exceptions to the ranking.

External confirmations may be used for a variety of audit purposes, including confirmations to:

- Banks regarding bank balances and related transactions
- Customers to verify A/R amounts and terms

- Vendors to verify accounts payable amounts and terms

- Warehouses to verify existence of inventories or other assets being held for the entity

- Brokers or investment firms to verify existence and balances of investment securities held on behalf of the entity

- Lenders to verify amounts due and terms

If management **refuses to allow** the auditor to perform external confirmation procedures, the auditor should seek evidence to determine if management's reasons are valid and reasonable. If so, the auditor will evaluate the effect on the RMM and apply alternative audit procedures.

If not, or if the auditor is not able to obtain sufficient appropriate audit evidence applying alternative audit procedures, the auditor should:

- Communicate with those in charge of governance

- Evaluate the implications on the audit and on the auditor's report

The auditor should tailor the confirmations to the specific audit objectives/assertions. Confirmations are most useful in addressing the **existence/occurrence assertion**. The auditor sends confirmation requests directly to the independent party; replies may be returned only directly to the auditor. Confirmation requests can be sent by mail, via the internet, or by other means.

 In the audit of a nonissuer, which of the following statements is correct regarding the use of external confirmations to obtain audit evidence?

- Management's refusal to allow an auditor to perform external confirmation procedures is considered a departure from GAAP sufficient to qualify the opinion

- Negative confirmations provide more persuasive audit evidence than positive confirmations

- A factor for an auditor to consider when designing confirmation requests is the assertion being tested

- Negative confirmations should be used only if a very high exception rate is expected

Management assertions, also called financial statement (F/S) assertions, are used to determine which substantive tests should be performed to gather the appropriate audit evidence. Each F/S account balance has one or more relevant management assertions.

For example, when testing **accounts receivable** (A/R), an auditor is most concerned with the **existence and valuation** assertions. Confirmations are a substantive test useful for addressing both assertions. The auditor should design A/R confirmation requests to provide evidence that customers owe the client money (existence) and that each customer's balance is correct (valuation).

If management refuses to allow external confirmations, the auditor should consider whether management's reasons for refusal are valid. For example, a client involved in litigation may wish to refrain from contacting large customers until resolution. Alternative audit procedures may be used without issuing a qualified opinion if the auditor is satisfied with management's explanation.

Negative confirmations provide *less persuasive evidence* than positive confirmations because they are returned only when there is a discrepancy. Because the auditor assumes the balances of unreturned negative confirmations are correct, those balances should not be used if issues are expected.

The circumstances under which a confirmation is received may lead to doubts about its authenticity. Confirmations received by email may not have originated from the email address indicated (ie, spoofing). Confirmations received indirectly (eg, through the client) may have been altered.

When there are doubts, the **auditor should verify the source** and content before accepting the confirmation. If the auditor can verify the contents with a phone call to the respondent (ie, client's customer), the confirmation should be accepted.

Customers are not legally obligated to reply to confirmation requests, meaning they are often ignored if it takes too much effort to respond. Including a list of the items or invoices and dollar amounts can improve confirmation response rates because it easier for customers to verify the amounts.

Accounts receivable confirmations: use of a statement of accounts

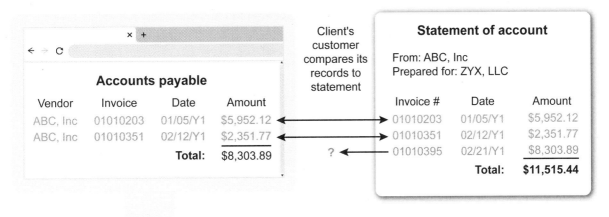

Types of Confirmations

Negative confirmations require the confirming party to reply only if the amount provided is *incorrect*.

Positive confirmations require a reply in either case (correct or incorrect amounts).

Blank confirmations are a type of positive confirmation that requires individuals to manually fill in an amount based on information given, such as "Please provide the balance for account number 123455."

Types of confirmations	
Blank positive	• Confirming party always required to respond • Fill in appropriate information
Positive	• Confirming party always required to respond • Verify information provided by auditor is correct
Negative	• Customers asked to respond only *if* the amount provided is *incorrect*

Effort

Alternative Procedures

Alternative (sometimes called "alternate") audit procedures are usually required when **no response** is received for a positive confirmation request:

- **Receivables**—The auditor would first look to see whether cash was received subsequent to the date of the confirmation request. Second best, the auditor would examine the documents underlying the apparent validity of the recorded transaction
- **Payables**—The auditor would usually verify subsequent cash disbursements as evidence of payment of the account

Accounts Receivable Confirmations

Using external confirmation procedures for accounts receivable is the generally accepted procedure to verify account balance, except when one or more of the following is applicable:

- The overall account balance is immaterial

- External confirmation procedures for accounts receivable would be ineffective

- The auditor's assessed level of risk of material misstatement at the relevant assertion level is low, and the other planned substantive procedures address the assessed risk. In many situations, the use of external confirmation procedures for accounts receivable and the performance of other substantive procedures are necessary to reduce the assessed risk of material misstatement to an acceptably low level"

Types of accounts receivable confirmations				
	Balance provided with request?	**Requires response?**	**Description**	**Suitable for**
Positive (with balance)	Yes	Yes	• Customer confirms amount provided	• High risk • Large balances
Positive (blank)	No	Yes	• Customer states amount per customer's records	• High risk • Large balances • Customer may not investigate
Negative	Yes	No	• Customer responds only if stated amount is incorrect	• Low risk • Small balances

Disclaimers

Some third parties will include disclaimers (ie, restrictions) in confirmations to protect themselves against litigation. Acceptable disclaimers are those that do not call into question the accuracy or completeness of the information in the confirmation. Unacceptable disclaimers are as follows:

- Information is obtained from electronic data sources, which might not contain certain information in the respondent's possession

- Information in the confirmation may not be relied upon by the recipient

- Information is not guaranteed to be accurate or current and could be a matter of opinion

AUD 19
Specific Matters That Require Special Consideration

19.01 Accounting Estimates

Overview

 Representative Task (Application): Recalculate and re-perform procedures to validate the inputs and assumptions of an entity's significant accounting estimates with a higher risk of material misstatement or complexity, such as fair value estimates.

 Representative Task (Analysis): Perform procedures (eg, reviewing the work of a specialist and procedures performed by the engagement team) to validate an entity's calculations and detailed support for significant accounting estimates, including consideration of information that contradicts assumptions made by management.

 Representative Task (Evaluation): Conclude on the reasonableness of significant accounting estimates with a lower risk of material misstatement or complexity in an audit.

AICPA Guidance

The relevant AICPA guidance is provided by AU-C 540, *Auditing Accounting Estimates, Including Fair Value Accounting Estimates and Related Disclosures*. The auditor's objective is to obtain sufficient appropriate audit evidence about whether the accounting estimates (including fair value accounting estimates) are reasonable and whether the related disclosures are adequate in view of the applicable financial reporting framework.

 Introductory sections related to Accounting Estimates are covered in Chapter 14.02, including: Auditing Approaches, Understanding Management's Process, Managemant Bias, and Assessing the Risks of Material Misstatements (RMM), along with PCAOB coverage on accounting estimates.

Procedures to Respond to RMM

Based on the assessed RMM with respect to estimates, the auditor will undertake one or more of the following **procedures**, considering the nature of the accounting estimate:

- Determine whether events up to the date of the auditor's report provide evidence regarding the estimate
- Test the methods and assumptions used by management and the data upon which they are based
- Test the operating effectiveness of controls over the development of accounting estimates
- Develop an expectation in the form of a point or range of estimates to use as a basis for evaluating management's estimate
- Re-perform or re-compute estimates using the same information and method used by management

When estimates represent **significant RMM**, the auditor will apply **additional procedures**:

- Address the effects of estimation uncertainty, including whether management has considered alternative assumptions and whether management's assumptions are reasonable

- Evaluate management's decision to recognize or not recognize accounting estimates and the basis used for measurement

Testing management's estimates

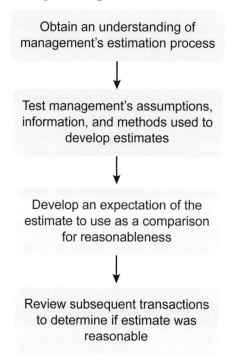

Documentation

The auditor should document the basis for the auditor's conclusions about:

- The reasonableness of estimates giving rise to significant risks
- Indicators of possible management bias

Disclosures

The auditor should obtain sufficient appropriate audit evidence as to whether the disclosures meet the requirements of the applicable financial reporting framework. For accounting estimates resulting in significant risks, the auditor should evaluate the adequacy of the disclosure of estimation uncertainty.

Fair Value Estimates—GAAS

The prior discussion related to auditing accounting estimates is also applicable to the discussion here related to auditing **fair value** accounting estimates, which is based on the same Statement on Auditing Standards. The focus here is on audit considerations that are **specific to fair value measurements** and disclosures.

Examples of accounting estimates

Involving fair value	NOT involving fair value
• Values of complex financial instruments that are not actively traded	• Allowance for credit losses (ie, bad debts)
• Share-based payments	• Inventory obsolescence
• Assets held for disposal	• Warranty obligations
• Assets/liabilities acquired in a business combination, identifiable intangibles and goodwill	• Depreciation methods, salvage values, and useful lives
• Nonmonetary exchanges	• Allowances recognizing the uncertainty of recoverability of certain investments
	• Results of long-term contracts
	• Financial effects of litigation

Risk-Based Audit Approach

Management is responsible for making the fair value measurements and disclosures included in the F/S as well as identifying the significant assumptions underlying fair value measurements and disclosures.

The **auditor evaluates** whether fair value measurements and disclosures, as determined by management, including the allocation of the acquisition cost relating to a business combination, are in conformity with the guidance in accounting technical literature.

In applying a risk-based approach to fair value estimates, the auditor should:

- **Obtain an understanding** of the requirements of the applicable financial reporting framework (AFRF), and how management makes the fair value accounting estimate (and data used), including how management assessed the effect of **estimation uncertainty**

- Evaluate the degree of **estimation uncertainty** involved and determine whether any of those fair value accounting estimates result in significant risks

- Determine whether management complied with the AFRF, and whether the methods used to make the fair value accounting estimate are appropriate and are consistently applied. The auditor should consider the need for **specialized skills or knowledge**

- Evaluate how management addressed estimation uncertainty; whether management's significant assumptions are reasonable; and, when relevant, whether management has the intent and ability to carry out specific actions

- Evaluate whether the fair value accounting estimates are **reasonable relative to the requirements** of the AFRF

- Obtain sufficient appropriate audit evidence as to whether the disclosures meet the requirements of the AFRF. The auditor should also evaluate the adequacy of disclosure of the estimation uncertainty for any identified significant risks

- Consider whether the fair value accounting estimates might indicate possible **management bias**
  - An example of an indicator of possible management bias would be the use of an entity's own assumptions for fair value accounting estimates that are inconsistent with observable market conditions

Estimation Uncertainty for Fair Value Accounting Estimates

High estimation uncertainty results in an **increased risk of material misstatement** when, for example:

- Fair value accounting estimates for derivative instruments are not publicly traded

- Fair value accounting estimates are based on a highly specialized entity-developed model or when the assumptions (inputs) cannot be observed in the marketplace

For fair value accounting estimates, **assumptions (inputs) affect estimation uncertainty** and vary as follows:

- **Observable Inputs**—Assumptions that market participants would use in pricing an asset or liability based on market data from sources independent of the reporting entity or

- **Unobservable Inputs**—An entity's own judgments about what assumptions market participants would use. Estimation uncertainty increases when the fair value estimates are based on unobservable inputs

 Which of the following would provide an auditor of a nonissuer with the best evidence of fair value pertaining to a client's investments in derivative instruments that are listed on a national exchange and disclosed at fair value?

- The client's personnel who trade the derivative instruments

- Quoted market prices

- Documents related to the original purchase of the derivative instruments

- Estimates of fair value provided by broker-dealers

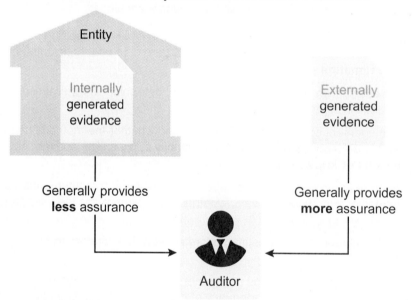

General assumptions about audit evidence

AICPA Professional Standards state that **published price quotations** generally are the most reliable indicator of fair value. Evidence from **external sources** is **less** likely to be **subject to management bias** than information obtained from internal sources. Therefore, such information is generally **more reliable** than information obtained from the client.

The auditor may decide to test how management made their estimate (and the data used) when the accounting estimate is a fair value accounting estimate using observable and unobservable inputs. This would include **evaluating the method of measurement**. Determining whether the method or model used by management is appropriate requires **professional judgment**.

Matters the auditor may consider in testing the model include determining whether:

- The model is validated for suitability prior to usage
- Appropriate controls exist over changes
- The model is periodically tested for validity (when inputs are subjective)
- Adjustments are made to the model's outputs
- The model is adequately documented, including key parameters and limitations

Another SAS (Statement on Auditing Standards) requires the auditor to communicate the auditor's views about the qualitative aspects of the entity's significant accounting practices, including accounting estimates. The auditor should determine that they are informed about the process used by management in developing sensitive accounting estimates, as well as the auditor's basis for conclusions about those matters.

Documentation

The auditor should document the **basis for the auditor's conclusions** about the reasonableness of fair value accounting estimates resulting in significant risks and their disclosure and any indications of possible management bias.

Fair Value Estimates—PCAOB

Guidance

PCAOB Auditing Standard No. 43 addresses accounting estimates, including **fair value measurements**. "In general, fair values of financial instruments based on trades of identical financial instruments in an active market have a lower risk of material misstatement than fair values derived from observable trades of similar financial instruments or unobservable inputs."

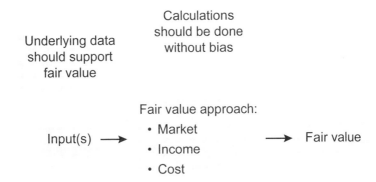

Auditing fair value

Underlying data should support fair value

Calculations should be done without bias

Input(s) ⟶ Fair value approach:
- Market
- Income
- Cost
⟶ Fair value

Using Pricing Information

The **reliability** of pricing information provided from a pricing service is affected by the pricing service's experience and expertise and whether the pricing service has a relationship with the company. The **relevance** of pricing information used as audit evidence is affected by the following:

- Whether the values are based on quoted prices in active markets for identical financial instruments
- When the values are based on transactions of similar financial instruments, the auditor should consider how those transactions were determined to be comparable

- When no recent transactions have occurred for the financial instrument being valued (or for similar financial instruments), the auditor should consider whether the inputs used are representative of the assumptions that market participants would use for valuation purposes. The auditor should perform additional procedures to evaluate the appropriateness of the method used by the pricing service

When using pricing information from **multiple pricing services**, less information is required when the following conditions are met:

- There are recent trades of identical or similar financial instruments
- The type of financial instrument is routinely priced by several pricing services
- Prices are reasonably consistent across the various pricing services
- The pricing information is based on inputs that are observable

When using pricing information from a **broker or dealer**, the relevance and reliability of the evidence provided depends on whether:

- The broker or dealer has a relationship with the company
- The broker or dealer is a "market maker" that deals in the same type of financial instrument
- The quote reflects market conditions as of the financial statement date
- The quote is binding on the broker or dealer
- There are any restrictions, limitations, or disclaimers in the quote

When **unobservable inputs** are significant to the valuation, the auditor should evaluate the reasonableness of the unobservable inputs.

When **changes are made to observable information**, the auditor should consider whether the assumptions used are consistent with what market participants would use for pricing purposes.

19.02 Investments in Securities

Fair Value Considerations

 Representative Task (Remembering & Understanding): Identify the considerations relating to the measurement and disclosure of the fair value of investments in securities in an audit.

 Representative Task (Application): Test management's assumptions, conclusions and adjustments related to the valuation of investments in securities in an audit.

AICPA Guidance

The relevant AICPA guidance is provided by AU-C 501, *Audit Evidence—Specific Considerations for Selected Items.* The objective of AU-C 501 is to **obtain sufficient appropriate audit** regarding the valuation of investments in securities and derivative instruments.

Risk

Estimation uncertainty is the susceptibility of an accounting estimate and related disclosures to an **inherent lack of precision** in its measurement.

- Estimation uncertainty **increases** with the increasing complexity of the financial instrument and with the increasing variability of the cash flows involved
- The risk of material misstatement (RMM) increases with estimation uncertainty

The Audit Guide introduced several additional concepts of risk.

- **Credit (or Counterparty) Risk**—The risk that one party to a financial instrument will cause a financial loss to another party by failing to discharge an obligation, and it is often associated with default
- **Market Risk**—The risk that the fair value or future cash flows of a financial instrument will fluctuate because of changes in market prices; examples include currency risk, interest rate risk, and commodity and equity price risk
- **Liquidity Risk**—The risk of not being able to buy or sell a financial instrument at an appropriate price in a timely manner due to a lack of marketability for that financial instrument
- **Operational Risk**—Operational risk relates to the specific processing required for financial instruments. Operational risk may increase as the complexity of a financial instrument increases, and poor management of operational risk may increase other types of risk

General Auditing Considerations

In the **planning stage**, auditors normally focus on:

- Understanding the accounting and disclosure requirements
- Understanding the purpose and risks associated with the financial instruments

- Determining whether specialized skills and knowledge are required, including possibly engaging an auditor's specialist to assist
- Understanding and evaluating the relevant internal controls
- Understanding management's processes for valuing the financial instruments
- Assessing and responding to the RMM for the financial instruments

The auditor should obtain an **understanding of the relevant internal controls** associated with financial instruments to properly assess the RMM to determine the nature, timing, and extent of further audit procedures.

The Audit Guide framed the discussion of **internal control issues** around the five components: (1) control environment, (2) risk assessment, (3) information and communication system, (4) control activities, and (5) monitoring.

- The discussion of control activities emphasized the importance of *segregation of duties*. Financial instrument activities may be segregated into these functions:
  - **Executing** the transaction (dealing)
  - **Initiating payments** or handling receipts (settlements)
  - **Sending out trade confirmations** and reconciling any differences
  - **Recording transactions** in the accounting records
  - **Monitoring risk** limits
  - **Monitoring positions** and valuing financial instruments

Assessing and Responding to the RMM

RMM increases with complexity (eg, having a high degree of uncertainty and variability of future cash flows); RMM is also affected by the volume, terms, and nature of the financial instruments. At the relevant assertion level, the RMM consists of inherent risk and control risk.

Characteristics that might affect inherent risk (and RMM)

1. **Management's objective**
   a. Indication of higher risk—Financial instruments used as hedges
   b. Indications of lower risk—Financial instruments held as investments
   c. Related assertion(s)—Rights and obligations, accuracy/valuation, classification, and presentation

2. **Management's intent and ability**
   a. Indication of higher risk—Accounting treatment based on intent and ability
   b. Indications of lower risk—Accounting treatment based on objective criteria
   c. Related assertion(s) —Accuracy/valuation, classification, and presentation

3. **Complexity of the financial instrument**
   a. Indication of higher risk—More complex (eg, futures contracts, swaps, etc.)
   b. Indications of lower risk—Less complex (common stock, U.S. Treasury securities, etc.)
   c. Related assertion(s)—Rights and obligations, accuracy/valuation, classification, and presentation

4. Whether there is an **exchange of cash** at inception of the financial instrument
   a. Indication of higher risk—No exchange of cash at inception
   b. Indications of lower risk—Cash exchanged at inception
   c. Related assertion(s)—Completeness, classification, and presentation

5. Whether the derivative is **freestanding versus embedded**

    a. Indication of higher risk—Embedded derivative

    b. Indications of lower risk—Freestanding derivative

    c. Related assertion(s)—Completeness, classification, and presentation

6. **Credit risk**

    a. Indication of higher risk—High counterparty credit risk

    b. Indications of lower risk—Low counterparty credit risk

    c. Related assertion(s)—Accuracy/valuation

7. **Market risk**

    a. Indication of higher risk—Volatile values or interest rates

    b. Indications of lower risk—Relatively stable values or interest rates

    c. Related assertion(s)—All

8. **Nature of security and related accounting principles**

    a. Indication of higher risk—Rapidly evolving

    b. Indications of lower risk—Relatively stable

    c. Related assertion(s)—All

9. **Assumptions about future conditions**

    a. Indication of higher risk—Significant subjective assumptions

    b. Indications of lower risk—Relatively objective and verifiable assumptions

    c. Related assertion(s)—All

Substantive Procedures

An auditor should design and perform substantive procedures for the relevant management assertions associated with investments in securities. The goal of these procedures is to provide sufficient appropriate audit evidence that the investments are reported according to the appropriate financial reporting framework (eg, GAAP).

When an entity invests in debt securities (eg, bonds), they must be classified into categories according to management's intentions:

- Held-for-trading securities are intended to be purchased and sold in the short term in order to generate a profit

- Held-to-maturity securities are intended to be held until they reach maturity

- Available-for-sale securities are those outside the other two categories

The entity must have evidence of ownership (rights and obligations assertion) and record all investments in debt securities (completeness assertion). The classification of debt securities (classification assertion) impacts their presentation on the balance sheet (ie, current versus noncurrent assets) and statement of cash flows (ie, operating versus investing activities). The classification also impacts the valuation of debt securities (valuation and allocation assertion)—that is, whether debt securities are carried at original cost or fair value—and how any valuation adjustments impact the income statement.

Examples of substantive procedures: Marketable debt trading security investments at FV

- Recalculating FV
- Inspecting documents reflecting FV
- Inquiring about procedures used to determine FV
- Confirming FV with external parties

In contrast, accounting for investments in equity securities (eg, stocks) is based on the amount of operating and financial control the investor has over the investee. An entity with a 20% to 50% controlling interest in an investee will account for the investment differently than when the controlling interest is 50% or more.

The auditor may test dividend income by calculating an expected dividend income amount and comparing it with the client's reported income amount.

The dividend amounts paid by publicly held companies are considered public information. Therefore, the auditor can **use** dividend-per-share **information** provided by reliable **investment advisory services** (eg, Bloomberg, Morningstar) to **calculate expected dividend income**. Reported dividend income will be considered reasonable if it is materially the same as the auditor's calculated dividend income amount.

Dividend or interest income validation

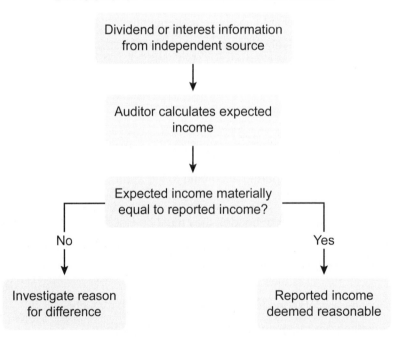

When an entity has a trading function for financial instruments, substantive tests alone may be insufficient as a basis for the auditor's conclusions; however, tests of control will not be sufficient by themselves.

Addressing the Valuation Assertion

The auditor is required to obtain an understanding of how **management makes its valuation**, including the **methodology used**, and to evaluate the reasonableness of that valuation relative to the requirements of the applicable financial reporting framework.

Valuation Methodology

When management uses a **model** to estimate fair value—

- Audit testing normally consists of either of two approaches: (1) evaluating the appropriateness of the model used by management, the reasonableness of the assumptions and data used, and the mathematical accuracy or (2) developing the auditor's own estimate and then comparing that with the entity's valuation (ie, an analytical procedures approach)

- When evaluating the reasonableness of management's assumptions, the auditor focuses on significant assumptions that might materially affect the valuation and those that are susceptible to bias

When management uses a **specialist** to estimate fair value, the auditor might evaluate the competence and objectivity of the specialist and obtain an understanding of the specialist's work, including the techniques used and assumptions involved.

FASB (Financial Accounting Standards Board) provides a **fair value hierarchy** that classifies *valuation inputs* into three levels. Note that **estimation uncertainty** (ie, an inherent lack of precision) and **RMM** *increase* as the financial instrument moves from level 1 to level 2 to level 3 (in other words, moving away from observable inputs toward unobservable inputs increases estimation uncertainty).

- **Level 1 inputs**—Quoted prices in active markets for identical financial assets or liabilities; usually viewed as sufficient appropriate evidence of fair value

- **Level 2 inputs**—Inputs other than quoted market prices (level 1) that are observable either directly (as prices) or indirectly (derived from prices); may involve similar assets or liabilities or markets that are not very active

- **Level 3 inputs**—Unobservable inputs for the asset or liability with little or no market activity at the measurement date

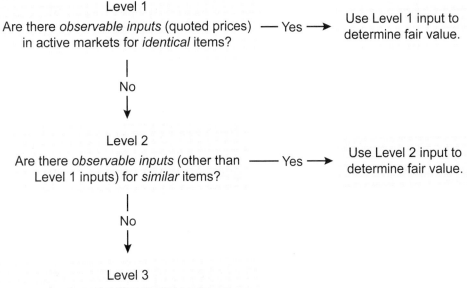

A client holds a debt security that is actively traded in the market. Which of the following indicators would be the preferable guide to the security's fair market value?

- The price at which the debt security was purchased

- Published price quotations in the market

- The cash flow model using discounted future cash flows

- Matrix pricing, in which published price quotations of similar debt securities are used to compute the fair market value

Published price quotations in the market (a Level 1 valuation input) are the **best guide** to determining a debt security's current **FMV**. When a published price is not available, there are two less reliable means of determining fair value. Level 2 valuation uses observable data from actual market transactions associated with similar, but not identical, securities (eg, matrix pricing). Level 3 valuation is largely based on management judgment (ie, unobservable inputs) and might involve a valuation technique such as discounted cash flows.

Third-party pricing sources may be used by smaller entities or those that have a relatively low volume of transactions for financial instruments. Third-party pricing sources fall into two categories:

- **Pricing services** consist of valuations that are based on *market data* and *prices* collected from a wide variety of sources to derive estimated fair values (often using level 2 inputs)

  - *Consensus* pricing services obtain pricing information about an instrument from *participating subscribers* who submit prices. The service returns to each subscriber the consensus price (usually an average after eliminating outliers); consensus pricing may be the best available data for some financial instruments, such as exotic derivatives

- **Broker quotes** (often used for instruments with level 3 inputs) may be "executable" or indicative: Executable quotes are strong evidence of fair value and represent a price at which the broker is willing to transact. Indicative quotes are a weaker evidence of fair value, since there is a lack of transparency of methods used

Impairment Losses

Applicable financial reporting frameworks may **require recognition of an impairment loss** when a decline in fair value is other than temporary. Examples of indicators of impairment include the following:

- Fair value is significantly below cost and the decline has existed for an extended period of time. The security has been downgraded by a rating agency

- The financial conditions of the issuer or counterparty have deteriorated

- Dividends have been reduced or eliminated, or scheduled interest payments have not been made

The auditor should **evaluate management's conclusions** about the need to recognize an impairment loss and obtain sufficient appropriate audit evidence regarding the recorded impairment loss

Additional Audit Considerations

Auditors focus on **disclosures** related to **risks and sensitivity analysis**, including the following:

- An entity's objectives and strategies for using financial instruments

- An entity's internal control framework for managing risk

- The risks and uncertainties associated with the financial instruments

Depending on the volume and complexity of financial instrument activities, additional specific **written representations** may be needed to support other audit evidence obtained.

Departures from the applicable financial reporting framework could arise from disagreements about the appropriateness of the valuation method or the reasonableness of significant valuation assumptions.

General matters to be **communicated to those charged with governance** include:

- Nature and consequences of significant assumptions used

- Degree of subjectivity involved in developing the assumptions

- Relative materiality of the items measured at fair value to the financial statements as a whole.

Audit Procedures for Traditional Investments (ie, Stocks and Bonds)

Other Audit Procedures

Other audit procedures may provide evidence related to the existence, completeness, and rights and obligations assertions as follows:

Examples of audit evidence supporting investments

- Confirmations with third parties (eg, investment issuer, broker)
- Board of directors' meeting minutes
- Documented management plans
- Market information (eg, stock exchanges, published values)
- Bank information
- Comparison with prior year
- Comparison of sources of interest income or dividends to investments

Existence Assertion

Auditors primarily use **inspection and confirmation**.

- Physically inspect securities in the possession of the client entity
- Confirm stocks and bonds held by an independent custodian

Completeness Assertion

Auditors primarily use **analytical procedures** to address the risk of omissions.

- Evaluate investment income or loss accounts:
  - *Verify revenue through confirmation when investments are held by an independent custodian*
  - *May trace recorded cash receipts to a bank statement*

- May recalculate the interest income on debt instruments or dividends received on stock investments

- Compare dividends, interest, or other investment income (loss) to prior year's work papers for reasonableness; dividends can be verified by consulting dividend record books produced by commercial investment advisory services

- Review the minutes of the meetings of those charged with governance for approval of any large investment-related transactions

Rights and Obligations Assertion

Auditors primarily use **inquiry and review**.

- Inquire of management about any restrictions applicable to investments (including any securities pledged as collateral for debt)
- Review cash receipts and cash disbursements subsequent to year end for any material transactions affecting investments, perhaps requiring disclosure

Classification and Presentation Assertions

Verify the appropriateness of the classification of investments in certain equity and debt securities.

- Investment in Equity Securities
  - **Fair value**—Equity investments when there is no significant influence and fair value is readily determinable; report at fair value with unrealized gains and losses included in earnings
  - **Cost**—Equity investments when there is no significant influence and fair value is not readily determinable; report at cost and test for impairment
  - **Equity method accounting**—Equity investments when there is significant influence; report using the equity method of accounting (can elect the fair value option if the entity chooses to do so)

- Investment in Debt Securities
  - Held-to-maturity—For debt securities when the entity has the intent and ability to hold the investment to maturity
  - Trading—For debt securities intended for sale in the near term

19.03 Inventory and Inventory Held by Others

AuNditing Inventories: Overview

 Representative Task (Evaluation): Test the ending inventory quantities in an audit by obtaining evidence regarding the existence and condition of inventory and inventory held by others (eg, inventory counting procedures, confirmation) and conclude whether inventory records accurately reflect count results.

AICPA Guidance

The relevant AICPA guidance is provided by AU-C 501, *Audit Evidence—Specific Considerations for Selected Items*. In obtaining evidence about inventories, the auditor will first evaluate whether there is reason to believe that inventories are misstated at the F/S element or account balance level.

Forms of Evidence

There are various *forms of evidence* the auditor may use in the audit of inventories. Some will be obtained from the client, some directly from outside sources, and some may result from the direct actions of the auditor.

- Material requisitions, purchase orders, vender invoices, and receiving reports indicating that the inventory was ordered and received
- Sales orders, shipping documents, and accounts receivable activity indicating the inventory was sold and paid for
- Agreements and confirmations from warehouses, consignees, and others that may be holding inventory on behalf of the entity
- Client inventory count sheets and reconciliations of perpetual inventory records to periodic physical counts taken by the client
- The auditor's personal observation of inventory, test count sheets, inventory tags

Inventory Testing Objectives

In obtaining evidence about inventories, the auditor will first evaluate whether there is reason to believe that inventories are misstated at the F/S element or account balance level. The auditor will consider the amount reported as inventory and apply analytical procedures to determine if the amount seems reasonable.

Based on the auditor's knowledge of the client's inventory policies (eg, reorder points, shelf lives, inventory turnover), the auditor will establish an expectation for the amount of inventory the client should have on hand. This amount will be compared to the amount reported by the client.

Observation of Physical Inventory

When inventory is material, the **auditor is required to attend** the physical inventory count for the purpose of obtaining evidence regarding the existence of inventory and its condition. The client counts the entire inventory, and the auditor observes the client's taking of the inventory (while taking independent test counts).

The auditor participates in this process for two primary reasons, referred to as **dual-purpose tests**:

- **To test existence of inventory**—The auditor should select items from the client's (final) inventory listing, which is essentially the subsidiary ledger for the adjusted general ledger balance. The auditor should agree those selected items to the underlying inventory count tags (and the auditor's own count sheets) that serve as source documents

- **To test completeness of inventory**—The direction of the test is just the opposite. The auditor should select items from the underlying inventory count tags (including the auditor's own count sheets) and agree those to the client's inventory listing to establish that there were no omissions from the client's inventory listing

While attending the physical inventory count, the auditor should:

- Evaluate instructions and procedures
- Observe the performance of count procedures
- Inspect inventory
- Perform test counts

Having obtained evidence about the accuracy of the inventory count, the auditor will also perform procedures to determine if the physical counts are accurately reported in the accounting records. If the count is performed on a date other than the date of the F/S, the auditor will also obtain evidence to determine that changes between the count date and the date of the F/S have been properly reflected.

When the auditor is **unable to attend** the physical count, alternate procedures should be applied, including the performance of test counts on alternate dates and applying audit procedures to transactions occurring between the count date and the date of the F/S.

When inventory that is in the **custody of third parties** is material, AU-C 501 requires the auditor to request confirmations from the third parties, perform an inspection of the inventory, or perform other procedures as the auditor considers appropriate under the circumstances.

To obtain assurance that all inventory items in a client's inventory listing are valid, an auditor most likely would trace

- Inventory tags noted during the auditor's observation to items listed in receiving reports and vendors' invoices
- Items listed in receiving reports and vendors' invoices to the inventory listing
- Inventory tags noted during the auditor's observation to items in the inventory listing
- Items in the inventory listing to inventory tags and the auditor's recorded count sheets.

Validate the inventory subsidiary ledger

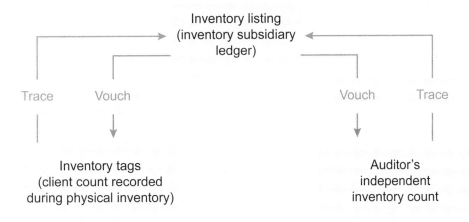

Here, the **goal** is to **validate** the **inventory listing**, which is a subsidiary ledger supporting the reported inventory asset on the balance sheet. To obtain assurance that the inventory listing is valid, items in the **inventory listing** would most likely be **compared with inventory tags** and the **auditor's** recorded **inventory count** sheets.

Goods in Transit

When a company buys or sells goods, the shipping terms will determine whether they are included in that entity's inventory while the goods are in transit. Although there are numerous factors that differentiate shipping contracts, most fall into one of two categories:

- **Shipping contracts, FAS** (free alongside), **shipping point, or FOB** (free on board), in which title transfers from the seller to the buyer when goods are delivered by the seller to a common carrier
- **Destination contracts, FAS destination or FOB destination**, in which title transfers from the seller to the buyer when goods are delivered by a common carrier to the buyer

FOB Shipping Point

- Title passes to the buyer when the seller delivers the goods to a common carrier (shipped)
- Included in buyer's books at year end

FOB Destination

- Title passes to the buyer when the buyer receives the goods from the common carrier
- Included in seller's books until received by buyer

FOB shipping terms

FOB = free on board

Simulation Example

Scroll down to complete all parts of this task.

Vine LLP is auditing the December 31, Year 1, financial statements of General Co., a nonissuer. The auditor obtained the client-prepared inventory reconciliation between the client's perpetual inventory records and the general ledger as of December 31, Year 1, below.

Consider the following observations:

- The reconciliation is mathematically accurate

- The client prepared the December 31, Year 1, reconciliation on January 15, Year 2

- The auditor observed the physical inventory count on December 31, Year 1, and agreed the test counts to those in the perpetual inventory system without exception

- All amounts are considered material

For each of the items in the table below, select the most appropriate audit procedure that the auditor should perform to test the client's balance and explanation.

Select an option below
Agree to the client's general ledger balance as of December 31, Year 1
Agree to the client's November 30, Year 1 final inventory reconciliation balance.
Agree to the client's perpetual inventory system report as of December 31, Year 1.
Trace to the client's general ledger balance as of December 31, Year 1.

	A	B	C	Audit procedure
1	Item	Amount	Client explanation	
2	Balance per perpetual inventory system	$1,555,550	N/A	
3	Inventory receipt #1992	20,332	Inventory in transit—FOB shipping point; was received January 2, Year 2.	
4	Inventory awaiting return to vendor	(14,346)	Inventory was approved for return to vendor on December 15, Year 1, and not shipped until January 6, Year 2.	
5	Scrap	(9,999)	Scrap inventory was identified on December 30, Year 1, and was included in the physical inventory count.	
6	Obsolete inventory	(55,454)	Obsolete inventory was identified by plant manager and included in the physical inventory count. The inventory was disposed of January 1, Year 2. The adjustment was recorded at year end in the general ledger.	
7	Price adjustment	8,765	Adjustment for clerical error in entering inventory cost. Error identified January 1, Year 2, and posted to the yearend general ledger.	
8	Balance per general ledger	$1,504,848	N/A	

Solution and Explanations

Balance per perpetual inventory system

Item	Amount	Client explanation	Audit procedure
Balance per perpetual inventory system	1,555,550	N/A	Agree to the client's perpetual inventory system report as of December 31, Year 1

Amounts listed on the inventory reconciliation are verified by agreeing the amount to the source document. Here, the balance per the perpetual inventory system listed on the reconciliation should be compared with the actual perpetual inventory report for December 31, Year 1.

Inventory receipt #1992

Item	Amount	Client explanation	Audit procedure
Inventory receipt #1992	20,332	Inventory in transit—FOB shipping point; was received January 2, Year 2.	Inspect vendor's bill of lading for proper shipping date and terms.

Inventory in transit that is sent FOB shipping point means that title to the inventory transfers from the seller to the buyer at the seller's shipping dock. Therefore, the auditor needs to review the vendor's shipping documents (ie, bill of lading) to determine the exact date the goods were shipped. If the goods were shipped prior to January 1, Year 2, they should be included in the Year 1 inventory balance.

Inventory awaiting return to vendor

Item	Amount	Client explanation	Audit procedure
Inventory awaiting return to vendor	(14,346)	Inventory was approved for return to vendor on December 15, Year 1, and not shipped until January 6, Year 2.	Inspect vendor's return authorization document to determine if item is properly excluded from inventory.

Inventory awaiting return to the vendor is no longer owned by the company. Once the return is approved by the vendor, the physical inventory should be segregated until shipped and excluded from the book inventory balance. The source document approving the return (ie, the vendor's authorization document) should be examined to verify that the inventory items were excluded from the physical count.

Scrap

Item	Amount	Client explanation	Audit procedure
Scrap	(9,999)	Scrap inventory was identified on December 30, Year 1, and was included in the physical inventory count.	Inspect the scrap inventory log and supporting documentation to verify the amount and the date the disposal was recorded.

The inventory account is generally adjusted (ie, reduced) for scrap at the time the scrap is identified (December 30, Year 1). Scrap is material left over from production and usually has little if any value. Therefore, the amount of scrap must be removed from the books (and is physically disposed of). To determine if the write-off was appropriate, the auditor will review the supporting documentation to verify that the inventory was indeed "scrapped" or disposed of, at no value.

Obsolete inventory

Item	Amount	Client explanation	Audit procedure
Obsolete inventory	(55,454)	Obsolete inventory was identified by plant manager and included in the physical inventory count. The inventory was disposed of January 1, Year 2. The adjustment was recorded at year end in the general ledger.	Review the plant manager's approval and corresponding journal entry recording the adjustment to the general ledger.

Obsolete inventory is inventory that is at the end of its product life cycle and is not expected to be sold. It should be written off in the period identified (not in the period of disposal). To ensure that the inventory really is obsolete (and not involved in theft or fraud), review the plant manager's approval and the corresponding journal entry to ensure that the general ledger was appropriately revised.

Price adjustment

Item	Amount	Client explanation	Audit procedure
Price adjustment	8,765	Adjustment for clerical error in entering inventory cost. Error identified January 1, Year 2, and posted to the year end general ledger.	Review vendor invoice and recalculate adjustment. Agree corresponding journal entry to the general ledger.

To verify that the price adjustment was correct, the auditor should review the vendor's original invoice and recalculate the adjustment. Once the adjustment is determined to be appropriate, the correction should be agreed to the final general ledger balance.

Balance per general ledger

Item	Amount	Client explanation	Audit procedure
Balance per general ledger	1,504,848	N/A	Agree to the client's general ledger balance as of December 31, Year 1.

The "balance per the general ledger" on the inventory reconciliation work sheet needs to be verified for accuracy (ie, all appropriate adjusting entries were properly recorded) by agreeing the amount to the general ledger balance as of December 31, Year 1.

19.04 Litigation, Claims and Assessments

Overview

 Representative Task (Application): Perform appropriate audit procedures, including inquiring of management and others, reviewing minutes and sending external confirmations, to detect the existence of litigation, claims, and assessments.

Auditor's Responsibilities

AICPA Guidance

The relevant AICPA guidance is provided by AU-C 501, *Audit Evidence—Specific Considerations for Selected Items*. This pronouncement states that the auditor's objective is "to obtain sufficient appropriate audit evidence regarding the completeness of litigation, claims, and assessments involving the entity" (among other matters specifically addressed by the SAS).

Contingencies

Contingencies represent gains or losses that may or may not **occur in the future** as a result of an event that has already occurred or an existing condition. Contingencies may result from asserted lawsuits as well as conditions that may result in a future lawsuit. If, for example, an entity is aware that it has sold a defective product, a condition exists that may result in future lawsuits and a future liability as purchasers become aware of the defects.

Contingent gains may not be accrued and are not required to be disclosed.

Contingent liabilities, however, are required to be accrued and disclosed when they are probable and estimable; disclosed without accrual if either they are probable but not subject to reasonable estimation or if they are reasonably possible; and neither accrued nor disclosed if remote.

Loss contingencies			
	Probabillity of occurring	**Disclose?**	**Accrue?**
Remote	Slight chance	No	No
Reasonably possible	More than remote, less than probable	Yes Full disclosure	No Fair presentation
Probable & estimable	Likely to occur	Yes	Yes
Probable & not estimable			No

Claims and Assessments

Asserted means that someone has already filed a claim or has at least announced the intention to make such a claim, which is synonymous with the AICPA's term "pending or threatened litigation." According to the American Bar Association, the lawyer should inform the auditor directly about any omissions of asserted claims in the lawyer's letter responding to the letter of inquiry.

Unasserted means that the entity has exposure to litigation, but no one has yet announced an intention to sue.

- The lawyer cannot (according to the American Bar Association's Statement of Policy Regarding Lawyers' Responses to Auditors' Requests for Information) inform the auditor directly about any omission of unasserted claims as identified in the letter of inquiry

- However, lawyers must tell their client about any such omissions and request that client management then inform the auditors

  o Note that this issue (whether the entity's lawyer has informed management of any omission of an unasserted claim that management should discuss with their auditors) is implicitly addressed in the management representations letter

- An unasserted claim must be disclosed according to GAAP if the following two conditions exist:

  o It is probable that a claim will be asserted, *and*

  o It is at least reasonably possible that a material unfavorable outcome will occur

Audit Procedures

Procedures designed to identify contingent liabilities, including litigation, claims, and assessments, include:

- Making inquiries of management and others within the entity, such as in-house counsel

- Obtaining from management a list of all litigation, claims, and assessments both existing at the date of the F/S or during the period between the date of the F/S and the date of the list, with a description and evaluation of each

- Reviewing minutes of meetings of the board of directors and others

- Reviewing documents regarding litigation, claims, and assessments received from management, including correspondence between the entity and its legal counsel

- Reviewing legal expenses and invoices for legal services

The auditor may determine that no actual or potential litigation, claims, or assessments exist that require accrual or disclosure in the F/S. If this is not the case, however, the auditor is required to seek direct communication with the entity's legal counsel. The auditor will also obtain a letter from each attorney with which the client did business relevant to any litigation, claims, or assessments involving the client.

Attorney Letter of Inquiry

An auditor arranges for a letter of inquiry to be sent to a client's legal counsel to obtain **corroborating evidence** (eg, description, likelihood of loss, estimated loss amount) when litigation, claims, and assessments (ie, contingencies) are considered material to the financial statements.

The attorneys' responses assist auditors in determining if:

- Probable contingencies are properly accrued

- Reasonably possible contingencies are adequately described/disclosed

- Remotely possible contingencies are neither accrued nor disclosed

To respect attorney-client privilege, letters of inquiry to attorneys are signed by client management, asking the attorneys to respond directly to the auditor. If the attorney replies with the statement, "I believe that the plaintiff will have problems establishing any liability," the auditor must **gather additional information**. Indicating that there may not be any liability is vague and does not state whether the likelihood of a loss is probable, reasonably possible, or remote.

An **attorney may refuse** to respond to a letter of inquiry. Before concluding that a scope limitation exists, the auditor may apply **alternative procedures** to obtain sufficient appropriate audit evidence corroborating management's information. If such evidence *is* obtained, the auditor may issue a report with an unmodified opinion.

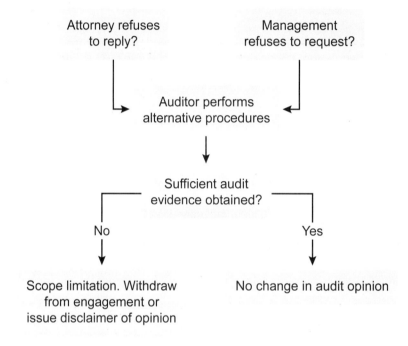

Attorney letter of inquiry

Which of the following procedures should an auditor perform concerning litigation, claims, and assessments?

- Inspect legal documents in the possession of the client's lawyer that are relevant to pending litigation and unasserted claims and assessments

- Discuss with the client's lawyer its philosophy of defending litigation, claims, and assessments that have a high probability of being resolved unfavorably

- Confirm directly with the client's lawyer that all litigation, claims, and assessments have been properly recorded in the financial statements

- Obtain assurance from management that it has disclosed all unasserted claims that its lawyer has advised are probable of assertion

Obtaining evidence of litigation, claims, and assessments

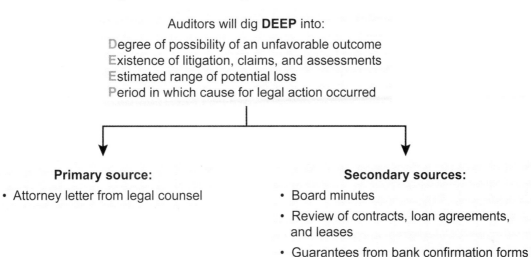

The **primary source** of evidence about litigation, claims, and assessments is the client's **management**. Even though legal counsel will be involved, attorney-client privilege prevents an attorney from directly providing an auditor with information about legal matters. Instead, the auditor will discuss with management the *procedures management used* to identity potentially material legal issues.

Management **provides assurance** in the **management representation letter** that all litigation, claims, and assessments with a material effect on the F/S have been disclosed to the auditor. Among other required information, the management representation letter should state that:

- There are no pending legal matters with a material impact on the F/S that have not been disclosed to the auditor (eg, pending lawsuits)

- Management believes all estimates (including accruals for contingencies) are reasonable

19.05 An Entity's Ability to Continue as a Going Concern

Going Concern Overview

 Representative Task (Remembering & Understanding): Identify factors that should be considered while performing planned procedures that may indicate substantial doubt about an entity's ability to continue as a going concern for a reasonable period of time.

AICPA Guidance and Objectives

The relevant AICPA guidance is provided by AU-C 570, *The Auditor's Consideration of an Entity's Ability to Continue as a Going Concern*.

Financial statements (F/S) are usually prepared on the assumption that an entity will remain in business for a reasonable period (ie, going concern assumption). If there is substantial doubt about the going concern assumption, the auditor considers management's plans (eg, selling assets) to alleviate that doubt and evaluates the **disclosure**. If the **disclosure** is **inadequate**, the auditor issues a **qualified** or **adverse** opinion, depending on the severity of the doubt and the wording of the disclosure.

Regardless of any disclosures, if the company will go out of business imminently, the **liquidation basis** should be used instead of the going concern basis (under liquidation accounting, assets are valued to reflect the cash proceeds expected from their sale, regardless of the entity's cost or accumulated depreciation).

Management's Responsibility

ASC 205 requires **management** to evaluate whether the entity has the ability to continue as a going concern for a reasonable time. The ability to continue as a going concern implies that the entity will be able to **meet its obligations as they come due**.

A **reasonable period of time** is considered **one year** from the date on which the F/S are issued, or, when appropriate, one year from the date on which they are available to be issued.

Auditor Requirements

During the performance of the risk assessment procedures applied by the auditor in obtaining an understanding of the entity and its environment, the **auditor should determine if management** has made a preliminary evaluation of whether events or conditions exist that raise doubts.

- If management has performed such an evaluation, the auditor should determine if management has identified events or conditions that raise substantial doubt. The auditor should understand management's plans to address them

- If management has not performed such an evaluation, the auditor should inquire of management whether such events or conditions exist

When events or conditions *have been identified*, the auditor is required to obtain sufficient appropriate audit evidence as to whether they, when considered in the aggregate, raise a substantial doubt about the entity's ability to continue as a going concern for a reasonable period of time, as well as any mitigating factors.

The auditor's procedures will include:

- Requesting management to make an evaluation if one has not already been made

- Evaluating management's plans in relation to the events and conditions to determine if it is probable that they can be implemented effectively and would mitigate the events and conditions that raise the doubt

- Evaluating a cash flow forecast and analysis, if one was prepared by management, including the reliability of the underlying data and determining if there is adequate support for assumptions made

- Considering whether additional facts or information have become available based on which management made its evaluation.

If, before considering management's plans, the auditor believes that substantial doubt exists as to the entity's ability to continue as a going concern, the auditor should **request written representations** from management. They should:

- Describe management's plans intended to mitigate the adverse effects of events or conditions contributing to the substantial doubt, including the probability that they can be implemented effectively

- Indicate that all relevant matters of which management is aware have been disclosed, including significant conditions and events, and also including management's plans

Going concern conditions (examples)

- Unable to pay debts as they come due
- Several years of operating losses and/or negative working capital
- Uneconomic long-term commitments
- Restructuring of debts
- Dividends in arrears
- Loss of key customers

Audit Procedures

Going concern issues might be indicated by the following circumstances:

- **Negative financial trends**—Recurring operating losses, negative cash flow from operations, adverse financial ratios, etc.

- **Other indications**—Already in default; entity is denied usual trade credit; cash dividends are in arrears; the entity is selling pieces of its business, etc.

- **Internal matters**—Facing work stoppages, dependence on a particular project or customer, etc.

- **External matters**—Uninsured casualty losses, significant litigation, changing technology, etc.

When conditions or events raise substantial doubt, then there may be a need for additional audit procedures (eg, analyzing and discussing the entity's latest interim F/S or relevant forecasts, determining the adequacy of support for planned disposal of assets, etc.).

Procedures to test going concern assumption (examples)

- Read loan agreements
- Read minutes of shareholder meetings
- Inquire of entity's attorney about litigation
- Confirm lines of credit
- Review reports of regulatory action

Management **plans** to **sell assets** may **indicate** a need to increase cash flows and potential **doubt** about the going concern assumption. However, the ability to sell those assets might **mitigate doubt** about the entity's ability to continue as a going concern. That ability might be restricted by loan covenants or the lack of a market for the assets.

Auditor Conclusions

When there is **substantial doubt** about an entity's ability to continue as a **going concern**, the F/S must **disclose that doubt in a footnote**. To decide whether the disclosure is adequate, an auditor determines whether there are conditions or events giving rise to substantial doubt. If there are, the auditor will evaluate management's **plans** to alleviate (ie, mitigate) the doubt.

Plans to mitigate going concern issues (examples)

- Dispose of business unit or major asset
- Cut or delay expenditures
- Borrow nore or restructure existing debt
- Increase ownership equity (eg, sell stock)

If management's plans are expected to mitigate the adverse effects, indicating that there is no longer substantial doubt as to the entity's ability to continue as a going concern, the disclosure should describe the events and conditions that created the doubt, management's evaluation of their significance, and management's plans that mitigated the adverse effects.

If management's plans are not expected to mitigate the adverse claims to the extent that they remove the doubt, the disclosure will be similar, except it will also indicate that there is substantial doubt. In addition, it will refer to management's plans that are intended to mitigate the effects, rather than indicate that the effects have been mitigated.

Communication with Those Charged with Governance

Such communications should include the following:

- Whether there are conditions or events that constitute substantial doubt for a reasonable period of time;
- Auditor's consideration of management's plans;
- Whether management's use of the going concern basis of accounting in its financial statements is appropriate;
- The adequacy of disclosures in the financial statements; and
- The implications of these going concern issues for the auditor's report.

Audit Documentation

The auditor should document the following:

- The conditions or events causing the auditor to have substantial doubt for a reasonable period of time;
- Elements of management's plans considered to be significant in mitigating those conditions or events;
- Audit procedures performed (and results obtained) to evaluate the significant elements of management's plans;
- Auditor's conclusion as to whether the substantial doubt remains or is alleviated and the evaluation of the adequacy of related disclosures; and
- Auditor's conclusion with respect to the effects on the auditor's report

Implications for the Auditor's Report

When the use of the going concern basis of accounting is **inappropriate**, the auditor should express an **adverse opinion** when liquidation is imminent and management's use of the going concern basis of accounting is inappropriate.

If **disclosure is inadequate**, the auditor should either express a qualified or adverse opinion, as appropriate.

If the auditor is **unable to obtain sufficient appropriate** audit evidence, they should either express a qualified opinion or disclaimer of opinion, as appropriate.

When there is substantial doubt about the entity's ability to continue as a going concern (but the use of the going concern basis of accounting is appropriate) and disclosure is adequate, the auditor should include a "Going Concern" section to the auditor's report (after the Opinion and Basis for Opinion sections).

The **SAS prohibits** using "conditional language" in expressing a conclusion about the existence of substantial doubt. For example, the SAS offered the following as inappropriate: "The Company has been unable to renegotiate its expiring credit agreements. Unless the Company is able to obtain financial support, there is substantial doubt about its ability to continue as a going concern."

Reporting when there is substantial doubt about the going concern assumption

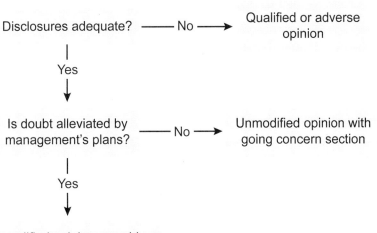

19.06 Uniform Guidance for Single Audits

Overview

 Representative Task (Application): Test transactions related to federal awards for compliance with statutes, regulations, and the terms and conditions of the federal awards.

 Additional topics related to Uniform Guidance for Single Audits is covered under Chapter 14.04. That coverage is related to understanding when an entity is required to have a single audit.

Reporting on single audits involves requirements in addition to a GAGAS financial audit. The auditor must also provide opinions on whether the schedule of federal awards expenditures is fairly stated and on the entity's compliance with laws, regulations, or grants that may affect the assistance program.

In addition, the audit report will include a schedule (ie, list) of findings and questioned costs. That schedule will include findings related to the financial statements that are required to be reported under GAGAS as well as a summary of all audit results.

 After performing a compliance audit of an entity that received federal funds, what conclusion would the auditor draw if the entity does not have adequate documentation to support $5 million in operating expenses paid from federal program funds?

- The entity spent $5 million in operating expenses that were not approved
- Questioned costs of $5 million for operating expenses have been identified
- The entity spent $5 million of government funds for services that were not required
- The entity submitted unauthorized invoices for expenses

The audit will include findings and questioned costs related to federal awards. Questioned costs are those costs singled out as problematic by the auditor. This may be, for example, because the costs seem unreasonable or were not adequately documented.

The fact that an auditor is unable to obtain adequate documentation for a disbursement would not necessarily lead to the conclusion that the expenses were not approved, authorized, or necessary. The auditor could only conclude that the costs are in question.

AUD 20
Misstatements and Internal Control Deficiencies

AUD 20: Misstatements and Internal Control Deficiencies

20.01 Misstatements and Internal Control Deficiencies

Misstatements

 Representative Task (Application): Prepare a summary of corrected and uncorrected misstatements.

 Representative Task (Analysis): Determine the effect of uncorrected misstatements on an entity's financial statements in an engagement.

AICPA Guidance

The relevant AICPA guidance is provided by AU-C 450, *Evaluation of Misstatements Identified During the Audit*. This pronouncement states that the auditor's objectives are to evaluate the effect of (1) identified misstatements on the audit and (2) uncorrected misstatements, if any, on the F/S.

Accumulation of Identified Misstatements

Misstatements are any difference between the way an amount, classification, presentation, or disclosure is presented on or with the F/S and how it should be presented on or with the F/S in order to be fairly presented in accordance with the applicable financial reporting framework (AFRF). Omissions of elements of financial reporting or required disclosures are also considered misstatements.

 Each of the following is a type of known misstatement, **except**

- An inaccuracy in processing data
- The misapplication of accounting principles
- Differences between management and the auditor's judgment regarding estimates
- A difference between the classification of a reported financial statement element and classification according to generally accepted accounting principles

GAAP recognizes that estimates are based on judgment. The auditor may **disagree with management**'s estimation process, but *both* parties' estimates must be based on GAAP. This disagreement does **not** immediately represent a deviation from GAAP and does not initially qualify as a known misstatement.

An **inaccuracy in processing data** is a type of **known misstatement** that can cause processed financial results to deviate from GAAP. For example, a material F/S misstatement could result from software that incorrectly calculates depreciation. Deviations from GAAP (such as the misapplication of accounting principles or a difference between the classification of a reported financial statement element and classification according to generally accepted accounting principles) are also examples of known misstatements.

The auditor should **accumulate all misstatements** identified during the audit (except for those that are *clearly trivial*, which means *inconsequential*). The auditor may wish to distinguish among the following three types of misstatements:

Categories of misstatement		
Type	**Definition**	**Example**
Factual	Misstatements about which there is no doubt	Miscalculation of depreciation expense
Judgmental	Misstatements arising from judgements of management that auditor finds unreasonable	Difference of opinion on estimation of an asset's useful life
Projected	Misstatements estimated based on results of a sample	Estimating a 5% error in the population based on a 5% error in a sample

In determining if misstatements are material, the auditor will consider both **quantitative** and **qualitative** factors. Some qualitative factors the auditor will consider will include whether misstatements affect:

- Trends of profitability
- Losses or income, or vice versa (ie, a flip from loss to income)
- Segment information
- Compliance with legal and contractual requirements

The auditor should determine whether the overall audit strategy and **audit plan need to be revised** as a result of the identified misstatements. That would be necessary if the aggregate of accumulated misstatements (and other misstatements that may exist) approaches what is considered to be material.

Communication

The auditor should communicate all misstatements accumulated during the audit on a timely basis with the *appropriate level* of management and **request they correct** the misstatements. The appropriate level is the one that has the authority to evaluate the misstatements and take necessary action.

- If management has examined a class of transactions or account balance at the auditor's request (eg, as a result of an audit sample that indicates a misstatement) and has made a correction, the auditor should **perform additional procedures** to determine whether any misstatements remain

Uncorrected Misstatements

If management **refuses to correct** some (or all) of the misstatements, the auditor should obtain an understanding of management's reasons and take that into consideration when evaluating whether the F/S are materially misstated.

In determining whether uncorrected misstatements are material, the auditor should consider (a) the size and nature of the misstatements and (b) the effect of uncorrected misstatements related to prior periods.

Circumstances affecting the **evaluation of materiality** also include the following:

- Compliance and regulatory requirements
- Debt covenants
- The effect on future periods' financial statements
- The effects on changes in earnings (such as changing income to a loss or vice versa) or other trends
- The impact on ratios

- The effects on segment information

- An effect that increases management compensation

- The omission of information important to users' understanding

- The misclassification between operating/non-operating items or recurring/non-recurring items

Other (undetected) misstatements may exist when a misstatement results from a break down in internal control, or when inappropriate assumptions or valuation methods have been widely used. The auditor should consider whether the detected and undetected misstatements might exceed materiality.

 Deviations from GAAP are considered known misstatements. An auditor of a nonissuer should request that management provide written representations regarding uncorrected misstatements in the financial statements that state

- The individual and cumulative differences between the auditor's point estimates and the recorded amounts for uncorrected misstatements

- Management's acceptance of responsibility for the auditor's opinion, if modified due to the uncorrected misstatements

- Whether management believes that the effects of uncorrected misstatements are immaterial, individually and in the aggregate, to the financial statements as a whole

- Management's rationale for not correcting misstatements noted during the course of the audit

Management representation topics	
Financial statements	• Fair presentation • Complete • Subsequent events • Estimates and assumptions • Related party transactions • Uncorrected mistakes
Internal controls	• Knowledge of existence of fraud
Legal issues	• Litigation and claims • Noncompliance with laws/regulations

The representation letter must address whether management believes the **effects of uncorrected misstatements are immaterial**, individually and in the aggregate, to the F/S as a whole. However, there is no requirement that management provide rationale for leaving these misstatements uncorrected. The letter should include a *summary of uncorrected misstatements*, but there is no requirement for this summary to reflect the difference between recorded and audit amounts.

Documentation

The auditor should document the following three matters in the audit documentation:

(1) The amount below which misstatements would be viewed as clearly trivial

(2) All misstatements accumulated during the audit and whether they have been corrected

(3) The auditor's conclusion (and the basis for that conclusion) about whether the uncorrected misstatements are material, individually or in the aggregate.

Internal Control Deficiencies

 Representative Task (Evaluation): Evaluate internal control deficiencies to determine potential impact on the nature, timing, and extent of audit procedures.

Definitions

Control Deficiency: When the design or operation of a control does not allow management or employees, in the normal course of performing their assigned functions, to prevent or detect misstatements on a timely basis.

Deficiency in Design: When a control necessary to meet the control objective is missing, or when the control objective is not always met, even if the control operates as designed.

Deficiency in Operation: When a properly designed control does not operate as designed, or when the person performing the control does not have the authority or competence to effectively perform the control.

Significant Deficiency: A deficiency (or combination of deficiencies) in internal control that is less severe than a material weakness, yet important enough to merit attention by those charged with governance.

Material Weakness: A deficiency (or combination of deficiencies) in internal control such that there is a reasonable possibility that a material misstatement of the entity's financial statements will not be prevented or detected and corrected on a timely basis.

Material weakness or significant deficiency

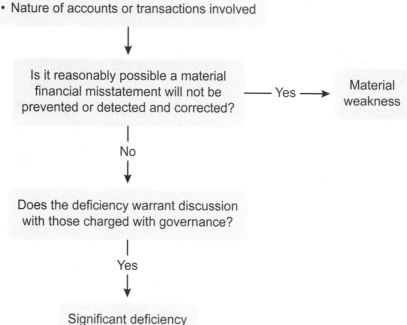

Internal controls deficiency factors

- Ineffective control oversight
- Issues noted in prior audit
- Size and complexity of entity
- Probability or size of material misstatement
- Volume of activity potentially impacted
- Nature of accounts or transactions involved

Is it reasonably possible a material financial misstatement will not be prevented or detected and corrected? —— Yes —→ Material weakness

No

Does the deficiency warrant discussion with those charged with governance?

Yes

Significant deficiency

Evaluating Control Deficiencies

A **nonissuer** client's internal control deficiencies may be identified in either a financial audit or integrated audit engagement that includes an examination of internal controls. The auditor must determine whether identified deficiencies are **significant deficiencies** or **material weaknesses**.

The auditor must also evaluate the client's resolution of any **prior material weaknesses or significant deficiencies**. If a prior deficiency still exists but is no longer material or significant due to changes in the client's internal control environment, it can be excluded from the current year written communications to the client.

In order to determine if current year items are significant deficiencies or material weaknesses, the auditor should consider both the **likelihood** and **potential magnitude** of misstatement in making that evaluation. Multiple control deficiencies affecting the same F/S item increases the likelihood of misstatement. When this occurs, the auditor must communicate, in writing, material weaknesses and significant deficiencies to client management and those charged with governance (eg, board of directors).

Risk factors that affect whether there is a reasonable possibility that a deficiency will result in a misstatement include the following:

- The nature of the accounts, classes of transactions, disclosures, and assertions involved
- The susceptibility of the related asset or liability to loss or fraud
- The subjectivity, complexity, or extent of judgment involved
- The interaction or relationship of the control with other controls
- The interaction among the deficiencies
- The possible future consequences of the deficiency

Specific indicators of material weaknesses include the following:

- Identification of any fraud involving senior management (whether or not material)
- Restatement of previously issued financial statements to correct a material misstatement due to error or fraud
- Identification of a material misstatement in the financial statements by the auditor that would not have been identified by the entity's internal control
- Ineffective oversight of the entity's financial reporting and internal control by those charged with governance

 An auditor determines that, due to accounting errors, a company's expenses and revenues are materially understated, both by approximately the same amount. What is the auditor's *most likely* course of action in response to these findings?

- Determine whether accounting policy control weaknesses allowed the errors to occur
- No further action is needed because net income is materially correct
- Request that management make adjusting entries to correct both expenses and revenues
- Issue an adverse audit opinion because the errors were not detected by management.

An auditor should **accumulate misstatements** that are more than trivial and determine their impact on the F/S. Incorrect revenues and expenses can distort financial ratios or other comparisons upon which management, investors, and analysts base decisions. In addition, if material misstatements are ignored, the audit opinion cannot state that the F/S fairly reflect, in all material respects, the results of operations. Therefore, the auditor should **request that management make adjusting entries to correct both expenses and revenues.**

Material misstatements are detected during substantive testing, the nature and extent of which is based on results from the test of controls. The auditor would have already tested controls (ie, accounting procedures) and thus determined whether any weaknesses needed to be considered when planning for and performing substantive tests.

The presence of material misstatements does not always warrant an adverse opinion. If management agrees to correct the misstatements and the results of operations are fairly reflected, in all material respects, the auditor may be able to issue an unmodified (nonissuer) or unqualified (issuer) report on the F/S.

Communicating Identified Control Deficiencies

The auditor must communicate the significant deficiencies and material weaknesses identified in the audit. Considerations related to this communication include:

Form of Communication: Identified significant deficiencies and material weaknesses must be communicated in writing to management and those charged with governance. Certain matters may not be communicated to management when communication would be inappropriate (eg, matters that raise questions about management integrity or competence). Lesser matters (not significant deficiencies) may be communicated to the appropriate level of operational management with the authority to take remedial action. Such lesser matters may be communicated either orally or in writing.

Timing: The required communication is best made by the report release date and should be made no later than 60 days following the report release date. The report release date is the date that the auditor grants the entity permission to use the auditor's report in connection with the audited financial statements.

- There is a slight difference as to timing between AICPA requirements and those of the PCAOB. The AICPA requires "timely" communication of these internal control matters (no later than the documentation completion date). The PCAOB requires such matters be communicated **prior to the release** of the auditor's report

- Early communication is permitted. The auditor may choose to verbally communicate certain significant deficiencies and material weaknesses during the audit (eg, to permit timely correction). However, all identified significant deficiencies and material weaknesses must still be communicated in writing no later than 60 days following the report release date, including those matters communicated orally during the audit

Contents: The written communication about significant deficiencies and material weaknesses should:

- State that the purpose of the audit was to express an opinion on the financial statements, not to express an opinion on the effectiveness of internal control

- State that the auditor is not expressing an opinion on the effectiveness of internal control

- State that the auditor's consideration of internal control was not designed to identify all significant deficiencies or material weaknesses

- Include the definition of the terms "material weakness" and "significant deficiency," as applicable

- Identify the matters that are considered to be material weaknesses and significant deficiencies, as applicable

- State that the communication is intended solely for the use of management, those charged with governance, and others within the organization (it should not be used by anyone other than those specified parties)

The auditor should not issue a written communication stating that no significant deficiencies were identified. However, the auditor is permitted to add a comment that no material weaknesses were identified, perhaps as requested to submit to a governmental authority.

Communication on I/C for audit of nonissuer F/S

- Provided in writing within 60 days of audit report date

- Addressed to and restricted for use by client management and those charged with governance

- Defines and explains identified significant definiciences and material weaknesses

- States audit was not designed to identify all significant deficiencies or material weaknesses

- Specifically expresses no opinion on I/C effectiveness

Management may issue a written response to the auditor's communication to indicate corrective action taken or planned or stating management's belief that the costs of correction exceed the benefits. If such a written response is included with the auditor's communication, the auditor should add a paragraph to disclaim an opinion on management's written response.

 Sample Written Communication about Internal Control Deficiencies

In planning and performing our audit of the financial statements of ABC Company (the "Company") as of and for the year ended December 31, 20XX, in accordance with auditing standards generally accepted in the United States of America, we considered the Company's internal control over financial reporting (internal control) as a basis for designing our auditing procedures for the purpose of expressing our opinion on the financial statements, but not for the purpose of expressing an opinion on the effectiveness of the Company's internal control. Accordingly, we do not express an opinion on the effectiveness of the Company's internal control.

Our consideration of internal control was for the limited purpose described in the preceding paragraph and was not designed to identify all deficiencies in internal control that might be significant deficiencies or material weaknesses and therefore, there can be no assurance that all deficiencies, significant deficiencies, or material weaknesses have been identified. However, as discussed below, we identified certain deficiencies in internal control that we consider to be material weaknesses (and other deficiencies that we consider to be significant deficiencies—*add this phrase only if applicable*).

A deficiency in internal control exists when the design or operation of a control does not allow management or employees, in the normal course of performing their assigned functions, to prevent, or detect and correct misstatements on a timely basis. A material weakness is a deficiency, or a combination of deficiencies, in internal control, such that there is a reasonable possibility that a material misstatement of the entity's financial statements will not be prevented, or detected and corrected on a timely basis. (We consider the following deficiencies in the Company's internal control to be material weaknesses:)

(*Describe the material weaknesses that were identified.*)

(A significant deficiency is a deficiency, or a combination of deficiencies, in internal control that is less severe than a material weakness, yet important enough to merit attention by those charged with governance. We consider the following deficiencies to be significant deficiencies in internal control:)

(*Describe the significant deficiencies that were identified.*)

This communication is intended solely for the information and use of management, (*identify the body or individuals charged with governance*), others within the organization, and (*identify any specified governmental authorities*) and is not intended to be and should not be used by anyone other than these specified parties.

Simulation

 Representative Task (Analysis): Determine the effect of identified misstatements on the assessment of internal control over financial reporting, individually and in the aggregate.

An accounting firm is performing the Year 2 audit of DDR Corp., a nonissuer. Consider the following:

- The auditor will rely on tests of controls for sales and cash receipts and purchasing and cash disbursements
- The amount in column C in the table below represents the potential misstatement as a result of the identified control deficiency
- The auditor will assess control risk as high for all other controls
- Materiality for each of the situations is $750,000

For each situation in column A:

- In column B, select the deficiency type: Design, Operational, None
- In column D, select the evaluation of deficiency: Deficiency, Material Weakness, Significant Deficiency, None
- In column E, select the communication requirement, if any, to those charged with governance
  - Oral or written, no later than 60 days following the audit report release date
  - In writing, no later than 60 days following the financial statement date
  - Oral or written, no later than 60 days following the financial statement date
  - Written, no later than 90 days following the audit report release date
  - No formal communication necessary

	Column A	Column B	Column C	Column D	Column E
	Situation	Deficiency type	Potential misstatement	Evaluation of deficiency	Communication required
1	The controller reviews and approves consolidating journal entries during the month end close. However, the auditor determined that the year end December consolidating journal entries were not properly reviewed. There are no compensating controls to mitigate the effects of this control deficiency.	Operation	$1,250,000	Material weakness	In writing, no later than 60 days following the audit report release date

This is a deficiency in operation. The control to review and approve journal entries is in place but is not being performed. It is a material weakness because there is a reasonable possibility that a *material* (ie, greater than the $750,000 materiality limit) misstatement will not be prevented or detected and corrected on a timely basis.

	Column A	Column B	Column C	Column D	Column E
2	The company does not have a process for matching invoices with purchase orders or receiving documents prior to payment. There are no other qualitative factors that would affect the deficiency evaluation.	Design	$725,000	Significant deficiency	In writing, no later than 60 days following the audit report release date

This is a deficiency in design. There is no process for matching invoices with purchase orders or receiving documents prior to payment. A risk exists that invoices that are in error (eg, goods never received) or fictious could be inappropriately paid. It is a significant deficiency because the potential misstatement (ie, $725,000) is considered immaterial (ie, below the $750,000 threshold). However, the control weakness was determined by the auditor to be important enough to merit attention by management. In addition, the potential misstatement is quite close to the materiality threshold, which makes this more than a mere deficiency.

	Column A	Column B	Column C	Column D	Column E
3	There is no physical security for a small portion of the company's inventory, and a warehouse employee stole $10,000 of the unsecured inventory in Year 1. The value of this inventory is inconsequential to the company's inventory balance. There are no other qualitative factors that would affect the deficiency evaluation.	Design	$50,000	Deficiency	No formal communication necessary

This is a deficiency in design. Strong I/C requires security over assets, including inventory. The lack of such a control creates the opportunity for theft. It is a deficiency because the amount of the theft is *immaterial*. Given that the deficiency is well below the materiality threshold of $750,000, and inconsequential to the inventory balance, it is considered just a deficiency (ie, not a significant deficiency).

AUD 21
Written
Representations

AUD 21: Written Representations

21.01 Written Representations

 Additional coverage on written representations is also presented in the relevant chapter (eg, Attestation Engagements).

Overview

 Representative Task (Remembering & Understanding): Identify the written representations that should be obtained from management or those charged with governance in an engagement.

AICPA Guidance

The relevant AICPA guidance is provided by AU-C 580, *Written Representations*. This pronouncement states that the auditor's objectives are

- To obtain **written representations** from management that they believe they have fulfilled their responsibility for the preparation and fair presentation of the financial statements and for the completeness of information provided to the auditor
- To support other audit evidence relevant to the financial statements by means of written representations determined necessary by the auditor

Document Verbal Responses to Auditor's Inquiries

An auditor is required to obtain **written representations** from management to corroborate management's verbal responses to important inquiries by the auditor. An important purpose of this letter is to **emphasize management's responsibility** for the F/S. Another is to provide the auditor with **some assurance** that management is not deliberately concealing any information that might have affected the auditor's opinion.

Should the auditor have some evidence of intentional misbehavior by management, the auditor will, of course, place less reliance on the representations made by management in the letter.

This letter from management is addressed directly to the auditors. The letter should be signed by those members of management with overall responsibility for financial and operating matters (ie, the chief executive officer (CEO) and the chief financial officer (CFO)).

- Any unwillingness by management to sign the management representations letterwould be a **scope limitation** probably resulting in a disclaimer of opinion or withdrawal from the engagement
- If any such representations are *contradicted by other evidence*, the auditor should investigate the circumstances and evaluate the implications to reliance on other management representations

The representations letter should cover **all periods** encompassed by the auditor's report. If current management was not present for all periods covered, tailor the representations to the circumstances. The representations letter should be dated the same as the **date of the auditor's report**.

If management refuses to provide written representations in the form of a management letter, the auditor should:

- Discuss the matter with management

- Disclaim an opinion or withdraw from the engagement

- Reevaluate management's integrity and the effect it has on the reliability of evidence obtained

- Consider modifying the auditor's opinion to indicate items affected

Management representation attributes

- Written affirmation of information provided during the audit

- Confirms management's responsibility for financial reporting

- Required audit documentation

- Addressed to the auditor

- Dated as of the audit report date

- Normally signed by the CEO and CFO

- Covers financial statements and periods referenced in the audit report

The **management representations letter** is a mandatory part of audit documentation. **Failure** to receive such a letter is considered a **scope limitation** sufficient to preclude an unqualified opinion on the financial statements. In the absence of such a letter, a **disclaimer of opinion** will be issued or the auditor may **withdraw** from the engagement.

Contents of the Letter

The content of the letter will, to some extent, depend on what has taken place during the audit prior to that point. In addition, the management representation [TJ6]letter clearly cannot have an impact on the gathering of evidence by the auditor during the audit, since it is obtained after the planning and performance of all other tests.

Certain representations, however, will be present in all such letters.

Regarding the Financial Statements

- That management is responsible for the fairness of the financial statements

- That management is responsible for internal control over financial reporting

- That management is responsible for internal control to prevent and detect fraud

- That significant assumptions used for any accounting estimates are reasonable

- That related party transactions have been properly accounted for and disclosed

- That subsequent events have been properly accounted for and disclosed

- That any uncorrected misstatements are immaterial

- That the effects of litigation and claims have been properly accounted for and disclosed

In obtaining written representations from management, materiality limits ordinarily would apply to representations related to

- Amounts concerning related party transactions
- Irregularities involving members of management
- The availability of financial records
- The completeness of minutes of directors' meetings.

Management must provide a written representation that all **related party** names, arrangements, and resulting transactions have been disclosed. When the **amounts** of related party arrangements have a **material impact** on the financial statements, written **representations** may also be **obtained from others** (eg, those charged with governance over these arrangements).

Regardless of materiality limits, irregularities involving management **must be disclosed** to the auditor. Additionally, management *must confirm* that the auditor had access to complete financial records and directors' meeting minutes.

Regarding the Information Provided

- That all relevant financial records and unrestricted access to personnel were made available to the auditor
- That all transactions have been recorded
- That management has made available the results of their assessment of fraud risks
- That regarding fraud, there is no fraud involving management or employees having significant internal control responsibilities, or others where the financial statement effect could be material
- That management has no knowledge of suspected fraud communicated by employees, former employees, or others
- That management has disclosed all instances of noncompliance with laws and regulations relevant to financial reporting
- That there are no (undisclosed) litigations, claims, and assessments relevant to the financial statements
- That management has disclosed all known related party relationships and transactions

An auditor of a nonissuer should request that management provide written representations regarding uncorrected misstatements in the financial statements that state:

- The individual and cumulative differences between the auditor's point estimates and the recorded amounts for uncorrected misstatements

- Management's acceptance of responsibility for the auditor's opinion, if modified due to the uncorrected misstatements

- Whether management believes that the effects of uncorrected misstatements are immaterial, individually and in the aggregate, to the financial statements as a whole

- Management's rationale for not correcting misstatements noted during the course of the audit

Management representation topics	
Financial statements	• Fair presentation • Complete • Subsequent events • Estimates and assumptions • Related party transactions • Uncorrected mistakes
Internal controls	• Knowledge of existence of fraud
Legal issues	• Litigation and claims • Noncompliance with laws/regulations

In some audit situations, other topics must be included in the representation letter. For example, should the audit disclose **uncorrected misstatements**, the **representation letter must address** whether management believes the **effects** of these misstatements are **immaterial**, individually and in the aggregate, to the F/S as a whole.

Supplementary Information

In some cases, the auditor will be expressing an opinion on *supplementary information* included with the F/S. When this is the case, the auditor is also required to obtain written representations indicating:

- Management's acknowledgment of its responsibility for the preparation and fair presentation of the supplementary information in accordance with applicable criteria

- Management's belief that the supplementary information is fairly presented in accordance with applicable criteria, including both its form and content

- That measurement and presentation methods either have not changed from the prior period or, if they have, the reasons for the changes

- Any significant assumptions or interpretations that affected the measurement or presentation of the supplementary information

Sample Management Representations Letter

 Management (Client) Representation Letter

(Date of the Auditor's Report)

(To Independent Auditor)

This representation letter is provided in connection with your audit of the financial statements of ABC Company, which comprise the balance sheet as of December 31, 20XX, and the related statements of income, changes in stockholders' equity, and cash flows for the year then ended, and the related notes to the financial statements, for the purpose of expressing an opinion on whether the financial statements are presented fairly, in all material respects, in accordance with accounting principles generally accepted in the United States (U.S. GAAP).

Certain representations in this letter are described as being limited to matters that are **material**. Items are considered material, regardless of size, if they involve an omission or misstatement of accounting information that, in the light of surrounding circumstances, makes it probable that the judgment of a reasonable person relying on the information would be changed or influenced by the omission or misstatement.

Except where otherwise stated below, immaterial matters less than $XXX collectively are not considered to be exceptions that require disclosure for the purpose of the following representations. This amount is not necessarily indicative of amounts that would require adjustment to or disclosure in the financial statements.

We confirm, to the best of our knowledge and belief, having made such inquiries as we considered necessary for the purpose of appropriately informing ourselves as of [*the date of the auditor's report*]:

Financial Statements

1. We have fulfilled our responsibilities, as set out in the terms of the engagement dated [insert date], for the *preparation and fair presentation of the financial statements in accordance with U.S. GAAP.*

   - We acknowledge our responsibility for the design, implementation, and maintenance (DIM) of internal control relevant to the preparation and fair presentation of financial statements that are free from material misstatement, whether due to fraud or error

   - We acknowledge our responsibility for the design, implementation, and maintenance of internal control *to prevent and detect fraud*

   - Significant assumptions used by us in making accounting estimates, including those measured at fair value, are reasonable

   - Related party relationships and transactions have been appropriately accounted for and disclosed in accordance with the requirements of U.S. GAAP

   - All events **subsequent to** the date of the financial statements and for which U.S. GAAP requires adjustment or disclosure have been adjusted or disclosed

   - The effects of uncorrected misstatements are immaterial, both individually and in the aggregate, to the financial statements as a whole. A list of the uncorrected misstatements is attached to the representation letter

   - The effects of all known actual or possible litigation and claims have been accounted for and disclosed in accordance with U.S. GAAP.

Information Provided

- We have provided you with:

    a. Access to all information, of which we are aware, that is relevant to the preparation and fair presentation of the financial statements such as records, documentation, and other matters;

    b. Additional information that you have requested for the purpose of the audit; and

    c. Unrestricted access to persons within the entity from whom you determined it necessary to obtain audit evidence.

- All transactions have been recorded in the accounting records and are reflected in the financial statements

- We have disclosed to you the results of our assessment of the risk that the financial statements may be materially misstated as a result of fraud

- We have [no knowledge of any] [disclosed to you all information that we are aware of regarding] fraud or suspected fraud that affects the entity and involves:

    a. Management;

    b. Employees who have significant roles in internal control; or

    c. Others when the fraud could have a material effect on the financial statements.

- We have [no knowledge of any] [disclosed to you all information that we are aware of regarding] allegations of fraud, or suspected fraud, affecting the entity's financial statements communicated by employees, former employees, analysts, regulators, or others

- We have disclosed to you all known instances of noncompliance with laws and regulations whose effects should be considered when preparing financial statements

- We [have disclosed to you all known actual or possible] [are not aware of any pending or threatened] litigation, claims, and assessments whose effects should be considered when preparing the financial statements

- We have disclosed to you the identity of the entity's related parties and all related party relationships and transactions of which we are aware

[Any other matters that the auditor may consider necessary]

(Name of Chief Executive Officer and Title)   (Name of Chief Financial Officer and Title)

AUD 22
Subsequent Events

AUD 22: Subsequent Events

22.01 Subsequent Events

Overview

 Representative Task (Application): Perform procedures to identify subsequent events that should be reflected in an entity's current period financial statements and disclosures.

AICPA Guidance

The relevant AICPA guidance is provided by AU-C 560, *Subsequent Events and Subsequently Discovered Facts*. This pronouncement states that the auditor's objectives are

- To obtain sufficient appropriate audit evidence about whether subsequent events are properly reflected in the F/S

- To respond appropriately to subsequently discovered facts

- For a predecessor auditor who is requested to reissue a previously issued report, to perform specified procedures to determine whether the previously issued report is still appropriate

Definitions

Subsequent Events: Events occurring between the balance sheet (B/S) date and the date of the auditor's report.

Subsequently Discovered Facts: Facts that became known to the auditor after the date of the auditor's report that, had they been known to the auditor at that date, may have caused the auditor to revise the auditor's report.

Types of Subsequent Events

Subsequent events are conditions or transactions that occur **after the** F/S date (eg, 12/31/Year 1) but **before the F/S are issued**. There are two types of subsequent events.

- **Type 1** events provide evidence that the condition existed at year end and must be **recognized in the F/S** (eg, an oil company has a spill in Year 1 and is fined in Year 2, before issuance of F/S)
  - A The filing of bankruptcy by a customer early in the period subsequent to year end may indicate that a receivable from that customer was not collectible as of the end of the period (ie, type 1 event) and should be written off

- **Type 2** events are not related to a condition that existed as of the F/S date and do not require recognition but may **require disclosure** if material
  - A large warehouse destroyed by a fire after year end is an example of a Type 2 event. Disclosing the event is important because it informs F/S users about the true conditions of the business as of the F/S issue date. F/S that exclude Type 2 disclosures are misleading

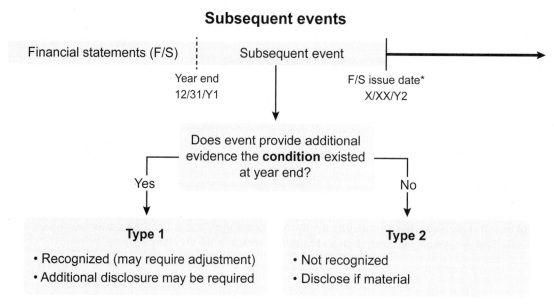

Subsequent events

Issue date applicable to public entities only; for all other entities, the available to be issued date is used.

Audit Procedures

The auditor's responsibility is to make certain that management has properly identified, evaluated, and recognized or disclosed, as appropriate, subsequent events up **through the date of the auditor's report**. There are several audit procedures occurring **after the B/S date** that may reveal evidence of subsequent events:

- Read minutes of meetings of the board of directors and other appropriate committees occurring after year end to determine if there is discussion of major events occurring in the subsequent period

- Make inquiries of the client's legal counsel to determine if there is litigation, or if there are claims or assessments arising or being settled after the B/S date

- Read interim reports prepared by management in the subsequent period to determine if they show unusual transactions occurring after year end

- Make inquiries of the client and obtain a management representation letter[TJ5] to determine if there were unusual transactions or major events occurring in the subsequent period

- Evaluate changes in long-term debt after year end to determine if there were major financial transactions occurring after the B/S date that affect the classification of liabilities and require adjustment of the B/S or may need to be disclosed to users

Which of the following procedures would an auditor generally perform regarding subsequent events?

- Inspect inventory items that were ordered before year end but arrived after year end
- Test internal control activities that were previously reported to management as inadequate
- Review the client's cutoff bank statements for several months after year end
- Compare the latest available interim financial statements with the statements being audited

Procedures to identify subsequent events

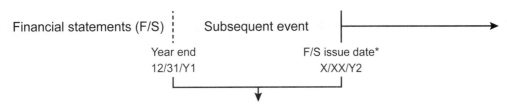

Issue date applicable to public entities only; for all other entities, the available to be issued date is used.

Required procedures to identify subsequent events **focus** on events that occurred **after year end** and are relevant to conditions that existed during the year under audit. Although management may provide auditors with information about how internal control deficiencies identified during the audit were corrected, it would not help identify subsequent events.

Comparing the *most recent* F/S (ie, interim) with the audited F/S would provide relevant information. If the information suggests that a material lawsuit that began in Year 1 was settled, then an adjustment and disclosure are required.

Cutoff procedures are used to test if transactions that occur *near* the end of the year are reported in the correct period. Inspection of inventory ordered before year end but that arrived after year end is used to verify that inventory was accounted for in the proper period. Similarly, a bank cutoff statement is used to verify that items on a bank reconciliation (eg, outstanding checks) clear the bank to confirm it was properly included in that period's cash balance.

Dating the Auditor's Report

The auditor's report should not be dated earlier than the date on which the auditor has obtained sufficient appropriate audit evidence to support the opinion. For a **subsequent event** that occurs after the completion of fieldwork but prior to the issuance of the auditor's report, and if the F/S are:

- Adjusted without any accompanying disclosure, the report should be dated whenever the auditor has obtained *sufficient appropriate audit evidence* (which may be the completion of fieldwork or later). In this case, there is no need to consider *dual dating*

- Adjusted along with additional footnote disclosure, or a disclosure is added without adjustment, then the audit report may be either:
  - Dual dated (using one date for the overall audit report and a later date to address a specific subsequent event)
  - The entire audit report may be dated as of the later date (which makes the auditor responsible, in general, for all subsequent events up to that later date).

 On March 18, an event came to the CPA's attention that should be disclosed in the notes to the financial statements. The CPA decided to dual date the auditor's report and dated the report March 18. The audit report was released on April 1. Under these circumstances, the CPA was taking responsibility for

- All subsequent events that occurred through April 1
- All subsequent events that occurred through March 12
- Only the specific subsequent event occurring on March 18
- All events that occurred through March 18

Changing report date vs. dual date

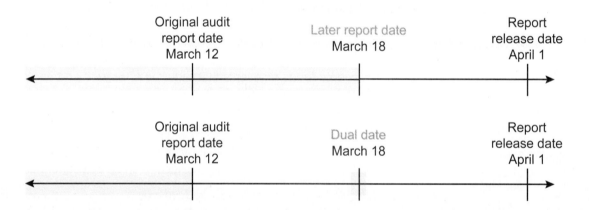

When **dual dating** an audit report such as "March 12, Year 2, except for the event described in Note J dated March 18, Year 2," an auditor indicates assuming responsibility for all subsequent events occurring before March 12, the last day of fieldwork, and is *taking responsibility* for *only* the single additional event occurring on March 18.

If a subsequent event occurs after the audit report date but prior to the release date of an audit report, resulting in management's revision of the financial statements of a nonissuer, then the auditor may do any of the following, **except**

- Maintain the original date of the report and state that the opinion is limited to the financial statements as they existed prior to the subsequent event

- Perform audit procedures necessary to obtain assurance about the revised financial statements

- Include an additional date in the audit report that is limited to the revision to the financial statements

- Revise the date of the audit report to reflect the necessity of additional audit procedures

Subsequent event: revised financial statements (F/S)

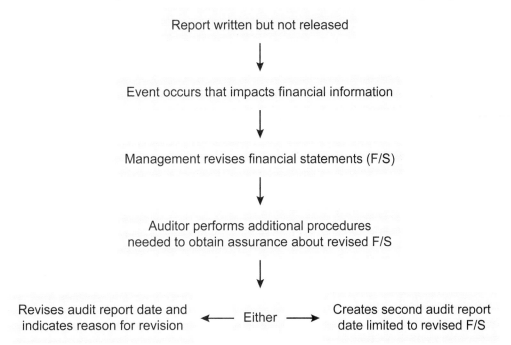

If a subsequent event requires F/S revision, and management appropriately makes the revision, the auditor should perform any additional audit procedures necessary to obtain assurance about the revised F/S. The auditor can either:

- include an additional date in the audit report that is limited to the F/S revision (ie, dual date the report) or

- revise the date of the audit report to reflect the necessity of the additional audit procedures

In this scenario, the **subsequent event** has enough impact to **warrant F/S revision**. Therefore, the auditor **cannot maintain** the **original** date of the **report** and state that the opinion is limited to the F/S that existed before the subsequent event was discovered. To do so would give F/S users an inaccurate view of the client's true financial results.

Task-Based Simulation

 Representative Task (Analysis): Determine whether identified subsequent events are appropriately reflected in an entity's financial statements and disclosures.

Below is a series of unrelated statements taken from various sections of the audit working papers. The menu contains a list of actions that the auditor might be required to take. Select, as the best answer for each item, the most likely action. An action may be selected once, more than once, or not at all.

Select an option below

Advise management to disclose the event in the notes to the financial statements.

Advise management to adjust the financial statements.

Discuss with management and determine whether the financial statements require revision.

Do nothing. The event does not need to be disclosed and the financial statements do not need to be adjusted.

	Situation	Auditor Action
1	A client acquired 25% of its outstanding capital stock after year end and prior to completion of the auditor's fieldwork. The auditor should: **Advise management to disclose the event in the notes to the financial statements.** *This is a type 2 subsequent event since the acquisition provided evidence of a condition which came into existence after year end. Therefore, the proper accounting approach would be to note disclosure rather than make an adjustment.*	
2	After issuing an auditor's report, an auditor becomes aware of facts that existed at the report date that might have affected the report had the auditor known of the facts at the time. The auditor should: **Discuss with management and determine whether the financial statements require revision.** *If the information is reliable and the facts existed at the date of the audit report, the auditor should discuss with management and determine whether the financial statements require revision. If so, the auditor should inquire as to how management will address the matter.*	
3	A loss on an uncollectible trade receivable recorded in year 1 was related to a customer that declared bankruptcy in year 2. The auditor should: **Advise management to adjust the financial statements.** *A loss on the trade receivable may be a Type 1 subsequent event requiring an adjustment if the customer was in a weak financial condition as of the end of year 1.*	

Situation	Auditor Action
4	A major drop in the quoted market price of a company's stock occurred after the end of the fiscal year under audit but prior to issuance of the auditor's report. The auditor should: **Do nothing. The event does not need to be disclosed and the financial statements do not need to be adjusted.** *A major drop in the quoted market price of the entity's stock would not have financial statement effects and need not be disclosed as a subsequent event.*	

Subsequently Discovered Facts

 Representative Task (Remembering & Understanding): Recall the impact of subsequently discovered facts on the auditor's report.

New information may come to an auditor's attention *after* the audit report date that is related to an event that occurred *before* the report date. Had auditors known about this event, they might have modified the audit report. This is known as a **subsequently discovered fact**.

This type of event is *not limited* to the subsequent events period between the balance sheet and report dates but could include events that occurred *at any time* during the year under audit. It can also include discovery that an important audit **procedure was omitted**. Omitted procedures are treated the same as a **subsequently discovered fact**.

The auditor should discuss the matter with management (and possibly those charged with governance) and determine whether the F/S require revision. If so, the auditor should inquire as to how management will address the matter.

If the discovery is found **before the report release date**, and if management:

- Revises the F/S, the auditor should perform appropriate audit procedures on the revision
- Does not revise the F/S, and the auditor believes that revision is necessary, the auditor should appropriately modify the opinion

If the discovery is found **after the report is released**, and management revised the F/S, the auditor should:

- Perform appropriate audit procedures on the revision
- Assess whether management's actions are timely and appropriate to ensure that users are informed
- If the opinion on the revised F/S differs from that previously expressed; add an emphasis-of-matter or other matter paragraph (that identifies the date of the previous report, the opinion previously expressed, and the reason for the different opinion now expressed)

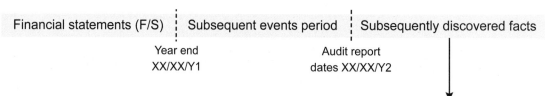

Subsequently discovered facts

Financial statements (F/S)	Subsequent events period	Subsequently discovered facts
Year end XX/XX/Y1	Audit report dates XX/XX/Y2	

- Relevant to published F/S
- After audit report issued
- Auditor action required
  - Discuss management steps taken
  - Determine if correction(s) needed
  - Prevent reliance on issued report if needed

If management **does not revise** the F/S, and the auditor believes that revision is necessary, the auditor should determine whether those F/S have already been **made available to third parties**.

- If the F/S have not been made available to third parties, the auditor should **notify management** and those charged with governance that the F/S should not be made available to third parties before making necessary revisions and a new audit report has been provided

- If the F/S have been made available, the auditor should **determine whether management** has taken timely and appropriate steps to ensure that users have been informed not to rely on those F/S

- If management does not take the necessary steps to inform the users, the auditor should **notify management** and those charged with governance that the auditor will try to prevent users' reliance on the auditor's report

Omitted Procedures (Subsequent Discovery of Facts)

After the report is issued, the auditor may discover that they **omitted procedures** that were considered to be *important* at the time of the audit. This could result from a miscommunication among the audit staff or the failure to note an item in the audit program.

This discovery **does not automatically** indicate that the audit was deficient or that there were misstatements in the F/S or notes. The auditor should first consider the **actual importance** of the omitted procedure to the auditor's opinion.

When this occurs, the auditor should:

- Assess the importance of the omitted procedure
- Determine tests to compensate for the omitted procedure (eg, subsequent receipts test for A/R)
- Perform tests
- Determine if there is a need to minimize reliance on the F/S (if so, notify the client, regulatory agencies, and anyone relying on the statements)

If the auditor decides that the omitted procedure is needed to support the opinion, then the client should be contacted and the procedure performed. Once completed, there is no need to notify parties relying on the report, since the auditor will once again feel they can support their opinion. Only if the client refuses to permit the auditor to perform the omitted procedure will it be necessary to withdraw the report and notify parties that they may not rely on it.

If the procedure leads to information affecting the statements and/or notes, this will be treated as a subsequent discovery of facts and handled in the manner discussed earlier in this section.

Predecessor Auditor Reissues the Auditor's Report

When a predecessor auditor is **requested to reissue** a *previously issued* report, the predecessor should perform the following procedures to determine whether the previously issued auditor's report is still appropriate:

- Read the F/S of the subsequent period (and compare those F/S with the ones previously audited and reported on to identify any significant changes)
- Inquire of and request written representations from management about any issues, including subsequent events, that might affect the previous representations from management
- Obtain a representation letter from the successor auditor about any known matters affecting the financial statements audited by the predecessor

If a subsequently discovered fact becomes known to the predecessor:

- The predecessor auditor should discuss the matter with management (and possibly those charged with governance) and determine whether the F/S require revision. If so, the auditor should inquire as to how management will address the matter
- If management revises the F/S and the predecessor auditor plans to issue a new auditor's report, the predecessor should:
  - Perform the procedures necessary to evaluate the revision (and date the audit report appropriately or dual date the report for the revision)
  - Assess steps taken by management to ensure that users do not rely on the erroneous financial statements
  - If the opinion on the revised F/S differs from that previously expressed, add an emphasis-of-matter or other matter paragraph (that identifies the date of the previous report, the opinion previously expressed, and the reason for the different opinion now expressed)

Omitted audit procedure subsequently discovered

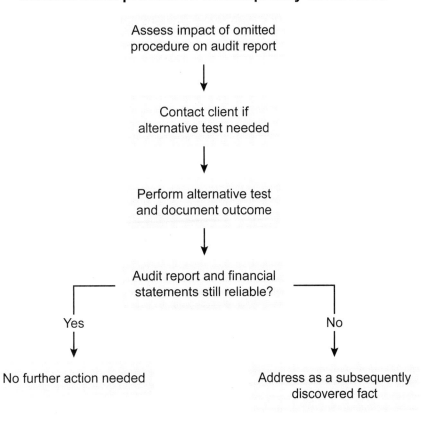

AUD

Area IV: Forming Conclusions and Reporting

AUD 23
Reporting on Audit Engagements

AUD 23: Reporting on Audit Engagements

23.01 Reporting on Audit Engagements

Introduction to Audit Reports

 Representative Task (Remembering & Understanding): Identify the factors that an auditor should consider when forming an opinion on an entity's financial statements.

 Representative Task (Remembering & Understanding): Identify the type of opinion (unqualified or unmodified, qualified, adverse, or disclaimer of opinion) that an auditor should render on the audit of an issuer or nonissuer's financial statements.

Remember that a **nonissuer** is a privately held entity that is not required to file with the SEC. Audits of nonissuers must adhere to **GAAS**. **An issuer** is a **publicly held entity** that files with the SEC. Audits of issuers must adhere to **PCAOB** auditing standards.

Comparison of external audits

Issuers   **Nonissuer financial audits**

- Audit governed by PCAOB
- Opinion expressed on internal control over financial reporting
- Auditor must test effectiveness of internal control

- Only independent CPA can perform audit
- Opinion expressed on fairness of financial statements
- Risk assessment due to fraud or error required
- Auditor must obtain an understanding of the control design and level of implementation

- Audit governed by GAAS
- No opinion expressed on internal control
- Auditor determines if testing control is necessary

Nonissuer (GAAS) Audit Reports—Overview

The relevant AICPA auditing standard is AU-C 700, *Forming an Opinion on Financial Statements*, which states that the auditor's objectives are to form an opinion on the financial statements (F/S) based on an evaluation of the audit evidence obtained and to clearly express that opinion through a written report.

The auditor must form an opinion as to whether the F/S are *presented fairly*, *in all material respects*, in accordance with the applicable financial reporting framework (AFRF). To do so, the auditor must determine whether *reasonable assurance* has been obtained that the F/S, taken as a whole, are *free of material misstatement*, whether caused by error or fraud.

The auditor issues an **unmodified report** if they determine the F/S are fairly presented. When the auditor determines that the F/S are **not fairly presented**, the auditor should discuss the matter with management. If the issue(s) cannot be resolved, the auditor must **modify the opinion**.

There are three types of modified audit reports:

- **Qualified opinion**—The auditor expresses one or more reservations about the:
  - Financial statement presentation (due to a departure from the requirements of the applicable financial reporting framework that is material but not pervasive)
  - Audit engagement (due to a scope limitation about a matter for which the auditor was unable to obtain desired audit evidence, the possible effect of which is material but not pervasive)

- **Adverse opinion**—The auditor states that the financial statements are not fairly stated due to one or more departures from the requirements of the AFRF that is/are material and pervasive

- **Disclaimer of opinion**—The auditor does not express any conclusion about the fairness of the entity's financial statements due to a scope limitation that is material and pervasive

	4 types of opinions	Will be expressed if . . .	Key report language
Unmodified* opinions	Standard "clean" opinion	F/S are fairly presented	"... [F/S] present fairly, in all material respects, ... in accordance with [GAAP]."
Modified opinions	Qualified opinion	F/S are fairly presented, except for...	"... except for ..., the [F/S] present fairly...."
	Adverse opinion	F/S are materially misstated	"... [F/S] do not present fairly..."
	Disclaimer of opinion	Sufficient appropriate audit evidence could not be obtained to conclude that F/S are fairly presented	"We do not express an opinion..."

Note that GAAS uses the term "unmodified" while the PCAOB standards (discussed later) use the term "unqualified."

Unmodified Audit Report

To issue an unmodified audit report, *all* of the following should be considered:

- Has sufficient appropriate audit evidence been obtained?
- Are uncorrected misstatements material, either individually or when combined?
- Have the F/S been prepared, in all material respects (quantitatively and qualitatively), in accordance with the AFRF (eg, GAAP)? This includes considering whether:
  - Management's judgments are biased (lack neutrality). For example, did management correct misstatements that increase earnings and disregard those that decrease earnings?
  - Accounting estimates are reasonable
  - Accounting policies applied are appropriate
  - The F/S appropriately disclose significant accounting policies

- Disclosures are adequate to allow F/S users to understand the effect of material transactions/events

- Information in the F/S is relevant, reliable, comparable, understandable, and complete

- F/S titles and terminology are appropriate

- The overall F/S presentation, structure, and content is appropriate. For example:

  - Does the presentation obscure useful information or result in misleading information?

  - Is the presentation consistent with industry practices?

- The F/S adequately refer to or describe the AFRF

The auditor's **unmodified report** typically consists of:

- **Title**—The title of the report must clearly indicate that it is the report of an independent auditor. Such a title as "Independent Auditor's Report" also emphasizes that the other pages of the annual report were prepared by the client, not the auditor

- **Addresses**—The addressees depend on the circumstances of the engagement, but generally the report is addressed to the party to which the auditor is reporting

  - This may be the entity, those charged with governance (eg, board of directors), or, in the case of an unincorporated entity, the owners. If a third party hired the auditor to audit an entity, the addressee may be that third-party client

  - It is not acceptable to address the report to members of the management team, since management is the party that the auditor is reporting on

- **Required sections**—An unmodified report will consist of at least four sections, each of which has certain requirements, including a specific title. The signature, location, and date follow this section, as shown below:

Standard unmodified audit report for nonissuers

Independent auditor's report

To: Addressee (eg, board of directors)

Opinion

Basis for opinion

Responsibilities of management for the financial statements

Auditor's responsibilities for the audit of the financial statements

Auditor's signature
Auditor's city and state
Date of report

- Express an opinion on financial statements (not internal control)
- Adhere to GAAS (eg, professional skepticism, risk assessment, examine evidence on test basis, understand internal controls, evaluate accounting principles and estimates)
- Evaluate entity's ability to continue as a going concern

Additional/Explanatory Sections for Unmodified Report

Additional sections and explanatory language may be added to an unmodified audit report. These additional items are *not considered modifications* of the report.

	Additional section/paragraph	Specified title?	Will be added if the auditor . . .	Applicable reports
Additional Sections	Substantial doubt about the entity's ability to continue as a going concern	Yes	Has such substantial doubt, which has *not* been alleviated	Unmodified
	Key audit matters	Yes	Is engaged to communicate such matters	Unmodified Qualified
	Other information (OI)	No	Needs to read OI that is included in an annual report for inconsistencies with the F/S	Unmodified Qualified Adverse
	Supplemental information (SI)	No	Has been engaged to audit SI that is presented with the F/S	Any type
	Required supplemental information (RSI)	No	Needs to apply limited procedures to determine whether RSI is complete and correct	Any type
	Report on other legal and regulatory requirements	No	Has reporting responsibilities in addition to those under GAAS	Any type
Explanatory Paragraphs	Emphasis of matter	No	Needs to draw attention to a matter that is *fundamental* to users' understanding of F/S	Unmodified Qualified
	Other matter	No	Needs to draw attention to matters *other than those presented/disclosed* in F/S that are *relevant* to users' understanding of the audit, auditor's responsibilities, or report	Unmodified Qualified

Substantial Doubt About the Entity's Ability to Continue as a Going Concern

F/S are usually prepared on the assumption that an **entity will remain in business** for a reasonable period (ie, going concern assumption). If there is substantial doubt about the going concern assumption, the auditor considers management's plans (eg, selling assets) to alleviate that doubt and evaluates the **disclosure**.

This section is required *only* if there is such substantial doubt that has not been alleviated.* It should:

- Draw attention to the F/S notes that disclose:
  - The conditions/events identified and management's plans to deal with these conditions/events
  - That these conditions/events indicate substantial doubt exists about the entity's ability to continue as a going concern for a reasonable period of time
- State that the **opinion is not modified** with respect to the matter
- Be presented directly after the Basis for Opinion section
- Be titled "Substantial Doubt About the Entity's Ability to Continue as a Going Concern"

When substantial doubt has been alleviated, the auditor may include an emphasis-of-matter paragraph instead.

Reporting when there is substantial doubt about the going concern assumption

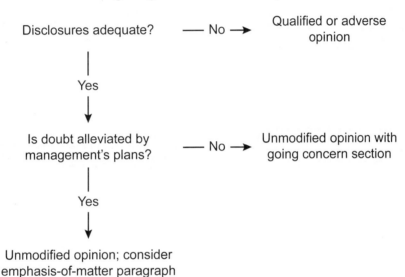

Key Audit Matters

Key audit matters (KAMs) are *matters communicated with those charged with governance* and, in the auditor's professional judgment, were of *most significance in the audit* of the current period F/S. This section is required only if the auditor is engaged to communicate key audit matters (KAMs).*

The KAM section should:

- Define what a KAM is
- State that these matters were addressed in the context of the F/S audit and a separate opinion is not expressed on the KAMs
- Include each KAM to be reported with:
  - An appropriate subheading
  - Reference to any related disclosures
  - A description of why the matter is a KAM
  - A description of how the matter was addressed in the audit
- Be titled "Key Audit Matters"

* *Unless required by law, the KAM section is prohibited when the auditor must issue an adverse opinion or disclaimer of opinion. (AU-C 701)*

In determining which matters to report as KAMs, the auditor must choose the most significant of all items requiring **significant auditor attention**, including:

- Significant risks, or areas of higher assessed risk of material misstatement (RMM)—eg, the risk of fraud in revenue recognition

- Areas involving significant *management* judgment, which in turn require significant *auditor* judgment, including accounting estimates with high estimation uncertainty

- Significant events/transactions occurring during the period and their effect on the audit

Determining which key audit matters (KAMs) to include in a report with a KAM section

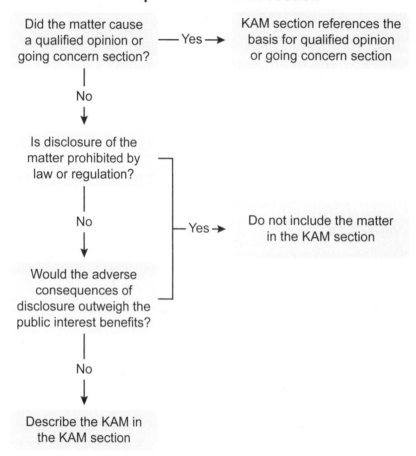

Certain KAMs **should not be included** in the KAM section when *any* of the following circumstances apply.

- Laws/regulations prohibit disclosure

- The adverse consequences of disclosure (eg, harm to the entity's competitive position) are likely to outweigh the benefits to the public

- The KAM is described in another section of the report and a reference to that section is appropriate. For example, one should:

  ○ Refer to the Basis for Qualified Opinion section when the matter results in a qualified opinion

  ○ Refer to the Going Concern section when there is substantial doubt about the entity's ability to continue as a going concern

If either or both of the above are the only KAMs to report, or there are no KAMs to report, the KAM section will be modified to say: "[*Except for the matter described in the Basis for Qualified Opinion section or Going Concern section*,] We have determined that there are no [*other*] key audit matters to communicate in our report."

Key audit matters sections (KAM) by report type

Adverse opinion	KAM should not be included (unless required by law)
Disclaimer of opinion	KAM should not be included (unless required by law)
Qualified opinion	KAM refers to basis of opinion section rather than describing the issue causing the modification
Unmodified opinion with going concern section	KAM refers to going concern section rather than describing the going concern issue

Audit documentation for KAMs should include *all* of the following:

- All matters that required significant auditor attention
- Rationale for why each matter is a KAM or not
- If applicable, the rationale for determining that there are no KAMs to report, or no KAMs other than those required to be reported in the Basis for Qualified Opinion or Going Concern sections
- If applicable, the rationale for determining not to include a KAM in the report due to possible adverse consequences

 Which of the following should be included in a key audit matters section when key audit matters are communicated in an audit report expressing an unmodified opinion?

- A reference to the basis for opinion section
- A description of communication on the matter with those charged with governance
- A statement that a separate opinion is not expressed on the matter
- A statement that the auditor was engaged to communicate key audit matters

Key Audit Matters

Key audit matters are those matters that were communicated with those charged with governance and, in our professional judgment, were of most significance in our audit of the financial statements of the current period. These matters were addressed in the context of our audit of the financial statements as a whole, and in forming our opinion thereon, and we do not provide a separate opinion on these matters.

A KAM section should be titled "Key Audit Matters" and include a definition of KAMs and a **statement that a separate opinion is not expressed** on them. A reference to the basis for opinion section is generally included in a KAM only when expressing a qualified opinion.

Although the subjects of KAMs must have been communicated to those charged with governance, that communication need not be described in the audit report. The fact that a KAM is included in an audit report only when the auditor has been engaged to include one is not stated in the KAM section.

Report on Other Legal and Regulatory Requirements

This section is required if the auditor has *other reporting responsibilities* in addition to those under GAAS. When this section is required, it should be:

- Titled appropriately, such as "Report on Other Legal and Regulatory Requirements"
- Segmented from the rest of the report by adding "Report on the Audit of the Financial Statements" as an overall heading to the main audit report

Emphasis-of-Matter and Other-Matter Paragraphs

 Representative Task (Remembering & Understanding): Identify the appropriate use of emphasis-of-matter and other-matter (explanatory) paragraphs.

 Representative Task (Application): Determine the appropriate form and content of an auditor's report for an engagement, including the appropriate use of emphasis-of-matter and other-matter (explanatory) paragraphs.

The AICPA auditing standard is AU-C 706, *Emphasis-of-Matter Paragraphs and Other-Matter Paragraphs in the Independent Auditor's Report*, which states that the **auditor's objective** is to draw the users' attention, as necessary, to:

- A matter, already appropriately presented/disclosed in the F/S, that is important to the users' *understanding of the F/S* (ie, **emphasis-of-matter paragraph**)
- Any other matter that is relevant to the users' *understanding of the audit*, the auditor's responsibilities, or the auditor's report (ie, **other-matter paragraph**)

Emphasis-of-Matter (EOM)

Matters that are of such importance that they are **fundamental to** the **users' understanding** of the F/S may warrant an additional EOM paragraph in the report. An EOM paragraph is appropriate when the client has **properly accounted for and disclosed** the item, but the auditor is concerned users might miss the information provided by the client.

An EOM paragraph should:

- Include a clear reference to the matter being emphasized and where the matter is addressed in the F/S
- Indicate that the auditor's opinion is not modified with respect to the matter
- Be included in a separate section of the report with an appropriate heading
  - Heading must include "Emphasis of Matter" if KAMs are also reported
  - Heading may be tailored to describe the nature of the matter (eg, "Emphasis of Matter—Litigation")
  - Placement of the section depends on the relative importance of the matters emphasized. When a KAM section is also presented, the emphasis of matter section should appear before or after the KAM section, as appropriate.

Emphasis of Matter

As discussed in Note X to the financial statements, subsequent to the date of the financial statements, there was a fire in ABC Company's production facilities. Our opinion is not modified with respect to this matter.

There are some circumstances in which the inclusion of such a paragraph is **mandatory:**

- A justified change in accounting principles affecting consistency
- F/S prepared in accordance with a special-purpose framework
- The auditor's opinion on revised F/S differs from the opinion previously expressed, although an other-matter paragraph may be used instead

In other situations, the auditor may choose to add an **optional** EOM paragraph:

- Substantial doubt about the entity's ability to continue as a going concern has been alleviated by management's plans
- Significant related-party transactions
- Material uncertainties (eg, an unresolved lawsuit)
- Important subsequent events
- A major catastrophe that had, or continues to have, a significant effect on the entity's F/S

 In which of the following should an auditor's report refer to the lack of consistency when there is a significant change in accounting principle that has been properly justified and disclosed?

- The auditor's responsibility section
- The opinion section
- An emphasis-of-matter paragraph
- The paragraph following the opinion section

Reporting on accounting changes		
	Appropriate report	**Example changes**
Justified change in estimate	• Standard unmodified opinion	• Useful life of an asset
		• Salvage value of an asset
Justified change in principle	• Unmodified opinion with emphasis-of-matter	• FICO to LIFO
		• Revenue recognition method

If the change in accounting principle (eg, from FIFO [first in, first out] to LIFO [last in, first out]) has a **material effect** on the comparability of the F/S from one period to the next, an auditor determines whether the change is **justified and properly disclosed**.

If the change is justified and properly disclosed, the auditor will issue an unmodified opinion with an emphasis-of-matter paragraph. The emphasis-of-matter paragraph will refer to the change (eg, the lack of consistency) and the note in the F/S discussing the change. If the change is not justified or is not properly disclosed, the auditor will issue a report with a qualified or adverse opinion.

Other Matter (OM)

An OM paragraph is used to communicate matters that are not otherwise reported or disclosed in the F/S, but are **relevant to users' understanding** of the audit, the auditor's responsibilities, or the auditor's report.

An OM paragraph should:

- Indicate that such matters are not required to be reported or disclosed

- Not include matters reported as KAMs
- Be reported in a separate section of the audit report with an appropriate heading, such as "Other Matter"
  - Heading may be tailored to describe the nature of the matter (eg, "Other Matter—Scope of the Audit")
  - Placement of the section depends on the relative importance of the matters presented
  - If the matter relates to other reporting responsibilities, it may be included in the Report on Other Legal and Regulatory Requirements section
  - If the matter relates to the entire audit report, it may be included in a separate section following the Report on Other Legal and Regulatory Requirements section

Certain circumstances require the auditor to include OM paragraph. Examples include when:

- The auditor's opinion on revised F/S differs from the opinion previously expressed, although an EOM paragraph may also be used
- The report of another auditor who reported on prior period F/S is not presented with comparative F/S
- The F/S are prepared in accordance with a **special-purpose framework** and are restricted to internal use
- The auditor is **reporting on compliance** with contractual agreements or regulatory requirements.

When F/S have been presented using certain **special-purpose frameworks**, an OM paragraph should be added to restrict the distribution of the auditor's report to specified parties when the F/S are based on:

- When the entity presents **supplementary information** with the F/S and the auditor does not issue a separate report on that supplementary information, the auditor should add an OM paragraph to address the supplementary information
- When auditing the F/S of an **employee benefit plan** subject to ERISA, the auditor should add an OM paragraph to address the supplemental schedules required by ERISA
- Prior periods presented in comparative F/S were reviewed or compiled, or they have not been audited, reviewed, or compiled

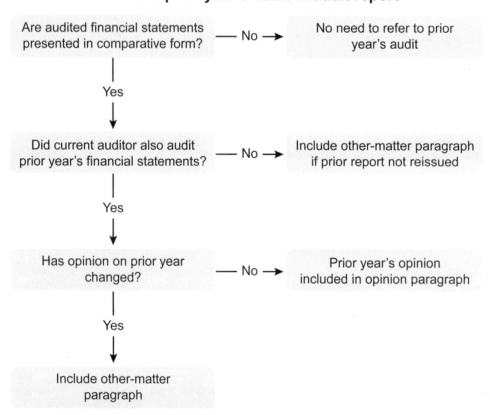

Reference to prior year's audit in audit report

An auditor has previously expressed a qualified opinion on the financial statements of a prior period because of a departure from generally accepted accounting principles. The prior-period financial statements are restated in the current period to conform with generally accepted accounting principles. The auditor's updated report on the prior-period financial statements should

- Express an unmodified opinion
- Be accompanied by the original auditor's report on the prior period
- Have the same date as the original auditor's report on the prior period
- Qualify the opinion concerning the restated financial statements because of a change in accounting principle

The auditor should indicate that the statements have been restated, and the auditor should **express an unmodified opinion** with respect to the restated financial statements. An other-matter paragraph is added to the report and should disclose (1) the date of the auditor's previous report, (2) the type of opinion previously expressed, (3) the circumstances or events that caused the auditor to express a different opinion, and (4) that the updated opinion differs from the previous opinion.

Example of an Other-Matter Paragraph:

Other Matter

In our report dated March 1, Year 2, we expressed an opinion that the Year 1 financial statements did not fairly present the financial position, results of operations, and cash flows of ABC Company in accordance with accounting principles generally accepted in the United States of America because of two departures from such principles: (1) ABC Company carried its property, plant, and equipment at appraisal values and provided for depreciation on the basis of such values, and (2) ABC Company did not provide for deferred income taxes with respect to differences between income for financial reporting purposes and taxable income. As described in Note X, the Company has changed its method of accounting for these items and restated its Year 1 financial statements to conform with accounting principles generally accepted in the United States of America. Accordingly, our present opinion on the restated Year 1 financial statements, as presented herein, is different from that expressed in our previous report.

Modified Audit Reports

As previously mentioned, there are four types of opinions under GAAS (AICPA) for nonissuers: one of them is the standard unmodified opinion discussed above, and the other three are modified opinions—**qualified, adverse, and disclaimer**—which **depend on the nature and severity** of the matters encountered during the audit.

Modified opinions	Will be expressed if ...	Key report language
Qualified opinion	F/S are fairly presented, except for...	"... except for..., the [F/S] present fairly...."
Adverse opinion	F/S are materially misstated	"... [F/S] do not present fairly..."
Disclaimer of opinion	Sufficient appropriate audit evidence could not be obtained to conclude that F/S are fairly presented	"We do not express an opinion..."

Nature of Matters

The nature of matters encountered during the audit fall into **two categories**:

- **Misstatements**—A misstatement is a difference between the reported amount, classification, presentation, or disclosure of a F/S item and the amount, classification, presentation, or disclosure that is required under the AFRF
- Such misstatements may be a result of one of the following **departures** from the AFRF:
  - Inappropriate selection of accounting policies
  - Improper application of accounting policies (eg, consistency, errors)
  - Inappropriate/inadequate F/S presentation or disclosure
- **Possible Misstatements**—The auditor was unable to obtain sufficient appropriate audit evidence to confirm the lack of misstatements. Thus, there may be undetected misstatements because the auditor's scope was limited, or in the case of uncertainties, the information was just unavailable

Severity of Matters

The severity of matters hinges on the materiality and pervasiveness of the effects of the matters on the F/S.

- **Materiality**, as previously discussed, is a matter of **professional judgment** as to whether misstatements and omissions, individually or taken together, are likely to influence the judgment of a reasonable F/S user
- **Pervasiveness** relates to the **extent of the effects** of a matter on the F/S. A matter is pervasive if the effects are:
  - Not confined to a specific element, account, or item of the F/S,
  - Could represent a substantial portion of the F/S, or
  - Relate to disclosures that are fundamental to the users' understanding of the F/S.

Modifying the Report

The following chart shows how the opinion must be modified considering the nature, materiality, and pervasiveness of the matters encountered in the audit.

Nature of matters	Severity of effects or possible effects on F/S		
	Immaterial	Material but not pervasive	Material and pervasive
Misstated F/S (Not AFRF/GAAP) • Inappropriate accounting policies selected • Improper application of accounting policies (eg, inconsistency, errors), or • Inadequate presentation/ disclosure	Unmodified	Qualified	Adverse
Scope limitation/uncertainties (Possible misstatements) Unable to obtain sufficient appropriate audit evidence		Qualified	Disclaimer*

When a scope limitation is management-imposed, the auditor may decide to withdraw from the audit instead, if allowable by law.

Qualified Opinion

The auditor must issue a qualified opinion when the nature of the matter is considered **material but not pervasive**. That is, a qualified opinion is required when either:

- **Known misstatements**, individually or in the aggregate, are material but not pervasive; or

- **Scope limitation**, due to possible undetected misstatements that could be material but not pervasive.

The same basic elements are required in an auditor's report expressing a qualified opinion as in an unmodified report; however, the headings and content of the opinion and basis for opinion sections will be modified as appropriate (see example report that follows).

- The opinion must include one of the following phrases depending on the nature of the matters:
  - **Material Misstatements:** "...except for the effects of the matter[s] described..." or
  - **Scope Limitation:** "...except for the possible effects of the matter[s] described..."

Reporting when evidence is unavailable (scope limitation)

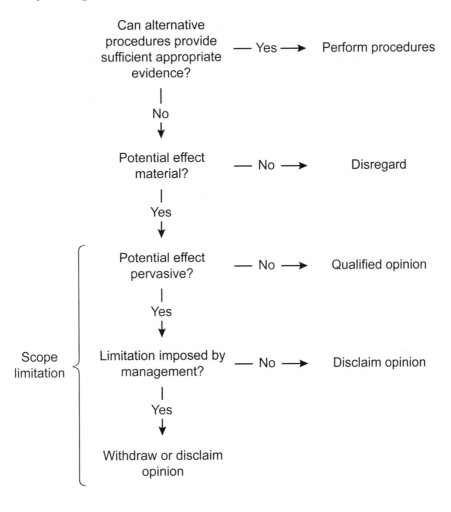

- The basis for qualified opinion section should:
  - Describe and quantify (or state that it is not practicable to quantify) the financial effects of any material misstatements on the F/S
  - Explain how any qualitative disclosures are misstated
  - Describe the nature of any omissions and include the information if it is reasonably obtainable (ie, the auditor should not be preparing the information)

○ Describe the scope limitation if the report is modified due to the inability to obtain sufficient appropriate audit evidence

○ State whether the audit evidence obtained is sufficient and appropriate to provide a basis for the opinion (appropriately modified for the type of opinion)

 A scope limitation sufficient to preclude an unmodified opinion always will result when management:

- Prevents the auditor from reviewing the working papers of the predecessor auditor

- Engages the auditor after the year end physical inventory is completed

- Requests that certain material accounts receivable not be confirmed

- Refuses to acknowledge its responsibility for the fair presentation of the financial statements in conformity with GAAP

Audit opinions, example situations	
Unmodified	• No scope limitation • Fairly stated
Qualified	• Scope limitation: Unable to confirm a material receivable • GAAP departure: A receivable is materially misstated
Adverse	• GAAP departure: Several material misstatements across accounts
Disclaimer	• Scope limitation: Management refuses to sign representation letter

Management acknowledges responsibility for the financial statements twice: before the audit begins (in the engagement letter) and at the end of the audit (in the management representation letter). **Management's acknowledgment is a key piece of audit evidence, the lack of which precludes an unmodified opinion.** This is because auditors are unable to judge solely on the basis of other evidence that management has fulfilled its responsibility for fair presentation of financial statements. When management is unwilling to acknowledge responsibility in the representation letter, **the auditor should disclaim an opinion or withdraw from the engagement.** This is because refusal to provide such acknowledgment constitutes a scope limitation that affects the financial statements as a whole and is therefore pervasive.

 An auditor's examination reveals a misstatement in segment information that is material in relation to the financial statements taken as a whole. If the client refuses to make modifications to the presentation of segment information, the auditor should issue a(n)

- Disclaimer of opinion

- Qualified opinion

- Unmodified opinion with an emphasis-of-matter paragraph

- Standard unmodified opinion

A misstatement in segment information would **not be considered pervasive** (ie, a segment generally does not represent a substantial proportion of the F/S); therefore, a **qualified opinion** (not an adverse opinion) would be most appropriate.

Adverse Opinion

An adverse opinion is required to be issued when **known misstatements**, individually or in the aggregate, are both **material and pervasive**.

The same basic elements are required in an auditor's report expressing an adverse opinion as in an unmodified report; however, the headings and content of the opinion and basis for opinion sections will be modified as appropriate (see example report that follows).

- The **opinion** must include the following language: "... *because of the significance of the matter[s] described* ... the accompanying financial statements *do not present fairly* ... in accordance with [GAAP]"

- The content requirements for the **basis for adverse opinion** section are the same as for a qualified opinion

- An audit report with an adverse opinion should not include a KAM section. A KAM section in an adverse report would distract the reader from the fact that the F/S are materially misstated

Disclaimer of Opinion

A disclaimer of opinion is required to be issued when either:

- There is a **scope limitation*** or **uncertainty** of such **magnitude** (ie, likely multiple uncertainties) that could result in undetected misstatements that are both material and pervasive; or

- The **auditor is not independent**, but is required by law/regulation to report on the F/S.

Note that it would be preferable to withdraw from an engagement when a scope limitation is imposed by management. However, it becomes more impractical to do so as the audit progresses. Thus, if the audit is nearly complete when the limitation is imposed, the auditor is more likely to issue a disclaimer of opinion.

 If a client will not permit inquiry of outside legal counsel, the auditor's report ordinarily will contain a (an):

- Adverse opinion
- Disclaimer of opinion
- Unmodified opinion with a separate explanatory paragraph
- Qualified opinion

In this scenario, the auditor cannot determine whether inquiries of the client's legal counsel would reveal ongoing legal actions that require the entity to accrue a liability with a material and pervasive effect on the F/S. Because the **scope limitation** imposed by management prevents the auditors from obtaining sufficient appropriate evidence and the potential effects are pervasive, they must either **withdraw or disclaim** an opinion.

Note that if the possible effects of a scope limitation are **material but not pervasive**, a **qualified opinion** is appropriate. If the possible effects are **material and pervasive**, auditors usually issue a **disclaimer of opinion** because the lack of such critical evidence makes it impossible to justify an opinion on the F/S as a whole.

The same basic elements are required in an auditor's report expressing a disclaimer of opinion as in an unmodified report; however, the headings and content of the opinion and basis for sections will be modified as appropriate.

- The **disclaimer of opinion** section must say:
  - "We do not express an opinion...", and
  - "Because of the significance of the matter[s] described ..., we have not been able to obtain sufficient appropriate audit evidence to provide a basis for an audit opinion on the [F/S]"
  - "We were engaged to audit the [F/S]..." instead of "We have audited the [F/S]..."

- The **basis for disclaimer** of opinion section should:
  - Not refer to the auditor's responsibilities section of the report (like the other reports do)
  - Not state that the audit evidence obtained is sufficient and appropriate (because the opposite is true)

    ○ Describe any known matters and their effects that would have required modification of the report

- The **auditor's responsibilities** section must be reduced to include only statements regarding:

    ○ The auditor's responsibility to conduct an audit in accordance with GAAS and to issue a report

    ○ The auditor's inability to obtain sufficient appropriate audit evidence due to the matters described in the Basis for Disclaimer of Opinion section

    ○ The auditor's requirement to be independent and to meet other ethical responsibilities

- An audit report with a Disclaimer of Opinion *should not include*:

    ○ A KAM section, as it would mislead the reader into thinking the F/S are more credible than they are with respect to KAMs discussed

    ○ An Other Information section regarding information included in an annual report other than the audited F/S and the auditor's report.

Evaluating Consistency

The relevant AICPA guidance is provided by AU-C 708, *Consistency of Financial Statements*. The standard states that the auditor's objectives are to (1) **evaluate the consistency** of the F/S for the periods presented and (2) **communicate** appropriately in the auditor's report when comparability has been materially affected (a) by a change in accounting principle or (b) by adjustments to correct a material misstatement in previously issued financial statements.

The auditor should evaluate whether the **comparability** between periods has been affected by either a material change in accounting principle or a material restatement of F/S. For a **change in accounting principle**, the auditor should evaluate whether the:

- Adopted principle is in accordance with the AFRF
- Method of accounting for the effect of the change is in accordance with the AFRF
- Disclosures about the change are adequate
- Entity has justified that the alternative adopted is *preferable*

When those four criteria are met, and the **change has a material effect** on the F/S, the auditor should include an *emphasis-of-matter* (EOM) paragraph in the auditor's report to describe the change and reference the footnote disclosure applicable to the change. The auditor should state that the auditor's opinion is not modified regarding the matter.

- Include the EOM paragraph in subsequent periods until the new principle is applied in all periods presented
- If the change is accounted for by *retrospective application* to the F/S, the EOM paragraph is only needed in the period of the change

If the criteria have not all been met, and the change has a material effect on the F/S, the auditor should evaluate whether the change results in a **material misstatement** and consider whether the auditor's report should be modified.

When a **change in the reporting entity** results in F/S that are essentially those of a different reporting entity, the auditor should include an EOM paragraph in the auditor's report describing the change in the entity and referencing the entity's disclosure. However, that is unnecessary when the change in entity results from a transaction or event, such as the purchase or disposition of a subsidiary.

When the **F/S are restated** to correct a **prior material misstatement**, the auditor should include an EOM paragraph in the auditor's report. (That paragraph need not be included in subsequent periods.) The auditor should state that the auditor's opinion is not modified regarding the matter.

- If the F/S disclosures relating to the restatement are not adequate, the auditor should evaluate the inadequacy of disclosure and consider whether the auditor's report should be modified

- A change from an accounting principle that is not in accordance with the AFRF to one that is in accordance is a **correction of a misstatement**

The auditor need not refer to consistency in the auditor's report unless there is an inconsistency due to a material change in accounting principle or restatement.

 Which of the following will result in an emphasis-of-matter paragraph as to consistency in the auditor's report, when the item is fully disclosed in the financial statements?

- A change in accounting estimate
- A change from an unacceptable accounting principle to a generally accepted one
- Changing the life of an asset from 8 to 5 years
- A change in classification.

A **change from an unacceptable accounting principle to an acceptable one** results in a consistency modification with the addition of an emphasis-of-matter paragraph. The remaining items do not require a consistency modification.

Sample emphasis-of-matter paragraph for a voluntary change in principle:

Emphasis of Matter

As discussed in Note X to the financial statements, the entity has elected to change its method of accounting for (*describe accounting method change*) in (*insert year(s) of financial statements that reflect the accounting method change*). Our opinion is not modified with respect to this matter.

Sample emphasis-of-matter paragraph for a restatement:

Emphasis of Matter

As discussed in Note X to the financial statements, the 20X2 financial statements have been restated to correct a misstatement. Our opinion is not modified with respect to this matter.

Piecemeal Opinions

A piecemeal opinion is the **inappropriate expression** of an **unmodified opinion** on a single financial statement or specific parts of a F/S in the same report as an adverse or disclaimer of opinion on the *F/S as a whole*.

Such piecemeal opinions result in a **contradictory effect**. While this type of combination of opinions is not allowed with respect to the same AFRF, the auditor can:

- In an initial audit, express an unmodified opinion regarding the financial position (B/S) and a disclaimer of opinion regarding the results of operations (I/S) and cash flows (eg, a scope limitation may prevent the auditor from obtaining sufficient appropriate audit evidence regarding an item that affects the I/S and cash flows but does not affect the B/S). The difference here is that the auditor is not disclaiming an opinion on the *F/S as a whole*
- Express an unmodified opinion on F/S prepared under one AFRF and express an adverse opinion on the same F/S under a different AFRF within the same report

Issuer (PCAOB) Audit Reports—Unqualified

Basic guidance as to the PCAOB's audit reporting model is provided in auditing standards: AS 3101, *The Auditor's Report on an Audit of Financial Statements When the Auditor Expresses an Unqualified Opinion.* Other PCAOB standards apply when an unqualified opinion cannot be expressed: AS 3105, *Departures from Unqualified Opinions and Other Reporting Circumstances.*

Audit reports prepared for a company that reports to the SEC (ie, **public companies/issuers**) are subject to the requirements of the Public Company Accounting Oversight Board (PCAOB); thus, such reports must be prepared differently under AS 3101 and 3105.

PCAOB audit guidelines

- Apply to issuers
- Require integrated audits
- Auditor must:
  - Obtain reasonable assurance that no material weaknesses exits in internal control over financial reporting (ICFR)
  - Express opinion about management's assessment of ICFR
  - Express opinion about fairness of the financial statements

For example, a "clean," unmodified report under the PCAOB standards is instead called an **"unqualified report,"** and the basis for the opinion must refer to "the standards of the Public Company Accounting Oversight Board (United States)," instead of "generally accepted auditing standards."

Unqualified Audit Report

The auditor's unmodified report (called an unqualified report for issuers) typically consists of the following sections along with a signature block:

Order of sections in audit report for issuers

- Opinion on the financial statements
- Basis for opinion
- Critical audit matters (if applicable placement/title is flexible
- Explanatory paragraph (if applicable and placement/title is flexible)

Critical Audit Matters (CAMs)

CAMs are any matter arising from the audit of the F/S that was communicated or required to be communicated to the audit committee and that relates to accounts or disclosures that are *material* to the F/S and involve especially **challenging, subjective, or complex auditor judgment**.

The PCAOB requires the following matters to be communicated to a company's audit committee:

- Significant risks the auditor identified;
- Relevant matters regarding the company's accounting policies and estimates;
- Significant unusual transactions;

- Matters regarding the auditor's evaluation of any related parties and transactions with those related parties; *and*
- Other matters identified that are significant to the oversight of the company's financial reporting process.

For each current-year identified CAM, the auditor's report should communicate the following:

- The identification of the specific CAM;
- A description of the considerations that caused the auditor to identify the matter as a CAM;
- A description of how the CAM was addressed in the audit; *and*
- Reference to the related financial statement accounts or disclosures.

Communication of CAMs in reports *not containing unqualified* opinions:

- **Qualified opinion**—Such a report should also include communication of CAMs, if applicable
- **Adverse opinion**—Such a report should not include any communication of CAMs, since the reason for the adverse opinion is most important
- **Disclaimer of opinion**—Such a report should not include any communication of CAMs, since the reason for the disclaimer is most important

When is a matter a critical audit matter? (CAM)

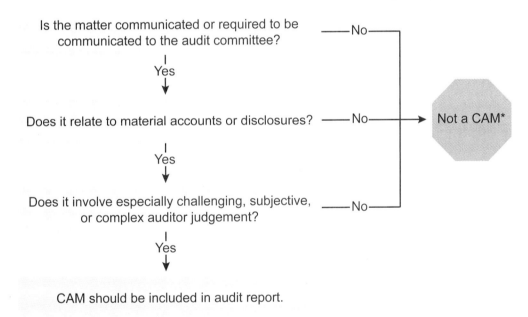

The CAM section will always be included in the report when a qualified or unqualified opinion is issued.

Explanatory Language

In addition to these basic elements and a CAM paragraph, an unqualified report may also **require explanatory language** in certain circumstances, when:

- There is substantial doubt about the company's ability to continue as a **going concern**
- The auditor **refers to the report of other auditors** as the basis, in part, for their own report
- There is a **change between periods in accounting principles** or in the method of application that has a material effect on the F/S
- There has been a **change in a reporting entity**

- A material misstatement in previously issued F/S has been corrected

- The auditor performs an **integrated audit** and issues separate reports on the company's F/S and internal control over financial reporting

- **Supplementary information** required by the AFRF has been omitted; the presentation of such info departs materially from the AFRF requirements; the auditor is unable to complete prescribed procedures with respect to such information; or the auditor is unable to remove substantial doubts about whether the supplementary information conforms to the requirements of the AFRF

- **Other information** in a document containing audited F/S is materially inconsistent with information appearing in the F/S

The auditor may also decide to **emphasize certain matters** even though they are **not required**, such as:

- Significant transactions (eg, related party transactions)

- Important subsequent events

- Accounting matters, other than changes in accounting principle, affecting the comparability of the F/S with those of the preceding period

- Uncertainties (eg, regarding significant litigation or regulatory actions)

- The entity's status as a component of a larger business enterprise

 A financial statement audit report issued for the audit of an issuer (public) company concludes that the financial statements follow:

- Public Company Accounting Oversight Board standards

- Generally accepted accounting principles

- International accounting standards

- Generally accepted auditing standards

While the audit is *performed* in accordance with PCAOB standards, the financial statements follow generally accepted accounting principles.

Issuer Audit Reports—Modified

Qualified Opinion

The same basic elements are required in an auditor's report expressing a qualified opinion as in an auditor's report expressing an unqualified opinion, including the communication of CAMs. The auditor should consider whether matters for which the auditor qualified the opinion are also CAMs.

- The opinion paragraph must include the words "except" or "exception" in phrases such as "except for" or "with the exception of"

- One or more paragraphs immediately following (after) the opinion paragraph should disclose all of the substantive reasons for the qualified opinion

- Where a qualified opinion results from a **scope limitation** or **insufficient evidence**, the auditor's report should describe the basis for departure from an unqualified opinion in a separate paragraph immediately following the opinion paragraph and refer to that description in both the Basis for Opinion section and Opinion on the Financial Statements section of the report

Adverse Opinion

When the auditor expresses an adverse opinion, the report must include the same basic elements as a report for an unqualified opinion, modified appropriately. However, a report containing an adverse opinion **does not include the CAM paragraph** as readers are more interested in knowing why an adverse opinion is expressed.

The auditor's report must describe in a separate paragraph(s) all the substantive reasons for the adverse opinion and the principal effects of the subject matter of the adverse opinion on financial position, results of operations, and cash flows, if practicable.

- If the effects are not reasonably determinable, the report should say so
- If the effects are disclosed in a note to the F/S, the explanatory paragraph should refer to the applicable note

Disclaimer of Opinion

When an auditor has not been able to perform sufficient procedures to form an opinion, the auditor must disclaim an opinion. In this case, the report must include the same basic elements of the unqualified option, modified as follows.

- The first section will be titled "Disclaimer of Opinion on the Financial Statements" and it will contain:
  - The name of the company whose F/S the auditor was engaged to audit
  - Identification of each financial statement and any related schedules that the auditor was engaged to audit
  - Statements that "we were engaged to audit," rather than "we have audited"
- The second section will be titled "Basis for Disclaimer of Opinion"
- The CAM section should be omitted. CAM requirements do not apply to disclaimers of opinions

Evaluating Consistency

When reporting on two or more periods, the auditor should **evaluate the consistency** between those periods and with the prior period, if that prior period is presented along with the F/S reported on. Note that the auditing requirements under PCAOB auditing standards are *substantially the same* as those of the AICPA's Auditing Standards.

There are **two types of issues** related to consistency that might affect the auditor's report:

- A change in accounting principle
- An adjustment to correct a misstatement in previously issued financial statements (ie, *restatements*)

Changes in accounting principle involve a change from one generally accepted accounting principle to another, including the situation where the accounting principle formerly used is no longer generally accepted.

- The PCAOB auditing standards point out that, when a company uses *retrospective application* to account for a change in accounting principle, the F/S generally will be viewed as consistent. (However, the previous years' financial statements will appear different from those that the auditor previously reported on)
- The auditor should evaluate whether (1) the newly adopted principle is GAAP; (2) the method of accounting for the effect of the change conforms to GAAP; (3) the disclosures related to the change are adequate; and (4) the company has justified that the alternative accounting principle is preferable
  - If the four criteria have been met, the auditor should add an explanatory paragraph to the auditor's report to identify the inconsistency
  - If the four criteria have not been met, the auditor should treat the matter as a GAAP departure and modify the audit report appropriately
  - When an investor uses the equity method and the investee has a change in accounting principle that is material to the investor's financial statements, the auditor should add an explanatory paragraph to emphasize the matter

- When there is a **change in accounting estimate effected by a change in accounting principle**, the auditor should evaluate and report on the matter like other change in accounting principle

- When there is a **change in the reporting entity** resulting from a transaction or event, such as the purchase or disposition of a subsidiary, it does not require recognition in the auditor's report. (However, if there is a change in the reporting entity that does not result from such a transaction or event, then an explanatory paragraph would be required)

Correction of a material misstatement in previously issued F/S should be recognized in the auditor's report by the addition of an explanatory paragraph.

- Restatements of previously issued F/S require related disclosures. The auditor should evaluate the adequacy of the company's disclosures

Changes in classification in previously issued F/S normally do not require recognition in the auditor's report (unless the change represents a change in accounting principle or the correction of a material misstatement).

- Accordingly, the auditor should evaluate a material change in F/S classification (and the related disclosure) to determine whether such a change is also a change in accounting principle or a correction of a material misstatement

Departure from a Generally Accepted Accounting Principle

The auditor should express a **qualified or adverse opinion** for a **departure from GAAP**. For a qualified opinion, the report should describe the **basis for departure** from an unqualified opinion in a separate paragraph **immediately following the opinion** paragraph and refer to that description in the Basis for Opinion section of the report.

Such a paragraph should also disclose the effects of the departure on the financial position, results of operations, and cash flows, if practicable. If not reasonably determinable, the report should say so. If disclosed in a note to the financial statements, the explanatory paragraph should refer to the applicable note.

Reference to the Use of a Specialist

An audit report may refer to the use of a specialist if such a reference will facilitate an understanding of a CAM, the reason for explanatory language, or a departure from an unqualified opinion. Otherwise, no reference should be made to the work of a specialist in the auditor's report.

Auditing Supplemental Information

Current PCAOB standards apply to supplemental information, whether it is required by regulatory authorities or provided voluntarily, when audited in connection with F/S audited under PCAOB auditing standards.

The auditor's objective is to obtain sufficient appropriate audit evidence to express an opinion on whether the supplemental information is fairly stated, in all material respects, in relation to the F/S as a whole.

The **auditor is required** to:

- Perform audit procedures specifically to test the supplemental information

- Evaluate (a) whether the supplemental information is fairly presented in relation to the audited financial statements and (b) whether the supplemental information complies with the relevant regulatory requirements (or other criteria, if applicable)

- Coordinate audit work on the supplemental information with audit work on the related financial statements

- Clearly report the auditor's responsibilities and conclusions when reporting on supplemental information

The **nature, timing, and extent** of the procedures to be applied to the supplemental information may vary with the circumstances, including the following: (1) the risk of material misstatement; (2) the applicable materiality levels relevant to the information; (3) the audit evidence obtained with respect to the financial statements; and (4) the type of opinion expressed on the financial statements.

In **performing procedures** on the supplemental information, the auditor should:

- Obtain an understanding of the purpose of the information and the criteria used by management for its presentation;

- Obtain an understanding of the methods used to prepare the information, evaluate the appropriateness of those methods, and determine whether those methods are consistent with those used in the prior period;

- Inquire of management about any significant assumptions underlying the presentation of the information;

- Determine that the information reconciles to the financial statements or other applicable records;

- Perform procedures to test the completeness and accuracy of the information (if not already tested in connection with the audit of the financial statements);

- Evaluate whether the information complies with relevant regulatory requirements (or other applicable criteria); *and*

- Obtain appropriate management representations: (a) that management acknowledges responsibility for the fair presentation of the information; (b) that management believes the information is fairly stated; (c) that the methods used have not changed from the prior period (if changed, state that the reasons for the changes are appropriate); (d) that the information complies with regulatory requirements or other applicable criteria; and (e) that management believes any underlying assumptions are appropriate.

As part of the auditor's evaluation of audit results, the auditor should:

- Evaluate whether the information is fairly stated in relation to the F/S, including whether the information is presented in conformity with regulatory requirements or other applicable criteria

- Communicate accumulated misstatements to management to give management a chance to make corrections

- Evaluate whether uncorrected misstatements are material (based on relevant quantitative and qualitative factors)

Reporting on supplemental information requires the following:

- Unless prohibited by regulatory requirements, the auditor may either issue a separate report on the supplemental information and the F/S or issue a combined report on both

- The auditor should evaluate whether any modification of the report on the F/S is relevant to the opinion to be expressed on the supplemental information

- The auditor should express a qualified opinion on the supplemental information if the basis for the overall audit report qualification also applies to the supplemental information

- The auditor should likewise express an adverse opinion (or disclaimer) on the supplemental information

Situation	Opinion	Basis for opinion	CAM*	Additional paragraph
Material departure	Qualified	Adequate basis for qualified opinion	Standard	Immediately after opinion paragraph
	Adverse	Adequate basis for adverse opinion	None	Immediately after opinion paragraph
Justified departure	Unqualified	Standard	Standard	Emphasis of matter— after CAM
Inconsistent— properly reported & justifiable (concur)	Unqualified	Standard	Standard	Emphasis of matter— after CAM

Situation	Opinion	Basis for opinion	CAM*	Additional paragraph
Inconsistent—not properly rep or not justifiable	Qualified	Adequate basis for qualified opinion	Standard	Immediately after opinion paragraph
	Adverse	Adequate basis for adverse opinion	None	Immediately after opinion paragraph
Inadequate disclosure (omitted disclosure)	Qualified	Adequate basis for qualified opinion	Standard	Immediately after opinion paragraph
	Adverse	Adequate basis for adverse opinion	None	Immediately after opinion paragraph
No statement of cash flows	Qualified	Adequate basis for qualified opinion	Standard	Immediately after opinion paragraph
	Adverse	Adequate basis for adverse opinion	None	Immediately after opinion paragraph
Other audit participants	Unqualified	Standard	Standard	Not required, location unspecified
Contingent liability	Unqualified	Standard	Standard	Emphasis of matter— after CAM Not required
Going concern doubts	Unqualified	Standard	Standard	Emphasis of matter— after CAM
Scope limit— Material but not pervasive	Qualified	Standard	Standard	Immediately after opinion paragraph
Scope limit— material and pervasive	Disclaimer	Inability to obtain evidence	None	Immediately after disclaimer paragraph
Scope limit— imposed by management	Disclaimer	Inability to obtain evidence	None	Immediately after disclaimer paragraph
Balance sheet only	Amended	Amended	Standard	Emphasis of matter— after CAM Not required

*Note, as applied in this chart, "Standard" does not differentiate between a CAM paragraph that states there are no CAMs and a CAM paragraph that lists CAMs; that is, they are both considered "Standard."

Internal Controls Audit—GAAS

 Representative Task (Remembering & Understanding): Identify the factors that an auditor should consider when forming an opinion on the effectiveness of internal control in an audit of internal control over financial reporting that is integrated with an audit of financial statements.

 Representative Task (Application): Determine the appropriate form and content of a report on the audit of internal control over financial reporting, including report modifications and the use of separate or combined reports for the audit of an entity's financial statements and the audit of internal control.

Guidance, Applicability, and Objectives

AICPA guidance is provided by **Statement on Auditing Standards (SAS) No. 130**, *An Audit of Internal Control Over Financial Reporting That Is Integrated with an Audit of Financial Statements* (AU-C 940).

AICPA guidance applies when an auditor is engaged to audit the internal control over financial reporting (ICFR) along with an audit of a **nonissuer's** F/S, known as an **integrated audit**. (Note: The AICPA guidance is closely aligned with the corresponding PCAOB Auditing Standards applicable to an integrated audit of an issuer.)

There are two objectives:

- To obtain reasonable assurance whether material weaknesses exist at the "as of" date in management's assessment of ICFR
- To express an opinion on the effectiveness of ICFR and communicate appropriately with management and those charged with governance

Concepts

If any (one or more) **material weaknesses** exist, then the entity's internal control cannot be considered effective. The auditor should plan and perform the audit of ICFR to obtain sufficient appropriate evidence to provide reasonable assurance whether material weaknesses exist as of the date specified by management's report.

The auditor is not required to search for deficiencies that are less severe than a material weakness (such as significant deficiencies or other lesser matters). The auditor should use the same suitable and available control criteria to perform the audit of ICFR that management uses for its assessment of the effectiveness of ICFR.

Internal control deficiency: **Design or operation of a control does not prevent or detect financial misstatements**

Material weaknesses	• Reasonable possibility of material financial misstatement
	• Indicators:
	   ○ Ineffective governance
	   ○ Prior year financial restatements due to error or fraud
	   ○ Material misstatements not detected by controls
	   ○ Fraud by senior management, material or immaterial

Internal control deficiency:

Design or operation of a control does not prevent or detect financial misstatements

Significant deficiency	• Less severe than material weakness • Merits attention by those charged with governance

Preconditions

Management must:

- Accept responsibility for the effectiveness of ICFR

- Provide the auditor with an assessment of ICFR using suitable and available criteria (eg, COSO's (Committee of Sponsoring Organizations of the Treadway Commission's) Internal Control-Integrated Framework)

- Support its assessment of ICFR with sufficient documentation

- Provide its written assessment about the effectiveness of ICFR in a report that accompanies the auditor's report. If management refuses to furnish a written assessment, the auditor should withdraw from the audit of ICFR

The auditor should plan and perform the integrated audit to achieve the objectives of both the F/S engagement and the ICFR engagement simultaneously—that is, design the tests of control to obtain sufficient appropriate evidence to support the auditor's:

- Opinion on ICFR at the "as of" date in management's report

- Control risk assessments for purposes of the audit of the F/S

Planning the ICFR Audit

In planning an ICFR audit, the auditor should use the same **materiality thresholds and risk assessment process** to focus attention on the areas of highest risk in the audit of ICFR and as those used for the entity's F/S.

Materiality is an amount that if omitted or misstated can affect decisions (eg, invest in a company, allow a company to borrow money) based on financial statements. Auditors must use professional judgment to determine what amount would affect such decisions if it were missing or omitted from financial information.

In an integrated audit, the auditor expresses opinions on both the fairness of the financial statements and the effectiveness of the internal control over financial reporting (ICFR). During the planning process, the auditor determines what amount of error (ie, measure of materiality) can occur without negatively affecting decisions based on the financial statements or the audit report. The **measure of materiality** must be the **same** for **tests** of both the **financial statements** and the **effectiveness of ICFR.**

Materiality determined by auditor

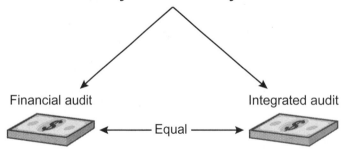

The auditor should also:

- Evaluate whether the entity's controls adequately address the risks of material misstatement (RMM) due to **fraud** as well as the risk of **management override** of controls

- Assess the RMM associated with the **various locations/business units** and correlate the amount of work with the degree of risk

- Assess the competence and objectivity of internal auditors when planning to use them either (1) to obtain audit evidence or (2) to provide direct assistance in the audit of ICFR. The need for the auditor to perform the work increases as the risk associated with a control increases

- Use a **top-down approach** by:
  - Beginning at the F/S level
  - Using the auditor's understanding of the overall risks to internal control
  - Focusing on "entity-level controls" (eg, the control environment, the entity's risk assessment process, monitoring controls, etc.)
  - Focusing on significant classes of transactions, accounts, disclosures, and relevant assertions that have a reasonable possibility of material misstatement to the F/S
  - Verifying the auditor's understanding of the risks in the entity's processes (includes performing walk-throughs)
  - Selecting controls for testing based on the assessed RMM to each relevant assertion

The size and complexity of the entity, its business processes, and the business units may affect the way in which the entity achieves its control objectives. Less control testing may be needed for smaller, less complex entities.

Top-down approach to evaluating internal controls over financial reporting (ICFR)

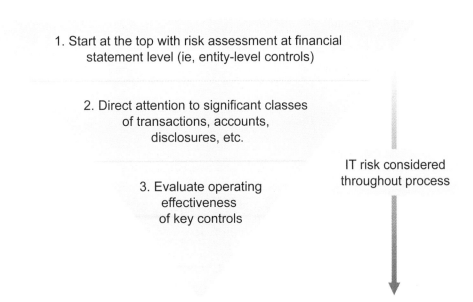

1. Start at the top with risk assessment at financial statement level (ie, entity-level controls)

2. Direct attention to significant classes of transactions, accounts, disclosures, etc.

3. Evaluate operating effectiveness of key controls

IT risk considered throughout process

The **evidence** that should be obtained through testing controls and evaluating identified deficiencies *increases* with the amount of overall identified risk. Remember, the objective is to express an opinion on ICFR overall, not on the effectiveness of individual controls.

To achieve this objective, the auditor will evaluate both the design and operating effectiveness of internal control.

- To evaluate **design effectiveness**, the procedures should include a mix of inquiry, observation of the entity's operations, and inspection of relevant documentation. A walk-through is usually sufficient to evaluate design effectiveness

- To test **operating effectiveness**, the procedures should include a mix of inquiry, observation of the entity's operations, inspection of relevant documentation, recalculation, and reperformance of the control. (Note that these procedures are presented in order of *increasing persuasiveness* of the resulting evidence.) Inquiry alone is insufficient for evaluating the operating effectiveness of controls

Selecting controls to test at a component in an integrated audit

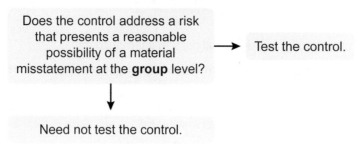

The **severity of a deficiency** depends on the magnitude of the potential misstatement and the degree of likelihood (whether there is a "reasonable possibility") of a failure; it does not require that an actual misstatement occur.

- **Risk factors** affecting whether a misstatement may occur include the:
  - Size and composition of the account
  - Susceptibility to misstatement
  - Volume of activity and complexity
  - Nature of the account, transactions, or disclosure
  - Accounting and reporting complexities associated with the account, transactions, or disclosures
  - Exposure to losses in the account
  - Possibility of significant contingent liabilities
  - Existence of related party transactions
  - Changes from the prior period

- **Multiple deficiencies** may cause a material weakness even though the deficiencies individually may be less severe

- **Compensating controls** may mitigate the severity of a deficiency, although they do not eliminate the deficiency entirely

- **Indicators of material weaknesses** include:
  - Discovery of any fraud involving senior management, whether material or not
  - Restatement of previously issued financial statements to correct a material misstatement
  - Identification of any material misstatement during the audit that was not detected by internal control
  - Ineffective oversight of reporting and controls by those charged with governance

Concluding Procedures

The auditor should:

- **Review the reports of others** (such as internal auditors) during the period that address internal control issues

- **Obtain written representations** from management specific to the audit of ICFR; management's failure to provide these representations is a scope limitation

- **Communicate** certain internal control matters identified during the integrated audit

  - **Material weaknesses and significant deficiencies** should be communicated in writing to those charged with governance and management by the report release date. For governmental entities only, the written communication must occur within 60 days of the report release date

  - **Lesser deficiencies** should be communicated in writing to management within 60 days of the report release date. The auditor should also inform those charged with governance of that communication

Reporting

The auditor's *separate* written report on ICFR should include the following elements:

- A title that includes the word "independent"

- An appropriate addressee

- **Opinion on ICFR** section that (a) identifies the entity involved; (b) states that ICFR has been audited; (c) identifies the applicable measurement criteria (eg, COSO); (d) expresses an opinion on ICFR; and (e) includes a paragraph that cross-references the auditor's report on the entity's F/S

- **Basis for Opinion** section that (a) references GAAS; (b) refers to the requirement to be independent and meet other ethical responsibilities; and (c) expresses the belief that sufficient appropriate audit evidence was obtained

Standard unqualified audit report on issuer's I/C over financial reporting

Report of Independent Registered Public Accounting Firm

To: Shareholders and the board of directors

Opinion on internal control over financial reporting

Basis for opinion

Definition and limitations of internal control over financial reporting

Audit firm's signature
Auditor's city and state
Date of report

- I/C is the responsibility of management
- Mention of management's report on I/C
- Auditor responsible for expressing opinion on I/C
- Audit employed PCAOB standards which require the auditor to obtain reasonable assurance
- Audit included:
  - Understanding I/C
  - Assessing risks of material weakness
  - Testing and evaluating design and operating effectiveness of I/C
- Auditor believes that the audit provides a reasonable basis for the opinion
- Auditor is registered with the PCAOB and is required to be independent

- **Responsibilities of Management for ICFR** section that identifies management's responsibilities for ICFR and references the title of the accompanying management report

- **Auditor's Responsibilities for the Audit of ICFR** section that identifies the objectives of the audit and defines reasonable assurance; and comments on the role of professional judgment, professional skepticism, and risk assessment

- **Definition and Inherent Limitations of ICFR** section that defines ICFR and includes a paragraph commenting on the inherent limitations of internal control

- The manual or printed signature of the auditor's firm

- The city and state where the auditor's report is issued

- The date of the auditor's report. The auditor's report on ICFR should not be dated *before* the auditor has obtained sufficient appropriate audit evidence to support the auditor's opinion, including evidence that the audit documentation has been reviewed

- The audit reports on ICFR and on the F/S should have the same date

Explanatory paragraph in report on issuer's F/S when I/C is reported on separately

- Immediately follows opinion paragraph

- States auditor has also audited I/C in accordance with PCAOB standards

- Identifies control criteria (eg, COSO) used to evaluate I/C

- Identifies as-of date for audit of I/C (typically balance sheet date)

- States date of report on I/C (same as date of report on F/S)

- States opinion expressed in report on I/C

Report Modifications

Reasons to depart from the usual unmodified wording in the auditor's report on ICFR include the following:

- **One or more material weaknesses**—The report should include the definition of "material weakness" and reference the description in management's report or point out that management's report did not identify the matter. The report should also determine the effect on the audit of the entity's F/S (state whether the opinion on the F/S was affected by adding an other-matter paragraph or commenting in the paragraph that identifies the material weakness)

- **Elements are incomplete or improperly presented**—If management does not revise its report, the auditor should add an other-matter paragraph to describe the reasons for the determination that elements of the report are incomplete or improperly presented

- **Scope limitations**—The auditor should either withdraw from the engagement or disclaim an opinion on ICFR (stating the reasons for the disclaimer) and consider the effect on the audit of F/S.

Opinions in audits of internal control over financial reporting

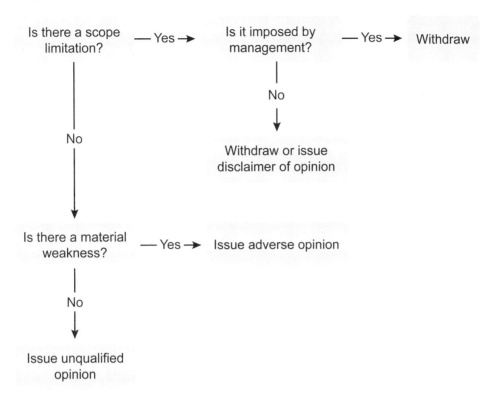

- **Reference to a component auditor**—The auditor *should not* make such a reference unless the component auditor has followed appropriate professional standards and has issued a report on a component's ICFR that is not restricted

- **Management's report includes additional information**—The auditor should add an other-matter paragraph to disclaim an opinion on the other information in management's report. If such other information is included in a document containing management's report, the auditor should read the additional information to evaluate whether there are material inconsistencies with management's report. (If there are, the auditor should try to persuade management to make appropriate changes to resolve any inconsistency)

Sample reports are provided in the Appendix.

Internal Controls Audits—PCAOB

Definitions

Control Deficiency—When the design or operation of a control does not allow management or employees, in the normal course of performing their assigned functions, to prevent or detect misstatements on a timely basis.

- **Deficiency in design**—When a control necessary to meet the control objective is missing or when an existing control is not properly designed so that, even if the control operates as designed, the control objective is not always met

- **Deficiency in operation**—When a properly designed control does not operate as designed or when the person performing the control does not possess the necessary authority or qualifications to perform the control effectively

Material Weakness—A deficiency, or a combination of deficiencies, in ICFR such that there is a *reasonable possibility* that a *material misstatement* of the company's annual or interim financial statements will not be prevented or detected on a timely basis. If one or more material weaknesses exist, the company's ICFR is not considered to be effective.

Significant Deficiency—A deficiency, or a combination of deficiencies, in ICFR that is *less severe* than a material weakness, yet important enough to merit attention by those responsible for oversight of the company's financial reporting.

Audit Process

The audit of ICFR should be **integrated** with the audit of the F/S (ie, the tests of controls should be designed to address both the objectives of the audit of ICFR and the audit of the F/S). Remember that **risk assessment** underlies the entire audit process, including the determination of significant accounts and disclosures and relevant assertions, the selection of controls to test, and the determination of the evidence necessary for a given control.

- There is a *direct relationship* between the risk of material weakness (RMM) and the amount of audit attention that is needed
- The *same materiality* considerations should be used in planning the audit of ICFR as for the audit of the company's annual F/S

The auditor may **use the work of others** to reduce the work the auditor might otherwise have to perform.

- This includes internal auditors, other company personnel, service auditors (when a service organization is involved), and third parties working under the direction of management or the audit committee. The auditor should assess the competence and objectivity of those whose work the auditor plans to use
- As the risk associated with a control increases, the auditor should take increasing responsibility for performing the work instead of using the work of others

Top-Down Approach

The PCAOB also uses a **top-down approach** which begins at the F/S level and with the auditor's understanding of the overall risks to ICFR. The auditor then focuses on *entity-level* controls and works down to significant accounts and disclosures and their relevant assertions.

The auditor must:

- Test those **entity-level controls** that are important to the conclusion about the effectiveness of ICFR. **Entity-level controls** include controls related to the control environment, controls over management override, the company's risk assessment process, controls to monitor results of operations or other controls, controls over the period-end financial reporting process; and policies that address significant business control and risk management practices
- Evaluate the **period-end financial reporting** process because of its importance to ICFR
- Identify significant accounts, disclosures, and their relevant assertions
  - **Relevant assertions**—Those F/S assertions that have a *reasonable possibility* of containing a material misstatement. PCAOB auditing standards specifically refer to the following assertions: existence or occurrence; completeness; valuation or allocation; rights and obligations; and presentation and disclosure
  - **Risk factors**—The auditor should consider risk factors relevant to the identification of significant accounts and disclosures and their relevant assertions, including the nature of the account or disclosure; size and composition of the account; susceptibility to misstatement, volume of activity, and complexity of transactions; and changes from the prior period, among others
- Understand likely **sources of misstatement**. To accomplish this, the auditor needs to:
  - Understand the flow of transactions related to the relevant assertions
  - Verify that the auditor has identified the points within the company's processes at which a material misstatement could arise

○ Identify the controls that management has implemented to address these potential misstatements

○ Identify the controls that management has implemented over the company's assets that could materially misstate the financial statements

- Perform walk-throughs, which encompass following a transaction from origination through the company's processes until reflected in the financial records. Walk-throughs are frequently the most effective way to achieve the objectives above

- Test those controls that are important to the conclusion about whether the company's controls sufficiently address the assessed risk of misstatement to each relevant assertion

Testing Controls

Test of controls (from least to most persuasive) includes: inquiry, observation, inspection of relevant documentation, and re-performance of a control:

- Testing design effectiveness procedures includes inquiry of appropriate personnel, observation of the company's operations, and inspection of relevant documentation (may be addressed by appropriate walk-throughs)

- Testing operating effectiveness procedures includes inquiry of appropriate personnel, observation of the company's operations, inspection of relevant documentation, and re-performance of the control

Testing controls over a greater period of time provides more evidence than testing over a shorter period of time; testing closer to the date of management's assessment provides more evidence than testing performed earlier in the year.

The more extensively a control is tested, the greater the evidence to evaluate the effectiveness of the control. When operating effectiveness has been tested at an interim date, the auditor should consider what additional testing for the remaining period may be necessary.

Evaluation and Communication of Identified Deficiencies

The auditor must evaluate identified control deficiencies to determine whether, individually or in combination, they constitute material weaknesses as of the date of management's assessment (based on whether there is a "reasonable possibility" that the controls will fail to prevent or detect a material misstatement, not whether a misstatement has actually occurred).

The auditor:

- Must communicate (in writing) to management and the audit committee all material weaknesses identified

- Must communicate (in writing) to the audit committee any other identified significant deficiencies

- Should communicate (in writing) to management all other identified deficiencies in ICFR and inform the audit committee that such a communication has been made

- Must communicate (in writing) to the board of directors any conclusion that the audit committee's oversight of financial reporting and ICFR has been ineffective

Communicating I/C issues: PCAOB rules

Applies to	Issuers
When to report	Prior to issuing audit report on internal control over financial reporting (ICFR)
Written report to management	All deficiencies in ICFR

Communicating I/C issues: PCAOB rules

Written report to audit committee	Material weaknesses, significant deficiencies
Notify audit committee	When management has received written report of all deficiencies

Reporting

The auditor may choose to issue a combined report on the F/S and on ICFR or separate reports

- **Combined Report**—An unqualified report on the F/S and on ICFR consists of five paragraphs: (1) introduction; (2) scope; (3) definition; (4) inherent limitations; and (5) opinion
- **Separate Reports**—An additional paragraph is added to the *audit report* on the F/S that references the report on ICFR. The auditor should add an additional paragraph to the *report on ICFR* that references the audit report on the F/S

**Explanatory paragraph in report on issuer's F/S
when I/C is reported on separately**

- Immediately follows opinion paragraph
- States auditor has also audited I/C in accordance with PCAOB standards
- Identifies control criteria (eg, COSO) used to evaluate I/C
- Identifies as-of date for audit of I/C (typically balance sheet date)
- States date of report on I/C (same as date of report on F/S)
- States opinion expressed in report on I/C

Title of report should include the word "independent" (eg, "Report of Independent Registered Public Accounting Firm").

If separate reports are issued, they should be dated the same (the date as of which the auditor has obtained sufficient competent evidence).

If one (or more) **material weakness exists**, the auditor must:

- Express an **adverse opinion** (unless there is a scope limitation)
- Include in the auditor's report the definition of a material weakness and refer to management's assessment of the material weakness.
- Determine the effect the adverse opinion on ICFR has on the opinion on the entity's F/S

If there is a **scope limitation**, the auditor should disclaim an opinion or withdraw from the engagement.

Sample reports on the effectiveness of ICFR are included in the Appendix.

Appendix of Sample Reports

 Standard Unmodified Opinion (GAAS)

INDEPENDENT AUDITOR'S REPORT

To: The Board of Directors of X Company (Those charged with Governance)

Opinion

We have audited the financial statements of ABC Company, which comprise the balance sheet as of December 31, 20X1, and the related statements of income, changes in stockholders' equity, and cash flows for the year then ended, and the related notes to the financial statements.

In our opinion, the accompanying financial statements present fairly, in all material respects, the financial position of ABC Company as of December 31, 20X1, and the results of its operations and its cash flows for the year then ended in accordance with accounting principles generally accepted in the United States of America.

Basis for Opinion

We conducted our audit in accordance with auditing standards generally accepted in the United States of America (GAAS). Our responsibilities under those standards are further described in the Auditor's Responsibilities for the Audit of the Financial Statements section of our report. We are required to be independent of ABC Company and to meet our other ethical responsibilities, in accordance with the relevant ethical requirements relating to our audit. We believe that the audit evidence we have obtained is sufficient and appropriate to provide a basis for our audit opinion.

Responsibilities of Management for the Financial Statements

Management is responsible for the preparation and fair presentation of the financial statements in accordance with accounting principles generally accepted in the United States of America, and for the design, implementation, and maintenance of internal control relevant to the preparation and fair presentation of financial statements that are free from material misstatement, whether due to fraud or error.

In preparing the financial statements, management is required to evaluate whether there are conditions or events, considered in the aggregate, that raise substantial doubt about ABC Company's ability to continue as a going concern for [*insert the time period set by the applicable financial reporting framework*].

Auditor's Responsibilities for the Audit of the Financial Statements

Our objectives are to obtain reasonable assurance about whether the financial statements as a whole are free from material misstatement, whether due to fraud or error, and to issue an auditor's report that includes our opinion. Reasonable assurance is a high level of assurance but is not absolute assurance and therefore is not a guarantee that an audit conducted in accordance with GAAS will always detect a material misstatement when it exists. The risk of not detecting a material misstatement resulting from fraud is higher than for one resulting from error, as fraud may involve collusion, forgery, intentional omissions, misrepresentations, or the override of internal control. Misstatements are considered material if there is a substantial likelihood that, individually or in the aggregate, they would influence the judgment made by a reasonable user based on the financial statements.

In performing an audit in accordance with GAAS, we:

- Exercise professional judgment and maintain professional skepticism throughout the audit.
- Identify and assess the risks of material misstatement of the financial statements, whether due to fraud or error, and design and perform audit procedures responsive to those risks. Such procedures include examining, on a test basis, evidence regarding the amounts and disclosures in the financial statements.
- Obtain an understanding of internal control relevant to the audit in order to design audit procedures that are appropriate in the circumstances, but not for the purpose of expressing an opinion on the effectiveness of ABC Company's internal control. Accordingly, no such opinion is expressed.
- Evaluate the appropriateness of accounting policies used and the reasonableness of significant accounting estimates made by management, as well as evaluate the overall presentation of the financial statements.
- Conclude whether, in our judgment, there are conditions or events, considered in the aggregate, that raise substantial doubt about ABC Company's ability to continue as a going concern for a reasonable period of time.

We are required to communicate with those charged with governance regarding, among other matters, the planned scope and timing of the audit, significant audit findings, and certain internal control–related matters that we identified during the audit.

[Auditor's signature]

[Auditor's city and state]

[Date of the auditor's report]

Standard GAAS Report with Examples of Additional Sections & Paragraphs

INDEPENDENT AUDITOR'S REPORT

To: Addressee

Report on the Audit of the Financial Statements

Opinion

***

Basis for Opinion

***

Substantial Doubt About the Company's Ability to Continue as a Going Concern

The accompanying financial statements have been prepared assuming that the Company will continue as a going concern. As discussed in Note X to the financial statements, the Company has suffered recurring losses from operations, has a net capital deficiency, and has stated that substantial doubt exists about the Company's ability to continue as a going concern. Management's evaluation of the events and conditions and management's plans regarding these matters are also described in Note X. The financial statements do not include any adjustments that might result from the outcome of this uncertainty. Our opinion is not modified with respect to this matter.

Emphasis of Matter — Litigation

As discussed in Note X to the financial statements, the Company is a defendant in a lawsuit [briefly describe the nature of the litigation consistent with the Company's description in the note to the financial statements]. Our opinion is not modified with respect to this matter.

Key Audit Matters

Key audit matters are those matters that were communicated with those charged with governance and, in our professional judgment, were of most significance in our audit of the financial statements of the current period. These matters were addressed in the context of our audit of the financial statements as a whole, and in forming our opinion thereon, and we do not provide a separate opinion on these matters.

[Description of each key audit matter]

Other Matter

The financial statements of the Company for the year ended December 31, 20X0, were audited by another auditor, who expressed an unmodified opinion on those statements on March 31, 20X1.

Responsibilities of Management for the Financial Statements

***

Auditor's Responsibilities for the Audit of the Financial Statements

***

Report on Legal and Regulatory Requirements

[The form and content of this section of the auditor's report would vary depending on the nature of the auditor's other reporting responsibilities.]

[Auditor's signature]

[Auditor's city and state]

[Date of auditor's report]

Qualified Opinion Due to Material Misstatement—Material but Not Pervasive (GAAS)

INDEPENDENT AUDITOR'S REPORT

To: Addressee

Qualified Opinion

We have audited the financial statements of ABC Company, which comprise the balance sheets as of December 31, 20X1 and 20X0, and the related statements of income, changes in stockholders' equity, and cash flows for the years then ended, and the related notes to the financial statements.

In our opinion, except for the effects of the matter described in the Basis for Qualified Opinion section of our report, the accompanying financial statements present fairly, in all material respects, the financial position of ABC Company as of December 31, 20X1 and 20X0, and the results of its operations and its cash flows for the years then ended in accordance with accounting principles generally accepted in the United States of America.

Basis for Qualified Opinion

ABC Company has stated inventories at cost in the accompanying balance sheets. Accounting principles generally accepted in the United States of America require inventories to be stated at the lower of cost or market. If the Company stated inventories at the lower of cost or market, a write down of $XXX and $XXX would have been required as of December 31, 20X1 and 20X0, respectively. Accordingly, cost of sales would have been increased by $XXX and $XXX, and net income, income taxes, and stockholders' equity would have been reduced by $XXX, $XXX, and $XXX, and $XXX, $XXX, and $XXX, as of and for the years ended December 31, 20X1 and 20X0, respectively.

We conducted our audits in accordance with auditing standards generally accepted in the United States of America (GAAS). Our responsibilities under those standards are further described in the Auditor's Responsibilities for the Audit of the Financial Statements section of our report. We are required to be independent of ABC Company and to meet our other ethical responsibilities, in accordance with the relevant ethical requirements relating to our audits. We believe that the audit evidence we have obtained is sufficient and appropriate to provide a basis for our qualified audit opinion.

Responsibilities of Management for the Financial Statements

[Same language as unmodified report]

Auditor's Responsibilities for the Audit of the Financial Statements

[Same language as unmodified report]

[Auditor's signature]

[Auditor's city and state]

[Date of the auditor's report]

Qualified Opinion Due to Scope Limitation—Material but Not Pervasive (GAAS)

INDEPENDENT AUDITOR'S REPORT

To: Addressee

Qualified Opinion

***

In our opinion, except for the **possible** effects of the matter described in the Basis for Qualified Opinion section of our report....

Basis for Qualified Opinion

ABC Company's investment in XYZ Company, a foreign affiliate acquired during the year and accounted for under the equity method, is carried at $XXX on the balance sheet at December 31, 20X1, and ABC Company's share of XYZ Company's net income of $XXX is included in ABC Company's net income for the year then ended. We were unable to obtain sufficient appropriate audit evidence about the carrying amount of ABC Company's investment in XYZ Company as of December 31, 20X1, and ABC Company's share of XYZ Company's net income for the year then ended because we were denied access to the financial information, management, and the auditors of XYZ Company. Consequently, we were unable to determine whether any adjustments to these amounts were necessary.

***

Responsibilities of Management for the Financial Statements

[Same language as unmodified report]

Auditor's Responsibilities for the Audit of the Financial Statements

[Same language as unmodified report]

[Auditor's signature]

[Auditor's city and state]

[Date of the auditor's report]

Adverse Opinion Due to Material Misstatement—Material & Pervasive (GAAS)

INDEPENDENT AUDITOR'S REPORT

To: Addressee

Adverse Opinion

We have audited the consolidated financial statements of ABC Company and its subsidiaries, which comprise the consolidated balance sheet as of December 31, 20X1, and the related consolidated statements of income, changes in stockholders' equity, and cash flows for the year then ended, and the related notes to the financial statements.

In our opinion, because of the significance of the matter discussed in the Basis for Adverse Opinion section of our report, the accompanying consolidated financial statements do not present fairly the financial position of ABC Company and its subsidiaries as of December 31, 20X1, or the results of their operations or their cash flows for the year then ended in accordance with accounting principles generally accepted in the United States of America.

Basis for Adverse Opinion

As described in Note X, ABC Company has not consolidated the financial statements of subsidiary XYZ Company that it acquired during 20X1 because it has not yet been able to ascertain the fair values of certain of the subsidiary's material assets and liabilities at the acquisition date. This investment is therefore accounted for on a cost basis by the Company. Under accounting principles generally accepted in the United States of America, the subsidiary should have been consolidated because it is controlled by the Company. Had XYZ Company been consolidated, many elements in the accompanying consolidated financial statements would have been materially affected. The effects on the consolidated financial statements of the failure to consolidate have not been determined.

We conducted our audit in accordance with auditing standards generally accepted in the United States of America (GAAS). Our responsibilities under those standards are further described in the Auditor's Responsibilities for the Audit of the Financial Statements section of our report. We are required to be independent of ABC Company and to meet our other ethical responsibilities, in accordance with the relevant ethical requirements relating to our audit. We believe that the audit evidence we have obtained is sufficient and appropriate to provide a basis for our adverse audit opinion.

Responsibilities of Management for the Financial Statements

[Same language as unmodified report]

Auditor's Responsibilities for the Audit of the Financial Statements

[Same language as unmodified report]

[Auditor's signature]

[Auditor's city and state]

[Date of the auditor's report]

Disclaimer of Opinion Due to Auditor's Inability to Obtain Sufficient Appropriate Audit Evidence About a Single Element of the F/S (GAAS)

INDEPENDENT AUDITOR'S REPORT

To: Addressee

Disclaimer of Opinion

We were engaged to audit the financial statements of ABC Company, which comprise the balance sheet as of December 31, 20X1, and the related statements of income, changes in stockholders' equity, and cash flows for the year then ended, and the related notes to the financial statements.

We do not express an opinion on the accompanying financial statements of ABC Company. Because of the significance of the matter described in the Basis for Disclaimer of Opinion section of our report, we have not been able to obtain sufficient appropriate audit evidence to provide a basis for an audit opinion on the financial statements.

Basis for Disclaimer of Opinion

ABC Company's investment in XYZ Company, a joint venture, is carried at $XXX on the Company's balance sheet, which represents over 90 percent of the Company's net assets as of December 31, 20X1. We were not allowed access to the management and the auditors of XYZ Company. As a result, we were unable to determine whether any adjustments were necessary relating to the Company's proportional share of XYZ Company's assets that it controls jointly, its proportional share of XYZ Company's liabilities for which it is jointly responsible, its proportional share of XYZ Company's income and expenses for the year, and the elements making up the statements of changes in stockholders' equity and cash flows.

Responsibilities of Management for the Financial Statements

[Same language as unmodified report]

Auditor's Responsibilities for the Audit of the Financial Statements

Our responsibility is to conduct an audit of ABC Company's financial statements in accordance with auditing standards generally accepted in the United States of America and to issue an auditor's report. However, because of the matter described in the Basis for Disclaimer of Opinion section of our report, we were not able to obtain sufficient appropriate audit evidence to provide a basis for an audit opinion on these financial statements.

We are required to be independent of ABC Company and to meet our other ethical responsibilities, in accordance with the relevant ethical requirements relating to our audit.

[Auditor's signature]

[Auditor's city and state]

[Date of the auditor's report]

Standard Unqualified PCAOB Report without Critical Audit Matters

REPORT OF INDEPENDENT REGISTERED PUBLIC ACCOUNTING FIRM

To the shareholders and the board of directors of X Company

Opinion on the Financial Statements

We have audited the accompanying balance sheets of X Company (the "Company") as of December 31, 20X2 and 20X1, the related statements of [*titles of the financial statements, eg, income, comprehensive income, stockholders' equity, and cash flows*], for each of the three years in the period ended December 31, 20X2, and the related notes [*and schedules*] (collectively referred to as the "financial statements"). *In our opinion*, the financial statements *present fairly*, in all material respects, the financial position of the Company as of [at] December 31, 20X2 and 20X1, and the results of its operations and its cash flows for each of the three years in the period ended December 31, 20X2, in conformity with [*the applicable financial reporting framework - AFRF*].

Basis for Opinion

These financial statements are the responsibility of the Company's management. *Our responsibility* is to express an opinion on the Company's financial statements based on our audits. We are a public accounting firm registered with the Public Company Accounting Oversight Board (United States) ("PCAOB") and are required to be independent with respect to the Company in accordance with the U.S. federal securities laws and the applicable rules and regulations of the Securities and Exchange Commission and the PCAOB.

We conducted our audits in *accordance with the standards of the PCAOB*. Those standards require that we plan and perform the audit to obtain *reasonable assurance* about whether the financial statements are free of material misstatement, whether due to error or fraud. Our audits included performing procedures to assess the risks of material misstatement of the financial statements, whether due to error or fraud, and performing procedures that respond to those risks. Such procedures included examining, on a test basis, evidence regarding the amounts and disclosures in the financial statements. Our audits also included evaluating the accounting principles used and significant estimates made by management, as well as evaluating the overall presentation of the financial statements. We believe that our audits provide a *reasonable basis* for our opinion.

Critical Audit Matters

Critical audit matters are matters arising from the current period audit of the financial statements that were communicated or required to be communicated to the audit committee and that: (**1**) relate to accounts or disclosures that are material to the financial statements and (**2**) involved our especially challenging, subjective, or complex judgments. We determined that there are no critical audit matters.

[Signature]

We have served as the Company's auditor since [year].

[City and State or Country]

[Date]

 Alternative paragraph for report with Critical Audit Matters

Critical Audit Matters

The critical audit matters communicated below are matters arising from the current period audit of the financial statements that were communicated or required to be communicated to the audit committee and that: (**1**) relate to accounts or disclosures that are material to the financial statements and (**2**) involved our especially challenging, subjective, or complex judgments. The communication of critical audit matters does not alter in any way our opinion on the financial statements, taken as a whole, and we are not, by communicating the critical audit matters below, providing separate opinions on the critical audit matters or on the accounts or disclosures to which they relate.

[Include critical audit matters]

Qualified PCAOB Report Example

REPORT OF INDEPENDENT REGISTERED PUBLIC ACCOUNTING FIRM

To the shareholders and the board of directors of X Company

Opinion on the Financial Statements

We have audited the accompanying balance sheets of X Company (the "Company") as of December 31, 20X2 and 20X1, the related statements of [titles of the financial statements, eg, income, comprehensive income, stockholders' equity, and cash flows] for each of the years then ended, and the related notes [and schedules] (collectively referred to as the "financial statements"). In our opinion, **except for** the effects of the adjustments, if any, as might have been determined to be necessary had we been able to examine evidence regarding the foreign affiliate investment and earnings, as described below, the financial statements present fairly, in all material respects, the financial position of X the Company as of December 31, 20X2 and 20X1, and the results of its operations and its cash flows for the years then ended in conformity with accounting principles generally accepted in the United States of America.

We were unable to obtain audited financial statements supporting the Company's investment in a foreign affiliate stated at \$_____ and \$_____ at December 31, 20X2 and 20X1, respectively, or its equity in earnings of that affiliate of \$_____ and \$_____, which is included in net income for the years then ended as described in Note X to the financial statements; nor were we able to satisfy ourselves as to the carrying value of the investment in the foreign affiliate or the equity in its earnings by other auditing procedures.

Basis for Opinion

These financial statements are the responsibility of the Company's management. Our responsibility is to express an opinion on the Company's financial statements based on our audits. We are a public accounting firm registered with the Public Company Accounting Oversight Board (United States) ("PCAOB") and are required to be independent with respect to the Company in accordance with the U.S. federal securities laws and the applicable rules and regulations of the Securities and Exchange Commission and the PCAOB.

Except as discussed above, we conducted our audits in accordance with the standards of the PCAOB. Those standards require that we plan and perform the audit to obtain reasonable assurance about whether the financial statements are free of material misstatement, whether due to error or fraud. Our audits included performing procedures to assess the risks of material misstatement of the financial statements, whether due to error or fraud, and performing procedures that respond to those risks. Such procedures included examining, on a test basis, evidence regarding the amounts and disclosures in the financial statements. Our audits also included evaluating the accounting principles used and significant estimates made by management, as well as evaluating the overall presentation of the financial statements. We believe that our audits provide a reasonable basis for our opinion.

Critical Audit Matters

[*Paragraph explaining CAM, if applicable, and list of critical audit matters or statement that there were no such matters.*]

[*Signature*]

We have served as the Company's auditor since [*year*].

[*City and State or Country*]

[Date]

Adverse PCAOB Report Example

REPORT OF INDEPENDENT REGISTERED PUBLIC ACCOUNTING FIRM

To the shareholders and the board of directors of X Company

Opinion on the Financial Statements

We have audited the accompanying balance sheets of X Company (the "Company") as of December 31, 20X2 and 20X1, the related statements of [*titles of the financial statements, eg, income, comprehensive income, stockholders' equity, and cash flows*] for each of the years then ended, and the related notes [and schedules] (collectively referred to as the "financial statements"). In our opinion, because of the effects of the matters discussed in the following paragraphs, the financial statements do not present fairly, in conformity with accounting principles generally accepted in the United States of America, the financial position of the Company as of December 31, 20X2 and 20X1, or the results of its operations or its cash flows for the years then ended.

As discussed in Note X to the financial statements, the Company carries its property, plant and equipment accounts at appraisal values, and provides depreciation on the basis of such values. Further, the Company does not provide for income taxes with respect to differences between financial income and taxable income arising because of the use, for income tax purposes, of the installment method of reporting gross profit from certain types of sales. Accounting principles generally accepted in the United States of America require that property, plant and equipment be stated at an amount not in excess of cost, reduced by depreciation based on such amount, and that deferred income taxes be provided.

Because of the departures from accounting principles generally accepted in the United States of America identified above, as of December 31, 20X2 and 20X1, inventories have been increased $_____ and $_____ by inclusion in manufacturing overhead of depreciation in excess of that based on cost; property, plant and equipment, less accumulated depreciation, is carried at $_____ and $_____ in excess of an amount based on the cost to the Company; and deferred income taxes of $_____ and $_____ have not been recorded; resulting in an increase of $_____ and $_____ in retained earnings and in appraisal surplus of $_____ and $_____, respectively. For the years ended December 31, 20X2 and 20X1, cost of goods sold has been increased $_____ and $_____, respectively, because of the effects of the depreciation accounting referred to above and deferred income taxes of $_____ and $_____ have not been provided, resulting in an increase in net income of $_____ and $_____, respectively.

Basis for Opinion

[*Same basic elements as the Basis for Opinion section of the auditor's unqualified report*]

[*Signature*]

We have served as the Company's auditor since [*year*].

[*City and State or Country*]

[*Date*]

Disclaimer of Opinion Example - PCAOB Report

REPORT OF INDEPENDENT REGISTERED PUBLIC ACCOUNTING FIRM

To the shareholders and the board of directors of X Company

Disclaimer of Opinion on the Financial Statements

We were engaged to audit the accompanying balance sheets of X Company (the "Company") as of December 31, 20X2 and 20X1, and the related statements of [titles of the financial statements, eg, income, comprehensive income, stockholders' equity, and cash flows], and the related notes [and schedules] (collectively referred to as the "financial statements"). As described in the following paragraph, because the Company did not take physical inventories and we were not able to apply other auditing procedures to satisfy ourselves as to inventory quantities and the cost of property and equipment, we were not able to obtain sufficient appropriate audit evidence to provide a basis for an audit opinion on the financial statements, and we do not express, an opinion on these financial statements.

The Company did not make a count of its physical inventory in 20X2 or 20X1, stated in the accompanying financial statements at $_____ as of December 31, 20X2, and at $_____ as of December 31, 20X1. Further, evidence supporting the cost of property and equipment acquired prior to December 31, 20X1, is no longer available. The Company's records do not permit the application of other auditing procedures to inventories or property and equipment.

Basis for Disclaimer of Opinion

These financial statements are the responsibility of the Company's management. We are a public accounting firm registered with the Public Company Accounting Oversight Board (United States) ("PCAOB") and are required to be independent with respect to the Company in accordance with the U.S. federal securities laws and the applicable rules and regulations of the Securities and Exchange Commission and the PCAOB.

[Signature]

We have served as the Company's auditor since *[year]*.

[City and State or Country]

[Date]

AUD 24
Reporting on Attestation Engagements

AUD 24: Reporting on Attestation Engagements

24.01 Examination or Review Engagements

Attestation Engagements: Overview

Attestation engagements are designed to evaluate how accurate data or information are when compared to a stated purpose (ie, provide assurance about the assertions or claims). The data are provided by *another party* (ie, the practitioner does not prepare the data).

Nonattest services are any services other than to issue a report to users of information on subject matter for which another party is responsible. A **consultation engagement** is a nonattest engagement because the CPA provides advice to a client but does not issue an opinion on any subject matter to external users.

Attest and nonattest services standards

	Examples	Standards
Attest services	• Audits • Review • Agreed-upon procedures	• Statements on Auditing Standards • Statements on Standards for Accounting and Review Services (SSARSs) • Statements on Standards for Attestation Engagements (SSAEs)
Nonattest services	• Consulting • Tax • Valuation	• Statements on Standards for Consulting Services (SSCSs) • Statements on Standards for Tax Services (SSTSs) • Statements on Standards for Valuation Services (SSVSs)

AICPA Guidance

Each attest engagement has a different set of standards with similar requirements, such as independence, objectives of procedures, and reporting. The standards establish requirements that enable a CPA to adequately report on the subject matter in question.

Types of Engagements

Attestation engagements consist of examinations, reviews, and agreed-upon (ERA) procedures, as follows:

- **Assertion-based examinations:** The responsible party measures or evaluates the underlying subject matter against the criteria and provides an assertion about the outcome of the measurement or evaluation. The practitioner expresses an **opinion** (reasonable assurance) about whether the underlying subject matter is in accordance with the criteria, or the responsible party's assertion is fairly stated, in all material respects.

- **Direct examinations:** The practitioner measures or evaluates the underlying subject matter against the criteria and performs other procedures to obtain sufficient appropriate evidence to express an **opinion** (reasonable assurance) that conveys the results of that measurement or evaluation. The responsible party does not provide an assertion.

- **Review engagements:** The responsible party measures or evaluates the underlying subject matter against the criteria and provides an assertion about the outcome of the measurement or evaluation. The practitioner expresses a conclusion with limited assurance (ie, negative assurance) in a report about whether the practitioner is aware of any material modifications that should be made to the subject matter to be in accordance with the criteria or for the assertion to be fairly stated.
- **Agreed-upon procedures engagements:** Practitioners issue a report on their findings (no opinion or conclusion) regarding specific procedures applied to the subject matter. The procedures will depend on the agreement made among the parties to the engagement.

 Which of the following activities would most likely be considered an attestation engagement?

- Consulting with management representatives of a firm to provide advice
- Issuing a report about a firm's compliance with laws and regulations
- Advocating a client's position on tax matters that are being reviewed by the IRS
- Preparing a client's tax returns

Attestation engagements (ERA)		
Engagement	**Examples**	**Type of report**
Examination*	• Examining internal controls at service organization (assertion required) • Examining information *other than* historical financial statements	Opinion **(positive assurance)**
Review	• Reviewing management discussion and analysis information • Reviewing information *other than* historical financial statements	Conclusion **(limited assurance)**
Agreed-upon procedures	• Verifying cash balances in bank statements • Checking security balances	Findings **(no assurance)**

*Can be an assertion-based examination or a direct examination

Attestation engagements provide users of information with an opinion, conclusion, or findings about the reliability of subject matter for which a third party is responsible. An examination of an entity's compliance with laws and regulations in which the CPA issues a report is an example of an attestation engagement. Nonattest services are any services other than to issue an opinion, conclusion, or findings on subject matter or assertions for which a third party is responsible. Examples include consulting services, tax advocacy, and tax preparation.

Definitions

Subject matter information: The outcome of the measurement or evaluation of the underlying subject matter against criteria. An assertion about whether the underlying subject matter is in accordance with the criteria is a form of subject matter information.

Underlying subject matter: In an examination or review engagement, the phenomenon that is measured or evaluated by applying criteria. In an agreed-upon procedures engagement, the phenomenon upon which procedures are performed.

The essential difference between an assertion-based examination engagement and a direct examination engagement is that:

- A written assertion from the responsible party is required for an assertion-based examination engagement, whereas such an assertion is not obtained for a direct examination

- The practitioner may report on either the assertion or the underlying subject matter for an assertion-based examination engagement, whereas the practitioner reports only on the underlying subject matter for a direct examination engagement.

Attestation Engagements: Common Concepts

 Representative Task (Remembering & Understanding): Identify the factors that a practitioner should consider when issuing an assertion-based examination, direct examination, or review report.

Preconditions for Acceptance

The following preconditions must be met prior to accepting an attestation engagement:

CPA requirements	• CPA must be *independent*
	• CPA must be competent and capable of performing services
	• CPA must have *access* to relevant information
	• CPA's opinion, conclusion, or findings must be *written* in a *report*
	• CPA must have reached a *common understanding* with engaging party regarding terms of engagement
Other requirements	• The responsible *party* must assume *responsibility* for *subject matter*
	• Subject matter must be appropriate (ie, *measurable* against criteria)
	• *Criteria* must be *suitable* and *available* to users

Note: Engagements on prospective financial information must contain a summary of significant assumptions

Purpose and Premise

The **purpose** of an attestation engagement is to provide users of information, generally third parties, with an opinion, conclusion, or findings regarding the reliability of subject matter or an assertion about the subject matter, as measured against suitable and available criteria.

An engagement in accordance with the attestation standards is conducted on the **premise** that the responsible party is responsible for:

- The subject matter (and, if applicable, the preparation and presentation of the subject matter) as well as assertions about the subject matter

- Measuring, evaluating, and, when applicable, presenting subject matter that is free from material misstatement, whether due to fraud or error

- Providing the practitioner with:
  - Access to all information of which the responsible party is aware that is relevant to the measurement, evaluation, or disclosure of the subject matter
  - Access to additional information that the practitioner may request from the responsible party for the purpose of the engagement

    ○ Unrestricted access to persons within the appropriate party (parties) from whom the practitioner determines it is necessary to obtain evidence.

A written assertion as to whether the subject matter is measured or evaluated according to suitable criteria is required when performing an assertion-based examination or a review engagement. A written assertion is not required when performing a direct examination engagement or an agreed-upon procedures engagement under the attestation standards.

- When the engaging party (ie, the party that hires the practitioner) is the responsible party and refuses to provide a written assertion for an assertion-based examination or a review engagement, the practitioner should withdraw from the engagement when that is permitted.

- When the engaging party (ie, the party responsible for the underlying subject matter) is not the responsible party and the responsible party refuses to provide a written assertion for an assertion-based examination or a review engagement, that refusal should be disclosed in the practitioner's report, and the report's use should be restricted to the engaging party.

Performance Responsibilities

In all services provided under the attestation standards, practitioners are responsible for:

- Having the appropriate competence and capabilities to perform the engagement,

- Complying with relevant ethical requirements,

- Maintaining professional skepticism

- Exercising professional judgment throughout the planning and performance of the engagement.

For an examination engagement: To express an opinion in an examination, the practitioner obtains reasonable assurance about whether the subject matter, or an assertion about the subject matter, is free from material misstatements, whether due to fraud or error. To obtain reasonable assurance, which is a high but not absolute level of assurance, the practitioner:

- Plans the work and properly supervises other members of the engagement team,

- Identifies and assesses the risks of material misstatement, whether due to fraud or error, based on an understanding of the subject matter, its measurement or evaluation, the criteria, and other engagement circumstances

- Obtains sufficient appropriate evidence about whether material misstatements exist by designing and implementing appropriate responses to the assessed risks. Examination procedures may involve inspection, observation, analysis, inquiry, reperformance, recalculation, or confirmation with outside parties.

For a review engagement: To express a conclusion in a review, the practitioner obtains limited assurance about whether any material modification should be made to the subject matter in order for it to be in accordance with (or based on) the criteria or to an assertion about the subject matter in order for it to be fairly stated. In a review, the nature and extent of the procedures are substantially less than in an examination.

To obtain limited assurance in a review, the practitioner:

- Plans the work and properly supervises other members of the engagement team

- Focuses procedures in those areas in which the practitioner believes increased risks of misstatements exist, whether due to fraud or error, based on the practitioner's understanding of the subject matter, its measurement or evaluation, the criteria, and other engagement circumstances

- Obtains review evidence, through the application of inquiry and analytical procedures or other procedures as appropriate, to obtain limited assurance that no material modifications should be made to the subject matter for it to be in accordance with (or based on) the criteria

For an agreed-upon procedures engagement: To report on the application of agreed-upon procedures, the practitioner applies procedures determined by the . . . parties . . . who are responsible for the sufficiency of the procedures for their purposes. As a result of the engagement, the practitioner reports on the results of the engagement but does not provide an opinion or conclusion on the subject matter or assertion. In an agreed-upon procedures engagement, the practitioner:

- Plans the work and properly supervises other members of the engagement team

- Applies the procedures agreed to . . . and reports on their results.

Other Considerations

Appropriate procedures related to acceptance and continuance of attestation engagements should be followed. Practitioners should not accept an attestation engagement unless they have reached an understanding with the engaging party as to the terms of the engagement.

Changing the terms of the engagement to a lower level of service requires reasonable justification.

- If there is *reasonable justification*, the practitioner's report should not reference the original engagement, any procedures that may have been performed, or scope limitations that caused the engagement to change.
   - A change in the nature of the engagement originally requested may not be considered reasonably justified if that change is motivated by an inability to obtain sufficient appropriate evidence regarding the underlying subject matter.

Using the work of other practitioner(s) requires the primary practitioner to:

- Obtain an understanding of whether the other practitioner understands and will comply with the ethical requirements relevant to the engagement (particularly independence),

- Obtain an understanding about the other practitioner's independence and competence,

- Communicate with the other practitioner about the scope and timing of the other practitioner's work; be involved with the work of the other practitioner when assuming responsibility for that work,

- Evaluate the adequacy of other practitioner's work for purposes of the engagement, and

- Determine whether to reference the other practitioner in the report.

Appropriate **engagement documentation** includes:

- Assembling the final engagement file no later than 60 days following the report release date.
   - After the documentation completion date, the practitioner should not delete or discard any documentation prior to the end of the retention period.
   - After the documentation completion date, additions may be made, but the practitioner must document the reasons for the additions as well as when and by whom the additions were made/reviewed.

- Adopting reasonable procedures to retain the documentation for a period sufficient to meet their needs and any legal/regulatory requirements.

- Adopting reasonable procedures to protect the confidentiality of the documentation.

When a **quality control review** is required, the engagement partner should discuss with the quality control reviewer the significant findings; the engagement partner should not release the report until the engagement quality control review is completed.

- The engagement quality control reviewer should evaluate the significant judgments and conclusions reached, including the following:
   - Discuss significant findings with the engagement partner
   - Read the written subject matter information or assertion and proposed report
   - Read selected documentation for significant judgments and conclusions reached
   - Consider whether the proposed report is appropriate.

Documenting the justification for departures from presumptively mandatory requirements and how alternative procedures met the intent of that requirement.

Unconditional	• Standards use the words *"must"* • Practitioners must comply with applicable standards

Presumptively mandatory	• Standards use the word *"should"*
	• Practicioners are expected to comply with standards if relevant, but:
	  ○ Rarely may depart from standards if deemed ineffective
	  ○ Alternative procedures must be performed and documented

Examination Engagements

AICPA Guidance

The guidance for examination engagements is provided in two sections of the SSAEs:

(1) AT-C 205, *Assertion-Based Examination Engagements*

(2) AT-C 206, *Direct Examination Engagements*

The practitioner is also required to comply with AT-C 105, *Concepts Common to All Attestation Engagements*, as well as any applicable subject matter sections. Compliance with these attestation standards is enforceable under the AICPA's Code of Professional Conduct (per the Compliance with Standards Rule of Conduct).

Terms of Engagement: Assertion-Based Examinations

In addition to the concepts applicable to all attestation engagements, all assertion-based examination engagements (eg, the examination of prospective financial information) are subject to another set of requirements specific to examinations under AT-C 205.

With this type of engagement, the practitioner should:

- Specify the terms of the engagement in an engagement letter, including:
  - The objective and scope of the engagement
  - Responsibilities of the practitioner
  - A statement that the engagement will be conducted in accordance with SSAEs
  - Responsibilities of the responsible/engaging party
  - Inherent limitations of the engagement
  - The criteria for measuring, evaluating, or disclosing the subject matter
  - An agreement by the engaging party (eg, those charged with governance) to provide a representation letter at the conclusion of the engagement
- Request a written assertion from the responsible party regarding measurement/evaluation of the subject matter.
- Establish an overall engagement strategy, which sets the scope, timing, and direction of the engagement and assists in the development of the engagement plan.
- Develop an engagement plan that includes the nature, timing, and extent of procedures to be performed, including risk assessment procedures.

- Obtain an understanding of the subject matter and relevant circumstances (including internal controls or I/C) over the preparation of the subject matter) to be able to:
  - Identify and assess the risks of material misstatement, and
  - Design procedures to respond to such risks and obtain reasonable assurance to support the opinion.
- Consider materiality for the subject matter when establishing the overall engagement strategy, and reconsider materiality if new information brings it into question.
- Obtain sufficient appropriate evidence to reduce attestation risk to an acceptably low level.
- Design and perform tests of controls if:
  - The practitioner intends to rely on the operating effectiveness of controls in determining the nature, timing, and extent of other procedures
  - If other procedures will not provide sufficient appropriate evidence alone or if the subject matter itself is I/C
- Design and perform tests of details or analytical procedures (unless the subject matter is I/C)
- Consider and inquire as to whether there are any indications of fraud or noncompliance with laws/regulations
- Consider and inquire about subsequent events (ie, events occurring after the period covered by the engagement up to the report date) and respond to subsequently discovered facts (ie, facts discovered after the report date)
- Request written representations (in the form of a letter to the practitioner as of the date of the report) from:
  - The responsible party regarding the assertion, relevant matters, their responsibilities, subsequent events, immaterial uncorrected misstatements, etc.; and
  - The engaging party (if a separate party) regarding the responsible party's responsibilities, their lack of knowledge of any material misstatements, subsequent events, etc.
- Read other information in the document that will contain the practitioner's report to identify any material inconsistencies or material misstatements of fact that exist in the other information, subject matter, assertion, or report.
- Evaluate the results of procedures, form an opinion, and prepare a written report.
  - If the practitioner was unable to obtain sufficient appropriate evidence or the subject matter is not in accordance with the specified criteria, in all material respects, and the effect of any such insufficiencies are material, the opinion should be modified and a separate paragraph describing such matters should be included in the report.
    - **Qualified opinion:** Effects are *material, but not pervasive*
    - **Adverse opinion:** Misstatements are *material and pervasive*
    - **Disclaimer of opinion:** Unable to obtain sufficient appropriate evidence (ie, scope limitation) and effects *could be material and pervasive*

Terms of Engagement: Direct Examinations

Direct examination engagements allow practitioners to use their skills and expertise to provide an opinion (*reasonable assurance*) for organizations about the results of measurements or evaluations of any subject matter (financial and nonfinancial) in relation to criteria. In this type of engagement, the responsible party does not provide an assertion.

For example, a practitioner may be engaged to evaluate the I/C over data security, processing, or confidentiality against the AICPA's Trust Services Criteria (ie, a SOC 2 engagement).

- Note, however, that direct examinations cannot be performed for subject matter falling under the following AT-C sections because an assertion is required to be provided:
  - AT-C 305, *Prospective Financial Information*

- ○ AT-C 310, *Reporting on Pro Forma Financial Information*
- ○ AT-C 315, *Compliance Attestation*
- ○ AT-C 320, *Reporting on an Examination of Controls at a Service Organization Relevant to User Entities' Internal Control Over Financial Reporting* (ie, SOC 1 engagements)
- ○ AT-C 395, *Management's Discussion and Analysis.*

In addition to the concepts applicable to all attestation engagements in AT-C 105, direct examinations are subject to many of the requirements in AT-C 205 (assertion-based examinations) and all of the requirements in AT-C 206 (direct examinations). If the rules in AT-C 205 cannot be applied due to the nature of the direct examination engagement, the practitioner should adapt and apply the requirement.

In some cases, AT-C 206 replaces or adds to certain requirements in AT-C 205. These differences relate to acceptance and continuance of the engagement, the terms of the engagement, the written representations that are required, and report requirements.

Prior to accepting/continuing a direct examination engagement, the practitioner should obtain an understanding of:

- The intended purpose of the engagement, how the report will be used, and why the engaging party wants a direct examination engagement
- Why the responsible party has not measured or evaluated the underlying subject matter against the criteria, if applicable
- Why the responsible party does not intend to provide an assertion when the responsible party has measured or evaluated the underlying subject matter against the criteria.

The engagement letter for a direct examination engagement should address all the same terms as an engagement letter for an assertion-based examination engagement. However, with respect to the responsibilities of the responsible party and the engaging party, when different, the following should be included:

- The responsible party is responsible for the underlying subject matter
- The responsible party or engaging party, as applicable, is responsible for:
  - ○ Selecting the criteria
  - ○ Determining that the criteria are suitable, will be available to the intended users, and are appropriate for the purpose of the engagement.

The practitioner should request written representations from the responsible party that:

- State that they have disclosed to the practitioner:
  - ○ All known matters contradicting the measurement or evaluation of the underlying subject matter, and any communication from regulatory agencies or others affecting the underlying subject matter
  - ○ All relevant deficiencies in I/C, any knowledge of actual, suspected, or alleged *fraud or noncompliance* with laws or regulations affecting the underlying subject matter, and other matters as the practitioner deems appropriate
  - ○ Any known *subsequent events* that would have a material effect on the underlying subject matter.
- Acknowledge their responsibility for the underlying subject matter, selection of the criteria (when applicable), and determining that such criteria are suitable, will be available to the intended users, and are appropriate for the purpose of the engagement
- State that they have provided the practitioner with all relevant information and access as agreed upon in the terms of the engagement

The practitioner's report for a direct examination engagement will differ from an assertion-based examination in that it should include statements that:

- Identify the practitioner's responsibility for:

- ○ Measuring or evaluating the underlying subject matter against the criteria
- ○ Expressing an opinion that conveys the results of the practitioner's measurement or evaluation of the underlying subject matter against the criteria
- ○ Presenting any subject matter information as part of the practitioner's measurement or evaluation, if applicable.

- AICPA standards require that the practitioner obtain reasonable assurance by measuring or evaluating the underlying subject matter against the criteria and performing other procedures to obtain sufficient appropriate evidence to express an opinion that conveys the result of that measurement or evaluation
- Describe the nature of a direct examination engagement
- Convey the results of the practitioner's measurement or evaluation of the underlying subject matter against the criteria.

Review Engagements

A review engagement is an attestation engagement in which the practitioner obtains limited assurance by obtaining sufficient appropriate evidence about the responsible party's measurement or evaluation of underlying subject matter against criteria in order to express a conclusion about whether any material modification should be made to the subject matter information in order for it to be in accordance with (or based on) the criteria or to the responsible party's assertion in order for it to be fairly stated.

AICPA Guidance

The guidance for review engagements is provided in AT-C 210, *Review Engagements*. In addition, the practitioner is required to comply with AT-C 105, *Concepts Common to All Attestation Engagements*, as well as any applicable subject-matter sections. Note that AT-C 210 specifically prohibits review engagements involving (a) prospective financial information; (b) I/C; or (c) compliance with the requirements of specified laws, regulations, rules, contracts, or grants.

Terms of the Engagement

The practitioner and the engaging party should agree on the terms of the engagement, which should be documented in an engagement letter (or other suitable form of written agreement). These terms should include the following:

- The objective and scope of the engagement
- The responsibilities of the practitioner
- The responsibilities of the responsible party and the engaging party if those are different
- A statement that the engagement will be conducted according to attestation standards established by the AICPA
- A statement that the level of assurance obtained in a review is substantially less than that of an examination and that, accordingly, no opinion will be expressed
- A statement identifying the criteria for measurement or evaluation of the subject matter
- Acknowledgment by the engaging party to provide the practitioner with a representation letter at the conclusion of the engagement.

Such an agreement should be obtained for each engagement, but, if the terms of the preceding engagement have not changed, the practitioner may simply remind the engaging party of the terms of the engagement (and document that communication).

Planning and Performing the Engagement

In planning and performing the review engagement, the practitioner should:

- Obtain a sufficient understanding of the subject matter and circumstances of the engagement to design and perform procedures to achieve the objectives of the engagement.

- Design and perform analytical procedures and make inquiries to obtain limited assurance.

  o Analytical procedures may not be applicable when the subject matter is qualitative instead of quantitative. In that case, the practitioner may need to perform other appropriate procedures (such other procedures might include inspection, observation, confirmation, recalculation, or reperformance, as applicable).

  o The suitability of specific analytical procedures should be determined (considering the subject matter and assessed risks of material misstatement); the reliability of data from which the expectation is developed should be evaluated; and an expectation that is sufficiently precise to identify material misstatements should be developed.

- Increase the focus in the areas of the engagement that have increased risks of material misstatement.

- Investigate significant differences from expectations by (a) inquiring of the responsible party and (b) performing any other procedures considered necessary.

The practitioner should inquire of the responsible party about the following:

- Whether the subject matter has been prepared according to (or based on) the criteria

- The practices used by the responsible party to measure and record the subject matter

- Whether the responsible party (a) has an internal audit function and (b) has used any specialists in preparing the subject matter

- Questions arising in connection with the other review procedures

- Communications from regulatory authorities or others, if any.

The practitioner should make inquiries to determine whether the applicable parties have any knowledge of fraud (including suspected or alleged fraud) or noncompliance with laws or regulations affecting the subject matter.

For incorrect, incomplete, or otherwise unsatisfactory information, the practitioner should perform additional procedures to obtain limited assurance as to whether any material modifications should be made to the subject matter.

When using the work of a practitioner's specialist or internal auditors, the practitioner should apply the same requirements stated in AT-C 205 (regarding examination engagements).

The practitioner should inquire whether the responsible party (and the engaging party, if different) is aware of any subsequent events up to the date of the report that could have a significant effect; if there are, the practitioner should perform appropriate procedures applicable to those events.

- There is no responsibility to perform additional procedures after the report date. If there are subsequently discovered facts that may have caused revision of the report if known at the report date, the practitioner should respond appropriately to those facts.

Written Representations

The practitioner should request written representations from the responsible party. The representations should address the subject matter and periods covered by the practitioner's report.

When the responsible party refuses to provide the requested written representations and the engaging party:

- IS the responsible party, the practitioner should withdraw from the engagement

- IS NOT the responsible party, the practitioner should make inquiries of the responsible party and seek oral responses. If satisfactory oral responses are obtained, the practitioner should restrict the use of the report to the engaging party.

If one or more of the requested representations are not provided (either in writing or orally), a scope limitation exists, and the practitioner should withdraw from the engagement, if possible.

The written representations letter should have the same date as the practitioner's report.

Documentation

The documentation should permit an experienced practitioner without any connection to the engagement to understand the work performed and the basis for the primary decisions.

The practitioner should prepare documentation sufficient to comply with AICPA Professional Standards and applicable legal and regulatory requirements, including the following matters:

- The identifying characteristics of the specific items tested
- Who performed the work and the date the work was completed
- The discussions with the responsible party (or others) about significant findings or issues, including the nature of the matters discussed (and when and with whom the discussions occurred)
- The actions taken when the engaging party is the responsible party and will not provide one or more of the required written representations (or when representations provided are not seen as reliable)
- The oral responses provided when the engaging party is not the responsible party and the responsible party will not provide the required written representations
- Who reviewed the work performed and the date it was reviewed.

The documentation normally addresses the following additional matters:

- Compliance with relevant ethical requirements, including applicable independence requirements
- Conclusions about acceptance and continuance of client relationships and engagements
- Conclusions about any consultations that occurred during the engagement.

If information has been obtained that is inconsistent with the practitioner's final conclusion about a significant matter, the practitioner should document how the practitioner dealt with the inconsistency.

Prospective Financial Information Engagements

AICPA Guidance

Guidance for examinations or agreed-upon procedures related to prospective F/S is provided in AT-C 305. Guidance for compilations and preparations related to prospective F/S appears in AR-C 70 and AR-C 80.

Prospective financial statement engagements			
Engagement	Assurance level	Procedures	Allowed?
Examination	Reasonable	Full testing on all material aspects	Yes
Review	Limited	Generally only inquiries and analytical procedures	No
Agreed-upon procedures	None	Only procedures requested by the parties	Yes
Compilation	None	Assist in the preparation of statements	Yes
Preparation	None	Full preparation of statements	Yes

Definitions

Financial Forecast: Prospective F/S that present, to the best of the responsible party's knowledge and belief, an entity's expected financial position, results of operations, and cash flows. A financial forecast is based on the responsible party's assumptions reflecting conditions it expects to exist and the course of action it expects to take. A forecast is for general or limited use.

Financial Projection: Prospective F/S that present, to the best of the responsible party's knowledge and belief, given one or more hypothetical assumptions, an entity's expected financial position, results of operations, and cash flows. A financial projection is based on the responsible party's assumptions reflecting conditions it expects would exist and the course of action it expects would be taken, given one or more hypothetical assumptions and is for limited use only.

Examination Preconditions

The practitioner should not accept an engagement to examine a:

- Forecast or projection unless the responsible party has agreed to disclose the significant assumptions

- Projection unless the responsible party has agreed to identify which of the assumptions are hypothetical and to comment on the limitations of the projection's usefulness

 Accepting an engagement related to a financial projection most likely would be inappropriate if the projection is to be distributed to

- The entity's principal stockholder, to the exclusion of the other stockholders

- Potential stockholders in an offering statement

- A financial institution in a loan application

- A state or federal regulatory agency.

Prospective financial information		
Forecast	• Shows where business is expected to go based on expected **general** conditions and the entity's expected course of action	For **general** or **limited** use
	• Example: forecasting future sales based on sales trends	
Projection	• Shows what management *believes* will occur given *specific* **hypothetical** assumptions (ie, what-if scenarios)	For **limited** use **only**
	• Example: projecting *what* would happen *if* an entity lost a major customer	

When accepting an engagement (eg, examination, compilation) in connection with projected F/S, CPAs must consider for whom the information is intended. It is acceptable to present a projection in connection with a loan application because the parties involved can discuss the nature of the projection in detail to obtain a comprehensive understanding. Likewise, it is acceptable to provide a projection to a single principal stockholder or a state or federal regulatory agency requesting the projection. However, it is inappropriate to accept an engagement if the projection is intended for a large group of users, such as potential stockholders (ie, general public) in an offering statement.

The practitioner should request a written assertion from the responsible party; if that party refuses, the practitioner should withdraw when that is permitted by applicable law or regulation.

The practitioner should establish an overall engagement strategy that guides the development of the engagement plan to determine the scope and timing of the work and should obtain an appropriate level of knowledge about the entity's industry (and accounting principles used) and the key factors underlying the prospective financial information.

Examination Procedures

The practitioner should perform the procedures considered necessary to report on whether the assumptions underlying the forecast (or projection) are suitably supported and provide a reasonable basis for the forecast (or projection).

The practitioner should evaluate the support for significant assumptions individually and in the aggregate. They are viewed as suitably supported if each significant assumption is supported by the preponderance of the information.

- For a **forecast**, the practitioner should evaluate whether there is a reasonably objective basis for the forecast and whether sufficiently objective assumptions can be developed for each key factor identified.

- For a **projection**, the practitioner should evaluate whether the hypothetical assumptions are consistent with the purpose of the projection; the practitioner need not obtain support for the hypothetical assumptions, however.

Management must include summary of significant assumptions

Assumptions can include:
- Expected sales or profits
- Obtaining financing from lenders
- Expected economic conditions
- Passing of certain laws or regulations

To evaluate the preparation and presentation of a forecast or projection, the practitioner should obtain reasonable assurance that:

- The presentation reflects the identified assumptions

- Any computations made are mathematically accurate

- Assumptions are internally consistent

- Accounting principles used are appropriate

- Information is presented according to the AICPA Guide

- Assumptions have been adequately disclosed.

Written Representations

The practitioner should request the required written representations from the responsible party (even if the engaging party is not the responsible party). There is no alternative to obtaining the requested representations, so the responsible party's refusal to furnish the representations is a scope limitation that may preclude an unmodified opinion and warrant withdrawal.

For a forecast, in addition to the representations required by AT-C 205 (regarding examination engagements), the practitioner should request the following from the responsible party:

- The forecast presents the expected financial statements and reflects expected conditions

- The underlying assumptions are reasonable and suitably supported

- If the forecast is expressed as a range, the range was not selected in a misleading manner.

For a projection, in addition to the representations required by AT-C 205, the practitioner should request representations from the responsible party that:

- Identify the hypothetical assumptions (and identify any of those that are considered to be "improbable")

- Describe the limitations of the usefulness of the presentation

- The projection presents expected financial information based on present circumstances, expected conditions, and the occurrence of the hypothetical events

- The assumptions (other than the hypothetical assumptions) are reasonable and suitably supported

- If the projection is expressed as a range, the range was not selected in a misleading manner.

Pro Forma Engagements

A practitioner may be asked to report on pro forma F/S that are derived from historical F/S. This refers to a presentation in which information is restated for an event that actually hadn't occurred. For example, a client that is considering a change in accounting principle might want to see how the F/S of the preceding year would have appeared had the change been made earlier.

As long as the F/S from which the pro forma statements were derived were audited, an examination engagement of this type is permitted. Similarly, as long as the F/S from which the pro forma statements were derived were audited or reviewed, a review engagement of this type may be performed.

Definitions

Pro Forma Financial Information: A presentation that shows what the significant effects on historical financial information might have been had a consummated or proposed transaction (or event) occurred at an earlier date.

Criteria for the Preparation of Pro Forma Financial Information: The basis disclosed in the pro forma financial information that management used to develop the pro forma financial information, including the assumptions underlying the pro forma financial information.

AICPA Guidance

Guidance is provided in AT-C 310, *Reporting on Pro Forma Financial Information* and applies to examination or review engagements involving pro forma financial information.

	Can be reviewed?	Standard
Annual financial statements (F/S)	✓	SSARS
Single financial statement	✓	SSARS
Pro forma F/S	✓	SSAE
Interim F/S (nonissuer)	✓	SAS/SSARS
Prospective F/S (projection or forecast)	✗	N/A
Internal control	✗	N/A
Compliance (eg, laws, contracts)	✗	N/A

Examination or Review Engagement Preconditions

In addition to preconditions identified in other relevant AT-C sections, additional preconditions include:

- The document containing the pro forma financial information should also include the historical F/S (or the historical F/S need to be readily available)

- For an examination, the historical F/S must have been audited

- For a review, the historical F/S must have been either audited or reviewed. They cannot express a higher level of assurance on the pro forma information than on the historical F/S

- The audit report or the review report on the historical F/S, as applicable, must be included in the document containing the pro forma financial information (or it must be readily available)

- The practitioner should obtain an appropriate level of knowledge of the entity's accounting and financial reporting practices to perform the necessary procedures to report on the pro forma financial information.

Assessing the Suitability of the Criteria

The criteria used by management are considered suitable when the criteria address the following matters:

- The financial information is extracted from the applicable historical F/S

- The pro forma adjustments are directly attributable to the transaction (event), are factually supportable, and consistent with the entity's applicable financial reporting framework and its accounting policies

- The pro forma financial information is appropriately presented, including adequate disclosures for users' understanding.

Examination and Review Procedures

The practitioner should apply the following procedures to the assumptions and pro forma adjustments for either an examination or a review engagement:

- Obtain an understanding of the underlying transaction (event)

- Obtain an understanding of the accounting and financial reporting practices of the entity (entities); if another practitioner performed the audit/review of the historical financial statements, the practitioner still should obtain this understanding

- Discuss with management their assumptions about the effects of the transaction/event

- Obtain sufficient appropriate evidence regarding the adjustments

- Evaluate whether pro forma adjustments are included for all significant effects

- Evaluate whether management's underlying assumptions are presented in a clear, comprehensive manner

- Evaluate whether the pro forma adjustments are consistent with each other and with the data used to make them

- Evaluate whether the computations of the adjustments are mathematically accurate and whether the pro forma column properly applies those adjustments to the historical financial statements

- Read the pro forma financial information and evaluate whether (a) the transaction/event, the underlying assumptions, and the pro forma adjustments (and any significant uncertainties) have been adequately described; and (b) the source of the historical financial information involved has been properly identified.

Written Representation in an Examination and a Review Engagement

The practitioner should request the following written representations (in addition to those identified in other relevant AT-C sections):

- Management is responsible for the underlying assumptions used

- The assumptions are factually supportable (meaning that they are supported by the "preponderance" of the information)

- The assumptions (a) provide a reasonable basis for presenting the significant effects, (b) the related adjustments properly reflect those assumptions, and (c) the pro forma amounts properly reflect those adjustments to the historical F/S

- The pro forma adjustments are consistent with the entity's applicable financial reporting framework

- The pro forma financial information is properly presented with proper disclosure of the significant effects directly attributable to the transaction/event involved.

Management's refusal to provide the requested written representations is a scope limitation sufficient to cause the practitioner to withdraw from the examination or review engagement. There is no alternative for obtaining the requested written representations from management for an engagement to examine or review pro forma financial information.

Other Attestation Engagements

Management's Discussion & Analysis (MD&A)

Publicly held entities are required to provide a set of disclosures referred to as Management Discussion and Analysis (MD&A) in accordance with certain rules prescribed by the SEC. In addition, some nonpublic entities prepare MD&A and management asserts that it is presented in accordance with SEC requirements.

A CPA may be engaged to perform either an examination or a review of MD&A for either type of entity (AT-C 395).

Such an engagement may only be accepted if the most recent period covered by the MD&A was audited by the CPA and all other periods covered by the MD&A were audited by either the CPA or a predecessor.

As a result of the engagement, the CPA will issue either an examination report or a review report, as appropriate. Both reports address the same issues:

- Does the MD&A include all of the required elements?

- Was the historical financial information included in MD&A accurately derived from the F/S?

- Do the underlying information, determinations, estimates, and assumptions provide a reasonable basis for the disclosures included in MD&A?

 Which of the following is an assertion embodied in management's discussion and analysis (MD&A)?

- Valuation

- Reliability

- Consistency with the financial statements

- Rights and Obligations

Assertions in management discussion and analysis (MD&A)	
Occurrence	The disclosed information has taken place during the period
Consistency with the F/S	The financial and nonfinancial information is aligned with F/S
Completeness	All information needing disclosure has been disclosed
Presentation and disclosure	Information is clearly presented and understandable

The attestation standards on MD&A indicate that **consistency with the financial statements** is an assertion. In addition, occurrence, completeness, and presentation and disclosure are embodied assertions.

Condensed Financial Statements or Selected Data

A client may wish to present condensed F/S or selected data in an advertisement, brochure, or other presentation that doesn't include the basic F/S and notes. The practitioner may issue a report on such information as long as they audited the basic F/S from which the condensed data are derived. The report on the condensed F/S must:

- Refer to the audit, providing the report date and type of opinion expressed.
- State whether the condensed data is fairly stated in all material respects in relation to the complete F/S.

Report on audit of an issuer's condensed financial statements

We have audited, in accordance with the standards of the Public Company Accounting Oversight Board (United States) ("PCAOB"), the consolidated balance sheet of X Company and subsidiaries as of December 31, 20X0, and the related consolidated statements of [*titles of the financial statements, e.g., income, comprehensive income, stockholders' equity, and cash flows*] for the year then ended (not presented herein); and in our report dated February 15, 20X1, we expressed an unqualified opinion on those consolidated financial statements. In our opinion, the informations et forth in the accompanying condensed consolidated financial statements is fairly stated, in all material respects, in relation to the consolidated financial statements from which it has been derived.

Source: PCOB AS 3315: Reporting on Condensed Financial Statements and Selected Financial Data

Attestation Engagement Reports

 Representative Task (Application): Determine the appropriate form and content of an accountant's report for an assertion-based examination, direct examination, or review for an attestation engagement.

Sample reports can be found in the Appendix.

Examination Reports

The paragraphs of an examination report are not labeled. The body of the examination report typically consists of four paragraphs (and a signature block) as follows:

- **Introduction:** This paragraph identifies the nature of the engagement and the assertion/subject matter (or underlying subject matter) involved; it also includes a brief statement as to the responsible party's responsibility and a statement as to the practitioner's responsibility.
- **Scope:** This paragraph refers to the attestation standards established by the AICPA; it describes the characteristics of an examination under those standards; and it includes a statement as to the practitioner's belief that sufficient appropriate evidence has been obtained to provide a reasonable basis for the opinion.
- **Independence:** A separate sentence (paragraph) acknowledges the requirement to be independent and meet other ethical responsibilities.
- **Opinion:** This paragraph expresses an opinion (on management's assertion, the subject matter, or underlying subject matter/subject matter information, as applicable, depending on the type of examination engagement).
- **Signature block:** This consists of (a) practitioner's signature (firm name); (b) practitioner's city and state (office responsible for issuing the report); and (c) date of practitioner's report.

Additional paragraphs may be added prior to the opinion paragraph. For example, a description of any significant inherent limitations or to emphasize certain matters related to the engagement/subject matter, and so on. An additional paragraph may also be added after the opinion paragraph to restrict the distribution of the report when appropriate.

Examination Reports: Unmodified

A standardized format for the examination report is not required for examination engagements (whether assertion-based or direct examination engagements). The report should include the identified basic elements but may be tailored to the circumstances of the engagement, including:

- A title that includes the word "independent"

- An appropriate addressee

- Identification of the applicable assertion or subject matter (or subject matter information), including the point in time or period of time involved

- Identification of the criteria against which the subject matter was measured or evaluated

- A statement that identifies (a) the responsible party and its responsibility and (b) the practitioner's responsibility to express an opinion

- A statement that: (a) the examination was conducted in accordance with attestation standards established by the AICPA; (b) those standards require the practitioner to plan and perform the engagement to obtain reasonable assurance (whether the subject matter is in accordance with the criteria in all material respects or whether the responsible party's assertion is fairly stated); and (c) the practitioner believes the evidence obtained is sufficient and appropriate to provide a reasonable basis for the opinion

- A statement regarding the requirement to be independent and meet other ethical responsibilities

- A statement that describes the nature of the examination engagement

- A statement describing any significant inherent limitations associated with the engagement

- An opinion on whether the responsible party's assertion is fairly stated in all material respects or whether the subject matter is in accordance with (or based on) the identified criteria in all material respects, as applicable

- A signature block that identifies (a) the practitioner's firm, (b) the city and state of the practitioner's firm, and (c) the date of the examination report.

Examination Reports: Modified Opinions

Examination reports may have a modified opinion due to:

- Presentation issues (subject matter is not in accordance with the criteria or is not fairly stated)

- Scope limitations (sufficient appropriate evidence has not been obtained)

Reporting when evidence is unavailable (scope limitation)

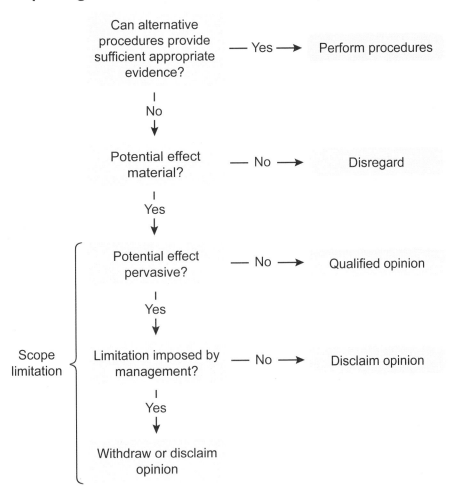

There are three types of modified opinions:

- **Qualified opinion:** Express a qualified opinion (a) when the possible effect of a scope limitation could be material but not pervasive; or (b) when the misstatement of the subject matter is material but not pervasive to the subject matter.

- **Adverse opinion:** Express an adverse opinion when the misstatement of the subject matter is both material and pervasive to the subject matter.

- **Disclaimer of opinion:** Express a disclaimer of opinion when the possible effect of the scope limitation could be both material and pervasive.

When modifying the opinion, a separate paragraph is added prior to the opinion paragraph to describe the reason(s) for the modification.

When modifying the opinion, the description of the practitioner's responsibility may need to be revised:

- When expressing a qualified or an adverse opinion, change the description of that responsibility to express the belief that the evidence obtained is sufficient and appropriate to provide a basis for the modified opinion.

- When expressing a disclaimer of opinion, change the first sentence of the report to say, "We were engaged to examine . . ...." instead of "We have examined . . ."; omit stating what the attestation standards require of the practitioner; omit expressing a belief that sufficient appropriate evidence was obtained; and omit the description of the nature of an examination engagement.

When expressing either a qualified or an adverse opinion (for an assertion-based examination engagement) due to a misstatement of the subject matter, express the opinion directly on the subject matter, not on the assertion (even if the assertion acknowledges the misstatement).

Examination Reports: Other Considerations

An alert to restrict the use of the report should be added when:

- The criteria used to evaluate the subject matter are appropriate only for a limited number of parties.

- The criteria used to evaluate the subject matter are available only to specified parties.

- The engaging party is not the responsible party, and the responsible party does not provide the requested written representation but does provide appropriate oral responses. In this case, the examination report should be restricted to the engaging party.

There should not be any reference to the practitioner's specialist in a report having an unmodified opinion. There may be a reference to the external specialist when the opinion is modified and reference to the specialist is relevant to understanding the reason for the modification.

Other Information (OI) may be presented along with the examination report. Responsibilities for addressing the OI include:

- Reading it to identify material inconsistencies relative to the examination engagement
- Discussing the matter with the responsible party and taking appropriate action if there is a material inconsistency (or if a material misstatement of fact exists in the other information)
  - Request that the responsible party change the other information to resolve the issue
  - Request that the appropriate party consult with a third party (such as legal counsel)
  - Communicate with third parties (such as a regulatory authority)
  - Describe the material inconsistency in the examination report.

Prospective Information Examination Report

After examining prospective F/S, a CPA issues a report expressing an opinion. Types of opinions on prospective F/S include:

Opinions on examination of prospective financial statements (F/S)	
Unmodified	• F/S are presented, in all material respects, in adherence with AICPA *presentation* guidelines, and
	• Underlying *assumptions* are reasonable for forecast or projection
Qualified or adverse*	• F/S materially depart from AICPA *presentation* guidelines
Adverse	• F/S fail to disclose significant *assumptions* or F/S misapply accounting principles, or
	• One or more significant *assumptions* is not suitably supported or does not provide a reasonable basis for the forecast or for the projection
Disclaimer	• The CPA cannot obtain sufficient appropriate evidence

*CPAs use professional judgement to determine significance of departure. Adverse opinions are more severe than qualified ones.

The report following an examination must include the following:

- A title that includes the word independent
- An appropriate addressee
- Identification of the prospective financial information being reported on and the time period it relates to
- An indication that the prospective financial information was evaluated against guidelines established by the AICPA
- A statement identifying the responsible party, indicating their responsibility for the preparation and presentation of the prospective financial information in accordance with the AICPA guidelines
- The practitioner's responsibility for expressing an opinion on the prospective financial information
- A statement that the examination was performed in accordance with the AICPA attestation standards, which require the practitioner to plan and perform the engagement to obtain reasonable assurance that the AICPA guidelines were followed and that the practitioner believes that the examination provided a reasonable basis for the opinion
- A description of the nature of an examination
- An opinion as to whether the statements conform to AICPA presentation guidelines and the underlying assumptions provide a reasonable basis for the presentation
- A warning (caveat) that the prospective results may not be achieved
- A statement that the practitioner has no responsibility to update the report for events occurring after the report date
- The manual or printed signature of the practitioner or the practitioner's firm
- The practitioner's city and state
- The date of the report.

For projections:

- A paragraph restricting the use of the report to specified parties (Remember, a projection is based on hypothetical conditions that are not necessarily expected to occur.)
- A separate paragraph with an indication of the limitations on the usefulness of the presentation.

Pro Forma Examination Report

The content should include the following:

- A title that includes the word "independent"
- An appropriate addressee
- Reference to the pro forma adjustments included
- Reference to management's description of the transaction (or event)
- Description of the pro forma financial information being reported on
- Identification of the criteria used to evaluate the pro forma financial information
- Reference to the financial statements from which the historical financial information is derived (refer to any modification of the auditor's report)
- Statement that the pro forma adjustments are based on management's assumptions
- A statement to identify management's responsibility and to identify the practitioner's responsibility to express an opinion
- A statement that the examination was conducted in accordance with attestation standards established by the AICPA and other statements describing the examination engagement
- A statement describing the objectives and limitations of pro forma financial information

- An opinion whether management's assumptions provide a reasonable basis for presenting the significant effects and whether the pro forma adjustments give appropriate effect to those assumptions and the pro forma amounts reflect the proper adjustments to the historical financial statement amounts
- The signature of the practitioner's firm
- The city and state where the practitioner practices
- The date of the report.

Review Reports

The paragraphs of a review report are not labeled. The body of the unmodified review report typically consists of five paragraphs (and a signature block) as follows:

- **Introduction:** This paragraph identifies the nature of the engagement and the assertion or underlying subject matter involved; it also includes a brief statement as to the responsible party's responsibility and a statement as to the practitioner's responsibility.
- **Scope:** This paragraph refers to the attestation standards established by the AICPA; it describes the characteristics of a review under those standards; and it includes a statement as to the practitioner's belief that sufficient appropriate evidence has been obtained to provide a reasonable basis for the conclusion.
- **Independence:** A separate sentence (paragraph) acknowledges the requirement to be independent and meet other ethical responsibilities.
- **Description of procedures performed:** This paragraph describes the work performed as a basis for the conclusion.
- **Conclusion:** This paragraph expresses a conclusion in the form of limited assurance on management's assertion or the underlying subject matter, as applicable.
- **Signature block:** This consists of (a) practitioner's signature (firm name); (b) practitioner's city and state (office responsible for issuing the report); and (c) date of practitioner's report.

Additional paragraphs may be added prior to the conclusion paragraph. For example, a description of significant inherent limitations or an emphasis of certain matters related to the engagement or subject matter. An additional paragraph may also be added after the conclusion paragraph to restrict the distribution of the report when appropriate.

Review Reports: Unmodified Conclusion

A standardized format for the review report is not required; however, the review report should include the identified basic elements tailored to the circumstances of the engagement.

When expressing an unmodified conclusion, the practitioner may report directly on either the subject matter or the responsible party's written assertion. When reporting on the assertion, that assertion should accompany the report (or be clearly stated within the report).

The following elements should be included in an unmodified review report:

- A title that includes the word "independent"
- An appropriate addressee
- Identification of the subject matter or the responsible party's assertion, as applicable, including the point in time or period of time involved
- Identification of the criteria against which the subject matter was measured or evaluated
- A statement:
  - Identifying the responsible party and its responsibility and the practitioner's responsibility to express a conclusion

- That the review was conducted in accordance with attestation standards established by the AICPA; those standards require the practitioner to plan and perform the engagement to obtain limited assurance whether any material modifications should be made (either to the subject matter to be in accordance with the criteria in all material respects or to the responsible party's assertion for it to be fairly stated); and the practitioner believes the evidence obtained is sufficient and appropriate to provide a reasonable basis for the conclusion

- That the level of assurance obtained in a review is substantially less than that of an examination—and disclaim an opinion

- Regarding the requirement to be independent and to meet other ethical responsibilities

- Describing any significant inherent limitations associated with the engagement.

- A description of the work performed as a basis for the conclusion

- A conclusion as to whether the practitioner is aware of any material modifications that should be made to the subject matter or to the responsible party's assertion, as applicable

- A signature block that identifies (a) the practitioner's firm, (b) the city and state of the practitioner's firm, and (c) the date of the review report.

Review Reports: Modified Conclusion

There are two types of modified conclusions for a review engagement:

- **Qualified conclusion:** Express a qualified conclusion when the misstatement of the subject matter is material but not pervasive to the subject matter

- **Adverse conclusion:** Express an adverse conclusion when the misstatement of the subject matter is both material and pervasive to the subject matter; the first sentence should state, "We have undertaken a review of. . ."

When modifying the conclusion, a separate paragraph is added prior to the conclusion paragraph to describe the reason(s) for the modification. The conclusion should be expressed directly on the subject matter, not on the assertion (even if the assertion acknowledges the misstatement).

When unable to obtain sufficient appropriate review evidence, the practitioner should withdraw from the review engagement without issuing a report, assuming that is permitted.

Review Reports: Other Considerations

An alert to restrict the use of the review report should be added following the conclusion paragraph when:

- The criteria used to evaluate the subject matter are appropriate for a limited number of parties or are available only to specified parties

- The engaging party is not the responsible party, and the responsible party does not provide the requested written representation but does provide appropriate oral responses. In this case, the review report should be restricted to the engaging party.

There should be no reference to the work of the practitioner's specialist in a report having an unmodified conclusion. There may be a reference to the external specialist when the conclusion is modified and reference to the specialist is relevant to understanding the reason for the modification.

OI presented along with the review report requires the following steps:

- Read the OI to identify material inconsistencies relative to the review engagement

- Discuss the matter with the responsible party and take appropriate action if there is a material inconsistency (or if a material misstatement of fact exists in the OI)

  - Request that the responsible party revise the OI to resolve the issue

  - Communicate with third parties (such as a regulatory authority)

- Describe the material inconsistency in the review report
- Withdraw from the engagement (when that is permissible).

Pro Forma Review Report

A review report contains all of the same information listed above for an examination report, except as follows:

- Reference to the financial statements from which the historical financial information is derived (the practitioner should state whether the F/S were audited or reviewed and identify any modification of such report)
- A statement to identify management's responsibility and to identify the practitioner's responsibility to express a conclusion
- A statement that the review was conducted in accordance with attestation standards established by the AICPA and other statements describing the review engagement

A conclusion whether the practitioner is aware of any material modifications that should be made to: (a) management's assumptions for them to provide a reasonable basis for presenting the significant effects, (b) the pro forma adjustments for them to give appropriate effect to those assumptions, and (c) the pro forma amounts for them to reflect the proper adjustments to the historical F/S amounts.

Requirements for presenting pro forma financial information

- Labeled as "pro forma" to distinguish from historical financial information
- Describes hypothetical transaction/event and the underlying historical information
- Describes significant assumptions and uncertainties
- States that it should be read in conjunction with the historical financial information
- States that it is not necessarily indicative of what would actually have happened

24.02 Agreed-Upon Procedures Engagements

Agreed-Upon Procedures Engagements: Overview

 Representative Task (Remembering & Understanding): Identify the factors that a practitioner should consider when issuing an agreed-upon procedures report for an attestation engagement.

AICPA Guidance

As previously discussed, an agreed-upon procedures engagement is one in which the practitioner issues a report on their findings (no opinion or conclusion) with regard to specific procedures applied to subject matter. AT-C 215 provides requirements applicable to agreed-upon procedures engagements in addition to the requirements applicable to all attestation engagements under AT-C 105.

Example of agreed-upon procedures engagement

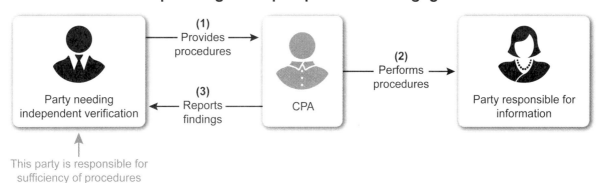

The engaging party that requires findings to be independently derived is the party responsible for the appropriateness of the procedures. For example, suppose Alpha, Inc. wants to purchase a subsidiary from Delta Co. Alpha can hire a CPA to verify that the cash balance associated with the subsidiary is what Delta claims, say $900,000. Alpha will direct the CPA to verify the total cash balance by reviewing bank statements.

In this scenario, Alpha is responsible for the sufficiency of the procedures (ie, ensuring that the procedures can effectively verify the cash balance), and Delta is responsible for the subject matter (ie, claiming that there is a $900,000 cash balance).

Preconditions

Agreed-upon procedures engagement

- CPA must be independent
- Parties involved (not CPA) are responsible for sufficiency of procedures
- List of procedures and findings is included in report

Terms of the Engagement

The practitioner and engaging party should agree upon the terms of the engagement, which are specified in an engagement letter (or other suitable written agreement) addressed to the engaging party. The agreed-upon terms should include the following:

- The nature of the engagement
- Identification of the subject matter and the responsible party
- The responsibilities of the practitioner
- A statement that the:
  - Engagement will be conducted according to AICPA attestation standards
  - Responsible party is responsible for the subject matter
  - Engaging party agrees to provide a written agreement and acknowledgment that the procedures performed are appropriate for the intended purpose of the engagement
  - Engaging party agrees to provide a representations letter (if the engaging party is not the responsible party, include a statement that written representations may be requested from the responsible party)
- If known at the start of the engagement, identification of any other parties that will be requested to agree to the procedures and acknowledge that the procedures are appropriate for their purposes
- Reference to the expected form and content of the AUP report, including any restrictions, if applicable
- Identification of any:
  - Disclaimers expected to be included in the report, if applicable
  - Assistance to be provided to the practitioner
  - Practitioner's external specialist to be used
  - Specified thresholds for reporting exceptions, if applicable.

Performing the Engagement

The practitioner should not agree to perform procedures that are vague or otherwise open to varying interpretations.

- Examples of unacceptable terms (due to vagueness) include the following: note, review, general review, limited review, evaluate, analyze, check, test, interpret, and verify
- Examples of acceptable terms include the following: inspect, confirm, compare, agree, trace, inquire, recalculate, observe, and mathematically check

When using the work of a practitioner's external specialist:

- Any involvement of a practitioner's external specialist should be agreed to by the engaging party
- The practitioner's report should describe any assistance provided by the practitioner's external specialist.

Only the engagement team (or other practitioners), not internal auditors, should perform the agreed-upon procedures referenced in the practitioner's report; internal auditors may prepare schedules and accumulate data for the practitioner's use.

The practitioner should obtain evidence from applying only the agreed-upon procedures; additional procedures beyond the scope of the engagement do not need to be performed.

Which of the following procedures is most likely to be an appropriate procedure when performed as an agreed-upon procedures engagement under the attestation standards?

- Evaluation of the competence or objectivity of another party

- Obtaining an understanding about a particular subject

- Performance of mathematical computations

- Interpreting documents

An agreed-upon procedures engagement is to present specific findings to assist users in evaluating management's assertions about an entity's compliance with specified requirements. An accountant may (1) compare procedures to written requirements, (2) discuss procedures to be applied with specified users, (3) review relevant contracts or communication from specified users to report on management's assertions, and/ or (4) perform mathematical computations. The engagement does not evaluate the competence or objectivity of another party. A CPA does not interpret documents; rather, they only use specific findings.

Written Representations

A written representation letter should be obtained from the engaging party stating:

- The responsible party is responsible for the subject matter

- If applicable, a statement that the engaging party has obtained from all necessary parties their agreement to the procedures and acknowledgment that the procedures are appropriate for the intended purposes

- The engaging party provided all relevant information and access, as agreed to

- The engaging party is not aware of any material misstatements in the subject matter

- The engaging party has disclosed all known subsequent events that would be material to the subject matter

- All known matters contradicting the subject matter and any communications from regulatory agencies or others relevant to the subject matter have been disclosed to the practitioner.

When the engaging party is not the responsible party, the practitioner should consider requesting written representations from the responsible party as well.

The written representations should be dated the same as the date of the practitioner's report.

If the requested written representations are not provided or are not reliable, the practitioner should discuss the matter with the appropriate parties and take appropriate action if the matters are not satisfactorily resolved (eg, if the responsible party refuses to provide requested written representations, that refusal should be identified in the practitioner's report).

Documenting the Engagement

The practitioner should document the following:

- The agreement with the engaging party regarding the procedures to be performed and the appropriateness of those procedures

- The nature, timing, and extent of the procedures performed to comply with AICPA attestation standards and applicable legal and regulatory requirements, including:

  - The identifying characteristics of specific items tested

  - Who performed the work and the date the work was completed

  - Matters related to situations when the appropriate party does not provide requested written representations or when those written representations do not appear to be reliable

  - Who reviewed the work performed and the date and extent of that review

- The results of the procedures performed and the evidence obtained.

Agreed-Upon Procedures Engagement Report

 Representative Task (Application): Determine the appropriate form and content of an agreed-upon procedures report for an attestation engagement.

Practitioners (ie, CPAs) who perform agreed-upon procedure engagements issue a written report of their findings based on procedures specified by the engaging parties. Agreed-upon procedure reports do not offer any form of assurance, and no opinion is issued by the practitioner or management. As such, the title of the report is simply "Independent Accountant's Report."

However, the report does state that the engaging parties agreed to and acknowledged the procedures performed were appropriate to meet the intended purpose of the engagement. There is also a statement that the report may not be suitable for any other purpose

 Which of the following statements is least likely to be included in a practitioner's report on agreed-upon procedures?

- The use of the report is not subject to specified restrictions.
- The subject matter is the responsibility of the responsible party.
- The report has provided limited assurance.
- The procedures performed were agreed to by the specified parties.

In this type of engagement, the CPA does not provide assurance and does not issue an opinion or conclusion. The statement least likely to appear in the AUP report is a statement about limited assurance being provided. A report on the findings of the engagement is issued. The report will include reference to restrictions, if any, responsibilities, and agreement on the procedures.

When reporting findings, practitioners accept responsibility for everything up to the report date.

Under certain circumstances, the report may include a restriction alert. The alert is a separate paragraph and restricts the use of the report, considering the understanding with the engaging party regarding the nature of the engagement. This is optional; reports are not automatically restricted.

Content of agreed-upon procedures report

- Title that includes the term "independent"
- Identification of engaging parties and subject matter
- Statement that the engaging party acknowledges the procedures performed were appropriate to the intended purpose of the engagement
- Description of each procedure performed and the findings from each procedure
- When applicable, a restriction alert concerning the procedures, findings, or report distribution

A nonissuer engaged a practitioner to perform agreed-upon procedures on specified matters. The date of the practitioner's report would ordinarily be determined by the occurrence of which of the following events?

- The receipt of the signed engagement letter from the client

- The completion of the agreed-upon procedures

- The client's review and approval of the contents of a draft report

- The delivery of the final report to the client

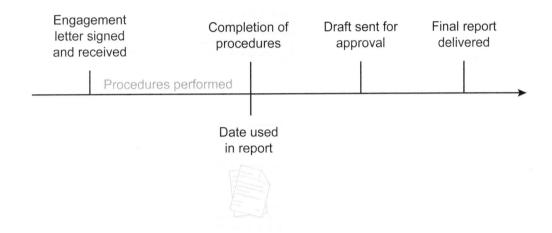

Suppose CPAs completed procedures to verify cash on 1/20/Year 2 but dated the report 1/30/Year 2. If the seller withdraws $15,000 from the cash accounts on 1/25/Year 2, CPAs could be liable for misrepresenting the validity of the cash account as of 1/30/Year 2, even if they were unaware of the withdrawal. Therefore, the date on the report would be the date the procedures are completed.

Prospective Information

Preconditions

The practitioner should not perform such an engagement on a forecast or projection unless the prospective financial information includes a summary of significant assumptions.

Content of Agreed-Upon Procedures Report

For agreed-upon procedures, the report must include the following:

- The findings of the practitioner resulting from the procedures

- A statement that the procedures applied may not be sufficient, and that the specified users accept responsibility for this fact

- A warning (caveat) that the prospective results may not be achieved

- A statement that the practitioner has no responsibility to update the report for events occurring after the report date

- A separate paragraph with an indication of the limitations on the usefulness of the presentation

- A summary of significant assumptions is also required.

Appendix: Sample Statements

 Assertion-Based Examination Report on Subject Matter – Unmodified Opinion

INDEPENDENT PRACTITIONER'S REPORT

To: Appropriate addressee

We have **examined** *[identify the subject matter, for example, the accompanying schedule of investment returns of XYZ Company for the year ended December 31, 20XX]*. XYZ Company's management is responsible for [identify the subject matter, for example, presenting the schedule of investment returns] in accordance with (or based on) *[identify the criteria, for example, the ABC criteria set forth in Note 1]*. Our responsibility is to express an **opinion** on *[identify the subject matter, for example, the schedule of investment returns]* based on our examination.

Our examination was conducted in accordance with **attestation standards** established by the American Institute of Certified Public Accountants. Those standards require that we plan and perform the examination to obtain reasonable assurance about whether *[identify the subject matter, for example, the schedule of investment returns]* is in accordance with (or based on) the **criteria**, in all material respects. An examination involves performing procedures to obtain evidence about *[identify the subject matter, for example, the schedule of investment returns]*. The nature, timing, and extent of the procedures selected depend on our judgment, including an assessment of the risks of material misstatement of *[identify the subject matter, for example, the schedule of investment returns]*, whether due to fraud or error. We believe that the evidence we obtained is sufficient and appropriate to provide a reasonable basis for our opinion.

[Include a description of significant **inherent limitations**, *if any, associated with the measurement or evaluation of the subject matter against the criteria.]*

[Additional paragraph(s) may be added to **emphasize certain matters** relating to the attestation engagement or the subject matter.]

In our opinion, *[identify the subject matter, for example, the schedule of investment returns of XYZ Company for the year ended December 31, 20XX or the schedule of investment returns referred to above]*, is presented **in accordance with** (or based on) *[identify* **the criteria**, *for example, the ABC criteria set forth in Note 1]*, in all material respects.

Asher P. Levy, CPA
Santa Ana, CA
March 1, 20XX

Assertion-Based Examination – Disclaimer of Opinion

INDEPENDENT PRACTITIONER'S REPORT

To: Appropriate addressee

We were engaged to examine *[identify the subject matter, for example, the accompanying schedule of investment returns of XYZ Company for the year ended December 31, 20XX]*, in accordance with (or based on) *[identify the criteria, for example, the ABC criteria set forth in Note 1]*. XYZ Company's **management is responsible** for *[identify the subject matter, for example, presenting the schedule of investment returns]*. **Our responsibility** is to express an opinion on [identify the subject matter, for example, the schedule of investment returns] based on conducting the examination in accordance with attestation standards established by the American Institute of Certified Public Accountants.

[Include a paragraph to describe scope limitations.]

Because of the limitation on the scope of our examination discussed in the preceding paragraph, the scope of our work was not sufficient to enable us to express, and **we do not express**, an opinion on whether *[identify the subject matter, for example, the accompanying schedule of investment returns of XYZ Company for the year ended December 31, 20XX, or the schedule of investment returns referred to above]* is in accordance with (or based on) *[identify the criteria, for example, the ABC criteria set forth in Note 1]*, in all material respects.

Darren Chris, CPA
Santa Ana, CA
March 1, 20XX

Direct Examination Report

INDEPENDENT PRACTITIONER'S REPORT

To: Appropriate addressee

We have **examined** *[identify the underlying subject matter, for example, the investment transactions of XYZ Company during the year ended December 31, 20XX]*. XYZ Company's management is responsible for *[identify the underlying subject matter, for example, its investment transactions during the year ended December 31, 20XX]* and maintaining a record of those transactions. Our responsibility is to obtain **reasonable assurance** by **measuring** (or **evaluating**) *[identify the underlying subject matter, for example, the investment transactions of XYZ Company during the year ended December 31, 20XX]* against *[identify the criteria, for example, the ABC criteria set forth in Note 1 of the accompanying schedule of investment returns]* to determine *[identify the subject matter information, for example, the rates of return on those investment transactions]* and performing other procedures to obtain **sufficient appropriate evidence to express an opinion that conveys the results of our measurement (or evaluation)** based on our examination. We have presented the results of our measurement in the accompanying schedule of investment returns.

Our examination was conducted in accordance with the attestation standards for a direct examination engagement established by the AICPA. Those standards require that we **obtain reasonable assurance by measuring (or evaluating)** *[identify the underlying subject matter, for example, the investment transactions of XYZ Company during the year ended December 31, 20XX]* against *[identify the criteria, for example, the ABC criteria set forth in Note 1 of the accompanying schedule of investment returns]* and performing other procedures to obtain sufficient appropriate evidence to express an opinion that conveys the results of our measurement or evaluation of *[identify the underlying subject matter, for example, the investment transactions of XYZ Company during the year ended December 31, 20XX]*. The nature, timing, and extent of the procedures selected depend on our judgment, including an assessment of the risks of material misstatement of *[identify the subject matter information, for example, the rates of return on those investment transactions for the year ended December 31, 20XX, as presented in the schedule of investment returns]*, whether due to fraud or error. We believe that the evidence we obtained is sufficient and appropriate to provide a reasonable basis for our opinion.

We are required to be independent of *[identify the responsible party, for example, XYZ Company]* and to meet our other ethical responsibilities, in accordance with relevant ethical requirements relating to our examination engagement. *[Include a description of significant inherent limitations, if any, associated with the measurement or evaluation of the underlying subject matter against the criteria.]*

[Additional paragraphs may be added to emphasize certain matters relating to the attestation engagement, the underlying subject matter, or the subject matter information.]

In our opinion, *[identify the subject matter information, for example, the rates of return on the investment transactions of XYZ Company during the year ended December 31, 20XX included in the accompanying schedule of investment returns of XYZ Company for the year ended December 31, 20XX,]*, are fairly presented in accordance with (or based on) *[identify the criteria, for example, the ABC criteria set forth in Note 1]*, in all material respects.

[Signature of the practitioner's firm]
[City and state where the practitioner's report is issued]
[Date of the practitioner's report]

Review Report on Subject Matter – Unmodified Conclusion

INDEPENDENT PRACTITIONER'S REVIEW REPORT

To: *Appropriate addressee*

We have **reviewed** *[identify the subject matter, for example, the accompanying schedule of investment returns of XYZ Company for the year ended December 31, 20XX]*. XYZ Company's management is responsible for *[identify the subject matter, for example, presenting the schedule of investment returns]* in accordance with (or based on) *[identify the **criteria**, for example, the ABC criteria set forth in Note 1]*. Our responsibility is to express a **conclusion** on *[identify the subject matter, for example, the schedule of investment returns]* based on our **review**.

Our review was **conducted in accordance with attestation standards** established by the AICPA. Those standards require that we plan and perform the review to obtain **limited assurance about whether any material modifications should be made** to *[identify the subject matter, for example, the schedule of investment returns]* in order for it to be **in accordance with** (or based on) **the criteria.** The procedures performed in a review vary in nature and timing from and are substantially less in extent than, an examination, the objective of which is to obtain reasonable assurance about whether *[identify the subject matter, for example, the schedule of investment returns]* is in accordance with (or based on) the criteria, in all material respects, in order to express an opinion. Accordingly, we **do not express such an opinion.** Because of the limited nature of the engagement, the level of assurance obtained in a review is substantially lower than the assurance that would have been obtained had an examination been performed. **We believe that the review evidence obtained is sufficient and appropriate to provide a reasonable basis for our conclusion**.

We are **required to be independent** and to meet our other ethical responsibilities in accordance with relevant ethical requirements related to the engagement.

[Include a description of the work performed as a basis for the practitioner's conclusion.]

[Include a description of significant inherent limitations, if any, associated with the measurement or evaluation of the subject matter against the criteria.]

[Additional paragraph(s) may be added to emphasize certain matters relating to the attestation engagement or the subject matter.]

Based on our review, **we are not aware of any material modifications that should be made** to *[identify the subject matter, for example, the accompanying schedule of investment returns of XYZ Company for the year ended December 31, 20XX]*, in order for it be **in accordance with** (or based on) [identify the criteria, for example, the ABC criteria set forth in Note 1].

Kristin Charberts, CPA
Santa Ana, CA
March 1, 20XX

Review Report on an Assertion – Unmodified Conclusion and Restricted

INDEPENDENT PRACTITIONER'S REVIEW REPORT

To: *Appropriate addressee*

We have reviewed management of XYZ Company's **assertion** that *[identify the assertion, including the subject matter and the criteria, for example, the accompanying schedule of investment returns of XYZ Company for the year ended December 31, 20XX, is presented in accordance with (or based on) the ABC criteria set forth in Note 1]*. XYZ Company's **management is responsible for its assertion**. **Our responsibility is to express a conclusion on management's assertion** based on our review.

Our review was **conducted in accordance with attestation standards** established by the AICPA. Those standards require that we plan and perform the review to **obtain limited assurance about whether any material modifications should be made to management's assertion** in order for it to be fairly stated. The procedures performed in a review vary in nature and timing from and are substantially less in extent than, an examination, the objective of which is to obtain reasonable assurance about whether management's assertion is fairly stated, in all material respects, in order to express an opinion. Accordingly, we do not express such an opinion. Because of the limited nature of the engagement, the level of assurance obtained in a review is substantially lower than the assurance that would have been obtained had an examination been performed. **We believe that the review evidence obtained is sufficient and appropriate to provide a reasonable basis for our conclusion**.

***

Based on our review, **we are not aware of any material modifications that should be made to management of XYZ Company's assertion** in order for it to be fairly stated.

This report is intended solely for the information and use of *[identify the specified parties, for example, ABC Company and XYZ Company]*, and is not intended to be, and should not be, used by anyone other than the specified parties.

[Practitioner's signature]
[Practitioner's city and state]
[Date of practitioner's report]

Review Report on an Assertion – Unmodified Conclusion and Restricted

INDEPENDENT PRACTITIONER'S REVIEW REPORT

To: Appropriate addressee

We have reviewed management of XYZ Company's **assertion** that *[identify the assertion, including the subject matter and the criteria, for example, the accompanying schedule of investment returns of XYZ Company for the year ended December 31, 20XX, is presented in accordance with (or based on) the ABC criteria set forth in Note 1].* XYZ Company's **management is responsible for its assertion. Our responsibility is to express a conclusion on management's assertion** based on our review.

Our review was **conducted in accordance with attestation standards** established by the AICPA. Those standards require that we plan and perform the review to **obtain limited assurance about whether any material modifications should be made to management's assertion** in order for it to be fairly stated. The procedures performed in a review vary in nature and timing from and are substantially less in extent than, an examination, the objective of which is to obtain reasonable assurance about whether management's assertion is fairly stated, in all material respects, in order to express an opinion. Accordingly, we do not express such an opinion. Because of the limited nature of the engagement, the level of assurance obtained in a review is substantially lower than the assurance that would have been obtained had an examination been performed. **We believe that the review evidence obtained is sufficient and appropriate to provide a reasonable basis for our conclusion**.

***

Based on our review, **we are not aware of any material modifications that should be made to management of XYZ Company's assertion** in order for it to be fairly stated.

This report is intended solely for the information and use of *[identify the specified parties, for example, ABC Company and XYZ Company]*, and is not intended to be, and should not be, used by anyone other than the specified parties.

[Practitioner's signature]
[Practitioner's city and state]
[Date of practitioner's report]

 Review Report on Subject Matter – Qualified Conclusion

INDEPENDENT PRACTITIONER'S REVIEW REPORT

To: Appropriate addressee

***

Our review identified [describe condition(s) that, individually or in the aggregate, resulted in a **material misstatement or deviation** from the criteria].

Based on our review, **except for the matter(s) described** in the preceding paragraph, we are **not aware of any material modifications** that should be made to *[identify the subject matter, for example, the accompanying schedule of investment returns of XYZ Company for the year ended December 31, 20XX]*, in order for it to be in accordance with (or based on) *[identify the criteria, for example, the ABC criteria set forth in Note 1]*.

Wendy Robson, CPA
Santa Ana, CA
March 1, 20XX

Agreed-Upon Procedures Report Example (with optional restriction alert)

INDEPENDENT PRACTITIONER'S REPORT

To: Appropriate addressee

We have performed the procedures enumerated below on *[identify the subject matter, for example, the financial accounts of the engaging party during the year ended December 31, 20XX]. [The responsible party]* is responsible for *[the subject matter]*.

[The engaging party] has agreed to and acknowledged that the procedures performed are appropriate to meet the intended purpose of *[identify the intended purpose of the engagement, for example, assisting users in understanding the financial accounts of the engaging party during the year ended December 31, 20XX]*. **This report may not be suitable for any other purpose.** The procedures performed may not address all the items of interest to a user of this report and may not meet the needs of all users of this report and, as such, users are responsible for determining whether the procedures performed are appropriate for their purposes.

The procedures and the associated findings are as follows:

*[Include paragraphs to describe the **procedures performed** detailing the nature and extent, and if applicable, the timing, of each procedure and to describe the **findings** from each procedure performed, including sufficient details on **exceptions found**.]*

We were engaged by *[the engaging party]* to perform this agreed-upon procedures engagement and conducted our engagement in accordance with **attestation standards** established by the AICPA. We were not engaged to and did not conduct an examination or review engagement, the objective of which would be the expression of an opinion or conclusion, respectively, on *[identify the subject matter]*. Accordingly, **we do not express such an opinion or conclusion**. Had we performed additional procedures, other matters might have come to our attention that would have been reported to you.

We are required to be **independent** of *[the responsible party]* and to meet our other ethical responsibilities, in accordance with the relevant ethical requirements related to our agreed-upon procedures engagement.

This report is intended solely for the information and use of *[identify the specified parties, for example, the engaging party and the State of XXX]*, and is not intended to be, and should not be, used by anyone other than these specified parties.

[Additional paragraphs may be added to describe other matters.]
Jae Evers, CPA
Santa Ana, CA
*March 1, 20XX**

---

* The report should be dated no earlier than the date on which the practitioner completed the procedures and determined the findings.

Examination Report of a Financial Forecast

INDEPENDENT PRACTITIONER'S REPORT

To: *Appropriate addressee*

We have **examined** the accompanying forecast of XYZ Company, which comprises the forecasted balance sheet as of December 31, 20XX, and the related forecasted statements of income, retained earnings, and cash flows for the year then ended, based on the guidelines for the presentation of a forecast established by the American Institute of Certified Public Accountants. XYZ Company's management is responsible for preparing and presenting the forecast in accordance with the guidelines for the presentation of a forecast established by the American Institute of Certified Public Accountants. Our responsibility is to express an opinion on the forecast based on our examination.

Our examination was conducted in accordance with **attestation standards established by the American Institute of Certified Public Accountants**. Those standards require that we plan and perform the examination to obtain reasonable assurance about whether the forecast is presented in accordance with the guidelines for the presentation of a forecast established by the American Institute of Certified Public Accountants, in all material respects. An examination involves performing procedures to obtain evidence about the forecast. The nature, timing, and extent of the procedures selected depend on our judgment, including an assessment of the risks of material misstatement of the forecast, whether due to fraud or error. We believe that the evidence we obtained is sufficient and appropriate to provide a reasonable basis for our opinion.

In our opinion, the accompanying forecast is presented, in all material respects, in accordance with the guidelines for presentation of a forecast established by the American Institute of Certified Public Accountants, and the underlying assumptions are reasonably supported and provide a reasonable basis for management's forecast.

There will usually be **differences** between the forecasted and actual results, because events and circumstances frequently do not occur as expected, and those differences may be material. We have **no responsibility to update** this report for events and circumstances occurring after the date of this report.

Jessica Daubson, CPA
Santa Ana, CA
March 1, 20XX

Examination Report on Pro Forma Financial Information – Unmodified Opinion

INDEPENDENT PRACTITIONER'S REPORT

We have **examined** the pro forma adjustments giving effect to the underlying transaction (or event) described in Note 1 and the application of those adjustments to the historical amounts in the accompanying pro forma condensed balance sheet of X Company as of December 31, 20X1, and the related pro forma condensed statement of income for the year then ended (pro forma financial information), based on the criteria in Note 1. The historical condensed financial statements are derived from the historical financial statements of X Company, which were **audited by us**, and of Y Company, which were audited by other accountants, appearing elsewhere herein [or "and are readily available"]. The pro forma adjustments are based on **management's assumptions** described in Note 1. X Company's management is responsible for the pro forma financial information. Our responsibility is to express an opinion on the pro forma financial information based on our examination.

Our examination was conducted in accordance with attestation standards established by the American Institute of Certified Public Accountants. Those standards require that we plan and perform the examination to obtain reasonable assurance about whether, based on the criteria in Note 1, management's assumptions provide a reasonable basis for presenting the significant effects directly attributable to the underlying transaction (or event), and, in all material respects, the related pro forma adjustments give appropriate effect to those assumptions, and the pro forma amounts reflect the proper application of those adjustments to the historical financial statement amounts. An examination involves performing procedures to obtain evidence about management's assumptions, the related pro forma adjustments, and the pro forma amounts in the pro forma condensed balance sheet of X Company as of December 31, 20X1, and the related pro forma condensed statement of income for the year then ended. The nature, timing, and extent of the procedures selected depend on our judgment, including an assessment of the risks of material misstatement of the pro forma financial information, whether due to fraud or error. We believe that the evidence we obtained is sufficient and appropriate to provide a reasonable basis for our opinion.

The objective of this pro forma financial information is to show what the significant effects on the historical financial information might have been had the underlying transaction (or event) occurred at an earlier date. However, the pro forma condensed financial statements are not necessarily indicative of the results of operations or related effects on financial position that would have been attained had the above-mentioned transaction (or event) actually occurred at such earlier date.

In our opinion, based on the criteria in Note 1, management's assumptions provide a **reasonable basis** for presenting the significant effects directly attributable to the above-mentioned transaction (or event) described in Note 1, and, in all material respects, the related pro forma adjustments give appropriate effect to those assumptions, and the pro forma amounts reflect the proper application of those adjustments to the historical financial statement amounts in the pro forma condensed balance sheet of X Company as of December 31, 20X1, and the related pro forma condensed statement of income for the year then ended.

***

AUD 25
Accounting and Review Service Engagements

AUD 25: Accounting and Review Service Engagements

25.01 Preparation Engagements

SSARS Overview (AR-C 60)

 The SSARS Overview information presented in this section applies to the entire chapter.

The **Statements on Standards for Accounting and Review Services (SSARS)** are issued by the AICPA's Accounting and Review Services Committee (ARSC) and are applicable to certain financial statement-related services that a CPA may provide to nonissuers.

SSARS No. 21, *Statements on Standards for Accounting and Review Services* is comprised of four sections:

- Section 60, General Principles for Engagements Performed in Accordance with [SSARS]
- Section 70, Preparation of Financial Statements
- Section 80, Compilation Engagements
- Section 90, Review of Financial Statements.

	Statements on Standards for Accounting and Review Services (SSARS)	
Engagement	**Description**	**Report Issued**
Review	• CPA performs inquiries and analytical procedures • *Limited assurance* provided • Independence required	Yes
Compilation	• CPA assembles and reads F/S • F/S used primarily by outside parties • Independence is *not* required, but must be disclosed	Yes
Preparation	• CPA prepares F/S or specified F/S elements (eg, balance sheet) • F/S used for internal purposes or by outside parties • Independence is *not* required and need not be disclosed	No

All SSARS engagements are required to be performed in accordance with AR-C 60, *General Principles for Engagements Performed in Accordance with Statements on Standards for Accounting and Review Services.*

General Principles (AR-C 60)

Ethical Requirements

The accountant is required to comply with all relevant ethical requirements, including those imposed by the AICPA Code of Professional Conduct, state boards of accountancy, or other applicable regulatory agencies.

Professional Judgment

Decisions are required to be made throughout an SSARS engagement and an informed decision can be made only by applying the accountant's knowledge and experience to the facts and circumstances. Informed decisions also may require consultation with others and should lead to judgments that reflect applications of SSARS and accounting principles that are both *competent and appropriate*.

Conduct of the Engagement

Conducting an engagement in accordance with SSARS requires the accountant to be familiar with, and apply, all relevant AR-C sections, including information provided in the application and other explanatory material sections.

In some cases, the accountant may be required to comply with requirements in addition to those of SSARS. This would be the case, for example, if laws or regulations imposed other requirements or the accountant is engaged to compile or review F/S in accordance with SSARS and some other set of standards, such as International Standards issued by the International Federation of Accountants.

As is the case in auditing standards, SSARS impose *two types of requirements*:

- An **unconditional requirement** is associated with the word *must* or the phrase *is required to*.
- A **presumptively mandatory requirement**, associated with the word *should*, is also required when relevant. In rare circumstances, however, the accountant may need to perform alternative procedures (eg, when a procedure presumptively required would be ineffective). In such cases, the accountant must document the reason for the departure and an indication of how the alternative procedures performed achieved the objectives of the requirement.

Engagement Level Quality Control

The engagement partner is responsible for:

- The overall quality of the engagement
- The engagement's direction, planning, supervision, and performance
- The report (if any)
- Compliance with the firm's quality control policies and procedures, including those related to client/ engagement acceptance or continuance, engagement team qualifications, and engagement documentation
- Identifying and communicating circumstances that may affect the client or engagement acceptance or continuance decision
- Being aware of potential noncompliance with ethical requirements.

Preconditions

Circumstances affecting acceptance and continuance of engagements in accordance with the SSARS include the following:

- The accountant should not accept an engagement to be performed in accordance with the SSARS if any of the following circumstances exist:
  - There is reason to believe that relevant ethical requirements (eg, independence requirements) will not be satisfied
  - Information that is needed to perform the engagement is unlikely to be either available or reliable
  - There is reason to doubt management's integrity.

- Prior to accepting an engagement to be performed in accordance with the SSARS, the accountant should perform the following actions:
  - Determine whether the financial reporting framework adopted by management is acceptable
  - Obtain an agreement that management acknowledges and understands its responsibilities for the following:
    - The selection of the financial reporting framework
    - The design, implementation, and maintenance (DIM) of internal control (I/C) relevant to the F/S
    - The prevention and detection of fraud
    - Compliance with applicable laws and regulations
    - The accuracy and completeness of the records, documents, and explanations, including significant judgments made by management for the F/S
    - Providing the accountant with access to all relevant information related to the fair presentation of the F/S, additional information requested by the accountant, and unrestricted access to personnel.

Downgrading an Engagement

Occasionally, an accountant will be in the midst of an audit of a nonpublic entity, and the client will request that the engagement be downgraded to a review or compilation. Similarly, an accountant performing a review may be asked to downgrade to a compilation.

In such circumstances, the accountant should use their professional judgment and consider:

- The **reasons** offered by the client for the downgraded engagement (change in circumstances or a misunderstanding of the nature of an audit, review, or compilation)
- The **additional cost and effort** needed to complete the original engagement. If the engagement is *almost complete* (or requires minimal cost to finish), the accountant should consider the appropriateness of the change request.

A CPA is engaged to audit the F/S of a nonissuer. After the audit begins, the client's management questions the extent of procedures and objects to the confirmation of certain contracts. The client asks the accountant to change the scope of the engagement from an audit to a review. Under these circumstances, the accountant should do each of the following, **except:**

- Consider the additional audit effort and cost required to complete the audit.
- Issue an accountant's review report with a separate paragraph discussing the change in engagement scope.
- Evaluate the possibility that F/S information affected by the limitation on work to be performed may be incorrect or incomplete.
- Consider the reason given for the client's request and assess whether the request is reasonable.

Downgrade in engagement

Client requests change
from audit to lower level of
assurance engagement

↓

Does reasonable
justification for
change exist?

Yes ← | → No

Yes:
Accountant and management should
agree on and document in writing
terms of the *new engagement*

↓

Accountant issues an appropriate
report with *no reference to original
engagement* (may include reference
to procedures performed)

No:
Accountant:

• Communicates circumstances to those
charged with governance

• Withdraws from engagement when possible

• Determines whether any obligation (legal or
contractual) exists to report circumstances
to other parties (owners)

Provided *reasonable justification* does exist, the CPA together with management document the change in a new engagement letter. Because significantly less work is performed in a review than in an audit, no mention of the change in engagement scope should be made in the review report.

If the request of the client is reasonable, the accountant will switch to the downgraded engagement. The report resulting from such an engagement makes no reference to the original engagement or the reasons for the downgrade, as it would only serve to confuse the reader as to the nature of the work performed by the accountant. If the reasons are not justifiable, the accountant should consider withdrawing from the engagement.

If, while auditing an entity's F/S, management refuses to allow the accountant to correspond with the entity's legal counsel, the accountant is generally precluded from changing to a review engagement.

Preparation Engagements (AR-C 70)

 Representative Task (Remembering & Understanding): Identify the factors that an accountant should consider when performing a preparation engagement.

As mentioned earlier, an engagement to prepare financial statements (F/S) is a **nonassurance, nonattest** engagement. In a preparation engagement, the accountant prepares F/S in accordance with an AFRF based on information provided by management.

AICPA Guidance

Preparation engagements requirements are documented in AR-C 70, *Preparation of Financial Statements.* As is true of all SSARS engagements, an accountant engaged to prepare F/S for a client is also required to adhere to the *General Principles for Engagements Performed in Accordance With SSARS* (AR-C 60).

In addition to preparing traditional F/S, this section also applies to preparation of the following:

- Specified elements, accounts, or F/S items

- Supplementary information and required supplementary information

- Pro forma financial information

- Prospective financial information (forecasts or projections).

AR-C 70 also applies when preparing:

- F/S prior to audit or review by another accountant

- F/S to be presented alongside the tax return

- Personal F/S for presentation alongside a financial plan

- Single F/S (eg, just a balance sheet) with substantially all disclosures omitted

- F/S using general ledger information outside of an accounting software system.

AR-C 70 does not apply to:

- Engagements to perform audit, review, or compilation services

- Preparing F/S for submission to taxing authorities

- Preparing F/S as part of personal financial planning

- Preparing F/S in connection with litigation services or business valuation services

- Performing bookkeeping services (ie, merely assisting with preparing financial statements rather than preparing).

Terms of the Engagement and Engagement Letter

The accountant and management should agree on the terms of the engagement, which should be documented in writing (typically in an engagement letter, but a contract would also be acceptable). The following should be documented:

Elements of a Preparation Engagement Letter

- Objective of engagement (ie, prepare F/S in accordance with AFRF)

- Responsibilities of management and the CPA

- Limits to the engagement (ie, prepare F/S only)

- Identification of applicable financial reporting framework (eg, GAAP)

- Expected conditions (eg, known AFRF departures)

- Management agrees that each F/S page states, "*No assurance is provided.*"

The agreement should be signed by the accountant (or firm) and management (or those charged with governance). If signed by those charged with governance, the accountant still should obtain management's agreement and understanding of its responsibilities.

Prepare the Financial Statements

- The accountant is required to obtain an appropriate understanding of the AFRF to be used and the significant accounting policies applicable to the F/S. If the F/S use a special purpose framework, the accountant should include a description of the AFRF on the face of the F/S or in a footnote.

- When assisting management with significant judgments, the accountant should discuss those judgments with management so that management understands those judgments and can take responsibility for them.

- When records, documents, or other information used in preparing the F/S are viewed as incomplete or inaccurate, the accountant should request additional or corrected information.

- When F/S contain known departures from the AFRF (including omission of some or all required disclosures), the accountant should discuss the matter with management and disclose those departures in the F/S. If management fails to provide the necessary information, the accountant should disclose the corrected information or withdraw from the engagement.

- The accountant may prepare F/S that omit substantially all disclosures required by the AFRF, provided the omission was not for the purpose of misleading users. The omission should, however, be disclosed in the F/S.

- Each page of the F/S should include a statement that no assurance is provided (or other words to that effect). The accountant's name (or firm) need not be identified. If that statement cannot be added to each page, the accountant should issue a disclaimer as to any assurance or perform a compilation engagement in accordance with AR-C 80 or withdraw from the engagement.

 An accountant prepared financial statements in accordance with SSARS. If the client does not agree to include a note on each page of the financial statements that no assurance is provided, the accountant may do each of the following except:

- Perform a compilation engagement.

- Issue the financial statements as is.

- Withdraw from the engagement.

- Issue the financial statements with a disclaimer.

Nonattest preparation of financial statement engagements

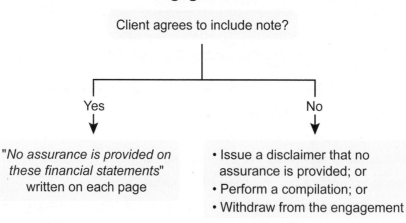

Each page of the F/S should include a note stating that "no assurance is provided" or "the financial statements have not been subject to audit, review, or compilation." *No assurance* means the accountant did not verify the accuracy or completeness of the information provided by management.

The note can only be included upon management's agreement. Should management decline, SSARS require the accountant clearly disclose their limited involvement to anyone who uses the F/S. The accountant may issue a disclaimer, perform a compilation, or withdraw from the engagement. To prevent misleading the public, issuing the F/S without cautioning the reader is not permitted.

Documentation

The accountant should document the preparation engagement in enough detail to clearly show the work performed and should include:

- The engagement letter (or other written documentation)
- A copy of the F/S prepared.

25.02 Compilation Engagements

Compilations (AR-C 80)

 Representative Task (Remembering & Understanding): Identify the factors that an accountant should consider when reporting on an engagement to compile an entity's financial statements

A **compilation engagement** involves assisting management in presenting the F/S (or other historical, pro forma, or prospective financial information) along with the accountant's accompanying report, which provides no assurance about those F/S (or other financial information).

AICPA Guidance

Guidance is provided in the AR-C 80, *Compilation Engagements*. The accountant is also required to comply with the requirements of AR-C 60, *General Principles*, including meeting the "preconditions" for accepting the compilation engagement. The accountant is not required to be independent for a compilation engagement because no assurance is provided.

AR-C 80 indicates that the objectives in a compilation engagement are to:

- Apply accounting and financial reporting expertise to assist management in the presentation of F/S

- Issue a report *without providing assurance* that there are no material modifications that should be made to the F/S for them to be in accordance with the applicable financial reporting framework (AFRF).

Objective	• Assist management in presenting financial information
Independence	• Is expected but **not** required • Lack of independence must be disclosed in the report
Responsibility	• Apply accounting expertise to assemble financial statements

Terms of the Engagement and Engagement Letter

The accountant must determine whether they are independent in relation to the entity. In addition, prior to accepting the engagement, the accountant should obtain the client's agreement that it understands and accepts its responsibility:

- For the preparation and fair presentation of the F/S

- To include the compilation report in any document containing the compiled F/S

The accountant is required to reach an agreement with the client on the terms of the engagement, which should be documented in an engagement letter that is signed both by the client and the accountant's firm. The agreement should include:

- The objective of the compilation engagement

- Management's responsibilities
- The accountant's responsibilities
- Limitations of a compilation engagement
- Identification of the AFRF and required informative disclosures
- The expected form and content of the compilation report

The engagement letter should also indicate circumstances under which the report may differ in form or content from that which is expected. For example, the engagement letter may indicate if the report will disclose a lack of independence.

The agreement should be signed by the accountant (or firm) and management (or those charged with governance). If signed by those charged with governance, the accountant should still obtain management's agreement and understanding of its responsibilities (associated with the "preconditions" for accepting an engagement).

Accepting and performing a compilation engagement

Conditions of **acceptance**:
- Management has integrity
- Management acknowledges responsibilities:
  - For the financial statements
  - To attach report to financial statements
- Signed engagement letter

⟶

Requirements for **performance**:
- Understand reporting framework (including its application in client's industry)
- Understand client's accounting policies
- Read financial statements and consider whether there are obvious errors

Performance Requirements

Performance requirements for the practitioner include the following:

- The accountant should obtain an understanding of the AFRF and the significant accounting policies applicable to the entity's F/S.
- The accountant should read the F/S to evaluate whether they are free of obvious material misstatements.
- If the accountant believes that the records or other information are incomplete or inaccurate, the accountant should request further or corrected information.
- If the accountant discovers a need for revision to the F/S, the accountant should propose appropriate revisions to management.

If management has failed to provide records or information as requested or if management does not make appropriate adjustments as proposed by the accountant, the accountant should withdraw (and inform management of the reasons for withdrawing).

An accountant has been engaged to compile the financial statements of a nonissuer. The financial statements contain many departures from GAAP because of inadequacies in the accounting records. The accountant believes that modification of the compilation report is not adequate to indicate the deficiencies. Under these circumstances, the accountant should

- Inform management that the engagement can proceed only if distribution of the accountant's report is restricted to internal use.

- Quantify the effects of the departures from GAAP and describe the departures from GAAP in a special report.

- Withdraw from the engagement and provide no further service concerning these financial statements.

- Obtain written representations from management that the financial statements will not be used to obtain credit from financial institutions.

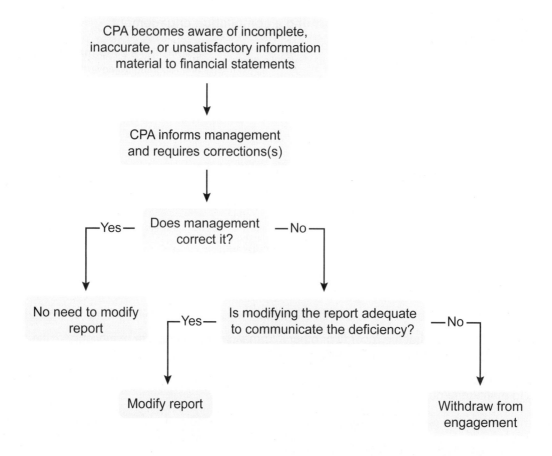

As discussed previously, compilations do not provide any level of assurance; therefore, no opinion or conclusion is issued. However, accountants are responsible for reading the F/S to identify obvious material misstatements, to determine if the F/S are appropriate in form, and to issue a report.

If accountants believe the F/S are *materially misstated* (ie, contain GAAP departures), they should notify management and request corrections. If management is unwilling to revise the F/S, the accountants should modify the report to inform users. However, if *modifying the report is not adequate* to communicate the deficiencies (eg, because misstatements are too pervasive), the accountants should withdraw from the engagement and provide no further services related to those F/S.

Reporting Responsibilities: Unmodified Report

 Representative Task (Application): Determine the appropriate form and content of an accountant's report for a compilation engagement.

The accountant's compilation report consists of a single paragraph and normally consists of the following:

- A statement that management (owners) of the identified entity is (are) responsible for the F/S and that identifies the F/S (and date/period) involved
- A statement that the compilation was performed in accordance with SSARS promulgated by the AICPA's Accounting and Review Services Committee
- A statement that the accountant did not audit or review the F/S, etc., and the accountant does not provide any assurance on them
- A statement that disclaims an opinion or any form of assurance
- The signature of the accountant (or the accountant's firm), along with the city and state of the office, and the date of the report.

The accountant may request that each page of the F/S state, *"See Accountant's Compilation Report."* Notice that the CPA is referred to as an accountant and **not** as an auditor since no audit was performed.

 An accountant's standard report issued after compiling the financial statements of a nonpublic entity should state that:

- The accountant was **not** aware of any material modifications that should be made to the accompanying financial statements.
- A compilation consists principally of inquiries of company personnel and analytical procedures.
- The accountant was **not** required to perform any procedures to verify the accuracy or completeness of the information provided by management.
- A compilation is substantially **less** in scope than an audit in accordance with GAAS, the objective of which is the expression of an opinion.

Key elements of nonissuer's standard complication report (CARD)

- Compiled: identify the compiled F/S or F/S elements
- AICPA standards: reference *Statements on Standards for Accounting and Review Services* (SSARS)
- Responsibility of management for the F/S
- Doesn't provide an opinion or any level of assurance

For a compilation, the report should state that the accountant did not audit or review the F/S and was not required to perform any procedures to verify the accuracy or completeness of the information presented. To ensure the nature of the service is understood, the report will also state explicitly that the accountant does not offer an opinion (as in an audit) or a conclusion (as in a review), or provide any assurance on the F/S.

Reporting Responsibilities: Modified Report

There are a number of reasons why the accountant may need to issue a modified report, including:

Reasons to modify a compilation report

- F/S prepared in adherence to special purposes FRF
- CPA lacks independence
- Omission of substantially all disclosures required by FRF
- Known departures from FRF (eg, inaccurate information)
- Supplementary information accompanying F/S
- FRF requires supplementary information

F/S = Financial statements   FRF = Financial reporting framework

Special-Purpose Framework Report

The accountant may be engaged to compile F/S that are prepared in accordance with an FRF other than GAAP.

- A general purpose framework is one that is widely recognized and about which it is reasonable to expect that users will be knowledgeable (eg, GAAP and International Financial Reporting Standards or IFRS).

- **Special purpose frameworks** (aka, Other Comprehensive Bases of Accounting, or OCBOAs) include the cash or modified cash basis, tax basis, contractual or regulatory basis, IFRS for SMEs (small to medium sized enterprises), or financial reporting framework (FRF) for SMEs promulgated by the AICPA.

When using a special purpose framework, the report should include a separate paragraph stating that the F/S are prepared in accordance with the particular special purpose framework and that refers to the note to the F/S describing the framework.

When the F/S are prepared using a regulatory basis or a contractual basis of accounting, the report should identify the purpose for which the F/S were prepared (or refer to a note that provides that information).

Unless the F/S omit substantially all disclosures, the accountant should modify the report when the F/S omit:

- A description of the special purpose framework
- A summary of significant accounting policies
- A description of how the special purpose framework differs from GAAP (although the differences need not be quantified)
- Appropriate informative disclosures.

Lack of Independence

When the accountant is not independent of the entity, the report will be modified to indicate the lack of independence, as follows:

- The last paragraph of the report should state that the accountant was not independent [either a single sentence without indicating the reason or with additional commentary indicating the reason(s) for the impairment].

- If stating any reason(s) for the impairment, the accountant should identify all applicable reasons for the lack of independence.

- If the accountant uses a title on the compilation report, it should not include the word *independent*.

Omission of Substantially All Required Disclosures

The accountant may compile F/S that omit substantially all disclosures required by the AFRF. The report will be modified by adding a separate paragraph indicating that:

- Management has elected to omit substantially all disclosures required by the AFRF.

- The information, had it not been omitted, may influence conclusions about the entity's performance or financial position.

- The F/S are designed exclusively for those knowledgeable about such matters.

The accountant may not report on F/S that omit disclosures if the omissions were *intended to mislead* the user. This might be the case, for example, if the client is trying to conceal a large potential loss due to a pending lawsuit from a potential lender.

If most disclosures are presented but selected disclosures are omitted, the report should identify the nature of the departure and any known effects.

Compiling financial statements (F/S): Disclosures omitted

Known Departures from AFRF

Material departures that are not disclosed in the notes should be reported in a modified compilation report in a separate paragraph. (If the accountant believes that modification of the report is not an adequate way to communicate the deficiencies, the accountant should withdraw.)

The effects of the departure should be disclosed if *known*. The accountant is not required to determine the effects, however, and can state in the report that management has not made such a determination.

The accountant should not add a statement to the report stating that the "F/S are not in conformity with [the AFRF]," which is equivalent to expressing a conclusion.

Supplementary Information

When supplementary information accompanies compiled F/S, the accountant will indicate that either the supplementary information was or was not compiled and if the accountant is reporting on the supplementary information.

When the AFRF under which the F/S were prepared requires supplementary information (RSI), the accountant's report will be modified to indicate:

- Whether the RSI is included, partially included, or omitted
- Whether or not the RSI that is included was compiled by the accountant and is being reported upon.

Comparative F/S

A CPA may be engaged to compile comparative F/S. The standard compilation report on comparative F/S is only different from the standard report on a single year's statement in that both dates are indicated and items are referred to in the plural, such as F/S and compilations.

When comparative F/S include statements from one or more prior periods that had been reviewed or audited, the report will include the same language as an unmodified compilation report on comparative F/S. An **explanatory paragraph** will be added, however, indicating:

- The prior F/S had been audited or reviewed.
- The date and type of report originally issued on the prior period F/S, and the reasons for a modification to the prior period report, if applicable.

Documentation

The accountant's documentation for a compilation engagement is required to include:

- The engagement letter
- A copy of the F/S
- A copy of the report

25.03 Review Engagements

Overview of Review Engagements (AR-C 90)

 Representative Task (Remembering & Understanding): Identify the factors that an accountant should consider when reporting on an engagement to review an entity's financial statements.

In a review of financial statements (F/S), the accountant expresses a conclusion regarding whether the entity's F/S are in accordance with an AFRF. The conclusion is based on obtaining limited assurance, primarily through the performance of inquiries and analytical procedures. The accountant is required to be independent for a review engagement since limited assurance is provided.

Review requirements

- Independent accountant must perform
- Scope is not limited
- Management accepts financial statement (F/S) responsibility
- Limited assurance regarding material modifications provided
- Evidence obtained through inquiry and analytical procedures
- Written management representation obtained
- Report reflects:
  - F/S reviewed
  - Period covered
  - Financial reporting framework

Review engagements for prospective information are not permitted because inquiry and analytical procedures are not expected to provide sufficient appropriate evidence to issue a review report. Review engagements may be performed in accordance with SSARS for annual F/S or single F/S (such as a balance sheet). They may also be performed on pro forma F/S under SSAEs.

Terms of the Engagement and Engagement Letter

An engagement to review F/S should only be accepted if the accountant:

- Is independent of the entity (ie, independence cannot be impaired).
- Has determined that there are no scope limitations on the ability to apply adequate review procedures.

The accountant and management should agree on the terms of the engagement, which should be documented in writing (typically in an engagement letter). The following should be documented:

- The engagement's objective

- Management's responsibilities

- The accountant's responsibilities

- The limitations of the engagement, including a statement that a review is substantially *less in scope than an audit* and does not contain an opinion on the F/S

- Identification of the AFRF

- The expected form and content of the review report (and a statement that, depending on circumstances, the actual report issued may differ from the expected report in form and content).

The agreement should be signed by the accountant and management (or those charged with governance). If signed by those charged with governance, the accountant should still obtain management's agreement and understanding of its responsibilities (associated with the "preconditions" for accepting an engagement).

	Can be reviewed?	Standard
Annual financial statements (F/S)	✓	SSARS
Single financial statement	✓	SSARS
Pro forma F/S	✓	SSAE
Interim F/S (nonissuer)	✓	SAS/SSARS
Prospective F/S (projection or forecast)	✗	N/A
Internal control	✗	N/A
Compliance (eg, laws, contracts)	✗	N/A

Review Procedures

In a F/S review, an accountant provides limited assurance that no material modifications are necessary for the F/S to conform to the reporting framework (eg, GAAP). Because reviews provide only limited assurance, the actions performed are likewise limited and primarily involve analytical procedures and inquiries of client personnel.

Materiality for the F/S as a whole should be determined and applied in designing and evaluating review procedures. Materiality should be revised if the accountant becomes aware of information that would have caused the accountant to set a different materiality level initially.

Review procedures

- Understand accounting practices in the client's industry
- Understand client's business, including its accounting practices
- Make inquiries
- Perform analytical procedures
- Obtain management representation letter
- Read F/S and consider whether they conform with GAAP

The accountant is required to design and perform analytical procedures and make inquiries to obtain sufficient appropriate evidence as a basis for the review report. Any significant differences relative to expectations should be further investigated by inquiring of management and performing other review procedures as needed.

An accountant's standard report issued after compiling the financial statements of a nonpublic entity should state: When conducting a review engagement of a nonissuer, each of the following is considered an analytical procedure, except a comparison of the current-year's financial information to:

- Expectations developed by the accountant.
- Financial statements of a comparable prior period.
- Supporting documentation.
- Industry benchmarks.

Substantive procedure	Examples
Substantive analytical procedures	<ul><li>Trend analysis</li><li>Ratio assessment</li><li>Information comparison</li><li>Estimate analysis</li></ul>
Tests of details	<ul><li>Bank confirmation</li><li>Invoice matching</li><li>Physical inventory observation</li><li>Management-targeted inquiries</li></ul>

Accountants follow three essential steps when following analytical procedures:

- Develop *expectations* using understanding of the industry, client knowledge, and general knowledge about business, accounting, and economics.
- Compare client's data to expectations and *industry benchmarks* to determine whether variances are within a reasonable range.
- Investigate significant differences by inquiring of management and performing other procedures such as ratio analysis.

Specific analytical procedures that the accountant should perform include:

- Comparing current period F/S data with prior period data
- Considering plausible relationships among financial and nonfinancial data
- Comparing disaggregated revenue data (eg, revenue reported by month).

Comparing financial information to supporting documentation is not an analytical procedure.

Inquiries should be made about the preparation and presentation of the F/S in relation to the AFRF. Additional inquiries required on every review are (list is not all-inclusive):

- Related party relationships and transactions
- Subsequent events
- Going concern issues
- Litigation, claims, and assessments
- Potential fraud.

 If, while performing a review engagement, an accountant has reason to believe that a material misappropriation of assets might have occurred, what should the accountant do?

- Assess whether controls are in place to deter similar misappropriations.
- Require an investigation to determine whether the misappropriation actually occurred.
- Disclose the potential misappropriation as supplementary information in the accountant's report.
- Document communications with senior management about the matter.

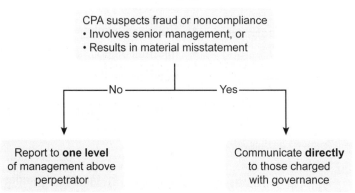

Review engagement

During a review, an accountant may become aware of **possible fraud** (eg, misappropriation of assets). If the fraud is *inconsequential*, it should be communicated to the next level of management above the perpetrator as soon as practicable. Fraud that may lead to a material misstatement should be communicated directly to senior management or those charged with governance.

Audits, not reviews, would require an investigation of fraud to determine if misappropriation actually occurred. In a review, the accountant would ask those charged with governance to provide information supporting that the F/S are not materially misstated due to fraud.

Finally, the accountant should request further or corrected information if the accountant believes that the records or other information is incomplete or inaccurate.

Review engagements

Accountant becomes aware of incorrect, incomplete, or unsatisfactory information

↓

Accountant requests that management consider the effect on F/S

↓

Accountant considers management's response to determine whether it indicates F/S may be materially misstated

If no indication of material misstatement, accountant proceeds as normal	If F/S may be materially misstated, accountant uses professional judgment to determine if additional procedures are needed

Written Representations from Management

The accountant is required to obtain written representations from management in the form of a representation letter addressed to the accountant. Representations are dated as of the date of the review report (ie, the date on which the accountant has determined that sufficient appropriate review evidence has been obtained).

- **Required representations** include that management:
  - Has fulfilled its responsibility to prepare and fairly present the F/S in accordance with the AFRF
  - Is responsible for the DIM of I/C relevant to reliable financial reporting (including the prevention and detection of fraud)
  - Has given the accountant access to all relevant information, as agreed upon
  - Has been complete and truthful in its responses to inquiries
  - Ensures that all transactions have been recorded and are reflected in the F/S (completeness)
  - Has disclosed any knowledge or suspicions of fraud, including allegations by others
  - Has disclosed known or suspected circumstances involving noncompliance with applicable laws or regulations that may affect the F/S
  - Believes that uncorrected misstatements are immaterial to the F/S, individually or in the aggregate (a summary of such items should be attached)
  - Has disclosed and appropriately accounted for known or threatened litigation and claims that may affect the F/S
  - Believes that significant assumptions used in preparing the F/S are reasonable
  - Has disclosed and appropriately accounted for all known related party relationships and transactions

- ○ Has disclosed all information relevant to using the going concern assumption in the F/S

- ○ Has adjusted for or disclosed subsequent events requiring recognition or disclosure.

- In addition, the accountant may require management to provide written representations regarding any matters that, in the accountant's professional judgment, are significant and relevant.

- If management does not provide the required representations, or there is reason to doubt the integrity of management and the reliability of the written representations, the accountant should withdraw from the engagement.

Unmodified Review Report

 Representative Task (Application): Determine the appropriate form and content of an accountant's report for a review engagement.

If nothing comes to the accountant's attention indicating that the F/S need material modification to conform with the AFRF, the accountant will issue an unmodified review report.

If the accountant determines that the F/S are materially misstated, the accountant should express a **modified conclusion**. When the accountant concludes that the effects of the matter(s) give rise to the modification are:

- Material but not pervasive to the F/S, a qualified conclusion is expressed

- Material and pervasive to the F/S, an adverse conclusion is expressed

Types of review conclusion		Expressed if the accountant...	Key report language
Unmodified	Standard conclusion	Has no reason to believe F/S are not prepared in accordance with [GAAP]	"...we are not aware of any material modifications that should be made to the... [F/S]"
Modified	Qualified conclusion	Has no reason to believe F/S are not prepared in accordance with [GAAP], except for...	"...**except for**..., we are not aware of any material modifications that should be made to the...[F/S]"
	Adverse conclusion	Believes F/S are not in accordance with [GAAP]	"...due to the significance of the matter(s) described..., the [F/S] are **not in accordance with** [GAAP]"

Note: Under certain circumstances, it may be appropriate for the accountant to withdraw from the engagement

The accountant's review report having an unmodified conclusion consists of the following:

- A title, such as "Independent Accountant's Review Report"

- An appropriate addressee

- An introductory paragraph (without a label) that identifies the F/S that were reviewed (and dates/periods involved), which states that a review consists primarily of analytical procedures and inquiries, and that states that a review is substantially less in scope than an audit (with a disclaimer of opinion)

- A section entitled "Management's Responsibility for the Financial Statements" that identifies management's responsibilities for the F/S and I/C

- A section entitled "Accountant's Responsibility" that references the SSARS promulgated by the ARSC of the AICPA and refers to limited assurance as a basis for reporting

- A section entitled "Accountant's Conclusion" that provides negative assurance on the F/S

- The signature of the accountant or the accountant's firm, the city and state where the accountant practices, and the date of the report.

Standard review report

- Introduction
- Management's responsibility
- Accountant's responsibility
- Accountant's conclusion (limited assurance)

  ... we are not aware of any material modifications that should be made to the accompanying financial statements in order for them to be in accordance with ...

  Joe Schmoe, CPA
  Dallas, TX
  March 29, Year 2

An **emphasis-of-matter paragraph** (EOM) is included in a review report to draw attention to a matter essential to understanding the F/S. EOMs refer only to matters properly presented or disclosed in the F/S. For example, material-related party transactions must be disclosed in a review as they may lack commercial substance or otherwise carry a risk of material misstatement.

The standard report issued by an accountant after reviewing the financial statements of a nonpublic entity should state that

- A review is limited to presenting in the form of financial statements information that is the representation of management.

- The accountant does not express an opinion or any other form of assurance on the financial statements.

- A review consists of inquiries of company personnel and analytical procedures applied to financial data.

- The accountant did not obtain an understanding of the entity's internal control or assess control risk.

Standard unmodified review report content (FAMILIAR)
Financial statements reviewed
AICPA standards (SSARS)
Management responsibilities
Inquiry and analytical procedures
Less in scope than an audit
Incapable of rendering an opinion
Assurance provided (ie, limited)
Refer to applicable financial reporting framework (AFRF)

An accountant expresses a **conclusion**, not an opinion, in a review of F/S. The conclusion addresses whether the entity's F/S are prepared in accordance with an applicable financial reporting framework. The conclusion is based on obtaining **limited assurance**, primarily through the performance of inquiries and analytical procedures.

The required components of a standard unmodified review report are reflected in the mnemonic FAMILIAR, shown above.

Modified Review Report

When the accountant determines the F/S are materially misstated, the accountant should express a(n):

Severity of Effects on F/S	Immaterial	Material but Not Pervasive	Material and Pervasive
Type of Conclusion	Unmodified	Qualified	Adverse

In the basis for conclusion paragraph, the accountant should:

- Describe and quantify the financial effects of the material misstatement, provided the misstatement relates to *specific amounts* in the F/S. If the effects are unknown, the accountant is not required to determine the effects and should state in the report that such determination has not been made by management.

- Explain how disclosures are misstated, if applicable.

- Describe the nature of any omitted information and include the omitted disclosures when feasible.

There are several reasons an accountant may modify a review report. Factors may include:

- A modified conclusion
- Comparative F/S
- Emphasis-of-matter and other-matter paragraphs
- Other reporting responsibilities

- F/S are prepared in accordance with a special purpose framework
- Restrictions on the use of the report
- Going concern considerations
- Subsequent events
- Work of other accountants
- Supplementary information accompanying reviewed F/S
- Required supplementary information

Special Purpose Framework (SPF)

When using a SPF, the report should include an EOM paragraph stating that the F/S are prepared in accordance with the SPF and referencing the note to the F/S describing the framework.

When the F/S are prepared using a contractual basis of accounting, the report should identify the purpose for which the F/S were prepared (or refer to a note that provides that information) and restrict the distribution of the report.

The accountant should modify the report when the F/S omit a description of the SPF, a summary of significant accounting policies, a description of how the SPF differs from GAAP (although the differences need not be quantified), and/or appropriate informative disclosures.

Comparative F/S

The report should refer to each applicable period for which F/S are presented as the type of engagement need not be the same for each period presented. For example, one period might be a compilation and another period might be a review; or one period might be a review and another period might be an audit.

If the prior period was audited and the audit report on the prior period's F/S is not presented, the review report should include an "other-matter" paragraph to indicate that the prior period's financials were audited; to identify the date of that audit report and the type of opinion expressed (and the reasons for any modifications); and to state that no audit procedures were performed after the date of the audit report.

The review report should include an other-matter paragraph to explain the removal of the previously reported departure.

Review Report

- Introduction
- Management's responsibility
- Accountant's responsibility
- Accountant's conclusion
- Emphasis of matter, if needed
- Other matter, if needed

Joe Schmoe, CPA
Dallas, TX
March 12, Year 3

Other matter

The **Year 1** financial statements were **audited** by another accounting firm and it expressed an **unmodified opinion** on them in a **March 1, Year 2 report**. **No auditing procedures** have been performed **since that date**.

Going Concern

When there is substantial doubt about the entity's ability to continue as a going concern for a reasonable period of time (and disclosure of those uncertainties are adequate), add a "Going Concern" section to the review report labeled, "Substantial Doubt About the Entity's Ability to Continue as a Going Concern." If disclosure is *not adequate*, the matter would be addressed in the "Basis for Qualified (Adverse) Conclusion" section of the review report.

The accountant may add an EOM paragraph to the review report to draw readers' attention to a matter that is appropriately reported or disclosed in the F/S. The accountant should add an EOM paragraph when the F/S have been restated to correct a misstatement in previously issued F/S.

The accountant may add an other-matter paragraph to the review report to draw readers' attention to a matter that is relevant to their understanding of the review, the review report, or the accountant's responsibilities.

Restricted Use

Under certain circumstances, use of an accountant's review report must be restricted to specified parties (ie, be issued with an alert). The alert should state that the report is intended solely for the information and use of the identified specified parties.

An example is performing a review of F/S prepared in adherence to a special purpose framework such as contractual basis accounting. The restriction is necessary to avoid misunderstanding or misuse by parties for whom the report *is not* intended. The report may, on the other hand, list specific parties for whom it *is* intended.

Once the report is issued, the accountant is *not responsible* for controlling its distribution because it would not be physically possible or practical to control what the client does with the report. Ideally, management will only distribute it to the specified parties, and the restriction would be sufficient to warn unintended users that the report should not be used by them.

Subsequent Events and Subsequently Discovered Facts

The accountant should request that management consider the appropriateness of the F/S treatment when subsequent events are identified.

For subsequently discovered facts *before* the report release date:

- The accountant should discuss the matter with management (and those charged with governance, as applicable) and determine how management intends to deal with the matter when the F/S require revision.

- If management revises the F/S, the accountant should perform review procedures on the revision and either change the date on the review report or "dual-date" the report.

- If management does not revise the F/S, the accountant should modify the review report appropriately.

For subsequently discovered facts *after* the report release date:

- The accountant should discuss the matter with management (and those charged with governance, as applicable) and determine how management intends to deal with the matter when the F/S require revision.

- If management revises the F/S, the accountant should perform review procedures on the revision, and either change the date on the review report or "dual-date" the report. The accountant also should determine whether third parties possess those released F/S and evaluate whether management is taking appropriate steps to inform them that the F/S should not be used.

- If management is not taking the appropriate steps, including revision, the accountant should notify management and take action to prevent the use of the accountant's review report. The accountant may wish to seek legal guidance in that event.

Work of Other Accountants

The accountant may rely upon the work of other accountants who may have performed reviews or audits on significant components of the reviewed F/S, such as consolidated subsidiaries. If the accountant decides not to take responsibility for that work, the report should reference the audit or review of the other accountant and indicate:

- That the accountant used the work of other accountants

- The magnitude of the portion of the F/S attested to by the other accountants

Note, however, that another accountant's report cannot be referenced if:

- It is restricted for limited use.

- The F/S are prepared based on a different FRF. Exceptions apply when:
  - The measurement, recognition, presentation, and disclosure criteria applicable to all material items in the component's F/S are similar to the criteria applicable to all material items in the reporting entity's F/S (eg, GAAP and IFRS would be considered similar); and
  - Sufficient appropriate review evidence has been obtained for purposes of evaluating the appropriateness of adjustments needed to convert the component's F/S to the FRF used by the reporting entity without assuming responsibility for, or being involved in, the work of the other accountants.

Documentation

The documentation should permit an *experienced accountant* with no prior connection to the engagement to understand the following:

- The nature, timing, and extent of review procedures performed in compliance with the SSARS

- The evidence obtained from the procedures performed

- Significant findings, conclusions reached, and significant professional judgments involved.

Specifically, the documentation should include the following:

- The engagement letter (or other written documentation)

- Communications with management about EOM or other-matter paragraph(s) in the accountant's review report

- Communications with management and those charged with governance about significant matters during the engagement

- Communications with other accountants associated with the F/S of significant components

- Any identified information that is inconsistent with the findings regarding significant matters (and how the inconsistency was addressed)

- The representation letter obtained from management

- A copy of the F/S and the review report.

Other Topics

Supplementary Information (SI)

When the accountant has reviewed the SI along with the F/S, the report should state that the:

- SI is presented for additional analysis and is not required as part of the F/S
- SI is the responsibility of management
- SI was subjected to the review procedures applied to the review of the F/S (and indicate whether the accountant is aware of any material modifications that should be made to it)
- Accountant has not audited the SI and does not express an opinion on it.

When the accountant has not reviewed the SI along with the F/S, the report should state that the:

- SI is presented for additional analysis and is not required as part of the F/S
- SI is the responsibility of management
- Accountant has not audited or reviewed the SI, and does not express an opinion, a conclusion, or any assurance on it.

Required Supplementary Information (RSI)

When RSI is relevant to F/S associated with either a compilation or review engagement, the accountant's compilation or review report should include an other-matter paragraph that comments on the applicable circumstances that:

- The RSI is included and the accountant *performed* a compilation or review engagement on it
- The RSI is included and the accountant *did not perform* a compilation, review, or audit on it
- The RSI is omitted
- Some RSI is included and some is omitted
- The accountant identified departures from the prescribed guidelines (established by the designated accounting standard-setting body)
- The accountant has doubts as to whether the information is presented in accordance with the prescribed guidelines.

Other Engagements

Pro Forma

Pro forma F/S are adapted from historical F/S to show how those F/S would have been affected if a given event or transaction had happened or not happened. For example, a client considering a change in accounting principle might want to see what effect the change would have had on the preceding year's F/S had it been made that year.

Pro forma F/S may be compiled, examined, or reviewed. To perform any of those engagements, however, it is necessary that the accountant understand the client's business and the AFRF. Because accounting practices vary by industry, even within the same AFRF (eg, GAAP), the accountant must also understand the client's industry.

If the accountant does not have that understanding prior to the engagement, the accountant can obtain that understanding after accepting the engagement; that way, the accountant need not issue a disclaimer or refer out the work. The accountant can consult industry publications (ie, trade journals), textbooks, or individuals knowledgeable about the industry to understand the client's industry

Obtaining an understanding of the reporting framework

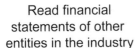

| Read financial statements of other entities in the industry | Consult AICPA guides, industry publications, textbooks, periodicals | Consult individuals knowledgeable about the industry or framework |

The accountant and the entity (management) should establish an understanding in writing (ie, an engagement letter) as to the nature and limitations of the services to be performed and the nature of the report to be issued.

- That understanding should specifically state that the engagement cannot be relied on to disclose errors, fraud, or illegal acts.

- That understanding also should state that the accountant will inform the appropriate level of management of any material errors and of any information coming to the accountant's attention that fraud or illegal acts may have occurred (excluding matters that are "clearly inconsequential").

Compilation report on pro forma F/S

Elements of standard compilation report (CARD)

- Compiled: identify the compiled F/S or F/S element

- AICPA standards: must reference SSARS

- Responsibility of management for F/S

- Doesn't provide an opinion or any level of assurance

- Reference to historical F/S from which pro forma F/S were drawn

- Statement that historical F/S were audited/reviewed/compiled and reference to any modification of the resultant report

- Description of pro forma F/S, including their limitations.

The accountant should read the compiled pro forma financial information (including the summary of significant assumptions) and consider whether that information appears to be free of obvious material errors. Reporting requirements include the following:

- The pro forma financial information should be clearly labeled in a manner that distinguishes it from historical F/S.

- Each page of the compiled pro forma financial information should include a reference such as "See Accountant's Compilation Report"

- The accountant is not required to be independent since no assurance is provided. If the accountant is not independent, the compilation report should indicate that fact.

- The accountant may "assist" with the preparation of pro forma financial information without issuing a compilation report (when the accountant has not been engaged to "compile" such information).

- The compilation report should not describe any other procedures performed by the accountant either prior to or during the compilation engagement.

Requirements for presenting pro forma financial information

- Labeled as "pro forma" to distinguish from historical financial information
- Describes hypothetical transaction/event and the underlying historical information
- Describes significant assumptions and uncertainties
- States that it should be read in conjunction with the historical financial information
- States that it is not necessarily indicative of what would actually have happened

Prospective Financial Information

The accountant may perform either a **preparation** engagement or a **compilation** of prospective financial information about the future (a review of such prospective financial information is not permitted). The information may be presented as complete F/S or limited to one or more elements, items, or accounts and can be in the form of either a financial forecast or a financial projection.

- **Financial forecast:** Prospective F/S that present, to the best of the responsible party's knowledge and belief, an entity's expected financial position, results of operations, and cash flows. A financial forecast is based on the responsible party's assumptions reflecting conditions it expects to exist and the course of action it expects to take.

- **Financial projection:** Prospective F/S that present, to the best of the responsible party's knowledge and belief, given one or more hypothetical assumptions, an entity's expected financial position, results of operations, and cash flows. A financial projection is sometimes prepared to present one or more hypothetical courses of action for evaluation, as in response to a question that begins for instance, "What would happen if ...?"

Assumptions in forecasts are general in nature (eg, expected sales based on previous trends). Therefore, a forecast is appropriate for either **general or limited use**. In contrast, a projection is based on a hypothetical scenario that may not be understood by the public. It is appropriate only for **limited use** by parties who understand the assumptions.

Prospective Financial Information

Forecast	• Shows where business is expected to go based on expected general conditions and the entity's expected course of action. • Example: Forecasting future sales based upon sales trends.	For general or limited use
Projection	• Shows what management believes will occur given specific hypothetical assumptions (ie, what-if scenarios). • Example: Projecting what could happen if the entity lost a major customer.	For limited use only

When engaged to prepare prospective financial information or issue a compilation report on prospective financial information:

- The accountant should not prepare (or issue a compilation report on) prospective financial information that omits disclosure of the summary of significant assumptions. The entity's F/S should also include a summary of significant accounting policies.

- The accountant should not prepare or issue a compilation report on a financial projection that:
  - Fails to identify the hypothetical assumptions
  - Omits a description of the limitations of the usefulness of the projection;

Any report on a projection should be restricted to specified users, consisting of third parties in direct negotiation with the responsible party (which allows them to ask questions about the presentation).

When issuing a compilation report on prospective financial information, the report should include statements that the:

- Forecasted/projected results may not be achieved
- Accountant assumes no responsibility to update the report for matters occurring after the date of the report.

(Any report on a "projection" must have restricted distribution; only a report on a "forecast" is permitted to have general distribution.)

AUD 26
Reporting on Compliance

AUD 26: Reporting on Compliance

Contractual & Regulatory Compliance Audits

AICPA Guidance

The relevant **AICPA guidance** is provided by AU-C 935, *Compliance Audits*. The standard states that the auditor's objectives are to:

- **Obtain sufficient appropriate audit evidence** to form an opinion and report whether the entity complied in all material respects with applicable compliance requirements (at the level specified in the governmental audit requirement)
- **Identify audit and reporting requirements** specified in the governmental audit requirements that are supplementary to GAAS and Government Auditing Standards and perform procedures to address those requirements

Audit Requirements

 Representative Task (Remembering & Understanding): Identify the factors that an auditor should consider when reporting on compliance with aspects of contractual agreements or regulatory requirements in connection with an audit of an entity's financial statements.

Compliance audits are often performed by or for governmental or regulatory organizations to determine if an entity is complying with applicable laws and regulations. Entities may be chosen for audit on a random basis or may be selected due to some indication that there may be one or more incidents of noncompliance (eg, tax returns with unusual deductions).

Material noncompliance is defined in authoritative literature as "A failure to follow compliance requirements or a violation of prohibitions included in the specified requirements that results in noncompliance that is quantitatively or qualitatively material, either individually or when aggregated with other noncompliance."

For a compliance audit, the auditor should:

- **Perform risk assessment procedures** to obtain an understanding of the applicable compliance requirements and internal controls over compliance
  - The nature and extent of the risk assessment procedures may vary with the circumstances (such as the complexity of the compliance requirements and the depth of the auditor's knowledge of internal control over compliance)
- **Assess the risks of material noncompliance** (whether due to fraud or error) for each applicable compliance requirement and consider whether any of those are pervasive to compliance
- **Perform further audit procedures in response** to the assessed risks, such as:
  - **Develop an overall response** to any risks that are pervasive to the entity's compliance
  - Perform appropriate **tests of details** and **tests of controls** when there is an expectation of operating effectiveness or when required to do so

The auditor should identify **supplementary audit requirements** (beyond GAAS and GAGAS) specified in the governmental audit requirement.

- Some governmental audit requirements specifically identify the applicable compliance requirements, whereas others provide a framework for the auditor to determine the applicable compliance requirements
  - The Office of Management and Budget provides a framework to determine the compliance requirements (ie, Uniform Guidance). Examples of supplementary audit requirements in the Uniform Guidance include requirements for the auditor to perform specified procedures to identify major programs, report on the current period schedule of findings and questioned costs, and follow up prior audit findings

In addition to supplementary audit requirements, the auditor should:

- **Obtain written representations** from management tailored to the entity and the governmental audit requirement
- **Perform procedures** up to the date of the auditor's report to identify **subsequent events** related to the entity's compliance (eg, reports from grantors regarding noncompliance or information about noncompliance obtained through other professional engagements for the entity). An example of a subsequent event warranting disclosure is the discovery of noncompliance causing the grantor to stop the funding

Evaluating the Evidence and Forming an Opinion

Most *governmental audit requirements* specify that the auditor's opinion on compliance is at the **program level** (and materiality is usually determined based on the program taken as a whole). As a result, the auditor should:

- Consider **likely questioned costs** (not just known questioned costs) and other noncompliance that may not result in questioned costs
  - *Known questioned costs* are those costs *specifically identified* by the auditor. The auditor reports known questioned costs that are greater than $25,000 for a major program
  - There may be other costs not actually identified. The auditor is charged with considering the best estimate of *total costs questioned*, not just the specifically identified costs
- Include a **variety of factors** in assessing the risk of noncompliance, including the:
  - Complexity of the compliance requirements
  - Length of time the entity has been subject to those compliance requirements
  - Degree of judgment involved in compliance
  - Entity's compliance in prior years

Reporting, Communication, Documentation, Reissuance

The auditor may **issue** (1) a separate report on compliance only; (2) a combined report on compliance and on internal control over compliance; or (3) a separate report on internal control over compliance.

The auditor should **communicate** the following matters with those charged with governance: the auditor's responsibilities under GAAS, GAGAS, and the governmental audit requirements; an overview of the planned scope and timing of the compliance audit; and any significant findings.

The auditor should **document** the risk assessment procedures performed, responses to the assessed risks of material noncompliance, the basis for materiality levels, and the auditor's compliance with applicable *supplementary audit requirements*.

When **reissuing** a compliance report, the auditor should add an **other-matter paragraph** describing why the report is being reissued and noting any changes from the previously issued report; if additional audit procedures are performed, the auditor's report date should be updated.

When an audit firm includes a report on compliance with aspects of contractual agreements in the auditor's report on the nonissuer's financial statements, in which section of the audit report should the report on compliance be included?

- Auditor's responsibilities section
- Opinion section
- Other-matter paragraph
- Emphasis-of-matter paragraph

Reporting on compliance in connection with audit of financial statements

	Noncompliance identified	Noncompliance not identified
Unmodified or qualified opinion on financials	Describe noncompliance	"Nothing came to our attention"
Disclaimer or adverse opinion on financials	Describe noncompliance	No reporting on compliance

In connection with an audit of a nonissuer's F/S, an auditor is sometimes asked to report on compliance with specific contractual agreements (eg, loans) or regulatory requirements. The auditor's findings may be included in an **other-matter paragraph** (OM) in the report or as a separate report. If the auditor identifies instances of noncompliance, each instance will be included in the report regardless of the opinion issued on the F/S.

If the auditor issues an unmodified or qualified opinion and finds no instances of noncompliance, the audit report will state that no instances of noncompliance came to the auditor's attention. If the auditor issues a disclaimer of opinion or an adverse opinion but finds no instances of noncompliance, the report will not include any assurance on compliance. This is because if the F/S are not fairly stated, auditors are unable to rely on them in making a judgment about compliance.

 Representative Task (Remembering & Understanding): Identify the factors that a practitioner should consider when reporting on an attestation engagement related to an entity's compliance with the requirements of specified laws, regulations, rules, contracts, or grants, and reports on the effectiveness of internal controls over compliance with the requirements.

AICPA Guidance

A practitioner may be engaged to report directly on the subject matter (compliance), on **management's assertion** about compliance, or on internal control over compliance. AT-C 315, *Compliance Attestation*, applies to examination or agreed-upon procedures reports related to compliance with specified requirements (or agreed-upon procedures related to internal control over compliance).

Examination Engagements

Preconditions

Preconditions require that management:

- **Provides** the practitioner written assertion(s). If management refuses to provide the assertions, the practitioner should withdraw from the engagement when that is permissible
- **Accepts responsibility** for compliance with specified requirements and the entity's internal control over compliance
- **Evaluates** the entity's compliance with specified requirements

Examination Procedures

The practitioner should obtain an **understanding of the specified requirements** through:

- Consideration of laws, regulations, rules, contracts, and grants relevant to the specified requirements
- Consideration of knowledge obtained through prior engagements and regulatory reports
- Discussion with appropriate personnel within the entity

When the entity involved has operations in several components, the practitioner should determine the nature, timing, and extent of testing at the individual components.

The practitioner should obtain an understanding of **internal control over compliance** and assess the risks of material noncompliance. They should also consider the kinds of potential noncompliance and design appropriate tests of compliance.

When compliance is related to **regulatory requirements**, the practitioner should review reports and communications involving the regulatory agencies, including inquiries of the regulatory agencies.

Written Representations

The practitioner should request written representations from management (in addition to those required by AT-C 205) that management has:

- Taken responsibility for internal control over compliance
- Performed an evaluation of the entity's compliance with specified requirements
- Provided its interpretation of any compliance requirements that are subject to different interpretations

Management's **refusal** to furnish the required written representations is a **scope limitation** sufficient to preclude an unmodified opinion and may warrant withdrawal when that is permitted; there is no alternative to obtaining the required written representations.

Content of the Practitioner's Report

Report contents should include:

- A title that includes the word "independent" and an appropriate addressee
- Identification of the compliance matters being reported on (or the assertion involved)
- Identification of the specified requirements; should also identify the criteria, if those criteria are not included in the compliance requirement

- A statement that:
  - Identifies management's responsibility for compliance and the practitioner's responsibility to express an opinion
  - Explains that the examination was conducted in accordance with attestation standards established by the AICPA and other statements describing the examination engagement
  - Describes the nature of an examination engagement
  - Describes any significant inherent limitations
  - Explains that the examination does not provide a legal determination
- An opinion whether the entity complied with the specified requirements, in all material respects, or whether management's assertion is fairly stated
- The signature of the practitioner's firm
- The city and state where the practitioner practices
- The date of the report.

Agreed-Upon Procedures Engagements

Preconditions

The preconditions requirement is that management:

- **Accepts responsibility** for compliance with specified requirements and the entity's internal control over compliance
- **Evaluates** the entity's compliance with specified requirements

Written Representations

The practitioner should request written representations from management (in addition to those required by AT-C 215) that management has:

- Taken responsibility for internal control over compliance;
- Performed an evaluation of the entity's compliance with specified requirements or internal control over compliance;
- Provided its interpretation of any compliance requirements that are subject to different interpretations; and
- Disclosed any known noncompliance occurring subsequent to the period covered by the practitioner's report.

Content of the Practitioner's Report

Report contents should include:

- A title that includes the word "independent"
- An appropriate addressee
- Identification of the specified requirements being reported on

- A statement that:
  - ○ Identifies management's responsibility for compliance with the specified requirements
  - ○ Identifies the specified parties
  - ○ States that the specified parties are responsible for the sufficiency of the procedures performed
  - ○ States that the agreed-upon procedures engagement was conducted in accordance with attestation standards established by the AICPA, and other statements pointing out that it was not an examination or a review and includes a disclaimer of opinion or any other conclusion

- A list of the procedures performed (or reference to them) and the findings

- A description of any agreed-upon materiality limits, if applicable

- A description of the assistance provided by a practitioner's external specialist, if applicable

- Any reservations about the procedures or findings, if applicable

- An alert that restricts the use of the report to specified users

- The signature of the practitioner's firm

- The city and state where the practitioner practices

- The date of the report

Mill, CPA, was engaged by a group of royalty recipients to apply agreed-upon procedures to financial data supplied by Modern Co. regarding Modern's written assertion about its compliance with contractual requirements to pay royalties. Mill's report on these agreed-upon procedures should contain a(n)

- Disclaimer of opinion about the fair presentation of Modern's financial statements

- List of the procedures performed (or reference thereto) and Mill's findings

- Opinion about the effectiveness of Modern's internal control activities concerning royalty payments

- Acknowledgment that the sufficiency of the procedures is solely Mill's responsibility

A practitioner performing an agreed-upon procedures engagement issues a practitioner's report of findings based on procedures that are specified by the engaging party. **No opinion or conclusion** is provided in the report.

The practitioner's report does include **a list (ie, description) of the procedures** performed and the **findings** for each procedure. An example of procedures and findings related to this scenario might be: "We obtained the contractual agreement and verified that payments were made on each payment period described for the correct amount. No exceptions were noted."

AUD 27
Other Reporting Considerations

AUD 27: Other Reporting Considerations

27.01 Comparative Statements and Consistency Between Periods

Comparative Statements

 Representative Task (Remembering & Understanding): Identify the factors (change in accounting principle, the correction of a material misstatement, or a material change in classification) that would affect the comparability or consistency of financial statements.

When the F/S of the previous year are shown alongside those of the current year, the auditor will have additional audit procedures to perform. If the auditor of the current year also audited the previous year, then the standard report will simply be updated so that both years are included in the audit report.

Required Procedures

When reporting on comparative F/S, the auditor is required to perform procedures in addition to those required when reporting on F/S for a single period. The auditor will determine whether the:

- Comparative F/S are presented in accordance with **applicable financial reporting framework (AFRF)** requirements.
- Comparative F/S and disclosures agree with those reported in the prior period, or they have been:
  - Restated to correct a departure in the prior period, or
  - Retrospectively adjusted for a change in accounting principle
- **Accounting principles and policies** applied in the comparative F/S and disclosures **are consistent** with those applied in the current period, or that there has been a change in accounting principles that has been properly accounted for and disclosed

During the current period's engagement, the auditor may become aware of a **material misstatement** in the comparative F/S. Upon performing procedures to determine if, in fact, such a misstatement does exist, and the comparative F/S are restated, the auditor should determine that the comparative F/S agree with the restated F/S.

When reporting on comparative F/S, the auditor will obtain **management representations** for all periods referred to in the report. The report requirements will vary, however, depending on whether the report:

- Includes a different opinion on prior period F/S than was previously expressed
- Covers prior period F/S audited by a predecessor auditor

Report Requirements—Prior Year Opinion Changed

In some cases, the auditor's opinion on the previous year will be different from the opinion expressed on those statements in the earlier report. One example might be if the previous opinion was qualified due to inadequate disclosure of a lawsuit, and the lawsuit was settled during the current year (or the client agrees to disclose the suit in the notes to the current comparative F/S).

When the auditor's opinion has changed, the opinion will reflect the current situation, but an **other-matter paragraph** will **refer to** the **earlier report** indicating:

- The date of the previous report

- The type of opinion previously expressed

- The substantive reasons for the different opinion

- That the auditor's opinion on the amended F/S differs from the previous opinion[SC2]

When reporting on comparative financial statements, an auditor ordinarily should change the previously issued opinion on the prior year's financial statements if the:

- Prior year's financial statements are restated to conform with the applicable reporting framework

- Auditor is a predecessor auditor who has been requested by a former client to reissue the previously issued report

- Prior year's opinion was unmodified and the opinion on the current year's financial statements is modified due to a lack of consistency

- Prior year's financial statements are restated following a change in reporting entity in the current year

Reporting on comparative financial statements (F/S): Same auditor, different opinion

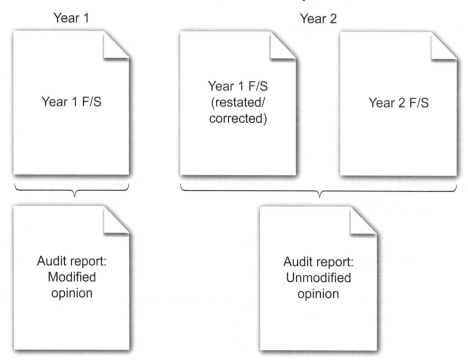

When the prior year's F/S are presented with the current year's (ie, comparative presentation), and the auditor of the current F/S also audited **the prior F/S, the report is updated to cover both years**.

For example, if the prior year's report included a qualified opinion but revisions have been made to the prior year's F/S to make them conform with the reporting framework, then the auditor can express an unmodified opinion on the restated F/S. In that case, the change is explained in an other-matter paragraph or emphasis-of-matter paragraph.

The reissuance of a previously issued report would not by itself be reason to change the opinion. The opinion on the current year F/S should not change the opinion issued on the prior year F/S. The restatement of a prior period's F/S due to a change in reporting entity might preclude an auditor from expressing an opinion on the prior F/S, but it would not require a change in any opinion previously expressed.

Report Requirements—Prior Period Audited by a Predecessor Auditor

When a predecessor auditor examined the F/S of the earlier year, the successor's comparative report of the current year can only express an opinion on the current year since that is the only year the successor audited. There are two ways of handling the earlier year.

1. Report Is Reissued

The predecessor's report can be reissued and included along with the successor's report. In this case, the predecessor must follow the responsibilities outlined in the following box.

Predecessor auditor's responsibilities when reissuing prior year report

- Read current year's financial statements (F/S)
- Compare prior period F/S with current period F/S
- Obtain updated management representation letter on prior period
- Obtain representation letter from successor on matters affecting prior F/S

When there is *no reason* to revise the report, the report will be reissued with the original report date.

It sometimes happens that the auditor of the current year discovers information requiring that the prior year's F/S be revised. For example, the prior year F/S may contain a material error or there may have been a subsequent change in accounting principles.

When this occurs, the successor auditor should request that management inform the predecessor auditor and arrange a discussion among the three parties. The successor auditor will, with **management's permission**, inform the predecessor of the relevant information.

Management will decide whether and how to restate the prior year's F/S, and the predecessor will decide whether the prior year report must be revised, given the subsequently discovered facts. Any revisions would result in the predecessor's report being dual-dated to refer to any new information obtained.

Client, successor, and predecessor auditor discuss revisions to prior year financial statements

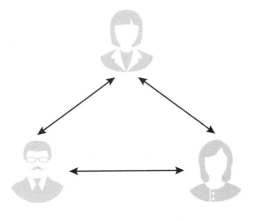

2. Report is not reissued

When the predecessor does not reissue their report, the successor will issue an **unmodified report** and add an **other-matter paragraph** that states the following:

- That the prior period F/S were audited by another auditor
- Date of predecessor's report
- Type of opinion
- Reasons for modification of the opinion, if applicable
- Nature of any explanatory paragraphs

 An entity's comparative financial statements include the financial statements of the prior year that were audited by a predecessor auditor whose report is not presented. If the predecessor's report was qualified, the successor should:

- Issue an updated comparative audit report indicating the division of responsibility
- Explain to the client that comparative financial statements may not be presented under these circumstances
- Express an opinion only on the current year's financial statements and make no reference to the prior year's statements
- Indicate the substantive reasons for the qualification in the predecessor auditor's opinion

---

**Other-matter paragraph* when predecessor's report
is not reissued (ie, not presented)**

- Statement that prior period was audited by another auditor
- Opinion of the predecessor auditor and basis for that opinion (if modified)
- Summary of any other-matter or emphasis-of-matter paragraphs in predecessor's report
- Date of predecessor's report

*For an issuer, this is called an explanatory paragraph

If the F/S of the prior period(s) were audited by a different auditor (ie, predecessor auditor) and the predecessor's report is *not reissued* with the comparative F/S, the auditor of the current F/S will include an **other-matter paragraph (OM)** in the audit report.

The OM will state that the current auditor *did not audit* the prior period F/S. It will explain the contents of the predecessor's audit report, including the predecessor's opinion, **substantive reasons for the qualification,** and contents of any emphasis-of-matter paragraph or OM. This provides the user of the comparative F/S with the information necessary to interpret and compare them with the current F/S.

Report Requirements—Prior Period Not Audited

In some cases, an auditor will audit the current period's F/S while the prior period's statements were **reviewed** or **compiled**. When that is the case, if the report on the prior period's F/S is not reissued, the auditor will provide an **other-matter paragraph** in the current period's audit report. It will state the following:

- The service performed in the prior period
- The date of the report on that service

- A description of any material modifications noted in the report
- When the service was a review, a statement that the service was substantially less in scope than an audit and does not provide the basis for the expression of an opinion on the F/S as a whole
- When the service was a compilation, a statement that no opinion or other form of assurance is expressed on the F/S

If **no audit, review, or compilation** was performed in relation to prior-period F/S, those F/S should clearly indicate their status. The report will include an **other-matter paragraph.**

Prior period not audited, reviewed, or compiled

Contents of other-matter paragraph:

- State that auditor has not audited, reviewed, or compiled prior period financial statements (F/S)
- State that auditor does not express any form of assurance on prior period F/S and takes no responsibility for them

Consistency between Periods

Consistency refers to the use of the *same accounting methods* for similar items or transactions from period to period. It does not refer to the consistent application of accounting principles across different situations within the same period. However, to avoid misleading users of F/S, **similar transactions** should be **accounted for similarly unless** there is a **valid reason** to do otherwise.

AICPA Guidance

The relevant AICPA guidance is provided by AU 708, *Consistency of Financial Statements*. The standard states that the auditor's objectives are to:

- Evaluate the consistency of the F/S for the periods presented
- Communicate in the auditor's report when comparability has been materially affected by:
  - a change in accounting principle
  - an adjustment to correct a material misstatement in previously issued F/S

Evaluating Consistency—Change in Accounting Principle

When the auditor's opinion covers two or more periods, the auditor should evaluate the consistency between such periods, as well as the consistency of the earliest period covered by the auditor's opinion with the prior period. Items that can affect consistency include a material change in an accounting principle or a material restatement of the F/S.

The auditor should evaluate a **change in accounting principle** in terms of the following four matters:

1. Whether the adopted principle is in accordance with the applicable financial reporting framework
2. Whether the method of accounting for the effect of the change is in accordance with the applicable financial reporting framework
3. Whether the disclosures about the change are adequate
4. Whether the entity has justified that the alternative adopted is **preferable**

Reporting on a change in accounting principles

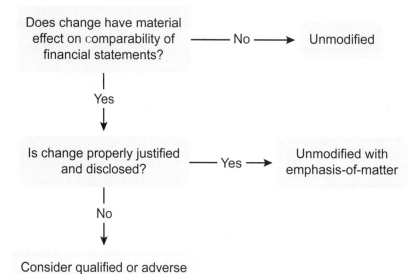

When those four criteria are met, and the change has a material effect on the F/S, the auditor should include an **emphasis-of-matter** paragraph in the auditor's report to describe the change and reference the footnote disclosure applicable to the change. The auditor should state that the auditor's opinion is *not modified* regarding the matter.

- Include the emphasis-of-matter paragraph in subsequent periods until the new principle is applied in all periods presented

- If the change is accounted for by retrospective application to the financial statements, the emphasis-of-matter paragraph is only needed in the period of the change

When those four criteria have not all been met (assuming the change has a material effect on the F/S), the auditor should evaluate whether the change results in a material misstatement and consider whether the auditor's report should be modified.

 Identify which of the following events would cause an auditor to issue a report that omits any reference to consistency:

- A change in the method of accounting for inventories
- A change from an accounting principle that is not generally accepted to one that is generally accepted
- A change in the useful life used to calculate the provision for depreciation expense
- Management's lack of reasonable justification for a change in accounting principle

	Reporting on accounting changes	
	Appropriate report	**Example changes**
Justified change in estimate	• Standard unmodified opinion	• Useful life of an asset • Salvage value of an asset
Justified change in principle	• Unmodified opinion with emphasis-of-matter	• FIFO to LIFO • Revenue recognition method

A change in an asset's estimated useful life is a change in estimate, not principle. Because changes in estimated amounts (eg, allowance for credit losses, salvage value) occur regularly, an auditor's report will not mention them unless they are so unreasonable as to constitute a material misstatement.

Evaluating Consistency—Change in Reporting Entity

When a change in the reporting entity results in F/S that are essentially those of a different reporting entity, the auditor should include an **emphasis-of-matter paragraph** in the auditor's report describing the change in the entity and referencing the entity's disclosure. However, that is unnecessary when the change in entity results from a transaction or event, such as the purchase or disposition of a subsidiary.

Evaluating Consistency—Correction on a Material Misstatement in Previously Issued F/S

There are three scenarios to consider in terms of a material misstatement in previously issued F/S:

- When the F/S are restated to **correct a prior material misstatement**, the auditor should include an **emphasis-of-matter paragraph** in the auditor's report. (That paragraph need not be included in subsequent periods.) The auditor should state that the *auditor's opinion is not modified* regarding the matter

- If the F/S disclosures relating to the restatement are not adequate, the auditor should evaluate the inadequacy of disclosure and consider **modifying the auditor's report**

- A **change from an accounting principle** that is not in accordance with the applicable financial reporting framework to one that is in accordance is a **correction** of a misstatement

Effect on the Auditor's Report

The auditor need not refer to consistency in the audit report unless there is an inconsistency due to a material change in accounting principle or restatement.

Sample paragraph for a voluntary change in principle

Emphasis-of-Matter

As discussed in Note X to the financial statements, the entity has elected to change its method of accounting for (*describe accounting method change*) in (*insert year(s) of financial statements that reflect the accounting method change*). Our opinion is not modified with respect to this matter.

27.02 Other Information in Documents with Audited Statements

Other Information (OI)

 Representative Task (Remembering & Understanding): Understand the auditor's responsibilities related to other information included in documents with audited financial statements.

Other information (OI) consists of *financial or nonfinancial* information (other than F/S and the auditor's report thereon) included in an entity's annual report. The **annual report** is a document or documents typically prepared by management in accordance with law, regulation, or custom.

- The **purpose** is to provide owners (or similar stakeholders) with information on the entity's operations and the entity's financial results and financial position as set out in the F/S
- An annual report **contains** the F/S and the auditor's report thereon and usually includes information about the entity's developments, its future outlook and risks and uncertainties, a statement by the entity's governing body, and reports covering governance matters

Examples of OI include the following:

- Chairman of the Board's statement
- Management report, management commentary, or operating and financial review
- Corporate governance statement
- Management's internal control and risk assessment reports
- Financial summaries or highlights, including financial ratios
- Employment data
- Names of officers and directors
- Selected quarterly data

Auditor's Responsibilities

The auditor should:

- **Obtain management's written acknowledgment** as to which documents are included in the annual report
- **Make arrangements** with management for the **timely receipt** of the final version of those documents
  - If any of those documents will not be available until after the date of the auditor's report on the F/S, then the auditor should request a written representation from management that the final version of such documents will be provided to the auditor prior to the documents' issuance

- **Communicate**:
  - The auditor's responsibility regarding the OI
  - The procedures performed regarding the OI
  - The results of those procedures

- **Read** the OI and consider whether there is a material inconsistency relative to the audited F/S or a material misstatement of fact regarding the OI
  - **Material inconsistency**—Involves differences between the OI and the auditor's knowledge obtained in the audit
  - **Material misstatement of fact**—Involves OI that is otherwise misleading

- **Discuss** with management when a material inconsistency appears to exist and determine whether a material misstatement of the OI (or a material misstatement of the F/S) exists

- **Respond** when the auditor concludes that a material misstatement of the OI exists
  - Request that management correct the OI. If management agrees, then verify that the correction has been made; if management refuses, communicate the matter to those charged with governance with a request to make the correction
  - If the OI has not been corrected after communicating with those charged with governance (prior to the date of the auditor's report), the auditor should take appropriate action (eg, withhold the audit report)
  - If the material misstatement in the OI is determined after the date of the auditor's report and
    - The OI has been corrected, perform the procedures necessary in the circumstances
    - The OI is not corrected (after communicating with those charged with governance), consider the legal rights and obligations of communicating with anyone in receipt of the auditor's report on the financial statements

Reporting Issues

The auditor should add a separate section in the auditor's report (after the "Auditor's Responsibilities" section) with an appropriate heading, such as "Other Information." The "Other Information" section should include the following:

- A statement that **management is responsible** for the OI
- An **identification** of the OI
- A statement that the **auditor's opinion** on the F/S does not cover the OI and that the auditor does not express an opinion or any form of assurance on it
- A statement that the **auditor is responsible** to read the OI and consider whether a material inconsistency exists between the OI and the F/S (or the OI otherwise appears to be materially misleading)
- A statement that, if the auditor concludes that an uncorrected material misstatement of the OI exists, the auditor is required to describe it in the auditor's report
  - If the auditor has concluded that an uncorrected material misstatement of the OI exists, the auditor should add a statement that an uncorrected material misstatement of the OI exists along with a description of it in the auditor's report

An auditor concludes that there is a material inconsistency in the other information in an annual report to shareholders containing audited financial statements. The auditor believes that the financial statements do not require revision, but the client is unwilling to revise or eliminate the material inconsistency in the other information. Under these circumstances, what action would the auditor most likely take?

- Disclaim an opinion on the financial statements after explaining the material inconsistency in a separate explanatory paragraph

- Revise the auditor's report to include a separate explanatory paragraph describing the material inconsistency

- Consider the situation closed because the other information is not in the audited financial statements

- Issue an "except for" qualified opinion after discussing the matter with the client's audit committee

Other information (OI) is **unaudited voluntary** data provided by management, such as a letter from the company president to shareholders. Although auditors do not express an opinion on OI, they are required to read it to determine whether it is consistent with F/S.

If material inconsistencies are discovered, auditors will request that management correct them. If management refuses, auditors will **revise the report with an explanatory paragraph** to inform users of the inconsistency. An example of a material inconsistency is if auditors issue an adverse opinion, but the president states that F/S are fairly stated.

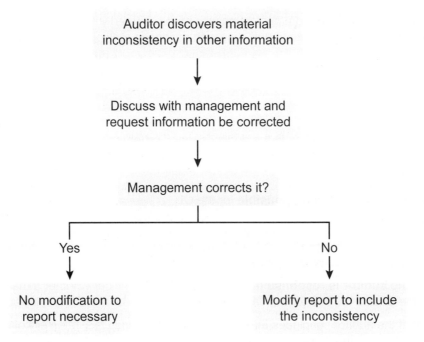

If the auditor issues a qualified or adverse opinion, they may need to modify the "Other Information" section of the auditor's report when the reason for the qualified or adverse opinion is relevant to the description of an uncorrected material misstatement of the OI.

If the auditor issues a disclaimer of opinion, the auditor's report should omit the "Other Information" section (providing such a section could overshadow the disclaimer of opinion).

27.03 Review of Interim Financial Information

Overview

Although the annual financial statements (F/S) of a **public** client (issuer) may be audited, the quarterly (interim) information typically is not. Instead, the auditor of the annual F/S will normally perform a **review of interim financial information** under PCAOB standards.

For **nonpublic entities**, these interim reviews are performed under GAAS (AU-C 930) when:

- The entity's latest annual F/S have been audited
- The auditor either:
  - Has been engaged to audit the entity's current year F/S
  - Audited the entity's latest annual F/S and expects to be engaged to audit the current year F/S
- The same AFRF used to prepare the annual F/S is used for the interim financial information

If all these conditions are not met, a review of interim financial information is required to be performed in accordance with SSARS (AR-C 90).

Engagement Acceptance

 Representative Task (Remembering & Understanding): Identify the factors an auditor should consider when reporting on an engagement to review interim financial information.

Before accepting an engagement to review the interim financial information, the auditor should:

- Determine whether the financial reporting framework to be applied is acceptable
- Obtain the agreement of management regarding the engagement terms

The auditor should agree upon the **terms of the engagement** with management (or those charged with governance) and record those terms in an engagement letter that includes the:

- Objectives and scope of the engagement
- Responsibilities of management
- Responsibilities of the auditor
- Limitations of a review engagement
- Identification of the applicable financial reporting framework

Engagement Procedures

Many of the procedures required for an interim review are similar to those of a review under SSARS. Some of the procedures that are more specific to interim reviews under GAAS and PCAOB standards include:

- **Obtaining an understanding** of the entity and its environment. This includes internal controls related to the preparation of annual and interim financial information which is sufficient to:
  - Identify the types of potential misstatements (and likelihood of occurrence)
  - Select the **inquiries and analytical procedures** for the auditor's basis for conclusion

    Obtaining (updating) understanding of entity and its environment for interim review

    - Read recent annual and interim financial information
    - Read documentation of previous audit and recent interim reviews
    - Consider results of audit procedures on current year's financial statements
    - Ask management about changes in business activities, internal control, related parties

- **Performing analytical procedures**: The auditor should apply analytical procedures to the interim information to identify unusual items that may indicate a material misstatement, including comparing:
  - Interim financial information with comparable information for the immediately preceding period and with the corresponding period(s) in the previous year;
  - Recorded amounts or ratios developed from recorded amounts to expectations; and
  - Disaggregated revenue data.

- **Making inquiries and performing other review procedures**: The auditor should make the following inquiries and perform the following other procedures:
  - Read the available minutes of meetings of stockholders, directors, and appropriate committees
  - Obtain reports from any component auditors related to reviews of significant components or inquire of those auditors if reports have not been issued
  - Inquire of management about the matters normally associated with a management representation letter
  - Obtain evidence that the interim financial information agrees with (or reconciles with) the accounting records
  - Read the interim financial information
  - Read other information in documents containing the interim financial information to see if any of it is materially inconsistent

- **Making inquiry concerning litigation, claims, and assessments**: The auditor should inquire of legal counsel if information about litigation, claims, and assessments does not appear to be presented in accordance with the applicable financial reporting framework

- **Considering going-concern issues**: If information indicates that there may be substantial doubt about an entity's ability to continue as a going concern, the auditor should inquire of management about plans for dealing with adverse effects and consider the adequacy of disclosure about such matters

- **Assessing the reasonableness and consistency of management's responses** (note that the auditor is not required to corroborate management's responses with other evidence)

The auditor should evaluate, individually and in the aggregate, misstatements to determine whether material modification should be made to the interim financial information.

The auditor should **obtain written representations** from management for all interim financial information presented as of the date of the auditor's review report. If management does not provide the written representation requested, the auditor should withdraw from the engagement to review the interim financial information.

Management representation letter for *review of interim financial information* (key points)

Management represents that it:

- Fulfilled responsibility for fair presentation of financial information
- Is responsible for internal control (I/C)
- Disclosed all significant defieincies and material weaknesses in I/C
- Provided auditor with all relevant information and access
- Disclosed all known sifnidicant fraud, noncompliance, litigation
- Disclosed all subsequent events that may require adjustment

Identify which of the following procedures would typically **not** be performed by an accountant during a review of interim financial information:

- Compare disaggregated revenue data
- Perform analytical procedures
- Make inquiries of management
- Obtain corroborating external evidence

As in other review engagements, reviews of interim F/S primarily involve analytical procedures and inquiries of management and result in reports expressing limited assurance. Comparisons of disaggregated revenue data should be among the analytical procedures performed. This might include comparing revenue by product line during the current period to comparable prior periods.

Because interim reviews require only limited assurance, not reasonable assurance, they do not require tests of controls, tests of details, or corroborating external evidence.

Procedures for interim reviews of financial statements (partial list)

- Make inquiries of client personnel
- Perform analytical procedures
- Understand the entity and its environment, including its internal control
- Read financial statements and compare to accounting records
- Read most recent audit documentation
- Read minutes of board directors' and shareholders' meetings

Reporting Requirements

The reports under SSARS, GAAS, and PCAOB standards are all a little different (see table below).

- The primary differences between the SSARS and GAAS reports are the **order of the report** and that the GAAS report has no Accountant's Responsibility section

- SSARS presents the **conclusion** in the last section while both GAAS and PCAOB standards put the conclusion in the first section of the report

	Differences between unmodified interim review reports		
Section	**SSARS**	**GAAS**	**PCAOB**
1	Introduction	Results of review of interim financial information (Includes introduction & accountant's conclusion)	
2	Management responsibilities*	Basis for review results	
3	Accountant's responsibility	Management responsibilities*	N/A
4	Accountant's conclusion	N/A	

*Shortened heading

The **PCAOB** report:

- Is generally the shortest as it has no management or accountant responsibilities sections

- Must be titled "Report of Independent Registered Public Accounting Firm"

- Must refer to "the standards of the Public Company Accounting Oversight Board (United States)," not SSARS or GAAS

 Review of interim financial information or F/S (Issuers)

REPORT OF INDEPENDENT REGISTERED PUBLIC ACCOUNTING FIRM

To the shareholders and the board of directors of ABC Company

Results of review of interim financial information

We have reviewed the accompanying [*describe the interim financial information reviewed*] of ABC Company (the "Company") and consolidated subsidiaries as of September 30, 20X1, and for the three-month and nine-month periods then ended, and the related notes [and schedules] (collectively referred to as the "interim financial information"). Based on our review, **we are not aware of any material modifications that should be made** to the accompanying interim financial information for it to be in conformity with accounting principles generally accepted in the United States of America.

Basis for review results

This interim financial information is the responsibility of the Company's management. We conducted our review in accordance with the standards of the **Public Company Accounting Oversight Board (United States)** ("PCAOB"). A review of interim financial information consists principally of applying **analytical procedures and making inquiries** of persons responsible for financial and accounting matters. It is **substantially less in scope** than an audit conducted in accordance with the standards of the PCAOB, the objective of which is the expression of an opinion regarding the financial statements taken as a whole. Accordingly, we **do not express such an opinion**.

Signature
City and State or Country
Date (completion of the review procedures)

27.04 Supplementary Information

Overview

 Representative Task (Remembering & Understanding): Identify the factors an auditor should consider when reporting on supplementary information included in or accompanying an entity's financial statements.

The relevant AICPA guidance is provided by AU-C 725, *Supplementary Information in Relation to the Financial Statements as a Whole*. The standard states that the auditor's objective is to evaluate the presentation of the supplementary information (SI) and report on whether it is fairly stated, in all material respects, in relation to the F/S as a whole.

SI is information presented **outside the basic F/S**, excluding required supplementary information (RSI). Such information may be presented in a document containing the audited F/S or separate from the F/S. The **auditor's objective** is to evaluate the presentation of the SI and report on whether it is fairly stated, in all material respects, in relation to the F/S as a whole.

Auditor's Responsibilities

Auditor Procedures

The **auditor should obtain management's agreement** that management has responsibility for:

- Preparing the supplementary information in accordance with applicable criteria
- Providing the auditor with written representations
- Including the auditor's report on the supplementary information in any document containing the supplementary information that references the auditor's association with it
- Presenting the supplementary information with the audited financial statements (or making the audited financial statements *readily available* to the intended users of the supplementary information)

When engaged to determine whether SI is fairly stated in relation to the F/S, the **auditor should determine** whether:

- The SI was derived from (or directly related to) the underlying records used to prepare the F/S
- The SI relates to the same period as the F/S
- The auditor served as the auditor of the F/S
- Either an unmodified or qualified opinion was expressed on the F/S (must not have issued an adverse opinion or disclaimer of opinion)
- The SI will either accompany the entity's audited F/S or the audited F/S will be made *readily available* by the entity

The **auditor should perform** the following procedures:

- Inquire of management about the purpose of the SI and the criteria used to prepare it

- Obtain an understanding about the methods used and whether those methods have changed (and if changed, the reasons for any changes)

- Compare and reconcile the SI to the F/S or to the underlying records used for the F/S

- Inquire of management about any significant assumptions used

- Evaluate the appropriateness and completeness of the SI in relationship to the audited F/S

- Obtain appropriate written representations from management

In its annual report to shareholders, Lake Co. included a separate management report that contained an assertion about the effectiveness of its internal control over financial reporting. Lake's auditor is expressing an unqualified opinion on Lake's financial statements but has not been engaged to examine and report on this management assertion. The auditor:

- Should add an explanatory paragraph to the report on the financial statements disclaiming an opinion on management's assertion

- Should request that Lake place the management report in its annual report where it will **not** be misinterpreted to be the auditor's assertion

- Should read the management report and consider whether it contains any material inconsistencies

In this scenario, it is suggested that the entity is a publicly held company because an unqualified opinion is issued; unmodified is issued for private entities. Publicly held entities are required to include management's assessment of the effectiveness of internal control over financial reporting (ie, RSI). Nonetheless, all supplementary information (OI, SI, or RSI) **requires auditors (through reading**, limited procedures, or audit procedures) to check for inconsistencies with F/S.

Reporting Requirements

The auditor may issue a **separate report** on the SI (in addition to the report on the audited F/S) or **combine the report** on the SI with the report on the F/S. (If the latter, then add a separate section labeled "Supplementary Information" regarding the SI.)

- If the auditor expressed an adverse opinion or a disclaimer of opinion on the F/S, the auditor is prohibited from reporting on the SI

If the SI is **materially misstated** in relation to the F/S, the auditor should discuss the matter with management and propose appropriate revision. If management does not revise the SI, the auditor should either appropriately modify the opinion on the SI or withhold the separate report on it.

Required Supplementary Information (RSI)

Required supplementary information (RSI) is information that a designated accounting standards setter requires to accompany an entity's basic F/S. RSI is not part of the basic F/S; however, a designated accounting standards setter considers the information to be an essential part of financial reporting for placing the basic F/S in an appropriate operational, economic, or historical context.

The auditor's objectives are to:

- Describe in the auditor's report whether RSI is presented

- Communicate when the supplementary information has not been presented in accordance with the established guidelines (or when material modification is necessary)